A History and Criticism

of

American Public Address

VOLUME III

A History and Criticism

of

American Public Address

PREPARED UNDER THE AUSPICES OF

The Speech Association of America

VOLUME III

MARIE KATHRYN HOCHMUTH

Editor

Associates

W. NORWOOD BRIGANCE   DONALD BRYANT

NEW YORK / RUSSELL & RUSSELL

Contents

Preface

In 1943 there appeared, under the sponsorship of the Speech Association of America, a two-volume work on the *History and Criticism of American Public Address*, edited by W. Norwood Brigance. The present volume is a companion piece to that work. It aims to continue the examination of men and women who, by oral discourse, have helped shape American ideals and policy.

Work for the volume began in 1946, at which time Professor A. Craig Baird of the University of Iowa, Bower Aly of the University of Missouri, W. Norwood Brigance of Wabash College, and Karl R. Wallace then of the University of Virginia and at present at the University of Illinois, constituted a committee for planning a volume designed to continue the series already begun. This committee supervised the selection of speakers to be included in the volume. It made this selection on the basis of advice from contributors to the earlier volumes, from members of the Committee on the History of American Public Address of the Speech Association of America, and counsel from men and women representing law, religion, politics, and other institutional areas.

In 1948, the present editorial staff was named. It has been responsible for selecting contributors to the volume and for planning and editing the manuscript. With fewer speakers to be included, we have sought more comprehensive treatment than was possible in the earlier volumes. We have also sought to employ techniques for analysis that, in some instances, represent developments since the appearance of the Brigance studies. For the cooperation and labor of the contributing authors we are deeply grateful. The patience and generosity with which they have responded to suggestions and to the whims of the editors has indeed been gratifying. To Wayne Brockriede of the University of Illinois we are deeply indebted for preparing the index.

To our publishers who, in every stage of preparation of the volume, have been our sympathetic and generous taskmasters and guides, may we express our warmest appreciation and deepest gratitude.

Editorial Committee:
Donald Bryant, Washington University
W. Norwood Brigance, Wabash College
Marie Hochmuth, University of Illinois

Marie Hochmuth
November 1, 1954

1

The Criticism of Rhetoric

by MARIE HOCHMUTH

"Show me," Walter Savage Landor makes Pericles remark, "how great projects were executed, great advantages gained, and great calamities averted. Show me the generals and the statesmen who stood foremost, that I may bend to them in reverence; tell me their names, that I may repeat them to my children... place History on her rightful throne, and, at the sides of her, Eloquence and war." [1] Pericles hoped that when the history of Athens from the invasion of Xerxes should be written, it would give "a fair and full criticism on the orations of Antiphon," [2] even at the expense of a narrative of the battle of Salamis.

Orators, of course, have been agents in history and, like all agents, must be supposed to have effects. Greece without Demosthenes, Rome without Cicero, England without Burke and Churchill, Germany without Hitler, and the United States without Patrick Henry and Lincoln would have been different. To believe otherwise is to succumb to the notion that human effort counts for little or nothing. Along with the other arts—painting, sculpture, drama, poetry—oratory has sometimes transformed abstractions into meaningful patterns and directives in our lives, has projected and given impetus to ideas that have become the values by which we live.

Ancient as an art form, the public speech in our age has gained new prominence as more and more public men appear on the television screen and in great public halls to "appeal directly to the people." One may legitimately question, I think, whether new prominence is accompanied by improved quality. Is there a promise of a new Golden Age of public speaking, or a threat of further deterioration in an art which once held a significant position among the arts? Will the somewhat casual ability to "say a few words" emerge in the form of a disciplined art, comparable to Athenian and Roman eloquence, the eloquence of eighteenth-century England, and the eloquence of the first half of nineteenth-century America?

[1] *Selections from the Writings of Walter Savage Landor*, arr. and ed., Sidney Colvin (London: Macmillan & Co., 1882), p. 277.
[2] *Ibid.*, p. 276.

I

American Public Address

I propose to deal here with the problem of evaluating human effort as it manifests itself in the making of speeches. Although I propose to deal chiefly with American speeches, I assume that the basic principles may be applied to the evaluation of speeches anywhere. I am concerned not merely with evaluating the speaking of present-day speakers, but also with the evaluation of past efforts of individuals whose lifework is best reflected in the body of speeches with which they are identified.

A sense of critical awareness is, I believe, a necessary prerequisite to achieving or maintaining high quality in any art. The degree of perfection manifested in any age is a response to ideals insistently proclaimed, recalled, or restated. Furthermore, it is through critical awareness that one discovers the implications of his art for his times.

Systematic criticism of any sort has no long and well-established heritage in America. In truth, it can hardly be said to have existed at all before the nineteenth century. As the literary critic, Van Wyck Brooks, once remarked, "There is nothing else in all modern history like the unanimity of praise and confidence with which, by its passengers, the American Ship of State was launched and manned. In all our long nineteenth-century past, there was scarcely a breath of dissent, doubt or censure...."[3] In the field of literary criticism the poverty of the nineteenth century has given way to the riches of the twentieth century, with critical warfare being one of its most distinctive features.

If one turns specifically to the records of speech-making, one finds little systematic criticism of the millions of words that have been uttered in the building of civilization. Early Colonial ministers, of course, sometimes examined the sermons of their fellows to find out if the sentiments were "correct," or for evidences of defection from generally accepted creeds. In the early part of the nineteenth century, in politics and religion, men like Everett, Webster, and Channing were praised for "great efforts" in the courts, town meetings, Congress, and the pulpit. British travelers in America surveyed the scene and placed our oratorical efforts against their great tradition of Parliamentary speaking.[4] People spoke of speech-making because it interested them. But as Wichelns observed as late as 1925, "We have not much serious criticism of oratory."[5]

[3] Van Wyck Brooks, *Sketches in Criticism* (New York: E. P. Dutton & Co., Inc., 1932), p. 11.

[4] Glenn Eugene Reddick, "Criticisms and Observations on American Public Address by British Travelers, 1785-1860" (Ph.D. dissertation, University of Illinois, 1954), pp. 40-87.

[5] Herbert A. Wichelns, "The Literary Criticism of Oratory," in *Studies in Rhetoric and Public Speaking in Honor of James Albert Winans* (New York: The Century Co., 1925), p. 182.

The Criticism of Rhetoric

The problem of criticism was sometimes complicated by literary men. They were uncertain of their genre, yet faced with a body of material that required consideration. Biographers and historians, with their own tools and preoccupations, likewise looked into the literature of speeches with some concern about how to use it. Surveying the body of critical comment on speeches for the last half of the nineteenth century, Barnet Baskerville has observed: "There is an absence of any prevailing critical temper in most of the literature. It is often eulogistic; it abounds in superlatives; it is impressionistic; it lacks system; it is personal rather than objective; it is frequently written in a style which manifests the same faults of verbosity, ostentatious erudition and gratuitous ornamentation which are attributed to the orators themselves." [6] A few exceptions may be noted in the critical commentaries of Channing, Emerson, Whipple, Godkin, and Goodrich.[7] Baskerville notes not only a lack of critical comment, but also apathy in regard to the need for systematic criticism, and concludes that such a "lack of speculation as to what criticism should be seems to indicate that critics of speaking had not yet become self-conscious.... Formulation of specific criteria, conscious efforts to establish a science of rhetorical criticism in America, were to come in a later period." [8]

In the criticism of speeches as in the criticism of literature generally, the twentieth century has yielded richer harvests. Wichelns in 1925,[9] Brigance in 1943,[10] and Thonssen and Baird in 1948 [11] focused attention on standards and methods for the evaluation of speeches as special genre. Spurred by the urgency of the world scene from the beginning of World War I through the period of present conflict, when misunderstanding is of the greatest concern, psychologists, linguists, aestheticians, semeioticians have been trying in good faith to advance our knowledge of the structure and use of language.

In the light of contemporary knowledge the problem of "giving fair and full criticism" to oratory may become somewhat more systematic. Our function here is not to write off previous attempts with a fine sense of superiority, but to set down in some brief form elements which must be considered when the speech as an art is being appraised.

---

[6] Barnet Baskerville, "A Study of American Criticism of Public Address, 1850-1900" (Ph.D. dissertation, Northwestern University, August, 1948), p. 314.

[7] *Ibid.*, p. 315.

[8] *Ibid.*, pp. 317, 318.

[9] *Loc. cit.*

[10] William Norwood Brigance (ed.), *A History and Criticism of American Public Address* (New York: McGraw-Hill Book Co., 1943).

[11] Lester Thonssen and A. Craig Baird, *Speech Criticism* (New York: Ronald Press, 1948).

What Is Criticism?

"Criticism, I hardly need point out," said John Dewey, "is not fault finding. It is not pointing out evils to be reformed. It is judgment engaged in discriminating among values. It is taking thought as to what is better and worse in any field at any time, with some consciousness of *why* the better is better and *why* the worse is worse." [12] Most of us will find little to disagree with in a concept of criticism whose minimal expectation is that of separation and division. Its biblical forebear is to be found in the New Testament: "But he said unto Him, Man, who made me a judge or a divider over you?" [13]

We need not haggle long over whether criticism arises because critics are frustrated speakers or writers. Nor need we add to the thousands of words already written on whether it is a science or an art. That it has not reached a standard of predictability common to the natural sciences should be obvious to all of us. Criticism, like anything else well-made, can achieve and sometimes has achieved artistic distinction. Of this much we are clearly aware: it is a universal practice, presumably fulfilling certain functions, and having values.

If we examine the critical process clearly, we may discern at least three aspects. It involves identification of what is to be evaluated; it recognizes what is to be evaluated as a cultural product of a particular time; it finally involves a judicial act of determining what is better or worse. In other words, a critic must necessarily be concerned with answering such questions as: What are we dealing with? When did the thing occur? In what relation does it stand to other similar cultural phenomena?

Let us note, for example, a typical case of identifying what one is dealing with. In it we may observe the precision with which Aristotle went about the process of naming his object, classifying, and differentiating:

Rhetoric may be defined as the faculty of observing in any given case the available means of persuasion. This is not a function of any other art. Every other art can instruct or persuade about its own particular subject-matter; for instance, medicine about what is healthy and unhealthy, geometry about the properties of magnitudes, arithmetic about numbers, and the same is true of the other arts and sciences. But rhetoric we look upon as the power of observing the means of persuasion on almost any subject presented to us; and that is why we say that, in its technical character, it is not concerned with any special or definite class of subjects.[14]

---

[12] *Construction and Criticism* (The First Davies Memorial Lecture, delivered February 25, 1930, for the Institute of Arts and Sciences [New York: Columbia University Press, 1930]), p. 12.

[13] Luke 12:14.

[14] *Rhetorica*, tr. W. Rhys Roberts, *The Works of Aristotle*, ed. W. D. Ross (Oxford: The Clarendon Press), XI, iii.2.1355[b].

Any critic, trained or untrained, goes through this process of identification in some way or other. Suppose a traveler walks into London's Hyde Park on Sunday afternoon and encounters a group of people surrounding a speaker uttering sounds to those who have stopped. Our traveler may previously have encountered someone quietly reclining on the grass, another absorbed in the Sunday paper, still another with brush and easel sketching the trees along the avenue. He may observe that the constituents which finally arrested his attention include the following: someone is speaking; others are listening; the event is taking place in a specific time; it is taking place in a particular locale; presumably there is some purpose; the utterance has some form; and the whole entity rests upon the natural condition that sound can be transmitted and received. If the traveler concludes that he is witnessing a unified whole different from any other unified whole which he has encountered, he will have performed the first analytic step in a total critical act, that of identifying his object and separating it from other cultural phenomena.

The traveler may go a step further. He may observe that what he is witnessing is an act bearing the marks of a culture at a particular time; the person doing the talking will have been conditioned by the culture of which he is a part; in purpose, matter, and manner the act will be a manifestation of the period of which it is a product. In fact, it will be the speaker's peculiar way of responding to the times. He will realize that time is not merely a physical fact, but a social fact. If the traveler recognizes the relations of the organic whole of which he is a witness to the cultural milieu of which it is a part, he will have performed a second analytic aspect of a critical act.

Our traveler may pass on and encounter similar behavior near by in the park. Unless he has encountered situations of a similar nature previously, or has an opportunity to witness at this time similar acts, he is in no position to perform the final aspect of judgment, for obviously what is "better or worse" involves an act of comparison. It is an act, in the main involving synthesis, in which the observer sees his object as a whole, and sees it in relation to similar cultural objects at the same or different times or places.

From time to time, critics have tended to single out for emphasis one or another aspect of the critical act. In the literary arts, we have tended at times to throw the emphasis on the person performing the act, and thus have written biography; at other times, we have tended to emphasize the cultural milieu of which the act was a part, almost to the exclusion of the act itself. In this respect, we have been sociological or historical. A concern with history or sociology, indispensable as preliminary aspects of criticism, sometimes obscures the fact that history and criticism serve different purposes. Whereas a concern for all these things is necessary, it does not represent criticism. As Edmund Wilson has enjoined the literary critics: "No matter how thorough and complete our

5

explanation of works of literature may be from the historical and biographical points of view, we must be ready to try to estimate the relative degree of success attained by the products of the various periods and the various person-alities....We shall not otherwise write literary criticism at all, but merely social or political history ... or psychological case histories from past eras, or ... merely chronologies of books that have been published." [15]

The criticism of speeches, like the criticism of all art, involves both analysis and synthesis. It is concerned with naming and identifying its object, locating its connections with the culture of which it is a part, and seeing it in relation to other similar phenomena. It is "discriminating among values."

The Constituents of the Rhetorical Act

The criticism of speeches must proceed from a clear conception of the nature of a speech. Whereas a speech may be easily differentiated from the graphic and visual arts on the basis of media and means, it is less easily differ-entiated from other verbal arts like poetry and prose writing generally. Tradi-tionally the speech has functioned both as an end in itself and as a means to other ends. Thus, Greek and Roman orators perfected the speech as a verbal form serving its own ends. On the other hand, the historian Thucydides, employed written forms of speeches in recording the political opinions of the day. Homer, Milton, Shakespeare, and numerous others have employed speeches as techniques for achieving particular effects within larger frameworks of verbal activity. Historically, the prose of the public speech was earliest to achieve artistic perfection; hence, the methods of the speech could be and sometimes were carried over into other forms of literary activity. All of this has been a source of confusion among critics who, at times, have mistaken the verbal record of the speaking event for the speech itself, and who just as often have applied the criteria of poetic to the evaluation of verbal activity demanding other criteria.

Two broad questions pertaining to the speech as a form have been tradi-tional: Is the speech an art form? Is the verbal record of a speech to be con-sidered literature? To the first question we may apply the ancient explanation that things come into being by luck, by nature, by spontaneity, or by art. [16] The records of speech-making indicate that principles and practices have entered into the making of speeches; speeches do not come into being by nature, nor are they typically the results of chance. More akin to architecture than to music as an art, the speech is primarily a practical art form. Just as the

[15] "The Historical Interpretation of Literature," in *The Intent of the Critic*, ed. Donald A. Stauffer (Princeton: Princeton University Press, 1941), p. 57.

[16] Aristotle *Metaphysica* in *The Works of Aristotle*, VIII, A. 3. 1070^a.

architect usually has functional ends primarily in mind in the construction of houses, office buildings, and even churches, occasionally he achieves far more than merely functional ends in a Cathedral of Chartres or of Cologne.

To the question: Are speeches literature? the answer, of course, depends on the breadth of definition. If we define literature as a "nation's mind in writing," obviously all verbal activity which is recorded is literature. If we define it as a qualitative factor in verbal activity, then the speech may or may not be literature. If we restrict the term to verbal activity whose primary purpose is to induce immediate pleasurable response, then the speech is clearly not primarily a literary form, although as an incidental aspect it may produce pleasurable response. In our age, the committee for awarding the Nobel Prize for literature chose Sir Winston Churchill in preference to Ernest Hemingway, Graham Greene, and other contenders for the award in literature for his "historical and biographical presentations and for the scintillating oratory in which he has stood forth as a defender of eternal human values." [17] Thus, he takes his place beside Kipling, Shaw, Galsworthy, T. S. Eliot, and others as a "literary" figure.

I am concerned here with evaluating that which the Greeks called rhetoric. One need be under no illusion about the difficulties involved in using the term. Modern critics use it in a variety of ways. [18] Some use it to refer chiefly to the blandishments in a prose piece. Others use it to refer only to the "purple patches." Its use often does not reflect any clear effort to come to grips with the term. Thus, the literary historian, Vernon L. Parrington, writes of Lincoln: "Matter he judged to be of greater significance than manner. Few men who have risen to enduring eloquence have been so little indebted to rhetoric. Very likely his plainness of style was the result of deliberate restraint, in keeping with the simplicity of his nature." [19] Here rhetoric seems to be correlated with "manner," particularly with a style which is not plain. It presupposes a clean division between matter and manner, as if thought and the manner of expressing it were completely separate entities. On the other hand, the literary scholar and editor of Lincoln's speeches, Roy Basler, writes of Lincoln: "It would be difficult to find in all history a precise instance in which rhetoric played a more important role in human destiny than it did in Lincoln's speeches of 1858." [20] The meaning of the term here is not

---

[17] *The New York Times*, October 16, 1953, p. 25, cols. 2, 3, 4.

[18] Donald C. Bryant, "Rhetoric: Its Functions and Its Scope," *The Quarterly Journal of Speech*, XXXIX (December, 1953), 402-7.

[19] Vernon Lee Parrington, *The Romantic Revolution in America* in *Main Currents in American Thought* (New York: Harcourt, Brace & Co., 1927-30), p. 158.

[20] *Abraham Lincoln: His Speeches and His Writings* (Cleveland: The World Publishing Co., 1946), p. 28.

clear. It appears to mean something "in" the speeches—but not necessarily the speeches themselves. Such a confusion leads two critics to come to completely opposite conclusions in evaluating Lincoln's indebtedness to rhetoric. At a pole opposite from many attempts to correlate rhetoric with style, lies the recent observation of Duhamel: "Cicero's style was influenced by his rhetoric." [21] Here rhetoric is a cause of style, not correlative with it.

Because of this troublesomeness, I. A. Richards has recommended that we "would do better just to dismiss it to Limbo," [22] unless the term can be revived to mean a "study of verbal understanding and misunderstanding...." [23] Kenneth Burke, on the other hand, recommends that a strong arm be used to reclaim a traditional province, once perfectly clear, but usurped by other disciplines. [24]

Doubtless no contemporary interpretation of the term throws more light on its proper use than that of the classical systematizers of the art. "Rhetoric may be defined as the faculty of observing in any given case the available means of persuasion," observed Aristotle. The ancients included in the term all the ingredients of persuasion, the impelling fact, the reasoned argument, the strategic ordering of details, no less than the well-wrought phrase. The art of rhetoric was the art of discovering arguments, adapting them, ordering them, expressing them in clear and proper words, and of using one's personal qualities to enhance the whole to the end of achieving persuasion in an audience. It was the whole rationale of persuasive discourse. [25] The term was so used by Cicero, and Quintilian, and by vigorous eighteenth- and nineteenth-century theorists, George Campbell, Richard Whately, and others. It is also used in this way by the contemporary critic, Burke, by the Chicago school of critics, and generally by critics whose writings regularly appear in the *Quarterly Journal of Speech* and in *Speech Monographs*.

I use the term "rhetoric," then, to apply to verbal activity primarily concerned with affecting persuasion, whether it be done by writing or speaking. Rhetoric operates in the area of the contingent, where choice is to be made among alternative courses of action. Its concern is with substance as well as with form, if any arbitrary distinction is to be made. In this essay I am concerned with evaluating persuasive efficacy as it manifests itself in *oral* verbal activity, the speech. "Typically, a speech is an utterance meant to be heard and

[21] P. Albert Duhamel, "The Function of Rhetoric as Effective Expression," *Journal of the History of Ideas*, X (1949), 346.

[22] I. A. Richards, *The Philosophy of Rhetoric* (New York: Oxford University Press, 1936), p. 3.

[23] *Ibid.*, p. 23.

[24] Kenneth Burke, *A Rhetoric of Motives* (New York: Prentice-Hall Inc., 1950), Introduction, xiii.

[25] See Donald C. Bryant, "Rhetoric: Its Functions and Its Scope," *op. cit.*, 401-24.

intended to exert an influence of some kind on those who hear it," remarks Wayland M. Parrish. "Typically, also the kind of influence intended may be described as persuasion." [26]

If we do not press the analogy too far, we may compare the speech with a multi-celled organism, whose units consist of speaker, audience, place, purpose, time, and form. In order to evaluate the speech, all these elements, verbal and nonverbal, must be examined.

First, consider the position of a speaker in the persuasive situation. In every instance, some specific "I" is doing the speaking. He may be familiar to us or quite unknown. If he is known, he may be known favorably or unfavorably. To the South during the Civil War, Lincoln was a "guerrilla"; to the North, in part, at least, he was "Honest Abe." Let us note for a moment the significance of the specific "I" in the speaking situation by referring to Emerson's characterization of Disraeli:

> Disraeli, the chiffonier, wastes all his talent on the House of Commons, for the want of character. He makes a smart cutting speech, really introduces new and important distinctions. . . . But he makes at last no impression, because the hearer asks, Who are you? What is dear to you? What do you stand for? And the speech and the speaker are silent, and silence is confession. A man who has been a man has foreground and background. His speech, be it never so good, is subordinate and the least part of him, and as this man has no planet under him, but only his shoes, the hearer infers that the ground of the present argument may be no wider.[27]

Whether Emerson's judgment of Disraeli is or is not vindicated by history is not in question. The point is that when one listens to speeches, the individual "I" is an element in the situation. It may matter little in the judgment of "The Last Supper" who painted it, or of the "Moonlight Sonata," who composed it, or of *Pisan Cantos* whether the poet was or was not a traitor, but there is no gainsaying the fact that when speeches are being evaluated the speaker is of paramount importance. One asks the question, then: What are the predispositions, if any, toward the man who is giving the speech? This is a cell in the organism; it may be healthy or in some way defective. Either because of previous acquaintance or because of signs during the speech itself, the audience comes to some conclusion about the speaker, and this plays a part in the judgment. In the political campaign of 1952, Adlai Stevenson, scarcely known at all at the beginning of the campaign, was being compared with a rival candidate whose name was favorably known to millions. This could hardly fail to be a factor in the ultimate decision. Not only the speaking, but the *man*

[26] Wayland M. Parrish and Marie Hochmuth, *American Speeches* (New York: Longmans, Green & Co., 1954), p. 3.

[27] *Journals of Ralph Waldo Emerson*, eds. Edward Waldo Emerson and Waldo Emerson Forbes (Boston: Houghton Mifflin Co., 1912), VII, 503.

9

who spoke was a factor. The critic needs to note and assess the persuasive effect of "echoes and values" attaching to the person and character of the speaker. Rarely is this a simple matter, for the man is not always to be seen as a single individual having his own merits only. Men and women derive force from the symbolic relations in which they stand among others. Thus, Eisenhower became the "man of action" speaking for a nation proud of its ability to "get things done"; Clarence Darrow, according to Maloney in a study in this volume, became a champion for the downtrodden, the underdog, and spoke as the representative of a class. Thus, the impetus given to ideas set in motion by the speaker is not merely the impetus deriving from the force of one man's character, but often from the whole class which he images.

Next, let us consider the audience as a cell in this complex organism. Audiences neither come from a vacuum nor assemble in one. They come with pre-established systems of value, conditioning their perceptions. As Susanne Langer has observed, "Every society meets a new idea with its own concepts, its own tacit, fundamental way of seeing things; that is to say, *with its own questions, its peculiar curiosity.*"[28] We are not without knowledge in regard to the role of perception. We know that perception is selective; we both see and hear with a previously established set of values, theoretical, economic, aesthetic, social, political, and religious.[29] Not only do we have general sets of values that predetermine our responses, we often also have specific predispositions regarding the subject being discussed. The rhetorician discovers his potentials for persuasion in a wise regard for the prevailing attitudes in the audience. Although he need neither compromise his integrity, nor bow in subservience to an audience, he does need to understand the operating forces in the audience and select arguments that induce persuasion. He must remember that his choices are conditioned by the audience. The poem may be written with the audience thrice-removed from the creator, for the poet creates from his experience with his subject. But the speech-maker must compose his speech from the available potentials in his audience. He aims to link his propositions to their value systems, and value systems differ with age, sex, educational development, economic class, social strata, political heritage, specialized interest, and so on. The speaker is a selecter. He must exclude certain arguments and include others. He must decide how to order details and the thought patterns into which material is to be cast. All this is determined by the audience for which the speech is designed. The critic who attempts to discriminate among values without reference to the audience is doing what a rhetorical critic really cannot

[28] Susanne K. Langer, *Philosophy in a New Key* (Mentor Books; New York: The New American Library, 1948), p. 4.

[29] Charles E. Osgood, *Method and Theory in Experimental Psychology* (New York: Oxford University Press, 1953), p. 292 ff.

do. Since the audience conditioned the speaker's choices in selecting the arguments, ordering them, and expressing them, the critic must inevitably consider whether the speaker chose wisely or ill in relation to the audience. The critic's necessary tool, then, is not personal whim but clear perception of the role of choice. He must know the mood of the audience. Was it hostile, neutral, or partisan? What tensions, if any, were to be released? Was it keyed up for any particular occasion? Daniel Webster long ago called attention to the significance of occasion and audience-tone in persuasion: "True eloquence, indeed, does not consist in speech. It cannot be brought from far. Labor and learning may toil for it, but they will toil in vain. Words and phrases may be marshalled in every way, but they cannot compass it. It must exist in the man, in the subject, and in the occasion." [30] Let the critic know, then, the audience for which the speech was intended.

Third, we must consider the function of *place*. Place, of course, is not merely a physical condition. It is also a metaphysical condition, an ideological environment. We hear much of the "industrial" East, the "conservative" Midwest, the "progressive" Far West, "rumor-ridden" Washington. Speeches take place in halls, to be sure, but halls are "sacred halls," "smoke-filled rooms," places "hallowed by the memory of the sacred dead." The church is an "atmosphere" as well as a place. Place conditions both the speaker's method and the audience's reaction. People do not react in a smoke-filled room the way they do in the restrained atmosphere of the Senate gallery.

I do not intend to minimize the purely physical aspect of place, for this is sometimes important, of course. Comfort and discomfort, audibility or inaudibility may take on considerable proportions. Webster, with 100,000 people milling over Bunker Hill could not have been expected to be talking to all of them, and an inaugural crowd in a chill wind is not likely to be giving itself completely to the speaker no matter how superlative his genius. No one would expect the playing of a concerto to produce the same effect in a run-down basement room of an apartment-hotel as it does in Carnegie Hall. And no one believes that a painting hung on just any wall will look well. In evaluating speeches, the aspect of place must be recognized as a conditioning factor. "The world will little note, nor long remember what we say here, but it can never forget what they did here," Lincoln observed at Gettysburg, and generations have murmured the words as they have explored the grounds.

Fourth, is the consideration of purpose. After examining the debates in the Constitutional Convention of 1787, the historians Samuel Eliot Morison and Henry Steele Commager concluded that "the main, central and determin-

---

[30] *A Discourse in Commemoration of the Lives and Services of John Adams & Thomas Jefferson, Delivered in Faneuil Hall, Boston, August 2, 1826* (Boston: Cummings, Hilliard & Co., 1826), p. 34.

ing consideration that appears throughout the debates, is to erect a government that would be neither too strong nor too shocking to popular prejudices for adoption, and yet be sufficiently strong and well-contrived to work." [31] This analysis highlights the significant role that *purpose* plays in evaluating speech-making. At the outset, it indicates that the finished Constitutional product did not represent anyone's notion of the perfect constitution, but what the Constitutional fathers thought they could get accepted. Presumably all language is uttered with some purpose, whether it be the salutation, "Good morning," or the frankly evangelistic sermon on Sunday. These purposes control choices of materials. Whatever the end the speaker has in mind, his specific purpose is to speak with persuasive effect toward that end; his available resources for persuasion are those which can be directed toward fulfillment of purpose.

The consideration of purpose undoubtedly misleads the critics more often than any other aspect of speaking. In an age oriented toward quick and tangible evidences of success, the critic has tended to make the specific accomplishment of ends the test of rhetorical effectiveness. The number of votes in the ballot box, the amount of money collected as a result of a promotion campaign are taken to be the measure of effectiveness. They are taken to represent the fulfillment of purpose. James Hadley noted the trend in the nineteenth century and expressed concern: "Some have a simple test, and that is persuasiveness; the best oration is the most persuasive, and *vice versa,* the most persuasive is the best; for it best fulfils the end of eloquence, which is persuasion." With shrewd good sense and discrimination, Hadley continued: "The eloquence of Mike Walsh has an effect as persuasive on the collective blackguardism of New York as the eloquence of Daniel Webster has on the collective dignity and learning of the Senate or the Supreme Court. Should we therefore decide that one is no higher than the other? Now persuasiveness... is indeed an indispensable element in true eloquence. But there is another element... and that is artistic perfection...." [32] In other words, the purpose of the speaker is to discover the available means of persuasion and the appropriate questions are: Did he discover them? What is their quality?

The critic who makes the fulfillment of specific purpose the only test of eloquence is not merely misguided, he is indeed attempting the impossible. As Leonard Bloomfield has observed, "persuasive and... powerful [as] ...effect may be, it is nearly always uncertain." [33] He further observes: "In the long

[31] Samuel Eliot Morison and Henry Steele Commager, *The Growth of the American Republic* (3rd ed.; New York: Oxford University Press, 1942), I, 281.

[32] James Hadley, "Is Ancient Eloquence Superior to Modern?" *Essays, Philosophical and Critical* (New York: Holt & Williams, 1873), p. 349.

[33] Leonard Bloomfield, "Linguistic Aspects of Science," *International Encyclopedia of Unified Science*, Vol. I, No. 4, pp. 16, 17.

run, anything which adds to the viability of language has also an indirect but more pervasive effect. Even acts of speech that do not prompt any particular immediate response, may change the predisposition of the hearer for further responses: a beautiful poem, for instance, may make the hearer more sensitive to later stimuli. The general refinement and intensification of human response requires a great deal of linguistic interaction. Education or culture, or whatever name we choose to give it, depends upon the repetition and publication of a vast amount of speech." [34]

Clearly, the speaker should not be judged by the fulfillment of specific purpose alone. Who can know how many sinners were "almost" saved as a result of a revival service of Billy Graham? The function of the preacher is to use his talents toward this end, and it is by the talents, not by the accomplishment of the end merely that he should be judged. The odds against the accomplishment of a specific end may be insurmountable. Was Lincoln's First Inaugural rhetorically inferior because it did not prevent the Civil War? The eye of the critic must be focused on the methods used by the speaker and not merely on the ends achieved. It is reason and judgment, not a comptometer, that make a man a critic.

Fifth, is the factor of time and timing. Just as civilizations rise, develop, and decline, so too problems rise, grow in dimension, yield to solution, and eventually give way to other problems. Time represents a stage in the life of problems. It reflects itself in both the proposition of the speaker and in his mode of handling the problem. It likewise represents a stage in the life of feelings toward a proposition. Anyone knows that he is more susceptible to argument and discussion at one time than at another. A man who has just had lunch is not likely to become excited over the promise of release from hunger. A solution presented either prematurely or tardily will be found wanting. The man with an answer at the time when people are searching for an answer is in a much more effective position rhetorically than the man who gives an answer after doubt has already been resolved, or who offers one before the problem has become acute.

But not only are the substance of a speech and the feelings of an audience conditioned by *time*, the mode of handling data is likewise conditioned. Mode of handling is a product of a culture at a given time. The critic who tends to write off the florid style of the nineteenth century is in effect saying that according to his "more enlightened" twentieth-century taste, the nineteenth-century mode of handling was inferior. Not many of us look with undimmed eyes upon the glories of nature and describe what we see. We look with eyes conditioned to see in terms of the language habits we have inherited. The ornate language of the nineteenth century was shared by a multitude of people

[34] Leonard Bloomfield, *Language* (New York: Henry Holt & Co., 1938), p. 41.

in the century, and there is little reason to suppose that it was not as persuasive as the language of the twentieth century. Tastes vary with the times. The real question for the critic is: Does the mode of handling represent the tastes of the time? Is it adjusted to the intellectual development and the habits of the hearer? Is it in harmony with aesthetic values of the time? In the poetic age of the translators of the King James Version of the Bible, the translators wrote in God's description of the battle horse to Job:

Hast thou given the horse strength? Hast thou clothed his neck with thunder? . . . The glory of his nostrils is terrible. . . . He saith among the trumpets, Ha, Ha.

Twentieth-century translators, heeding the injunction to produce a Bible "written in language direct and clear and meaningful to people today" write as follows:

Do you give the horse his might? Do you clothe his neck with strength? . . . His majestic snorting is terrible. . . . When the trumpet sounds, he says, 'Aha! [35]

In both cases, presumably, we have the language of the people, designed to have an impact on the readers in their own centuries. Does anyone really believe the new rendering of the passage is superior? A rhetorical critic may note differences in quality, to be sure, but the scale by which one determines persuasive effect must be a scale adjusted to the time in which the product was made.

In our discussion so far we have, in the main, been concerned with a consideration of the extra-verbal aspects of persuasion. We come now to the verbal instrument itself. According to George Campbell, astute eighteenth-century rhetorical theorist and practitioner of the art of rhetoric, "there are two things in every discourse which principally claim our attention, the sense and the expression; or in other words, the thought and the symbol by which it is communicated. These may be said to constitute the soul and the body of an oration. . . ." [36]

Both ancient and contemporary thought might question the dichotomy between "the sense and the expression" as indicated by Campbell. From Aristotle to modern times competent critics have recognized that "there can be no distinction drawn, save in reflection, between form and substance. The work itself *is* matter formed. . . ." [37] The contemporary philosopher, Jordan,

[35] See Dwight MacDonald, "The Bible in Modern Undress," *The New Yorker* (November 14, 1953), pp. 179, 187.

[36] *The Philosophy of Rhetoric* (New ed., with the Author's Last Additions and Corrections; Edinburgh: Neill & Co., for Archibald Constable & Co., and John Fairbairn, Edinburgh; and T. Cadwell & W. Davies, London, 1816), I, 82, 83.

[37] John Dewey, *Art as Experience* (New York: Minton, Balch & Co., © 1934), p. 109.

14

notes that "At the point of the abstract ultimate what is said . . . and the way it is said . . . may be the same thing. . . ." [38] Experience, of course, reveals that so united are matter and form that when a speaker struggles to make his thoughts clear but fails, he in fact says something else.

Recognizing the inseparability of matter and form in any art, we may, nevertheless, in "reflection," consider the work in terms of constituents, arguments, broad structural pattern, and particular stylistic features.

Let us first look at the substance of a speech. Persuasion requires choices among alternatives. The speech presumably will consist of persuasions to induce acceptance of the speaker's point of view. Presumably this point of view is directed toward some ultimate Good. Hence, the speaker's persuasions represent directly or by implication his philosophic outlook and commitment. These persuasions will be revealed verbally in statements of fact and of opinion. "Facts cannot be selected without some personal conviction as to what is truth," [39] observes the historian, Allan Nevins. Likewise, Karl Wallace notes: "Truth is a word I shall use to describe the moment of certainty, or commitment, or decision which signals the resolution of doubt. The decision is revealed verbally as a statement of opinion or value, or as a statement of fact." [40] Accordingly, Richard Weaver remarks: "there is no honest rhetoric without a preceding dialectic," [41] that is, without an attempt to discover truth. Thus, the critic is brought face to face with the necessity of understanding and discriminating among the ideas or the truths to which the speaker has committed himself. But to evaluate the speaker's philosophy involves the critic in a discrimination of ethical values. The warning of Baskerville is well taken: ". . . today's critic often side-steps inquiry into the basic soundness of the speaker's position, offering the excuse that truth is relative, that everyone is entitled to his own opinion, and that the rhetorical critic's task is to describe and evaluate the orator's skill in his craft and not to become entangled in complex ethical considerations." [42]

The simple fact is that audiences do not respond alike to any and every opinion, that whereas the critic may think it not his function to tangle with the problem of truth and the weight of ideas, audiences which determine the

[38] E. Jordan, *Essays in Criticism* (Chicago: University of Chicago Press, 1952), p. 193.

[39] Allan Nevins, *The Gateway to History* (Boston: D. C. Heath & Co., 1938), p. 38.

[40] Karl R. Wallace, "The Field of Speech, 1953: An Overview" (A Speech, Delivered July 17, 1953, Summer Speech Conference, University of Michigan, Ann Arbor, Michigan [MS University of Illinois, Department of Speech]), p. 10.

[41] Richard M. Weaver, *The Ethics of Rhetoric* (Chicago: Henry Regnery Co., 1953), p. 25.

[42] Barnet Baskerville, "Emerson as a Critic of Oratory," *The Southern Speech Journal*, XVIII (March, 1953), 161.

degree of persuasion do so involve themselves with these matters. Ideas are a means of persuasion. Emerson responding to Webster's 7th of March speech was keenly aware of Webster's philosophic position: "Nobody doubts that there were good and plausible things to be said on the part of the South. But this is not a question of ingenuity, not a question of syllogisms, but of sides." [43] For Emerson there was always "the previous question: How came you on that side? Your argument is ingenious, your language copious, your illustrations brilliant, but your major proposition palpably absurd. Will you establish a lie?" [44] In evaluating a sermon of an American churchman, a critic recently observed: "His arguments were specious, but his rhetoric was good." That rhetoric can consist of specious arguments as well as sound ones no one will question. But that the validity and the truth of the argument has nothing to do with pronouncing the rhetoric "good" is, indeed, dubious.

The critic's function is to examine the speaker's premises, stated or implied, and to examine the truth of those premises. Inevitably he must ask such questions as: Does the orator argue from an abiding concept of the "nature of things"? from a conception of expediency? from the authority of history? from similitude? from transcendental grounds?

There are conventional means for evaluating the quality of premises. Does the premise presented "correspond" to data which may be revealed to the senses of observers? Does the truth of a premise yield to a pragmatic test? Is the truth of a premise "believed" by the many? Is the truth of a premise "self-evident"? [45] However much the critic may wish to escape discriminating among values, as an effective rhetorical critic he cannot do so.

This may not be the place to argue for any of the particular criteria of truth used through the ages. One may say that great and good men have from time to time used all of these tests, depending upon their general philosophic position. We do not ask too much when we ask a critic to reveal his philosophic position by his choice of criteria for evaluating premises. In fact, we may be paving the way for critical commentary vastly richer and more cogent than if the bases of evaluation were ignored.

Nor is the argumentative substance of the speech the critic's only concern. Persuasion represents deliberate manipulation of symbols. Symbols contain not only rational meanings. They contain experience also and represent attempts to create and release emotional tensions. Woven into the substance of argument are directives to action, terms of interpretation and valuation. Persuasion rec-

---

[43] *The Complete Works of Ralph Waldo Emerson*, ed. Edward Waldo Emerson (Centenary ed.; Boston: Houghton Mifflin & Co., 1903), XII, 225.

[44] "Eloquence," *ibid.*, VIII, 131.

[45] See C. J. Ducasse, "Propositions, Truth, and the Ultimate Criterion of Truth," *Philosophy and Phenomenological Research*, V (September—June, 1943, 1944), 317-40.

ognizes men to be creatures of desire; it also recognizes that desire provides a basis for action. Hence, the speaker's persuasions represent techniques for awakening and satisfying desire. Furthermore, within every culture are values that have authority. Thus, "virtue" was the ultimate Good for the Greeks; "courage," an ultimate Good for the Romans; "duty," an ultimate Good in early American Christian civilization. The critic examines the texture of persuasive compositions for those symbols of authority designed to evoke response. The perceptive critic must observe that since motives are not fixed, these authoritative symbols change from age to age. Whereas an early Christian civilization responded to appeals to action, presented in the name of "duty," a later civilization is activated to a greater degree by the promise of earthly "progress." On an ethical scale, we may find considerable difference between the lowest motive and the highest motive to which men will respond. The discerning critic must not only assess both extremes but he must locate the center of gravity. He need not deny the persuasive value of low motives, but he has no moral obligation to sanction the use of such motives under the label of "good" rhetoric.

"The most minute study, the widest experience in the investigation of human actions and their motives," says Gamaliel Bradford, "only make us feel more and more the shifting, terrible uncertainty of the ground under our feet." [46] The difficulty of the task gives no warrant to the critic to shirk his responsibility. Surveying the rhetoric of Hitler's *Mein Kampf*, Kenneth Burke notes: "Here is the testament of a man who swung a great people into his wake. Let us watch it carefully, and let us watch it, not merely to discover some grounds for prophesying what political move is to follow Munich, and what move to follow that move, etc.; let us try also to discover what kind of 'medicine' this medicine-man has concocted, that we may know, with greater accuracy, exactly what to guard against, if we are to forestall the concocting of similar medicine in America." [47] Such an observation suggests the responsibility of the critic. His place should be in the vanguard, not in the rear—wise-after-the-fact. He should be ready to alert a people, to warn what devices of exploitation are being exercised, by what skillful manipulations of motives men are being directed to or dissuaded from courses of action. James G. Randall asks: Was the willful manipulation of men's minds by the wily a factor in the cause of the Civil War? Is it a factor in most wars? [48] The care-

---

[46] Cited in Allan Nevins, *op. cit.*, p. 327.

[47] "The Rhetoric of Hitler's 'Battle,'" in his *The Philosophy of Literary Form* (Baton Rouge, Louisiana: Louisiana State University Press, 1941), p. 191.

[48] J. G. Randall, "A Blundering Generation," in his *Lincoln, The Liberal Statesman* (New York: Dodd, Mead & Co., 1947), pp. 36-64.

ful examination of motives must not merely furnish an amusing pastime for the critic; it is his urgent responsibility.

Pursuing our examination of aspects of form, we turn "in reflection" to the aspect of structure. Literary art, like all art, observes Daiches, "communicates significance through patterns." [49] A tragedy unravels through a pattern of exposition, complicating circumstances, climax, and denouement. A detective story lays down premises and takes its deductive course. The speech also is a structured organism and this structure must be a concern of the critic. By structure we mean, as Whitehead has suggested, "that eye for the whole chessboard, for the bearing of one set of ideas on another." [50] In speech-making this has traditionally been called *dispositio*. Aristotle defined it as "the arrangement of that which has parts, in respect of place, or of potency or of kind." [51]

Probably all people need forms, for "We take delight in recognition." [52] Whether we speak a word, a sentence, or a whole speech, intelligibility depends on form. To borrow an ancient illustration, we recognize a bronze pitcher only after it has taken form from a mass of bronze and *become* a bronze pitcher. [53] In the laboratory, speech takes on a visual shape, as is shown by spectograph readings. In ordinary communication, meanings are in part determined by organization. Thus, "an rhetoric art is" yields intelligibility by assembling the elements: Rhetoric is an art.

The critic must observe the contribution made by thought pattern to the effectiveness of the whole. A thought pattern is something more than external manifestation of a beginning, a middle, and an end. It is a functional balancing of parts against each other, a determination of the relative strength of arguments. It is reflected in proportion and placing. The speaker who sandwiches weak arguments between strong arguments has at least considered force as a factor in persuasion. Structure reveals the speaker's assessment of his audience in the placement of parts, whether they are partisans, neutrals, or opponents, or are a significant mixture of two or more. To that extent, at least, it represents the psychology of the audience rather than the psychology of the speaker. [54]

We come finally to that most elusive of all aspects of the speaking act—style, still another aspect of form. Thonssen and Baird, referring to a rhetorical critic of the last century, have remarked, "Jebb is more deeply concerned

[49] David Daiches, *A Study of Literature for Readers and Critics* (Ithaca, New York: Cornell University Press, 1948), p. 77.

[50] A. N. Whitehead, *The Aims of Education & Other Essays* (New York: The Macmillan Co., 1929), p. 18.

[51] *Metaphysica, op. cit.,* Δ. 19. 1022^b.

[52] Donald A. Stauffer, "Introduction: The Intent of the Critic," *op. cit.,* p. 24.

[53] Aristotle *Metaphysica, Λ.* 3. 1070^a.

[54] See Kenneth Burke, "Psychology and Form," in *Counter-Statement* (2nd ed.; Los Altos, California: Hermes Publications, 1953), p. 31.

18

with the orator's style than are most present-day critics. In this regard, he is, perhaps, less the rhetorical and more the literary critic." [55] Rhetorical critics unfortunately tend to be less interested in style than they ought to be, for, as Lasswell has noted, "style is an indispensable feature of every configuration of meaning in any process of communication." [56]

Partly because of the difficulty, and partly because of confusion with the function of literary critics, contemporary rhetorical critics have given the matter little attention. Preoccupation with trying to distinguish written from oral style has often yielded results both fruitless and misleading. "Not only are contemporary critics...unable to distinguish oral from written style," observes Schrader, "but they are also confused as to the nature of style itself." [57] "Their statements are often based on untenable assumptions, and their conclusions are even contradictory." [58]

If, as Wichelns has remarked, the problem of the orator is "so to present ideas as to bring them into the consciousness of his hearers," [59] the neglect of style becomes serious, and mistaken notions about it equally hazardous.

It is significant that the two living orators who have achieved greatest distinction for their oratory are both sensitive stylists. Churchill has a feeling for the nobility of the English sentence, and Stevenson's style became a campaign issue in the election of 1952. In general, the style of our orators has been so undistinguished as to escape the notice of listeners, but this may in part account for the lack of impact that many speakers have had on their age. It does not justify the neglect of style by rhetorical critics. If the testimony of the centuries to the importance of style needed support, we could find it in an unsuspected source—from one of the great atomic scientists of the twentieth century. Said J. Robert Oppenheimer:

The problem of doing justice to the implicit, the imponderable and the unknown is, of course, not unique to politics. It is always with us in science, it is with us in the most trivial of personal affairs, and it is one of the great problems of writing and of all forms of art. The means by which it is solved is sometimes called style. It is style which complements affirmation with limitation and with humility; it is style which makes it possible to act effectively, but not absolutely; it is style which, in the domain of foreign policy, enables us to find a harmony between the pursuit of ends essential to us, and the regard for the views, the sensibilities, the aspirations of

[55] Lester Thonssen and A. Craig Baird, *op. cit.*, p. 257.

[56] Harold Lasswell, Nathan Leites, and Associates, *Language of Politics* (New York: George W. Stewart, Publishers, Inc., 1949), p. 38.

[57] Helen Wheatley Schrader, "A Linguistic Approach to the Study of Rhetorical Style" (Ph.D. dissertation, Northwestern University, 1949), p. 17.

[58] *Ibid.*, p. 15.

[59] "The Literary Criticism of Oratory," *op. cit.*, p. 190.

those to whom the problem may appear in another light; it is above all style through which power defers to reason.[60]

Thus, in its simplest manifestation, style is a mode of "ingratiation"; [61] in its most complex aspect it is the "ultimate morality of mind." [62] It is an "aesthetic sense" says Whitehead, "based on admiration for the direct attainment of a foreseen end, simply and without waste." It is an index of a preference for "good work." [63]

That audiences have value systems pertaining to style is well known. Two thousand years ago Aristotle called attention to reaction tendencies of listeners in regard to stylistic matters: "The effect which lectures produce on a hearer depends on his habits; for we demand the language we are accustomed to, and that which is different from this seems not in keeping but somewhat unintelligible and foreign because of its unwontedness.... Thus some people do not listen to a speaker unless he speaks mathematically, others unless he gives instances, while others expect him to cite a poet as a witness. And some want to have everything done accurately, while others are annoyed with accuracy, either because they cannot follow the connexion of thoughts or because they regard it as pettifoggery." [64]

Aristotle's statement has been proved valid by the test of centuries. The language of persuasion must be conditioned by the needs of the audience, and the needs of the audience differ considerably. As we remarked earlier, the ideals of any age, regarding style, may differ. The late John Livingston Lowes said of the King James Version of the Bible: "Its phraseology has become part and parcel of our common tongue—bone of its bone and flesh of its flesh. Its rhythms and cadences, its turns of speech, its familiar imagery, its very words, are woven into the texture of our literature, prose and poetry alike.... The English of the Bible... is characterized not merely by a homely vigour and pithiness of phrase, but also by a singular nobility of diction and by a rhythmic quality which is, I think, unrivalled in its beauty." [65] The twentieth-century revisers of the Bible were enjoined to "combine accuracy with the simplicity, directness, and spiritual power" of the King James Version, as well as to make it "more readable for the American public of today." [66]

[60] "The Open Mind," *The Bulletin of the Atomic Scientists*, V, No. 1 (January, 1949), 5.

[61] Kenneth Burke, *Permanence and Change* (New York: The New Republic, 1935), p. 71.

[62] A. N. Whitehead, *op. cit.*, p. 19.

[63] *Ibid.*, p. 19.

[64] *Metaphysica*, a. 3. 995^a.

[65] "The Noblest Monument of English Prose," in his *Essays in Appreciation* (Boston: Houghton Mifflin Co., 1936), pp. 3-5, *passim*.

[66] Dwight MacDonald, *op. cit.*, p. 175.

Style is in no sense magic. It is rather a manifestation of a speaker's or writer's temper and outlook. It has the capacity to name objects, to evaluate them, and to incite feelings toward them. In its objective manifestations it pertains to the selection of words and the ordering of them, and in this a preference for "good work" may be shown.

"Style to be good must be clear," notes Aristotle, "as is proved by the fact that speech which fails to convey a plain meaning will fail to do just what a speech has to do." [67] Beyond clearness, of course, lie other properties: appropriateness, distinctive language constructions, rhythm. All of these have concern for the analyst of rhetorical style, for they are means by which the orator reaches the minds of the listener. They are means by which he seeks identification and ingratiation.

For want of better methods, the rhetorical critic sometimes satisfies himself with a simple enumeration of stylistic devices of the speaker. Unless the enumerations are particularizations of the pervasive tones and effects sought by the speaker, such enumeration probably serves little purpose. We need to ask: What is language doing to further the end of ingratiation or identification? If, for instance, the prevailing tone of a speech is "humorous," we might expect language to behave in such a way as to produce humor. Hence, the rhetorical critic would look to language constructions, the diction, the characteristics of rhythm which contribute to the prevailing tone. If style is the man himself, then a close scrutiny of the details of style should tell us what manner of man is doing the speaking, and in what relationship he conceives himself to be with his audience. If it is style which "complements affirmation with limitation and with humility"; if it is style which "makes it possible to act effectively, but not absolutely"; if it is style which "in the domain of foreign policy, enables us to find a harmony between the pursuit of ends essential to us, and the regard for the views, the sensibilities, the aspirations of those to whom the problem may appear in another light"; if it is style "through which power defers to reason"—then, to look to style for manifestations of the groundswells and tensions of our times, for manifestations of healthy states and unhealthy ones must become the imperative task of the critic concerned with the implications of his art for the nation and the world. May not the simple metaphor be the harbinger of death and destruction, or the cock's crow of an era of good feeling as well as a literary tool in the grammar books?

These are the ingredients of the rhetorical situation which must be examined for their contribution to the persuasive efficacy of the whole. As one may observe, some of them are verbal aspects, others are nonverbal. Just as in drama many elements are harmonized to give delight to an audience, so too

---

[67] *Rhetorica*, iii. 2. 1404[b].

in the rhetorical situation many elements contribute to the end of persuasion. The total organism is the concern of the critic.

Evaluating Speeches of the Past

Whether the efforts of the critic are focused on speaking events in which he is a participant or on speaking events of the past, the problem is essentially the same. His aims are to evaluate rhetorical effort or to account for effectiveness or ineffectiveness in rhetorical situations. When the critic centers his attention on events of the past, he discovers that his problem increases considerably. He is confronted with the task of trying to see the orator perfecting a strategy to encompass a situation in which he himself is an actor. Not only do the speeches of public men represent the aspirations of the nation, they foreshadow the shape of things to come. Everyone recalls the majestic peroration of Lincoln's address at Gettysburg, "that this nation, under God, shall have a new birth of freedom—and that government of the people, by the people, for the people, shall not perish from the earth." It was not only a summing-up, it was a direction for the future. "Seated on the roaring loom of time," says Nevins, "for six thousand years man has woven a seamless garment. But that garment is invisible and intangible save where the dyes of written history fall upon it, and forever preserve it as a possession of generations to come." [68]

When a student concerns himself with the speeches of the past, he tries to obtain a view of the conditions, limitations, and potentialities of the leadership of speakers in all spheres, political, economic, social, cultural. He tries to discover the ideas which have been generated, the conditions of their acceptance or rejection, the scope, dimension, and intensity of concerted action. The critic of rhetoric must endeavor to see events in terms of their yet unactualized future, free from all events which were subsequent. To recover the implications of time, place, attitudes of both speaker and audience, the symbolic fitness of the speaker, the level of cultural development and taste becomes an almost insurmountable task. Not only are the nonverbal aspects of the situation capricious, but the verbal aspects are also fraught with difficulties. What was said on any given occasion may become quite blurred by the passing of time, or by the editorial hand of publishers and relatives of speakers who often want to make the speaker appear in light other than that which glowed at the time. The critic must search for the authentic record, however stony the path which leads to its discovery. If one is not evaluating the original, he is obviously evaluating something different from the original. The crumbling ruins of the Parthenon, however suggestive they may be of the beauty of the original

[68] Allan Nevins, *op. cit.*, p. 5.

structure, leave the spectator with something to be desired, and the Elgin marbles in the British Museum are not a satisfying substitute.

Rhetoric being essentially a process whereby means are adapted to ends, it is imperative that the critic not only know what the ends were but what resources were available at the time to secure these ends. To the extent that the critic is able to determine this, he may function effectively.

"Our common humanity is best studied in the most eminent examples that it has produced of every type of human excellence," [69] observed the historian H. W. C. Davis. Human excellence has sometimes manifested itself in speechmaking. Human effort has sometimes been directed to the end of giving clearer vision and safer passage into an unknown future. In this, the orator has shared eminently. Sometimes asserting or reasserting human values, sometimes helping to resolve conflicts of national or international scope and dimension, the speaker has through his art attempted to point the way to a better life. In searching for effective methods for evaluating the impact of words, we search for methods whereby we may criticize present assumptions about human behavior and the forces which have operated to produce our culture.

[69] Cited in Morris R. Cohen, *The Meaning of Human History* (La Salle, Illinois: Open Court Publishing Co., 1947), p. 224.

Alexander Hamilton

by BOWER ALY

Alexander Hamilton was born on the island of Nevis in the West Indies. The date of his birth is a vexed question; most of his biographers accept January 11, 1757. After somewhat desultory schooling in Christianstadt and some experience working in a country store, Hamilton went to the mainland in October, 1772.* In preparation for college entrance he attended the grammar school kept by Francis Barber at Elizabethtown, New Jersey, and entered King's College in the fall of 1773. Apparently Hamilton pursued his studies with diligence but not without attention to the controversy then raging between the colonies and Great Britain. In 1775, he quit his studies to enter the revolutionary army. As captain of artillery and later as aide-de-camp to Washington, he gave distinguished service to the American forces. During the war Hamilton was married to Elizabeth, the daughter of General Philip Schuyler, a leader in political, social, and business affairs in the State of New York. Following his marriage he entered into the practice of law, which was thereafter his profession and means of livelihood; but his practice was subject to interruptions occasioned by public service. Hamilton was a member of the legislature of the State of New York; of the Annapolis Convention (1786); of the Constitutional Convention (1787); and of the New York Convention which ratified the Constitution (1788). Under Washington he was the first Secretary of the Treasury and after his retirement continued to exert a primary influence on public affairs, including the policies of the Adams administration. Recognized leader of the Federalists, he found his political fortunes declining with the fall of that party from favor; but the direction which he had given the new government, particularly in policy and administration, continues to this day. He died in New York on July 12, 1804, following a duel with Aaron Burr, and is buried in Trinity Churchyard in Manhattan.

So far as the record goes, Alexander Hamilton's career as a public speaker began on July 6, 1774, when as a young collegian he addressed the citizens of New York at a meeting in the "Fields," now City Hall Park. The career

* Concerning the circumstances of Hamilton's life, this statement follows the conventional biographies. But for a revision of the received account of his early years, see among others the article by Harold Larson, "Alexander Hamilton: The Fact and Fiction of His Early Years," *The William and Mary Quarterly*, Third Series, Vol. IX, No. 2 (April, 1952), 139-51.

was ended only with his death. In the tumultuous years intervening, Hamilton witnessed and participated in the rebellion against the British government in North America, in the formation of "The League of Friendship," in the establishment of free and independent commonwealths under the Continental Congress, in the measures taken during the critical years 1783 to 1789, in the formation of the federal union, in the founding of a national government, and in the fateful decisions governing national administrative policy. He was a major force in the Federalist party and observed apprehensively the rise of the partisans of democracy under the leadership of Aaron Burr in New York and Thomas Jefferson in Virginia. Looking abroad, he watched as closely as a busy man could the course of affairs in Europe: the origin and progress of the revolution in France and the rise of Napoleon Bonaparte; the preparations made and the measures executed in Britain for her survival; and the power of Spain diminishing relative to that of other European states. Talleyrand observed that Hamilton "...had divined Europe." [1] Hamilton's generation was obviously one of change and of developing contention and controversy. It was also a generation in which Hamilton "...more than any other man, did the thinking of the time." [2]

In what rhetorical atmosphere did Hamilton breathe and live? What kind of man was he? What were his ways of persuasion and what were the results of his efforts to influence public opinion?

The Rhetorical Atmosphere

A popular conception, shared to a degree even by some persons who should know better, is that the American Revolution was generated by a mass of patriots who united to cast off the yoke of a foreign tyrant and immediately instituted by public acclaim the government under which the American people have lived ever since. Insofar as public discussion was required, it proceeded in a gentle spirit of sweetness and light permeated by the love that brothers bear each other. This conception could hardly be more mistaken.

The sources disclose that the American Revolution was begun by a small band of men who believed themselves to be struggling for the rights of Englishmen. Only by degrees did they come to assert the right to independence and then only over the objections of a highly influential and vocal group of their fellow citizens. During the Revolution the leaders were constantly beset by

---

[1] Charles Maurice de Talleyrand-Perigord, *Étude sur la république...*, p. 192. Quoted in George Shea, *The Life and Epoch of Alexander Hamilton: A Historical Study* (Boston: Houghton, Mifflin & Co., 1881), p. 35.

[2] Statement by Judge Ambrose Spencer. Quoted in Henry Cabot Lodge, *Alexander Hamilton* (Boston: Houghton, Mifflin & Co., 1882), p. 277.

opposition to the movement, by apathy in the populace, and by disagreements among their supporters. After the defeat of the British forces, controversy continued. Such allegiance to a national state as had developed during the war of independence tended to disintegrate. Commonwealths disagreed with each other. A new national constitution and government were proposed and formed only against the strong opposition of such outstanding leaders as Willie Jones of North Carolina, Patrick Henry of Virginia, and George Clinton of New York. When, in spite of protest, the new government was finally erected, disagreements immediately arose; and differences of opinion, far from being expressed uniformly in the sedate language appropriate to the forum, were often couched in violent terms both in speeches and in the press.

Perhaps fortunately, the good that men said in those days lived after them; their evil words were often interred with their bones. But anyone who needs to understand the public discussion of Hamilton's generation should face the facts: it was frequently coarse, crude, and violent. Only in a highly charged atmosphere could George Washington have been called a patron of fraud, a hypocrite, and an impostor. Only at the lowest level of scurrilous doggerel could Thomas Jefferson have been accused of cohabiting with his own slaves to produce children for sale in the markets. Only in a time of unrestrained language could a newspaper have published the statement that "...as far as his maternal descent can be traced [Alexander Hamilton] was the son of an Irish Camp Girl." [3] Yet the statements were made; and they describe a level at which some public discussion took place in Hamilton's time. When the adoption of the Constitution was under debate, charges and counter-charges of lying and of bearing false witness were made and printed in the public press. The proposed Constitution was referred to by its opponents as a trap baited with illustrious names to catch the liberties of the people. [4] Those who favored the new Constitution declared that their opponents were circulating handbills fraught with sophistry and falsehood. [5] In an account not remarkable for its felicity, one controversialist reported a dream in which he observed his opponent's venerable shape changed "into a bladder of wind, which laid before the fire of criticisms, instantly burst, and left nothing but small stink and garbage behind!" [6]

Perhaps no better description of some of the levels of public discourse employed during Hamilton's lifetime can be found than the one which he provides in the pamphlet wherewith he destroyed his private reputation in defense of his honor as a citizen and public man:

[3] *Aurora and General Advertiser*, March 17, 1798.
[4] *New York Journal and Weekly Register*, November 1, 1787.
[5] *Daily Advertiser*, December 4, 1787.
[6] *Daily Advertiser*, March 1, 1787.

A principal engine, by which this spirit endeavours to accomplish its purposes is that of calumny. It is essential to its success that the influence of men of upright principles, disposed and able to resist its enterprises, shall be at all events destroyed. Not content with traducing their best efforts for the public good, with misrepresenting their purest motives, with inferring criminality from actions innocent or laudable, the most direct falsehoods are invented and propagated, with undaunted effrontery and unrelenting perseverance. Lies often detected and refuted are still revived and repeated, in the hope that the refutation may have been forgotten or that the frequency and boldness of accusation may supply the place of truth and proof. The most profligate men are encouraged, probably bribed, certainly with patronage if not with money, to become informers and accusers. And when tales, which their characters alone ought to discredit, are refuted by evidence and facts which oblige the patrons of them to abandon their support, they still continue in corroding whispers to wear away the reputations which they could not directly subvert.[7]

An understanding of the rhetorical atmosphere of Hamilton's time accounts for some of the anomalies in the history of his reputation and suggests some of the values of his contribution to public discussion in his generation.

Hamilton's Character and Reputation

Most of the great men of Hamilton's generation have outlived the slanders current in the polemic of their day. Even Jefferson, whose reputation suffered an eclipse following the Civil War, is now restored to public favor. But Hamilton, while respected by some and admired by a few, is still sometimes distrusted as an enemy of the common man, a friend only of the rich and well-born. That this misconception should endure is unfortunate not only for Hamilton's memory but for the public welfare.

Hamilton's philosophy comprehended a profound belief in the virtue and efficacy of personal liberty. No less than Jefferson, Hamilton was the enemy of every form of tyranny over the mind of man. In his belief in freedom, Hamilton was not remarkably different from the other children of the Enlightenment; he was different from many of them in understanding clearly, as he thought, the means by which freedom can be obtained and kept. Only under a government strong enough to maintain both itself and the liberty of every citizen could free men be secure. In a state of anarchy no man is free; all are subject first to nameless fears and eventually to the tyrants who play upon them. Did Hamilton, as was charged, respect the British political society? Then it was primarily because the British people, above all others, had learned

[7] Alexander Hamilton, *Observations on Certain Documents Contained in No. v & vi of "The History of the United States for the Year 1796," in which the Charge of Speculation against Alexander Hamilton, Late Secretary of the Treasury, is Fully Refuted* (Philadelphia: Printed for John Fenno, by John Bioren, 1797), pp. 3-4.

27

to maintain a strong government, able at once to restrain itself and to protect the individual man against infringement of his rights. In Hamilton's opinion the dignity of the free man was simply not compatible with a state of anarchy. Hamilton disbelieved profoundly in all dictatorships, including that of the proletariat.

How is a government strong enough to protect both itself and its citizens to be established and maintained? Obviously, by some means that would gain the allegiance of all classes of people and so divide its own powers that no one element could become tyrannical. Before pragmatism, Hamilton was a pragmatist. His instinct was for the practical, for what works. No visionary, he could nevertheless prevision circumstances and establish courses to work naturally toward desirable ends. Possessed of rare insight into probable courses of action, he had the gift of imagining not fantasy but fact. Hamilton assumed, as did Aristotle in an earlier and Madison in a contemporary time, that men could be safely counted on for the long run to act only in their own interest or in what they conceived to be their interest. The self-interests of men should be so employed as to work for rather than against the common good. Without being original in the idea, Hamilton saw men divided into two classes: those who own property and those who do not. He observed that those who own and those who do not behave in different ways in political and social groups. Eager to obtain the allegiance of all classes for a central government, he sponsored measures to obtain the support of men of property—the assumption of the state debts, the founding of a national bank, the raising and maintaining of the public credit. These measures are remembered and have sometimes served to stigmatize Hamilton as the friend of the mercantile and the moneyed classes.

Yet Hamilton was eager also to gain the allegiance of men without property to a central government strong enough to maintain the ordered liberty which he cherished. Accordingly, he sponsored public education as a foundation of responsible government. In a day when the proposal was considered extreme, Hamilton advocated manhood suffrage—not so much because of theoretical conceptions as because the right to vote would provide every citizen with an attachment to the government. Significantly, at that troubled point where the rights of men and the rights of property met most urgently—in the system of slavery—Hamilton stood for abolition.

Hamilton's Method

As a public man Hamilton employed every avenue to influence opinion. His pamphlets and addresses to the editors of the newspapers were speeches in print, rhetorical adaptations to the means available. No one can understand

Hamilton's public address from a study of his speeches alone. Far less than other celebrated speakers was he a professional orator. He was first of all a man of strong motivation, of energetic opinion, and of great aptitude for the management of public business. His power of effective statement he exercised at will in public speaking or in the public press as a means to an end. From his first pamphlets, which were written as *apologia* for the American Revolution, to his last extensive publication attacking President Jefferson's message to Congress, he demonstrated a capacity for surveying an argumentative field, for analyzing a persuasive problem, and for discovering a method of statement that will bear comparison with any discourse in the history of America. In *The Continentalist*, precursor both of *The Federalist* and of the Constitution, Hamilton supplied one of the happiest examples of his gift for analysis and of his ability to employ disjunction as a means of demonstration. In the penultimate paragraph he states succinctly his political creed:

There is something noble and magnificent in the perspective of a great Federal Republic, closely linked in the pursuit of a common interest, tranquil and prosperous at home, respectable abroad; but there is something proportionably diminutive and contemptible in the prospect of a number of petty States, with the appearance only of union, jarring, jealous, and perverse, without any determined direction, fluctuating and unhappy at home, weak and insignificant by their dissensions in the eyes of other nations.[8]

As in *The Continentalist* so in *The Federalist* Hamilton exemplified the power of cogent reasoning operating upon evidence observed and events foreseen. Long the object of study by the political scientist and the jurisconsult, *The Federalist* is of no less interest to the rhetorician. Two aspects of the work considered as polemic require mention:

1. In conception and in execution the papers raised the level of controversy concerning the proposed constitution to a place not often reached in political argument. In *The Federalist,* Hamilton and his collaborators followed faithfully the Aristotelian advice:

In a political debate the man who is forming a judgment is making a decision about his own vital interests. There is no need, therefore, to prove anything except that the facts are what the supporter of a measure maintains they are.[9]

[8] *The Works of Alexander Hamilton,* ed. Henry Cabot Lodge (12 vols.; Federal Edition; New York and London: G. P. Putnam's Sons, 1904), I, 286-87. (Referred to hereinafter as *Works*, Lodge.)

[9] Aristotle, *Rhetoric*, 1354b.

Hamilton wrote most of the eighty-five issues of *The Federalist*. See Douglas Adair, "The Authorship of the Disputed Federalist Papers," *The William and Mary Quarterly,* Third Series, Vol. I, No. 2 (April, 1944), 97-122; No. 3 (July, 1944), 235-64.

2. In addressing an argument at high level to the American people, the authors of *The Federalist* paid their fellow citizens a high compliment; for they assumed members of an audience able to follow a reasoned description and willing to free themselves from the difficulties common to hearers generally. In this again they followed an Aristotelian principle:

The right thing in speaking really is that we should be satisfied not to annoy our hearers, without trying to delight them: we ought in fairness to fight our case with no help beyond the bare facts: nothing, therefore, should matter except the proof of those facts.[10]

Just as Hamilton's pamphlets are speeches adapted to print, so his speeches are the pamphlets stated for a listening audience. His basic conceptions did not change. From a mature and well-rounded system of thought and theory of action Hamilton drew central ideas to expound as occasion demanded in writing and speaking.

Some of Hamilton's most significant and perhaps most effective speeches were addressed to audiences of one—to those who received the letters that now and again he chose to write on matters of grave concern to himself and to his conception of national welfare. In an amazing letter composed while he was aide-de-camp to Washington and subject to all the distractions that office involved, Hamilton set forth to James Duane, then a member of the Continental Congress, a remedy for the difficulties of the Articles of the Confederation. In 1780, while he was still in the army, he wrote to Robert Morris a remarkable letter in which he set forth the argument for the essential principles later embodied in the national banking system. In letters to James McHenry, then Secretary of War, he set forth in great detail opinions and counsels concerning the military establishment. To Thomas Jefferson he wrote concerning coinage and the mint. To George Washington he wrote on many questions including, for example, the maintenance of the national credit, the behavior of the French envoy, and the correct policy to pursue toward Great Britain. His letters, like his pamphlets, are distinguished by acute observation, cogent reasoning, and characteristic judgment, of which the following is an example:

It is necessary, then, to reflect, however painful the reflection, that gratitude is a duty, a sentiment, which between nations can rarely have any solid foundation. Gratitude is only due to a kindness or service, the predominant object of which is the interest or benefit of the party to whom it is performed. Where the interest or benefit of the party performing is the predominant cause of it, however there may result a debt, in cases in which there is not an immediate adequate and reciprocal advantage, there can be no room for the sentiment of gratitude. Where there is

[10] Aristotle, *Rhetoric*, 1404a.

30

such an advantage, there is then not even a debt. If the motive of the act, instead of being the benefit of the party to whom it was done, should be a compound of the interest of the party doing it and of detriment to some other, of whom he is the enemy and the rival, there is still less room for so noble and refined a sentiment. This analysis will serve as a test of our true situation in regard both to France and Spain.[11]

In fact, Hamilton's pamphlets and letters deal with every one of the main matters on which all men deliberate and on which statesmen make speeches: ways and means, war and peace, national defense, imports and exports, and legislation.

One major difference existed between the conduct of argument by letter or pamphlet and the address to a listening audience. Both the letter and the pamphlet had to effect the writer's proposition without the assistance of his presence. An occasional letter and all the pamphlets appeared without the help—or hindrance—of the writer's name. Merely to list the pseudonyms which Hamilton employed, after the custom of his time, to disguise his authorship is to suggest the extent of his engagement in the controversy of his day:

A Sincere Friend to America, Publius, Civis, Fact, Observer, Phocion, Pacificus, No Jacobin, Americanus, Camillus, Horatius, Titus Manlius, Detector, Americus, Pericles, Tully, An American, Catullus, Metellus, A Plain Honest Man, and Lucius Crassus.

Argument in Person: *Hamilton's Presence*

When Hamilton sought to adapt his ideas to a listening audience, he discovered both opportunities and problems.

Paradoxically, one of the problems he sometimes encountered was his own reputation for ability at persuasion. Men who valued their own opinions and wished never to change them were reluctant to subject their arguments to Hamilton's power of penetration or themselves to his personal charm. To lay one's opinions open to Hamilton's inspection was to run the risk of having to modify or reject them, a possibility not attractive to persons of settled mind. Doubtless a fear of Hamilton's eloquence thus entered into the decision of the House of Representatives to decline his request to appear personally before that body in order to present his plan for support of the public credit. Even some of Hamilton's friends, thinking that his presence might be disturbing, preferred to have his report in writing. If read from the printed page or by a clerk, the report would stand on its own merits, divested of the persuasive influence that Hamilton's presence would add. Accordingly, even though Elias

[11] *Works*, Lodge, IV, 322.

Boudinot suggested that the members of the House might not be able to comprehend the matter without oral presentation, Elbridge Gerry, Fisher Ames, and the other members of the House were all for having a written report. They thus unwittingly established a precedent which related the Cabinet more closely to the executive than to the legislative branch of the federal government.

Hamilton's reputation for brilliance, allied to that of his eloquence, also created a problem for him as an orator. Ingenious men, it was thought, may say ingenious things. Hamilton's experience recalls the demagogic oration attributed by Shakespeare to Mark Antony:

> I come not, friends, to steal away your hearts:
> I am no orator, as Brutus is;
> But, as you know me all, a plain blunt man. . . .[12]

Although he might steal away hearts, Hamilton could never have assumed the character of a plain man. In the tradition of British and American politics he was thus suspect; for many of the voters and their representatives preferred a man to be dull and safe rather than brilliant and disturbing.

Yet Hamilton's oratory also suffered from his bluntness, from his unwillingness always to be tactful. Gouverneur Morris, who knew Hamilton well, suggested that his want of hypocrisy was his greatest liability. A firm believer in free, representative, and responsible government, Hamilton despised the demagogue and all his works. Many instances could be cited in which his expressions revealed at least a trace of sentiments which, like the following from his pen, are hardly calculated to win friends in great numbers:

For my part, I am not much attached to the *Majesty of the multitude* . . . I consider them in general as very ill qualified to *judge* for themselves what government will best suit their peculiar situations; nor is this to be wondered at:—The science of Government is not easily understood.[13]

Hamilton's skepticism concerning human virtues was not limited to the poor. The rich also had their characteristic vices, as Hamilton suggested in one of his speeches at the New York Convention for the Ratification of the Constitution:

Experience has by no means justified us in the supposition that there is more virtue in one class of men than in another. Look through the rich and the poor of the community, the learned and the ignorant. Where does virtue predominate? The difference indeed consists, not in the quantity, but kind, of vices which are incident to various classes; and here the advantage of character belongs to the wealthy. Their

[12] *Julius Caesar*, Act III, Scene ii.
[13] *Daily Advertiser*, October 17, 1787.

vices are probably more favorable to the prosperity of the state than those of the indigent, and partake less of moral depravity.[14]

After the disagreement with Madison, when Hamilton came more and more to be regarded as the protégé—or patron—of the rich and well-born, his reputation doubtless suffered among those who regarded themselves as poor and perhaps not particularly well-born. Hamilton's membership in the Society of the Cincinnati, his kinship by marriage to the patrician Schuyler family, his rapid rise to power and his position of pre-eminence in the federal government all made him subject to attack by political enemies. Doubtless many a veteran who had sold his pay at distress prices was not well pleased to learn that under Hamilton's policy the speculator who bought it had received payment at face value. Opposition to the funding of the state debts, suspicion of speculation in the state funds by persons known to Hamilton, sympathy for the unfortunate victims of the Whiskey Rebellion—all these were factors in public opinion which must have affected Hamilton's appeal to an audience.

Yet in the elements of weakness there was strength. Hamilton had risen to power under the aegis of George Washington, respected by nearly all Americans as the hero, the modern Fabius. If Hamilton was powerful, power attracts as well as repels. If the action in the Whiskey Rebellion was unpopular in some quarters, it was lauded in others; and furthermore it was reminiscent of Hamilton's service to the Revolution—as, indeed, was his membership in the Society of the Cincinnati.

Among Hamilton's unqualified assets was his characteristic appeal to reason. Even men who could not follow a close argument were doubtless flattered to have one addressed to them. Hamilton's reputation for logic, for cogency, and for reasoned argument increased his personal standing, which in turn aided him in obtaining a full and favorable hearing.

Another of Hamilton's assets must surely have been his personal appearance.[15] In his mature years he was a well-built and handsome man of fine address. Not large—he was about five feet seven inches in height—he was lithe and graceful in all his movements, without the affectation of self-importance which sometimes afflicts the orator and public man. His erect bearing betrayed perhaps a trace of his military experience, but apparently the dignity of manner to which his command of his subject matter entitled him never

---

[14] Jonathan Elliot, *The Debates in the Several State Conventions on the Adoption of the Federal Constitution* ... (Philadelphia: J. B. Lippincott Co., 1901), II, 257.

[15] A number of likenesses of Hamilton exist, including the portrait by Trumbull, probably the best-known. Other likenesses were done by Pine, by Sharpless, and by Robertson. The statue by Partridge, which now stands near Hamilton Hall on the campus of Columbia University, is thought to be well executed. The iconography of Alexander Hamilton has not received the systematic study that it deserves.

33

became stereotyped into the pomposity of the pseudo-orator. His speeches were delivered consistently with notable directness, energy, and grace.

Hamilton's countenance, which could be severe in repose, was animated in speaking. In private discourse it was sometimes merry. He had a Roman nose, a strong chin, a fair complexion, and reddish-brown hair. The most notable aspect of his countenance was his deep-set, deep-blue eyes. On occasion he was said to captivate a group with an engaging smile. Hamilton followed the fashions of his day. Neither slovenly nor foppish, he was careful of his personal appearance.

Conflicting testimony exists concerning Hamilton's delivery. One who heard him in the Constitutional Convention in Philadelphia thought his voice was weak. But contrary evidence suggests that his voice was agreeable in the highest degree. He spoke with energy and normally employed forceful gestures. William Pierce described Hamilton as "... rather a convincing speaker than a blazing orator."[16] James Kent described Hamilton's appearance before the Bar of New York in *Livingston* v. *Hoffman* as "... fluent, argumentative, ardent, and accompanied with great emphasis of manner and expression."[17]

Argument in Person: Hamilton's Composition

In appearing before an audience, Hamilton never relied solely on his charming presence and engaging manner. His speeches uniformly demonstrated an active intelligence energetically at work. Among the marked characteristics of his oral style were the attention given to transitions, the tendency to amplify, and the use of the direct question addressed to his hearers. Although the extant texts of his speeches are perhaps inadequate to justify strong conclusions concerning the minutiae of his style, they provide clear evidence of his understanding of the needs of the listener: to be forewarned of a change in direction, to have a central idea expanded meaningfully, and to hear questions as well as answers.

Hamilton's speeches reveal many instances of clear transition. If the line of the argument was not immediately perspicuous, he introduced such a phrase as "Without dwelling any longer on this subject, I shall proceed to the question immediately before the committee."[18] Or, on concluding one part

[16] William Pierce, "Character Sketches of Delegates to the Federal Convention," Max Farrand, ed., *The Records of the Federal Convention of 1787* (New Haven, 1911), III, 89.

[17] James Kent, "Address before the Law Association," New York, October 21, 1832. Extract quoted in George Shea, *op. cit.*, p. 436.

[18] Elliot, *Debates*, II, 235.

of his covering of the subject, he turned with proper notice to his audience to a second: "But, dismissing these reflections, let us consider how far the arrangement is in itself entitled to the approbation of this body. We will examine it upon its own merits."[19] On still another occasion he provided a characteristic transition simply by announcing the new subject: "I now proceed to consider the objection with regard to the number of representatives, as it now stands."[20] No listener giving reasonably thoughtful attention to Hamilton could ever have been in doubt concerning the tenor of the argument. Always Hamilton exercised great care in restating the *immediate* proposition.

The tendency to meaningful amplification is so marked throughout Hamilton's speeches as to suggest the possibility of his conscious following of Quintilian's advice on repetition with a variant. In any event his method of complete investigation can hardly be overlooked in the study of his speeches, nor was it unnoticed by his hearers. William Pierce observed:

Colo. Hamilton ... enquires into every part of his subject with the searchings of phylosophy, and when he comes forward he comes highly charged with interesting matter, there is no skimming over the surface of a subject with him, he must sink to the bottom to see what foundation it rests on.[21]

If the reporters can be trusted, and there is no apparent reason to distrust their reports at this point, Hamilton's composition was notable for the extent to which he developed his proof not merely by assertion, by pounding his hearers over the head with arguments, but with the calculated question. Far from being rhetorical, in the sense that no answer was intended, Hamilton's questions must surely have provoked a response and must sometimes have led to a conclusion—the conclusion which Hamilton had adopted in the premises. Rather than to assert, for example, that "we have all been witnesses..." he called upon the members of his audience to testify, as indubitably they must, to the experience of noncompliance with requisitions made by the Constitutional Congress on the states: "Have not all of us been witnesses to the unhappy embarrassments which resulted from these proceedings?"[22]

Not content with a single question, Hamilton could on occasion pile question upon question, each directed toward the next ensuing and all conjoined to lead toward an overwhelming conclusion:

What must be the final issue of the present state of things? Will the few States that now contribute, be willing to contribute much longer? Shall we ourselves be long content with bearing the burthen singly? Will not our zeal for a particular system,

[19] *Ibid.*, p. 237.
[20] *Ibid.*, p. 238.
[21] "Character Sketches ...," Farrand, *op. cit.*
[22] Elliot, *op. cit.*, p. 231.

soon give way to the pressure of so unequal a weight? And if all the States cease to pay, what is to become of the Union? It is sometimes asked, Why do not Congress oblige the States to do their duty? But where are the means? Where are the fleets and armies, where the Federal treasury to support those fleets and armies, to enforce the requisitions of the Union? All methods short of coercion, have repeatedly been tried in vain.[23]

Argument in Person: Hamilton's *Refutation*

As a legislator and a lawyer, Hamilton had to think on his feet. His greatest speeches were delivered not on fixed occasions but in the changing conditions of debate. Here his comprehensive grasp of major policy, his understanding of basic issues, and his ability to adapt himself quickly to attack made him formidable to any opposition. Hamilton's fixed habit of refutation appears to have been, first, to state the opponent's proposition; second, to analyze it; third, to offer counterargument as to evidence, reasoning, or assumptions; and finally, to review the matter. The introduction to his speech on Acceding to the Independence of Vermont illustrates his characteristic method of beginning a refutation:

The counsel for the petitioners has entered into a large field of argument against the present bill. He has endeavored to show that it is contrary to the Constitution, to the maxims of sound policy, and to the rights of property. His observations have not been destitute of weight. They appear to have the more force, as they are to a certain degree founded in truth. But it is the province of the committee to distinguish the just limits of the principles he has advanced; how far they extend, and where they terminate. To aid the committee in this inquiry shall be my endeavor, and following the counsel for the petitioners through the different heads of his argument, I hope to be able to show, that neither of the objections he has urged stands in the way of the measure proposed, and that the Constitution permits, policy demands it, and justice acquiesces in its adoption.[24]

In refutation as in constructive argument, Hamilton was likely to raise his devastating questions. In the speech on acceding to the independence of Vermont, for example, he let daylight into the debate by advancing two refutatory questions and a single formidable answer:

Are we now in a situation to undertake the reduction of Vermont; or are we likely speedily to be in such a situation? Where are our resources, where our public credit, to enable us to carry on an offensive war?

[23] *The Works of Alexander Hamilton; Comprising His Correspondence and His Political and Official Writings* . . . ed. John C. Hamilton (7 vols.; New York: Charles S. Francis & Co., 1851), II, 366. (Referred to hereinafter as *Works*, J. C. Hamilton.)
[24] *Works*, J. C. Hamilton, II, 375-76.

We ought to recollect, that in war, to defend or attack, are two different things: to the first, the mountains, the wilderness, the militia, sometimes even the poverty of a country will suffice. The latter requires an *army* and a *treasury*.[25]

In refutation Hamilton was quick to seize on any inconsistency developed by his opposition. He endeavored, though not always successfully, to expose and exploit the inconsistency without giving personal offense. In the New York Convention for the Ratification of the Constitution he thus set forth the inconsistency of the Antifederalists as a justification of his own elaboration of the question at issue:

This day, sir, one gentleman has attempted to answer the arguments advanced by my honorable friend; another has treated him as having wandered from the subject. This being the case, I trust I shall be equally indulged in reviewing the remarks which have been made.[26]

Continuing in the vein of exposing inconsistency, Hamilton declared:

Sir, it appears to me extraordinary, that while gentlemen in one breath acknowledge, that the old Confederation requires many material amendments, they should, in the next, deny that its defects have been the cause of our political weakness, and the consequent calamities of our country. I cannot but infer from this that there is still some lurking favorite imagination that this system, with corrections, might become a safe and permanent one. It is proper that we should examine this matter.[27]

In refutation Hamilton was always alert to look for the specific fact, the pointed citation required to puncture a presumption. In Hamilton's employ such evidence was likely to be a point of law easily documented or such an item of common knowledge as the following:

Gentlemen have said that the non-compliance of the States has been occasioned by their sufferings. This may in part be true. But has this State been delinquent? Amidst all our distresses, *we* have fully complied. If New-York could comply wholly with the requisitions, is it not to be supposed that the other States could in part comply?[28]

Hamilton as an Epideictic Orator

Although Hamilton's career as a speaker was pre-eminently in forensic and deliberative oratory and debate, on one occasion he delivered a ceremonial address that has been preserved and is still worthy of study.

[25] *Ibid.*, p. 378.
[26] *Ibid.*, pp. 427-28.
[27] *Ibid.*, p. 428.
[28] *Ibid.*, p. 429.

One of Hamilton's closest friends was Major General Nathanael Greene. Among the military heroes of the Revolution, Greene was probably second only to Washington in public esteem and in the devotion of his comrades. After Greene's death in 1786, Hamilton was invited by the Society of the Cincinnati to deliver a eulogy in his behalf and did so on July 4, 1789.

Hamilton's eulogy of Greene follows a fairly conventional pattern. It expresses the speaker's readiness to join in praise of the hero, declines to exhibit any fault in him, and proceeds to an enumeration of his great accomplishments as a patriot, a statesman, and a soldier. Even in this epideictic address, however, a casual reader may observe Hamilton's characteristic analytical procedure. Each of Greene's accomplishments is discussed adequately in turn and provided with illustrations. A notable feature of the speech is the specific reference to events doubtless familiar to all the members of the audience. The Heights of Monmouth, the defeat at Camden, the misfortune of Gates, the military operations in the southern states all pass in review and reveal Hamilton's predilection not only for rhetorical but also for military arts. In his conclusion Hamilton displays again his penchant for the provocative question:

But where, alas, is now this consummate General; this brave Soldier; this discerning Statesman; this steady Patriot; this virtuous Citizen; this amiable Man? Why could not so many talents, so many virtues, so many bright and useful qualities, shield him from a premature grave? Why was he not longer spared to a country he so dearly loved; which he was so well able to serve; which still seems so much to stand in need of his services? Why was he only allowed to assist in laying the foundation, and not permitted to aid in rearing the superstructure, of American greatness? Such are the inquiries which our friendly, yet short-sighted regrets, would naturally suggest. But inquiries like these are to be discarded as presumptuous. 'Tis not for us to scan, but to submit to the dispensations of Heaven.

Let us content ourselves with revering the memory, imitating the virtues, and, as far as we dare, emulating the glory of the man, whom neither our warmest admiration, nor our fondest predilection, could protect from the fatal shaft. And as often as we indulge our sorrow for his loss, let us not fail to mingle the reflection, that he has left behind him, offspring who are the heirs to the friendship which we bore to the father, and who have a claim from many, if not from all of us, to cares not less than parental.[29]

Hamilton as a Forensic Speaker

Hamilton was certainly one of the foremost lawyers of his day. Chancellor James Kent, who knew all the leading attorneys of New York during Hamilton's time, believed that Hamilton was indisputably pre-eminent among them.

[29] *Ibid.*, pp. 494-95.

The Chancellor was impressed also with Hamilton's gentle, kind, and courteous manner and with his clear and fluent style. These qualities, together with Hamilton's profound penetration, power of analysis, integrity of character, innate dignity and melodious voice, caused Hamilton, in Chancellor Kent's opinion, to soar far above all competition at the Bar of New York.[30]

Judge Ambrose Spencer, who served as opposing counsellor and judge in cases where Hamilton was concerned, compared Hamilton's forensic abilities with those of Daniel Webster:

In power of reasoning, Hamilton was the equal of Webster; and more than this can be said of no man. In creative power Hamilton was infinitely Webster's superior.[31]

According to the custom of his day, Hamilton engaged in the general practice of law and was thus concerned at one time or another in almost every kind of action requiring lawyer, judge, or jury. A successful practitioner, he was able to win for his clients satisfying verdicts. In his most famous cases, however, which involved political questions of the highest order as well as matters of law and equity, even his forensic talents did not gain the verdict.

1. Rutgers v. Waddington

The first of the two great politico-legal questions in which Hamilton was concerned arose out of the disorders accompanying and following the Revolution. In New York perhaps more than in any other commonwealth, the Revolution had been a war among citizens as well as a colonial struggle against Britain. In certain areas of the state the Loyalists had been in the majority; and everywhere many good people had steadfastly maintained their loyalty to the King and to their British country as they understood it. Many Tories who had lived out the war in districts under British occupation had enjoyed prosperity while the followers of the Continental Congress were subjected to persecution. Under the active leadership of Governor George Clinton, who openly and doubtless honestly declared his bitter hatred of all Tories, the legislature of New York in 1779 passed an act confiscating the property of all persons who adhered to the enemy, i.e., to the old order. With the coming of peace the hatred of the Tories did not abate, and the opportunities for confiscation under the act of 1779 enormously increased. On the withdrawal

---

[30] "Chancellor Kent's Memories of Alexander Hamilton." James Kent to Mrs. Elizabeth Hamilton, December 10, 1832. *Memoirs and Letters of James Kent, LL.D.* ..., ed., William Kent (Boston: Little, Brown, & Co., 1898), p. 291.

[31] Allan McLane Hamilton, *The Intimate Life of Alexander Hamilton* ... (New York: Charles Scribner's Sons, 1910), p. 198.

of British troops from the City of New York, confiscation of Tory property became a major, a lucrative, and a satisfying enterprise to those who had suffered for the patriot cause.

As a young lawyer just entering practice, Alexander Hamilton found immediate opportunity in the postwar troubles. The opportunities were increased for him and for such other soundly patriotic young lawyers as Aaron Burr and Rufus King, because many of the leading lawyers of New York had been loyal to the British and were therefore disbarred. Doubtless the legal business of the Schuyler enterprises, for which Hamilton was the attorney, could have occupied him fully. But with his usual systematic expenditure of energy, Hamilton found time for additional legal business which often involved considerable sums.

With characteristic energy, Hamilton had been faithful during the war in the prosecution of every military objective against armed forces; but he had been strongly opposed to harsh and retaliatory measures against civilians not actively aiding the enemy. The war being over, he believed all the more firmly that the proper policy to pursue toward British sympathizers was one of forgiveness, of conciliation. Doubtless he was the more persuaded of the rightness of his views because many of the luckless Tories were among the "respectable characters" whom Hamilton regarded as aids to good government; and he was appalled at the stupidity of policies which were driving into exile some good men merely because they had once held bad opinions. On going to Nova Scotia, these men would take with them talents and fortunes badly needed in New York.

Hamilton's convictions as well as his superior talents thus made him a natural choice for those Tories who, standing in danger of having their estates confiscated, were in need of an able attorney of impeccably patriotic antecedents. The Act of Confiscation passed in 1779 made troubles enough for such men, but in 1783 the Trespass Act passed by the legislature compounded their disasters. In brief, the Trespass Act provided that any citizen whose property had been seized and used during the British occupancy might sue the user thereof for damages of trespass. Even an order of the British military forces would not be competent to afford relief.

Apparently the first action brought under the Trespass Act was that of Elizabeth Rutgers, a widow who, with her son, had fled with the patriot army when the British took Manhattan. Mrs. Rutgers and her son owned a brewery on Maiden Lane in New York. When the British occupied the city in 1776, they took over the brewery and eventually, in 1778, they rented it to Benjamin Waddington and a partner. The partner seems to have had the discretion to flee with the British forces when they left New York, but Waddington remained and was clearly subject to a suit under the Trespass Act. If the suit against Waddington should result in a verdict for the plaintiff, many other interested parties would be encouraged to seek damages.

To the unsophisticated layman here was an open and shut case. The law was clear; the facts were demonstrated. Waddington had used the brewery for more than four years. It was admittedly the property of the Widow Rutgers and her son. The law stipulated that such use was trespass and provided for the recovery of appropriate damages by action at law. Moreover, the matter was heavily involved in public opinion. Mrs. Rutgers, as a widow and a patriot, would naturally enlist the sympathies of the populace. Waddington, as a Tory, was in the prevailing opinion an enemy of the people, a traitor who still claimed to be a British subject. Besides, he was reputed to be wealthy. The case of the poor patriot widow against the rich British brewer could hardly have been better calculated to excite tumult.

Yet Hamilton took a brief for the defendant Waddington; and in company with Brockholst Livingston and Morgan Lewis, he undertook to raise the case from the level of a mere action for trespass to one implicit with the principles of international law. When the case was tried in the Mayor's Court of New York City, Hamilton submitted a demurrer, i.e., he admitted the allegations, but pleaded that the law was insufficient and unavailing to support the claim. The first aspect of his plea declared that the law of nations— which was never very far removed from Hamilton's legal system—gave the British Army the right to seize and hold the property of the Widow Rutgers during the occupation; the right to rent the property to Waddington flowed therefrom. The second aspect of Hamilton's case was solidly grounded on the Treaty of Peace with Great Britain, a treaty providing that no claims for damages were to be honored, either by the nations themselves or on behalf of individuals.

Egbert Benson, the opposing counsel, replied that the State of New York, a full sovereign, could not be bound either by the so-called law of nations or by a treaty passed by the Congress. The statutes of New York were clear, the facts were admitted, and the law and the facts required judgment for the plaintiff.

Here, even before the adoption of the present Constitution of the United States, the issue between statute and treaty, between state legislature and national policy, was clearly joined. Hamilton appropriately appeared as advocate for a national and international as opposed to a parochial point of view. Yet although his operation was successful, his patient died. The court decided that the congressional treaty had in fact supervened upon the New York statute. Therefore, the statute was presumably void. But in the instant case, the court held for the plaintiff on the ground that the license from the British authority to Waddington, the brewer, had been imperfectly executed and that in consequence he was in fact a trespasser. The widow was thus entitled to damages which she later recovered.

If James Duane, the judge, had sought to effect a palliating compromise, he did not succeed. The state legislature voted a censure of Duane, and mass meetings denounced him as well as Hamilton. The issue was released from the courtroom to the public forum and the legislature. One immediate consequence of the case was Hamilton's writing of the "Letters from Phocion" (1784), which appealed "to the considerate citizens of New York on the politics of the times in consequence of the peace."[32] These letters brought forth from the Clintonians a reply upholding the sovereignty of New York. Although Hamilton's letters to Phocion bristled with cogent arguments which were hardly to be answered, the controversy was still rife while he was a member of the legislature of New York in 1787. At that time he argued on the ground of expediency for the repeal of all acts inconsistent with the Treaty of Peace:

He urged the committee to consent to the passing of the bill, from the consideration that the State of New York was the only State to gain anything by a strict adherence to the treaty. There was no other State in the Union that had so much to expect from it. The restoration of the western posts was an object of more than £100,000 per annum. Great Britain, he said, held those posts, on the plea that the United States have not fulfilled the treaty, and which we have strong assurances she will relinquish, on the fulfillment of our engagements with her.[33]

The legislature of 1787 was not responsive, however, and not until the Federalists gained control of the legislature in 1788 did New York repeal the statutes inconsistent with the Treaty of Peace with Britain.

2. THE CROSWELL CASE

The second of Hamilton's great politico-legal cases was tried at the close of his career, just a few months before his death in 1804.[34] It supplies an interesting sequel to the Sedition Act which the Federalists, contrary to the judgment of Hamilton, had pushed through the Congress during the administration of John Adams. The act had provided that any person convicted of uttering false, scandalous, or malicious statements against the government, the Congress, or the President of the United States, with intent to defame them or bring them into disrepute, should be imprisoned or fined. Doubtless designed

[32] *Works*, Lodge, IV, 230-90.

[33] *Ibid.*, p. 291.

[34] A text of Hamilton's speech in the case of the *People* v. *Croswell* is given in *Works*, Lodge, VIII, 387-425.

to curb sedition in anticipation of a war with France, the act was applauded by the Federalists and attacked by the Jeffersonians. Ironically, the Jeffersonians after having employed the Sedition Act as an issue in the campaign of 1800, and after having been instrumental in preventing its re-enactment in 1801, thought it necessary to use the concept of seditious libel on which it was based to chastise one of the more uninhibited of the Federalist editors. The country was thus presented with a political paradox. The Federalists, who had formerly upheld action against seditious libel, now decried such action by the New York Jeffersonians, who defended their recourse to a principle they had formerly declared contrary to the Constitution and to the public interest.

The Jeffersonians chose to make an example of Harry Croswell, the editor of *The Wasp*, a local paper published at Hudson, New York. The case for the action against Croswell was his reprinting, with a few comments of his own, a statement attributed to one Callender, a notorious mudslinger. The statement declared that Jefferson had paid Callender for slandering Washington and Adams.

On September 9, 1802, Croswell was indicted for libel. Hamilton was immediately importuned to appear as counsel, but he was then too busy to take the case. The trial proceeded with Morgan Lewis, who had been of counsel with Hamilton in *Rutgers* v. *Waddington*, sitting as justice. The prosecution exhibited the alleged libel and demonstrated that Croswell was the editor of the paper in which it was printed, whereupon Croswell's attorneys requested a subpoena for Callender so that he might testify to the truth of the libel alleged. Judge Lewis ruled, in effect, that Callender's testimony would be irrelevant on the ground of "The greater the truth the greater the libel." In short, the judge's ruling left the jury no choice. A verdict of guilty was found, and an appeal was taken to the Court of Errors sitting in Albany. At this point Hamilton entered the case for Croswell.[35]

Ambrose Spencer, the attorney general, appeared for the prosecution, and the case was heard by the four justices of the Court of Errors—Chief Justice Morgan Lewis, from whose decision the case had been appealed, and Justices Kent, Livingston, and Thompson. Both of the leading attorneys were assisted by counsel who presented the case for and against the appeal. But the final and most brilliant speech in behalf of Croswell and a free press was that of Alexander Hamilton. Chancellor Kent regarded Hamilton's argument in this case as the greatest forensic effort Hamilton ever made. The Croswell case provided an occasion for Hamilton to eulogize Washington, to appeal for liberty of the press, and to declare the rights of the jury. Doubtless the

[35] For a judicious account of Hamilton's relations with the Press, see Frank L. Mott, *Jefferson and the Press* (Baton Rouge, Louisiana: Louisiana State University Press, 1943), pp. 11-13.

gravity of the issues, as well as the deep convictions of the speaker on questions of tyranny and freedom, enabled him so to speak as to justify Chancellor Kent's opinion that Hamilton "... never, in any case at the bar, commanded higher reverence for his principles, or equal admiration of the power and pathos of his eloquence." [36] In one of the most stirring passages of the speech, Hamilton endeavored to define the service of a free press to a free people:

We have been careful that when one party comes in it shall not be able to break down and bear away the others. If this be not so, in vain have we made constitutions; for if it be not so, then we must go into anarchy, and from thence to despotism and to a master. Against this I know there is an almost insurmountable obstacle in the spirit of the people. They would not submit to be thus enslaved. Every tongue, every arm would be uplifted against it; they would resist, and resist, and resist, till they hurled from their seats those who dared make the attempt. To watch the progress of such endeavors is the office of a free press—to give us early alarm, and put us on our guard against the encroachments of power. This, then, is a right of the utmost importance; one for which, instead of yielding it up, we ought rather to spill our blood. [37]

But in the immediate case, even Hamilton's eloquence did not avail. By a divided vote, the court declined the appeal and Croswell's conviction stood. As in *Rutgers* v. *Waddington*, however, Hamilton's arguments eventually had profound consequences. The legislature next ensuing passed a bill permitting the truth to serve as a sufficient defense in a charge of libel. Eventually, after Hamilton's death, the State of New York acquired a new constitution embodying the principle for which Hamilton had argued.

Hamilton as a Parliamentarian

As a deliberative orator, Hamilton spoke chiefly to legislature, congress, and convention. When he addressed or attempted to address mass meetings or informal groups, he appears to have spoken in circumstances that may well have deepened his antipathy to lynch law, to violence, and to mob rule. One of his earliest speeches defended Dr. Myles Cooper, the Tory president of King's College, from a patriot mob that threatened him. Cooper escaped while Hamilton engaged the attention of the mob, but no existing evidence suggests that the speech offered more than a diversion. In later years, Hamilton came to the defense of a merchant named Thurman against the so-called Travis Mob. On still another occasion Hamilton is said to have headed a group

---

[36] James Kent, "Address before the Law Association," New York, October 21, 1836. Extract quoted in George Shea, *op. cit.*, p. 436.

[37] *Works*, Lodge, VIII, 422.

of men who attempted to suppress a riot growing out of supposed body-snatching proclivities of young medical students. In the quelling of this riot, John Jay, who was a member of Hamilton's party, was injured. Other references extant suggest that Hamilton sometimes made speeches to the voters gathered at the polls or elsewhere on election day. But insufficient evidence exists to justify a judgment concerning his method or his effectiveness. One point is clear, however: Hamilton had a number of unfortunate encounters with mobs. These encounters may well have deepened his distrust of *democracy*, a term that connoted to him, as to other men of his time, a kind of government quite unlike that suggested by *democracy* today. A strong believer in representative and responsible government, Hamilton never wavered in his opposition to mob rule.

If Hamilton despised mobs and had perhaps no great ability to deal with them, he respected assemblies and knew how to address them. In deliberative speech, Hamilton was an orator in the tradition of Pitt, Fox, and Burke. He would have been perfectly at home in the British Parliament. His theory of government would doubtless have been compatible with that of Burke. His understanding of men and his grasp of affairs, together with his quickness in refutation would have made him a worthy ally—or rival—of Fox.

Hamilton's career as a parliamentarian was unusual in at least one respect: he completed it as a young man, at an age when many speakers have hardly begun public appearances. Prior to his last first-hand experience in legislative debate in 1788, Hamilton had served in five parliamentary posts. His first legislative or quasi-legislative post was that of receiver of taxes from the State of New York for the Continental Congress. His duty was to negotiate with the legislators to obtain the sums due the national government from the State of New York, with the opportunity to develop support for the idea of a strong central government. Hamilton was influential in persuading the legislature to appoint a recess committee to study ways and means for a more effective system of taxation. His first legislative post led to his second, for he was elected as a delegate from New York to the Continental Congress.

During Hamilton's membership the Continental Congress considered important measures: the restoration of the national credit, the reduction of the public debt, the disbanding of the army, the conclusion of a treaty of peace with Great Britain, and plans for a peacetime government. Hamilton set forth his views, which centered on a strong national government. He wished to obtain for the Confederation the right to levy taxes on citizens rather than to requisition funds from the several states; but only three of the states, besides New York, were willing to grant such power to the central government.

Hamilton was a moving spirit in the Annapolis Convention of 1786, and it was he who phrased the resolutions addressed to the legislatures of Virginia,

Delaware, Pennsylvania, and New York. The resolutions proposed the meeting which developed into the Constitutional Convention of 1787.

In the same year (1786) Hamilton undertook his fourth legislative assignment, that of membership in the Assembly of the State of New York. When he took his seat in January, 1787, he immediately began to pursue his favorite subject, i.e., a strong national government. His membership in the state legislature continued through the session which convened in January, 1788. Meanwhile, however, he had served as one of three delegates from New York to the Constitutional Convention which met in Philadelphia from May to September, 1787.

Hamilton's participation in the great convention of 1787 was limited by two factors: the open and decisive opposition of Yates and Lansing, his colleagues from New York, to any substantial proposal for a new system; and his obligation to his clients as well as to himself to continue his thriving law practice in New York. In consequence Hamilton undertook both to maintain his practice and to be as effective a member of the convention as possible in the circumstances. He was in attendance when the convention opened on May 25, 1787, and he remained until the end of June, when he went back to New York. He returned to Philadelphia on September 2 and remained until the close of the convention.

In addition to occasional contributions to the debate, Hamilton made at least two noteworthy speeches in the Philadelphia convention. The first, delivered on June 18, 1787, was declared by Gouverneur Morris to be the greatest speech he ever heard. Hamilton spoke for some five or six hours to set forth his proposal for a central government based on the British model. During the course of his speech, he revealed his strong beliefs in national strength and individual freedom:

The members most tenacious of republicanism are as loud as any in declaiming against the vices of democracy. This progress of the public mind leads me to anticipate the time when others as well as myself will join in the praise bestowed by Mr. Neckar on the British constitution, namely, that "it is the only government in the world which unites public strength with individual security."

In every community where industry is encouraged, there will be a division of it into the few and the many. Hence, separate interests will arise. There will be debtors and creditors, etc. Give all power to the many, they will oppress the few. Give all power to the few, they will oppress the many. Both, therefore, ought to have the power, that each may defend itself against the other. To the want of this check we owe our paper-money instalment laws, etc. To the proper adjustment of it the British owe the excellence of their constitution. Their House of Lords is a most noble institution.[38]

[38] *Works*, Lodge, I, 389.

Hamilton did not expect to see his plan adopted. Evidently his intention was to influence the "tone" of the proposed new government; and his conservative model was doubtless offered as a provocation to thought and as a counterweight to the New Jersey plan, which would have modified the Articles of Confederation without setting up as strong a national government as Hamilton or the Virginians preferred. The effect of Hamilton's speech is thus difficult to determine, for while it excited admiration and favorable comment, it gained no adherents. Yet it may well have been influential, since it advocated measures that by comparison made the Virginia plan appear less revolutionary than it would have otherwise; and in the end the convention adopted a proposal which Hamilton was able to support, though his fellow delegates from New York were not.

Hamilton's second major speech in the convention was given at its close, when he urged every member to sign the document then being presented for signature. As Madison reported:

Mr. Hamilton expressed his anxiety that every member should sign. A few characters of consequence, by opposing, or even refusing to sign the Constitution, might do infinite mischief by kindling the latent sparks that lurk under an enthusiasm in favor of the convention, which may soon subside. No man's ideas were more remote from the plan than his own were known to be; but is it possible to deliberate between anarchy and convulsion on one side, and the chance of good to be expected from the plan on the other? [39]

How many delegates were influenced by Hamilton's plea cannot be known. Randolph, Mason, and Gerry held firm in their opposition and declined to sign. Yates and Lansing, the other delegates from New York, had long since departed from Philadelphia in protest against the actions of a convention which had exceeded its grant of authority. Alexander Hamilton alone signed for New York and thus indicated his willingness to accept for the general good a form of government less central, less energetic, and less national than he would have preferred.

1. THE RATIFICATION

When Hamilton signed the draft constitution, the proponents of the new order were assured of a powerful advocate. Putting aside his doubts, Hamilton immediately set to work to do all he could in behalf of a constitution which, though imperfect in his eyes, yet offered a substantial improvement over the existing conditions. He explained and expounded, he wrote letters and articles for the paper, he brought his personal influence to bear wherever possible. In New York he endeavored to obtain the election of delegates of like mind to

[39] *Ibid.*, I, 420-21.

attend the convention called to consider the draft constitution. In the latter enterprise he and his friends signally failed. In the election of delegates to the New York Convention scheduled to be held at Poughkeepsie, an election in which the adoption or rejection of the proposed constitution was the sole issue, the voters of New York returned nineteen delegates pledged to the new constitution and forty-six opposed. Only the City of New York and environs were unmistakably Federalist. Governor George Clinton, able opponent of the new constitution, had won an outstanding victory. Hamilton and his Federalist friends had failed. All this was clear to Hamilton; yet he had no thought of acknowledging defeat or of surrender.

2. HAMILTON's TACTICS

As the acknowledged leader of the Federalists at the Poughkeepsie convention which met on June 17, 1788, Hamilton's first objective was to keep the convention in session. Nothing would have been easier or on the face of the matter more reasonable than for the delegates to convene, to vote, and to go home. Indeed, that is precisely what some of the Antifederalists supposed would be done. They reckoned without Hamilton, whose first endeavor was to get the draft constitution debated thoroughly and well, not only because he thought the result of the labors at Philadelphia deserved serious consideration but also because he was persuaded that events were moving in favor of a ratification. If the convention could be held in session, changing conditions might well require an approval that the delegates would be loathe to give on an early ballot.

His keen analysis of the parliamentary situation was confirmed by events. In the first period of the convention, until the news of the ratification by New Hampshire, the debate was on the merits of the constitution. But New Hampshire's ratification being the ninth, the new government was actually formed. The issue thus became not: Should New York help to form a new central government? It was rather: Should New York refrain from joining a new government already established? Despite the protestations of Antifederal men, the conditions of the debate were vastly changed. Even so, the debate continued in a thorough consideration of the new constitution, with arguments pro and con on such questions as taxation and the rights of the states, until news was received of the ratification by Virginia. Events again had come to Hamilton's rescue, as he had hoped. Now indeed the position of the Antifederalists in New York seemed increasingly untenable. Still, they would not assent to ratifying the draft constitution as it stood; they insisted on a contingent ratification, qualified by the requirement of certain amendments. Only when Hamilton brought forth an opinion by an eminent gentleman of Virginia (James Madison) that a conditional ratification would be inadmissible did some of the leading Antifederalists capitulate and agree to vote for the ratification. The final vote of 30-27 for ratification, with eight absences or abstentions, marked the end of a parliamentary contest that will always be fascinating for students of legislative debate in America, for it demonstrated in its technical aspects the possibilities open to a parliamentarian even in what might appear to be a hopeless situation. Hamilton's contribution to the decision was made not only in his speeches but also in his envisioning of the course of events and in his parliamentary management.

But his speeches also were notable contributions to the result. Although the leading ideas were mostly to be found in *The Federalist,* the speeches added to the arguments already current the powerful persuasion of Hamilton's person. They permitted him to bring valid emotional appeals to bear on the major issues and to re-enforce argument with ethical proofs. All in all, Hamilton's speeches at Poughkeepsie deserve the high praise they have received from critics of contemporary and later times and would appear to have justified the judgment of James Kent, later Chancellor of New York, who as a youth heard the speeches delivered:

> Mr. Hamilton maintained the ascendency on every question, and being the only person present who had signed the Constitution, he felt and sustained the weight of the responsibility which belonged to his party. He was indisputably preeminent, and all seemed, as by a common consent, to concede to him the burden and the honor of the debate.[40]

Hamilton did not go unnoticed in the celebration that followed the adjournment of the Poughkeepsie convention. The victory of the Federalist forces was regarded as a personal triumph for Alexander Hamilton. His name was heard in the songs of celebration. His name was given to the "Federal Ship" that graced the parade in the victory march of the Federalists in New York City. To Hamilton was accorded the honor of conveying the ratification by the state of New York to the Congress. With the public acclaim, Hamilton thus ended a career, hardly yet begun, as a parliamentary speaker and turned to the treasury, to the law, and to administration.

Hamilton's Place in the History of Oratory

Although Hamilton was thought by many of his contemporaries to be the greatest orator of his day, he has not been remembered primarily for his speeches. The reasons are not hard to find. Oratory was to Hamilton an instrumental art. He employed it, as he employed his pen, as naturally as a soldier turns to arms or a financier to credit. He was not greatly interested in

[40] Kent, *Memoirs and Letters,* pp. 304-5.

the means. To him the hearer was the speech's end and object; yet he saw beyond the immediate hearer to others out-of-doors, and perhaps to those yet to come. Without speaking to posterity, he nevertheless was so heavily engaged in developing universal principles that his speeches more than most have a pervasive and a permanent quality. The immediate circumstances forgotten, the body of principles remains, even if deprecated, as the statement of a keen intelligence actively at work, for Hamilton went beyond the obligation of the orator to interpret and to expound ideas and feelings. He is to be numbered among the few orators who, like Burke, have been the creative spirits of their time. In the *Federalist Papers*, as in the texts of his speeches, Hamilton leaves the evidence of his power to find and to invent ideas that were effective in their day and profoundly influential in time to come.

Such a man deserves well of his countrymen; and Hamilton, as orator and good citizen, merits a recognition that he has not had, partly no doubt because he has been misunderstood. The rich have thought him their special friend. The poor have thought him their special enemy. Both have been mistaken. Profoundly skeptical of the virtues of human beings, he wished so to order events as to employ even their vices in their own interest. A conservative statesman, a conservative orator, he voiced his hopes and fears with equal eloquence and in his characteristic utterances disdained to resort to the demagogic appeals sometimes thought necessary to maintain wealth within the commonwealth.

BIBLIOGRAPHICAL NOTE

The bulk of the Hamilton papers are in the Library of Congress. Microfilm of the holdings of the Library of Congress is available in the libraries of Columbia University and the University of Missouri. In the collection are Hamilton's legal papers: pleas, indentures, depositions, miscellaneous items, and briefs, including those of *Rutgers* v. *Waddington* and *People* v. *Croswell*. The Library of Congress also has Hamilton's Notes, an outline of material presented in speeches at the convention in Poughkeepsie (1788), as well as his Sketch, an account of the speeches (chiefly those of the opposition) at the convention. The New York Public Library has a file of Hamilton papers and also the Abraham Yates papers, the Olin Collection, and the Gilbert Livingston papers, including the Report of the Poughkeepsie Convention. The New York Historical Society has the DeWitt Clinton papers, the John Lamb papers, and the John McKesson papers. (McKesson served as secretary of the Poughkeepsie convention.) The New York State Library has some Hamilton manuscripts, and some papers relevant to Hamilton in the Melancton Smith papers, the George Clinton papers, and the Philip Schuyler letters and papers, as well as various items of correspondence of the Clintons, the Livingstons, and other leaders of the commonwealth. The Huntington Library has some Hamilton items and others concerning George Clinton. The Library of Columbia University has a great many of the papers of DeWitt Clinton. The Library of Hamilton College has some of Hamilton's notes.

Hamilton has not been the subject of a definitive modern biography, and there is no adequate bibliography. Paul Leicester Ford's *Bibliotheca Hamiltoniana: A List of Books Written by or Relating to Alexander Hamilton* (New York, 1886) is the usual approach to bibliography. At the time of his death the late James Callendar had almost completed a typewriten Bibliography and Iconography of Alexander Hamilton.

Treatment of certain phases of Hamilton's speechmaking will be found in Bower Aly, *The Rhetoric of Alexander Hamilton* (New York: Columbia University Press, 1941). This work also includes a selected bibliography (pp. 199-213) of primary and secondary sources concerning Hamilton. Since 1941 the following biographies of Hamilton, each containing a bibliography, have appeared: Nathan Schachner, *Alexander Hamilton* (New York: D. Appleton-Century Co., Inc., 1946), vi + 488 pp.; and Johan J. Smertenko, *Alexander Hamilton: Man of Action* (New York: Julian Messner, Inc., 1941), viii+336 pp.

·· 3 ··

Thomas Hart Benton

by NORMAN W. MATTIS

Born March 14, 1782, near Hillsboro, North Carolina, Thomas Hart Benton was the oldest son of Jesse Benton, a prosperous lawyer, farmer, and land speculator, and Ann Gooch Benton. His father died in 1790, leaving the mother with eight children and a large but somewhat encumbered estate. Tutored at home in his early years, Thomas later attended a Hillsboro school and, for a few months in 1799, the University of North Carolina, but his education came largely from the books in his father's fine library. In early 1801 the family moved to Tennessee, settling on a huge tract south of Nashville. In 1804, Benton left the farm to read law and teach school at Duck River; he was licensed to practice law and admitted to the Williamson County bar in 1806. In 1808, he published a series of articles on the Tennessee judiciary, and a series on the presidential election of 1808, in the *Impartial Review and Cumberland Repository*. Elected to the state senate in 1809, he served one term notable for his successful promotion of judicial reform. He recruited volunteers to serve under Jackson in 1812, commanded one of the regiments raised, and was eventually regularly commissioned as lieutenant colonel in the Thirty-Ninth Infantry, but saw no combat. In 1815, he moved to St. Louis, where he practiced law, edited the St. Louis *Enquirer* (1818-20), and worked for Missouri statehood. Elected senator in 1820, he took his seat in 1821 and served for five terms. He was a member of the House of Representatives, 1853-55, tried unsuccessfully to regain a Senate seat in 1854, and ran unsuccessfully for governor in 1856. He died at Washington, April 10, 1858.

In the national Capitol stands the statute of Thomas Hart Benton, flanked by his enemies Henry Clay, John C. Calhoun, and Daniel Webster. One hand grasps a roll of manuscript. The other rests on an open book.

The book and the manuscript are appropriate symbols. Benton, senator from a frontier state, a rough-hewn champion of the little man, and a pugnacious leader of Jacksonian Democracy, was an erudite man. "What are the facts?" he asked of every legislative proposal. He ferreted them out, wherever they might be found, learned the history of the question, sought the analogies of other lands and other times. And then he wrote all down, to the last remorseless detail, and uttered what he had written to the last syllable before his impressed but weary colleagues.

This granite-faced, imperious man had his imaginative insights, his flights of fancy, his visions of the future, but his bent of mind was primarily factual and utilitarian. When he proposed a highway from the Mississippi to the Pacific, where scarcely a trail existed, he saw a right-of-way a mile wide with a whole series of parallel roads: one for steam engines ("If that should prove practicable"), one for coaches, and one, free of tolls, for the humble wayfarer. A fantastic notion, spawned by demagogy and nourished to catch votes, thought the Whigs and anti-Benton Democrats. Benton, however, turned at once from the vision to its implementation—to the gradient of the slopes, the depth of snow in mountain passes, the financing of the project.[1] The chief bias of his mind, said his son-in-law John Charles Frémont, was to utilize material. He touched only what he could assimilate and apply to the affairs of the nation.

This eminently practical legislator relied on his speeches to influence his own generation and to win the plaudits of posterity. He recognized, to be sure, certain limitations to the power of public address. He knew that some movements were beyond both persuasion and legislation, that measures could be promoted or thwarted by "secret springs and hidden machinery" that reason and eloquence could not affect, and that the "practical, sensible, upright business men" of an assembly often helped more than the brilliant rhetoricians to shape laws and secure their adoption. These reservations did not, however, weaken his conviction that the statesman of a democracy had to depend on the spoken word, multiplied and preserved by the printing press, if he wished to attain national leadership and an honored place in the history of his country.[2]

Benton, "the great Missouri demagogue" to conservatives like Philip Hone, held lofty and even idealistic views of the nature and function of the political speaker. These views grew naturally from confidence in man as a rational and moral being whose highest attribute is what Benton called "judgment." "Judgment" might be glossed as reasoning power, but it included more than dialectical skill. It was intellectual ability of a high order plus common sense, or reasoning power rooted in reality. He defined a great speaker, on whom the national spotlight focused, as one who combined superior judgment with "the faculty of fluent and copious speech." Men of excellent judgment who lacked fluency became the valuable "business" legislators who were known only to their colleagues and constituents. Men of little judgment who

---

[1] In the Senate, December 16, 1850. *Congressional Globe*, 31st Cong., 2d sess., 56-58. In references to the Congressional records, "In the Senate" is to be understood except when "In the House" is specified.

[2] [Thomas Hart Benton] *Thirty Years' View* (New York: D. Appleton & Co.. 1854-1856), I, Preface, v; 144; 187-90; II, 176, 467.

had been capriciously blessed with command of words might become nationally notorious by "addresses to popular interests, the conciliation of the interested passions, [and] the gratification of cupidity," but did not achieve enduring influence or fame. In a moment of unaccustomed modesty Benton might class himself with the businessmen of the Senate, but these moments were rare. He certainly aimed at national leadership, and justly thought that he had attained it.[3]

How, through his speeches, did this democratic statesman with the admirable conception of the ethics of persuasion attempt to make his will prevail? The answer to that question is the burden of this essay.[4] Before turning, however, to the complicated matters that are relevant to the inquiry, let us observe him in action at a happy moment.

[3] *Ibid.*, I, 94, 369.

[4] Most of Benton's speeches are available only in the records of Congress, although dozens of them were also published as pamphlets and a few, plus long excerpts from many, were reprinted in the *Thirty Years' View*. A number delivered outside Congress have survived, the most important being: (1) A St. Louis speech of July 18, 1835, reported in *Niles' Weekly Register*, August 29, 1835. (2) The famous "appeal from the instructions," printed without date at St. Louis as "Speech of the Hon. Thos. H. Benton, delivered at the Capitol at Jefferson City, May 26th, 1849." (3) An exposition of his considered views on slavery extension, the Wilmot Proviso, and Calhoun, published as *Speech ... Delivered at Fayette, Howard County, Missouri, Saturday the First of September, 1849* (Jefferson City, 1849). (4) A Boston address of December 20, 1854, on "The Physical Geography between the States of Missouri and California, with a View to Show its Adaptation to Settlement, and to the Construction of a Railroad," published as a Boston Mercantile Library Association pamphlet titled, "Discourse of Mr. Benton of Missouri." (5) "Remarks of Thomas H. Benton at the New England Celebration in New York," printed in the *National Intelligencer* for December 25, 1856.

In the main, the texts represent Benton as he wished to be represented. Ordinarily, he submitted his manuscript to the printer, or edited the reporter's version. This care depended, however, on the printer's cooperation, and practice varied. On December 18, 1834, he denounced the *Register* for suppressing his speech on the Bank veto and reducing his six-hour speech on the bill to recharter to one paragraph! (*Register of Debates*, 23d Cong., 2d sess., 26). On February 12, 1835, he declared that the *Register* of the preceding session contained not a paragraph that was not "more or less a downright falsification of what he said." (*Ibid.*, 414.) On March 2 of the same year he added that the printers no longer submitted their reporters' copy for correction. (*Ibid.*, 700.) Despite these and other complaints, Benton's desire to censor the copy, his capacity to create trouble for the printers if they did not cooperate, and the fact that most of his allegations of misrepresentation relate to a relatively short period, give reasonable assurance that his speeches were printed in substantially the form that he preferred.

Few of the Missouri campaign speeches have survived, but contemporaries indicate that he exercised similar care to insure accurate reporting of them, and liked to furnish the newspapers with at least a summary of his arguments. See Daniel M. Grissom, "Personal Recollections of Distinguished Missourians," *Missouri Historical Review*, 18 (1924), 139; John F. Darby, *Personal Recollections* (St. Louis: G. I. Jones & Co.,

"Solitary and Alone"

Early in 1834 a combination of Whigs and Calhoun Democrats drove through the Senate a resolution censuring President Jackson for ending the deposit of public funds in the Bank of the United States. Benton fought vainly against the coalition and announced, when the Senate refused to receive Jackson's temperate remonstrance, that he would introduce a resolution to expunge the censure from the journal, and prosecute it until it passed or he ended his political life.[5] On February 27, 1835, he delivered his first major speech on expurgation,[6] hoping to influence the elections of the following summer. As the Senate still consisted of the members who had passed the original censure, he had no intention of bringing his resolution to a vote, but the opposition outmaneuvered him. On the last day of the session, Clayton of Delaware moved to take it up, and White of Tennessee instantly moved to strike out the word "expunge" and insert a milder retraction. Astonished by the defection of Jackson's old friend White, Benton reluctantly assented, only to suffer the mortification of hearing Webster exultantly move to lay the amended resolution on the table, where it went by the almost standard anti-Jackson vote of 27 to 20. Webster's speech, said Benton, "made a man of me again," and he promptly submitted anew the original resolution, "with the peremptory declaration that I would never yield it again to the solicitations of friend or foe."[7] In March, 1836, he returned to the attack with an enormous speech in which he reviewed all the complex controversies that had arisen out of Jackson's war on the Bank.[8] Ten months later he was confident of his power. Some hostile senators had been involuntarily retired; others had been instructed by their legislatures to vote for the expurgation. On January 12, 1837, he made his final speech on the subject.

The Senate in 1837 met in the handsome chamber now called the Old Supreme Court Room. Though large enough for the forty-eight senators, visitors often crowded the floor. The gallery accommodated only a fraction of those who wished to attend when excitement ran high, and the legislators made room among themselves for the fashionable ladies of Washington. At

---

1880), p. 187; Charles P. Johnson, *Personal Recollections of Some of Missouri's Eminent Statesmen and Lawyers* (n.p., n.d.), p. 7.

Presumably the manuscripts of Benton's speeches were destroyed when his Washington home burned in 1855.

[5] 17 April 1834. *Register of Debates*, 23d Cong., 1st sess., 1347-55; *Thirty Years' View*, I, 428-32.

[6] *Register of Debates*, 23d Cong., 2d sess., 631-59.

[7] 3 March 1835. *Ibid.*, 723-27; *Thirty Years' View*, I, 549-50.

[8] 18 March 1836. *Register of Debates*, 24th Cong., 1st sess., 877-933.

one time, few came to hear the senator from Missouri, and even his colleagues turned to their correspondence when he made a speech.[9] Henry Clay had once remarked, somewhat indelicately, that although he could not define what the chamber was filled with when Benton spoke, he could testify that the galleries were empty! [10] But all listened now to the man who had initiated a movement and carried it to completion against the united opposition of Clay, Calhoun, and Webster.

Nearly three years ago, he said in substance, when I moved to expunge the resolution of censure, I expressed confidence in the outcome. That confidence sprang from my reliance on the justice of the American people, and it has been justified. The complection of the Senate has altered. The Bank of the United States, which took the initiative in accusing the President, now musters but a slender phalanx of friends in the two Houses of Congress. In the recent election Mr. Van Buren, an advocate of expurgation, was exalted to the lofty honors of the American Presidency. The verdict of the people thus expressed should be binding on us, and I shall not re-open the argument they have settled.

It remains, however to review President Jackson's administration as it ends. The political existence of this great man draws to a close. Whatever motive the servile and time-serving may have had for raising the altar of adulation to him no longer exists. He becomes a character for historical contemplation, and historically I shall view him. And first, I ask, was there ever a magistrate of whom so much evil was predicted and so much good come? He is said to have destroyed our liberties, endangered the peace, delivered the streets of the cities to grass and weeds, robbed labor of its reward, ruined the currency, and plunged an innocent people from the summit of felicity to the depths of misery.

What are the facts? We are at peace with the world. No nation wrongs us, many make reparation for old wrongs, and even the Malays of Sumatra have been taught that an American citizen, like a Roman in the great days of the Republic, has an inviolable passport throughout the whole habitable globe. At home, the public debt has been paid; taxes reduced; national defense promoted; our States freed of their Indian population. Industry flourishes. The Bank has been cast down, and the only constitutional justification for its existence has been destroyed by President Jackson's demonstration that it is not "necessary" to the conduct of government, and that a gold currency is all we need. To detail specific acts which adorn this great Administration would be inconsistent with this rapid sketch, but we cannot pass over his removal of the public funds from the Bank, whereby he rescued an empire from the fangs of a merciless, revengeful, greedy, insatiate, implacable moneyed power. Even those who had supported his veto of the bill to recharter quailed at this

[9] Ben: Perley Poore, *Perley's Reminiscences of Sixty Years in the National Metropolis* (Philadelphia: Hubbard Bros., 1886), I, 350.

[10] 13 July 1832. *Register of Debates*, 22d Cong., 1st sess., 1293.

drastic action; but he knew that the veto would be unavailing, and a new charter eventually coerced, if the Bank remained the depository of the immense Federal revenues.

But why specify? Jackson came into office the first of generals; he goes out the first of statesmen. The City of Washington has been to the American politicians who assailed him what New Orleans was to the British generals. Great is the influence, great the power, which he has acquired over the public mind. And how has he acquired it? First, by an intuitive sagacity which, leaving all book learning immeasurably behind, enabled him to do the right thing at the right time. Next, by moral courage. Last, and chiefest, by honesty of purpose, disinterestedness of motive, and devoted patriotism. Let those who envy his influence and popularity envy also, and emulate, if they can, these qualities.

And now, sir, I finish the task which, three years ago, I imposed on myself. Solitary and alone, and amidst the jeers of my opponents, I put this ball in motion. The people have taken it up, and I am no longer anything but a unit in the vast mass which propels it. In the name of that mass I speak. I demand the execution of the people's edict.[11]

Thus did Old Bullion honor Old Hickory. Pompous he may have been, but as Claude Bowers observes, in his most extravagant praise he spoke the language of his heart.[12] To posterity, the occasion may not seem to have warranted such thundering, and the whole campaign to write "Expunged" across a few lines of the Senate journal may look like much ado about nothing. Expurgation had, however, attained immense symbolic value in the struggle for power, and to Benton victory on the issue was almost as sweet as Van Buren's victory at the polls. The leaders of the opposition did not conceal their bitterness. Calhoun detected in the result not the voice of the people but the voice of executive patronage corruptly employed. He reminded the senators that there had been a "universal giving way of conscience" when the measure was first introduced, "so that the Senator from Missouri was left alone," and not to be outdone in the appeal to antiquity, declared that the removal of the deposits might have been perpetrated in the days of Pompey or Caesar, but the expurgation could not have been accomplished until the times of Caligula and Nero. Clay, in a peroration that Benton dryly remarked "lacked nothing but verisimilitude to have been grand and affecting," advised the country that henceforth a President might "snatch from its lawful custody the public purse, command a military detachment to enter the halls of the Capitol, overawe Congress, trample down the constitution, and raze every bulwark of freedom." Webster, less effervescent, spoke a shade more moder-

[11] 12 January 1837. *Register of Debates*, 24th Cong., 2d sess., 382-91. Complete text also in *Thirty Years' View*, I, 719-27.
[12] *Party Battles of the Jackson Period* (Boston: Houghton Mifflin Co., 1922), p. 463.

ately. He regretted the exercise of executive power to dominate the Senate, and resigned himself "to look on, in silence, while a scene is exhibited which, if we did not regard it as a ruthless violation of a sacred instrument, would appear to us to be little elevated above the character of a contemptible farce." [13] Perhaps Webster, Calhoun, and Clay were better judges than posterity of the rhetoric appropriate to the occasion. If Benton erred, he erred in excellent company.

"Benton and the People Are One, Sir"

Benton appeared on the national scene in 1820 as senator from the newly-organized State of Missouri. He remained at his post for thirty consecutive years or, as he put it, for six Roman lustrums. During that time, "The bare enumeration of the measures of which he was the author, and the prime promoter, would be almost a history of Congress legislation," he said of himself with more truth than modesty. [14] For nearly a third of a century he placed his stamp on every issue that agitated the country. He earned his nickname of "Old Bullion" by taking a commanding position in the fight for the Jacksonian financial reforms. He identified himself even more closely with attempts to liberalize the policies governing the distribution of the public lands. He instigated unnumbered bills to encourage the exploration, settlement, and defense of the nation, pressed our claim to the Columbia Valley when most Americans knew little and cared less about that distant land, and became in his old age the chief protagonist of a transcontinental highway and railroad. To the constitutional argument finally settled by civil war he made a notable contribution on behalf of the Union. Whatever may be the subject of historical inquiry—extinction of Indian claims, protection of the fur trade, bankruptcy acts, imprisonment for debt, direct election of the President, the Seminole War, French Spoliations, the Ashburton Treaty, Texan Annexation, the Mexican War—the trail of Benton must be followed through the endless columns of the congressional journals.

Benton's leading ideas, and the position he occupied in our national life, may be conveniently though incompletely summarized under four headings. He was (1) a radical democrat, (2) a Westerner, (3) an expansionist, and (4) a Unionist.

[13] 16 January 1837. *Register of Debates*, 24th Cong., 2d sess., 417-18; 429-40; 499-502. For a description of the exciting midnight scene on January 16, 1837, when the resolution passed and the censure was actually expunged, see the *Thirty Years' View*, I, 727-31. William E. Seelen has brought together many eye-witness accounts in "Thomas Hart Benton's Expunging Speech," *Speech Monographs*, VIII (1941), 58-67.

[14] "Auto-Biographical Sketch," in the 1903 edition of the *Thirty Years' View* (New York: D. Appleton & Co.), I, iv.

1. A Jeffersonian democrat in the equalitarian rather than the State-rights line of descent, Benton had unwavering faith in the wisdom of the people. In his old age he wrote of their "instinctive sagacity... which is an over-match for book learning; and which being disinterested, is always honest." [15] Thirty years earlier, about the time Harriet Martineau was contemptuously calling him a "temporary People's man" whom nature had designed to be a barber,[16] he told the Senate that "the body of the people are always sincerely devoted to the interests of their country, and their honest mistakes are less dangerous to liberty than may be the artful designs of a small and select body." The United States, he added, had demonstrated the great moral truth, that "under a free Government, the power of the intellect is the only power which rules the affairs of men; and virtue and intelligence the only passports to honor and preferment." [17] The people might be temporarily misled or thwarted by the force or fraud of powerful minorities, but in the long run the judgment of the majority will be right and must prevail. Perhaps, as Theodore Roosevelt said, Benton rode loose in the saddle when on his democratic hobby.[18] The weakness, if it is one, is an amiable element in the character of an American statesman.

Translated into action appropriate to his times, this democratic faith made Benton a leader in the Jacksonian struggle to redress the balance of economic and political power. When he went to Washington the Federalist program had triumphed although the party was moribund. With the Supreme Court dominated by John Marshall, broad constructions of the Constitution had prevailed. Under the pressure of exigencies created or revealed by the War of 1812, the Jeffersonians had sanctioned a series of Hamiltonian measures, so that by 1820 the nation had a Bank of the United States, a public debt, a protective tariff, a restrictive land policy, and an ambitious program of internal improvements. When the Era of Good Feeling came to a crashing end in 1824 and party lines were slowly reforged, Benton moved to the front of those who proposed to end the dominance of Federalist principles and business interests.[19] The program evolved slowly and without doctrinaire formulation, yet it had a high degree of internal consistency. Pay the debt, reduce income to the level required by an economical, strict-constructionist government, make revenue paramount and protection secondary in revising the tariff, restrict

---

[15] *Thirty Years' View*, I, 228.

[16] *Retrospect of Western Travel* (London: Saunders & Ottley, 1838), I, 179.

[17] 3 February 1824. *Register of Debates*, 18th Cong., 1st sess., 180, 185.

[18] *Thomas H. Benton* ("American Statesmen Series" [Boston: Houghton Mifflin & Co., 1899]), p. 114.

[19] "There are but two parties; there never has been but two parties ... founded in the radical question, whether people, or property shall govern?" Benton at St. Louis, July 18, 1835. Reported in *Niles' Register*, August 29, 1835.

internal improvements to those of great national importance, let the Second United States Bank dissolve with the expiration of its charter in 1836, sever all connections between the finances of the nation and the banks, use gold and silver for the ordinary currency, and open the public lands freely to all: these were the main items. Taken together, they constituted a revolution in the orientation of the United States government.

2. Though not a native of the West, Benton made himself the special guardian of that vast region. In return, as Senator Sevier remarked, the Westerners named their counties, their towns, and their children for him. He knew the immensity and richness of our empty spaces, and believed that nothing but an illiberal land policy could hinder the rise of great commonwealths in the Mississippi Valley. By 1819, he was prophesying in his St. Louis *Enquirer* that the wealth of the Orient would flow to America through the West Coast—though he thought it might have to be transported over the Sierras on dog sleds! He sponsored measures to mark and protect the road to Santa Fe, to abolish the Indian Factory System, to fortify the Oregon Trail, to legalize the Spanish and French land grants, to construct a highway to the Pacific, and to do a dozen other constructive things. The Western outlook also gave impetus, edge, and urgency to many Bentonian measures, such as reform of the land system and abolition of the salt duties, that in a more fundamental sense were part of the general Jacksonian economic program.

3. As an expansionist or imperialist and early disciple of the doctrine of manifest destiny, Benton read history as the march of the white race westward, with the Anglo-Saxons in the vanguard. The Americans spearheaded the Anglo-Saxons, and to maintain American primacy he would fight our British comrades-in-destiny as readily as he would fight the lesser breeds. He opposed the Convention of 1818 with England, which consented to joint occupation of the Columbia; the Spanish Treaty of 1819, which gained Florida but gave up Texas; and the Ashburton Treaty, which compromised territorial claims in the Northeast and ignored Oregon. Jingoistic he sometimes sounded, but he never urged a militant front unless convinced that we had superior claim in both law and equity. To the discomfiture of many in his own party, who would have left the British lion with no spot on the American Pacific to rest his paw, he rejected contemptuously their slogan of "Fifty-four Forty or Fight," and to the annoyance of President Polk he accepted the Nueces as the historic boundary of Texas.

4. Benton was a ,Unionist who set himself against all separatist tendencies from the moment he recognized, rather tardily, the implications of the South Carolina doctrine of nullification. Adopting as his formula for slavery "no extension and no agitation," he opposed both the abolitionists and the Southern extremists, who were alike in placing their special values above the

Union, and who, like the two halves of a pair of shears, could not cut until joined together. From 1835 on he thought of the South, and especially of John C. Calhoun, as the aggressors. On February 18, 1847, when Calhoun presented his resolutions asserting that Congress had no power to bar slavery from the territories, Benton promptly labeled them "firebrand." Calhoun observed that he had expected to find the representative of a slave state at his side. "I shall be found in the right place—on the side of my country and the Union," retorted Benton. When his state legislature instructed him to vote for the resolutions, or their equivalent, he "appealed from the instructions," waged a campaign on the issue, and went down to defeat; but twelve years later, when Missouri by a narrow margin remained within the Union, his lingering influence played an important part.

To define Benton as a democrat, a Westerner, an expansionist, and a Unionist is not, of course, to explain him fully or to account for his position on all the issues that a senator of 1820-50 had to meet. It was, however, by his attempts to extend economic and political democracy, to foster the development of the West, to expand the country to its present continental dimensions, and to preserve the United States as an indivisible whole, that he made his greatest impact upon the nation. To determine how he attempted to make his will prevail in these great areas of legislation it will be convenient to examine first his lifelong efforts on a single issue, reform of the land laws, confining the inquiry principally to his appraisal of the persuasive problem, the arguments he used, and the motives to which he appealed. Then, casting the net in a wider circle, it will be enlightening to range over his entire career to discover how he employed all the elements that contribute to the effectiveness of a speaker.

"*The People Go for Land*"

Shortly before Benton entered the Senate, the government altered the policy that had for a generation governed the sale of the public lands. The new law established a minimum price of $1.25 an acre, provided that newly-surveyed land opened for settlement should first be offered for sale at public auctions, and required payment in cash. Acreage unsold to competitive bidders remained indefinitely on the market at the statutory minimum.[20]

In Benton's view, this system, though superior to the one it superseded, was wrong in principle. It treated land as an ordinary commercial asset of the Federal Treasury, ignoring the great truth that God created all natural resources for those who could use them. It prevented poor people from becoming independent farmers although the nation owned hundreds of millions of

[20] *Thirty Years' View*, I, 12, 103-7.

acres untouched by the plow. A wiser policy, based on the understanding that real wealth comes not from the sale but the cultivation of the soil, would be to distribute unoccupied land as rapidly as possible to those who would make it fruitful on whatever terms would assure the widest diffusion of private ownership.

For thirty years Benton embodied these principles in bills that varied in scope and detail but may be characterized generally as having four main provisions. First, they provided for "graduation," or periodical reduction in price according to the number of years the land had been on the market, thereby making allowance for difference in quality and insuring that the less desirable tracts would eventually attract purchasers. Second, they permitted donation of a limited acreage to those who could not pay even the lowest contemplated price. Third, they granted pre-emptive rights to first settlers, so that those who moved into the wilderness and hewed out farms before the area had been opened for settlement (the "squatters") could not be outbid at the auctions and perhaps lose their homesteads. And fourth, they established a preferential price for actual settlers, giving the man buying for his own use an advantage over investors and speculators. Often they also authorized the federal government to cede to the states land that stubbornly remained unclaimed either as a gift or a purchase over a long period. The program, although Jeffersonian in spirit, did not originate in theory. Benton thought he might have received his first inkling of correct policy when he learned in childhood how the Israelites divided the promised land, or when he saw families flourishing in Tennessee on the 640-acre headrights bestowed by North Carolina. When a youthful member of the Tennessee Senate he "was fully imbued with the doctrine of donations to settlers," and supported the pre-emption claims of the settlers on "Big and Little Pigeon, French Broad and Nolichucky." Not until 1826, when he was preparing his first important speech on the subject, did he find high authority for his opinions. He found it then in Edmund Burke's speech on the Crown Lands, where Burke had asserted that the selling price of the royal forests and mines was as nothing in comparison with the revenues that would accrue in perpetuity, through the "political secretions" of the state, when the properties had been developed by private initiative.[21]

The persuasive problem in its broadest aspects remained the same from the initiation of Benton's campaign to the end of his legislative life. The western states where the public domain was located could be counted on generally to support his bills, and the admission of each new state strengthened his hand. But the West unaided could not pass legislation, and he had to find allies among the seaboard states that had no federally-owned land, including those

[21] *Ibid.*, I, 102-4.

that had originally ceded a large part of the western acreage to the central government. He could (1) stress the humanitarian foundations of his policy, and its consistency with established principles of political economy, appealing chiefly to those who could rise above sectional or class interest and act for the increased prosperity, population, and stability of the entire nation. Or (2) he could angle for the support of the less prosperous people, in all parts of the country, who had the greatest stake in free access to the western lands, and hope that their potential political power might eventually become actual. Or (3) he could aim at sectional alliances, using Western voting power as a make-weight in the struggle between the North and the South in return for support of his land bills. Obviously these possibilities were not mutually exclusive, and Benton tried all of them.

He introduced his first graduation bill so late in the session of 1824 that he knew there would be no opportunity to discuss it, explaining that he wanted to give public opinion a chance to crystallize on the subject before pressing it to a vote.[22] In 1826, he presented a new version of his proposals and delivered his first major speech in support of them. The bill called for successive annual reductions (beginning when the land had been on the market at $1.25 for five years) until the price reached 25¢, when the unsold residue could be given, in eighty-acre allotments, to actual settlers. Benton divided his constructive argument into two parts, speaking first as a financier interested in current revenues, and then as a statesman looking to the permanent health, wealth and stability of the republic.

History, he said, revealed the need of a reduction in price even if we concerned ourselves only with Treasury balance sheets. The compacts of cession which had transferred ownership of the western lands from the seaboard states to the central government had pledged the receipts from sales to payment of the Revolutionary War debt. Hamilton, backed by Washington, proposed a price of 20¢ an acre as calculated to produce the maximum income. A political combine which included speculators in the public debt defeated Hamilton, arguing that to pay interest on the debt while waiting for a rise in land values was better than to sell so cheaply. The speculators had brought up the certificates of indebtedness from the old soldiers at 2s.6d. in the pound, converted their cheap investment into 20-shilling certificates by funding the debt (Benton neglected to say that Hamilton also sponsored the funding!), and then aimed to make the debt eternal by restricting the land sales on which its payments depended. They did this by fixing the minimum price at $2.00 per acre, "and the People were unblushingly told, that a national debt was a national blessing, because it would create a powerful moneyed interest, to support the Government." The policy had been disastrous: land sales had languished, and the nation was still saddled with a debt of $80,000,000.

[22] 28 April 1824. *Register of Debates*, 18th Cong., 1st sess., 582-83.

Graduation, by letting lands automatically classify themselves and sink to their true value, would so accelerate sales that this sum could be discharged in eight years, the tariff-derived sinking fund of $10,000,000 being devoted to retirement of the principal, and the augmented land revenues taking care of the constantly-diminishing interest payments.

Having established that graduation should be approved for financial reasons, Benton turned happily to the statesmanlike view of natural resources. The power of a republic is in its population; the basis of population is agriculture; and the most productive agriculturist is the freeholder, who is also the most loyal supporter of a free government. Pass the land cheaply to the People; give to those who cannot pay. What is so given is sold for the best of prices, "a race of virtuous and independent farmers."

After adverting briefly to the ways in which the Federal jurisdiction over vast areas in the West impaired state sovereignty, Benton turned to the objections to the bill. Would the Atlantic states lose population under its operation? Ireland illustrates the truth that no country fit for habitation can be depopulated by emigration. If some poverty-stricken parts of the East are deserted, so much the better, for it is foolish to keep people scratching in pine woods and sandy wastes when they might migrate to where "there is neither count, nor weight, nor measure, for anything that is given to man or beast to eat." Would Eastern landlords lose their tenants, and factory owners their laborers? In our country, every man may try to better himself; no landlord or employer has a "right" to a free American. Would Eastern States lose political influence? Perhaps; but destiny, not legislation, determines the westward movement of power.

The second objection is that speculators will profit. They will not, because the vastness of our empty acreage will baffle them. And even if they do buy up inferior land when the price falls to 25¢, they will never be able to sell for as much as the government now charges. The third objection, that the bill will create monopolies, is baseless. With abolition of the laws of entail and primogeniture, baronial estates cannot be preserved even if they are founded. The fourth objection, that earlier purchasers at higher prices will be injured, has no force, for they too will have the benefit of the new law and can round out their holdings and buy farms for their children. They are, indeed, ardent supporters of the bill. The fifth objection comes from those who want to "wait for a rise." The history of thirty-five years should convince us that no rise will occur in any lifetime short of Methusaleh's. At the present rate of sales, it will be hundreds of years before even the lands now on the market are sold! The sixth objection, that the bill is incompatible with the pledge to apply land receipts to the Revolutionary debt, is relevant only to the donation clause. The legality of donations must be conceded, for every Congress has made them—to General Lafayette, to insane asylums, to French viniculturists. The only question, therefore, is of expediency, and what could be more expedient than to transform the indigent into prosperous citizens? The proposed grants, culled over five times and unsalable at 25¢ per acre, are niggardly in quantity, but even they will save many families from poverty and vice. Eighty acres may currently cost only $100, but innumerable honest men have never had, and never will have, $100 in cash.

In concluding, Benton reviewed his financial argument and stressed the burden resting on the Western farmers, who had to pay their share of the customs plus the sums required for land purchase. This injustice was the more remarkable in that the whole government revenue came from the farmers, whose exported produce paid for the imports on which the duties were levied. "Surely a wise and paternal Government would cherish, not kill, the goose which lays such golden eggs . . . [and] . . . gratuitously bestow upon every citizen that would work it, as much land as he would take. . . . Land must cease to be treated as an object of revenue. . . . Shall [this Government] have no eyes to see, no ears to hear, no heart to feel, no bowels of compassion to yearn over the misfortunes of the naked and houseless? . . . We may . . . embrace the entire circumference of the globe . . . and everywhere (save in these United States,) we shall find LAND, the gift of God to man, bestowed by the Governors of the earth . . . upon those who will work it." [23]

At whom had Benton aimed his speech? The Senate of 1826 had many distinguished members, and he studded his address with compliments to their wisdom, disinterestedness, and patriotism. Assuredly he hoped to impress them favorably. He could not, however, have been working for an immediate response in senatorial action, for he had called up his bill too late in the session to expect it to come to a vote. Unquestionably he was still primarily interested in the formation of public opinion, with special reference to opinion in Missouri, where he distributed the speech in pamphlet form. Administration stalwarts, diagnosing him as a parochial politician currying favor with the Western farmers to insure his own re-election, furnished wry or unintentional evidence that he was hitting the target they attributed to him. Barton, Benton's hostile colleague, revealed the trend more truly by his bitterness than by his words when he asserted that the Missourians were not disaffected and that no man, not even one endowed with all the qualities of a traitor, could seduce them from their loyalty to the government.[24] Alarmed by the "frenzy" Benton had stimulated, Missouri's solitary representative, John Scott, proposed that Adams adopt graduation as an Administration policy. "Treasonous!" thought the badgered man in the White House. In November, 1826, D. P. Cook, an Illinois representative who had failed of re-election, reported to the President that his opposition to graduation had been partly responsible for his defeat, and Adams noted that Benton's speech had excited "hopes among

[23] 16 May 1826. *Register of Debates,* 19th Cong., 1st sess., 720-49.
[24] *Ibid.,* 749-53.

the Western people that they can extort the lands from the Government for nothing." [25]

These contemporaries, distressed by the immediate effect of the speech and of the bill itself, missed a significant fact: if Benton was winning an election, he was also launching a crusade, and had no reason for attaching a Western label to a measure that must win national support. A remarkable feature of the address is not that he paid so much attention to his own region's vested interests, but that he paid so little. The farmers could tell a hawk from a handsaw and did not need to be argued into supporting a bill that would make a clear title easier to obtain. Nor did Benton weight heavily the pleas to the poorer people who had most to gain from cheap land. By humanitarian apostrophes, incidental remarks, the character of his illustrations, and the passionate peroration he revealed his social sympathies, but the speech did not significantly accentuate class consciousness. He referred, for example, to industrial workers only when replying briefly to those who said his reforms would deplete the labor force of factory owners.

At whom, then, was Benton aiming? The answer seems to be that he was trying to find arguments that would appeal to all judicious Americans. The stated objectives of the bill—to increase the revenues and promote the production of real wealth—were about the least debatable of all that might have been formulated. He was functioning as an educator, explaining the principles of a wise policy and supplying facts that would enable the people to pass judgment on both the existing and proposed systems. It was therefore appropriate for him to rely chiefly on reasoning, supported by a wealth of factual information not adequately revealed by our summary. His own deep feelings on the subject erupted occasionally (perhaps often enough to weaken the speech by arousing the suspicion that he would be delighted to distribute the public domain on even more liberal terms than he was currently proposing), but he had fair justification for asserting that he had confined himself "chiefly to facts, leaving conclusions to the Senate." Eight statistical tables buttressed the indictment of past policy. The history of the question served not only to clarify the issues but also to furnish support for Benton's position and to make the Founding Fathers his allies. Personal experience and observation contributed to documentation so exhaustive that even Senator Barton spoke of the speech as "evidently the product of much labor."

In late December, 1827, Benton again introduced his bill, with a significant addition. He now proposed to cede to the states, for education and internal improvements, land that could neither be sold nor donated. In an introductory

---

[25] *Memoirs of John Quincy Adams*, ed. C. F. Adams (Philadelphia: J. B. Lippincott & Co., 1874-77), VII, 367.

speech he tried to weaken the impression that his program would benefit only the Western states, arguing that it was truly national because, by hastening discharge of the debt, it would make tariff reduction possible and thereby minimize a dangerous source of sectional dissension.[26] In his main address he said that he wished to increase revenue and secure for the states complete jurisdiction over their own territory within a reasonable time. He stressed the quantity (nearly eighty million acres) of land that had been on the market for five or more years without finding a buyer, and showed how the old states, the new states, and the nation as a whole would profit from his proposals. Even Congress would benefit, by getting free of a question which bedeviled truly national business more appropriate to a great legislature than the huckstering of property! The donation and cession clauses received rather helter-skelter treatment near the end of the speech, indicating perhaps that Benton himself recognized that the arguments in favor of them did not fit too well into a case for graduation in price.[27]

These speeches showed little advance in Benton's thinking on land policy, but they marked a tentative stride forward in adaptation to political realities. He had now decided to press his measure to a vote, and was actively seeking allies. New England, adapting to a protective tariff it had opposed, was industrializing rapidly and political control was passing from the mercantile to the factory interests. Benton could have little hope of winning converts there. In the South, fear of centralized power and resentment against the protectionist system gave him leverage. Cession would reduce Federal influence and patronage, and bigger revenues from the land would weaken the argument that tariffs must be high because the Treasury needed the money. Benton was not yet making an overt bid for Southern support, giving up New England as hopeless,[28] but the necessities of the situation were pushing him in that direction.

In debate this session Benton displayed a conciliatory spirit. He opposed an amendment proposed by Webster to restrict graduation to acreage that had been on the market for ten years, saying that it would be unfair to the slave states, where most of the land had been offered for sale more recently than in Ohio, Indiana, Illinois, and Michigan Territory. But he gave up the clause applying graduation to future offerings in deference to those who wanted to try the principle experimentally on what had already been surveyed. He surrendered the cession clause, and accepted an amendment providing for

[26] 24 December 1827. *Register of Debates*, 20th Cong., 1st sess., 23-27.
[27] 9 April 1828. *Ibid.*, 609-28.
[28] Twice Benton took pains, in itemizing the tariff reductions he would favor, to show that they would not affect manufactures. Evidently he was still striving for national support.

67

a nominal charge of 5¢ an acre for the land that he wanted to donate. All these concessions proved useless, and the Senate defeated the bill 21 to 25.

That Benton was growing in political sophistication is shown by some resolutions that he introduced late in 1828. Two resolutions recommended technical financial measures to expedite payment of the debt. A third demanded that the Bank of the United States pay interest on public funds deposited with it. Two others, merely declaratory, stated that the debt could be discharged within four years by appropriate congressional action, and that the customs could then be reduced by ten millions annually without sacrifice of "adequate" protection for manufacturers. In a speech on these resolutions he connected them with his land bill: payment of the debt and subsequent tariff reduction depended on increasing the revenues from the sale of land and decreasing expenses by declaring a moratorium on internal improvements.[29] Evidently he was moving toward the complex Jacksonian program, with even the attack on the Bank foreshadowed by a casual sideblow at one of its privileges. Here also is the first significant indication of hostility to internal improvements. To J. Q. Adams, one of the most important political facts of the time was the scheme, hatched by Benton, to trade the West's interest in the tariff and internal improvements for Southern votes on the land bills.

For five years, beginning in 1824, Benton had been on the offensive. On December 29, 1829, the opposition attacked. Senator Foote of Connecticut introduced his famous resolution instructing the Committee on Public Lands to inquire into the expediency of limiting the sale of lands to those already on the market and abolishing the office of the Surveyor General. Benton promptly branded the resolution as an order "to inquire into the expediency of committing a great injury" and in his first speech against it said that its practical effect would be to resign vast areas to the beasts and savages. It was unjust to the West, and to the poor workers of the Northeast, and when linked with the protective tariff became part of "A most complex scheme of injustice, which taxes the South to injure the West, to pauperize the poor of the North." He then attempted to show, by analysis of the historical record, that the South had always been sympathetic to the West, and the North antagonistic. He concluded that the West, too weak to stand alone, knew aid would come from the solid phalanx of the South, plus a few scattering Northerners.[30]

Benton was now bidding boldly for the Southern alliance toward which he had been moving for several years, and was striving also to protect the Jacksonian party in the North by distinguishing between the dominant Federalists and the laboring masses. On the day after Benton spoke Senator

[29] 6 January 1829. *Register of Debates*, 20th Cong., 2d sess., 18-22.
[30] 18 January 1830. *Register of Debates*, 21st Cong., 1st sess., 22-27.

Hayne made a mildly-worded address calculated to encourage hopes of Southern support. He agreed that the land should be distributed on nominal terms to get the country settled, attacked those who would retain a docile laboring class by discouraging emigration, and favored managing both the land and the tariff in a way that would keep revenues low and hinder the growth of centralized power.

Hayne's words about centralized power evoked Webster's celebrated First Reply, and the debate widened until it covered, during the five months it occupied the Senate, nearly every conceivable subject of constitutional or historical import. Benton's part in it may be best understood by remembering (1) that he bitterly resented the Foote Resolution, which came from New England; (2) that he needed Southern support to pass his graduation bill; and (3) that he failed to detect disunionist sentiments in Hayne's speeches.[31] Having no notion that his Southern friends were contemplating nullification in the South Carolina sense of 1832, he looked on Webster's defense of the Union as an ingenious evasion of the true issues. He therefore paid little attention to the constitutional aspects of the debate, and concentrated his fire on Webster's claim that New England had always been friendly to the West, which he regarded as an attempt to destroy the West-South alliance he had been fostering. He started to reply on the spur of the moment but quickly checked himself "in an effusion, in which feeling was at least as predominant as judgment, with the reflection that issues of fact, between Senators, were not to be decided by bandying contradictions across this floor," and sat down with the intention of beginning anew, "cooly and regularly," as soon as he could refresh his memory with dates and references.

Benton delivered the bulk of his main speech, which occupied portions of four Senate sittings, after Webster and Hayne had completed their work.[32]

[31] For an analysis of the debate, see Wilbur Samuel Howell and Hoyt Hopewell Hudson, "Daniel Webster," in *A History and Criticism of American Public Address*, ed. W. N. Brigance (New York: McGraw-Hill, 1943), II, 692-711. This lucid account is perhaps somewhat unfair to Benton. Would victory for his position have created an America in the image of Europe, "with continental security the object of a game of alliance and counter-alliance among geographical units?" Or would it have created an America much as it is today, with diverse interests coalescing to accomplish special purposes, and by a process of mutual accommodation making for unity rather than disunity? And did Benton aim at "securing sectional independence by creating a division of opinion at points where sectional differences, class hatreds, and partizan rivalries existed"? "Sectional independence" was so far from Benton's mind that he could not conceive that Hayne meant by nullification anything more than remonstrance or the privilege of working among the states to secure the majority required for constitutional amendment.

[32] The entire speech is printed in the entries for 2 February 1830. *Register of Debates*, 21st Cong., 1st sess., 95-119.

He had already sounded the keynote in his first brief attack: the South and the democracy of the North had always been friendly to the West, and the dominant party of New England had always been inimical. He also dealt with slavery, blaming Webster for its "extraordinary introduction" into the debate, and with the latter's conception of judicial supremacy, which Benton said would place the South in a sad plight if, at some future time, Congress passed, and the Supreme Court upheld, a law making slavery illegal.

Benton's strategy in the debate on the Foote Resolution fitted fairly well the political realities of the moment. Even after the elections of 1828 only one New England senator could be classed as a Democrat, and the only hope of winning support there lay in nurturing Jacksonian strength among the workers who were as hostile as Benton himself to the dominant Federalists.[33] The South had no vested interest opposed to more liberal land distribution, and was ripe for any combination that would arrest the centralization of power, end federally-financed internal improvements, and reduce the tariff. The South, however, was an uneasy ally, with the thinking of those led by Calhoun turning more to nullification as a remedy for grievances than to establishment of coalitions within the Federal framework. In less than two years this trend alienated Jackson and Benton, and it must be written down as a defect in vision and sagacity that the latter was trying in 1829-30 to cement an alliance with forces that two years later were lined up against the Administration. Moreover, in wooing the South, and attacking Webster at every point, he took positions on extraneous issues that later embarrassed him. His remarks on slavery began mildly enough with the statement that few in the South approved it in theory, but soon passed into a different key with a denunciation of those who, unconnected personally with the institution, and far from perfect themselves, denounced it as morally indefensible. These observations, plus his forebodings about judicial tyranny, plagued him twenty years later when Calhoun, Atchison, Foote of Mississippi, and others quoted them to prove that he himself had thought at one time that the Northern attitude toward slavery was potentially dangerous to the South.

Whatever reservations we may have about Benton's strategy when viewed in the long run, it placed the sponsors of the Foote Resolution on the defensive, and makes credible his own belief that Webster's motion for indefinite postponement (made at the end of his First Reply to Hayne) was a "signal of retreat and dispersion to his entangled friends." Within the framework of his plan of attack, he displayed erudition and ingenuity in analyzing ancient issues from a specialized (and partisan!) point of view. Relying heavily on the journals of the old Confederation, on the congressional records, and on the minutes of

[33] The major party opposed to the Democrats might call itself National Republican or Whig, but it was Federalist to Benton!

committees, he exhaustively documented his case against New England. The rehearsal of events long past and the exhumation of legislative records long forgotten sometimes grew tedious, but circumstantial detail, odd bits of recondite information, occasional purple passages, and the sarcastic correction of Websterian errors kept interest fairly well sustained. The correspondent of Isaac Hill's *New Hampshire Patriot* was, however, voicing a highly partisan opinion when he described Benton's speech as "a splendid display of eloquence, and every way superior to Mr. Webster's."

When the debate on the Foote Resolution finally dragged toward a close, the Senate resumed consideration of the graduation bill, now a staple on the senatorial market. This year it applied only to "refuse" lands—those that had failed for five or more years to find a purchaser. These were to be reduced 25¢ per acre each year, with actual settlers permitted to buy at 25¢ less than the general price until it reached 25¢, when the settler could buy for a nominal nickel. The bill also included the familiar provision for donations to the excessively poor and a clause granting pre-emption rights to squatters, but Benton seems to have included them simply for the record, or to give him something to bargain with; he himself termed them "subsidiary provisions" and did not discuss them. In his speech of this year he argued that competition between general purchasers and settlers with their 25¢ preference would keep both from waiting for desirable acreage to fall below its true value. He also amplified his proof that existing prices kept thousands of Westerners from owning their own farms, and explained in greater detail than hitherto why sober, industrious people might never accumulate cash in a new country.[34] Despite these additions, and the newly-limited character of the bill itself, friendly senators began to amend it. Led by Hayne, and Woodbury of New Hampshire, Benton's leading Southern and solitary New England ally against the Foote Resolution, the Senate converted the bill into a simple proposal to reduce the price of lands that had been on the market for five years to $1.00, with a 25¢ differential for settlers. Benton yielded with good grace; indeed, he could not easily do otherwise, as the amendments came from senators whose votes he needed. At length he for the first time got a favorable verdict: the emasculated bill (done to death by its friends, said the hostile Clayton) passed to a third reading, 24-22. It was lost in the House.

A man wilier than Benton at welding coalitions now took a hand in the game, and the opposition bluntly embodied in the Foote Resolution assumed a more insidious form. Henry Clay returned to the Senate in 1831 and began pondering ways to prevent the imminent extinction of the debt from affecting the protective tariff. Seeking an excuse to keep revenues high even though expenses dropped, he hit upon a plan to distribute to the states the proceeds

[34] 3 May 1830. *Register of Debates*, 21st Cong., 1st sess., 405-8.

from the land sales. The measures implementing his scheme varied from time to time, but provided typically that 10 per cent of the profits should be divided among the public land states in proportion to the acreage sold in each, and the remainder distributed among all the states by a formula based on congressional representation. Benton, caught off-guard, confessed that he hardly knew what to say about a bill so novel and so mischievous. Rallying quickly, he demonstrated a double connection between distribution and special favors for the manufacturers: as an excuse for keeping the tariff up, the Treasury must be kept empty, and to discourage laborers from migrating, land must remain expensive.[35] It is, however, difficult to vote against a distribution of money. Clay's bill passed, 26 to 18, and met defeat in the House by only a narrow margin. In the next session, it passed both Houses, and only Jackson's veto defeated it. Clay, who could be as stubborn as Benton, kept the plan alive even after he had presumably accomplished its real purpose in 1836 by passing the act to distribute the Treasury surplus in the guise of a "deposit." It kept Benton on the defensive and in conjunction with the time-engrossing war on the Bank of the United States compelled him to hold in abeyance the energetic prosecution of his own plans during most of the thirties.

In 1841-42 a curious set of political circumstances gave Clay the appearance and Benton the substance of a great victory. In the short session of Congress between the election of Harrison and his inauguration, Benton put through the Senate a measure that he shrewdly called a "Log Cabin Law" establishing the right of pre-emption as a permanent part of our system of land administration. It failed in the House, and then Harrison's death brought Tyler to the presidency. Tyler, worried about the finances of the states, many of which had been unable to meet their obligations since the Panic of '37, intimated that he would sign a bill to distribute the proceeds from land sales if its operation did not compel Congress to raise the 20 per cent ad valorem tax to which all duties, by the Compromise Tariff of 1833, were to be reduced after June, 1842. Clay, to meet Tyler's requirements and at the same time command a majority in Congress, ended by conceding to the West a pre-emption amendment resembling Benton's Log Cabin Bill of the preceding session, and to the South a guarantee that distribution would cease if the duties were raised above the 20 per cent ad valorem level. In the event, the duties *were* raised in 1842, distribution lapsed, and only pre-emption, which Clay disliked, remained![36]

[35] 28 June 1832. *Register of Debates*, 22d Cong., 1st sess., 1145-54. Clay delivered his major speech 20 June 1832. *Ibid.*, 1095-1119.

[36] Frederic L. Paxson, *History of the American Frontier, 1763-1893* (Boston: Houghton Mifflin Co., 1924), pp. 386-91. Benton delivered an ironical speech when introducing his bill. (14 December 1840. *Congressional Globe*, 23d Cong., 2d sess., 14-15).

In December, 1850, Benton entered upon his last tour of duty as senator. The second session of the Thirty-First Congress had barely convened when he served notice of his intention to introduce a bill "to accelerate the sales of the public lands and pay the public debt, and to extinguish the Federal title to lands within the new States, and to grant donations and preëmption rights to actual settlers, and to cede the refuse lands to the States in which they lie." One suspects that the Old Roman, rejected by his state in the preceding election after thirty years of service, wanted the record to show his perseverance on this issue. On December 30 he uttered for the last time in the Senate his favorite arguments on his favorite subject, with a twist suitable to the times. Our debtless days under Jackson had been of short duration, and we now had a debt of $74,000,000. Warrants for millions of acres had been bestowed as bounties on Mexican War veterans, who were selling their warrants for 45¢ per acre less than the federal minimum. Unless the government lowered its price, it would sell no land at all. And once again, Benton explained that the argument he stressed most was not the best argument, assured his colleagues that the income from sales meant little in comparison with the regular revenues that would accrue when settlers brought the land into production, and paid Edmund Burke his usual tribute.

Benton's bill ended this year by being attached as an amendment to one introduced by Walker of Wisconsin to cede, under stringent conditions, all the land to the states, and the misshapen product never came to a vote. Less than twelve years later, on May 20, 1862, President Lincoln signed the Homestead Act, and Benton's ghost must have saluted him with stately gravity. New forces had come into operation. The Southerners were meeting in a Congress of their own, and the measure passed with votes that Benton never even hoped to win. The manufacturers had discoverd an abundant supply of labor in the immigrants from Europe, and were forging a coalition with the West that kept Benton's party out of power for a quarter of a century.

A number of conclusions about Benton as a rhetorician emerge from this survey:

1. He had an intelligent understanding of the total situation. He recognized from the beginning that his greatest problem was to reconcile those who wanted to distribute the land on whatever terms would promote private ownership with those who regarded it as a Treasury asset. He attempted to solve this problem by combining his democratic, humanitarian, and agrarian propositions with proof that reduction in price would actually increase revenues by increasing sales. But land is a non-renewable commodity, and to accelerate sales would be to hasten the day when there would be nothing left to sell. To offset this weakness (and for other purposes) he adopted Burke's theory that revenue from sales is negligible in comparison with the revenues that accrue

when citizens have developed a natural resource and created taxable wealth. His case was coherent, consistent, and comprehensive. It did not, to be sure, deal directly with the motivations of those who feared that easier access to the land would reduce their political power by encouraging migration from their regions, and increase the bargaining power of labor by giving the worker an alternative to remaining on the job. These gentlemen were not, however, amenable to persuasion; at best, they could be neutralized by disclosure of their animus, and this Benton normally undertook in refutation.

2. Excellent as the case was, its development in specific speeches revealed that Benton was temperamentally incapable of keeping its parts in equilibrium. Burke's theory of the sources of national wealth evoked little interest, perhaps because it demanded a too-long and too-altruistic look into the future. This indifference to Burke made the question of current revenues from sales supremely important, as it was through them that the states that had no public domain could profit from its disposition. Benton recognized this in determining the proportions of his speeches. But the emotional drive behind his reforms had little to do with profits, and no matter how much he elaborated his "financial" arguments, his sympathies broke through and created the suspicion that he would happily sacrifice the Treasury receipts if necessary to achieve wide distribution. His bills confirmed that impression. Had they included just graduation, preference, and pre-emption, each provision might have been defended under all the headings of his case. Actually, the bills usually provided also for donation and cession, and these were of no help in raising current revenues. That Benton was aware of the problem is shown by his tendency to discuss these clauses in what might almost be regarded as afterthoughts or appendices to his speeches. Awareness did not, however, produce a solution, and the fact is that Benton regularly undercut a major portion of his argument, addressed to those whose support he needed, by delightedly dwelling on his vision of the landless poor becoming a prosperous yeomanry, and by persistently introducing bills with provisions that were incompatible with his bid for seaboard support.

3. Throughout his campaign, Benton displayed skill in adapting his arguments to changing circumstances. In major strategy, this adaptation took the form of relating his proposals to other measures that commanded wide support, such as debt retirement and tariff reduction. In tactics, his adaptation may be illustrated by reference to his argument for graduation. When only "picked-over" land was available, the price should be reduced, he said, until it attracted a purchaser. When millions of prime acres granted to Mexican War veterans were flooding the market at cut rates, the price should be reduced to meet the competition!

4. Benton's program, no matter what it owed to his exigencies as a Missouri politician, rested on humane, republican, and economically-valid prin-

ciples. The motives that impelled him, and to which he appealed, were among man's noblest: sympathy for the poor, confidence in humanity, justice for the backwoodsman, pride in the nation's growth, and respect for the independence and freedom of the man who owns his own farm.

5. The method was rational: Benton relied on the facts, logically grouped and interpreted, to justify his criticism of existing policy, and on reasoning to establish the probability that his program would attain its intended ends. His ultimate premises were, however, hardly susceptible of rational demonstration. One cannot imagine how J. Q. Adams could be convinced that an American unable to amass $100 for the purchase of an eighty-acre farm could turn into an efficient, tax-paying farmer if he were given the eighty acres. At this point, therefore, Benton tended to fall into exclamatory declamation. He had, and he presented, justification for his confidence in the ordinary man; but he sensed that he could accomplish little with those who did not share his views, and aimed chiefly at inspiring those who were already with him. His praise of the average man often came late in his speeches, as part of his discussion of donation, or in the perorations, and is largely responsible for the impression that he failed to keep his total case in a nice equipoise.

It is obviously impossible to determine what influence Benton had on the determination of so complex a subject as national land policy. It may fairly be said, however, that he was the pre-eminent proponent of the principles that were finally adopted. He took the initiative, devised the program, and promoted it in fair and foul political weather. He read the minds of the Western farmers, taught them how their needs could be translated into legislation, and became their supreme spokesman. Operating on the national level, he showed how the interests of the West coincided with the general good, and educated the nation in the applicable theories of political economy and the realities of frontier settlement. His sweeping measures were never enacted into law, but by his ceaseless agitation he helped to push through Congress almost numberless acts to accomplish for a limited time or locality one or more of the objectives he strove to incorporate in a total reform. By an irony, the most important land law passed between 1820 and 1862 (the general, prospective Pre-emption Act of 1841) went through as part of a Henry Clay compromise; but Clay would never have sponsored the measure had it not been for the strength of Benton's forces.

"The Little Boys Study His Speeches"

The zeal for facts that has been detected in Benton's speeches on the land, and the respect for reason that led him to define a great speaker as an articulate man of superior "judgment," dominated all his persuasive efforts. His financial reforms, he observed, had called for "pulling down, as well as building up,"

And, to do this, many speeches were to be digested and delivered; and speeches of a different kind from those which the rhetoricians teach us to pronounce. We live in an age of intelligence and activity, and when the public mind is powerfully directed to objects of utility. In speaking to such a people, I concluded that, of the six parts of the regular oration, four parts might be thrown away: that I could dispense with all except the facts, and the application of the facts, cemented and enforced by reason. . . . My speeches were stripped of ornament, stinted of phrases, and crowded with material. They were brimfull of facts and reasons; and this was a compliment to the intelligence of the age in which I lived. The compliment was not misapplied.[37]

Even in rebuttal he tried to keep the debate on the rational level he had established by ignoring "imaginary exhibitions, rhetorical flourishes, vehement declamations, general praise, general censure" and attending only to what "the mind could lay hold of, and present to the people as a proposition susceptible of proof, or disproof . . . by the touchstone of evidence, and the laws of logic." [38] No doubt Nicholas Biddle had a different notion of the part played by logic in the polemics against the Bank, but Benton did indeed rely primarily on "the facts, and the application of the facts, cemented and enforced by reason," for the substance of his speeches.

In the analysis of a question Benton used intellectual power of a high order to resolve complex subjects into their relatively simple components. Just how his mind worked at this stage of the preparation of a speech connot be determined, but two techniques or practices recur so frequently that they are worth special mention. (1) Normally he examined exhaustively the origin of the question, finding there clues to the current issues. (2) He liked to reduce a Proposition of Policy to a Proposition of Fact, either by a process of reasoning of his own, or by taking advantage of admissions of his opponents. When he took the floor on May 22, 1846, for his great speech on Oregon, the debate had boiled down to the question, "Is the American claim to the entire Northwest superior to the British claim?" Benton was in his element in settling a dispute of this type. He defined "a superior claim" as one bottomed on priority of discovery, actual settlement, and continuous occupation. He then divided the disputed land into three great natural areas, the Columbia Basin, the Frazer's River Basin, and the coastal islands, applied to each the criteria of a "superior claim," and emerged with the convincing conclusion that our right to the Columbia was unquestionable, that the British right to the Frazer was equally unquestionable, and that no one had unequivocal right to

---

[37] 16 January 1840. *Congressional Globe,* 26th Cong., 1st sess., Appendix, 119.

[38] Speech on the removal of the deposits. Quoted by Thomas R. Lewis, "Persuasive Techniques of Thomas Hart Benton as a Congressional Debater" (Ph.D. dissertation, State University of Iowa, 1948), pp. 205-6.

the islands, which should therefore follow the fate of the land masses adjacent to them.[39]

This liking for the Proposition of Fact adumbrates an important truth about Benton. Though competent in analysis, his great superiority in the logical department of rhetoric lay in the massing of evidence to support the assertions that analysis produced. With scholarly instinct he sought primary sources, caring little for "books compiled in closet... [which] were generally shallow, of no use to the informed, and dangerous to the uninformed, whom they led astray, and to the indolent, who would trust to their superficial glosses, without going to the fountain head." Benton went to the fountain-head, which consisted of treaties, geographies, maps, annals of explorers, government reports and statistical tables, legislative records, diplomatic correspondence, official journals and minutes, speeches, letters, memoirs, constitutions, laws, and judicial opinions. No pains dismayed him when he wished to equip himself to legislate intelligently or even to track down a single fact. How should the land grants made by Spain in territories now a part of the United States be handled? Benton hired a teacher and learned Spanish so that he could read the relevant charters and royal decrees. When he wanted to know all the circumstances surrounding the single senatorial precedent for his expunging resolution, he could find no account in the annals of Congress. He then fruitlessly searched the manuscript journal from which the printed Register had been made. Finally he sent a friend, with a clerk, to ransack the garret rooms of the Capitol, and there they found the loose minutes of 1806. The minutes told him what had been expunged, but not why; he had to learn that from the records of the House of Representatives! [40]

To support his intensive study of particular public issues, Benton could draw upon knowledge stored from a lifelong habit of miscellaneous reading. His father's library ranged from Homer through Shakespeare and Cervantes to Madame de Sévigné. He was introduced to Greek at the age of five; his mother used the British State Trials as primers when teaching him to read, and under her guidance he was soon delving into Plutarch's *Lives* and the Scriptures. Forty years later he and his daughter were reading the *Odyssey* together when they rested during tramps through the Virginia hills. Poetry, fiction, and philosophy attracted him less than history, geography, political economy, biography, oratory and constitutional law, but he ignored nothing.[41]

[39] 22, 25 May and 6 June 1846. *Congressional Globe*, 29th Cong., 1st sess., 851-55; 857-62; 913-20.

[40] 18 March 1836. *Register of Debates*, 24th Cong., 1st sess., 888-91.

[41] The scattered information about Benton's schooling and early reading has been brought together by William N. Chambers in "As the Twig Is Bent," *North Carolina Historical Review*, XXVI (1949), 385-416, and in "Thomas Hart Benton in Tennessee, 1801-1812," *Tennessee Historical Quarterly*, VIII (1949), 291-331. These articles, plus

Few among his contemporaries rivaled him in the range and accuracy of his historical knowledge. The British parliamentary records fascinated him, and he found in them many a precedent for American legislators. With the aid of a tenacious memory, he made himself a veritable walking library—more crammed with facts than with wisdom, thought his critics.

The fruits of his industry Benton packed into speeches that often exhausted both the subject and the audience. In his first speech on Recision of the Treasury Circular, he referred to, and usually quoted, Clay, Webster, Ewing, Biddle, Jackson, Adam Smith, McCulloch, ("present head of the Adam Smith school") the Althorpe Committee of the House of Commons, the *Federalist,* Hamilton, the rules and reports of the United States Bank, Bicknell's *Counterfeit Detector,* Treasury reports, a table of imports and exports of coin and bullion, 1821-36, and the laws of the United States.[42] When speaking against the plan for a "Federal Exchequer," he cited Smollett's continuation of Hume, the Statutes of George III, the Index to British Statutes at Large, McCulloch's "commercial dictionary," a history of the Constitutional Convention, Gallatin, W. M. Gouge, Appleton (once president of the Boston branch of the Bank), several of Webster's speeches, a number of Treasury tabulations, Hamilton's 1791 report on a National Bank, John H. Sargent's 1837 pamphlet on a "Print Mint," a private letter from Lowell Bicknell—and Sancho Panza and the *Vicar of Wakefield!* [43] In his speech on the revival of the gold currency, he alluded to Voltaire, Hamilton, Gallatin, the "member from Louisiana," Webster, Quincy's Treasury report, the statutes of the first Congress, and the monetary systems of Mexico, Peru, Assyria, Persia, Egypt, Carthage, Rome, France, Spain, and Portugal.[44] These speeches on finance are weighted especially heavily with the results of historical, legal, and economic research, but they are not atypical. In a discussion of February 2, 1843, on our northwestern boundaries, he made many references to maps and cited the provisional treaty of 1782, the Treaty of 1783, Jay's Treaty of 1794, King's Treaty of 1802 (rejected by the Senate), Monroe's Treaty of 1807, the Treaty of Ghent, the Convention of 1818, the Ashburton Treaty, Jay's correspondence, seven partners and clerks of the British Northwest Company (more than 2,500 words from these!), the minutes and correspondence of the Ghent negotiators, a letter of William McGillivray, and the Ashburton-Webster letters.[45]

---

four others by the same author (see the bibliography) have completely superseded the biographies as sources of information about Benton's life to 1820.

[42] 19 December 1836. *Register of Debates,* 24th Cong., 2d sess., 21-64.

[43] 13 January 1842. *Congressional Globe,* 27th Cong., 2d sess., Appendix, 62-72.

[44] List compiled by Lewis, *op. cit.,* p. 305.

[45] *Congressional Globe,* 27th Cong., 3d sess., Appendix, 132-38. Benton was very

Although Benton never felt more comfortable than when entrenched behind a fact certified by competent printed sources, the bookish and scholarly aspects of his speeches must not be exaggerated. He was also an active, observant man of broad experience, curious about the practical operations of trade and industry, interested in mechanical skills, a snapper-up of unconsidered trifles. To supplement the research of the library, he could draw upon a reservoir of information acquired at first hand, or from those who had it at first hand. To prove the iniquity of the salt tax, he might rely heavily on the findings of a Royal Commission, but he could also tell precisely why the Western farmers needed alum salt and could use no other, and how many pounds should be fed to a pig.[46] He needed no books to tell him that the indigent might prosper if granted farms: he had known Granny White in Tennessee. She could never have bought an acre, but on donated land (so hilly that she had to stake the pumpkins to keep them from rolling into the road) she established with her orphaned grandchildren a self-respecting, tax-paying family.[47] If he did not travel in the Far West, he at any rate knew those who did. He conversed with the traders who took their caravans to Santa Fe, dined with the archbishop to whom the missionaries reported, entertained Kit Carson at his home (where Kit wondered uneasily if the ladies knew he had been married to an Indian), and received reports from the wide-ranging Frémont before the government did.[48] As the years of his Washington service lengthened, he became a primary source for the history of which he had himself been a part, and few questions came before the Senate that he could not elucidate from his memories of past debate and action.

Benton's respect for history, his practical bent, indeed the whole cast of his mind made him couch his proofs normally as straightforward assertions supported by precedent, authority, example, analogy, statistics, and personal observation, but he did not lack versatility in argument. Often he combined testimonial evidence with reasoning from generally-accepted premises, as he

---

accurate in his citations. Hunter compared the references in four speeches, scattered over thirty years, with their sources. He could find only a few minor errors and these did not substantially affect either the spirit or the letter of the originals. See Charles Francis Hunter, "Four Speeches of Thomas Hart Benton" (Ph.D. dissertation, Cornell University, 1942), II, *passim*.

[46] 8 February 1831. *Register of Debates*, 21st Cong., 2d sess., 120-48, and especially, 136-38.

[47] *Thirty Years' View*, I, 105-6.

[48] John Charles Frémont, *Memoirs of My Life* (Chicago & New York: Belford, Clarke & Co., 1887), I, 74; Allan Nevins, *Frémont, the West's Greatest Adventurer* (New York: Harper & Brothers., 1928), II, 367; Jessie Benton Frémont, "Sketch of the Life of Senator Benton in Connection with Western Expansion," in Frémont, *Memoirs*, I, 8-9.

did when he proved that graduation of the public lands would not halt all sales while people waited for the lowest price by showing that this had not happened in Tennessee, where the principle had already been applied to state-owned land, and that it ought not to happen, because no sensible person would risk losing a desirable tract by delaying purchase after it had fallen to a fair price. He was especially ingenious in refutation, and clever at couching an argument in one of the forms embarrassing to opponents. He liked, for example, to "turn the tables." When Clay, attacking Jackson's use of the veto, remarked that the French at the beginning of the Revolution called the King and Queen "M. and Mme. Veto," Benton promptly showed that Louis XVI had used his vetoes in behalf of justice, moderation, and compassion! Allied to this device was the use of a man's words against himself. In urging an increase in the army (to 12,000 men!) Benton said that he would quote Calhoun, Secretary of War under Monroe against the Senator Calhoun of 1837, and then having used this *argumentum ad hominem,* would turn to the *argumentum ad judicium* and present his case on the basis of the country's needs. He delighted also in unveiling the unintended implications of an argument. Nicholas Biddle, testifying that the Bank of the United States had never injured the independent bankers, enhanced the reputation of his institution for civic virtue and self-restraint by asserting that it could easily have destroyed the independents had it wished. Benton recognized at once that Biddle had given the game away, for he had admitted Benton's main contention, which was that the Bank had the power, insufferable in a democracy, of life or death over its competitors. In ways too numerous to illustrate further Benton supported his propositions so comprehensively that the opposition could not easily find any point of special weakness. He worked like a military engineer, said Oliver Dyer, placing his batteries, redoubts, fosses, and ambuscades so skillfully that one supported the other and made the whole impregnable to assault.[49]

This reliance on reasoning did not blind Benton to the importance of the non-logical modes of persuasion. He himself was a man of passion and conviction, and he knew, even though in moments of theorizing he regretted, that people are swayed by their emotions and by their reactions to the reputation and personality of a speaker. A closer look at his personal qualities will furnish a foundation for appraisal of his capacity to stir men, to motivate them to action, and to win their good will.

Even his enemies commonly conceded that Benton brought industry and learning to bear on every legislative duty. Generally recognized also were his honesty, sobriety, and devotion to his family. In an age of violent partisan-

[49] *Great Senators of the United States Forty Years Ago (1848 and 1849)* (New York: Rob't. Bonner's Sons, 1889), p. 261.

ship his honesty could not completely escape impeachment, but in the main his scrupulous care to avoid even the appearance of having a private motivation for his public conduct bore rich dividends in public recognition.[50] His personal habits and domestic virtues exacted respect. He did not drink, smoke, or gamble, attributing his abstemiousness to the lessons of his mother, who lived to the age of eighty in St. Louis. His social life revolved around the home, where he liked to entertain and bring his children into the circle of his distinguished friends. His wife, Elizabeth McDowell of Virginia, was incapacitated in varying degrees by illness from the mid-forties to her death in 1854, and pleasant stories of her husband's attentiveness abound. On fine afternoons he could be seen, truant from the Senate for an hour, hovering over her wheel chair in the Capitol grounds and gathering nosegays for her.[51]

No one questioned his courage. Though nurtured in a home of refinement and piety, he had come to maturity in the rough atmosphere of the frontier and had become adept at the bare-knuckled fighting of highly personal politics. He had killed Charles Lucas in a St. Louis duel, and he went to Washington notorious as the man who had engaged in a bloody Nashville brawl with Andrew Jackson. Translated to the moral sphere, his self-reliance and indifference to danger enabled him to maintain a position no matter how unpopular or politically inexpedient it might be. To William M. Meigs, he attained the heights of disinterestedness when, on the eve of the 1844 election, he attacked a Texan policy overwhelmingly approved by the Missouri Democracy;[52] to Theodore Roosevelt, he rose to moral grandeur when he set himself against his state by opposing the extension of slavery.[53] This same independence and moral courage also led to his persistence in a cause even when it seemed hopeless. "He never gave up, even when defeated," remarked Nathan Sargent, who had watched him in action.[54] Hamlin of Maine once incautiously remarked, with reference to a minor Bentonian measure, "... if this thing is to be pressed." Benton, ironically noting that he and the Senator had been ac-

---

[50] Benton had a skeleton in the closet. When sixteen years old he entered the University of North Carolina. Before the end of his first term, he was expelled for stealing. William N. Chambers, who has illuminated an episode long shrouded in obscurity, thinks that the humiliation and the consciousness that he had betrayed his mother's standards may have produced the almost "compulsive" honesty he ever afterwards displayed. *North Carolina Historical Review*, XXVI (1949), 409-14.

[51] Varina Howell Davis, *Jefferson Davis: A Memoir by His Wife* (New York: Belford Co., 1890), I, 279.

[52] *The Life of Thomas Hart Benton* (Philadelphia: J. B. Lippincott Co., 1904), pp. 356-57.

[53] *Thomas H. Benton* ("American Statesmen Series" [Boston: Houghton Mifflin & Co., 1899]), pp. vii and 282-85.

[54] *Public Men and Events* (Philadelphia: J. B. Lippincott Co., 1875), p. 298.

quainted for only a short time, not more than six or seven years, said that nothing in their acquaintance authorized the interposition of that word "if." The Senate laughed, perhaps ruefully.[55] Truly, he said, in 1844, he was in a position to begin most speeches with "Twenty years ago." He added good-naturedly that no doubt some of his colleagues wrote him down as one who learned nothing and forgot nothing.[56]

There was, however, something almost more than life-size about the dimensions of Thomas Hart Benton, and his admirable qualities tended to be exaggerated until they lost some of their attractiveness. His persistency could sometimes lead to what appeared to be mere obstructionism. His courage and self-reliance had as their counterpart an aggressiveness that often embroiled him with his associates. "There is a lie in his throat," he shouted once of Senator Butler of South Carolina. "I will cram it down or choke it out," and started to rise from his seat. Other senators intervened, an investigating committee was appointed, and eventually both Butler and Benton were put under heavy bonds to preserve the peace.[57] Episodes almost as violent were not uncommon during his legislative career. Oliver Dyer reports that when a senator spoke of a quarrel in which Benton had engaged, the latter retorted that the senator was mistaken. "I never quarrel, sir; but I sometimes fight, sir; and whenever I fight, sir, a funeral follows, sir!"[58] Whether the words are Benton's or not, they reflect the public's impression that the "masterful, overbearing spirit of the West" found full expression in the Missourian.

Benton's excellent qualities were also vitiated in some measure by his awareness of them. Americans were accustomed to senators who made little distinction between themselves and the sovereign states they represented, but Benton outdid most in consciousness of his own importance and merit. "When God Almighty lays his hand upon a man, sir, I take mine off, sir," he said after Calhoun's death; and that the weights of the hands were not incommensurable seems to be clearly implied.[59] His vanity attained such heroic proportions that eventually, when he assumed the status of an Elder Statesman, people began to delight in it: there is more good humor than malice in the report that he was seen strolling down the avenue while keeping up a gentle remonstrance with himself for being so much greater than the rest of the world.[60] Perhaps, as he grew older, he even deliberately fostered such anecdotes. N. P. Willis

[55] 31 December 1850. *Congressional Globe*, 31st Cong., 2d sess., 149.

[56] *Thirty Years' View*, II, 626.

[57] Meigs, *op. cit.*, 377-78.

[58] *Op cit.*, 200.

[59] Margaret L. Coit, *John C. Calhoun* (Boston: Houghton Mifflin Co., 1950), p. 513.

[60] Varina Howell Davis, *op. cit.*, I, 271.

detected a twinkle in his eyes that told much about the man behind the monolithic façade.[61] Could the twinkle have been present when he wrote that little boys from the seaboard cities to the lonely frontier cabins studied his career when an honorable ambition to serve the country stirred in their bosoms? [62] Or when he told his publishers, who had asked for an estimate of the probable sale of the *Thirty Years' View,* that the census would tell them how many people could read?[63] Whatever the status of the stories, they were psychologically true: Benton's pride and self-assurance exceeded normal bounds and drastically affected his relations with people. "[Colonel Benton] is apt to think that nothing is done properly that he is not consulted about," grumbled President Polk, who was not alone even among the Democrats in finding Old Bullion an intractable customer.[64]

The violence of Benton's temperament and his capacity for anger colored his speeches and tempered their pervasive intellectualism. The critic who said that he mistook getting very angry for being deeply convinced shot wide of the mark, but was right in saying that he sounded angry a good part of the time. Prevailingly he invoked the harsher, more aggressive passions, disdaining the "softer lenitives to persuasion" and seeking to steel the people to fighting determination. Expansion and digression produced imagination-kindling and emotion-rousing pictures; an excellent vocabulary furnished a stock of vivid or loaded words; opponents were pilloried and their policies ridiculed. Often he employed a cumbersome apparatus of descriptive, hyperbolical, objurgative, and ejaculatory passages to rouse the people and give vent to his indignation. In a speech on the Ashburton Treaty he moved to strike out the article that obligated the United States to maintain a naval squadron in African waters to help suppress the slave trade, and then burst out: "If I fail in my motion to strike out ... I do not say, tear up the Declaration of Independence! But I do say, Take it down; dislodge it from its conspicuous place on our wall; carry it away; hide it in a dark chamber; cover it with a black veil; and let it hang in shame, shrouded in gloom and mourning, until some new *Jacksonian* President shall retrieve his country's disgrace, break the chains which bind us to England, and let America again be free." [65] To heighten the effect of his proof that New England had given niggardly support to measures to control

---

[61] *Hurry-Graphs: or, Sketches of Scenery, Celebrities and Society* (New York: Charles Scribner, 1851), p. 179.

[62] *Auto-Biographical Sketch,* iv.

[63] Dyer, *op. cit.,* p. 209.

[64] *The Diary of James K. Polk during his Presidency, 1845 to 1849,* ed. M. M. Quaife (Chicago: A. C. McClurg & Co., 1910), III, 367.

[65] Delivered in secret session 18 August 1842. Printed, *Congressional Globe,* 27th Cong., 3d sess., Appendix, 1-27.

the Indians, he painted a lurid picture of frontier massacres—and even called on a living witness, a senator whose family had been slain, to corroborate his description! [66] To swell national pride and militant ardor, he drifted from a plea for land grants to Oregon emigrants into a vision of 30,000 men liberating Ireland and an American general marching through London! [67] Such passages were so congruous with his temperament that no one can tell whether they originated as eruptions of his own feelings or as calculated attempts to rouse the people and induce an attitude favorable to acceptance of his views.

In his persuasive efforts Benton could not rely on kindling that affectionate responsiveness that makes people believe a man merely because they like him. His best qualities evoked respect rather than love, and when he called attention, as he often did, to his industry, consistency, foresight, and adherence to the facts, he managed merely to sound self-righteous. His contemporaries amply recognized his defects of manner and attitude. Shortly after he entered the Senate the old Federalist Rufus King, whom he greatly admired despite the divergence of their political views, gently told him that when heated by opposition he assumed an authoritative manner, and a look and tone of defiance, that sat ill upon the older members. Touched by the friendliness of the admonition, Benton suppressed the speech and resolved to study moderation and forbearance. [68] That he had indifferent success he himself admitted. "The Senator from South Carolina complains that I have been arrogant and overbearing in this debate, and dictatorial to those who were opposed to me," he said in 1844. "So far as this reproach is founded, I have to regret it, and to ask pardon.... I have, indeed, been laboring under deep feeling; and while much was kept down, something may have escaped." [69] Such apologies were rare; that they might well have been more numerous his friends testify as freely as his enemies. John Wentworth, almost a disciple, admitted that Benton's "raging" distressed his supporters as much as it angered his foes. [70] Alexander K. McClure said that his arrogance weakened him, and suggested that it might have been developed while he was evolving a technique for dominating his "rude and variegated" Missouri consistency. [71] Many shared the opinion of H. S. Foote (no friend, to be sure), who thought that he was always more eager to crush the opposition than to win it over. [72] Old men

[66] 2 February 1830. *Register of Debates,* 21st Cong., 1st sess., 99-100.

[67] 12 January 1843. *Congressional Globe,* 27th Cong., 3d sess., Appendix, 78.

[68] *Thirty Years' View,* I, 57-58.

[69] 15 June 1844. *Congressional Globe,* 28th Cong., 1st sess., Appendix, 610.

[70] *Congressional Reminiscences* (Chicago: Fergus Printing Co., 1882), pp. 46-50.

[71] *Recollections of Half a Century* (Salem: Salem Press Co., 1902), p. 272.

[72] *The Bench and Bar of the South and Southwest* (St. Louis: Soule, Thomas & Wentworth, 1876), p. 161.

recollecting his later canvasses of Missouri spoke almost unanimously of his haughty reserve and blank indifference to all conciliatory art.[73] He insisted, for example, on addressing his constituents simply as "Citizens." No complimentary flourishes, not even "Fellow Citizens," just "Citizens." No doubt the Old Roman thought he was complimenting his people with their proudest title, but men could and did say that he simply refused to admit that the members of a mass meeting were "fellows" of his.

His egotism and a somewhat humorless pedantry produced a condescension that was perhaps more irritating than his belligerence. It found typical expression in the correction of errors. Let a man slip on even a minor matter, and Benton sent the page boys scurrying to the library for the books that would convict the culprit. This propensity had its innocent aspects, and Henry Clay, in fine fettle, could twit him good-naturedly about it. "There is no man whom we could not better spare—our arithmetic, our grammar, our geography, our dictionary, our page, our date, our ever-present library, our grand labor-saving machine." [74] To smile was easy when Benton politely dispatched the books, relevant passages marked, to the erring member. More often he trumpeted his corrections to the world. When General Cass incautiously offered to retire from the fight for 54-40 if shown proof that the Utrecht line of 49 between the French and British possessions had ever been extended to the Pacific, Benton produced the required proof "to vindicate history, and the intelligence of the Senate," and then baited Cass: "The Senator's occupation is gone. 'War, inevitable war,' can no longer be the burden of his song. War is now evitable. ... It is peace that is now inevitable! and henceforth we must hear that dulcet sound." [75] Cass, who had been born (as had Calhoun, Webster, and Van Buren) in the same year as Benton, resented the treatment but could make only a feeble rejoinder to "Professor Benton's" history lesson. During the debate on the Foote Resolution Benton observed that he must remove some ornamental work and some rubbish that Webster had placed in the way "either to decorate his own march, or to embarrass mine." He then skillfully demolished Webster's notion that Nathan Dane had originated the Ordinance of 1787, but what he gained by the demolition he probably lost by a boastfulness and sarcasm that fitted no prescription for winning friends.

Benton's oral presentation did little to ingratiate him with his auditors or to mitigate the impression of his arrogant indifference. He had, to be sure, some of the characteristics of a fine speaker. He made himself heard, speaking

[73] E.g., Daniel M. Grissom, *op. cit.*, pp. 131 and 142; John F. Darby, *op. cit.*, pp. 184-85; L. T. Collier, "Recollections of Thomas Hart Benton," *Missouri Historical Review*, 8 (1913), 136-41.
[74] Quoted by Wentworth, *op. cit.*, p. 50.
[75] 1 April 1846. *Congressional Globe*, 29th Cong., 1st sess., 581-83.

deliberately and emphatically, and he caught the eye of all with his massive figure, majestic carriage, and formal, unvarying dress of frock coat, white waistcoat, and high neck cloth. Certain idiosyncrasies, such as the bulletlike repetition of "Sir," and the unexpected explosion, with each word hammered out energetically, no doubt helped to hold attention. But his appearance and deportment, however commanding, created the impression of dignity without amiability, and a gravelly voice, in which some detected the whirr of the tomahawk and others an exasperating squeal, had in it no conciliatory qualities.[76]

Clearly, Benton functioned without benefit of those "magnetic" qualities commonly attributed to democratic politicians. His handicaps must not, however, be exaggerated. His talents, traits, and virtues might not arouse the enthusiasm so easily generated by Henry Clay, but they commanded respectful attention, and attention was what he wanted. Let the people listen to him, and he would abide the result without worry about their affections. Nor should those characteristics that embroiled him with his colleagues be regarded as total liabilities. Countless Americans of our hot-tempered National Era liked a fighter who neither gave nor asked quarter. Modesty, moderation, and a mild demeanor paid few premiums on the frontier, and were not typical even of the senators who debated nullification, the Bank, the Mexican War, and the extension of slavery. A suave, gracious Benton striving to get on common ground with his enemies might have won some votes that never came his way. He might also have lost some that did come his way!

The nature of Benton as a human being accounted for the character of his speeches. He gave priority to reasoning and restricted himself to just a few octaves of the gamut of emotions because he was a certain kind of man, with great powers significantly limited in some directions. He was, however, a political speaker, not a lyric poet. He wanted specific responses from those who heard or read his speeches, and was well aware of the doctrine that the audience governs the construction of rhetorical discourse. No matter how

[76] His daughter thought he had a beautiful voice—"full, round and sustained and full of inflexions." Jessie Benton Frémont, "Sen. Thomas Hart Benton," *The Independent*, 55 (1903), 243. She was, however, almost alone in her admiration. For descriptions of his platform manner and delivery, see the memoirs already cited (Grissom, Darby, Johnson, Poore, Dyer, Foote, Davis, McClure, Wentworth, Collier) and Henry S. Foote, *Casket of Reminiscences* (Washington: Chronicle Pub. Co., 1874), p. 338; William C. Todd, *Biographical and Other Articles* (Boston: Lee & Shepard, 1901), pp. 93-94; Charles W. March, *Reminiscences of Congress* (2nd ed.; New York: Baker & Scribner, 1850), pp. 97-99; Meigs, *op. cit.*, 456-58. For a sympathetic portrait drawing on some other sources, see Arthur M. Schlesinger, Jr., *The Age of Jackson* (Boston: Little, Brown and Company, 1948), pp. 59-61.

independent or courageous he might be, he had to frame his speeches with reference to his understanding of the American scene.

As a senator, every time he prepared a speech he had to determine when to deliver it, how to fit it into the existing parliamentary situation or debate, and whether to address himself primarily to the Senate or to the public at large. That he made such decisions by reference to the political complexion of the Senate, the dating of elections, the novelty or immediacy of an issue, and the state of public opinion might be demonstrated by scores of citations. That he on the whole made them wisely is shown by the legislative history of his times. His knowledge of the nation also operated more pervasively, dictating strategy in its largest sense, suggesting the motivations to be used, and helping to shape even the logical argument. We have already traced his adaptations to changing circumstances as he pursued his unchanging aims for the public domain. In his futile fight against the Ashburton Treaty, he addressed himself to the East, which had been injured by the Northeastern boundary adjustments; to the South, whose grievance against the British for freeing slaves from coastal vessels driven by storms into colonial harbors had been ignored; and to the West, which had suffered by exclusion of Oregon from the agenda. Psychology, not logic, inspired the decision, when firing the first salvos against the Bank, to "avoid the beaten tracks of objection, avoid all settled points, avoid the problem of constitutionality—and take up the institution in a practical sense, as having too much power over the people and the government." [77] The speeches on finance contained arguments that would appeal with special force to each element that could be rallied against the Bank: to those who believed that the Charter was unconstitutional, to State-rights men who disliked its centralizing tendency, to independent bankers who feared its competition, to democrats who resented its aristocratic bias, and to wage earners who thought it made the rich richer and the poor poorer. [78] The intelligent analysis of the national audience must also have been responsible for his success in enlisting in behalf of one proposal the driving forces behind others. Land reform got linked with tariff reduction; opposition to distribution of the Treasury surplus to national defense.

Benton's knowledge of human nature did not quite equal his understanding of the main currents of public opinion, but he was by no means deficient as a practical psychologist. Self-interest and fear, he once said, are the most powerful passions of the human heart, and profit and loss the strongest principles of human action. [79] He used this perception more often, however, in analyzing

---

[77] *Thirty Years' View*, I, 187.

[78] See Thomas R. Lewis, "Thomas H. Benton's Analysis of His Audience," *Quarterly Journal of Speech*, 35 (1949), 441-47.

[79] Speech on Reciprocal Trade, *Thirty Years' View*, I, 153.

the motives of his enemies than in framing his constructive appeals to the people. In them, relying on his democratic faith in man, he prevailingly emphasized that his goals were justice, honor, freedom, and national security or prestige. That he did not adapt easily to people in many respects has already been almost overstressed, but his failures arose less from imperceptiveness than from inability to incorporate his insights into his speeches.

Did Benton deliberately analyze his audience when preparing a speech and mold his material in the light of his analysis? Perhaps, in some cases, but it seems unlikely that that was his general practice. He could follow his own inner light, firm in the conviction that "The People and Bane-ton are One, Sir," and with his exhaustiveness, his ingenuity in tracing the ramifications of a subject, and his general social sympathies, produce his speeches without dividing "The People" into classes and slanting his case to win the support of a winning combination. The question of deliberation is not, however, of great moment. His knowledge of the country was part of his total intellectual equipment, consciously or unconsciously influencing him at every step in the preparation of his speeches.

Benton's knowledge, logic, and insight into public affairs were not, unfortunately, consistently displayed to the best advantage in his completed speeches. Though not gravely deficient in any aspect of composition, he fell short of the highest order of skill in marshaling his ideas and expressing them in words. To say that his speeches were formless and marked by a "vast irrelevance" is to exaggerate grossly, but it is true that the pattern of organization often failed to reveal clearly the analytical foundation or to give the supporting detail its maximum impact. That he was not incapable of tightly-knit, systematic development is shown by some of his best speeches. That he was not indifferent to it is shown by his just remark about Jackson, who, he said, "had vigorous thoughts but not the faculty of arranging them in a regular composition, either written or spoken," and by the formal scaffolding he gave to most of his speeches, with the proposition stated, the main heads of the argument, and often the subheads, enumerated, and transitions carefully marked. Sometimes the enumeration was far from inclusive, and sometimes an initially clear outline was disrupted by the superimposition of a secondary pattern based on the several provisions of a bill, but on the whole little fault is to be found with the stripped framework. The weaknesses lie less in the conception of the whole than in the treatment of the parts.

The chief reason for the impression of formlessness is that the speeches contain too much. Depending more upon weight and amplitude than on architectonic neatness, Benton hated to leave anything unsaid. Three pages from Hansard befuddled when the pointedness of a half-page might have been unescapable. Restatement and amplification piled up until they confused more than they clarified. After reaching a proper conclusion, he could not believe that he had said all that needed to be said, and kept circling the subject. Tenuous associational links introduced favorite themes, including the historical retrospects and geographical panoramas in which he delighted. A speech on a transcontinental highway became the vehicle of a eulogy on the road-building achievements of the Incas. Mention of New Orleans in a speech on Mississippi navigation produced an excursus on the city's eponym, Marcus Aurelius, whose proudest achievement was an order to the Roman legions forbidding them ever to levy a tax on salt! Rhetorical justifications for such passages can usually be found, but they slowed progress, impaired logical unity, and obscured the main line of development. In combination with the excited, ejaculatory, even intemperate paragraphs that he often injected into sober argument or exposition, they hindered the achievement of climax and contributed to the impression that he was rambling.

The net effect was to make Benton's speeches cumbersome and slow-moving. He ground at his task like a bulldozer. Backing and filling, pushing hither and yon, he demonstrated impressive power to the patient; but the impatient would not linger to see the field smoothed by the clattering juggernaut.

The Bentonian style was spotty. At his worst, he handled the language like a man insensitive to rhythm and careless even of grammar. Sentences break in the middle, pronouns do not refer clearly to their antecedents, clause is piled on clause until the beginning has been forgotten before the end is reached. Preposterous remarks like, "Look at the case of Mr. Jefferson, a man than whom no one that ever existed on God's earth were the human family more indebted to," are not uncommon. Statistical tables and quotations sometimes make the speeches look like documented essays with the footnotes incorporated in the text.

At his average level, however, Benton was clear, and at his best he was tough, lively, and pungent. He delighted in balance and contrast, often whittled to antithetical sharpness. Denouncing Webster for failing as Secretary of State to obtain satisfaction from the British for the burning of the *Caroline,* he summed up his indictment: "McLeod is given up because he is too weak; the Queen is excused because she is too strong; propitiation is lavished where none was offered; the statute of limitations pleaded against an insult, by the party which received it! And the miserable performers in all this drama of national degradation expect to be applauded for magnanimity, when the laws of honor and the code of nations stamp their conduct with the brand of cowardice." Restatement plus contrast, metaphor, and alliteration could make a striking passage. Speaking against rescinding the Treasury Circular that required specie payment for public land, he said of the bill: "I

89

separate myself from it; I wash my hands of it; I oppose it. I am one of those who promised gold, not paper. I promised the currency of the constitution, not the currency of corporations. I did not join in putting down the Bank of the United States, to put up a wilderness of local banks. I did not join in putting down the paper currency of a national bank, to put up a national paper currency of a thousand local banks. I did not strike Caesar to make Anthony master of Rome." An appealing homeliness might rivet a general argument, as when he drove against tax systems that brought in more money than was needed: "The pockets of the citizens are the best treasuries which the Government can have for its spare revenues. They are the safest; for every citizen is the keeper of his own. They are the cheapest, for these keepers have no salaries; they are the most beneficial, for they are the only treasuries of which the keeper may always use the contents without blame, and with profit to himself and the country." A pithy generalization might sum up much reasoning. "I never purchase as a concession what I hold as a right, nor accept an inferior title when I already hold the highest," he said when pointing out that the Compromise of 1850 offered to the South only what she already possessed, the constitutional right to reclaim fugitive slaves.

Often a sort of rhetorical exuberance infected this sober statesman. A tariff, he pointed out, raises the price of a product by more than the amount that the government collects, because the merchant's mark-up is based on his total cost, including the duty. Having stated the point, he drove it home: "The amount of this superincumbent, superstructive, and, I believe I might say, supercrescential tax ... cannot be less than ... eight or ten millions upon our present Customhouse revenue." The hodge-podge Compromise of 1850 opened "a new chapter in legislative ratiocination. It substitutes contiguity of territory for congruity of matter, and makes geographical affinities the rule of legislative conjunction." The repeal of the Missouri Compromise, proposed by the Kansas-Nebraska Act, was demanded not by the people in the territories concerned, "but upon a motion in Congress—a silent, secret, limping, halting, creeping, squinting, impish motion—conceived in the dark—midwifed in a committee room, and sprung upon the Congress and the country in the style in which Guy Fawkes intended to blow up the Parliament House...." The monstrosity called "territorial sovereignty," when first broached in the Senate, was "received as nonsense—as the essence of nonsense—as the quintessence of nonsense—as the five-times distilled essence of political nonsensicality."

Analogies came easily. The privilege of presenting a bank draft issued at St. Louis for payment at Philadelphia was to most men "equivalent to the privilege of going to Mecca to sue the successors of Mahomet for the bones of the prophet." A ludicrously inadequate tariff reduction was "in the Western vernacular, 'the little end of nothing sharpened,'" and bore as little relation to the revision needed as one hair of a horse's tail bears to the whole horse! Names could not alter things, and "it is as idle to call a gift a deposit, as it would be to call a stab of the dagger a kiss of the lips." Had it not been for intriguing American politicians Texas would have entered the Union with no more need for plots and tricks than there was "for some old hag of a match-making beldame, with her arts and allurements, her philters and her potions, to get Eve into Adam's bosom."

The enthusiasm for classical allusion that marked our National Period came to full flower in Benton. A proposal for a Pan-American Congress on the Isthmus of Panama evoked "cherished recollections" because the Greeks had assembled on the Isthmus of Corinth. His twelve-year fight against the salt tax had lasted two years longer than the Trojan War. Calling a bank a "fiscal corporation" was like calling the rape of the Sabines a marriage. Eumenes, secretary of Alexander the Great, originated the weird notion that a national debt is a national blessing because it binds the rich to the state. When his master died, he borrowed hugely to raise an army, laid claim to Cappadocia and Paphlagonia, and forced his creditors to support him to insure repayment of their loans. To Benton, one proper way to defend the veto was to trace a far-fetched resemblance between the powers of the president and those of the Roman tribunes, and one way to praise Sam Houston was to point out that he was the first self-made general to take the commander of the enemy army and the head of the enemy government captive in battle since Mark Antony captured King Antigonus—a distinction that probably astonished General Houston when he learned of it.

The light touch did not come easily. When Clay convulsed the galleries with a picture of the Senator from Missouri warbling "Refuse lands, Refuse lands, Refuse lands" from the west side of the Mississippi until the governor of Illinois, enchanted with a tune so sweet to the electorate, converted the refrain into a duet, Benton sourly retorted that the duet was a solo, sung only in the Senate, by a performer whose studied gayety had been puffed in advance by the *National Intelligencer*. When Dickerson of New Jersey wondered if future Oregon congressmen would reach the Potomac by doubling Cape Horn, following a new route laid out under the North Pole, or climbing mountains whose summits presented twelve feet of snow to the July sun, Benton grimly observed that wit was useful to embellish an argument or to conceal the lack of one, and he would not say for which purpose the Senator had indulged in it. When he himself essayed a humorous flight the machinery creaked. In a discussion of unsuitable articles purchased by the government for sale to the Indians, he came to the item of jew's-harps. They reminded him that music hath charms to soothe the savage heart, that a musician of old charmed a woman out of hell, and that although jew's-harps did not in

91

his opinion discourse very excellent music, *De gustibus non disputandum.* They were at any rate innocent instruments, specifically exempted from a Hartford ordinance that banned drums and fifes, and without them the tawny-colored Corydons and Amaryllises, *recubans sub tegmine fagi,* could make no progress in the delightful dalliance of love. He did better when, opposing an appropriation for a riding academy at West Point, he poked fun at the military jargon that turned "learning to ride on horseback" into "exercises in equitation," and was at his humorous best when, resisting a motion to distribute some documents, he observed that they might be useful to the grocers if the leaves had not been cut. Servants in the boardinghouses had told him that the plethora of government publications had depressed the market for waste paper to two cents per pound. "The gentleman ... smiled; but if he would take his little children to a shoe store and buy a pair of shoes, he would find that they would be wrapped up in public documents."

In his own day Benton enjoyed a reputation for wit. Little survives in the published speeches, and the anecdotal material suggests that what passed for wit would now be classed as irony, sarcasm, and ridicule. Irony was a telling weapon, as he showed when the Whigs won the election of 1840 with the slogans and symbols of a hitherto unsuspected zeal for the poor man and he called on them to prove their sincerity by passing a pre-emption law. "The gentlemen of this party have betaken themselves to the love of log-cabins ... with the fury and incontinence of a sudden and romantic affection. They build them with their own hands, and piously dedicate them—they sing, dance, drink and speak in them ... they decorate them with appropriate trappings, with gourds, coon skins, buck horns, beaver traps, and whatever else denotes the real cabin of the ... pre-emptioner. ... Like Pygmalion, they become madly enamored of the work of their own hands. ..." Heavy-handed ridicule often delighted those whose ox was not gored. When the Whigs, with one eye on President Tyler's constitutional scruples, attempted to revive the old Bank of the United States in the guise of a "Fiscal Corporation," Benton expressed his views with good-natured contempt. A steamboat named *La Belle Creole* that everybody called *The Owl,* the Aesopian black cat that fooled her prey by rolling herself in a meal tub, the Meal-Tub plot against Charles II, Praise God Barebone, the meaning of "shakepoke," and equally unlikely topics were loosely woven together and given a droll, mocking relevance to the "corporosity." When the efforts to revive the Bank took the form of a "Federal Exchequer" he also adopted a mocking tone, but apologized: "It is not my custom to speak irreverently of official matters; but there are some things too light for argument—too grave for ridicule—and which it is difficult to treat in a becoming manner."

In the main, Benton's style adequately represented the man himself.[80] One suspects, however, that sheer pressure of business must often have prohibited the revisions that might have improved the syntax and pruned the redundancies. He never had a clerk, not even a copyist. His researches took endless hours, and he busied himself with every topic of public interest. In one session of Congress he complained about the suppressions of the *Register*, and the printers in reply revealed that more than one hundred pages, five times the average for each senator, had been devoted to his speeches. Even the *Thirty Years' View* had to be composed under pressure. He was already afflicted with the cancer that killed him; fire destroyed part of his manuscript; and he had committed himself to newspaper publication by installments in the New York *Evening Post*.

Evidently Benton does not belong with those select few who managed to speak to posterity as well as to their own age and their own people. His speeches are a part of the historical record rather than a part of literature. Judged by the less exacting standards of ordinary political speaking, he exhibited in his style a mixture of weakness and strength. He lacked precision, grace, economy, and ease; he sometimes seemed to fluctuate between flat pedestrianism and bombast; even the minimum essential of clarity often eluded him. On the other hand, he had great merits. His expansiveness insured ultimate clarity despite occasional syntactical ambiguity. Contrasts, exclamations, questions, exhortations, illustrations, analogies, repetitions, and restatements helped to liven the dead weight of exhaustive factual evidence and to sustain interest at a high level. The classical allusions, attributable not to an "ostentation of learning" but to the respect paid by a young and in some respects insecure republic to its ancient prototypes, were a convention of the times and constituted a form of literary adornment more appreciated then than now.

The pattern of this essay has not permitted an attempt to trace Benton's growth as a statesman and speaker. His maturity when he first went to Washington and the bold cast of his personality insured that he would be in 1850 essentially the man he was in 1820; but he was a seeker and a learner, one who could profit from experience. This capacity for growth revealed itself strikingly in style. Francis Blair wrote that prior to 1850 Benton was more

---

[80] That is, the style of the speeches adequately represented the stern, aggressive public figure. The gentler, more compassionate side of Benton's character, known so well to his family, found admirable expression in the notices of deceased contemporaries to be found in the *Thirty Years' View*. Had space permitted, these notices (there are about thirty) might well have been quoted to show that he had, when inspired by respect or affection, or by a generous appreciation of greatness, the literary talent to express himself with moving simplicity and to paint memorable portraits of men that we ought not to forget.

impressive when read than when heard; after that, the contrary was true. Retaining his primary characteristics, he trimmed his speeches of some of their pedantry and achieved a directness, force, and simplicity that could be found only in sporadic passages of his earlier efforts. Increasingly after 1845 he was engaged in the task of preserving the Union, and it is perhaps not fanciful to suggest that the greatness and urgency of the work combined with the realization that he was fighting for his political existence to give new life to his language.

Conclusion

It is a striking fact that no Jacksonian legislative leader earned an enduring reputation as a great speaker. Benton, Van Buren, Buchanan, Cambreleng, and Polk are unlikely candidates for canonization in the anthologies. With Jackson they wrote the history of an age, but their defeated opponents have been enshrined in the national consciousness as our most eloquent men.

A great many explanations of this apparent paradox may be offered, and in each may be a kernel of truth. One of these partial explanations is suggested by an inspection of the relations between Jackson and Benton. Jackson, no speaker or writer, attracted to himself the affection and enthusiasm of the people; his was the pivotal personality usually so necessary to a successful mass movement. Benton formulated, systematized, expounded, and justified the intuitions of the President. Functions of leadership that Franklin D. Roosevelt united in himself during the New Deal were severed during the Jacksonian Revolt.

For his own work Benton's merits were great and his weaknesses superficial. The American people, by recognition of his intelligence, honesty, and devotion to the common good, showed themselves worthy of the compliments he paid them.

SELECTED BIBLIOGRAPHY

Books, Pamphlets, Unpublished Theses, Speeches

BENTON, THOMAS HART. *Abridgment of the Debates of Congress from 1789 to 1856.* 16 vols. New York: D. Appleton & Co., 1857-61.
———. *Discourse of Mr. Benton of Missouri.* Boston: Boston Mercantile Library Association, 1854.
———. *Examination of the Dred Scott Case.* New York: D. Appleton & Co., 1857.
———. *Selections of Editorial Articles from the St. Louis Enquirer, on the Subject of Oregon and Texas, as Originally Published in That Paper, in the Years 1818-19.* St. Louis: Missourian Office, 1844.
———. *Speech of the Hon. Thos. H. Benton, Delivered at the Capitol at Jefferson City, May 26th, 1849.* St. Louis: Union Job Print, n.d.
———. *Speech ... Delivered at Fayette, Howard County, Missouri, on Saturday, the First of September, 1849.* Jefferson City, 1849.

BENTON, THOMAS HART. *Thirty Years' View*, 2 vols. New York: D. Appleton & Co., 1854-56.

DARBY, JOHN F. *Personal Recollections*. St. Louis: G. I. Jones & Co., 1880.

DAVIS, VARINA HOWELL. *Jefferson Davis: A Memoir by His Wife*. 2 vols. New York: Belford Co., 1890.

DYER, OLIVER. *Great Senators of the United States Forty Years Ago*. New York: Rob't. Bonner's Sons, 1889.

FOOTE, HENRY S. *Casket of Reminiscences*. Washington, D. C.: Chronicle Pub. Co., 1874.

————. *Bench and Bar of the South and Southwest*. St. Louis: Soule, Thomas & Wentworth, 1876.

FAGG, THOMAS JEFFERSON CLARK. *Thomas Hart Benton: The Great Missourian and His Times Reviewed*. n.p., 1905.

FRÉMONT, JOHN CHARLES. *Memoirs of My Life Together with a Sketch of the Life of Senator Benton . . . by Jessie Benton Frémont*. Chicago & New York: Belford, Clarke & Co., 1887.

HUNTER, CHARLES FRANCIS. "Four Speeches of Thomas Hart Benton." Edited with Notes and an Introduction. 2 vols. Unpublished Ph.D. dissertation, Cornell University, 1942.

JOHNSON, CHARLES P. *Personal Recollections of Some of Missouri's Eminent Statesmen and Lawyers*. n.p., 1903.

LEWIS, THOMAS R. "Persuasive Techniques of Thomas Hart Benton as a Congressional Debater." Unpublished Ph.D. dissertation, University of Iowa, 1948.

MCCLURE, ALEXANDER K. *Recollections of Half a Century*. Salem: Salem Press Co., 1902.

MEIGS, WILLIAM M. *Life of Thomas Hart Benton*. Philadelphia: J. B. Lippincott Co., 1904.

POLK, JAMES K. *The Diary of James K. Polk during his Presidency, 1845 to 1849*, ed. M. M. QUAIFE. Chicago: A. C. McClurg & Co., 1910.

POORE, BEN: PERLEY. *Perley's Reminiscences of Sixty Years in the National Metropolis*. 2 vols. Philadelphia: Hubbard Bros., 1886.

ROGERS, JOSEPH M. *Thomas H. Benton*. Philadelphia: Geo. W. Jacobs & Co., 1905.

ROOSEVELT, THEODORE. *Thomas H. Benton*. ("American Statesmen Series.") Boston: Houghton Mifflin & Co., 1899.

SARGENT, NATHAN. *Public Men and Events*. 2 vols. Philadelphia: J. B. Lippincott Co., 1875.

TODD, WILLIAM C. *Biographical and Other Articles*. Boston: Lee & Shepard, 1901.

WENTWORTH, JOHN. *Congressional Reminiscences*. Chicago: Fergus Printing Co., 1882.

Periodicals

BIDSTRUP, DUDLEY J. "The Background of Public Speaking in Missouri, 1840-1860," *Missouri Historical Review*, XXXVI (1941-42), 133-59.

CHAMBERS, WILLIAM N. "As the Twig Is Bent: the Family and the North Carolina Years of Thomas Hart Benton, 1752-1801," *North Carolina Historical Review*, XXVI (October, 1949), 385-416.

————. "Thomas Hart Benton in Tennessee, 1801-1812," *Tennessee Historical Quarterly*, VIII (1949), 291-331.

————. "Thwarted Warrior: The Last Years of Thomas Hart Benton in Tennessee, 1812-1815," *East Tennessee Historical Society's Publications* (Knoxville), 22 (1950), 19-44.

95

CHAMBERS, WILLIAM N. "Young Man from Tennessee: First Years of Thomas H. Benton in *Missouri Historical Society Bulletin,* IV (July, 1948), 199-216.

————. "Thomas Hart Benton: Editor," *Missouri Historical Review,* XLVI (July, 1952), 335-45.

————. "Pistols and Politics: Incidents in the Career of Thomas H. Benton, 1816-1818," *Missouri Historical Society Bulletin,* V (October, 1948), 5-17.

COLLIER, L. T. "Recollections of Thomas Hart Benton," *Missouri Historical Review,* VIII (April, 1913), 136-41.

FRÉMONT, JESSIE BENTON. "Senator Thomas Hart Benton," *Independent* (New York), 55 (1903), 240-44.

GRISSOM, DANIEL M. "Personal Recollections of Distinguished Missourians," *Missouri Historical Review,* XVIII (January, 1924), 129-45.

LEWIS, THOMAS R. "Thomas H. Benton's Analysis of His Audience," *Quarterly Journal of Speech,* XXXV (1949), 441-47.

McCLURE, C. H. "Early Opposition to Thomas Hart Benton," *Missouri Historical Review,* X (April, 1916), 151-96.

Niles' Weekly Register and *Niles' National Register* (Baltimore, Washington), 1818-49.

SEELEN, WILLIAM E. "Thomas Hart Benton's Expunging Speech: An Analysis of the Immediate Audience," *Speech Monographs,* VIII (December, 1941), 58-67.

STEVENS, WALTER B. "A Day and a Night with 'Old Davy'," *Missouri Historical Review,* XXXI (January, 1937), 129-39.

Documents

Annals of Congress, 1819-24.
Register of Debates in Congress, 1824-37.
The Congressional Globe, 1833-58.

Susan B. Anthony

by Doris Yoakam Twichell

Susan Brownell Anthony was born in Adams, Massachusetts, on February 15, 1820, the fourth of the six children of Daniel Anthony, pioneer cotton manufacturer. The family moved to Battenville, New York, in 1826, and to Hardscrabble, New York, in 1839. Susan attended a district school and later the school established by her father at home for his own and neighborhood children. She spent two years at Deborah Moulson's Boarding School near Philadelphia. Family misfortunes, caused in part by events leading to the Panic of 1837, turned her to teaching, a career she followed until around 1849. She then went to the Rochester, New York, farm to which her family had moved in 1845, and aided with its management in order to help her father, who had become a regional agent for the New York Life Insurance Company. She called Rochester her home for the rest of her life. Here she entered the popular reform movements of mid-nineteenth century America. From Rochester she went forth to work for the woman's rights movement, and to the struggle for woman's improvement and suffrage she devoted the rest of her life. She died on March 13, 1906.

In view of the fact that Susan B. Anthony was not acclaimed by friends, critics, and contemporary press as a public speaker of the outstanding ability of such women as Lucy Stone, Elizabeth Cady Stanton, Anna E. Dickinson, and Anna Howard Shaw, it may seem strange to find her name listed as a woman representative in a volume on American public address. She was, however, one of the most prominent among women in American history, and as such her career upon the public platform is a subject worthy of study. But just what was her standing as a public speaker? How effective was she? The first step in answering these questions is a brief review of her life and work.

The circumstances of Susan B. Anthony's birth undoubtedly conditioned her future. The daughter of Daniel and Lucy Anthony, Quakers, she was taught the doctrines of the Society of Friends. These doctrines emphasized equality of the sexes and encouraged women to participate in spiritual and temporal matters.[1] As a citizen of New York State in the early nineteenth

---

[1] Auguste Jorns, *The Quakers as Pioneers in Social Work* (New York: The Macmillan Co., 1931), p. 42.

century she was subjected to the reform spirit which was evidenced in the many organized movements for social and economic improvement.

The question of whether Susan would follow the predilections of her environment was soon resolved. As a child she was precocious.[2] She learned to read at four, and before long demanded to be taught such aspects of arithmetic as "long division," then regarded as unnecessary for girls. She was influenced greatly by her father, a man considered radical among the Quakers, and a reformer whose ideas encompassed improvement in housing for the workers in his factory, and no trade with slaveholders.

A reversal in family fortunes taught Susan to face realities and to shoulder serious responsibilities. In order to earn her own living and to help the family recover from the financial crisis, she turned to teaching, filling positions first in New Rochelle and then near Hardscrabble, New York. For a while she served as governess for a family near Fort Edwards, New York, and here she found the opportunity to read current periodicals and to take more and more interest in national politics.

As principal of the girls' department of the Canajoharie Academy in Canajoharie, New York, a position she accepted in 1846, she gained influence and the reputation of being both a very able teacher and a popular young woman. She dropped the Quaker plain speech, the Quaker garments, and, until she found them too dull, participated in social events, going to parties, the theater, and the circus.[3] In this community she conquered the obstacles of the local teaching profession. She saw her father reinstated in a salaried position, and she came to lead for the only brief time in her career, a life of self-interest and moderate luxury. Soon she found this insufficient, deadening, boring.

The Reformer

Susan B. Anthony began her work for reform while teaching in Canajoharie. She joined a local woman's organization called the Daughters of Temperance and soon became its secretary. On March 1, 1849, as speaker of the evening at a village supper sponsored by the Daughters, she gave her first public speech, reading from manuscript to a two-hundred person audience a plea for support of the temperance movement. Her appeal was directed especially to the women for, as she said, "In my humble opinion, all that is needed to produce a complete Temperance and Social reform in this age of

[2] Rheta C. Dorr, *Susan B. Anthony* (New York: Frederick A. Stokes Co., 1928), pp. 12-13.

[3] *Ibid.*, p. 34.

Moral Suasion, is for our Sex to cast their United influences into the balance." [4]
She concluded:

Ladies! there is no Neutral position for us to assume. If we sustain not this noble enterprise, both by precept and example, then is our influence on the side of Intemperance. If we say we love the Cause, and then sit down at our ease, surely does our action speak the lie. And now permit me once more to beg of you to lend your aid to this great Cause, the Cause of God and all Mankind. [5]

It was inevitable that soon Susan Anthony should develop into a fullfledged reformer. Upon her return to the family farm near Rochester, New York, in 1850, she listened to the discussion of leading events and issues that took place at Sunday dinners when her father was at home, and the Anthony farm, a favorite meeting place of liberal-spirited men and women, had as guests such prominent reformers as Garrison, Pillsbury, Phillips, Channing, and Frederick Douglass.

Susan read. She attended reform meetings. She longed to take a more active part in the two great reforms of temperance and antislavery which were absorbing public attention at the time. Her mother gave her sympathy. And her father encouraged her, giving her financial backing when necessary and moral support upon all occasions.

Having brought her credentials from the Canajoharie temperance organization she was soon at work in Rochester. In 1851 she began to demonstrate unusual executive ability in organizing a number of temperance societies in towns close to Rochester, and in raising funds through a series of local suppers and festivals. In 1852 and 1853 she was among the women temperance workers who disturbed temperance meetings in Albany, Syracuse, and New York City by attempting to speak and take part in the proceedings. She was prominent in the women's meetings held immediately upon the opposition of the general conventions. [6]

Susan Anthony undertook arrangements for the temperance convention held in Rochester on April 20, 1852, at which five hundred women assembled and formed the first Woman's State Temperance Society. She opened this meeting, reading the Call which urged women to initiate "associated Action"

---

[4] Ida H. Harper, *The Life and Work of Susan B. Anthony* (3 vols.; Indianapolis: Hollenbeck Press, 1898-1908), I, 53.

[5] *Ibid.*, I, 53. Cf. also Harriett E. Grim, "Susan B. Anthony, Exponent of Freedom" (Ph.D. thesis, University of Wisconsin, 1938), III, Appendix, pp. 10-16, for a slightly different version of the same speech. Both are copied from the original.

[6] Cf. *The Liberator* (Boston), July 9, 1852, May 20, September 9 and 16, 1853; *The Lily* (Seneca Falls, New York), July, 1852, pp. 60-61; *The Una* (Providence, Rhode Island), June, 1853, pp. 73-75; September, 1853, p. 131; October, 1853, p. 154.

to protect their interests and those of society at large which "too long had been invaded and destroyed by legalized intemperance." [7]

With three other women she traveled throughout New York State during the summer of 1852, holding meetings, organizing temperance societies, and trying to rouse women to come out of seclusion and work for temperance. [8] And by 1854 she had increased her sphere of labor to the point that she was receiving such notices as the one listed in *The Liberator* on April 14th, announcing her appearance before the "Marion Temperance Society" of Baltimore.

After hearing her speak in Canajoharie, New York, in 1854, and upon learning that she was being urged to return there to teach, her uncle Read emphatically stated, "No, some one ought to go around and set the people thinking about the laws and it is Susan's work to do this." [9]

During the 1850's she joined the ranks of the abolitionists. She attended meetings and was converted to the radical sentiments of the Garrisonites. In April of 1851 she helped sponsor a meeting in Rochester conducted by Stephen and Abby Kelley Foster, among the most fearless and persecuted of the antislavery leaders. [10] As a result of this meeting she accompanied them for a week on their tour of meetings in adjoining counties and was urged by them to go actively into this reform. [11]

By 1854 she was urging the importance of bringing antislavery papers before the people at the Pennsylvania Anti-Slavery Convention. [12]

She served as general agent for the National Anti-Slavery Society for New York State in 1856 and 1857, and according to Parker Pillsbury, proved very able in planning meetings, marking out routes, and keeping three companies of speakers constantly employed. [13]

Her name appeared frequently in the "Announcement of Meetings" section of *The Liberator* for the next few years. She was advertised as holding meetings with such abolitionists as Aaron M. Powell, William Wells Brown, Parker Pillsbury, Marius R. Robinson, and Wendell Phillips. [14]

During the Civil War her work for antislavery continued. She planned and attended conventions, and took as her sole theme in 1862 "Emancipation

[7] Harper, *op. cit.*, I, 68.

[8] Elizabeth C. Stanton *et. al.*, eds., *The History of Woman Suffrage* (Rochester, New York: Charles Mann, 1887), I, 488-89.

[9] Harper, *op. cit.*, I, 121.

[10] Blake McKelvey, "Susan B. Anthony," *Rochester History*, VII (April, 1945), 6.

[11] Harper, *op. cit.*, I, 63.

[12] *The Liberator*, November 3, 1854.

[13] Harper, *op. cit.*, I, 157.

[14] Cf. *The Liberator*, January 23 and April 10, 1857; January 27, February 24, and March 2, 1860.

the duty of the government."[15] Another of her activities was administrative work in the Woman's Loyal League. She and Elizabeth Cady Stanton called a mass meeting for May 14, 1863, in Dr. Cheever's church in New York City, and the league was formed. Its special purpose was to awaken public sentiment through writing and speaking, and to secure signatures to a petition to Congress demanding a Federal amendment abolishing slavery in the United States. Miss Anthony was able to say that by August, 1864, "nearly 400,000 signatures to petitions for emancipation were secured and Charles Sumner and Henry Wilson wrote us repeatedly that these petitions formed the bulwark of their demand for congressional action to abolish slavery."[16]

From shortly after the Civil War until her death on March 13, 1906, Susan B. Anthony's chief purpose was to elevate the social and economic condition of women. She was well qualified to assume leadership of the woman suffrage movement, for her activities during the first decade of her reform work had included a great deal of effort for woman's rights. She had first become aware of discrimination against women when, as a teacher, she had seen the variance in salaries paid to men and women, and the docile manner in which women accepted their inferior condition. In 1852, while canvassing for temperance, she happened into a teacher's convention in Elmira, New York. Here she determined to demand for women all the privileges then claimed by men.[17] At the State Teacher's Convention in Rochester in 1853, she fought for the privilege of speaking. By 1856 she was an invited speaker at the convention in Troy. Her subject was "Educating the Sexes Together," a speech she also gave upon several other occasions.[18] In 1859 she submitted to the convention in Poughkeepsie a report of the committee upon "Declamation and Discussion for Girls," and advocated the teaching of these subjects.[19]

Susan Anthony encouraged New York women teachers to fight their own battles. She argued for equal pay for equal services, and she advocated improvements in methods of teaching and in the sanitary conditions of school buildings.[20] By 1860 she was encouraged to see that there was no further need to urge the women to take part in meetings. She had succeeded in arousing them to demand justice and to become aware of their opportunities and responsibilities.[21]

[15] Harper, *op. cit.*, I, 222.

[16] Susan B. Anthony, "Woman's Half Century of Evolution," *North American Review*, CLXXV (December, 1902), 806-7.

[17] Harper, *op. cit.*, I, 71-72.

[18] Cf. *National Anti-Slavery Standard* (New York), February 6, 1858.

[19] *The Daily Press* (Poughkeepsie, New York), August 4, 1859.

[20] Stanton *et al.*, *op. cit.*, I, 513.

[21] Nanette B. Paul, *The Great Woman Statesman* (New York: Hogan-Paulus Corp., 1925), p. 17.

Enthusiasm for the woman's rights movement manifested itself among the members of Susan's own family. She came home for a vacation in July, 1848, and found that her father, mother, and sister Mary had just attended the first Woman's Rights Convention in Seneca Falls, had signed a declaration demanding equal rights, and were enthusiastic over the subject and the leaders who had taken part in the convention. In 1849 she read Lucretia Mott's "Discourse on Woman," which explained the equality intended for women as shown by careful reading of the Scripture, justified the reasons why women needed and wanted to enlarge their sphere, defined the inequality of existing laws, and pleaded for encouragement and aid in elevating women to their rightful place as responsible citizens.[22] In 1850 her consciousness was fully awakened by reading the favorable account of the Worcester, Massachusetts, Woman's Rights Convention which appeared in the *New York Tribune.* The next year she met Elizabeth Cady Stanton, who was to become her lifelong friend and colleague.[23]

Susan B. Anthony's active work for woman's rights began at a convention in Syracuse, New York, in September of 1852. By 1854 she was acting as general agent for the state association whose program included holding a series of conventions in all of the counties and chief cities of the state in order to enlighten the people on the actual claims of the movement. The state association also prepared petitions to present to the state legislature to secure property and other rights for women.[24] In 1860 she was a prominent participant in the New York state convention in Albany. In October of that year she was invited to make a speech representing women at the Fair of the Union Agricultural Society in Dundee, New York.[25]

After the Civil War all of Miss Anthony's energies were devoted to the battle for the rights of women. By this time she was so convinced that a constitutional amendment was the only method, and that full suffrage for women was the only guarantee of equality that she never deviated from direct agitation to secure these ends.[26] She objected to the word "male" in the Fourteenth Amendment, and sought to add the word "sex" to the Fifteenth. She agitated for a constitutional amendment that would give suffrage to citizens without discrimination based on sex. She tried to educate the people of the United States to understand the rights of women and to act for women's enfranchisement.

[22] Anna D. Hallowell, *James and Lucretia Mott, Life and Letters* (Boston: Houghton, Mifflin & Co., 1884), pp. 487-506.

[23] Anthony, *op. cit.,* p. 806.

[24] Stanton *et al., op. cit.,* I, 619, 856.

[25] Cf. *The Liberator,* March 2, 1860; Susan B. Anthony Scrapbooks (33 vols.; Rare Book Room, Library of Congress), I, 123.

[26] Cf. Stanton *et al., op. cit.,* II, 91-151.

One of her chief activities was that of organizing and supervising woman suffrage associations. She was a leader in the organization of the National Woman Suffrage Association in 1869, attended its yearly conventions with the exception of two, from the first one held in Washington, D.C., in 1869, through the 1906 convention, a month before her death. She held such offices as treasurer, secretary, and vice-president frequently, and was national president from 1892 until 1900. Yearly she served on such committees as the finance, the executive, the business, or the resolutions. She aided in the formation and encouraged the work of local and state woman suffrage groups throughout the United States. An article appearing in "Photographs of Our Agitators" in *The Hearth and Home* of January 22, 1870, said:

She is the Bismarck; she plans the campaigns, provides the munitions of war, organizes the raw recruits, sets the squadrons in the field. Indeed, in presence of a timid lieutenant, she sometimes heads the charge; but she is most effective as the directing generalissimo. . . . She presides over the treasury, she cuts the Gordian knots, and when the uncontrollables get by the ears at the conventions, she is the one who straightway drags them asunder and turns chaos to order again. In every dilemma, she is unanimously summoned.

Work for suffrage reform resulted in Miss Anthony's speaking before audiences all over the United States. She made her first tour through Missouri, Illinois, Wisconsin, and Ohio in 1869, traveling with Elizabeth Cady Stanton, and holding meetings that were felt to have valuable results in rousing women who had been absorbed in war work to renew their efforts in their own behalf as citizens.[27] Throughout her career she appeared at state conventions, attending them from Maine to Oregon and from Minnesota to Louisiana.

When state constitutions were under revision or when state legislatures were considering woman suffrage bills, she was usually on the scene and in the midst of the campaigns. She was prominent in state canvasses not only in her own State of New York, but in Kansas, Michigan, Colorado, Nebraska, Indiana, South Dakota, California, and others.[28]

She presented the woman suffrage question to legislative groups, both state and national. She spoke to such legislative groups as those in Nebraska in 1871, New Hampshire in 1881, Indiana and New York in 1897. She appeared before congressional committees yearly, usually in hearings occurring during or after the national woman suffrage convention in January or February. She and Mrs. Stanton gave the arguments on woman suffrage before the first congressional hearing granted on the question on January 26,

[27] Stanton *et al.*, *op. cit.*, II, 367.
[28] *Ibid.*, Vols. I-IV.

1869,[29] and she presided at the hearing in 1904 in her frequent role as chairman, introducing the other women speakers, and making the closing address.[30]

Susan B. Anthony attended political conventions and endeavored to enlist the aid of political parties for woman suffrage. In addition to the Republican national conventions from 1872 to 1892, she attended Democratic conventions, National Prohibition conventions, National Liberal conventions, Greenback Labor conventions and others.

Trips to Europe were included in her journeys. In 1888 she presided over eight of the sixteen sessions of the International Council of Women, and she again appeared at the International Women's Conferences in 1899, 1902, and 1904. Her chief interest in traveling abroad was not in sight-seeing but in meeting reformers, in studying social conditions, and in furthering international organization among women.

In her program to educate the public she appeared at many general meetings and conventions and asked for resolutions supporting woman suffrage. She spoke at meetings of the South Dakota Farmer's Alliance in 1889 and 1890, the Ladies' Library Association in Ann Arbor, Michigan, in 1889, the American Federation of Labor in Indianapolis in 1899, and the Bricklayer's and Mason's International Union, Rochester, New York, in 1900. She talked to Negro audiences from Rochester to San Francisco to New Orleans. She appeared before student groups in high schools, teachers' colleges, and universities. On the long list of her appearances were those at the Woman's College of Brown University, the University of Nevada, San Jose Normal School, Atlanta University, Tuskegee Institute, and many others.[31]

Miss Anthony went on lecture tours, appearing alone or with other speakers, lecturing under private auspices, under sponsorship of a bureau, and sometimes under her own arrangement. In 1867 she and Elizabeth Cady Stanton undertook a lecture tour in company with George Train, and spoke in towns from Kansas to New York City. In 1870 she substituted for Mrs. Stanton for a month while the latter was ill, and proved so acceptable to the New York Lyceum Bureau that she was engaged by it, and spoke in Pennsylvania, Ohio, Indiana, Illinois and Michigan. From 1870 to 1876 she accepted all the lecturing dates she possibly could in order to earn money for paying the debt incurred by *The Revolution*, a woman's rights paper she ran from 1868 until it succumbed financially in 1870. She spoke for the Star Course

[29] Harper, *op. cit.*, I, 313-14.
[30] Elizabeth C. Stanton *et al.*, eds., *The History of Woman Suffrage* (New York: J. J. Little & Ives Co., 1922), V, 110.
[31] Cf. Harper, *op. cit.*, Vols. I-III; Susan B. Anthony Scrapbooks.

in 1870, and the Dime Lecture Course in 1875 and 1876. She lectured under contract with the Slayton Lyceum Bureau in 1876, 1877, 1885, and 1888.

In reviewing her work for an article appearing in the *Chautauqua Assembly Herald* on August 9, 1892, Miss Anthony said that between 1870 and 1880 she spoke in public on the subject of woman suffrage on an average of nearly two hundred nights each year. From Seattle, Washington, she wrote on November 4, 1871, "I have traveled 1,800 miles in fifty-six days, spoken forty-two nights and many days...." [32] In the Michigan campaign of 1874 she spoke in thirty-five places in forty days and also took three days out to attend the Illinois Woman Suffrage Convention in Chicago.[33] She told the audience at the National Woman Suffrage Convention in May, 1879, that she had already spoken in 140 places that year, and said that if there were a man in the house who had gone through that amount of physical endurance she would like to see him.[34] On a "brief lecture tour" in 1893, and at the age of seventy-three, she made nine evening addresses, attended several receptions, and traveled more than a thousand miles in twelve days. In response to a question asked her in 1897 regarding the extent of her work, she said:

It would be hard to find a city in the northern and western States in which I have not lectured, and I have spoken in many of the southern cities. I have been on the platform over forty-five years and it would be impossible to tell how many lectures I have delivered; they probably would average from seventy-five to one hundred every year.[35]

When in Washington she talked with individual congressmen, seeing them both at the Capitol and in their homes. She interviewed Presidents Grant, Johnson, Arthur, McKinley, and Theodore Roosevelt. She accepted invitations to dinners and receptions when she saw the opportunity of influencing prominent people for woman suffrage. She called herself a lobbyist without the two necessary requisites—she neither accepted money nor had any to pay out.

Throughout her whole career Susan carried on a voluminous correspondence, and wrote letters to everyone from the most modest housewife to the most prominent politician. By way of illustration, there were nine hundred letters from all parts of the world addressed to her on her seventy-seventh birthday, and she spent three months of 1897 answering these.[36] Her letters were full of concrete and hopeful suggestions.

[32] Harper, *op. cit.*, I, 400.
[33] *Ibid.*, I, 459.
[34] *St. Louis Globe-Democrat*, May 8, 1879.
[35] Harper, *op. cit.*, II, 925.
[36] McKelvey, *op. cit.*, p. 20.

The records of her experiences, which came to fill thirty-three volumes of old ledgers, and her daily journal aided in the writing of *The History of Woman Suffrage*. She spent years helping to write, finance, and publish the first four volumes of this work. And she aided Ida Harper in the writing of the first two volumes of her biography, which in itself is a partial history of the suffrage movement.

She published tracts and wrote articles, drafted resolutions and circulated petitions. She urged women to read suffrage pamphlets and the equal rights' papers, and she passed out literature at the end of her lectures.[37] At a meeting in Huron, South Dakota, in 1889, for example, she presented the Beadle County Suffrage Association with a gift of three volumes of the *History*, and she left a basket full of suffrage literature at the door. The literature disappeared so quickly that the leaders felt that ten times as much could have been used purposefully at the close of the meeting.[38]

Knowing the value of the press, Miss Anthony was cordial to newspaper reporters. She was eager to get as much as possible about woman suffrage into the papers, and personally she had an admiration for the faithful and industrious people who earned their living at newspaper work. She ordered a thousand copies of a Sunday edition during the 1883 national convention when she learned that the paper was going to give space to the convention, and she announced in the meeting that she would send to the address of any friend in the audience a copy free of charge.[39]

She believed that her own paper, *The Revolution*, exerted a tremendous influence for woman's rights in its short lifetime. When the paper could no longer continue because it was too expensive to run and too radical in its sentiments to be very popular, she gave it up with reluctance, and felt that the indebtedness of $10,000 which she personally assumed was not too big a price to pay for the good it had done.

In trying to demonstrate woman's rights she followed practical leads. In one attempt to verify the belief that women had the right to vote under the Fourteenth and Fifteenth Amendments she stood as the test case when she and fifteen other women were arrested for trying to vote in Rochester in 1872.[40] She lectured in her defense before the trial in 1873, and was still describing the events in 1899.

Susan Anthony insisted that women should be represented at the National

---

[37] Cf. *The Revolution* (New York), January 6, 1870, for a typical list of woman suffrage reading material.

[38] *Daily Huronite* (Huron, South Dakota), November 14, 1889.

[39] Stanton *et. al.*, *op. cit.*, III, 259.

[40] Cf. Anonymous, *An Account of the Proceedings on the Trial of Susan B. Anthony* ... , pp. 1-150.

Centennial Celebration in Philadelphia on July 4, 1876, in spite of the refusal of the committee in charge. Leading a small group of women to the platform during the ceremony, she presented to the chairman a "Woman's Declaration of Rights," and thus inscribed women's activities as a part of the program of that momentous occasion.[41]

The Individual

At the time of her death in 1906, Susan B. Anthony was acclaimed one of the most remarkable women of her age. Obituary notices praised her as a reformer, crusader, and woman.[42] Thirty-nine years after her death her home was declared a shrine and preparations were made for its restoration. A question at once arises in the mind of the reader. What were the qualities for which this woman gained fame?

First, there was her consecration to her cause. She probably gave more time and thought to the specific issue of woman suffrage than any other person. To it she devoted most of the years of her long life. Other suffragists married and had families, and Susan had ample opportunity to do this, but she was not interested in a personal life; she was interested in helping all women toward better living. Other women leaders followed professions in addition to their suffrage work. Susan hewed so closely to her single purpose that the responsibility for care of her home and even for the selection of her clothes was largely delegated to her sister Mary, without whom she said she could not have pursued her public career. Her concentration on her work earned for her such titles as "The Apostle of Woman's Rights," "The High Priestess of Woman's Suffrage," and the "Napoleon," "the Moses," and the "Sir Galahad" of the movement. "What Gladstone has been to the home rule," said the Albany, New York, *Evening Journal* of March 14, 1894, "Miss Anthony has been to woman suffrage."

She was always available, and no task was too great. If a speaker fell ill or was unable to reach a meeting, Susan filled in. If a suffragist could not complete the arrangements for a convention, or finish writing a report, Susan completed the job. If a suffrage campaign needed someone to advertise meetings, distribute tracts, see to the personal comforts of the workers, and attend to the drudgery behind the scenes, Miss Anthony would take care of it all.

---

[41] Stanton, *op. cit.*, III, 944-45.

[42] Around two hundred obituary notices were placed in the appendix of Volume III of the Harper biography. The achievements she made possible for women during her career were discussed in the majority of these. Her consecration to her cause was stressed. Mention of her ability as a public speaker appeared in less than twenty of these notices.

This was well exemplified in 1867 in Kansas when she managed the campaign from Lawrence, while Elizabeth Cady Stanton and others stumped the state and received the publicity.[43]

As an unmarried woman she could legally assume debts for an organization that a married woman could not undertake, and this she sometimes did. When the Woman's Loyal League had overspent its treasury by $5,000 in 1863, Secretary Anthony assumed the responsibility, devised and executed means for paying it. Her undertaking of the $10,000 debt incurred in the publishing of *The Revolution*, when she could have declared bankruptcy, brought her widespread respect and was considered a good lesson in proving woman's pecuniary independence.[44]

She solicited contributions from every possible source, but accepted money for her own expenses only when absolutely necessary. She used personal bequests for the Woman Suffrage Association, and friends finally had to arrange an annuity for her so that she would not use the lump sum for the movement. In order to help the women of Michigan with their 1874 campaign she gave up lecture offers which would have helped materially to lessen the debt on *The Revolution*. She was the only speaker in the South Dakota campaign in 1890 who refused pay for her services. And in 1896 she donated her services to the California campaign, where her speeches even at twenty-five dollars an appearance would have contributed over $3,000 to the suffrage cause, not including parlor and club addresses.[45]

She did not fail an engagement, no matter what the risk or expense. In announcing her availability as a lecturer in 1877, the Slayton Bureau praised her dependability by stressing that she could lecture every night, that she did not object to night rides between appointments, and that "nothing but an Act of God" would prevent her from fulfilling an engagement.[46]

Anna Howard Shaw, who traveled seven thousand miles and gave twenty lectures during a two-week period in 1892, sometimes had trouble keeping up with her energetic friend. She liked to tell of a night during a meeting of the Woman's International Council in Chicago in 1888 when Miss Anthony, after a busy day but still "as fresh and full of enthusiasm as a young girl," came into Miss Shaw's room to talk the night away. Miss Anthony then continued with the next day's convention program with no sleep and with little attention to food.[47]

[43] Stanton *et. al.*, *op. cit.*, II, 253-54.

[44] Cf. May Wright Sewall in *Our Herald*, in Scrapbooks (1884), VII, 344-49.

[45] Cf. Harper, *op. cit.*, I, 459; II, 694-95, 892.

[46] *Ibid.*, I, 486-87.

[47] Anna Howard Shaw, *The Story of a Pioneer* (New York: Harper Brothers, 1915), pp. 189-90.

Of the women leaders, only Clara Barton and Frances Willard paid as little attention to physical needs. Susan believed in living a simple life and in eating simple foods. Her favorite exercise was long walks, and she liked to walk before bedtime, talking over issues with an accompanying friend who might have to hurry to keep up with her.

She was seldom ill, and then stayed in bed only as long as she was forced to do so, being up and on her way before friends could admonish her that she needed more time for recuperation. After an apoplectic stroke in 1900 she was warned by her physician to take care of herself, and particularly to avoid crowds and the cold. She decided to "die in the harness" and ignored his admonitions. Always rebellious against physical limitations, she attended public meetings until a month before her death.

Susan B. Anthony's physical appearance was distinctive. She was tall, slim, "Patrician-like," with strong features frequently called Grecian, firm set mouth, straight nose, and ample forehead. She had dark hair which turned a becoming gray, and deep-set gray-blue eyes which were keen and bright. Her carriage was erect, and she walked with a firm tread; she kept her toes straight ahead, and she was straight as an arrow. The *Washington Star* said of her in 1889:

She is one of the remarkable women of the world. In appearance she has not grown a day older in the past ten years. Her manner has none of the excitement of an enthusiast; never discouraged by disappointment, she keeps calmly at work, and she could give points in political organization and management to some of the best male politicians in the land. Her face is strong and intellectual, but full of womanly gentleness. Her gold spectacles give her a motherly rather than a severe expression, and a stranger would see nothing incongruous in her doing knitting or fancy-work.[48]

Many pen-and-ink sketches of her appear in her Scrapbooks.[49] On the whole they seem to be very solemn. But they uphold the statement of the *St. Louis Daily Globe-Democrat* of May 7, 1879, that she commanded attention anywhere at a glance. Of the many pictures appearing in the three volumes of the Harper biography, and on the walls of the Anthony home in Rochester, the majority seem sad. The one taken when she was forty-eight years of age is one of the most appealing.[50]

Susan Anthony was an individualist. She had courage to uphold her convictions and she followed the course she thought right regardless of the beliefs of others. At a time when divorce was scarcely countenanced, she staunchly defended it, and emphasized women's need for the right to divorce. She

---

[48] Cited in Harper, *op. cit.*, II, 660.
[49] Cf. Susan B. Anthony Scrapbooks (1893), Vol. XVI; (1894), Vol. XVII.
[50] Harper, *op. cit.*, I, 302.

argued that the World's Fair should be kept open on Sundays, and answered local clergymen by saying that young men might learn more at the Fair than at some of the churches in Chicago. She was tolerant of Carrie Nation because she felt that women had no legitimate means of enforcing their wills, although she emphasized that the hatchet was a barbarian weapon and that the ballot is the weapon of the civilized.

In conventions she fought to keep the aims and goals of the woman suffrage organization unfettered. For example, she opposed all efforts to pass resolutions concerning the reinterpretation of the Bible from woman's point of view, contending that contests on account of religious theories only set back the hands on the dial of suffrage reform.[51] She opposed such resolutions as one which proposed to place the National Woman Suffrage Association on record as abhorring "free loveism," stating that such a resolution had no place in a woman's convention because it might imply that some of the members were in favor of free love.[52] In the smallest of issues she was persistent, as in her argument that women should follow the dictates of etiquette and address audiences as "Gentlemen and Ladies."[53] As a reporter of the 1894 national suffrage convention wrote in *The Chicago Journal* of February 20th:

Susan B. Anthony is one of the most remarkable products of this century. She is not a successful writer; she is not a great speaker, although a most effective one; but she has a better quality than genius. She is the soul of honesty; she possesses the gift of clear discrimination—of seeing the main point—and of never-wavering loyalty to the issue at hand. . . .

Miss Anthony had a youthfulness of spirit which remained with her even in her old age. Upon receiving an invitation to attend the Buffalo Bill show at the Chicago World's Fair in 1893, she took a group of women with her and entered wholeheartedly into the spirit of the occasion. At seventy-eight she attended her first football game and felt that she had spent "a pleasurable and profitable afternoon."[54] In 1900 a Chicago reporter commented that it was hard to believe that she was eighty years of age, and added:

Talking with her and realizing how closely her fingers are upon the pulse of the world, that fact is still harder of belief. Her mantle in the movement for equal suffrage has fallen to younger shoulders, but her heart and life are in the work.[55]

[51] Cf. Stanton *et. al., op. cit.,* IV, 263-64.
[52] *Ibid.,* II, 389-90.
[53] *Ibid.,* II, 384, 388. Cf. also Scrapbooks (1874), Vol. V.
[54] *Chicago Democrat and Chronicle,* November 20, 1898.
[55] *Chicago Tribune,* June 25, 1900.

Miss Anthony's greatest attribute, according to Carrie Chapman Catt, who assumed presidency of the national organization in 1900, was "her utter unselfishness and lack of self-consciousness."[56] If complimented by a chairman introducing her to an audience, Susan would remark that she preferred to have her obituaries spoken after her demise, and that now it was time to get down to the important business at hand.[57] She asked the guests at her fiftieth birthday reception to join her in demanding congressional and legislative action on woman suffrage if they wished to honor her personally.[58] She could only express gratitude for the improvement in public opinion toward the woman's movement when she was feted in Portland, Oregon, in 1905.[59] And when informed at one meeting that she was joining in with the applause for herself she continued to clap, and insisted that the praise was really intended for the cause.[60]

Her chief bias was that woman suffrage was the cure-all for social evils. As early in her career as 1852 she evidenced this tendency in a letter written to Amelia Bloomer on June 28th, saying,

Oh! if women would but speak out—if they would but rise *en-masse*, and demand that their interests be truthfully represented in our legislative halls, then would man no longer inflict upon us, and upon society, the vile curse of the liquor traffic.[61]

She was a deeply religious woman, a Quaker turned liberal, and she attended the Unitarian church in Rochester as regularly as her travels would permit. But she considered that her true religion lay in her work. Work was a panacea for physical, mental, and spiritual ills and a refuge in time of sorrow.

Although Lucretia Mott might be said to be the "soul of the woman's rights movement," and Mrs. Stanton the "swift, keen intelligence," Grace Greenwood, a writer and correspondent, emphasized that Miss Anthony, "alert, aggressive and indefatigable," was its "nervous energy, its propulsive force."[62] And the *Boston Globe* commented in 1881,

The young women of the day may well feel that it is she who *has made life possible* to them; who has trodden the thorny paths and, by her unwearied devotion, has opened to them the professions and higher applied industries; nor is this detracting from those who now share with her the labor and the glory. Each and all recog-

---

[56] Stanton, *et. al.*, *op. cit.*, V, 40-41.
[57] *The Revolution*, January 27, 1870.
[58] Harper, *op. cit.*, I, 342.
[59] *Ibid.*, III, 1365.
[60] Shaw, *op. cit.*, p. 208.
[61] *The Lily*, July, 1852, p. 59.
[62] Stanton *et. al.*, *op. cit.*, II, 361-62.

nize the individual devotion, the purity and singleness of purpose that so eminently distinguish Miss Anthony.[63]

One can give but a glimpse of the praise bestowed upon Susan B. Anthony by both contemporary and present-day writers. Criticism and ridicule were heaped upon her as a strong-minded woman and a creature so masculine as to step outside the confines of woman's sphere, but the censure was because of the inacceptable quality of her cause to those who upheld tradition, and not because of the individual.[64]

The Speaker and Her Speeches

In spite of the wealth of material concerning the personality and accomplishments of Miss Anthony, one does not easily gain a picture of her ability as a public speaker. Testimonials from her friends were no doubt influenced by personal contact. Newspaper accounts during the early years of her career emphasized the subject of woman's rights and all its implications in a world of confusion, politics, and reform, and briefly mentioned that another reformer was presenting nonconformist ideas. Later, when she had become nationally known as a woman suffragist, press accounts were so taken with her sterling qualities that they often failed to mention audience reactions or her speaking style. With the spreading of her fame the discussion of suffrage issues expanded until newspaper accounts such as those reporting her California tour in 1896 filled many columns. Few of them, however, discussed her manner of speaking. An analysis of forty-two newspaper articles selected at random and covering a variety of occasions between 1869 and 1895 reveals thirty-eight résumés of subject content, seventeen descriptions of the personality of the speaker, and ten comments on speaking style.

Miss Anthony frequently appeared on the platform as one of a group of speakers, a custom popular in days when travel was not easy, and when an evening's listening was happily extended to three to five hours. She must have profited not only from practice but from listening to other speakers with whom she appeared, including Henry Ward Beecher, Wendell Phillips, Robert G. Ingersoll, Ralph Waldo Emerson, and William Lloyd Garrison.

There is little doubt that her speaking was influenced by the people with whom she worked. In the 1850's she shared audiences with such excellent women speakers as Amelia Bloomer, Antoinette Brown Blackwell, and Ernestine L. Rose. In later years she traveled extensively with Dr. Anna Howard Shaw, famous minister, physician, and public speaker.

[63] Cited in Harper, *op. cit.*, II, 534.
[64] Cf. *The New York Tribune*, in Scrapbooks, (1871), III, 336; *New York Herald*, May 15, 1874.

She was aided and directed by Elizabeth Cady Stanton, with whom she worked closely for the majority of the years of her career, and whose excellence in speech composition and brilliance in conversation were widely acclaimed. Miss Anthony often attested that Mrs. Stanton was the intellectual center of the woman suffrage movement, while she herself was merely its hands and feet. Dr. Shaw insisted:

... [The] two women worked marvelously together, for Mrs. Stanton was a master of words and could write and speak to perfection of the things Susan B. Anthony saw and felt but could not herself express.[65]

Amelia Bloomer said in an article written for Chicago's *New Era* in November, 1885:

... without the push of Miss Anthony, Mrs. Stanton would probably never have gone abroad into active work or achieved half she has done; and without the brain of Mrs. Stanton, Miss Anthony would never have been so largely known to the world by name and deeds. They helped and strengthened each other, and together they have accomplished great things for humanity.

Susan Anthony did not consider herself an effective speaker. She began to speak in public when she could find no one else who would or could do it. She continued to speak because the public platform was the most accessible as well as the most popular medium of education and entertainment of the time. In 1870 she said that "so soon as cultivated women come up and are ready to do the speaking, I shall fall back. My work is that of subsoil plowing...."[66] She told a newspaper reporter in 1896:

I never could think up points, and I can't write a speech out. I must have an audience to inspire me. When I am before a house filled with people I can speak, but to save my life I couldn't write a speech.[67]

And after what she considered an evening's failure before an audience in Geneva, New York, in March, 1899, she stated:

I always feel my incapacity to give a "set" address—I can when in the best condition make a few remarks, but a sustained speech was, is and always will be an impossibility. Alas, that the friends will forever press me into a position where I must attempt it.[68]

The value of her existing speeches may be questioned. Before 1858 she tried to memorize or to speak from prepared manuscripts and these samples

---

[65] Shaw, *op. cit.*, p. 240.
[66] *The Revolution*, February 24, 1870.
[67] *Rochester Democrat and Chronicle* (Rochester, New York), February 4, 1896.
[68] Harper, *op. cit.*, III, 1126.

seem stilted and labored. For the rest of her career she spoke from notes or completely extemporaneously. Reports of these speeches are given in résumé or abridged synopsis, and frequently in third person. Probably the complete speeches have lost much of their flavor for they are, at least in part, the result of attempts by Miss Anthony or a confederate to write out the addresses from memory after their delivery.[69]

The most reliable part of Susan B. Anthony's role as a public speaker was the consistency of her purpose and subject matter. If she were lecturing on temperance, she would also show how much more weighty would be the influence of women if they had the ballot. And a suffrage lecture sometimes included appeals to women to take higher standards for temperance reform. Her purpose in her long speeches, which usually ran from one and a half to two hours, was to stimulate thought and actuate change for social improvement.[70]

Frequently she described unhappy existing social conditions, presented solutions, and made appeals for action. Sometimes she traced the history of the franchise and established need for further reform. She often talked of the importance of the ballot and of the necessity for every citizen to possess the right to vote. She described the degradation of women and demonstrated their need of the ballot for the protection of their persons and interests. And as time went on she chronicled the legal and professional gains of women during the nineteenth century, pointed out that enfranchisement was inevitable, and appealed for continued work for woman suffrage.[71]

The available samples of her speeches are filled with words and phrases that had emotional meaning for the people of her time. Appearing frequently are the expressions: "Resistance to tyrants is obedience to God"; "The price of liberty is eternal vigilance"; "Truth will prevail"; "Taxation and representation are inseparable"; and "Governments derive their just powers from the consent of the governed." The ballot she referred to as "a shield," "a symbol of equality," "a weapon," and "the right protective of all other rights." The black reality of the "upas of disfranchisement," "woman's slavery," "oppression" and "degradation" was lined with the silver hope of "justice,"

---

[69] In telling of the 1876 Illinois Woman Suffrage Convention, Elizabeth Boynton Harbert commented: ". . . I wish to emphasize the great loss to women in the fact that as Miss Anthony's speeches were never written, but came with thrilling effect from her patriotic soul, scarce any record of them remains, other than the intangible memories of her grateful countrywomen." Cf. Stanton *et. al.*, *op. cit.*, III, 580.

[70] Cf. *The Detroit Free Press*, November 30, 1889; *The Sentinel* (Indianapolis, Indiana), December 11, 1878.

[71] In selecting sixteen speaking situations at random from 1875 to 1900 it was found that thirteen dealt with the theme of the progress of women, two with the history of the franchise, and one with constitutional argument.

"equality," "freedom," "democracy," and "enfranchisement." The words "peer" and "citizen" were often used.

Miss Anthony spoke to the reason of her listeners and upheld her issues with facts, figures, and examples.[72] Her recorded speeches are crowded with statistics and direct quotations from authorities, law, and history. A good memory enabled her to give her speeches on "Constitutional Argument" and "The New Situation," both composed largely of legal and constitutional references, with the aid of only a few notes.[73]

In "Constitutional Argument,"[74] a good example of the repletion of her information, she first stated that she stood before her audience under indictment for the alleged crime of having voted in the last presidential election, and said that it was her work of the evening to prove that in voting she exercised her rights as a citizen. She then proceeded to analyze the Declaration of Rights, the Constitution, and laws discriminatory to women. She quoted authorities including President Grant, Chief Justice Daniels, Attorney General Bates, Charles Sumner, and others. She defined citizenship and discussed its implications. She established by syllogistic reasoning the right of women to vote under existing statutes. She concluded with a statement that upon the proof given in her address she and the women of the National Woman Suffrage Association intended to vote and to demonstrate their rights. She asked support of their program.

The *Daily Nebraska State Journal* of January 8, 1887, in reviewing the previous evening's address in Lincoln, stated that Miss Anthony spoke "evidently from inexhaustible resources of knowledge upon her subject. Her auditors followed her with the closest attention and her logical address shows her to possess a most statesmanlike insight into the affairs of the nation and society." And a report in the Terre Haute, Indiana, *Express* of February 12, 1879, concerning a recent lecture given in that city attested that "There are not half of our public men who are nearly so well posted in the political affairs of our country as she, or who, knowing them can frame them so solidly in argument."[75]

Susan B. Anthony excelled in argument. She stated issues and defended them, making frequent use of the rhetorical question, sarcasm, and "withering invective." The recorded speeches show logical reasoning, with many "therefores," and "if-this-is-true, then that-is-bound-to-be-so." She put her basic

---

[72] Cf. *New York Democrat*, May 13, 1871; *The Commercial Gazette* (Cincinnati), February 11, 1889.

[73] Cf. Grim, *op. cit.*, pp. 441, 468-69; also, Harper, *op. cit.*, I, 380.

[74] Cf. Harper, *op. cit.*, II, 977-92.

[75] This lecture was given under the auspices of the Young Men's Occidental Literary Club, of which Eugene V. Debs was president and one of the founders.

115

premises succinctly, pointed to generally entrenched beliefs, and emphasized the new ideas that must necessarily be accepted.

In her address on "Social Purity," [76] first given during the spring of 1875, she insisted that the efforts of man had been insufficient to suppress the evils of intemperance. Man's legislative attempts have proved equally ineffective. Women's prayers and petitions had been futile. The solution to the problem pointed toward enfranchisement of women. She further remarked:

... the tap-root of our social upas lies deep down at the very foundation of society. It is woman's dependence. It is woman's subjection. Hence, the first and only efficient work must be to emancipate woman from her enslavement. The wife must no longer echo the poet Milton's ideal Eve, when she adoringly said to Adam "God, thy law; thou, mine!" She must feel herself accountable to God alone for every act, fearing and obeying no man, save where his will is in line with her own highest idea of divine law.[77]

How could anyone doubt the power of the ballot? If, for one example, the 18,000 Chicago women, with the tens of thousands they represented, had been able to go to the ballot box at the next election, was there any doubt that respect rather than ridicule would have been shown them by the members of the Common Council, when they had presented their petition to retain the Sunday Liquor Law in that city? She insisted that it was futile for women to hope to battle successfully against the evils of society until they were armed with weapons equal to those of the enemy—votes and money:

Archimedes said, 'Give to me a fulcrum on which to plant my lever, and I will move the world.' And I say, give to woman the ballot, the political fulcrum, on which to plant her moral lever, and she will lift the world into a nobler and purer atmosphere.[78]

To the audience of the Universalist convention held in Rochester in 1901 she said, among other things:

I want you women to realize what a power you might be if you were enfranchised. Women constitute three-fourths of the church membership and for that reason ministers have small influence in politics. The Catholic priesthood commands considerable respect from politicians because of the large number of men in its congregations, but the Protestant ministers are not respected by them any more than are the women who compose their congregations. The same is true of the schools— three fourths of the teachers women—and thus churches, schools and homes are all practically disfranchised.[79]

[76] Cf. Harper, *op. cit.*, II, 1004-12.
[77] *Ibid.*, II, 1011.
[78] *Ibid.*, II, 1012.
[79] *Rochester Democrat and Chronicle* (Rochester, New York), July 12, 1901.

She often spoke of the injustice of allowing any class of people to have control over another. Cruelty and unfairness resulted from allowing the rich to rule the poor, the white to rule the black. Women undoubtedly would be just as unfair as men, had they been at the controls at the beginning of nations and governments. She asserted in her lecture "Woman Wants Bread, Not the Ballot," [80] given many times between 1870 and 1890:

... there never was, there never can be, a monopoly so fraught with injustice, tyranny and degradation as this monopoly of sex, of all men over all women. Therefore I not only agree with Abraham Lincoln that, 'No man is good enough to govern another man without his consent;' but I say also that no man is good enough to govern a woman without her consent, and still further, that all men combined in government are not good enough to gꞏvern all women without their consent. There might have been some plausible excuse for the rich governing the poor, the educated governing the ignorant, the Saxon governing the African; but there can be none for making the husband the ruler of the wife, the brother of the sister, the man of the woman, his peer in birth, in education, in social position, in all that stands for the best and highest in humanity.[81]

It was no wonder that the "white male" class was cruel to the Negro, she said in her address on "Reconstruction," [82] for men could not be trusted:

... [They cannot be trusted] even to legislate for their own mothers, sisters, wives and daughters. The cruel statutes in nearly all the States, both slave and free, give ample proof. In scarcely a State has a married woman the legal right to the control of her person, to the earning of her hands or brain, to the guardianship of her children, to sue or be sued, or to testify in the courts, and by these laws have suffered wrongs and outrages second only to those of chattel slavery.[83]

If any lawyer doubted the legal inequality of women, she emphasized to audiences during the spring of 1873, she would remind him that the Common Law of England prevailed in every state but two except where the legislatures had enacted special laws annulling it.[84]

In her closing address at the 1884 National Woman Suffrage Convention she commented:

... the reason men are so slow in conceding political equality to women is because they cannot believe that women suffer the humiliation of disfranchisement as they would. A dear and noble friend, one who aided our work most efficiently in the early days, said to me, "Why do you say the 'emancipation of women?' " I replied,

[80] Cf. Harper, *op. cit.*, II, 997-1003.
[81] *Ibid.*, II, 1000-1001.
[82] Delivered in Ottumwa, Kansas, July 4, 1865; Cf. Harper, *op. cit.*, II, 960-67.
[83] *Ibid.*, II, 965.
[84] *Ibid.*, II, 989.

"Because women are political slaves!" Is it not strange that men think that what to them would be degradation, slavery, is to women elevation, liberty?[85]

How could taxation without representation be any less humiliating to women of the nineteenth century than it was to the Fathers of our country a century earlier?

The suffragists did not oppose men, she insisted; they opposed the statute books.

She argued for correct interpretation of standing statutes. If women were considered to be "persons," they had a right to vote under the constitutional amendments. Even the popular contention that our laws were written with the masculine pronoun, which in itself excluded women from voting, was disproved by the decision of the Supreme Court in the case of *Silver* v. *Ladd* in 1868, in which it was said that the term "single man" embraced that of "unmarried woman." Moreover, if women were excluded from voting by masculine pronouns, why were they not also exempted from taxation?

That the members of her audiences were believers in good government she took for granted. In order to insure good government there must necessarily be good citizens, and if there was a need to improve the caliber of the voting populace, she told Joseph T. Alling's Sunday school class in Rochester in September, 1899, it was obvious that the best way to do it was to add the vote of women.[86] To improve society, one must have rights and powers, she argued in 1901 at the national suffrage convention held in Minneapolis:

I am a full and firm believer in the revelation that it is through women the race is to be redeemed. For this reason I ask for her immediate and unconditional emancipation from all political, industrial, social and religious subjection. It is said, "Men are what their mothers made them," but I say that to hold mothers responsible for the characters of their sons while denying to them any control over the sons' lives is worse than mockery, it is cruelty. Responsibilities grow out of rights and powers. Therefore before mothers can rightfully be held responsible for the vices and crimes, for the general demoralization of society, they must possess all possible rights and powers to control the conditions and circumstances of their own and their children's lives.[87]

Speaking to the convention of the Bricklayers' and Masons' International Union in Rochester in 1900, she said:

Women should vote for the sake of the home. By working to give your wives and daughters the ballot you would be working to double the representation of

[85] Elizabeth C. Stanton *et al.*, eds., *The History of Woman Suffrage* (Indianapolis: The Hollenbeck Press, 1902), IV, 27.

[86] Harper, *op. cit.*, III, 1148-49.

[87] Stanton *et al.*, *op. cit.*, V, 4-5.

the home in government; for the lowest men—the men who make up the slum vote, the floating vote, the vote that can be bought by anyone for any measure—these men seldom have homes and women in them whose votes could be added to theirs. It is the honest, hard-working men, with homes and families, those who have done most to build up this country and who are the bone and sinew sustaining it today, who have most to gain from women's getting the ballot. But the best argument of all is justice—the sister should have the same rights as her brother, the wife as her husband, the mother as her son....[88]

At times Miss Anthony's speeches seem very argumentative. Those available for reading appeal often to the sense of duty. Some of them seem to assert and demand rather than to persuade. The reader cannot help occasionally asking "Why?" and "What for?" and wondering if audience prejudices could accede to demands without more appeal to sentiment.

"The Demand for Party Recognition" [89] is a speech that prompts such a query. After a good introduction by which Miss Anthony established a bond between herself and the audience in talking about their common work, she went on to a detailed chronicle of past events, of women's work during the war, in previous suffrage campaigns and during political elections. She used negative suggestion in asking if the unhappy events of the past were going to be repeated in the impending campaign, and threatened to disown women who supported the Republican party unless it had a plank for woman suffrage. To a present-day reader the speech seems harsh. Yet a resolution for the support of woman suffrage which was the conclusion of the talk elicited unanimous approval.

She had a habit of calling for a show of hands from her audiences concerning their approval of her contentions and of woman suffrage, and usually she found approval.[90]

In writing about a debate between Miss Anthony and Professor E. C. Hewitt at the State Normal School in Bloomington, Illinois, in March, 1870, Emily L. Boynton observed that in spite of the popular professor's quick repartee and wit in condemning woman suffrage, Miss Anthony carried the honors of the day and won the applause of the audience.[91] A member of the Detroit audience of more than five hundred who heard her refute Rev. J. B. Fulton's speech upholding woman's sphere felt that "if cheering of the audience

---

[88] Harper, *op. cit.*, III, 1161-62.

[89] Delivered in Kansas City, Kansas, May 4, 1894. Cf. Harper, *op. cit.*, II, 1015-21.

[90] Cf. *The Daily Republican* (East Saginaw, Michigan), October 30, 1874; *The Chronicle* (Muskegon, Michigan), October 8, 1874; *St. Louis Globe-Democrat*, May 11, 1879; *Rochester Morning Herald* (Rochester, New York), December 29, 1882.

[91] *The Revolution*, March 31, 1870.

is any indication she must have been gratified at her success in demolishing his arguments." [92]

The general organization of the available speeches is good, although for the sake of clarity in supporting details she might profitably have rearranged subordinate ideas and changed expressions from passive to active voice.

The introductions to her speeches were brief, often a statement of fact that was thought-provoking or unusual. A clear statement of the purpose of the address followed immediately. In introducing "Constitutional Argument," for example, she said:

Friends and Fellow Citizens: I stand before you under indictment for the alleged crime of having voted at the last presidential election, without having a lawful right to vote. It shall be my work this evening to prove to you that in thus doing, I not only committed no crime, but instead simply exercised my citizen's right, guaranteed to me and all United States citizens by the National Constitution beyond the power of any State to deny.[93]

In "Woman Wants Bread, Not the Vote," she began:

My purpose tonight is to demonstrate the great historical fact that disfranchisement is not only political degradation, but also moral, social, educational and industrial degradation. . . .[94]

In opening the meeting of the International Council of Women in Washington, D. C., in 1888, she stated:

Forty years ago women had no place anywhere except in their homes; no pecuniary independence, no purpose in life save that which came through marriage. From a condition, as many of you can remember, in which no woman thought of earning her bread by any other means than sewing, teaching, cooking or factory work, in these later years the way has been opened to every avenue of industry, to every profession, whereby woman to-day stands almost the peer of man in her opportunities for financial independence.[95]

The conclusions of her speeches were equally brief and usually forceful. Upon the formation of the Woman's Loyal League in May, 1863, she concluded her speech asking for cooperation by saying,

And now, women of the North, I ask you to rise up with earnest, honest purpose, and go forward in the way of right, fearlessly, as independent human beings, responsible to God alone for the discharge of every duty, for the faithful use of every

[92] *Ibid.*, December 16, 1869.
[93] Harper, *op. cit.*, II, 977.
[94] *Ibid.*, II, 997.
[95] Stanton *et al.*, *op. cit.*, IV, 133.

gift the good Father has given you. Forget conventionalisms; forget what the world will say, whether you are in your place or out of your place; think your best thoughts, speak your best words, do your best works, looking to your own conscience for approval.[96]

She ended a speech, "Social Purity," by observing,

Two great necessities forced this nation to extend justice and equality to the Negro:

First, Military necessity, which compelled the abolition of the crime and curse of slavery, before the rebellion could be overcome.

Second, Political necessity, which required the enfranchisement of the newly-freed men, before the work of reconstruction could begin.

The third is now pressing, Moral necessity—to emancipate woman, before Social Purity, the nation's safeguard, ever can be established.[97]

Her closing words to a Baltimore audience in 1894 were:

Women of Maryland, that is what the negro got out of it. Cannot we get the same? We've never had any flag, never had any country. Let us get both. Only prejudice stands in the way. Education, reason, judgment has nothing to do with the opposition. It's only prejudice.

There is an old saying that if you give a woman an inch she'll take an ell. Women of Maryland—we've got the inch.[98]

Press reports often remarked that she spoke "more concisely" than the average speaker and that she did not put much ornamentation into her speeches.[99] Her metaphors included homely phrases. She noted that money was "the wood and water of the engine" of reform. Again, she remarked that the woman suffragist organization would gladly do the work if people would only give generously to "oil the machinery." Her illustrations were simple stories of actual experiences faced by herself and others. In telling of the need for woman's enfranchisement, she narrated the story of the failure of the Collar Laundry Women's Union in Troy, New York, in its attempt to improve working conditions. In describing woman's ineffectiveness before the law, she quoted the case of the farmer's wife who could not testify that her false teeth were unsatisfactory when an uncooperative dentist brought suit against her husband for their payment.

In analyzing Miss Anthony's speaking style, May Wright Sewall, a

[96] *Ibid.*, II, 57-58.
[97] Harper, *op. cit.*, II, 1012.
[98] *The Sun* (Baltimore, Maryland), February 14, 1894.
[99] Cf. *Daily Oregonian* (Portland, Oregon), September 9, 1871; *The Evening Post* (Toledo, Ohio), November 18, 1884; *New York World*, November 5, 1899.

suffragist speaker in her own right, wrote for *Our Herald* from Indianapolis, February 12, 1884:

I am inclined to think that in the days when her own style was forming, the gravity and seriousness of the objects for which she spoke so impressed her that ornament seemed incongruous to her honest mind. Perhaps unconsciously she set rhetorical decoration aside as fit only for poetry, romances and critical essays, and the habits of "plain, unvarnished" speech remain, although she has the readiest admiration for the witty, poetical, or polished sentence of another.

Susan B. Anthony's appearance upon the platform was one of modesty, calmness, and dignity. She came forward with an "easy grace which none are so capable of assuming as those who for years have stood night after night before the footlights." [100] She stood quietly behind or beside the speaker's stand, moved around very little and made few gestures. At times she leaned forward toward her audience as if to try to bridge the distance between it and the platform.

Her contemporary biographer insisted that she was one of the most perfectly dressed women on the platform, although her tastes were very plain and simple. She usually dressed in black silk or satin, and relieved the severity of the color with a collar of rose point lace, a stomacher of white lace, a gold neck chain and pendant, or a delicate bit of jewelry such as a cameo brooch or an agate pin. She delighted her friends at a meeting in Portland, Oregon, by wearing a pink bow at her throat and a narrow pink ribbon in her hair to go with her gray silk dress. In later years she sometimes added a soft white shawl or a red crepe shawl to her costume. And on very special occasions she wore a garnet velvet dress that received widespread praise.

She always wore her hair plainly, brushed back smoothly over her ears and arranged in a knot at her neck. The Baltimore *Sun* of February 14, 1894, noted that her hair had "the same simple, old-fashioned twist that she has given to it for years and years." The paper hastened to add that she was a progressive woman in other ways than politics for the women in her audience had quickly noticed that her "puffed sleeves and wide sloping skirt were respectively as big and broad and sloping as that of the most devoted disciple of Dame Fashion."

She believed that the appearance of the woman suffragists should attract no special attention to itself, and for this reason she gave up wearing the Bloomer dress after a few months. She tolerated but could not approve of the platform ostentation of such women as Elizabeth Oakes Smith and Victoria Woodhull.

The factor in Susan Anthony's delivery most frequently appraised by

[100] *Labor Advocate* (Shelbyville, Illinois), April 14, 1886.

contemporary reports was her voice. She could be heard easily even in very large halls. The report of her first woman's rights convention by the Syracuse, New York, *Journal* of September 10, 1852, said that "Miss Anthony has a capital voice and deserves to be made clerk of the Assembly." During one appearance in New Orleans in March of 1885, *The Daily Picayune* remarked that "her voice was full, musical and sonorous." On January 22, 1895, *The Picayune* emphasized that her voice was "singularly sweet and clear." And during the International Council of Women held in London in 1899, Ida Harper remarked:

... at nearly 80 years of age, her voice still has the best carrying quality of any of the fine voices which have been heard during the meetings. Even in these large halls, filled with thousands of people, she has been able to reach the farthest corner without apparent effort.[101]

Many felt that much of her effectiveness in speaking stemmed from the fact that she could be understood. Her utterance was rapid, and she made few pauses, but so good was her articulation that the attentive listener did not lose a word. She especially "enforced her remarks by the inflections of her voice." [102]

She was complimented for her "emphatic earnestness," and for making addresses "full of fire and prophecy." But she was also accused of being so serious as to seem solemn and so earnest as almost to become tearful.

Susan B. Anthony's audiences were usually large, numbering over three thousand at such meetings as the one in Framingham, Massachusetts, on July 4, 1862, and those of the women suffrage meetings in New York State during the summer of 1903. In 1874 her meetings throughout the state of Michigan were crowded and as many as a thousand people were unable to gain admission. The national woman suffrage meetings practically always filled whatever building they used.

Her audiences included prominent reformers, the interested, the apathetic, and the hostile. In increasing numbers were women predominant, including enthusiastic suffragists, those sincerely interested in learning about the reform and those merely curious. Newspaper comments emphasized that the woman suffrage conventions were composed of women of refinement and culture, of standing and position in society. Miss Anthony spoke especially highly of her audiences in the West, commenting on the fine pioneer character of the people and on the fact that they came many hard miles in wagons and buggies, crowding into lecture halls with enthusiasm for knowledge of the suffrage cause.

[101] Harper, *op. cit.*, III, 1138.
[102] Cf. Scrapbooks (1885),Vol. VIII; *Detroit Free Press*, November 30, 1889; *Los Angeles Evening Express*, June 13, 1895.

The hardships and obstacles she faced in speaking before the public were similar to those experienced by other reformers.[103] She spoke in churches, schoolhouses, wigwams, saloons, pool rooms, polling booths, out-of-doors, and on train platforms. She cheerfully endured the hardships and discomforts common to itinerant lecturers during the nineteenth century. There were disturbances created by adults and annoyances from crying babies. She experienced the difficulties common during the critical days of the antislavery movement in the 1850's and early 1860's, which meant speaking above hisses, shoutings, and booings, and which might mean hurrying out stage doors when meetings were broken up by mobs.[104] The opposition toward antislavery carried over into antagonism toward woman's rights and the women's meetings were also disturbed. But because she began her work in the 1850's, she did not have to go through the severe demonstrations endured by such reformers as Frances Wright in the 1830's, and Abby Kelley Foster and Ernestine L. Rose in the 1840's. By the mid-nineteenth century audiences had recovered at least a little from the initial shock of seeing women on the American public platform. And by 1871 the days of the novelty of hearing women speak were said to be over. Advice was given to young ladies at this time not to enter the profession of lecturing unless they had "brains and ability, culture and fitting preparation," because audiences in the hamlet as well as in the city were awake and critical.[105]

Miss Anthony faced formidable opposition throughout her career. Her propaganda was radical and it hit the defenders of the *status quo*. Opposing her were many of her own sex, and the ministry, press, and political figures in great numbers. She was accused of trying to break up the American home, of preaching doctrines which were calculated to degrade and debauch society, of being a shrew and a revolutionist.[106]

To offset the opposition and to cheer her along her way, she found friends throughout the nation who opened their homes and their hearts to her. And as her fame grew she became more and more an honored personage. During the 1897 national suffrage convention in Des Moines, Iowa, many men in the audience left when she had finished speaking, having come only to listen to her.[107] In 1896 she walked ankle-deep in roses upon California platforms.

[103] Cf. William Norwood Brigance (ed.), *A History and Criticism of American Public Address* (New York: McGraw-Hill Book Company, Inc., 1943), I, 153-92.

[104] Cf. *Evening Telegraph* (Utica, New York), April 28, 1853; January 15, 1861.

[105] *The Revolution*, April 13, 1871.

[106] Cf. Scrapbooks (1867), II, 60; (1882), VI, 373; *The Revolution*, November 18, 1869; *Detroit Free Press*, December 10, 1869; *Union and Advertiser* (Rochester, New York), May 8, 1873.

[107] Stanton *et al., op. cit.,* IV, 270.

Susan B. Anthony

As a participant in meetings and conventions Susan B. Anthony assumed a stellar role. As chairman she presided with what the *Washington Chronicle* of January 28, 1883, called "inspiring dignity." In reporting the suffrage convention of 1890 the *Washington Star* remarked:

> She does not make much noise with her gavel, nor does she have to use it often, but she manages to keep the organization over which she presides in a state of order that puts to shame many a convention of the other sex. Business is transacted in proper shape, and every important measure receives its due share of attention. . . . If any of those who have not attended the meetings of the association are of the opinion that serious breaches of parliamentary usage are committed through ignorance or with intent, they are laboring under a decided delusion.[108]

She insisted that speakers be heard and saw to it that freedom of speech was upheld. She kept meetings informal, but directed the discussion so that it progressed toward a goal. In general, she seemed a genial, lively leader. In telling of the events of the woman's meeting in New York, the *World* of April 21, 1888, emphasized that "if ever there was a gay-hearted, good-natured woman it is certainly Miss Anthony." And the *Sentinel* report of her appearance in Indianapolis meetings in 1899 observed that "Miss Anthony has a delightful smile, the smile and laugh of real enjoyment; her love of fun bubbles all through her talk. She will pause in the most serious conversation to laugh at a joke and her sense of humor is very keen." [109]

She did a good deal of oral reading of reports, resolutions, letters, and other papers. In 1852 she read a letter from Mrs. Stanton in "a most emphatic manner." Instead of giving a set speech at the session honoring Mrs. Stanton's eightieth birthday in 1895, she paid an eloquent tribute to the "Pioneers," and then read the most important of the one hundred telegrams of congratulation. The New York *Sun* commented that "in ordinary hands this task would have been dull enough, but Miss Anthony enlivened it with her wit and cleverness and made a success of it." [110]

Her introductions of speakers were brief and colorful, bright and spicy. Audiences liked them. When introducing Kate Field, who was known to have opposing views on the suffrage question, at the 1894 national convention, Miss Anthony said, "Now Friends, here is Kate Field, who has been talking all these years against woman suffrage. She wants to tell you of the faith that is in her." [111]

[108] *Washington Star* (Washington, D.C.), February, 1890, cited in Stanton *et al.*, *op. cit.*, IV, 173.
[109] Cited in Harper, *op. cit.*, III, 1154.
[110] *Ibid.*, II, 848.
[111] Stanton *et. al.*, *op. cit.*, IV, 235.

She introduced Henry Blackwell, husband of Lucy Stone, at the 1900 national convention by saying,

Here is a man who has the virtue of having stood by the woman's cause for nearly fifty years. I can remember him when his hair was not white, and when he was following up our conventions assiduously because a bright, little, red-cheeked woman attracted him. She attracted him so strongly that he still works for woman suffrage, and will do so as long as he lives, not only because of her who was always so true and faithful to the cause—Lucy Stone—but also because he has a daughter, a worthy representative of the twain who were made one." [112]

In 1902 she remarked, "He [is] the husband of Lucy Stone; I don't think he can quite represent her but he will do the best he can." [113]

Susan B. Anthony was adept at thinking quickly on her feet. She could make quick responses to speakers from the audience, and she seemed to know the right thing to say at the right moment. There was singing at the close of the 1883 national convention. Miss Couzins and Mrs. Shattuck sang the stanzas of the "Star-Spangled Banner," and Mr. Wilson of the Foundry M.E. Church, led the audience in the chorus. Miss Anthony quipped that the audience could see how much better it was to have a man help, even in singing. The quip "brought down the house." [114]

During a discussion on the divorce question in 1860, a minister thought he could stop her with "You are not married, you have no business to be discussing marriage." "Well, Mr. Mayo," she replied, "You are not a slave, suppose you quit lecturing on slavery." [115]

In the question period that followed Mrs. Stanton's address at a committee hearing of the legislature in Albany in 1867, Mr. Greeley asked, "Miss Anthony, you know the ballot and the bullet go together. If you vote, are you ready to fight?" Instantly she rejoined with "Yes, Mr. Greeley, just as you fought in the late war—at the point of a goose-quill." [116]

In a lively session following lectures given by Susan and George Francis Train to an audience in Rahway, New Jersey, on January 6, 1868, a prominent visitor from Kansas addressed the speakers saying, "You did a good work in Kansas, Miss Anthony, but you should not charge the Republican *party* as opposing woman's suffrage. It was only individual Republicans." Miss Anthony answered promptly:

[112] *Ibid.*, IV, 357.
[113] *Ibid.*, V, 33.
[114] *Ibid.*, III, 260.
[115] Harper, *op. cit.*, I, 196.
[116] *Ibid.*, I, 278.

The reverse of that is true. It was only individuals who helped us. Your State Committee declared themselves neutral, and then sent out, as agents, all the prominent anti-female suffrage men and not one prominent advocate of the Cause in the whole State.[117]

Mr. Train immediately changed the subject of the discussion.

During the South Dakota suffrage campaign of 1890 an intoxicated man kept interrupting speeches with loud remarks. Several men cried, "Put him out!" "No, gentlemen," said Miss Anthony, "he is a product of man's government, and I want you to see what sort you make."[118]

When someone quietly reminded her that the national suffrage convention of 1896 had started without the opening prayer, she said without the slightest confusion:

> Now, Friends, you all know I am a Quaker. We give thanks in silence. I do not think the heart of anyone here has been fuller of silent thankfulness than mine, but I should not have remembered to have the meeting formally opened with prayer if somebody had not reminded me. The Rev. Anna Howard Shaw will offer prayer.[119]

Clearly, Miss Anthony had presence of mind and general affability in the handling of audiences. As the *History of Woman Suffrage* emphasizes,

> Miss Anthony seldom made a stated address either in opening or closing, but throughout the entire convention kept up a running fire of quaint, piquant, original and characteristic observations which delighted the audience and gave a distinctive attraction to the meetings. It was impossible to keep a record of these and they would lose their zest and appropriateness if separated from the circumstances which called them forth. They cannot be transmitted to future generations, but the thousands who heard them during the fifty years of her itineracy will preserve them among their delightful memories. Perfectly at home on the platform, she would indulge in the same informality of remarks which others use in private conversation, but always with a quick wit, a fine satire and a keen discrimination. Words of praise or criticism were given with equal impartiality, and accepted with a grace which would have been impossible had the giver been any other than the recognized Mentor of them all. Her wonderful power of reminiscence never failed, and she had always some personal recollection of every speaker or of her parents or other relatives. She kept the audience in continuous good-humor and furnished a variety to the program of which the newspaper reporters joyfully availed themselves.[120]

[117] *The Revolution*, January 8, 1868.
[118] Harper, *op. cit.*, III, 693.
[119] Stanton *et al.*, *op. cit.*, IV, 252-53.
[120] *Ibid.*, IV, 238.

Conclusion

For more than a half-century Susan B. Anthony appeared upon the public platform to promote the cause of woman's emancipation. People thronged to hear her speak, and went away filled with admiration for the speaker. And yet a careful study of her life, work, and speeches reveals no satisfactorily clear picture of her speaking ability. Careful, detailed reports found about other women speakers are lacking for Miss Anthony.

Contemporary reports gave other women speakers approbation by calling them "orators," "popular lecturers," and "noted female talkers." They devoted paragraphs to method of delivery, style, and elocution, and described the women as being "eloquent," "persuasive," and "silver-tongued." Susan was referred to as a worker, an organizer, and a reformer, and was said to speak plainly. During a lecture tour from Kansas to New York in 1867, she was accompanied by Elizabeth Cady Stanton and George Francis Train. The Louisville, Kentucky, *Journal* of November 28th observed simply that Miss Anthony had been before the public for years and always had won "the applause of the multitudes in whose cause she has been a standing champion." The same article noted that Mrs. Stanton was "one of the greatest and noblest women of our country," who "addresses all her audiences with the most thrilling power and effect." Mr. Train was said to be an orator in his own peculiar way, having "dashing eloquence, resistless humor and fertility of resource." The views of the three speakers were equally radical and outspoken.

In discussing the National Woman Suffrage Convention of 1899, the *Washington Post* of January 22nd especially commended the address made by Mrs. Lillie Devereux Blake which captivated the large audience, and added that the lady in question occupied an enviable place among her sex upon the lecture platform. She elicited continuous applause on this evening as "she threw her shafts of wit and satire with electrical rapidity." The meeting was closed by a short and interesting talk by Miss Anthony "in her own inimitable style" and the audience dispersed.

In 1871 popular lady lecturers were compared. Mrs. Elizabeth Cady Stanton was considered the most dignified, Mrs. Mary Livermore the most eloquent, Mrs. Lillie Devereux Blake the wittiest, Miss Anna Dickinson the fieriest, Miss Kate Field the spiciest, Miss Olive Logan the jolliest, and Miss Lillian Edgarton the handsomest of the lecturers. Miss Anthony was not mentioned.[121]

An article on "Platform Honors," appearing in the same paper on April

---

[121] *The Revolution*, March 30, 1871.

13, 1871, stated that "we have yet no one more logical than Mrs. Stanton, more earnest than Miss Anthony and more persuasive and clear-headed than Lucy Stone." Among the newer speakers "Anna Dickinson stands always first and foremost for eloquence and fire. Miss Field, Miss Logan, and others are distinguished in different ways...."

A report of the Fort Wayne, Indiana, *Daily Sentinel* of February 26, 1873, which was fringed with disapproval of the woman's rights movement, insisted that "Susan B. Anthony has not the dash and sparkle of Anna Dickinson, nor the pleasing oratorical grandeur of Cady Stanton. She does not thrill an audience like Mrs. Livermore with the humorous and pathetic...."

And the *Boston Herald* of February 17, 1890, in describing noted "female talkers" remarked that it was a distinct loss to the platform when Anna Dickinson left it. She and Mary Livermore were the most magnetic of the women speakers of the day. Kate Field, with her exquisite pronunciation, fine humor and wit, brought the drawing room to the audience. Lucy Stone and Julia Ward Howe had choice of language that was wonderful to hear. Elizabeth Cady Stanton's "well rounded periods" were "those of the orator rather than of the talker." And Susan Anthony, "the kindliest soul that ever lived" had "few graces of oratory," but could "strike out from the shoulder in a most vigorous fashion," was never unpleasantly assertive, and spoke as if she were talking to a room full of friends and not to an audience.

In his article on "Great Orators and the Lyceum," J. B. Pond noted that Elizabeth Cady Stanton was usually ranked higher in the list of woman suffragists than Miss Anthony, although the latter had done more work. He emphasized that Mrs. Stanton was unquestionably the ablest orator and the most scholarly woman in the movement.[122]

Of the younger speakers, Dr. Anna Howard Shaw was considered beyond question to be the "leading woman orator" of her generation.[123] When they reviewed the history of suffrage reform, Carrie Chapman Catt and Nettie Rogers Shuler explained that while Susan Anthony was the "greatest souled woman" of the movement, it was Dr. Shaw who was the "master orator," and who "stood unchallenged throughout her career as the greatest orator among women the world has ever known."[124]

There is no doubt that Miss Anthony was a master of group discussion and of impromptu speaking. She probably would have become a famous woman even if she had not appeared upon the platform as a lecturer, just as did

[122] James B. Pond, "Great Orators and the Lyceum," *The Cosmopolitan*, XXI (July, 1896), 247-56.

[123] Stanton *et al.*, *op. cit.*, IV, 149.

[124] Carrie Chapman Catt and Nettie Rogers Shuler, *Woman Suffrage and Politics* (New York: Charles Scribner's Sons, 1926), pp. 260, 268.

Dorothea Dix who was not a public speaker but gained renown as a reformer in the treatment of the insane.[125]

An obituary notice in the *Des Moines Register and Leader* of March 15, 1906, concluded:

Miss Anthony was not an orator, but her addresses did more for the advancement of woman than those of any dozen women of her time. She said the things that needed to be said at the particular time in which she was speaking. Not every man who listened to her was converted, but every man who heard her realized that she knew her business and was making a formidable appeal. The net outcome of her work and of her example it would be difficult to estimate. The status of woman has changed more in the three-quarters of a century of her active labors than it had in the nineteen centuries that preceded. In the field of mechanical invention there has been nothing to astonish the world which compares with the change in the thought of the world with regard to woman's capacities and woman's sphere. . . .

Susan B. Anthony was an effective public speaker, but probably not a great one. Perhaps the anonymous clipping found in her Scrapbook for 1890 gives the most adequate conclusion.[126] This article depicts her appearance before an audience in Aberdeen, South Dakota, on an evening when Anna Howard Shaw was unable to fill the engagement, and declares:

. . . those who were disappointed at missing the rhetoric of Dr. Shaw were well satisfied to listen to a social talk from the old campaigner. Miss Anthony is no orator; in fact it is difficult, in listening to her, to conceive that she has stood upon the platform thousands of times in the past fifty years.

Judged critically she is angular in gesture and uncouth in phraseology. But when you remember who she is—that you are listening to a woman who has fought a noble and successful battle for half a century in behalf of her sex—that her intelligence is as keen as her persistence is laudable, you cease to criticize the orator and remember only the woman.

Enigmatic as Susan B. Anthony's power as a public speaker may remain, one thing is certain. She was a classic example of the importance of the individual in public speaking.

SELECTED BIBLIOGRAPHY

Unpublished Material

Susan B. Anthony's Scrapbooks. 33 vols. Rare Book Room, Library of Congress, Washington, D. C. The Scrapbooks cover a period from 1837-1900. In them are programs and proceedings of conventions and of congressional hearings on woman

---

[125] Cf. Francis Tiffany, *Life of Dorothea Lynde Dix* (Boston and New York: Houghton Mifflin & Co., 1890).

[126] Scrapbooks (1890), Vol. XIII.

suffrage. There are also propaganda leaflets, handbills announcing lectures, and abstracts of speeches given by Elizabeth Cady Stanton, Lucy Stone, Henry Ward Beecher, and others. Hundreds of newspaper clippings pertaining to political activities, suffrage, and personal activities are also included.

GRIM, HARRIETT E. "Susan B. Anthony, Exponent of Freedom." Unpublished Ph. D. dissertation, University of Wisconsin, 1937-38.

YOAKAM, DORIS G. "A History of the Public Speaking Activity of Women in America." Unpublished Ph.D. dissertation, University of Southern California, 1935.

Biographies

ABBOTT, WILLIS J. *Notable Women in History.* Philadelphia: The John C. Winston Co., 1913.

ANTHONY, KATHARINE. *Susan B. Anthony: Her Personal History and Her Era.* Garden City, New York: Doubleday & Co., Inc., 1954.

BENNETT, D. M. *The World's Sages, Infidels and Thinkers.* New York: Liberal and Scientific Publishing House, 1876.

BLACKWELL, ALICE STONE. *Lucy Stone.* Boston: Little, Brown & Co., 1930.

BLOOMER, D. C. *Life and Writings of Amelia Bloomer.* Boston: Arena Publishing Co., 1895.

BROWN, OLYMPIA. *Acquaintances, Old and New, among Reformers.* 1911.

BRYAN, FLORENCE HORN. *Susan B. Anthony, Champion of Women's Rights.* New York: Julian Messner, Inc., 1947.

CHADWICK, JOHN (ed.). *A Life for Liberty: Anti-Slavery and Other Letters of Sallie Holley.* New York: G. P. Putnam's Sons, 1899.

CHESTER, GIRAUD. *Embattled Maiden, The Life of Anna Dickinson.* New York: G. P. Putnam's Sons, 1951.

COLMAN, LUCY N. *Reminiscences.* Buffalo: H. L. Green, 1891.

DORR, RHETA CHILDE. *Susan B. Anthony.* New York: Frederick A. Stokes Co., 1928.

DOUGLASS, FREDERICK. *Life and Times of Frederick Douglass.* Hartford, Conn.: Park Publishing Co., 1884.

GARRISON, WENDELL PHILLIPS, AND GARRISON, FRANCIS JACKSON. *William Lloyd Garrison.* 4 vols. New York: The Century Co., 1885-89.

HALL, FLORENCE HOWE. *Julia Ward Howe and the Woman Suffrage Movement.* Boston: Dana Estes & Co., 1913.

HALLOWELL, ANNA DAVIS (ed.). *James and Lucretia Mott: Life and Letters.* Boston: Houghton, Mifflin & Co., 1884.

HANAFORD, PHEBE A. *Daughters of America.* Augusta, Maine: True & Co., 1883.

HARPER, IDA HUSTED. *The Life and Work of Susan B. Anthony.* 3 vols. Indianapolis: The Hollenbeck Press, 1898-1908.

HOWE, M. A. DEWOLFE. *Causes and Their Champions.* Boston: Little, Brown & Co., 1926.

LIVERMORE, MARY A. *The Story of My Life.* Hartford, Conn.: A. D. Worthington & Co., 1899.

LUTZ, ALMA. *Created Equal, A Biography of Elizabeth Cady Stanton.* New York: The John Day Co., 1940.

PARTON, JAMES, et al. *Eminent Women of the Age.* Hartford, Conn.: S. M. Betts & Co., 1869.

PAUL, NANETTE B. *The Great Woman Statesman.* New York: Hogan-Paulus Corp., 1925.

SHAW, ANNA HOWARD. *The Story of a Pioneer.* New York: Harper & Brothers, 1915.

STANTON, ELIZABETH CADY. *Eighty Years and More.* New York: European Publishing Co., 1898.

STANTON, THEODORE, AND BLATCH, HARRIOT STANTON. *Elizabeth Cady Stanton as Revealed in Her Letters, Diary and Reminiscences.* 2 vols. New York: Harper & Brothers, 1922.

STOWE, HARRIET B., *et al. Our Famous Women.* Hartford, Conn.: A. D. Worthington & Co., 1884.

TIFFANY, FRANCIS. *Life of Dorothea Lynde Dix.* Boston and New York: Houghton, Mifflin & Co., 1890.

General Accounts

BJORKMAN, FRANCES M., AND PORRITT, ANNIE G. (eds.). *Woman Suffrage.* New York: National Woman Suffrage Publishing Co., Inc., 1917.

BROCKETT, L. P. *Woman's Work in the Civil War.* Philadelphia: Zeigler, McCurdy & Co., 1867.

CATT, CARRIE CHAPMAN, AND SHULER, NETTIE ROGERS. *Woman Suffrage and Politics.* New York: Charles Scribner's Sons, 1926.

FARMER, LYDIA H. (ed.). *What America Owes to Women.* New York: Charles Wells Moulton, 1893.

MEYER, ANNIE NATHAN. *Woman's Work in America.* New York: Henry Holt & Co., 1891.

ROBINSON, HARRIET H. *Massachusetts in the Woman Suffrage Movement.* Boston: Roberts Bros., 1883.

SEWALL, MAY WRIGHT (ed.). *The World's Congress of Representative Women.* Chicago and New York: Rand, McNally & Co., 1894.

STANTON, ELIZABETH CADY; ANTHONY, SUSAN B.; GAGE, MATILDA J.; AND HARPER, IDA H. (eds). *The History of Woman Suffrage.* 6 vols. Rochester, New York: Charles Mann, 1887, Vols. 1-3; Indianapolis: The Hollenbeck Press, 1902, Vol. 4; New York: J. J. Little & Ives Co., 1922, Vols. 5-6.

Periodicals

"A Hint to Our Female Agitators," *The Nation,* IX (December 2, 1869), 479-80.

HIGGINSON, THOMAS W. "American Audiences," *The Atlantic Monthly,* XCV (January, 1905), 38-44.

LONSDALE, MARGARET. "Platform Women," *The Nineteenth Century,* LXXXV (March, 1884), 409-15.

"Lyceums and Lecturing in America," *All the Year Around,* V (March 4, 1871), 317-21.

POND, JAMES B. "Great Orators and the Lyceum," *The Cosmopolitan,* XXI (July, 1896), 247-56.

———. "The Lyceum," *The Cosmopolitan,* XX (April, 1896), 595-602.

"The Lyceum Lecture," *The Nation,* VIII (April 8, 1869), 271-72.

Newspapers

The Liberator (Boston). 1831-65.

The Lily (Seneca Falls, New York). 1849-56.

The Revolution (New York). 1868-71.

The Una (Providence, Rhode Island). 1853-55.

The Woman's Journal (Boston). 1870-1917.

The Woman's Tribune (Washington, D.C.). 1890-1909.

5

George William Curtis

by CARROLL C. ARNOLD

Born in Providence, R. I., February 24, 1824, George William Curtis attended private schools near Boston and Providence until he moved with his family to New York City in 1839. Here he studied under private tutors and worked briefly as a clerk until, with his brother, he enrolled as a student and boarder at Brook Farm (1842-43). Subsequently, the brothers attached themselves to Emerson's circle at Concord (1844-45). While traveling in Europe and the Middle East (1846-50), George William began writing for *The New York Tribune* and after his return to the United States he continued on the staff of that paper until he established himself as a contributor to various periodicals and as a lyceum lecturer. In 1853, he began to contribute to "The Editor's Easy Chair," a monthly department of *Harper's Magazine*, and he was solely responsible for this feature from 1859 until his death. In 1863, he also became editor of *Harper's Weekly*. In addition to several volumes of essays Curtis published *Nile Notes of a Howadji* (1851) and *The Howadji in Syria* (1852); two novels: *Prue and I* (1857) and *Trumps* (1861); and edited *The Correspondence of John Lothrop Motley* (1889). From 1851 until illness forced him to discontinue the activity in 1874, he regularly appeared on lyceum platforms as a lecturer on literary, moral, and political subjects. After he ceased lecturing, he remained in great demand as an occasional and ceremonial speaker. He was active in Republican politics from 1856 until 1880 and in the Independent Republican and reform movements from 1880 until his death. He held important offices in the Republican party and in civic organizations and in addition he served as a member of the Board of Regents of the State of New York (1864-90), member of the New York State Constitutional Convention (1867-68), member of President Grant's Civil Service Commission (1871-74), President of the American Social Science Association (1873-74), President of the National Civil Service Reform League (1881-92), and Chancellor of the University of the State of New York (1890-92). He died at his home on Staten Island, August 31, 1892.

In 1884, James Russell Lowell described the social and political prospect toward which many educated Americans of his time looked with quiet confidence. Said he, "In the scales of the destinies brawn will never weigh so much as brain. Our healing is not in the storm or in the whirlwind, it is not in monarchies, or aristocracies, or democracies, but will be revealed by the still small voice that speaks to the conscience and the heart, prompting us

133

to a wider and wiser humanity." [1] Thus Lowell epitomized the creed which William Dean Howells styled "the Socinian graft of a Calvinist stock." [2] It was a creed which postulated the ultimate triumph of social goodness through the power of personal morality, devotion to duty, and self-reliance. It was derived in part from Emerson and the transcendentalist movement and in part from the expansive optimism of the time. It was the keystone of the New England idealism which touched and deeply marked George William Curtis, publicist, literary commentator, and guardian of political morality for the century's declining half.

Curtis was literally a child of New England and, though the greater portion of his life was spent in New York, he seems always to have resided, intellectually, near Boston. Unquestionably, the experiences that did most to mold his thought and character were those he encountered in his nineteenth, twentieth, and twenty-first years, when he was a boarder and student at Brook Farm and a farmhand and intellectual pilgrim in the vicinity of Concord. In the words of James Burrill Curtis, George's elder brother and companion, the impact of these three years "proved to be the cardinal event of our youth; and I cannot but think that the seed then sown took such deep root as to flower continuously in our later years, and make us both the confirmed 'Independents' that we were and are, whilst fully conscious at the same time of the obligation of living in all possible harmony with our fellows." [3] Neither brother surrendered himself unreservedly to the Brook Farm way of life, but each was deeply influenced by the philosophical ideas which he found there and, after about two years, the brothers moved from Brook Farm to Concord in order to absorb at first hand the ideas of Emerson and his circle.

For George William, "a willing captive to Emerson's attractions, and to the incidental attractions of the movement of which he was the head," [4] these were his college days. A year of study at home and two years of travel in Europe completed his preparation for a career as writer, editor, and speaker.

From Brook Farm, where he daily observed the workings of collectivist reform, Curtis wrote to his father in 1843:

No wise man is long a reformer, for Wisdom sees plainly that growth is steady. . . . Reform is organized distrust. It says to the universe fresh from God's

---

[1] Address on "Democracy," delivered on assuming the presidency of the Birmingham and Midland Institute, Birmingham, England, October 6, 1884. Thomas B. Reed (ed.), *Modern Eloquence* (New York: The University Society, 1900), VIII, 807.

[2] *Literary Friends and Acquaintance* (New York: Harper & Brothers, 1900), p. 117.

[3] Edward Cary, *George William Curtis* (Boston: Houghton Mifflin & Co., 1894), p. 16.

[4] *Ibid.*, p. 17. James Burrill Curtis quoted.

hand, "You are a miserable business; lo! I will make you fairer!" and so deputes some Fourier or Robert Owen to improve the bungling work of the Creator.[5]

And a year later, when a friend decided to join formally with the Brook Farm Association, Curtis defended his own independent position saying,

> There is indeed a latent movement, badly represented by these reforms, and that is the constant perception of the supremacy of the Individual. . . . I can reach other men only through myself. So far as you have need of association you are injured by it.[6]

His travels in Europe at the time of the generally ill-fated revolutions of 1848 seem to have affected his political and social sensitivities very little if at all.[7] It is clear that in this period, as in the early years of his career as a writer, his critical interests were as yet confined to the aesthetic aspects of art, literature, and manners.

In 1851, a year after his return from Europe, Curtis published *Nile Notes of a Howadji* and *The Howadji in Syria*, wrote regularly on art, literature, and music for *The New York Tribune*, and delivered his first lyceum lectures. In 1852, he published a third volume of travel notes—this time treating the American scene under the title, *Lotus Eating*. During the next year, his *Potiphar Papers*, a series of satirical essays on New York and Newport society, appeared. Meanwhile, Curtis had also become a regular contributor to *Putnam's Magazine*, *Harper's Magazine*, and *Harper's Weekly* and had achieved the status of a "regular" in Eastern lyceums. He appeared to be fashioning a pleasant and profitable, if undistinguished, career as a littérateur; but *The Potiphar Papers* and his early "Easy Chair" essays reveal that contemplation of aesthetic problems in literature, manners, and art could not alone satisfy the urgings of his New England conscience.[8] Although he had

---

[5] *Ibid.*, pp. 25-26.

[6] George Willis Cooke (ed.), *Early Letters of George Wm. Curtis to John S. Dwight* (New York: Harper & Brothers, 1898), p. 159.

[7] Cary quotes liberally from Curtis' letters from Europe, but none contains any significant comment on the revolutionary developments of the time. See Cary, *op. cit.*, pp. 39-51; also Cooke, *op. cit.*, pp. 258-73.

[8] Donald G. Mitchell and Curtis served as joint occupants of "The Easy Chair" from 1853 until 1859; *Harper's Magazine*, 201 (1950), 20.

Among the essays which clearly came from the hand of Curtis in 1854-55 there are three which condemn the hypocrisy and extravagance connected with charity concerts, bazaars, and similar functions, one demanding better building practices to end the loss of life by fires, a mild argument against attempts to control the sale of liquors by unrealistic laws, an extended plea for the extension of the rights and privileges of women, and a number of incidental complaints against the tendency to elevate financial success above personal integrity in the scale of social values. See *ibid.*, 9 (1854), 120, 122-23, 551-53; 10 (1854-55), 549-50; 11 (1855), 123-24, 268-69, 412-14.

begun his career as a mere commentator on matters of taste and morality, his basic assumptions concerning the nature and functioning of a democratic society directed his attention increasingly toward the necessity for elevating and improving the morals and the tastes of his fellow citizens without resort to the experiments in social reorganization which he had learned in his youth to distrust.

The Speaker and His Premises

On the lecture platform Curtis succeeded as literary commentator, social critic, and advocate of civil service reform. He was, in some quarters at least, much admired as a political speaker. As an occasional speaker he became the favored eulogist of public and private virtues and of self-reliant men. He successfully presided over and spoke for the American Social Science Association, the National Civil Service Reform League, and numerous lesser civic and reformist bodies. It is somewhat startling, then, to discover that this man who was so widely applauded and who won admiration with nearly every subject he chose, spoke from a remarkably limited store of rhetorical topics. Almost from the beginning of his public career he addressed himself to a single theme: the power, place, and function of conscience in public life.

Although Curtis apparently delivered his first formal lectures during the winter of 1850-51,[9] his first widely acclaimed address was "The Duty of the American Scholar to Politics and the Times," delivered in 1856 to the literary societies of Wesleyan University, Middletown, Connecticut.[10] In this speech the assumptions that shaped the thinking of his mature years were set forth in considerable detail. These views were the natural extensions of the transcendentalist, neo-Federalist creed which Curtis together with Lowell, Godkin, Aldrich, and others had consciously or unconsciously come to accept in varying degrees. Not collectivism nor other reorganizations of patterns for living, not some vague "progress" indigenous to democracy or to America, not revolt, nor even the extension of general education were likely to vitalize and elevate American life, thought these Eastern intellectuals. They were skeptics and individualists enough to reject the reform movements which emphasized social or political reorganization, but they were still utopians enough to believe in prescriptive cures for social ailments. They, and Curtis with them, turned away from the reform movements with which they had

[9] Cary, *op. cit.*, p. 74.

[10] Charles Eliot Norton (ed.), *Orations and Addresses of George William Curtis* (New York: Harper & Brothers, 1894), I, 1-35. The address was delivered on August 5, 1856. It was published in *The New York Weekly Tribune* of August 16, thus gaining, according to Norton, a circulation of 173,000 copies. It was also issued in pamphlet form.

grown up and placed their faith in the ability of men of their own class to provide society with wisdom and rectitude which, thus provided, might then filter through to the lower strata of society until all public life should in the end be prompted to the "wider and wiser humanity" which Lowell anticipated.[11]

At Wesleyan University, Curtis developed fully his interpretation and application of this creed. The scholar, he said, is the "representative of thought" and the "public conscience by which public measures may be tested; the scholarly class, therefore, to which now, as of old, the clergy belong, is the upper house in the politics of the world." In opposition to this saving force stands "selfish trade" which in "its eagerness for peace constantly lowers the moral ideal." But conscience being society's ennobling force, and scholars being "the priests of the mind," those educated men who accept their true obligations are duty-bound to form "the conservative party of intellectual and moral freedom." To live nobly and to defend honesty and liberty at all costs, as Milton did, thus become the scholar's general duties to politics, said Curtis.

Having developed these general principles, Curtis turned to their meaning for 1856. American history, he alleged, was the record of a continuous struggle between slavery and liberty. In 1856, the duty of the American scholar was: "To know that freedom always has its Thermopylae, and that his Thermopylae is called Kansas." Thus, "the intelligent exercise of political rights" was the immediate duty of the scholar and, by indirection, Curtis made it abundantly clear that this obligation could only be fulfilled by joining the Republican, antislavery political forces in supporting General Frémont against the proslavery Democrats and their presidential candidate, Buchanan.

It is essential for an understanding of Curtis' addresses on political and social themes, and in smaller degree for an understanding of his lectures on literary subjects, that the assumptions expressed in this early speech be kept always in mind. From even so brief a summary as that just given, it can be seen that four basic premises furnish the sources for each important line of argument:

1. That moral truths are discernible and absolute;
2. That the proper exercise of intellect is the discovery of these truths;
3. That those who have gained the "upper house" of education and intellect have, by that fact, incurred an obligation to society which they can only

[11] Herbert W. Schneider has explained the emergence of this pattern of thinking thus: "After the failure of ... [the] utopian schemes American transcendental philosophy became increasingly individualistic, culminating in Emerson's gospel of self-reliance. As a consequence American transcendentalism was confined to a limited group whose chief aim was to be spiritually free and culturally elect." "Transcendentalism," *The Encyclopædia of the Social Sciences* (New York: The Macmillan Co., 1935), XV, 76-77.

fulfill by infusing into the social and political system the truths which they alone can fully discern;

4. That the American political system must, under the leadership of the intellectual and moral elite, be made a system energized by moral truth or it will die.

Except for those arguments which he used to prove that American history could be read as a story of conflict between slavery and liberty, Curtis offered his Wesleyan University audience no lines of reasoning which did not spring from one or more of these premises. But what is more significant to a full understanding of Curtis as an American orator is the fact that important lines of argument not traceable to these propositions rarely appear in any of his addresses.

Speaking to the Union College graduating class of 1857, Curtis analyzed the nature and need of patriotism. Again, he came to the same general conclusions he had offered at Wesleyan University the previous year:

If we believe that our country embodies any principle ... and that as moral agents and self-respecting men we have something to do in America besides turning the air and water and earth into wealth, we shall need to cling to no principle so strongly as this, that no possible law can bind us to do a moral wrong. ... What excuse is it for my lying and thieving and murdering, for my trampling upon conscience, which is God in me, that the law ordered it? [12]

The men at Wesleyan had been urged simply to support Frémont against the proslavery elements, but since then Frémont had been defeated by Buchanan and the Dred Scott decision had been pronounced by the Supreme Court. Educated men who recognized the absolute, moral evil of slavery now found it still more difficult to translate their perceptions into social and political action. In response to this situation Curtis intensified his original theme. The intellectual elite must now be prepared to resist immoral laws such as the Fugitive Slave Act and decisions such as that given in the Dred Scott case. Such resistance would be the highest form of patriotism. The premises for Curtis' arguments had changed in no way.

The same fundamental beliefs also appeared in "The American Doctrine of Liberty" which Curtis delivered to the Phi Beta Kappa Society at Harvard and to other audiences in 1862. Here he insisted, "the real patriot in this country is he who sees most clearly what the nation ought to desire, who does what he can by plain and brave speech to influence it to that desire, and then urges and supports the laws which express it." The American doctrine of liberty he defined as "the equality of human rights based upon our common humanity." And who were the patriots capable of leading in the rediscovery

[12] "Patriotism," delivered July 20, 1857; Norton, *op. cit.*, I, 55.

and defense of this doctrine? The familiar answer is evident enough in such passages as,

In a system like ours, where almost every man has a vote and votes as he chooses, public opinion is really the government. *Whoever panders to it is training a tyrant for our master. Whoever enlightens it lifts people toward peace and prosperity.*[13]

When he considered Thackeray as a literary figure, he dwelt on the "tenderness, the sympathy, the simplicity which were combined with that noble leonine hatred of hypocrisy and sham," and he praised Thackeray for firing "hot shot upon his Sebastopol of sham, which was society."[14] And when he spoke of Dickens, the familiar postulates emerged still more clearly. "The story-teller," he told a Providence audience in 1870, "takes his place with the statesman and the orator.... Of this tendency and purpose Dickens is the great representative." His tales, said the lecturer, are "batteries opened against great wrongs." One involuntarily thinks of Dickens as a reformer, he went on, but "we do not lessen the greatness of an artist when we say he does men good. He is the great street preacher of to-day."[15] The inference that Curtis would have thought less highly of Dickens had he been a still greater artist but a poorer reformer is corroborated by the fact that his eulogy of Lowell contains no notice of Lowell's scholarship and only the following observation regarding that portion of his poetry which was least didactic:

The happy young scholar at Elmwood, devoted to literature and love, and unheeding the great movement of public affairs, showed from time to time that beneath the lettered leisure of his life there lay the conscience and moral virility that give public effect to genius and accomplishment. Lowell's development as a literary force in public affairs is unconsciously and exquisitely portrayed in the prelude to "Sir Launfal" in 1848.[16]

Whether he commented upon literature, war, or politics, Curtis sought out and used arguments drawn from the premises set forth above. To this there is no exception among his published speeches. These were assumptions which at once directed and circumscribed his rhetorical invention from the time of his first important address at Wesleyan University to the eulogy of Lowell which was his last. These assumptions concerning man's relationships

---

[13] *Ibid.*, p. 111. Italics mine.

[14] Lecture on "Thackeray" delivered at Providence, Rhode Island, January 29, 1864, and elsewhere. See summary of the lecture, *Providence Daily Journal*, January 30, 1864, p. 2.

[15] *Ibid.*, November 17, 1870, p. 1.

[16] "James Russell Lowell," delivered before the Brooklyn Institute, February 22, 1892; Norton, *op. cit.*, III, 375.

to man in a democratic society were pivotal factors in his rhetorical successes, but at the same time they seriously limited the circumstances in which he could succeed.

Curtis and His Audiences

It was on the lecture platform that Curtis first gained fame as a speaker. Although he became a regular occupant of the lecturer's desk through financial necessity, there can be little doubt that he would, in any case, have made extensive use of this instrument for public enlightenment.[17] Indeed, as early as 1854—several years before his financial reverses—he was planning a two-month lecture tour and hoping to earn two thousand dollars at the rate of fifty dollars per lecture.[18]

The lyceum of the fifties and sixties offered Curtis an ideal opportunity to enlighten the unenlightened and to arouse the educated to their social duties. In its early period the lyceum had been primarily an instrument for adult education. The subjects discussed were informative rather than controversial or inspirational and the speakers and demonstrators, whether scholars or laymen, undertook to teach their listeners rather than to arouse them.[19] In the lyceum's second period, beginning about 1845, it became increasingly an instrument for awakening America's social conscience. The system is said to have become "a branch of that national institution 'the stump.' "[20] It is probable, however, that a more precise and accurate description of the purposes of the lyceum in its second phase is that offered by J. G. Holland: the melioration of prejudices, the improvement of public taste, and the championing of liberty.[21] It is clear in any case that American lecturing and the expectations of the lecture-going audience made it easy and appropriate for Curtis to bring his convictions to the lecturer's desk.

As an essayist and commentator on literary as well as political and social issues, Curtis was perfectly fitted to meet the demands of lecture committees who sought to temper controversy with the improvement of public

[17] Curtis and his father-in-law suffered severe financial losses in the failure of Dix, Edwards and Company, publishers of *Putnam's Monthly*. Curtis, characteristically, assumed debts for which he was not legally liable and committed himself to extensive lecture tours in order to repay them. Cary, *op. cit.*, pp. 106-7.

[18] *Ibid.*, p. 90.

[19] See Waldo W. Braden, "The Lecture Movement: 1840-1860," *Quarterly Journal of Speech*, 34 (1948), 206-12.

[20] Thomas W. Higginson, "The American Lecture System," *Every Saturday*, 5 (April 18, 1868), 492. Higginson adds that lyceum audiences demanded "a glimpse at every public man, and especially every prominent reformer."

[21] "The Popular Lecture," *Atlantic Monthly*, 15 (1865), 362-71.

taste.[22] Since, in the first fifteen years of his career, Curtis was interested in elevating the moral tone of society rather than in agitating for a specific reform, it was easy for him to satisfy the eclectic tastes of lecture committees with a variety of themes. That he satisfied his audiences and the lecture committees is attested by the number of his invitations and his reappearance upon the same platforms in successive seasons.[23]

Of what sort were these thousands who heard Curtis lecture? What expectations and inclinations did they bring to the lecture hall? "You will find," said an anonymous writer who may have been Curtis himself, "that the lec-

[22] The lecture "courses" advertised in such newspapers as the *Providence Daily Journal*, the *Albany Daily Argus*, *The New York Times*, *The New York Daily Tribune*, and numerous smaller papers make it clear that few courses of long standing offered programs that were either entirely literary or entirely social and political. There were, however, a few courses which offered exclusively religious or scientific programs.

[23] The following is a partial list of Curtis' lecture subjects preceding and during the Civil War period:

In 1855, Mary A. Dodge ("Gail Hamilton") heard him speak on "Success" at Hartford, Connecticut; H. Augusta Dodge (ed.), *Gail Hamilton's Life in Letters* (Boston: Lee and Shepard, 1901), I, 83. Andrew D. White records that he heard Curtis in lyceum lectures on modern literature, but the exact year to which he refers is unclear. Since it was after White had begun his Junior year at Yale, the time must have been in 1852 or 1853; *Autobiography* (New York: The Century Co., 1905), I, 29. In 1857, Curtis delivered an address on "Patriotism" at the Union College commencement exercises; Norton, *op. cit.*, I, 38. In his letters of 1858, he mentions two subjects which may be variant titles for the same lecture, delivered at the University of Michigan, Antioch College, before a teachers' institute at Newport, Rhode Island, and probably elsewhere. These titles were "The Democratic Principle and Its Prospects in Our Country" and "Democracy and Education"; Cary, *op. cit.*, pp. 118-19. The latter speech was also delivered in Brooklyn, New York; *The New York Times*, December 1, 1858, p. 1. In all he lectured at least sixty times during this season; Cary, *op. cit.*, p. 120. When he delivered one of the Plymouth Lectures at Plymouth Church, Brooklyn, in 1859, his subject was "The Present Aspect of the Slavery Question"; *The New York Times*, October 19, 1859, p. 5. Since the same lecture was also delivered in Boston and Philadelphia, there is reason to believe this was his chief subject for the 1859-60 lecture season; Norton, *op. cit.*, I, 62-63. His chief lecture for 1860-61 was "The Policy of Honesty"; Cary, *op. cit.*, p. 138. In October, 1861, he was preparing a lecture on "National Honor" which apparently was the subject he used for 1861-62 lectures; *ibid.*, p. 151. During 1862-63, "The American Doctrine of Liberty" was the subject most frequently used; Norton, *op. cit.*, I, 96. I was unable to discover Curtis' main topic for the 1863-64 season, but on at least one occasion his subject was "Thackeray"; *Providence Daily Journal*, January 30, 1864, p. 2. For 1864-65, he prepared his famous lecture, "Political Infidelity," which was delivered some fifty times; Cary, *op. cit.*, p. 185. This lecture marked the shift of his attention to the problems of political administration and the civil service which were his primary concern for the remaining twenty-eight years of his life.

ture audience is composed mainly of young people, and largely of women." [24] Later, Curtis recorded his belief that those who gathered in the lecture halls were "all profoundly interested in the moral principles which were involved in the political situation." [25] In both judgments Curtis' views have modern support. The general desire for self-culture, which characterized the age, "was often associated with a somewhat vague feeling that the acquisition of culture was in itself a satisfaction and that it further enhanced the value of living," according to Curti.[26] And another student of the time has added a qualification which is also reflected in the observations appearing in *Putnam's* and the "Editor's Easy Chair":

The American's attitude toward culture was at once suspicious and indulgent. Where it interfered with more important activities, he distrusted it; where it was the recreation of his leisure hours or of his womenfolk, he tolerated it. For the most part, he required that culture serve some useful purpose.[27]

The nineteenth-century lecture hall was at once a monument to cultural aspiration and a public forum. Those who purchased tickets for the lecture "courses" did so, at least in part, out of a yearning for significant knowledge. By an act of will they presented themselves before the lecturer. They expected some reward for their efforts. Some sought release from their uncertainties, some desired reinforcement for their predispositions, some desired solace for their feelings of cultural inadequacy; others undoubtedly sought no more than satisfaction for their curiosity or relief from a humdrum existence. Almost none, however, could be satisfied by an offering of either culture for culture's sake or entertainment for entertainment's sake.[28] The lyceum, in its second phase, was what *Putnam's* observer called it: "a week-day church a little humanized." [29] Its members expected enlightenment and inspiration.

George William Curtis met perfectly the expectations of such audiences as

[24] "Lectures and Lecturing," *Putnam's Monthly Magazine*, 9 (1857), 321. The style of the essay closely resembles Curtis' and since the article appeared a month before the failure of Dix, Edwards and Company under whose management Curtis was an associate editor, he may well have been the author. See also Cary, *op. cit.*, pp. 78 and 104.

[25] "Editor's Easy Chair," *Harper's Monthly*, 40 (1869-70), 920. Curtis was the sole occupant of this department from 1859 until 1892; *ibid.*, 201 (1950), 20.

[26] Merle Curti, *The Growth of American Thought* (New York: Harper & Brothers, 1943), p. 597.

[27] Henry Steele Commager, *The American Mind* (New Haven: Yale University Press, 1950), p. 10.

[28] Those who arranged the lyceum programs soon discovered that their patrons disliked speakers who were professional lecturers and nothing else. Men and women of affairs, however, retained their popularity if they were competent speakers. See Holland, *op. cit.*, p. 369.

[29] "Lectures and Lecturing," *op. cit.*, p. 320.

these. His own view of what a lecture should be coincided exactly with what lyceum audiences seem to have demanded. Said he,

> An American popular lecture is a brisk sermon upon the times. Whatever its nominal topic may be, the substance of the discourse is always cognate to this people and this age. It may be a critical, a historical, or a moral discourse; but it is relished by the audience just in the degree that it is applied to them. . . .
> The Lyceum in this country has been emphatically what it has been so often called—lay-preaching.[30]

One may choose at random from among Curtis' lyceum and occasional lectures and, whether the subject be "Sir Philip Sidney," "The Genius of Dickens," "The Position of Women," "Political Infidelity," or "The Present Aspect of the Slavery Question," it will always be found that the speaker offered a facile array of information about his subject and a timely application thereof. The ticket-holder received the information and the inspiration he expected. He was never harried or discomfited by a zealot's plea for sudden change; instead, he was comforted by the speaker's assurance that truth was not elusive, that taste was prescribed by tradition, and that honest sentiment together with conscience could mold a social order. Furthermore, Curtis gratified his audiences because he was a man of affairs and of influence in both journalism and politics and because he possessed charm of person and manner. Considering all of these factors, one is not greatly surprised to read such comments as, "The mere announcement of the name of the lecturer, as might be expected, was sufficient to fill the hall to overflowing." [31]

As Non-Resident Professor of Recent Literature at Cornell University, Curtis also delivered lectures to the students, faculty, and guests of that institution.[32] This arrangement was, interestingly enough, the direct result of the impression which Curtis' literary lectures in the New Haven lyceum had made upon Andrew D. White and of subsequent discussions between the two men.[33]

[30] "The Editor's Easy Chair," *Harper's Monthly*, 24 (1861-62), 266.

[31] *Providence Daily Journal*, November 21, 1862, p. 2. This observation occurs in a news account concerning Curtis' appearance in the Franklin Lyceum Series to deliver his lecture on "The American Doctrine of Liberty," November 20, 1862.

[32] His subjects were: "A Review of Modern Literature," "The Novel," "Dickens," "Thackeray," "Women in Literature," "George Eliot," "Carlyle," "Robert Browning," "Elizabeth Barrett Browning," "Tennyson," "American Literature," and "Nathaniel Hawthorne." These lectures were first delivered in the spring trimester of 1869 and what appears to have been the same series was repeated in the spring of 1871. Waterman T. Hewett, *Cornell University, a History* (New York: The University Publishing Society, 1905), I, 135.

[33] White had now become the first president of Cornell University and had created the system of non-resident professorships as a means of offering Cornell's students the

Among students and townsmen Curtis' Cornell lectures aroused great enthusiasm and some of the reasons are perhaps to be found in the comments of *The Ithaca Journal's* reporter:

> Mr. Curtis is one of our most thorough scholars, polished, genial and manly. He is a finished orator, master of whatever subject he takes up, abounding in wit, flashing and keen in satire, and possessing a voice under complete control, rich and mellow. . . . He is in short the model American gentleman, cultivated, natural and the highest type of the manly scholar.[34]

The lectures themselves have not been preserved, although essays and lyceum lectures on the same subjects are in some instances available. There is no reason to believe, however, that Curtis changed his treatment of these topics markedly when he published his opinions on them or spoke of them on the lyceum platform. To have done so would have been entirely contrary to his usual practice, as will be shown below. One may suppose, then, that the Cornellians and Ithacans of 1869 and 1871 heard Thackeray praised for the same qualities which had been singled out in 1864 [35] and that Dickens was praised as having replaced Scott as England's great storyteller and because "as Forster said of Goldsmith, he reconciles us to human nature." [36] That Curtis approached these academic, literary lectures with the same didactic intent that gratified his lyceum audiences is evident from his remark to a friend concerning the lecture, "American Literature":

> I have written a lecture upon American Literature to the effect that what we have belongs to the great English stock, as Ovid was a Roman, though upon the Euxine, and Theocritus a Greek, though a Sicilian. The undertone is friendliness for England.[37]

James Russell Lowell, Non-Resident Professor of General Literature, was also on the Cornell campus in 1869 and one may catch the scholar's view of the two lecturers' relative merits in the observations of Professor Hewett:

> Professor Lowell's subjects, while more critical and remote than those of Mr. Curtis, possessed . . . charm of composition, . . . ample knowledge, . . . [and] grace and delicacy of humor. . . . Mr. Curtis, whose graceful style and pleasant discursive

---

kind of stimulation which he had found in the lyceum while a student at Yale. White, *op. cit.*, I, 337.

[34] May 25, 1869, p. 1.

[35] Thackeray, Curtis had said, took life as he found it, like the preacher or Luther "repeating to us . . . 'I can do no other, God help me.'" *Providence Daily Journal*, January 30, 1864, p. 2.

[36] These were the themes developed in Curtis' lyceum lecture on "Dickens." *Ibid.*, November 17, 1870, p. 1.

[37] Cary, *op. cit.*, pp. 202-3.

criticism charmed for so many years the readers of *Harper's Monthly*, won an enthusiastic reception from the student world.[38]

The reasons for Professor Hewett's gentle distinction between the critical faculties of the two lecturers are clear. Curtis discoursed gracefully upon men and motives, drawing illustrations from recent literature; he made of literary criticism, social comment. Nor did he disturb his hearers by demanding an exact and disciplined foreknowledge of his subject. But Lowell dared, from time to time, to pursue knowledge for its own sake. The students and honest citizens of 1869 preferred Curtis' commentary to Lowell's criticism and in so doing they identified themselves with the lecture audiences of their time.[39]

In the lyceum and in academic halls Curtis was fortunate in finding audiences generally interested in what he wanted most to give them—genteel sermons on the times. As a political speaker he was not always equally fortunate.

The antislavery cause drew Curtis into Republican party politics almost as soon as the party was formed. He served as a Republican committeeman, speaker, and candidate from 1856 until 1879. In the latter year he began to doubt that political machines could be destroyed from within either party and he, therefore, began to make his way, via the Independent Republican movement, into complete political independence.[40]

Because of the premises from which he invariably argued it is hard to believe that Curtis was ever entirely at home before unculled, mass audiences. His lines of argument and his style required audiences possessing literacy and an initial concern for morality in public conduct. Auditors like the well-tailored, well-educated, New England-born Nathaniel P. Willis were deeply impressed by the arguments Curtis offered them [41] but the same arguments and appeals

[38] Hewett, *op. cit.*, I, 136-37.
[39] An unidentified reporter for the *New York Evening Post*, who was in Ithaca during the spring lecture courses of Lowell, Curtis, and Theodore W. Dwight of the Columbia Law School, enumerated what he thought were the lectures "most noticeable thus far." In so doing he, perhaps unwittingly, revealed the pattern of lecture-audience preferences. He cited four lectures by Curtis, two by Lowell ("The Troubadours" and "On Wit and Humor"), and one by Dwight ("The Origin of Our Constitution"). Quoted in *The Ithaca Journal*, June 8, 1869, p. 1.
[40] Speaking of the plight of individual Republican voters in 1880, Curtis said, "But they are only befooled. They can buy the machine or they can frighten it, but they cannot conciliate it; and while they suppose that they are placating it for their own purposes, they are as dead as Hector dragging at the chariot-wheels of a scornful Achilles." "Machine Politics and the Remedy," an address to the Independent Republicans in Chickering Hall, New York City, May 20, 1880. Norton, *op. cit.*, II, 152.
[41] Willis wrote that when he was fifty-four he heard Curtis speak in behalf of Frémont's candidacy. At first he thought Curtis "too handsome and too well dressed a boy for popular oratory. And I continued to think so, for five minutes or so ... and

must have had much less immediacy for the impoverished or the ill-educated. Such auditors would, for example, have had considerable difficulty with the somewhat remote allusions of his speech in behalf of Cleveland, in which he contended:

> ... [Independent Republicans had to] sacrifice conscience to party or bolt; and they bolted. [Loud applause.] ... And then there was one scream of dude, Pharisee, bolter, kicker. And then there came the heavier wind instruments [Laughter]— dishonorable, traitor, deserter; and then, the scattering scream of sentimentalists, Britishers, free traders, soreheads; assistant Democrats, fools, idiots, scoundrels; and then, the English language giving out, mugwumps. [Laughter, applause, and three cheers for the mugwumps.] As Mrs. Malaprop says in the play, here was a "nice derangement of epitaphs." [42]

This speech was received with "the wildest enthusiasm" and much waving of handkerchiefs [43] but it could hardly have been so had the audience been composed of persons who were little read or of men who already believed that the other great issue of the campaign, revision of the tariff, actually transcended in importance the simple "question of honesty in government" which Curtis offered as the principal matter to be settled by the election.

There is evidence of a more specific sort which confirms the judgment that Curtis did not have unqualified success as a campaign orator. In the New York campaign for state offices in 1863, although "big names" were not numerous on the speakers' roster of the Union party, Curtis' name appears only twice during the entire campaign in the state committee's lists of speaking assignments. With two others he was assigned to address a party rally in his home county of Richmond and on another date he was scheduled to speak at tiny Roslyn, Long Island. [44] Yet at this time Curtis was the political editor

---

then, to tell the truth, I forgot all about it! He engrossed me so completely with his subject that I lost sight of what I was to criticize." Willis' letter concluded with praise for Curtis' self-possession, logic, *ethos*, and eloquence. "It comes natural to the boy! He was born to be an orator," said the observer. It is important to notice, however, that Willis resolved to cast his "virgin vote" for Frémont because Curtis had convinced him that the times were so serious that leadership could not be entrusted to *any* candidate, and that "by nature and culture" and by "the training and discipline to fit him for his work" Frémont was fitted for the presidency as Buchanan was not. From a private letter first published in *The New York Evening Post* and quoted in *The New York Times*, October 8, 1856, p. 2. The speech in question was delivered at Newburg, N. Y.

[42] Campaign speech delivered at the Brooklyn Rink, as reported in *The New York Times*, October 31, 1884, p. 1. This account purports to give the entire address excepting only a section devoted to sketching Blaine's past record in politics.

[43] *Ibid.*

[44] Announcements of such meetings throughout the state were regularly published by the State Committee. *Ibid.*, October 23, 1863, p. 5.

of *Harper's Weekly* and was sufficiently high in party councils to be chosen a delegate to the Republican National Convention in the following year and to receive the unpropitious nomination for congressman in his district.

Men sharing less common ground with the speaker than did N. P. Willis must have found it difficult to forget in a few minutes the many ways in which Curtis always showed that he was and wished to be the spokesman for the social and moral views of a class. James Ford Rhodes has probably drawn an accurate description of Curtis' potentialities as a campaign speaker and, by implication, specified his limitations in this form of public address. Says the admiring Rhodes, referring specifically to the Wesleyan University speech cited above:

> To college men, and men who read much, it spoke with mighty accents. The sincere and thoughtful orator had an earnest purpose; he looked upon politics from a lofty plane. ... The voter who was influenced by that argument must have felt that he had been borne into a political atmosphere which was freed from foul exhalations.[45]

In short, if one may judge from his Wesleyan University speech, from his address in behalf of Cleveland's candidacy, and from news reports and other accounts of his campaign speaking, it appears that he consistently addressed himself to the same classes of men who were his admirers in the lecture halls. With that segment of his campaign audience, and probably with that segment only, he was eminently successful.

In addressing political conventions Curtis won a few clear successes and some moral victories, but the qualities of mind and manner which set him apart from the man in the street also separated him from most practical politicians. At the second Republican National Convention he achieved considerable notice by opposing those party leaders who wished to conciliate doubters by adopting a platform which made no specific reference to the equality of men.[46] Curtis had been active in politics for scarcely four years but on this

[45] *A History of the United States from the Compromise of 1850* (rev. ed.; New York: The Macmillan Co., 1920), II, 170.

[46] Cary calls Curtis' speech a "most brilliant and unexpected assault" and cites confirming evidence from a recollection apparently written twenty years after the event. *Op. cit.*, pp. 132-35. Rhodes also devotes considerable space to Curtis' speech and parliamentary maneuver which, he says, "was greeted with deafening applause" and assured Lincoln of the support of the abolitionists in the election of 1860. *Op. cit.*, II, 463-64. The Republican *New York Times*, however, treated the incident as shrewd parliamentary strategy by which Curtis secured a second vote on an amendment previously defeated. The *Times* did not comment on the speech in support of the renewed amendment, only reporting that Curtis' amendment was unanimously accepted. See issue of May 18, 1860, pp. 1 and 4. I have found no full report of the speech itself nor any adequate body of data on which to judge the true temper of the audience. It seems

occasion he set forth the future pattern of his relationships with party regulars. In any conflict between political expediency and what Curtis liked to call "the right side" of a question, he was willing to settle for nothing less than the whole of his principle.

At the New York State Republican Convention of 1877, Curtis again enhanced his reputation for integrity but his demand for a formal statement approving the administration of President Hayes was defeated. Curtis proposed that the convention endorse in its platform Hayes' "pacification" policies and his civil service reforms. The question, he contended, was not *whether* New York Republicans would take a stand concerning these policies, but what stand they would take. To make no statement was to repudiate the administration, he said. This was, of course, precisely the problem which practical politicians preferred not to discuss, for they were well aware of a division in their party. Curtis' proposal was as disagreeable practically as it was sound morally. But the most significant feature of his two speeches in behalf of his proposition is that he made no effort to prove that any election advantages could be won by making a positive statement concerning the Hayes administration. His moral absolutes, it appears, led him to discount the one common concern of all listeners—the outcome of the forthcoming state elections. Practical considerations triumphed over Curtis' amendment to the platform even after Roscoe Conkling had delivered a savage diatribe against Curtis which drove unexpected votes into support of the Curtis-led faction.[47]

Twice during the Republican National Convention of 1884 Curtis took the floor, again in the interest of principles. Once he was eminently successful and once he seems to have missed the arguments to which his auditors were most likely to respond. When a Blaine delegate offered a resolution that would have bound all delegates to support actively the convention's ultimate choice, Curtis made a passionate speech against the proposal. "A Republican and a free man I came to this convention, and by the grace of God, a Republican and a free man I will go out of it," he began. He called attention to the rejection of such moves by previous conventions, invoked the shades of Lincoln and Garfield, begged delegates to act in the spirit of the party which was born to defend the rights of all individuals, and pressed home the argument that the resolution would strip every delegate of his freedom of action and judgment. His appeals seem to have had a strong effect on the delegates,

---

doubtful, however, that rhetorical power alone could have produced so complete a reversal in the voting.

[47] A full report of the convention's proceedings is to be found in *The New York Times*, September 27, 1877, pp. 1-2. Curtis' speech was apparently very poorly reported. See letter from Curtis to Norton; Cary, *op. cit.*, pp. 257-58.

for he was vigorously applauded and those supporting the resolution, seeing that it could not carry, withdrew it.[48]

But when the Blaine forces sought to elect Powell Clayton as temporary chairman of the convention, Curtis and Theodore Roosevelt supported the candidacy of John R. Lynch, a Negro from Mississippi. Both spoke in Lynch's behalf, Curtis developing the theme that the nation was watching the Republicans and the convention must live up to the party's past. Roosevelt, however, argued a theme more likely to influence the calculating politicians. "Let us elevate the race we freed," he cried, and argued that voting on the issue at hand must be by individuals rather than by states so that each delegate would "stand accountable to those whom he represents." Lynch was selected, but it was Roosevelt rather than Curtis who had diagnosed and rhetorically aroused his audience's strongest motives for action.[49]

It seems hardly possible that Curtis could have functioned comfortably among the "practical politicians." Certainly, it is clear that he was somewhat at odds with the leaders of his party from the very beginning of his political career. He was happier and more effective in such deliberative assemblies as the New York State Constitutional Convention of 1867-68 and the Board of Regents of the University of the State of New York, for in such assemblies the presumptions controlling discussion were less favorable to crass expediency. When, for example, Curtis proposed to the New York Constitutional Convention that suffrage be extended to women, he was defeated by a vote of 51 to 20, but he successfully focused the two-day debate on the principles involved and the question was discussed without any of the levity usually accorded the topic in the sixties. Said *The Albany Daily Argus* in discussing its own opposition to Curtis' proposal,

> The fullness and candor of the argument, of which the reader can judge as well as the audience, . . . gave it [Curtis' speech] its force. It raised the speaker and the subject in the estimation of the Convention.[50]

Here, as in the lecture room, Curtis' urbane manner and moral intensity were appropriate and acceptable to the audience.

---

[48] *The New York Times*, June 5, 1884, p. 1. The *Times'* reporter in Chicago called Curtis' address "the best speech of the day." News reports give no hint that the resolution in question would have been adopted had Curtis remained silent but they do imply that his speech forestalled a vote which might have destroyed what little unity there was in this convention.

[49] *Ibid.*, June 4, 1884, p. 1. The *Times'* reporter asserted that it was Roosevelt's speech which actually influenced the convention's vote although he called the remarks by Curtis the "most impressive speech of the day."

[50] July 24, 1867, p. 1. The record of the full debate is published in the July 23, 24, 25, 26, and 27 issues of this paper.

For Curtis, politics was not "the art of the possible" but rather, the means of achieving perfection. In a legislative assembly he would undoubtedly have become the admired conscience of the council; but practical politics offered too little room for purely moral suasion and Curtis appealed to the secondary motives—if, indeed, they were motives at all—of his listeners while he ignored their practical and immediate concerns. Probably no political party could have held Curtis' allegiance permanently; certainly the machine-ridden Republican party carried on its business in a language Curtis could never learn. In a sense he left the Republican party to create a party of his own. It was the party of civil service reform and it had but a single plank in its platform—civic morality. It was a party whose members were of the genteel tradition and Curtis was its natural leader as its members were his natural audience. Curtis understood their motivations as he had never understood the drives of the practical politicians.

Curtis' first address on civil service reform was delivered to the American Social Science Association in October, 1869; and the same speech, somewhat altered in structure but not in materials or theme, became his lecture for the 1869-70 lyceum season. Between 1871 and 1874, Curtis served as a member of President Grant's Civil Service Commission and, hence, he avoided public addresses on the subject. In 1878, he spoke on the subject to the Unitarian Conference at Saratoga, New York, having concentrated during the preceding four years on achieving reform through political action within the Republican party. It was with the formation of the New York Civil Service Reform Association in 1880, however, that he found a permanent forum in which to discuss his "radical remedy" for political corruption.

Excepting his ceremonial addresses, his most important speeches after 1880 were his annual addresses as president of the National Civil Service Reform League, which was formed in 1881, and his occasional speeches delivered as a leader in the movement for improvement of the civil service.

Those who, after 1870, heard Curtis discuss reform of the civil service were chiefly professional men interested in arousing others like themselves to a crusade.[51] These gentlemen, and often their ladies, gathered in small, dignified groups to hear Curtis report, expound, and praise the movement which, for the most part, they already supported. The American Social Science Association had a New York City membership of seventy-three when Curtis addressed it in 1869.[52] National Civil Service Reform League meetings were

[51] See John Howard Thatcher, "Public Discussion of Civil Service Reform, 1864-1883" (Ph.D. dissertation, Cornell University, 1939), p. 211.

[52] *Journal of Social Science*, No. 1, June, 1869, p. 199. The association also had members outside New York City, some of whom undoubtedly attended the New York general meeting. The association was, nonetheless, a small and select organization.

held annually at Newport, Rhode Island, until 1888 after which date they rotated from city to city. At its first meeting delegates were present from each of the thirty municipal and state associations which formed the league.[53] The *Times* reported that a "large audience of ladies and gentlemen" heard Curtis' second annual address in 1883,[54] and in 1885 "over fifty members were present from all parts of the country."[55] In 1886, a large audience "of prominent citizens and Summer visitors" received Curtis' address "enthusiastically."[56] Perhaps even more descriptive of the movement and the annual assemblies, however, was the complaint of Senator W. D. Foulke of Indiana who, while reporting the progress of reform in his state, added that he "thought the various associations in the country were not sufficiently popularized. The cause of Civil Service reform was a poor man's cause. The associations were regarded as aristocratic institutions."[57]

When the seventh annual meeting of the league was held in New York City in May, 1888, the size of the audience was increased but its essential character was apparently unchanged. The audience that filled the seats, the aisles, and the rear portion of Chickering Hall was admitted by ticket only. Those attending were, according to the reporter for the *Times,* people "whose appearance indicated that they were thinking men and women," and when Curtis concluded his address they gave him cheers and long applause.[58]

Of the other audiences that heard Curtis speak on civil service reform the Unitarian Conference, the Brooklyn Reform Association, and the "small but enthusiastic audience" that heard him close a series of Saturday Night Free Lectures at Cooper Union are typical.[59] Those who attended these meetings were persons very much like the delegates and visitors at reform league meetings; indeed, in a few identifiable instances they were the same people.[60]

[53] *The New York Times,* August 3, 1882, p. 3.
[54] *Ibid.,* August 2, 1883, p. 2.
[55] *The New York Daily Tribune,* August 6, 1885, p. 5.
[56] *The New York Times,* August 5, 1886, p. 3.
[57] *The New York Daily Tribune,* August 5, 1886, p. 4.
[58] See accounts of the meeting in *The New York Times,* May 30, 1888, p. 5, and *The New York Daily Tribune* for the same date, p. 7.
[59] He addressed the American Social Science Association for a second time in 1881. The text of this address appears in Norton, *op. cit.,* II, 173-96. For an account of the Cooper Union address which was later repeated for the Brooklyn Reform Association see *The New York Daily Tribune,* March 27, 1881, p. 2, and *The New York Times,* same date, p. 5.
[60] For example, Dorman B. Eaton, reputed author of the Pendleton Act establishing the civil service merit system, also addressed the Unitarian Conference of 1878 over which the Reverend Henry W. Bellows was presiding officer. Both were active in the National Civil Service Reform League after it was founded.

These audiences were composed of persons possessing the very qualities of mind and attitude which Curtis exemplified. Speaker and audience alike have been admirably described in the following characterization of the late nineteenth-century reformers:

Good government, they believed, would follow axiomatically from the merit system and the participation of gentlemen in politics, and when they thought of gentlemen they thought of each other. . . . They could deplore corruption but they could not explain it, for they understood neither its motivations nor its implications nor, for that matter, its consequences. They looked upon the spoils system or bribery or the pollution of the ballot box as moral delinquencies—which indeed they were—and they were reluctant to associate with bosses. But they did not understand that corruption was more than a personal manifestation of depravity. . . .[61]

Those who came to hear Curtis did so because, like the speaker, they saw in themselves and their class the nation's political conscience. With him they were ready to cry out,

Happily there is a conservative and patriotic public intelligence which is the sure and invincible bulwark of popular institutions, because it saves popular impulse from its own excesses. When that intelligence fails, the republic ends. But that it is not failing our recent history shows. It has already extorted from party a profession of reform. It will presently compel a policy of reform, unless, as Goldwin Smith suggests, party can be maintained only by corruption and the bribery of place. But that is not yet the American faith.[62]

Like the lecture audiences in the lyceum's second period, those whom Curtis addressed in the reform movement expected a sermon on the times— in this case a sermon on the application of morality to political administration. Already firm in their faith, they were gratified by Curtis' gentle exhortations to remain so; it is even possible that they would not have supported a leader who strongly urged them to engage in vigorous and ungenteel agitation against corruption in all its public forms. As it was, they believed with Curtis that "the duty . . . [of reform advocates] is to appeal constantly . . . to intelligent and patriotic public and private opinion."[63] Like Curtis, they were "too Utopian and too unsophisticated to appreciate the tragic complexity— the mingling of good and evil—in all human affairs."[64] Such listeners were

[61] Commager, *op. cit.*, pp. 318-19.

[62] "The Situation and Prospects of Reform," delivered at the eighth annual meeting of the National Civil Service Reform League, Philadelphia, October 1, 1889. Norton, *op. cit.*, II, 412.

[63] Editorial, *Harper's Weekly*, 22 (May 11, 1878), 366.

[64] Henry Bamford Parkes, *The American Experience* (New York: Alfred A. Knopf, 1947), p. 256. See also Thatcher, *op. cit.*, pp. 179-84 on the reformers' tendency to take a too simple view of the causes and cures for corruption in government.

satisfied with the addresses and leadership Curtis offered, for he gave dignity and plausibility to accepted values. Indeed, one may reasonably doubt that any leader-orator could have formed a truly popular movement, comparable to that which narrowly missed installing Henry George as mayor of New York in 1886, out of the nineteenth-century reform leagues and associations. Nor is it likely that any leader could have retained the support of the intellectuals in a program of agitation for such comprehensive reforms as were being demanded by the Anti-Monopoly party in 1884.[65] Certainly Curtis made no attempt to enlarge the scope of the civil service reform movement in any such ways. He sustained the movement as it was, but he did nothing rhetorically or otherwise to make it appeal to those who were neither intellectuals nor moralists.

The relationship which Curtis established with those who heard him on ceremonial occasions was akin to that which he established with his audiences in the reform associations. In fact those who came to hear him commemorate events and the lives of eminent men brought with them attitudes and expectations comparable in some important ways to those which prevailed in the meetings of the reform groups.

In general, those who wait upon ceremonial speakers are drawn from their habitual haunts by a sense of duty, a personal involvement in the occasion, a lively curiosity, or—perhaps most often—by a desire to hear a preachment upon the present significance of the occasion. And the ceremonial speaker, freed from the exactions of opposition, from knottily worded propositions, and from the necessity of counseling detailed and immediate action, is usually at liberty to view the celebrated event in its most symmetrical cosmic attitude. Listener and speaker are intent upon contemplating together the relation of the occasion to the received values honored by all parties. The celebrants may differ with those outside their bethel, but differences among themselves are usually excluded by tacit agreement.

These sanctions of ceremonial address have probably never been more scrupulously observed in America than in the latter half of the nineteenth century, and George William Curtis was peculiarly qualified by habit of mind and manner to fulfill them. Moreover, since most of his ceremonial addresses were delivered in New York and New England, where the values he habitually praised had most admirers, his success was often preordained. To be sure

[65] The Anti-Monopoly party supported Benjamin F. Butler for the presidency, calling for regulation of corporations, graduated income taxes, direct election of senators, and the prohibition of grants of public lands to corporations. Together with the Greenback party, which also supported Butler, the Anti-Monopolists polled only 175,370 votes. Nelson P. Mead, *The Development of the United States since 1865* (New York: Harcourt, Brace & Co., 1935), p. 142.

153

not all New Yorkers and New Englanders admired these values, but those who did not were unlikely to attach themselves to assemblies bent upon commemorating the men and events of the past.

When, for example, Curtis addressed the New York Historical Society's memorial meeting in honor of William Cullen Bryant, the auditorium of the New York Academy of Music was crowded with distinguished holders of the society's tickets of admission. Among the honored guests on the auditorium's temporarily enlarged stage sat President and Mrs. Hayes, General William Tecumseh Sherman, and Secretary of State William Evarts. The band employed for the event played "Hail Columbia," the audience of nearly five thousand applauded the dignitaries and the spirit of the occasion, an invocation which "alluded eloquently to the poet in whose honor the great throng was called together" was pronounced, and with the mood of the occasion thus formally set Curtis was introduced as the orator of the evening.

The language and the substance of one reporter's account admirably convey the pervading spirit of ceremony and the speaker's easy adjustment to it:

He advanced with his oration in his hand, spread it upon the desk, and began his address in a low impressive voice, and with an allusion to the missing figure of the venerable Bryant that immediately commanded the close attention of the audience. This attention was not relaxed from the moment the address was begun until it ended. There was much of the oration that was merely narrative, and which called for no expression of approval. Still, some of the more eloquent analyses of the poet's lines were applauded while the interest felt was apparent in every face. The passages in the oration which set forth the devotion of Bryant to high political principles, several of which were full of poetic fire, aroused the enthusiasm of the audience, and the declaration that the best President was he who "served his country best" was approved by warm and continued plaudits.

• • •

The last word of the orator was spoken, there was a moment's silence, as if the audience waited and wished to listen longer, and then the approval of the assemblage found expression in a tumult of applause.

When the assembly had voted its thanks to the orator, the invited guests left the platform in files to be received at the home of Frederic De Peyster where wine was provided "in unstinted quantities." [66] Only Governor Samuel Tilden

[66] This account of the address is based upon reports published in *The New York Times,* December 31, 1878, pp. 1-2, and in *The New York Daily Tribune* of the same date, pp. 1-2 and 4. Direct quotations are from the *Times.* Editorially, the *Tribune* concluded that the greatness of the address lay in "the justness of its comments, the dignity of its tone, the felicity of its style, and the manly sympathy which shines through its vivid and graceful phrases." P. 4.

seems not to have surrendered himself to the spirit of the occasion for "toward the latter part of the address he moved his chair to a remote corner of the box." [67] One may suppose that the sight of Hayes, more than the words of the speaker, accounted for his indifference.

Unerringly, if not involuntarily, Curtis built his eulogy of Bryant around the virtues which were unquestioningly accepted by nineteenth-century intellectuals. When Bryant wrote "Thanatopsis," Curtis told his audience, he emerged as the "first adequate poetic voice of the solemn New England spirit." He had possessed "the impenetrable armor of moral principle," but his greatest virtue was that "he reconciled, both in fact and popular imagination, the seeming incompatibility of literary taste and accomplishment and superiority with constant political activity." It was thus that he had "illustrated the scope and the fidelity of republican citizenship." [68]

The applause of the audience, the accounts of the reporters who attended, and the editorials in the morrow's newspapers demonstrate that Curtis had placed his subject in precisely the right relation to his listeners' time and values.[69] It could hardly be otherwise, for he was addressing his own kind.

Five years later Curtis delivered his most famous toast, "Puritan Principle and Puritan Pluck," at the annual dinner of the New England Society of the City of New York. Again, with men of his own sort as his hearers, he established immediate and complete rapport.

About two hundred and fifty "smiling gentlemen in evening dress passed two-and-two beneath a huge shield of roses over the door of Delmonico's large dining room" for the dinner. With Curtis, at the head table, sat former Secretary Evarts, General Ulysses S. Grant, Mayor Low of New York City, Chauncey M. Depew, Henry Ward Beecher, and others. The orchestra, it is recorded, received special applause for playing "Yankee Doodle" and "The Old Oaken Bucket." Dignified, responsible fellowship was the dominant tone and Curtis' address perfectly suited the occasion.

The dinner ended and a toast having been drunk to the absent President Arthur, Grant rose "amid deafening applause" and spoke very briefly and generally. Curtis was the third speaker, following Evarts who discussed

[67] *The New York Times*, December 31, 1878, p. 1.

[68] See Norton, *op. cit.*, III, 323-63 for text of the address.

[69] Note, for example, Commager's generalization concerning the uses of philosophy in the nineteenth century: "It had work to do and was required to pay its way. It had to fortify the American for the experience that he was to embrace, justify his effort and his hazards, give meaning to his history, and guarantee his destiny. It had to prove that the happiness of man was dependent on virtue, enterprise, freedom, and the sovereignty of moral law." *Op. cit.*, p. 27. Curtis' eulogy interpreted Bryant's life by the light of precisely these received values.

Mormonism as a political problem; he was "greeted with loud cheers as he arose" and "on sitting down, was applauded for several minutes and, in conclusion, three rousing cheers were given for him." [70] Others also spoke, but reports agree that the most successful speech of the evening was that by Curtis.

Here, as in the hall of the Academy of Music, Curtis perfectly related his theme to the values to which both he and his auditors paid willing homage. Puritan pluck became enterprise and devotion to duty; its principle was "unswerving fidelity to the individual conscience." These values Curtis applied to matters of special interest to his hearers: the separation of Church and State, the acceptance of loyalty to law as a civic obligation, and the elimination of corruption from politics.[71] In short, the speaker gave meaning to the ritual of ancestor worship by discovering contemporary applications for ancestral values. His audience of Protestant civic leaders applauded and cheered because they found the suggested applications familiar, urgent, and real.

Whether he commemorated the anniversary of Burgoyne's surrender, dedicated a statue of Burns in Central Park, or eulogized Sumner, Garfield, Wendell Phillips, or Lowell, Curtis invariably made the occasion and the subject reinforce his listeners' veneration for moral integrity and the fulfillment of civic duty. Even the story of Burns' life had its moral: "He knew better than we the pathos of human life. We know better than he the infinite pathos of his own." [72]

If one may generalize at all on so broad a scale, it can be said that devotion to duty, self-reliance, and personal integrity were among the virtues which the nineteenth century honored most in the relationships of individuals. It was true, of course, that these excellencies did not always determine the personal and social behavior of even the most distinguished citizens of the time, but only the heretical dared openly to question their righteousness and importance. Moreover, the intellectuals, the idealists, the distinguished citizens who gathered to hear Curtis comment upon men and events came, for the most part, to join in honoring the "older, liberal, humanitarian, and individualistic type of patriotism" in which many good men of the time hoped to find an answer to the materialism and chauvinism which they saw about them.[73] And even the exponents of manifest destiny and spread-eagle patriotism could find

[70] *The New York Times*, December 23, 1883, pp. 1-2. The address by Curtis was reprinted in full.

[71] For text of this speech see Norton, *op. cit.*, I, 251-60.

[72] Address at the unveiling of Burns' statue in Central Park, New York, October 2, 1880. Norton, *op. cit.*, III, 321.

[73] Merle Curti, *The Roots of American Loyalty* (New York: Columbia University Press, 1946), p. 205. Professor Curti points to Lowell's admiration for Curtis as a convenient illustration of this stream of thought.

no quarrel with the "older" emphasis on individual responsibility so long as it was not offered as a substitute for what they took to be larger and more inclusive obligations.

The Substance and Method of the Speeches

Given audiences who were, for the most part, favorably disposed toward his premises, Curtis needed to amplify and vitalize his principles of judgment and conduct and, if possible, to impel his listeners to act upon these principles with vigor and without delay. To have translated latent belief into action would have been his ultimate rhetorical achievement, and the extent to which he attained this goal was necessarily governed to a considerable degree by the proofs which he adduced to support his urgings and by the manner in which he applied those supports.

Enough has already been said to show that most of Curtis' speeches were properly described by the term which he often used, "lay-sermons." It was not, however, revelation but rationalism that characterized his inventive processes in speech-making. Indeed, if we except for the moment his purely political speeches, it is demonstrable that he preferred to rest his important propositions upon historical and biographical narratives and examples. These materials, arranged in chronological sequence or in topical order, formed the supports which he commonly gave to the social and moral principles he sought to apply to contemporary life. To complete the homiletic figure, his sermons were more doctrinal than evangelical.

In his first address to the American Social Science Association, Curtis devoted half his time to narration and development of historical and contemporary analogies, incidents, and examples.[74] Twelve years later, when he addressed the same organization on the same subject, he shortened his standard account of the history and growth of the spoils system but still spent slightly more than two-fifths of his total time in developing historical examples and analogies to support his case for reform.[75] And, as one would expect, his commemorative addresses ordinarily contained an even higher proportion of historical and biographical evidence. The supporting materials in his eulogy of Wendell Phillips, a typical example, were divided approximately as follows: historical narratives and analysis, 33 per cent; biographical narratives and analysis, 37 per cent; other modes of development and support, 30 per cent.

[74] "Civil Service Reform," delivered in New York City, 1869; Norton, *op. cit.*, II, 3-28.
[75] "The Spoils System and the Progress of Civil Service Reform," delivered at Saratoga, New York, 1881. *Ibid.*, pp. 173-96.

"Fair Play for Women" [76] is one of the speeches in which Curtis placed least reliance upon historical evidence, yet the following outline of the body of this speech reveals how frequently such supports appeared even in such cases:

I. The denial of equal rights to women has always been a form of tyranny and usurpation;
   A. Gibbon and Montaigne point to the historical truth of this fact and Edward Lear has cited an example illustrating its contemporary validity;
   B. Greek and Roman societies illustrated the tyranny of such a denial;
   C. Contemporary examples demonstrate the presence of the same quality of oppression;

II. Only if she has true liberty of action can woman's proper "sphere" be discovered and protected;
   A. Analogical reasoning applied to Nature supports the truth of this generalization;
   B. The lives of famous women from Joan of Arc to Mrs. Stowe show how impossible it is to prescribe nicely limited "spheres" of activity and interest in which women properly and profitably function;

III. No amount of "virtual influence" in the affairs of society constitutes true justice and equality for those denied rightful, direct influence;
   A. This was the truth taught by the American Revolution but denied by present laws and practices toward women;
   B. All the arguments previously used for extending manhood suffrage apply equally to its extension to women;

IV. Completion of woman's historic progress from degradation in ancient societies to ultimate self-realization demands the grant of suffrage;
   A. Women's agitation for suffrage reveals their anxiety and preparedness for this right;
   B. The woman-suffrage movement is analogous to the abolition movement which was also scorned but eventually triumphed because of its undeniable justice.

Of the twenty-one pages which this speech occupies in Norton's collection, six are filled by historical narratives and analogies, three with narratives and analogies based on contemporary incidents and events, and twelve by reasoning, assertion, and other nonnarrative and nonhistorical forms of support. Thus, even in a speech using comparatively few biographical and historical supports, one finds each of the four major propositions resting in some degree

[76] An address delivered to the American Woman-Suffrage Association meeting at Steinway Hall, New York, May 12, 1870. The text of the address may be found in Norton, *op. cit.*, I, 217-38.

on such evidence, two-sevenths of the total speech taken up with historical narratives, and one-seventh with narration of contemporary incidents.

Curtis' political·speeches were in some ways exceptions to the generalization that he found his favorite forms of proof in events which would lend themselves to narration. Of his campaign speeches only one incomplete text is available for study [77] and in general it conforms to the pattern just described. However, the texts and summaries of his speeches to political conventions suggest that in such circumstances he reasoned from, rather than toward, generalizations and that he consequently depended less upon narration. The facts remain, however, that the addresses which won him fame rested largely on narration of historical, biographical, and contemporary events and that to understand the quality of his success one must understand the rhetorical effects of this mode of development.

Curtis' use of narration involves much more than is comprehended in the ancient conception of *narratio*,[78] yet much of what the ancient rhetoricians said of *narratio* and its effects upon the listener applies with equal force to the narrative methods which Curtis used. Thus, when Quintilian observed that "a statement of facts is not made merely that the judge may comprehend the case, but rather that he may look upon it in the same light with ourselves," [79] he spoke specifically of the *narratio* or statement of the case; yet he as accurately described the rhetorical purpose of the speaker who at any point offers his listener an interpretative account of past or present events. Such a speaker insinuates into his narration his beliefs concerning causative forces, hoping to make his listeners at once comprehend the facts and accept his interpretation of their meaning.

Those who heard Curtis recount the rise of the slaveholders' political power, recall the history of the spoils system, or tell the stories of Bryant, Burns, Sedgwick, or the Revolutionary skirmish at Concord found listening easier and meaning more comprehensive because of the speaker's method. Genung, among others, has aptly described the rhetorical advantages of this mode of presentation:

When we inquire what ordinary men ... are interested in and talk about, we find it is almost sure to be some manifestation of action.... Such things can be

[77] Speech in behalf of Cleveland delivered at the Brooklyn Rink, October 30, 1884; *The New York Times*, October 31, 1884, p. 1. His address to the literary societies of Wesleyan University was also in some sense a campaign speech but the occasion was not purely political.

[78] See Charles Sears Baldwin's remarks on the narrow meaning of *narratio* as compared with the modern concept of narrative. *Ancient Rhetoric and Poetic* (New York: The Macmillan Co., 1924), pp. 34-35 and 68.

[79] *Institutes of Oratory*, trans. J. S. Watson, iv. 2. 21.

observed without learning and without painful thought; moreover, the very progress of them is a stimulus to sustained attention. The spirited account of such things, accordingly, is the kind of literature that appeals most easily to all classes of men.[80]

And the appeal and interest value of this rhetorical method could only increase the acceptability of the moral interpretations with which Curtis studded his narratives. Even when, for example, he sacrificed historical accuracy to thematic consistency—if Themistocles sometimes led "the educated Athenians at Salamis" and at other times Marathon and Salamis were "battles...won by slaves"[81]—the smooth progress of the narration hurried the listener along, uncritically, toward the speaker's predetermined conclusion.

An excerpt from Curtis' eulogy of Charles Sumner admirably illustrates his skill in combining narration with evaluation:

The hour in which Mr. Sumner wrote those words, the hour of his entrance upon public life, was the darkest of our history. . . .

What, then, was the political situation when Mr. Sumner entered the Senate? Slavery had apparently subdued the country. Great juries in the Northern States presented citizens who, in time of peace, wished to discuss vital public questions, as guilty of sedition. The legislatures were summoned to make their speeches indictable offences. . . . Every committee in Congress was the servant of slavery, and when the Vice-President left his seat in the Senate it was filled by another like himself. . . . Meanwhile, at the very moment of his [Sumner's] election, the horrors of the Fugitive-slave Law had burst upon thousands of innocent homes. Mothers snatched their children and fled, they knew not whither. Brave men, long safe in recovered liberty, were seized for no crime but misfortune, and hurried to their doom. . . . The man who impatiently exclaimed that of course the law was hard, but it was the law, and must be obeyed, suddenly felt the quivering, panting fugitive clinging to his knees, guilty of no crime, and begging only the succor which no honest heart would refuse a dog cowering upon his threshold; and, as he heard the dread power thundering at the door, "I am the law, give me my prey!" in the same moment he heard God knocking at his heart, "Inasmuch as ye have done it unto the least of these my little ones, ye have done it unto me!"

Those days are passed. That fearful conflict is over; and the flowers just strewn all through these sorrowing States, indiscriminately upon the graves of the Blue and the Gray, show how truly it is ended. Heaven knows I speak of it with no willingness, with no bitterness; but how can I show you Charles Sumner if I do not show you the time that made him what he was? This was the political and moral situation of the country when he took the oath as Senator, on December 1, 1851. The famous

---

[80] John F. Genung, *The Practical Elements of Rhetoric* (Boston: Ginn & Co., 1892), p. 354.

[81] See eulogy of Sumner and address at the centennial celebration at Northfield, New York. Norton, *op. cit.*, III, 207 and 126.

political triumvirate of the former generation was gone. Mr. Calhoun, the master-will of the three, had died in the previous year. . . .[82]

The purpose Curtis had for examining the past, he expressed simply and directly to the Unitarian Conference at Saratoga:

I cannot help feeling that I am doing something to bring morality and politics nearer together when I am telling this story to so many of those who, more than any other class in the community, influence the moral and intelligent sentiment of the country.[83]

And when, as was often the case, the narratives of past and present events dramatized values and tendencies which the audience was already anxious to discover, the listeners were all the more inclined to enjoy the storyteller's art, to praise his invention, to admire his insight as refreshing, and to become his captives as he set in motion familiar and honored principles.

Curtis' arguments usually dealt with social and moral forces and it was seldom that they could rest upon discrete and isolated facts; they required proofs demonstrating the existence of universal tendencies. And how might the speaker better establish the existence of natural laws of public morality than by offering a narrative view of their operation? By this method he could present a body of data, incidents, and statements neatly correlated and synthesized to make his conclusions about their significance seem unquestionable. The listener who neither added discordant items to Curtis' narratives and analogies nor discounted any of the items he chose to include was compelled to take Curtis' view of the case.

But some weaknesses were also inherent in the speaker's method. Even those who accepted his judgments could not be moved to vigorous action by the contemplation of past events alone. Moreover, the events of the hour—which might have aroused listeners to seek actively the correction of immediate and pressing wrongs—were almost never treated in his addresses. One is, for example, astonished to find no reference to the insurrection at Harper's Ferry in the text of an address on "The Present Aspect of Slavery," delivered at Plymouth Church on October 18, 1859.

The New York newspapers had that day headlined the early news of John Brown's raid and carried hourly dispatches from Washington, Baltimore, and smaller cities in the area, yet neither the published version of Curtis' address nor the news reports concerning it indicate that the speaker

[82] "Charles Sumner," delivered before the Legislature of Massachusetts, June 9, 1874. *Ibid.*, III, 216-19.

[83] "The Relation between Morals and Politics," September 20, 1878, Norton, *op. cit.*, II, 120.

in any way recognized this new and dramatic aspect of the slavery question.[84]

Two months and six days after President Garfield had been shot, Curtis included a reference to the event and its influence upon public interest in civil service,[85] but even such allusions are rarely found in his addresses. One can only conclude that Curtis did not adjust his supporting materials to meet changing situations even when adaptations might have enhanced the persuasiveness and immediacy of his arguments. His arguments consistently looked backward—toward the recent or the remote past—for their supports. Through them the speaker induced his listeners to judge what had been and what ought to be but never to act with vigorous and decisive effort to remake the future by controlling the real, if unpleasant, present.

To analyze the logical structure of Curtis' argument would shed little light upon the speaker's undeniable success. His hearers did not analyze his logic; instead, they reacted to implicative arguments as past events were unfolded before them. Perhaps a truer sense of Curtis' thought-in-process can be gained from examining a representative section of an important yet typical address such as "The Public Duty of Educated Men." [86] Here, one can discern the balance of abstract reasoning, examples, analogies, and narration which is to be found in most of the speaker's addresses:

> It is especially necessary for us to perceive the vital relation of individual courage and character to the common welfare, because ours is a government of public opinion, and public opinion is but the aggregate of individual thought. We have the awful responsibility as a community of doing what we choose, and it is of the last importance that we choose to do what is wise and right. In the early days of the

[84] *The New York Times* for October 18 carried the first-page headline, "Servile Insurrection" with subheadings reading: "The federal arsenal at Harper's Ferry . in possession of the insurgents; General stampede of slaves; United States troops on their march to the scene." News accounts reported "about two hundred white men engaged in the insurrection. Everything had been plundered and all appeared determined to fight." A Baltimore dispatch stated that at Frederick "all the principal citizens are imprisoned, and many have been killed."
On the following day the *Times* reported that Curtis had reviewed the Founders' opinions on slavery in answering Douglas and the Supreme Court. "The lecture," concluded the account, "was written in the elegant and piquant style which has made Mr. Curtis so popular an author, and was read with a graceful and effective delivery. Mr. C.'s voice is wonderfully musical, and well modulated with remarkable skill." The report contains no hint that the revolt of white men and slaves, still occupying a large portion of the paper's first page, had entered into the evening's discussion. See the *Times*, October 19, 1859, p. 5.

[85] "The Spoils System and Civil Service Reform," delivered to the American Social Science Association, September 8, 1881, ten days before Garfield's death. See Norton, *op. cit.*, II, 175.

[86] Delivered at Union College, June 27, 1877. Norton, *op. cit.*, I, 263-85.

antislavery agitation a meeting was called at Faneuil Hall, in Boston, which a good-natured mob of sailors was hired to suppress. They took possession of the floor and danced breakdowns and shouted choruses and refused to hear any of the orators upon the platform. The most eloquent pleaded with them in vain. They were urged by the memories of the Cradle of Liberty, for the honor of Massachusetts, for their own honor as Boston boys, to respect liberty of speech. But they still laughed and sang and danced, and were proof against every appeal. At last a man suddenly arose from among themselves and began to speak. Struck by his tone and quaint appearance, and with the thought that he might be one of themselves, the mob became suddenly still. "Well, fellow-citizens," he said, "I wouldn't be quiet if I didn't want to." The words were greeted with a roar of delight from the mob, which supposed it had found its champion, and the applause was unceasing for five minutes, during which the strange orator tranquilly awaited his chance to continue. The wish to hear more hushed the tumult, and when the hall was still he resumed, "No, I certainly wouldn't stop if I hadn't a mind to; but then, if I were you, I *would* have a mind to!" The oddity of the remark and the earnestness of the tone held the crowd silent, and the speaker continued: "Not because this is Faneuil Hall, nor for the honor of Massachusetts, nor because you are Boston boys, but because you are men, and because honorable and generous men always love fair play." The mob was conquered. Free speech and fair play were secured. Public opinion can do what it has a mind to in this country. If it be debased and demoralized, it is the most odious of tyrants. It is Nero and Caligula multiplied by millions. Can there then be a more stringent public duty for every man—and the greater the intelligence the greater the duty—than to take care, by all the influence he can command, that the country, the majority, public opinion, shall have a mind to do only what is just and pure and humane? [87]

Neither here nor anywhere else in "The Public Duty of Educated Men" did Curtis adequately support the basic inference that wisdom and righteousness in public policy are peculiarly dependent upon the influence exerted by educated men. This inference rests upon the assumption that public opinion has no creative power and no qualitative nature of its own, that public opinion is passive until either debased and demoralized by tyranny or inclined toward righteous policy by a vigorous intelligentsia. The rank and file elements of society must, for the validity of this argument, be assumed to be fickle and without will; yet as proof of the underlying assumption a single example is adduced and no attempt is made to show that even that example is representative.

In this instance, as in so many others, the logical proof which Curtis used is specious. His historical analogies are consistently open to the charge that the

[87] *Ibid.*, pp. 280-82. It is interesting to note how closely the first two and the final four sentences of this passage parallel the thought which Curtis had expressed fifteen years before in "The American Doctrine of Liberty."

elements of dissimilarity are more significant than the elements of similarity. What careful historian, for example, would say that the New England preacher, anathematizing Jefferson as an atheist, displayed a partisan spirit of the same sort as that which possessed the political bosses of the seventies or that the peaceful settlement of the Hayes-Tilden election of 1876 was a test of American patriotism greater than the Colonial declaration of independence? [88] Nor is it difficult to discover generalizations which are vitiated by the fact that atypical, doubtful, and insufficient instances are their only support.

But to dwell on these logical inadequacies would be to miss the heart of Curtis' persuasiveness. Except in his annual reports to the National Civil Service Reform League and in a few other speeches on civil service reform, the persuasive power of his addresses lay in their pathetic proofs. The students and faculty of Union College were unlikely to identify themselves with the shouting sailors in Faneuil Hall when Curtis offered the passage cited above. It is clear that Curtis expected each listener to find his own image in the commanding speaker rather than in the unruly mob, and this each undoubtedly did. That a vacuous public opinion desperately needed their wise counsel was not a displeasing possibility. It did not need logical demonstration; it needed only to be suggested. Pride would dispose the listeners to accept the speaker's implication and to take his single example as proof. In "The Public Duty of Educated Men," as in most of Curtis' addresses, the persuasive force lies in the speaker's power to fuse his own counsel with the listener's wish by dramatizing both in apt and vivid narratives.

On the other hand, some reservations must be registered concerning these generalizations when one speaks of the reports on the progress of civil service and a selected few of his other addresses. While a heavy dependence upon emotional proofs is characteristic of his ceremonial, lyceum, and occasional speeches, what may be termed his official utterances often display a tighter logic.

Again a typical passage from such an address will best illustrate the forms of proof and the kinds of data and evidence characteristic of these speeches. Speaking to the Reform League in 1886, Curtis attacked a proposal for the re-establishment of four-year terms for appointive offices in government. He said in part:

> The third chief incident in the annals of reform for the year is the bill recently introduced in the Senate by Senator Edmunds. . . . [T]wo of its provisions demand our most careful attention, for while this League seeks the repeal of the four years' law, the Edmunds bill proposes to re-enact it; and while the League would leave

[88] Both of these assertions appear in "The Public Duty of Educated Men." See *ibid.*, pp. 275 and 277.

the power of removal to the appointing officer and destroy the motives for its unjust exercise, the Edmunds bill would confer that power upon the United States judges. The passage of this bill would confirm and perpetuate one of the most mischievous abuses in the government. Miss Salmon, in her "History of the Appointing Power of the President," is not extravagant in saying of the four years' law, "Never in the whole history of the legislation of a hundred years affecting the appointing power has so disastrous a measure been enacted." It practically places the whole body of important subordinate offices . . . at the disposal of the President during his term. It enables him to change the entire force of the Civil Service without the odium of arbitrary removal. It was, indeed, the four years' law that introduced the practice of such removals and began the sophistication and corruption of public sentiment which are revealed in the familiar assertion that a clean partisan sweep of the public service is the intentional and logical result of an election. The truth is otherwise. Mr. Randall, the biographer of Jefferson . . . [says] that even after Jefferson's election minor offices were understood to be held upon the constitutional tenure of good conduct; and Mr. Calhoun, in 1835, states that arbitrary removals were of recent date, that is since 1820, when the four years' law was passed. Mr. Benton said truly that the expiration of the term was regarded as the creation of a vacancy to be filled by a new appointment, and in 1826, six years after the passage of the law, the select committee of the Senate recommended its repeal. . . .

The forecasts of Jefferson and Madison in regard to the mischievous results of the four years' law have been amply verified by experience. . . . In 1882 I pointed out that, of 825 officers whose terms had expired in nine months of the late administration, nearly half had been dropped from the service. If 825 offices, nearly one quarter of the 3400 or 3500 subject to executive nomination . . . had not been vacated by law within the space of nine months, is it probable that the President would have vacated them within that time either by his own act or by an appeal to a judge? Is it conceivable that of those 825 officers nearly one half were unfit for their positions? . . . A limited term for the minor appointive offices is a direct incitement to intrigue and fraud and falsehood. It is a folly unknown in private business, and it deprives public employment of that incentive to diligence and efficiency, and destroys that mainspring of honorable self-respect, the peaceful consciousness that success depends upon merit and not on favor. . . .[89]

This passage is typical of the argumentative method which Curtis used in his defenses and refutations. The assertions, the arguments from historic tendencies and causes, the use of historical authorities, the dilemmas and analogies, and the steady emphasis upon the moral significance of the policy in question are all standard features of his speeches for or against specific policies. And, as in the case of his suggestive and pathetic proofs resting on examples and narratives, the chain of reasoning which the speaker develops here is a strong

[89] "The Situation," August 4, 1886. Norton, *op. cit.*, II, 305-29. Excerpted portions, pp. 317-19.

and persuasive one when offered in the absence of an opponent who might question the truth or representative character of the evidence.

The extent to which Curtis repeated the same arguments in successive speeches is also illustrated by the passage quoted above. Jefferson's resistance against pressures for political spoils had formed a leading feature in his historical narratives in seven earlier speeches on civil service reform. The delegates to the convention of the National Civil Service Reform League had, in fact, heard him discuss the incident in much the same way in each of the three annual reports preceding that of 1886.[90] The contrast between business and governmental practice had also been developed in the reports of 1883 and 1884.[91] The select committee of 1826 had been quoted to the league delegates in 1883 and 1884 as well as now.[92] Two years before the address from which the passage above is taken, the delegates had heard him quote Calhoun's comment of 1835.[93] And only the previous year, 1885, the delegates had heard Curtis speak as follows:

> Indeed, to facilitate the abuse was the very object in substituting a four years' term *for the constitutional tenure of honesty and efficiency. It was to place the whole Civil Service at the absolute disposal of the President, and enable him politically to change all incumbents without the odium of arbitrary removal.*[94]

It was not in speaking of civil service reform alone that Curtis regularly repeated himself, however. His historical analogies and illustrations, like his historical authorities, were used again and again in lectures and occasional speeches. Milton was the exemplar of the politically conscious scholar; Sir Philip Sidney, the prototype of the true gentleman. Pym and Hampden were the great resisters of tyranny and the Stuarts exemplified tyranny. Luther's revolt against the Church was repeatedly taken as the historic prototype of all reform. The American Revolution was regularly linked with the spirit of the Protestant and English Reformations. And the list of favored analogues and allusions could be extended to cover almost every topic on which Curtis touched in his many speeches.

Curtis almost never spoke extempore. It was his practice to write his addresses well in advance and to deliver them from manuscript or to commit them to memory. If he relied upon a relatively small body of arguments, proofs, evidence, and allusions and if he repeated them frequently, it cannot have been because he was calling to the service of the moment whatever

---

[90] *Ibid.*, pp. 243, 261, and 292.
[91] *Ibid.*, pp. 248 and 266.
[92] *Ibid.*, pp. 244 and 258.
[93] *Ibid.*, pp. 244 and 245-46.
[94] *Ibid.*, pp. 296-97. Italics mine.

familiar materials came easily to mind as he completed the process of rhetorical invention at the speaker's desk. Moreover, his practice in his annual addresses to the Reform League seems, with reference to repetitions at least, to have been the same as that which he followed in his lectures and occasional speeches. One suspects, therefore, that his tendency to use the same materials repeatedly is indicative of a certain superficiality in the study and treatment of his subjects.

The modern reader of his addresses senses a kind of insularity in this reliance upon a few familiar arguments and supporting materials. Curtis seems to have had but a single avenue of approach to many of his topics. It does not appear that he searched widely for fresher, stronger, and more immediate proofs once a single, serviceable proof or mode of development had been found. To read his speeches consecutively is to invite a vision of Curtis, preparing his next address, with his file of former speeches spread before him.[95]

But the charge of insufficiency in invention was never leveled against Curtis by his contemporaries. In fact, the editor of his speeches praises him for having achieved a considerable variety in his treatments of the civil service question.[96] To find an explanation for this disparity between the modern judgment and the reactions of those who actually heard Curtis, one must turn again to the attitudes and predispositions of his auditors.

Parrington has argued that in the culture of the seventies the unity of an older, aristocratic tradition had been lost and,

... three diverse strands of cultural impulse remained, each of an individual fabric that could not easily be woven into a harmonious pattern: a decadent Federalistic culture that occupied the seats of authority in New England and wherever New England opinion was respected; the body of social aspiration that had come from the French Enlightenment, from which individual dreamers still drew nourishment; and the vigorous individualism of the frontier that bit so deeply into the psychology of the age.[97]

In George William Curtis the first and second of these cultural strands were joined, even though they were not always compatible. So, too, were those who heard him in the lecture halls and on special occasions more receptive to one or the other of these cultural patterns than to the less retrospective spirit of the West. And it is even more certain that the Unitarians, the civil service reformers, and the members of the Social Science Association were the intellectual children of Puritanism and French skepticism.

[95] The essays published in "The Easy Chair" seem to me to lend added support to these generalizations regarding Curtis' invention.

[96] Norton, *op. cit.*, II, iv.

[97] Vernon L. Parrington, *The Beginnings of Critical Realism in America* (New York: Harcourt, Brace & Co., 1930), pp. 49-50.

If, therefore, Curtis usually defended the revolt of conscience with allusions to Luther, Wycliffe, Cromwell, Pym, and Hampden, he used the authorized parallels of the Puritan and neo-Federalist streams of thought which colored the judgments of his listeners. Or if his testimony to the saving power of an individualistic, reformist faith took much the same form in successive meetings, the faithful did not object provided the speaker maintained, as Curtis did, a critical attitude toward contemporary events even while he gazed somewhat uncritically at the past. If Curtis succeeded with such arguments and evidence as have been described—and he did succeed in a considerable degree—it must have been because he gave dignity and attractiveness and significance to lines of thought toward which his listeners were already favorably disposed. Perhaps, had his inventive powers been greater and more original, he might have discovered fresher and stronger arguments that could move his listeners to act more and to decry less; but to reach beyond the mere reinforcement of beliefs,' to translate beliefs into energetic action, seems to have been either beyond his rhetorical power or outside his purpose. He was, in short, a ceremonial speaker capable of giving an acceptable dignity and moral tone to almost any theme or occasion. If he did not place a high value upon freshness in argument or upon originality in interpretation, his supporting materials still had a familiar and therefore authoritative ring to those already inclined to accept his propositions. Such listeners were only the more disposed to praise his skill in exalting received values, for they missed not at all the arguments and evidence with which another speaker might have sought to create belief in the unbelieving and turn dissatisfaction into action among the believers.

The Adornment of the Speech

Curtis was admired and sought after as a speaker because he fulfilled in manner, thought, and word his time's image of the gentleman orator. The impressions carried away by that part of America which loved him and came repeatedly to hear him celebrate mutually admired virtues are concisely expressed by his biographer, personal friend, and colleague in the movement for civil service reform:

> The more important of the orations were written out and read, though they did not seem to the hearer to be read. Some of them were committed to memory, but the memorizing was complete and the delivery without hesitation, so that in each case the personal impression of the orator was the same, and the impression was very strong. The matter was prepared with the audience constantly in mind, and nothing was neglected which could arouse or hold them; but the essential thing with the orator was the substance, the thought, which the form must serve. . . .

In the immediate impression made by the oratory of Mr. Curtis his personality counted for much. .... His charm was felt the moment he rose. His form was manly, powerfully built, and exquisitely graceful. .... His forehead was square, broad, and of vigorous lines; his eyes of blue-gray, large, deep-set under strong and slightly shaggy brows, lighted the shadow as with a flame, now gentle and glancing, now profound and burning. His voice was a most fortunate organ, deep, musical, yielding without effort the happy inflections suited to the thought. .... His gestures were very few and simple. .... The speaker seemed absorbed by the expression of his thought, unheeding the eyes, seeking the judgment and the heart, of his auditors.[98]

That Curtis omitted nothing which might have aroused his listeners is not supported by the evidence offered in this essay, but in other respects Cary's description of the speaker in action and of the sources of his influence is in every way corroborated by the testimony of other contemporaries.

Newspaper accounts reflect at once the values of his time and place and the source of his popularity by applying again and again to both speaker and speech the adjectives "manly," "thoughtful," and "graceful." There was nothing vigorous or dramatic about his delivery; rather, there was dignity, intensity, and unquestionable sincerity. Howells, listening to Curtis, was struck by the speaker's effortless presentation but above all he rejoiced that such a man had "the heart to feel the wrongs of men so little befriended." His strength, said Howells, lay in the fact that he was "the neighbor, the contemporary, and the friend of all who read or heard him." [99]

It was only when he spoke in behalf of civil service reform that he needed to strengthen his ethical position deliberately. And even here his task was the simple one of reminding listeners that both he and the reform associations had always been scrupulously nonpartisan in their approach to problems connected with the civil service. Elsewhere he had little need for invented ethical supports of a verbal sort, since his widely known integrity and the earnestness of his manner were sufficient in speeches which questioned no defensible social norms and attacked no honorable traditions. Where Wendell Phillips might have irritated with studied art, Curtis called upon the latent nobility and common sense of Everyman to strike down offending tendencies; where Ingersoll attacked shams with ridicule, Curtis described them with regret and dwelt upon the happier prospects of governance by intelligence and conscience. Whenever he spoke, Curtis stressed the potential power of honesty and independence and he had little need of added words to prove that he was a proper man to plead such a cause.

Perhaps, a sharp, intense, or impassioned style might have enabled a

[98] Cary, *op. cit.*, pp. 325 and 329-30.
[99] Howells, *op. cit.*, pp. 109 and 111.

speaker of Curtis' reserve to move his listeners deeply, but his utterance did not possess these attributes. The informal, often whimsical and always precise style of his essays is not to be found in his speeches; but the cadenced and luxuriant prose of his addresses still suggests an observer's forbearance rather than a participant's involvement. Parrington has said of his addresses, "The rich context of his speeches, elaborated with formal dignity and embellished with literary allusions, hit to a nicety the taste of a generation that still delighted in oratory and preferred dignity to informality." [100] It would be difficult, indeed, to express more succinctly the quality and significance of Curtis' oral style.

That Curtis sought to achieve only dignity and embellishment in speaking seems unlikely if one may judge from the qualities he admired in others. He reserved his warmest praise for Wendell Phillips:

... [Phillips made use of] the apt quotation, the fine metaphor, the careful accumulation of intensive epithet to point an audacious and startling assertion, the pathos, the humor. ... It was consummate art, and as noble a display of high oratory as any hearer or spectator had known.

Phillips' address at Harvard in 1881, he concluded, was "one of the most charming discourses that were [*sic*] ever delivered in the country." [101] It was not until Phillips' death that he was willing to grant to Beecher, the orator possessing the greatest emotional power since Patrick Henry in Curtis' view, the rank of the greatest orator of his own time. [102]

Curtis, himself, never achieved the sharpness of speech and manner which he praised in Phillips nor did he attain the lush emotional force he admired in Beecher. The reason is not far to seek. He could not handle facts and ideas without adjusting them to fit his own none-too-precise or systematic moral creed. This had been his difficulty when, at the beginning of his career, he had sought in *The Potiphar Papers* to emulate the social satire of his literary model, Thackeray. He could not take life as he found it; he blurred his observations with sentiment and his judgments therefore wanted precision and an internal consistency. Neither could he abandon himself to pure agitation as Phillips had done. To damn the consequences, to cast off the cultural moorings of a lifetime, to dare even irresponsibility were impossible for Curtis. He could never stand, as Phillips stood, playing "his polished rapier with a

[100] *Op. cit.*, p. 150.

[101] George William Curtis, "Wendell Phillips at Harvard, 1881," in *From the Easy Chair* (New York: Harper & Brothers, 1893), pp. 133-34 and 137.

[102] George William Curtis, "Henry Ward Beecher," in *Other Essays from the Easy Chair* (New York: Harper & Brothers, 1893), pp. 110 and 116.

flexible wrist." [103] Instead of precision and flexibility, Curtis attained dignity; instead of brilliance, embellishment and adornment.

Perhaps the same want of precision in expression accounts in part for the lack of urgency and specificity which one often senses at crucial points in his addresses. Thus, the logical and emotional climax of "The Public Duty of Educated Men" is weakened by a remote allusion which suggests, though it does not assert, that the reformation of politics need occupy only a little of the citizen's attention:

> The remedy for the constant excess of party spirit lies, and lies alone, in the courageous independence of the individual citizen. The only way, for instance, to procure the party nomination of good men, is for every self-respecting voter to refuse to vote for bad men. In the mediæval theology the devils feared nothing so much as the drop of holy water and the sign of the cross, by which they were exorcised. The evil spirits of party fear nothing so much as bolting and scratching. *In hoc signo vinces.* . . . If we would have good men upon the ticket, we must scratch bad men off. . . . The evil spirits must be taught by means that they can understand.[104]

Not only is the proffered remedy anticlimatic following an extended narrative filled with specific and compelling instances of "the brutal spirit" of partisanship and its effects, but the listener's sense of concern and personal involvement cannot be strengthened and may be vitiated by the suggestion that political corruption may be magically ended. The example is in no way extreme; the language of immediacy was consistently missing in the otherwise clear, forceful, and felicitous style which Curtis used.

Curtis did not seize, control, and redirect the thoughts of his audiences; he magnified and adorned beliefs already shared by his listeners and himself. Though his powers of invention were no more than second-rate, he found a class of auditors who demanded, not illumination of the scene about them, but the delineation of an image of it. His rhetorical skill was equal to this assignment. His command of language was facile if not impelling. His acquaintance with the worlds of literature, art, politics, and moral philosophy was wide though not intimate, and his allusions gave a cultured air to all that he said. His character was transparently good and his sympathy, generous. Said an obituary notice published in *The Literary World*, "Few writers have known so well how to sugar the pill of moral discourse as the always courteous and never censorious 'Easy Chair.' " [105] The comment might as easily have been applied to Curtis' addresses as to his writings. He aspired to be the voice of "the

---

[103] *Ibid.*, p. 116.
[104] Norton, *op. cit.*, I, 280.
[105] 23 (September 10, 1892), 308-9.

moral and intelligent sentiment of the country," and by zeal, talent, and character he became not only its voice but its paradigm.

Conclusion

What Curtis once wrote of the minor literary figures of New England, the twentieth century might well apply to him:

> Fame does not retain the name of every minstrel who passes singing. But to say that Fame does not know them is not dispraise. They sang for the hearers of their day, as the players played. Is it nothing to please those who listen, because those who are out of hearing do not stop and applaud? [106]

The voice of George William Curtis pleased those who listened, but it fails to reach across the "watershed of the nineties" which Commager has envisaged.[107] On our side of the divide the view is taken that the society he sought to purify had even in his own time ceased to be governed, as he imagined, by the simple interplay of many individual consciences. The twentieth-century social critic says with Parrington that his was "a tiny note of criticism" destined to "run into a blind alley of moral indignation, overlooking the major issues and leaving the vital factors of the problem unconsidered." [108]

The rhetorical judgment of Curtis' achievements supplements, and in some small sense emends, the broader social and historical judgment of the man in his own time. Rhetorical analysis of his public discourses confirms history's verdict that his thinking rested upon a narrow, oversimplified conception of operative social forces; but the same analysis supplies the further reminder that Curtis left unused many of the available means of persuasion. To the extent that this is true his social and political suggestions were denied a full and complete trial. Their whole strength—whether great or tiny—was never tested, for he did not or could not motivate large-scale action in their behalf.

One is tempted to believe that Curtis' place in his own time and in history might have been somewhat higher had he expounded the practical as well as the moral toll of public corruption, if he had shown his fellow Republicans that the party machines and party policies were causing an electoral as well as a moral erosion. And even after he had abandoned practical politics for the purer but weaker instrumentalities of political independence and reform, could not his

---

[106] "Oliver Wendell Holmes," *Harper's Magazine*, 83 (1891), 220.

[107] *Op. cit.*, chap. 2.

[108] *Op. cit.*, p. 137. Parrington here speaks of the general characteristics of social criticism in the seventies.

reformist and occasional audiences have been stirred to more vigorous and productive activity if he had sought to move them as well as to please them? Theodore Parker and Henry Ward Beecher, through speech and deed, helped to make religion a dynamic influence in the politics of their day. Wendell Phillips and Robert Ingersoll won no such universal affection as did Curtis, but they followed the logic of their premises relentlessly and in consequence they disturbed their hearers enough to have marked the thought of their own and later times. Erratic men like Horace Greeley and Henry George successfully mobilized mass support behind themselves and their panaceas while agitation for civil service reform remained weak or strong in proportion to the energy and vigor of local association leaders. George William Curtis left the values and the practices of his time much as he found them, for his was always a ceremonial rhetoric and never the rhetoric of agitation or even of pleading. He appealed exclusively to the interests of a class which lacked instruments of effective and vigorous social action. His arguments were neither as strong nor as varied as even his restrictive premises permitted. His style and his delivery were courtly and dignified but without a zealous passion. If his name is only just retained by Fame, it is not alone because he held a narrow conception of democracy's meaning and its way to perfection; it is also because he did not use fully the tools of suasion, because he won but a partial hearing and a half-hearted, sporadic application to public life of the New England creed.

SELECTED BIBLIOGRAPHY

Books, Unpublished Theses, Speeches

CARY, EDWARD. *George William Curtis*. Boston: Houghton Mifflin Co., 1894.

COMMAGER, HENRY STEELE. *The American Mind*. New Haven: Yale University Press, 1950.

COOKE, GEORGE WILLIS (ed.). *Early Letters of George Wm. Curtis to John S. Dwight*. New York: Harper & Brothers, 1898.

CURTIS, GEORGE WILLIAM. *Ars Recte Vivendi*. New York: Harper & Brothers, 1898.

———. *From the Easy Chair*. New York: Harper & Brothers, 1893.

———. *Other Essays from the Easy Chair*. New York: Harper & Brothers, 1893.

———. *From the Easy Chair*. 3rd series. New York: Harper & Brothers, 1894.

———. *Literary and Social Essays*. New York: Harper & Brothers, 1894.

———. *The Potiphar Papers*. New York: Harper & Brothers, 1856.

HOWELLS, WILLIAM DEAN. *Literary Friends and Acquaintance*. New York: Harper & Brothers, 1900.

NORTON, CHARLES ELIOT (ed.). *Orations and Addresses of George William Curtis*. 3 vols. New York: Harper & Brothers, 1894.

PARRINGTON, VERNON LOUIS. *The Beginnings of Critical Realism in America*. New York: Harcourt, Brace & Co., 1930.

RHODES, JAMES FORD. *A History of the United States from the Compromise of 1850*. 8 vols. New York: The Macmillan Co., 1920.

American Public Address

THATCHER, JOHN HOWARD. "Public Discussion of Civil Service Reform, 1864-1883." Unpublished Ph.D. dissertation, Cornell University, 1943.

Periodicals

CHADWICK, JOHN W. "Recollections of George William Curtis," *Harper's Magazine*, 86 (1892-93), 469-76.

CURTIS, GEORGE WILLIAM. "The Editor's Easy Chair," a monthly department of *Harper's Magazine* written entirely or in part by Curtis from 1853 to 1892.

———(?). "Lectures and Lecturing," *Putnam's Monthly Magazine*, 9 (1857), 317-21.

HOLLAND, J. G. "The Popular Lecture," *Atlantic Monthly*, 15 (1865), 362-71.

SCHURZ, CARL. "George William Curtis, Friend of the Republic," *McClure's Magazine*, 23 (1904), 614-23.

Newspapers

Albany Daily Argus, July 23 and 24, 1867.

The New York Times, Dec. 23, 1876; Sept. 27, 1877; Dec. 31, 1878; March 27, 1881; Dec. 23, 1883; Oct. 31, 1884; Feb. 23, 1892; Sept. 1, 1892.

The New York Daily Tribune, Sept. 27, 1877; Oct. 18, 1877; Sept. 21, 1878; Dec. 31, 1878; May 21, 1880; March 27, 1881; April 19, 1884; Sept. 1, 1892.

Providence Daily Journal, Nov. 21, 1862; Jan. 30, 1864; Dec. 7, 1866; Nov. 17, 1870.

Lucius Q. C. Lamar

by DALLAS C. DICKEY AND DONALD C. STREETER

Lucius Q. C. Lamar, Mississippi lawyer, teacher, representative and senator in Congress, Cabinet member, and member of the United States Supreme Court, was born in Putnam County, Georgia, September 17, 1825. He was graduated from Emory University in 1845, and was admitted to the Georgia bar in 1847. After his marriage to Virginia Longstreet in 1849, he followed his father-in-law, A. B. Longstreet, to Mississippi where he practiced law and served as adjunct professor of mathematics at the University of Mississippi. In 1852 he went back to Georgia and served in the 1853 state legislature. He returned to Mississippi in 1855 where he entered politics. Elected to Congress in 1857 and re-elected in 1859, he acted with the Southern Democrats on the slavery issue and drafted the Mississippi ordinance of secession. During the Civil War he was a lieutenant colonel in the Confederate Army and was appointed special commissioner to Russia, although he did not get beyond London. He returned to Richmond in 1864 and supported the Davis administration against its critics. Following the war, he practiced law in Oxford, Mississippi, and taught law at the University of Mississippi. He was elected to Congress in 1873 and in 1874 delivered his significant eulogy on Charles Sumner which attracted wide attention and which did much to soften bitterness between the North and South. Elected to the Senate in 1876, Lamar continued in numerous debates to speak for the South as he championed reconciliation and good will between the sections. He was appointed Secretary of the Interior by Grover Cleveland in 1885 and was made an associate justice of the United States Supreme Court in 1888. He died January 23, 1893.

In 1861, Lucius Q. C. Lamar resigned from Congress to serve the Confederacy. In 1873, he resumed his place to become the greatest public voice from the South in behalf of understanding and reconciliation. A Southerner by heredity and environment, Lamar's formative and first public years were spent in the period when Southerners grew increasingly to doubt their security within the Union. As one of Mississippi's representatives, he was an ardent defender of Southern institutions, even to the point of being an active secessionist. His early radicalism might well have led him to lifelong vindictiveness. Instead, lawyer, scholar, reflective thinker—even dreamer—that he was, Lamar gave his services to the Confederacy, suffered the depression of its

175

defeat, and bore the agonies of Radical Reconstruction and misrule. Eventually, the opportunity came for him to serve in Congress as representative and later as senator. One of the first Southerners after the war to be invited into a President's Cabinet, he finally became a member of the Supreme Court and interpreted the Constitution he once rebelled against. Certain of his utterances in the years prior to, during, and following the Civil War reflect his early radical impulses, his fervor for the Southern cause in the darkest days of the struggle, his acceptance of the inevitable upon defeat, and his sentiments and aspirations once he perceived the ultimate direction his public life should take.

In the last years before secession Lamar placed himself on record as one of the staunch defenders of slavery and Southern rights when he said to Northern agitators in Congress:

The Southern people demand that this organized "irrepressible conflict" shall stop— that the institution of slavery shall be maintained as an existing fact in the Confederacy. The sentiment is rapidly approaching to unanimity among them, that any attempt to impair its property value, or a single political privilege which it confers, or any of the constitutional rights by which it is guaranteed, or to place over them the party which arrogates to itself the right to do any of these things will be a fatal blow to the peace and stability of this great country.[1]

The election of Lincoln, secession, and the organization of the Confederacy found Lamar sharing the early hopes of the Southern people for independence. He made clear his allegiance, stating publicly his support of the new government and his willingness to fight to sustain it. In 1861, Lamar, by then a colonel in the Confederate Army, was present at Richmond, Virginia, at a serenade for Jefferson Davis. Along with Davis, Henry Wise, and others, Lamar spoke from the balcony of the Spotswood Hotel and told the assemblage, "This very night I look forward to the day when this beloved country of ours—for, thank God! we have a country at last—will be a country to live for, to pray for, to fight for, and if necessary, to die for." [2] His feeling for the Southern cause led him to declare further that the Southern armies would "drive back the invader from the hallowed soil of Virginia; he shall not continue to hover around the sacred tomb of Washington." [3]

Lamar's was not to be a military contribution, however. Illness required him to leave the service. Lamar was in Europe during a large part of the war, having been appointed envoy to Russia; he never got beyond England and Paris. He returned to find Southern morale low. In contrast to certain South-

---

[1] *Congressional Globe and Appendix*, 36th Cong., 1st sess., p. 117.

[2] Edward Mayes, *Lucius Q. C. Lamar: His Life, Times, and Speeches* (Nashville: Publishing House of Methodist Episcopal Church, South, 1896), p. 96.

[3] *Richmond Daily Examiner*, June 3, 1861.

erners such as Alexander Stephens, Joseph E. Brown, and even Robert Toombs who, in opposition to Davis, were contributing to Southern defeat, Lamar assumed the task of cooperation. The extreme action of the Confederate government in suspending the writ of habeas corpus was a severe blow to President Davis' prestige. It was this severe measure which brought home to multitudes with shorter vision the fact that the new government could prove more tyrannical than the former one. Lamar reflected that extreme measures were the price of war and victory, telling an audience in Atlanta:

> O my countrymen, cease your repinings; and when you bend your knee to God thank him for giving you such a country and your children such a heritage. If you love that country, do not complain because she cannot in this moral struggle to give you liberty, give you also ease and luxury and gold. Let not the world be deceived as to your true sentiments by these seeming dissensions; but rise like true brothers, as you are, and show that you have the courage to strike for the right a braver blow than your enemy dare to strike for the wrong.[4]

Lamar knew well the cost of the Civil War and the price of defeat. Not only did he observe its consequences as he journeyed from Appomattox back to Mississippi, but in his university town of Oxford he was to see that there was but "one business house left standing."[5] Disfranchised, he believed his public life was over. For five years he was publicly silent, turned to law, and became a professor of law at the University of Mississippi. When virtually forced to resign in 1870 because the university came under the "radicalized" political control of the state, Lamar told his students at a commencement occasion, "And now, young gentlemen, as you go home I pray that you may have prosperity and happiness through life, with just enough of sorrow to remind you that this earth is not your home."[6]

Lamar had experienced sorrow. Many of his closest friends, including Jefferson Davis, had languished in prisons. His beloved father-in-law, Judge Augustus B. Longstreet, died, leaving him profoundly affected. The suffering around him distressed him and made him feel helpless. He wrote:

> The country is in a deplorable state, and the people, with all their sacred convictions scattered to the winds, are absorbed in the prosaic details of making a living. Our public men have become bewildered in the wreck of all that they considered permanent and true, and know not what to do or advise. There is a perfect anarchy of opinion and purpose among us. . . .

[4] Mayes, *Lamar*, p. 656.
[5] E. Merton Coulter, *The South during Reconstruction, 1865-1877* (Baton Rouge: Louisiana State University Press, 1947), p. 3.
[6] Mayes, *Lamar*, p. 127.

We feel that the fate of our section is not in our hands; that nothing we can *do* or *say* will affect the result.[7]

But there were to be opportunities to alleviate sufferings and injustices. Radical Reconstruction policies could not endure forever; more important, Lamar, who entered the Civil War a sectionalist, became, by 1870, a Unionist. The change was a result of considerable mental struggle. A friend told him in those days, "Do you know that your character has been greatly improved by what you have gone through: softened, rounded, made sympathetic? I think so, and congratulate you."[8] Years later, Henry Adams referred to Lamar as a man who had grown to be one of the "calmest, most reasonable and most amiable Union men in the United States."[9] Adams gave a partial explanation for the transformation of Lamar when he referred to him as never questioning "the soundness of the Southern system until he found that slavery could not stand a war."[10] Much is implied in Adams' statement. It was not so much the doom of slavery that the South could not afford. Rather, it was the aftermath of Radical Reconstruction and misrule that subjected the Southern system to more than it could endure. With Lamar, then, it was a period of waiting and enduring—enduring carpetbaggers and radical rule until measures of hate and war psychoses should spend themselves. It was also a season of tempering a naturally reflective and sensitive mind. Fortunately, by 1872, when the malice and zeal of the radicals had abated somewhat, the call came for Lamar to run for Congress. Still disfranchised and without assurance he would be seated if elected, Lamar received the unanimous vote of the Mississippi Democratic Convention, entered into a three-way political contest against two Republicans, received numerous Republican votes in spite of his severe denunciations of carpetbaggerism, and won. Thus the way was prepared for Lamar to begin his uninterrupted period of public service.

What course did Lamar chart as he anticipated his congressional career? The national temper had modified to a degree, but reconciliation had by no means been effected. Lamar's meditations are significant. He asked, "Will the North listen to a Southern man with patience and respect? Is it possible for a secessionist from the South to convince a Northern audience that there is a common ground on which the two sections can stand and live in harmony?" He reflected further:

I only know enough to observe that so far the utterances of Southern men, whether they be Jeff Davis or Toombs or Stephens on the one hand, or Lee on the other,

[7] Lamar to Charles Reemelin, Sept. 11, 1870, quoted, *ibid.*, p. 130.

[8] Henry Craft to Lamar, n.d., quoted, *ibid.*, p. 168.

[9] *The Education of Henry Adams: An Autobiography* (Boston: Houghton Mifflin Co., 1918), p. 185.

[10] *Ibid.*, p. 246.

not only fail to conciliate ... but generally inflame ... irritated feelings. And yet such conciliation has become indispensable to the security and tranquillity of Southern society. In my opinion the two sections are estranged simply because each is ignorant of the inner mind of the other, and it is the policy of the party in power to keep up and exaggerate the mutual misunderstanding.

Lamar continued to ponder the problems of the brave but defeated South, and the problems of the North flushed with victory. Surely there was something that could bring an end to misunderstanding:

But is not this an appalling spectacle? On the one hand a brave, impulsive, but too sensitive people full of potent life and patriotic fire, ready—aye, eager—to abide with knightly honor the award of the bloody arbitrament to which they appealed; and yet, as if dumb, unable to speak intelligibly their thought and purpose. On the other hand a great and powerful section ... flushed with victory and success, but full of generous and magnanimous feeling toward their vanquished brethren; and they too, as if under some malign spell, speaking only words of bitterness, hate, and threatenings.

He indeed would be a patriot and benefactor who could awake them from their profound egotism, and say to them with effectual command: "My countrymen, *know* one another." For then nature herself with her mighty voice would exclaim: "*Love* one another." [11]

What Lamar needed most as he assumed his congressional duties was the opportunity to express these sentiments in a public address. The opportunity came in the death of Charles Sumner, March 11, 1874. On April 27, the Senate heard a series of speeches of tribute by Northern colleagues. The following day the House resolved that additional tributes be paid to him in that body. This was Lamar's opportunity. Knowing the sentiment of the South against Sumner for his advocacy of the Civil Rights Bill, but recognizing also Sumner's concern for amnesty toward the Southern people, and anxious above all else for the cause of harmony and reconciliation, Lamar rose to second a resolution and thereupon delivered the most important speech of his life. In the words of one historian, "The eulogy which Lamar delivered had all the essentials of a great oration. If words alone could reconcile, it would have made the sections one." [12]

All that Lamar had reflected previously was presented. Moreover, the dramatic setting occasioned further refinement of his premeditations. While the great message of the eulogy was a plea for understanding, Lamar faced, also, the task of saying those precise things about Sumner which the North would endorse and which the South would not disapprove. Hence, Lamar praised

[11] Lamar to Reemelin, July 15, 1872, quoted in Mayes, *Lamar*, p. 182.
[12] Paul H. Buck, *The Road to Reunion, 1865-1900* (Boston: Little, Brown & Co., 1938), p. 128.

the high intellectual qualities of the departed leader, dwelt extensively on the ideal of freedom which motivated him and recognized elements of graciousness toward the South in Sumner. He expressed regret that he had forfeited the opportunity of personal acquaintance and friendship until, "Suddenly, and without premonition, a day has come at last to which, for such a purpose, there is no to-morrow." Then, he asked:

Shall we not, over the honored remains of this great champion of human liberty, this feeling sympathizer with human sorrow, this earnest pleader for the exercise of human tenderness and charity, lay aside the concealments which serve only to perpetuate misunderstandings and distrust, and frankly confess that on both sides we most earnestly desire to be one; one not merely in community of language and literature and traditions and country; but more, and better than all that, one also in feeling and in heart?

High purpose required that still more be said. His concern was to find the answer to the further question: "Do the concealments of which I speak still cover animosities which neither time nor reflection nor the march of events have yet sufficed to subdue?" Lamar's reflections on this question, put in writing two years before, were now presented anew, and in still more refined words for this singular occasion:

The South—prostrate, exhausted, drained of her lifeblood, as well as of her material resources, yet still honorable and true—accepts the bitter award of the bloody arbitrament without reservation, resolutely determined to abide the results with chivalrous fidelity; yet, as if struck dumb by the magnitude of her reverses, she suffers on in silence. The North, exultant in her triumph, and elated by success, still cherishes, as we are assured, a heart full of magnanimous emotions toward her disarmed and discomfited antagonist; and yet, as if mastered by some mysterious spell, silencing her better impulses, her words and acts are the words and acts of suspicion and distrust.

Would that the spirit of the illustrious dead whom we lament to-day could speak from the grave to both parties to this deplorable discord in tones which should reach each and every heart throughout this broad territory: "My countrymen! *know* one another, and you will *love* one another." [13]

More than words were required for reconciliation; nevertheless, Lamar had taken this vital step and established himself as a spokesman for conciliation and national welfare. Although the radical Wendell Phillips referred to this and other of Lamar's addresses as "pretty speeches...even if not absolute hypocrisy...only drops of rose-water flung on the mad surface of Southern

---

[13] For versions of the speech, see Mayes, *Lamar*, pp. 184-87; *Congressional Record*, 43rd Cong., 1st sess., pp. 3410-11; Edwin A. Alderman *et al.*, *Library of Southern Literature* (17 vols.; Atlanta, 1909), VII, 2968-72.

hate,"[14] equally severe Northern critics recognized Lamar's influence and wholesome contribution. The *New York Times* called it "a speech of great frankness and admirable temper."[15] The Washington *National Republican* in a lengthy review of the speech interpreted Lamar as saying, "Mr. Sumner believed in life that the time had come when all bitterness between the sections should pass away, and now over his grave the same sentiment should prevail on all sides."[16] Lamar knew no more formidable opponent in Congress than James G. Blaine. Blaine declared of Lamar's eulogy:

> A singular interest was added to the formal eulogies of Mr. Sumner by the speech of Mr. Lamar. . . . It was a mark of positive genius in a Southern representative to pronounce a fervid and discriminating eulogy upon Mr. Sumner, and skillfully to interweave with it a defense of that which Mr. Sumner . . . believed to be the sum of all villanies. Only a man of Mr. Lamar's peculiar mental type could have accomplished the task. He pleased the radical anti-slavery sentiment of New England: he did not displease the radical pro-slavery sentiment of the South. . . . There is a certain Orientalism in the mind of Mr. Lamar, strangely admixed with typical Americanism. He is full of reflection, full of imagination; seemingly careless, yet closely observant; apparently dreamy, yet altogether practical.[17]

Lamar had made his commitments and declarations. "I felt that the time had come for me to stake my political life,"[18] he observed. While he rejoiced in the praise which he received, he was also pained at the adverse criticism which resulted, particularly in the South. To one friend and critic Lamar tried to explain at length his purposes and hopes in delivering the eulogy:

> When I got to Washington and observed the indications of the temper of the Northern Representatives, I saw that what the Southern members said Never Reached The Masses of the North. Indeed they were not listened to by the Republican side, unless one should allow himself to be betrayed into intemperate and imprudent language. This would be caught up and circulated at the North to produce new irritations, and inflame old passions.

To counteract this situation, which was aggravated particularly during the debates on the Civil Rights Bill, Lamar declared he "mingled freely with the Northern Representatives and talked with them often to find out . . . whether there was any point upon which they could be approached successfully by the South, to ascertain if there was any ground upon which harmony, concord,

---

[14] Wendell Phillips, "The Outlook," *North American Review*, 27 (1878), 100.

[15] *New York Times*, April 28, 1874.

[16] *National Republican* (Washington, D. C.), April 28, 1874.

[17] James G. Blaine, *Twenty Years of Congress: From Lincoln to Garfield* (2 vols.; Norwich, Conn.: Henry Bill Co., 1886), II, 546.

[18] Lamar to Clement C. Clay, Jr., September 3, 1874, in the Clement C. Clay Papers (MSS in Duke University Library, Durham, N. C.).

peace and justice between the sections could be established." The results were both discouraging and reassuring. One group, "the New Englanders and a few North Westerners [were] egotistical, monstrously harsh and proud, with souls shut against everything like commiserations, tenderness and charity; cynical, inexorable and contemptuous for the suffering people of the South." On the other hand, he was encouraged that "such was not the spirit of even the Republicans in the North-west," and there were "some exceptions" among New Englanders. Even so, these "were apprehensive and distrustful," because they feared "the negroes will be put into a position of legal and civil insubordination and an alliance formed with the Northern Democrats to reverse the results of the war." Lamar tried to "assure them that the results of the war were fixed beyond the power of reaction," and stressed how the South had supported Horace Greeley in 1872.

Such efforts of Lamar to win Northern sympathy, however, were too slight, for, as he said, "the Northern mind was fixed." Thus he declared:

What was wanted was an occasion on which they would Listen, and listen with something of a feeling of Sympathy. I thought the death of Sumner was such an occasion. He was a man who had perhaps the largest personal following in the country. Every Word Said About Him, On the Occasion of His Funeral, Would Be Read All Over The North, Especially Among Those Classes Who Have Never Given Us A Hearing.

To Southern critics who believed that he had, in a great sense, betrayed the South, in so eulogizing a New Englander, Lamar supplied his motivations. "If the Southern people wish them not," he declared, "They Are Valueless To Me. For her wishes are my wishes, my honors are her honors, and what She refuses to accept, I decline to wear." He did insist, however, "I believe I have converted resentments into kind feelings and prejudices into sympathies." Also, Lamar could not forgo telling his Southern critics that many in his position would have acted similarly because "I believe your Love of the South is stronger than any feeling of Resentment," and because, also, when a man is placed in a public situation he may "have the largeness of mental vision to See More when an opportunity for extended observation is before you, than one can possibly see at home in the South." [19]

[19] *Ibid.* This extended letter from Lamar to Clay resulted in Mrs. Clay's writing that his explanations for giving the speech were so persuasive that she and her husband desired his permission to have the letter published in Southern newspapers. Lamar refused to give his consent, saying, "After all my Sumner Speech must be 'justified by faith' rather than by any reasons formally set forth. Those who *know* me, understand what I intended to accomplish. Those who do not know me and believe in me cannot be made to approve it. So let it stay with you and Mr. Clay *unpublished.*" Lamar to Mrs. C. C. Clay, December 20, 1874, in Clay Papers (MSS in Duke University Library).

Lucius Q. C. Lamar

To understand the man who spoke thus, one must know the training that he had and the resources that were developed.

Background, Training, and Methods

The earliest records of Lamar's forebears named two brothers, Thomas and Peter Lamore, who came to the province of Virginia sometime before 1663.[20] Included in the sixth generation of descendants of Thomas, was Lucius Quintus Cincinnatus, the subject of this essay, whose family became established in Georgia. Among the outstanding relatives whose activities probably were discussed in the boy's hearing were many planters, four ministers, two Supreme Court justices, one state justice, a president of the Republic of Texas, two doctors, a governor, a lieutenant colonel, and a senator.[21]

Besides these people whose names were familiar to him, there were three persons who directly influenced his life: his father, his mother, and Augustus B. Longstreet.

Lamar's father, the first in the family to have the name Lucius Quintus Cincinnatus, was an outstanding young lawyer in Georgia. At thirty-four he became judge of the Okmulgee Circuit, a position comparable to a judgeship on the Supreme Court of Georgia.[22] Under the strain of melancholy, however, on July 4, 1834, before young Lucius had reached his ninth birthday, his father took his own life. In his letters and speeches Lamar never mentioned the circumstances of his father's death. Occasionally, however, Lamar mentioned his father in terms of praise. In 1852, when he was considering returning from Mississippi to Georgia to live, he wrote to his friend, Robert Harper:

There is one circumstance which alone is sufficient to endear me to Georgia above all other places. In her bosom rests the sacred dust of my honored father whose blood, whose name, whose very temperament, whose everything (save his shining virtues and surprising genius) I have inherited. Such things have greater influences on my action than on most men.[23]

On another occasion, years later, in the United States Senate, Lamar referred to his father's influence: "Mr. President...I belong to that class of public

[20] Clarinda Pendleton Lamar, *Joseph Rucker Lamar* (New York: Knickerbocker Press, 1926), p. 5.

[21] Edward Mayes, *Genealogy and History of Lamar and other Related Families* (Jackson, Miss., 1928), *passim.*

[22] There was actually no supreme court in Georgia until 1848, fourteen years after the judge's death. Mayes, *Lamar,* p. 17.

[23] Lamar to Robert Harper, February 8, 1852, in Lamar-Harper Papers (Georgia Department of Archives and History, Atlanta, Ga.).

men who were secessionists.... But sir, that conception is gone; ... Another one has taken its place; ... The elements of it were planted in my heart by my father; ... may I tell you what it is, Sir? ... It is that of one grand, mighty, indivisible Republic...." [24]

In addition to the personal influences of the elder Lamar, the father's library was important. Once, in 1870, Lamar mentioned it in a speech:

> Books? I was surrounded with books. My father's library was unusually large and varied for those times. The first book I remember having put into my hands by my mother, after juvenile books, was Franklin's Autobiography. The next was Rollin's History. Then came Plutarch's Lives, which I keenly enjoyed. Then Mrs. Hemans' innocent poems were entrusted to me, and Young's Night Thoughts. As an antidote, or at least a foil, for these, came Byron, which I devoured with eagerness. It was not till later years that I discovered that I had read an expurgated edition— 'Don Juan' had been carefully cut out. After this was Robinson's America, Marshall's Life of Washington, Locke on the Understanding, Stuart's Mental Philosophy, Brown's Lectures on the Intellect, and, after a while, Cousin's Psychology.[25]

His mother put a book into his hand for the first time. Her interest in his reading and education influenced him most in his early years. When widowed she was fortunate in being left considerable property, and was able to send her three sons through college.

Before reaching college, Lamar attended several schools. While his father lived, he was a pupil at Scottsboro and Midway, two communities in the neighborhood of Covington. After his death, the mother moved, devout Methodist that she was, to Covington, where the Georgia Conference Manual Labor School was located. To this school Lucius, a diminutive, pale, and dyspeptic child, was sent for three years, 1835 to 1838. Of these valuable years, he said:

> I was a delicate boy, never so athletic as my two brothers, and being put to work strengthened and toned up my whole system. We all had to work three hours every day at the ordinary work of a plantation—plowing, hoeing, cutting wood, picking cotton and sowing it, pulling fodder, and every item of a planter's occupation. When we left that school we could do not only this ordinary drudgery in the best way, but the most expert could shoe a horse, make an ax helve, stock a plow, or do any plain bit of blacksmithing and carpentry. It was a great training for us all, for we became perfectly versed in the details of the work of a farm. Many of Georgia's most distinguished men were reared there.[26]

[24] *Congressional Record*, 47th Cong., Special Senate sess., April 1, 1881, p. 159.
[25] Commencement Address, Emory College, July, 1870, quoted in Mayes, *Lamar*, p. 28.
[26] *Ibid.*, p. 29.

Lamar did manual work for which he was paid, although not according to the amount of work accomplished.[27] Here he was also introduced to public speaking. The boys were required to "declaim, every week or two, such selections of prose or poetry as they might fancy."[28]

Concurrently, Lamar began to demonstrate his interest in the speaking of others. Georgia was a center of Southern Methodist activity. Since prominent Methodists were frequent guests in his home, and because the same men frequently spoke at the school, he had opportunities to hear sermons, orations, and discussions.

When the Manual Labor School was moved to Oxford, Georgia, to become part of Emory College, Mrs. Lamar moved her home to that place. There, in 1841, Lamar entered the freshman class; he was graduated in 1845.

While her son was in college, Mrs. Lamar placed before him another source of reading, *The Ladies' Repository*. Of it Lamar wrote many years later:

> Much of my practical success in life among men is due to the principles I imbibed from the speeches of your father [Rev. Edward Thomson] when he was President of a Western College which I read during the formative state of my intellect and character. Those speeches were published in a magazine entitled the Ladies' Repository, and my attention was called to them by my widowed mother, who was at a Methodist college in the South educating her sons.[29]

The articles by the Reverend Edward Thomson, to which Lamar referred, included "Close Thought." In this article the author advised his readers to consider "one thing at a time" with a "fixedness of concentration of mental energy," all of which demands "patient, laborious research." He argued that a speech should be carefully prepared. He illustrated the point with an account of a preacher who, when he delivered a long, learned, and involved sermon, would say that "he had not time to prepare a short and simple one."[30]

In another article on "Originality," Reverend Thomson claimed that "there may be bombast, and noise, and declamation, without perspicuity, but not eloquence." He also urged that the speaker analyze his audience with reference to "age, the education, the habits, and the state of feeling." Another admonition was that a speaker should use the extempore method in order to

---

[27] Henry Morton Bullock, *A History of Emory University* (Nashville: Parthenon Press, 1936), p. 34ff.

[28] Mayes, *Lamar*, p. 30.

[29] Lamar to Rev. Edward Thomson, May 13, 1887, in Lamar Papers (Mississippi Department of History and Archives, Jackson, Miss.).

[30] Rev. Edward Thomson, "Close Thought," *The Ladies' Repository*, 1 (March, 1841), 80.

"take advantage of every little circumstance which may occur." [31] Such writings doubtless left their impact on young Lamar.

While at Emory, Lamar came to know Augustus Baldwin Longstreet, his future father-in-law, a man who influenced him profoundly. This man of many interests—lawyer, politician, orator, judge, farmer, teacher, newspaper editor, preacher, author of Southern humor, musician, carpenter, and sportsman—had just become president of Emory. His first influence on Lamar may have been through the course of study which the boys followed. Longstreet, a Yale graduate, patterned the curriculum after that of his alma mater, and included Blair's *Rhetoric*, Cicero's *de Oratore*, Plato's *Gorgias*, and Hedge's *Logic*.[32]

To what extend did Plato, Cicero, and Blair leave lifelong imprints? Evidence is not available to know the precise answers. Nevertheless, ultimate forces operated. Eventually Savoyard was to proclaim Lamar a "Wizard of the English tongue." [33] Bishop Charles Galloway, at the time of Lamar's death eulogized: "at times he had the classic diction of Edward Everett, and again he could rival the peerless periods of Edmund Burke.... For majestic utterances and forensic eloquence he had no peer in all our borders." [34] And Chauncey M. Depew noted "Johnsonian periods and the lofty style of Edmund Burke" [35] in Lamar's writing and speaking. Even such a critical Northern newspaper as the Chicago *Times* referred to his Centennial Controversy speech in Congress as "the most clearly put and the most coherent recently delivered in either house." [36] Possibly the best insight into what Lamar himself thought of style was given in his analysis of Calhoun, whose speaking revealed elevation of language, soaring imagination, and force of logic. Calhoun gave "the true impression of a profound and elevated mind, communicating its thoughts and feelings to the minds of others in words plain and clear and sentences simple and natural." [37]

Lamar worked to achieve perfection in the composition of his own speeches. His notebook, which contains about a hundred pages of hand-written texts of speeches delivered in Mississippi, indicates many instances of attempts

[31] *Ibid.*, p. 82.

[32] Emory College Catalogue for 1848, pp. 10-11, quoted in Bullock, *op. cit.*, p. 104.

[33] Savoyard [Eugene W. Newman], *Essays of Men, Things, and Events* (New York, 1904), p. 186.

[34] Rev. Charles B. Galloway, Bishop of the Methodist Episcopal Church, South. See *Appeal Avalanche* (Memphis), January 25, 1893; *Daily Clarion Ledger* (Jackson, Miss.), January 25, 1893.

[35] Chauncey M. Depew, *My Memories of Eighty Years* (New York: Charles Scribner's Sons, 1924), p. 387.

[36] *Daily Times* (Chicago), quoted in Jackson *Daily Clarion*, February 1, 1876.

[37] Speech on the unveiling of the Calhoun monument, April 26, 1887.

to achieve a style "plain and clear," and "simple and natural." For example, he began the introduction of one speech: "Fellow citizens of Marshall County: Though utterly exhausted from unusual labors and so hoarse that I fear I cannot command this audience, it gives me the greatest pleasure to appear upon this occasion." As he wrote he changed "unusual labors" to "continuous labors." Then he apparently reconsidered the expression and struck it out completely. He also thought over the words, "I cannot command this audience," and changed them to read "my voice will not be heard," possibly because he feared a misinterpretation of the word "command." He also substituted "meet you" for "appear." Thus the first sentence read: "Though utterly exhausted and so hoarse that I fear my voice will not be heard, it gives me the greatest pleasure to meet you upon this occasion." [38]

Moreover, in his attention to style, Lamar, though inclined toward Anglo-Saxon words, used ones of various origin, including French and Latin. He did not resort to slang or vulgarisms, and employed relatively little humor. [39] Likewise, to achieve the "simple sentence" Lamar averaged about thirty-one words per sentence, though sentences varied widely as to length, complexity, and form. Certain passages are distinctly ornate. His fondness for alliterative adjectives can be illustrated by the closing sentence of one of his speeches: "Insolent, oppressive, imbecile, dishonest, false, and abject in spirit,—it shows in every trait its servile character." [40]

Longstreet influenced Lamar's preparation and delivery of speeches. The students were required to "deliver original orations in the College Chapel, several times during the year, in addition to the usual exercises at Commencement." [41] Longstreet was interested in these speeches, and often invited the students to his home for criticisms before they spoke. The commencement orations, with large audiences in attendance, were supervised by Longstreet and showed evidence of his hand "standing out all over them." [42] Lamar appeared at one of the commencements at which Longstreet presided, speaking on the subject, "Religion Came, and Where Proud Science failed, She bent her knee to Earth, and over Man prevailed." [43]

While Lamar probably memorized the speeches in college which were

[38] "Lamar Notebook," pp. 52ff., in Lamar Papers (Mississippi Department of Archives and History).
[39] Humor and slang characterized certain of his letters. He wrote to Bob Harper, saying that a speech he had just given was a "rip-snorter." See Lamar to Harper, December 3, 1853, in Lamar-Harper Papers.
[40] "Lamar Notebook," pp. 27-28, in Lamar Papers.
[41] Bullock, *op. cit.*, p. 109.
[42] John Donald Wade, *Augustus Baldwin Longstreet* (New York: Macmillan Co., 1924), p. 265.
[43] Program for Senior Exhibition, Emory College, 1845.

closely supervised by Longstreet, he changed his habits in time. In describing his mature habits, he observed:

As to never speaking on any occasion without committing my speech to memory: I am now forty-eight years old, and have not done such a thing but once or twice (on literary occasions) since I was twenty-one. *I cannot write a speech.* The pen is an extinguisher upon my mind and a torture to my nerves. I am the most habitual extemporaneous speaker that I have ever known. Whenever I get the opportunity I prepare my argument with great labor of thought, for my mind is rather a slow one in constructing its plan or theory of an argument. But my friends all tell me that my offhand speeches are by far more vivid than my prepared efforts.[44]

That Lamar could not write a speech may be true; that he did not try, however, is false, for his notebook contains many sections of texts of speeches. A more complete interpretation of his methods may be gained from his advice "never attempt to speak when you are unprepared":

I try not to speak unless I am prepared. I don't write my speeches; my practice is, when preparing a speech, after having determined what subject to discuss, to form my sentences in my mind; to turn each sentence over and over until I get it in shape to suit me, and then to repeat it to myself until it is thoroughly impressed on my mind, and then to go to the next sentence; so that when I am through with my preparation, I not only know what I am going to say, but the very gesture that will accompany every word of it.[45]

Another source of training while at Emory was Lamar's membership in the Phi Gamma Literary Society. Apparently he was only moderately active in the society, but following his graduation and during the years from 1845-47 at Macon where he was reading law, he returned to speak at least twice to the society. Once he discussed a subject vital to him years later: "Should Senators be instructed in Congress?"[46] On another occasion he spoke on "Should Southern Youth be Educated at the North?"[47]

The influences of Longstreet continued all the years of Lamar's life, for in 1847 he married Longstreet's daughter, Virginia. At almost the same time Longstreet moved to Oxford, Mississippi, where he became chancellor of the State University. Within two years Lamar also moved to Oxford where he began teaching mathematics while practicing law with Longstreet. Politics

[44] Lamar to John C. Butler, quoted in *The Green Bag*, V (April, 1893), 153.
[45] Quoted by Walter B. Hill, *ibid.*, p. 160.
[46] Phi Gamma Minutes, November 21, 1846 (Emory University Library, Atlanta, Ga.). The secretary of the society recorded the following in regard to Lamar's speech: "He entertained the Society with a short but beautiful, instructive, and highly entertaining address."
[47] *Ibid.*, January 30, 1847.

soon became an absorbing interest, too, and by 1850 Lamar became active in the Mississippi State Rights Association. He spoke for the group,[48] took an active part in business meetings,[49] and was sent to Jackson as a delegate to the state convention.[50]

Earlier Georgia ties were not easy to break, however, and in 1852 Lamar wrote to his friend, Robert Harper, in Georgia: "When I deliver a speech that elicits applause and praise, my first thought is...what of it, what good does it do, *Bob* will not hear of it, my *mother* knows nothing about it, *none* of my Georgia friends will know it."[51] But political sentiments were being crystallized and, with Longstreet nearby urging him to vigorous activity for Southern rights,[52] Lamar became concerned. In his letter to Harper, he continued:

> It is high time ... to show ... Southern spirit ... standing aloof from all conventions with Free-soilers, anti-slavery men, and enemies of the South. ... My party has quit its principles and is begging to get admission into a National party which we denounced as thoroughly corrupted on the slavery question.

Because sentiments and ambitions continued to beckon, Lamar returned to Georgia. He located at Covington, practiced law with Harper, and was elected to the Georgia Legislature. Disillusioned after being defeated for Congress, and realizing that ties established in Mississippi with Longstreet were more firmly rooted than he realized, Lamar then returned to Mississippi. There his political fortunes rose rapidly, and at the age of thirty-two he was elected to Congress.

Pre-Civil War Congressional Speaking

During Lamar's early years in Congress a reporter for the *New York Times* observed: "Mr. Lamar has a rather tall and full figure...with a large high forehead bulging out over his face, long, sleek and plentiful brown hair, combed back behind his ears, a reddish-brown beard only shaved on the upper lip, blue eyes with a red tinge in them, and a nose of the average size, which at no place stands out on a line with his overhanging forehead." Lamar's speaking came within the purview of the reporter's comments: "As a speaker, he is extremely fiery, and inclined to raise his voice; but his portraiture and

[48] *Organizer* (Oxford, Miss.), November 16, 1850.

[49] *Ibid.*, April 5, 1851.

[50] *Ibid.*, May 17, 1851.

[51] Lamar to Robert Harper, February 8, 1852, in Lamar-Harper Papers.

[52] Longstreet was a vigorous proponent and follower of Calhoun's policies. He spoke openly against practices of the North. See Willie D. Halsell, "Prelude to a Career: L. Q. C. Lamar Tries Politics," *Journal of Mississippi History*, VII (April, 1945), 75-90.

descriptions are graphic and poetical, extensively colored with Southern war-paint, and heightened to an interesting point by many romantic exaggerations."[53]

Lamar entered Congress in 1857, at a time when Southerners were threatening open revolt if a Republican should be elected President. Because of his utterances in those years, which the *New York Times* considered "extremely fiery," Lamar has been termed a radical and uncompromising secessionist, even a rabid Southern fire-eater. He was a secessionist. He did not, however, crusade for secession as did Yancey or Rhett. The statement of one writer that he was a "moderate rebellionist,"[54] is more nearly the truth. Certain Southerners even feared his mildness on the slavery question.[55] For example, Mrs. Jacob Thompson, wife of the Secretary of the Interior under Buchanan, wrote to Mrs. Howell Cobb: "He is very reasonable on the secession question, does not go as far as your husband or mine...."[56] Nevertheless, Lamar was no submissionist. Probably the most accurate statement of Lamar's position is that given by himself, albeit spoken years later:

I belong to that class of Southern men who were secessionists. Every throb of my heart was for the disunion of these States.... I confess that I believed in the right of secession and that I believed in the propriety of its exercise. I will say further that it was a cherished conception of my mind: that of two great free Republics on this continent, each pursuing its own destiny and the destiny of its own people and their happiness according to its own will.[57]

Actually, however, it is difficult to believe otherwise than that Lamar hoped for a peaceful solution to the last. He feared the consequence of civil strife, and wrote in early 1860:

The sectional war rages with unabated violence. No one started out with more of honest indignation than I felt. But I begin to hope that there exists a mutual misunderstanding between the two sections, brought about by ultra party leaders and deluded fanatics. I think I can see, through all the rancor and madness of this struggle, the slow evolution of right principles. What is now the greatest need is some one man, one *true* man, who will present the whole controversy in its true light —who, rising above the passions and prejudices of the times, will speak to both

[53] *New York Times*, December 26, 1859.

[54] Percy Lee Rainwater, *Mississippi: Storm Center of Secession* (Baton Rouge: Louisiana State University Press, 1938), p. 207.

[55] Wirt Armistead Cate, *Lucius Q. C. Lamar: Secession and Reunion* (Chapel Hill: University of North Carolina Press, 1935), 54-55.

[56] Mrs. Jacob Thompson to Mrs. Howell Cobb, December 15, 1860, quoted in U. B. Phillips (ed.), "The Correspondence of Robert Toombs, Alexander Stephens, and Howell Cobb," *American Historical Association Annual Reports for 1911*, p. 523.

[57] *Congressional Record*, 47th Cong., Special Senate sess., p. 159.

sections in a spirit at once tolerant, just, generous, humane, and national. No one has shown himself to be that man yet.[58]

Although there is considerable truth in the statement that Lamar "does not love slavery any more than Sumner does," [59] Lamar's pre-Civil War speeches defended the institutions peculiar to the South. Quoted as saying, "Slavery is too heavy a load for us to carry," [60] he nevertheless was devoted to that which was Southern. From the time of his election until he joined his Southern colleagues in secession, Lamar delivered no less than seven speeches defending the South. In two speeches particularly, one on January 13, 1858, on the admission of Kansas, and a second, two years later, February 21, 1860, on "Slavery and Southern Rights," Lamar expressed cogently the views he espoused at that time.

The most important political issue before Congress when it convened in December, 1857, was the admission of Kansas to statehood. The Lecompton Constitution which would have made Kansas a slave state and enabled the South to regain numerical equality with the free states was sent to Washington for approval. Hence there began in both Houses one of the most heated debates in American history.

Lamar's Lecompton speech was his maiden effort in defense of Southern sentiment.[61] In the words of one writer, this speech "exemplified the first stage in Lamar's political development when his views and sympathies were narrowly and even unpleasantly sectional." [62] Illustrative of Lamar's temper was an introductory remark: "If I could do so consistently with the honor of my country, I would plant American liberty, with Southern institutions, upon every inch of American soil." Likewise, before developing his specific issues, Lamar left no doubt as to his Southern position:

> Before I consent to any new schemes of territorial acquisition, to be effected, as usual, by the prowess of southern arms, and the contributions of southern blood and treasure, I desire the question of the South's right to extend her institutions into territory already within the Union, practically and satisfactorily settled by the legislation of this Congress. These territorial acquisitions, so far, have been to the South like the far-famed fruit which grows upon the shores of the accursed sea, beautiful to sight, but dust and ashes to the lips.

[58] Lamar to F. A. P. Barnard, n. d., in Mayes, *Lamar*, p. 81.

[59] Ben Ames Williams (ed.), *A Diary from Dixie* (Boston: Houghton Mifflin Co., 1949), p. 70.

[60] *Ibid.*, p. 151.

[61] To a great extent it followed the pattern of the speeches delivered by numerous other Southerners on the legality of the Constitution. Often they were oblivious to the errors or flaws in their contentions. See Allan Nevins, *The Emergence of Lincoln* (2 vols.; New York: Charles Scribner's Sons, 1950), I, 280-81.

[62] Cate, *op. cit.*, p. 57.

Lamar assumed the task of proving that Kansas should be admitted into the Union under the Lecompton Constitution. He approached it by saying, "I propose to examine into the grounds upon which this violation of plighted faith is attempted to be justified. . . . The question now presents itself: do the circumstances attending the application of Kansas for admission into the Union present such a case?" His answer was an unequivocal denial: "I hold that it was a convention of the people called by the regularly constituted authority, and with the previous assent of Congress. I hold that the Kansas bill was an enabling act, vesting the Territorial Legislature with the power to call such a convention."

To establish these assertions he reviewed the previous congressional action enabling the people of Kansas to draft the constitution in convention, argued that it was drawn in accordance with all rules and regulations for such documents, and quoted Robert J. Walker in his inaugural address as governor of Kansas as saying of the Lecompton Convention, " 'That convention is now about to be elected by you, under the call of the Territorial Legislature created, and still recognized by the authority of Congress, and clothed by it, in the comprehensive language of the organic law, with full power to make such an enactment. The Territorial Legislature, then, in assemblying this convention, were fully sustained by the Act of Congress.' "

Thus, Lamar denied the contentions of Douglas and others that the constitution was irregular, illegal, and unacceptable merely because the majority of the people voted to allow slavery in Kansas. More important, the speech was a plea for the equality of all sections of the United States. In an attempt to accomplish this goal, Lamar was particularly severe in his indictment of Stephen A. Douglas.

To the charge of Douglas that the Lecompton Constitution was irregular, Lamar stated, "It is rather late in the day for this gentleman to begin to rectify such irregularities." This he based on the activities of Douglas in 1850 for the admission of California. Circumstances there, he contended, were far more irregular in allowing her admission:

We need go no further back than California. She was begotten by a military general, and forced into the family of States by the Caesarean operation of an executive *accoucheur.* [Laughter.] Yes, sir, without any previous assent of Congress, without even the authority of a Territorial Legislature, without any census, a band of roaming adventurers was lugged into the Union over all law and precedent, as the coequal of the oldest State of this Union, because it happened to be a free State. . . .

The fact that Douglas in 1850 was exasperated that Congress did not act with more dispatch to admit California and in 1858 was acting to retard statehood for Kansas, Lamar could view in only one light:

There is but one solution, and every day is riveting it in the Southern mind; and that is, where a State, with a constitution excluding slavery, applies for admission, no irregularity can be too enormous, no violation of precedent too marked, no disregard of constitutional procedure too palpable, no outrage too enormous, for its admission as a State into the Union; but when a State, with slavery in its constitution, applies for admission, no excuse can be too trivial, no pretense too paltry and ignoble, to keep her out. Sir, the direct tendency, and with some avowed object, of all this opposition, is to delay the admission of Kansas until she becomes a free State. I do not charge this on that gentleman; but why does he pursue this course? It is but an offshoot of that damnable policy which has been preying upon the vitals of the South for the last forty years: that of buying peace for the turbulent and fanatical at the expense of the quiet and orderly. . . .

Such language was but little milder than that employed by the most rabid of Southerners. The "preying upon the vitals of the South" began in earnest, Lamar contended, in 1820 when Missouri applied for admission, and "For peace's sake Congress overleaps the constitution, and marks out a line beyond .which slavery shall not go." Then "Abolitionism raves to be heard in Congress about slavery generally, and for the sake of peace Congress allows it to fill the Capitol with abolition petitions which it has no power on earth to grant." Finally, the Kansas incident was the climax to everything:

Abolitionism hires armed bands to go and drive slave-holders out of Kansas; and Robert J. Walker, for peace's sake, would hand it over to them. . . . And Stephen A. Douglas, who was for lassoing California and dragging her into the Union over all law and precedent and the violated rights of fifteen of the sovereign States of this Union, would now subject Kansas to all the rigors of the Inquisition to keep her out of the Union.

Lamar's was a categorical denial of the charges of irregularity and illegality in Kansas. To him the convention had acted in a legal and orderly manner. The Lecompton Constitution embodied slavery because the delegates had willed it so. Because slavery was allowed in Kansas there was no altering it by Congress in its obligation to admit Kansas. Thus Lamar declared as he drew his speech to a close:

It is no longer a Territory of these United States; she has, by your own authority and permission, thrown off the habiliments of territorial dependence, and stands now a State . . . and asks admission as an equal in this noble confederation of sovereignties. . . . To remand her to her territorial condition, you cannot, anymore than you can roll back to their hidden sources the waters of the Mississippi. Kansas is a separate, organized, living State, with all the nerves and arteries of life in full development and vigorous activity.[63]

[63] For versions of the speech, see *Congressional Globe and Appendix*, 35th Cong., 1st sess., pp. 49-52 and Mayes, *Lamar*, pp. 609-18.

The repudiation by the House of the Lecompton Constitution and the subsequent circumstances of admitting Kansas as a free state, together with the rise of Republican strength opposing extension of slavery meant that all further efforts of Southerners in Congress were doomed to failure. Lamar could not alter circumstances; he could only do his part by speaking for Southern rights and institutions.

Two years later, Lamar delivered his most ardent and determined speech on Southern rights and slavery. Congress, in a Committee of the Whole, was deliberating on the President's annual message which had given rise to a succession of antislavery and proslavery speeches. The message was only the occasion, not the cause, for events were speeding the crisis. The raid of John Brown at Harper's Ferry had precipitated angry and frightened speeches by abolitionists and Southern partisans. Helper's *Impending Crisis*, read with completely opposite reactions in the North and South, became an object of defense and attack in Congress. Conventions for the nomination of presidential candidates were soon to meet. Within a week from the time Lamar delivered this speech Lincoln proclaimed at Cooper Union his concept of what the "Fathers" had interpreted as their rights and duties in regard to the extension of slavery. Because Lamar feared the imminence of actual disunity, he was torn between devotion to the Union and his loyalty to the South. Even two years earlier he wrote to a friend in Mississippi: "Dissolution cannot take place quietly: the vast ... machinery of this government cannot be divided without general tumult and, it may be, ruin. When the sun of the Union sets it will go down in blood." [64] Such forebodings doubtless influenced him to plead for honorable reconciliation without in any measure suggesting submission by the South.

The early part of the speech was eminently ethical in appeal. Lamar believed himself and the state of Mississippi to be beneficiaries of the federal government. He described the precise nature of the mind of the people he represented:

> My object to-day is to inquire how far my constituents and the people with whom they are associated are responsible for the existing condition of things. Mississippi, sir, has grown up under this Federal Union. . . . Her noble university, and her common schools are all established by donations from the public domain, which she has received in common with all the new States. . . . Nor will she be driven from her devotion, except by causes which she has not created and by consequences for which she is not responsible. Mississippi has never declared herself in favor of disunion, *per se*. She will not make that declaration until she becomes convinced that her sister States North are deliberately determined to endanger her

[64] Lamar to B. S. Rozell, March 8, 1858, quoted in Mayes, *Lamar*, p. 73.

internal and social institutions, or to impair her dignity and equality as a Confederate State.

Now, sir, I should not be candid if I did not say that there are many, perhaps a majority, in my State who do not speak with the same reserve and caution as I am doing on this occasion. The obvious and unmistakable tokens of design in the long-continued and crafty agitation of this slavery question have produced alienation and distrust. It is a unanimous sentiment in the South that the existence of this Republican organization is a standing menace to her peace and security, and a standing insult to her character.

Harper's Ferry and Helper's *Impending Crisis* were blamed for causing undue agitation. As Lamar took up these matters, he found himself replying to Thomas Corwin on how "can a small book like the Helper Compend endanger your proud institutions?" He replied: "Sir, a million of such books could not for an instant affect the South, but for the conviction that it represents and embodies the sentiments of a large class of the Northern people." Since Northern sentiment was dedicated to exterminating slavery, and was part and parcel of all the theological and political thinking, Lamar could only conclude: "Now, sir, this is a portentous fact; for a moral sentiment thus diffused among the majority of a great people will work itself out into practical action, and the law, fundamental or statute, which obstructs its progress to development must yield before it or be overborne by it." This was true, he held, because "institutions and constitutions and laws and governments are at last but external structures whose roots are in the moral and intellectual life of the people for whom they exist; and any revolution in that moral and mental life must have its corresponding effect upon institutions subject to its influence."

The tragic nearness of disunion was explained by just one thing—"misunderstanding." Because of it, he asked: "Is it strange, sir, that our people should think of withdrawing their imperiled institutions from the sweep of this fanatical revolution?" Regrettably he declared: "Sir, the calamity of the times is that the people of the North do not understand the people of the South, and it is to the interest of a certain class of politicians to perpetuate the misunderstanding." To ameliorate feelings in the North, and to state the case for the South, became Lamar's task, albeit with arguments not new after years of intense discussion of a problem for which there appeared no solution. Nevertheless, he refuted the claims of Northern abolitionists, defended slavery on constitutional grounds, and presented biblical and social arguments revealing thought and careful composition.

First and fundamentally, Lamar argued the constitutionality of slavery as he refuted the contentions that it was in violation of "natural rights." To the statement of Corwin that "it was the policy of the founders of our Republic to prevent the establishment of slavery in new communities," Lamar replied: "In my opinion, a greater error was never committed upon this floor. My own State is a standing refutation of the proposition. Sir, slavery exists this day in Mississippi by the encouragement—certainly with the consent—of this Federal Government when it was in the hands of the founders of our Republic." Certainly, too, the failure of the Wilmot Proviso after the Mexican War was evidence that the nation must accept slavery as "an integral and live element in her social system, interfused with the social relations, the industrial pursuits, the investments of capital, and the political forms of her people." Thus he declared:

Gentlemen, I ask, have you the right—I do not mean the constitutional power—have you the moral right, is it just, is it tolerant, to reverse the action of this government and embark it in a career of hostility to an institution which the action of this government has made the basis upon whose durability our social and political order is constituted?

More constructive defenses of slavery were presented as Lamar continued to refute Northern contentions that slavery was "hateful to God and unjust to man," and repugnant to an "enlightened conscience." Lamar's positive position was that the Negro in America was in no wise ready for the responsibilities of freedom. His lot was better by far than that of the felons who must be confined to cells "because the order and well-being of society require that they shall be deprived of that liberty and equality which, in our hands is such a priceless, peerless blessing." Moreover, he argued that the Negro was by no means the only individual deprived of full political liberty for "all the young men of the country under twenty-one years of age are reduced to that condition...." They are deprived "not because their rights are not natural, inherent, and inalienable, but simply because the interests of society require that they should be kept under this personal restraint until they are fitted for political and social equality." The same principle was true with respect to women. Thus, "one half of the adult population" was disfranchised. He added:

Now I put the question, and I want it answered, whether female dependence or the immaturity of youth constitute any better reason for the privation of social and political equality, for the infliction of civil disabilities and personal restraints, than the ignorance, superstition, the mental and moral debasement, which centuries of barbarism have entailed upon a servile race?

With such arguments presented, Lamar was in a position to draw a basic conclusion which may be considered the central thesis of the speech:

Mr. Chairman, the mistake of these gentlemen is this: that men are to be governed by certain fixed, inflexible, invariable rules deduced from natural reason; and that a government which is applicable to a race of intelligent white men can be forced upon States consisting of two distinct races opposite in color, and differing as widely in character, disposition, moral and mental habits, as are the opposing characteristics of barbarism and civilization.

Still other justifications and defenses were advanced. The biblical ones were to Lamar, as to many Southerners, a ready source of argument. Dr. Wayland, author of *Elements of Moral Science*, was used extensively in tracing biblical arguments for slavery from Moses to Christ. Accordingly, Lamar quoted him: " 'The *duty of slaves* is also explicitly made known in the Bible...not, however, on the grounds of *duty to man*, but on the ground of *duty to God.*' "

More pressing political and social arguments were brought to bear. He delineated the benefits received by "three hundred thousand negroes" in America in contrast to the savages in Africa. He contrasted the Negro with American Indians who were driven back "by the advancing wave of European civilization to continually contracting circles, with diminished means of subsistence into degradation, wretchedness, and extinction." "The African," Lamar declared, "with all its foulness, with all its prosaic vulgarities, domesticated and disciplined, has been by that same wave borne up higher and higher, until now it furnishes inspiration for Northern song, heroes and heroines for Northern romance, and is invited by Northern statesmen into their charmed circle of political and social equality." In addition, Lamar contended that when all slaves were freed and returned to Africa, they retrogressed, that in spite of slavery in the South there were actually 40,000 more free Negroes in the South than in the North. He asked, "what has humanity to complain against the institution?"

He discussed the extension of slavery in terms of morality. To the Northern contention that all new territories should be free because "free labor is dishonored by its contact with slave labor," Lamar supplied one of his strongest answers. He relied on a picture of the great masses of non-slaveowners in the South who far exceeded the "three hundred and twenty-thousand slaveholders," all of whom exercised "universal suffrage":

...each one of the five million nonslaveholders has one vote, and no less. These... have the overwhelming majority. Sir, the institution is in the hollow of the hand of the nonslaveholder of the South.... Sir, if these effects were degrading, why not throw it off, when he could do it by simply depositing a ballot in a senseless urn? I will tell you why he does not do it.... It is because there is no class among whom negro slavery secures such wide-spread blessings.... There has never been a race of men more maligned and lied about than that very class of freemen in the South.... I have lived among them, and have felt the heart-warm grasp of their strong hands.... It is impossible, from the very nature and constitution of Southern society, that it should be otherwise.

A great portion of these people were landowners. Hence Lamar retorted to the abolitionists, "You talk about free labor at the North, and free soil, as if it did not exist in greater purity in the South than anywhere else."

But the Southern slaveholding planter received an even greater defense. His was a salutary influence over his slaves. Moreover, his industry in growing cotton was the source of the prosperity of Northern manufacturers. Negro labor, so basic to cotton culture, was directed and protected by him. Qualities of character in the planter "have enabled him to take a race of untamed savages, with no habits except such as inspire disgust, with no arts, no information, and out of such a people to make that the finest body of fixed laborers the world has ever seen." Likewise his ability to penetrate "the dense forest," and his habits of making "daily and yearly provision for a large body of domestics and dependents for whom he has to think," were the very ones which qualified him. He was well qualified "to fill the county court or to become a member of his State Legislature, to discharge the duties of local magistracy, or to take his place in the national councils." Washington, Jefferson, Madison, Monroe, Jackson, Calhoun, Polk, Davis, Lee, Quitman, and Taney were all evidence of this.

Lamar's defense of slavery was thus presented. His conclusion was: "I do not pretend to say that we have arrived at a standard of ideal perfection; but I do say that there is a reach of thought and a maturity of judgment brought to bear upon this subject in the South which is always adequate to evolve the greatest good. We certainly can learn nothing from the enemies of our institutions and conspirators against our peace." Thus he declared to his auditors, "The Southern people demand that this organized 'irrepressible conflict' shall stop." [65]

But it did not stop. As with the advent of a storm, the ominous threatenings grew louder and louder. Starting with the election of Lincoln late that year and ending with the firing on Fort Sumter, the Southern delegations gathered their belongings and went home. As Blaine noted:

> The members from Mississippi 'regretted the necessity' which impelled their State to the course adopted, but declared that it met 'their unqualified approval.' The card was no doubt written by Mr. L. Q. C. Lamar, and accurately described his emotions. He stood firmly by his State in accordance with the political creed in which he had been reared, but looked back with tender regret to the Union whose destiny he had wished to share and under the protection of whose broader nationality he had hoped to live and to die. [66]

[65] For versions of the speech, see *Congressional Globe and Appendix*, 36th, Cong., 1st sess., pp. 113-17, and Mayes, *Lamar*, pp. 624-33.

[66] Blaine, *op. cit.*, I, 243.

House and Senate Speaking after the War

Lamar's eulogy of Sumner (the first speech he delivered in Congress after the war) revealed the idealism which characterized his speaking in the eleven years he was to serve in the two chambers. Taken as a whole, Lamar's post-Civil War speeches embodied three basic premises: (1) the battle had been fought, the North had won, the issue was decided; (2) understanding would reunite the North and the South; and (3) the progress of both the South and the North depended upon the welfare of each. The first two premises were stated in the Sumner eulogy. The third was expressed often as time went on and as he reiterated the others.

Lamar became a genuine realist after the war. He saw the need of cooperation and collaboration with Northern Democrats and Republicans to secure economic benefits for the South in the way of railroad building, construction and improvement of levees along the Mississippi River, and the investment of capital for greater industrialization of the region. The year 1876 marks, to a large degree, the end of carpetbag control and the restoration of the state governments in the South to the hands of Southern whites. For years the ante-bellum white leaders had been powerless. The Radical Reconstruction policy held sway. But in the early years of the seventies there developed, even among Northern Republicans, a belief that native whites could best serve as leaders in the restoration of the Southern states. Many of the native whites had been active Whigs, allied in national interests, before the war. Southern leaders, made up of numerous old-line Whigs, but including also such lifelong Democrats as Lamar, constituted a body known as "The Redeemers." Among them were such individuals as Robert Toombs, Joseph E. Brown, Wade Hampton, and many others.[67] In the election of 1876, such Southerners as Lamar helped to bring about a Republican victory, believing that under a Republican administration restoration of white supremacy in the South would be assured and appropriations for such projects as the Texas and Pacific railway would be secured. The election of Hayes rather than Tilden made possible by what has been designated as "The Unknown Compromise," brings clearly to light the fact that such men as Lamar, chastened by the war, but determined also on practical ends for the South, played roles embodying, superficially at least, practical expediency.[68]

[67] For an enlightening treatment of "The Redeemers," see C. Vann Woodward, *Origins of the New South, 1877-1913* (Baton Rouge: Louisiana State University Press, 1951), pp. 1-22.

[68] This interpretation of Lamar, as well as a treatment of the election of 1876, is admirably developed in C. Vann Woodward, *Reunion and Reaction, The Compromise of 1877 and the End of Reconstruction* (Boston: Little, Brown & Co., 1951), *passim.*

The ways and means employed to restore the South often seemed contradictory. There was incongruity in the alliance of "The Redeemers" and Republicans to oppose the Northern Democrats following 1876. By the 1880's Lamar's position seemed fraught with contradiction. Although he represented an agrarian state, he adhered to the Eastern and hard-money faction of the Democratic party and opposed the silverites of the Northwest who sought to influence the Southern agricultural states to accept their more radical measures for the agrarian ills of that decade. Although Lamar was one of "The Redeemers," he was also a conservative Democrat, finding his reward ultimately in a Cabinet post in the Cleveland administration. As one writer has expressed it, "It was plain that the road to reunion was a forked road, that the right fork led to the East and the left fork to the West. Beween the right-forkers and the left-forkers the debate raged for months." [69]

The practical and expedient in Lamar did not, however, obscure his idealism. He labored for harmonious relations. His character, actions, and speeches are evidence of this. A perusal of congressional debates in which he was involved indicates that he was usually silent until any controversy was well under way. While not a frequent speaker, Lamar sought opportune moments to aid in the fulfillment of his goal of reconciliation.

Shortly after the Sumner speech, June 8, 1874, Lamar participated in a congressional debate, delivering his "Misrule in the Southern States" speech. The circumstances of the Louisiana election controversy precipitated it. The immediate issue was whether the Negro, Pinchback, supported by the carpetbaggers, would be seated in the House over G. A. Sheridan, the fusion candidate of the Democrats and Reform-Republicans. Repeated countings of the Louisiana returns indicated the election of Sheridan, but these results were denied by congressional radicals. The problem of free elections, the right of the Southern people to elect their state and national representatives, was one which Lamar saw to be transcendent over the Louisiana incident.

While exposition and portrayal of facts in the Louisiana controversy characterized much of the speech, the occasion was used for a wider plea. Injustices toward the South were delineated, consequent sufferings were presented, and the submission of the Southern people to the results of the war was stated:

They fully recognize the fact that every claim to the right of secession from this Union is extinguished and eliminated from the American system, and no longer constitutes a part of the apparatus of the American Government. They believe that the institution of slavery . . . is dead, extinguished, sunk into a sea that gives not up

[69] C. Vann Woodward, *Origins of the New South*, p. 49.

its dead. They cherish no aspirations or schemes for its resuscitation. With their opinions on the rightfulness of slavery unchanged by the events of the war, yet as an enlightened people, accepting what is inevitable, they would not, if they could, again identify their destiny as a people with an institution that stands antagonized so utterly by all the sentiments and living forces of modern civilization.

Hence, he could plead for Northern magnanimity:

Mr. Speaker, my heart has on more than one occasion thrilled under the tributes of applause paid by Northern members, who were Federal officers in the war, to the valor of Southern troops and the fortitude of Southern people during the war. Sir, if the conquest over self is the greatest of all victories, then that people deserve a still higher meed of praise for their conduct in peace; for, sir, they have borne unprecedented indignities, wrongs, oppressions, and torture, with unexampled patience and dignity.[70]

This speech and the Sumner eulogy, coming in such close succession, gave Lamar a reputation far beyond that which he previously enjoyed. The speeches were printed and commented upon extensively,[71] and the way was paved for alert interest in what he would say on future occasions. Especially was this significant, for Lamar could not hope to continue speaking in an atmosphere free from debate. Controversial matters soon were to bring him into clashes with political opponents, notably James G. Blaine.

The first clash occurred in early January, 1876, as the House debated whether it had authority to appropriate money for the proposed Centennial celebration in Philadelphia. Townsend of New York and Blaine attacked the South and Jefferson Davis. They alluded to the assault of Brooks upon Sumner years earlier. Lamar rose to speak. His was the task of rebuking, even while he pleaded for reconciliation. His answer was virtually another eulogy on Sumner whom he quoted in respect to the incident: " 'Never while a sufferer did anyone hear me speak of him in unkindness.' " But more important was Lamar's plea for harmony:

But in the political as well as in the natural world the agencies which are the most powerful are not the noisiest. Violence, passion, fanaticism, and animosity, can always find voice and rend the air with their ... clamors; while deep and earnest conviction lies unspoken in the heart of a people. The currents of passion and of feeling may flow hither and thither under extraneous influences and forces, like the dash and roar of waves lashed to fury by the storm, while the great sea, the unsounded

[70] For versions of this speech, see *Congressional Record and Appendix,* 43d Cong., 1st sess., pp. 426-31; Mayes, *Lamar,* pp. 659-69.

[71] See *New York Tribune,* June 13, 1874, for comments and quotations from the Richmond *Dispatch,* and June 15, 1874, for comments from the Syracuse *Journal.*

depths of a common humanity, a common hope, a common interest, and a common patriotism, lies voiceless but almighty beneath.[72]

The result of his effort was described as follows:

Blaine, tightly squeezed between both hands until nothing but hair, nose, and mouth were discernible, colored visibly, dropped his eyes before Lamar's gaze, and moved restlessly in his seat. Townsend, whose face is naturally a flame, coughed irresolutely, turned in his seat, and looked the very picture of discomfort. Judged by its effect on the House and the comment of the town, the speech was the most masterful in moderation, exhaustive in argument, and captivating in method so far delivered. It told on every soul.[73]

Such encounters with Blaine were to continue through the years, and were even more vigorous when the two men moved from the House to the Senate.[74]

Actually, however, Lamar and Blaine, in spite of repeated political combats, became relatively good friends. Too, Lamar's conflicts in debate were not limited to Blaine, for others, particularly Hoar and Roscoe Conkling, experienced similar rebukes. One occasional method of Lamar was the severe reprimand. Just as Blaine received one early, so Hoar, after Lamar had moved to the Senate, was one time a recipient. Hoar referred. to Jefferson Davis as being another Aaron Burr or Benedict Arnold, only to have Lamar reply:

Sir, it required no courage to do that; it required no magnanimity to do it; it required no courtesy; it only required hate, bitter, malignant sectional feeling and a sense of personal impunity. The gentleman, I believe takes rank among Christian statesmen. He might have learned a better lesson even from the pages of mythology. When Prometheus was bound to the rock, it was not an eagle—it was a vulture—that buried his beak in the tortured vitals of the victim.[75]

Such severe reprimands were, however, never a basic characteristic of Lamar's speaking. They were few rather than numerous. Lamar could not

[72] For versions of the speech, see *Congressional Record,* 44th Cong., 1st sess., pp. 630-31; Mayes, *Lamar,* pp. 670-74. The importance of this speech and its extensive notice are reviewed fully in Cate, *op. cit.,* pp. 239-44.

[73] Chicago *Times,* n. d., quoted in Mayes, *Lamar,* p. 277; Cate, *op. cit.,* p. 242.

[74] Doubtless the most notable conflict between Lamar and Blaine during their years in the House together centered around Belknap, Secretary of War in Grant's administration, who was accused of accepting bribes. This encounter was related only incidentally with the problem of North-South reconciliation; therefore, it is being passed over in the treatment of Lamar, notwithstanding the fact that it contributed to the reputation of Lamar and did discredit to Blaine's personal integrity. It weakened the power of the Radical Republican party and made easier the development of Democratic strength and the restoration of Southern rights.

[75] *Congressional Record and Appendix,* 45th Cong., 3d sess., p. 2228.

serve out his days in Congress by delivering speeches comparable to the Sumner eulogy or by making generalized pleas for understanding. Controversial matters of policy arose, particularly in 1876-77, as he approached the termination of his House career. Two major speeches, one on the "Policy of the Republican Party in the South," and the other, an address on the "Electoral Commission" which grew out of the disputed Hayes-Tilden election, illustrate the extent to which Lamar defended the South.

The last year of Lamar's period in the House was 1876. In the presidential election he supported Tilden, hoping thereby to end Reconstruction in the South. He was not unaware of the campaign promises of Hayes that policies toward the South would be softened. He was doubtful about the promises, though, and told Congress:

But their significance must be measured, not by what he is willing to promise as a candidate, but by what he will be permitted to perform as a President. Sir, rarely in history have we seen the man who had the courage and resolution to put down the exacting tyranny of his own party, to impose upon it the impress of his own will, to infuse into it a higher life, and say to the selfish and ambitious politicians who had chosen him as their tool: 'Behold your master!'

These words were spoken at a time when Lamar arose in the House to deliver a carefully prepared and philosophical speech against the policy of the Republican party toward the South. The speech was a campaign effort for Tilden as opposed to Hayes. Its thesis was that the solution to Southern problems was local autonomy. Northern apprehensions that the South would plot to gain control and undo the effects of the war were answered by his saying that "no such hallucination inflames the imagination of the South." He emphasized the desire of the South to participate wholeheartedly in the national welfare and condemned the policy of Republican domination resulting in unhealthy sectionalism. "As Southern men," he declared, "they know that to keep up the high moral standard of a high-spirited people, obedience must emanate from patriotic love, and not from ignoble fear." Moreover, they have "no aspirations not bounded by the horizon of that Union, no purpose adverse to the national instincts, no scheme that looks to the disturbance of the elective franchise as it exists in the constitution."

The hope of the South naturally depended upon a Democratic victory in 1876. Lamar reviewed Southern sufferings under Republican rule. Victory for the Democrats "as must be seen by consulting statistics of population, will be national, and not sectional," he concluded. Lamar stated that he was reviewing Republican misrule with reluctance, but hastened to add that without complete realization of it there would be no hope for the necessary reconciliation. Party politics, not "unlawful ambitions" of Southerners was to blame. Again he spoke for the South:

All that we ask, in common justice to the South, is that you will reflect and act upon the fact that the governments you contrived have, by your own testimony, proved to you and to the world their utter incompetence to solve peaceably and prosperously a problem the difficulty of which we do not deny. When you point me to acts of violence, I acknowledge and deplore them; but I ask you, who has governed the States where this violence occurs, for the last ten years? ... Who have taxed us, controlled our legislatures, filled our courts, received the patronage of the Federal Government, ruled over us at home, and represented us here?

The peroration was a still stronger plea:

The motive which prompts their co-operation is not the expectation of filling cabinets and directing policies, but simply to get an administration which will not be unfriendly to them; an administration which, in place of the appliances of force, subjugation, and domination, will give them amnesty, restoration to the privileges of American citizenship; ... Give them that, give them local self-government, and you will then see at last what will be the dawn of prosperity in all the industries and enterprises of the North; you will see, sir, a true Southern *renaissance*, a real grand reconstruction of the South in all the elements of social order, strength, justice, and equality of all her people. Rising from her confusion and distress, rejoicing in her newly recovered liberty, prosperous, free, great, her sons and daughters of every race happy in her smile, she will greet your benignant Republic in the words of the inspired poet: "Thy gentleness hath made me great." [76]

When an electoral commission was proposed for the presidential deadlock which could not be broken in the House, it was necessary for Lamar to make one of the major decisions of his life. Tilden with more popular votes than Hayes, but lacking one electoral vote, was seemingly the choice of the nation. Unless, however, the House concurred and should rule that he was the choice, the result would be four more years of Republican control. All things considered, and as a means of avoiding election results in which one party or the other would be compelled to accept the principle of submission, Lamar, acting in opposition to a great portion of his Mississippi constituency, accepted the commission as the solution.[77] It was an alternative that appealed

[76] For versions of the speech, see *Congressional Record and Appendix*, 44th Cong., 1st sess., pp. 5087-94; Mayes, *Lamar*, pp. 682-97.

[77] See Woodward, *Reunion and Reaction*, pp. 166-85, *passim*. Woodward's thesis is that the Southern Democrats allied with Hayes's supporters to assure a Republican victory. For Southern support Hayes agreed to restore the South to her native leaders and to aid in such coveted projects as the Texas and Pacific railroad. One significant statement of Woodward is: "To account for the action of the Southerners without reference to patriotism and the more statesmanlike motives would be to adopt a deplorably

to him. In any instance, and notwithstanding the fact that Lamar was a partner to the agreement of Southern Democrats to join with the Northern Republicans to assure a victory for Hayes, one of Lamar's significant postwar congressional speeches was his support of the commission. His thesis was that fifteen men (five from the House, five from the Senate, and five from the Supreme Court) could be found who would put "devotion to the country" above "devotion to the party." The five men from the Supreme Court, he felt, could be counted upon to exercise judicial impartiality. Said Lamar: "I do know that in the dark hour of our distress it was from that court, just as it is now constituted, and from it alone of all the departments of this Federal Government, that we of the South have had protection against the legislation that forgot the Constitution in the vengeful spirit of its harsh and oppressive provisions. Its decisions in the Slaughter-house and other cases jusified us in believing that there was one refuge for those who claimed that protection." [78] Lamar's brief speech was not without results and influence. In the opinion of one Republican it made possible the commission: "Mr. Lamar put his powerful influenc and saved the peace of the country." [79]

The decisions of the commission seating Hayes may or may not have justified his faith, but his hope that the Hayes administration would be milder toward the South proved to be justified. Simultaneously with the election of Hayes, Lamar moved to the Senate, having been elected from Mississippi the previous autumn. From August, 1876, as Lamar spoke in Mississippi, he anticipated that questions of tariff and currency would be foremost before the Senate. In view of this, perhaps his most important accomplishment during the campaign was the preventing of the Mississippi Committee on Platform from including a free-silver plank. He was, thereby, enabled to go to Washington without being committed to any resolutions.

Lamar spoke infrequently during his years in the Senate. His basic concerns were, as always, reconciliation and national welfare. Successive issues gave Lamar additional opportunities to continue to counsel. The later speeches differ

---

cynical interpretation of human conduct. On the other hand, to offer such motives as the complete explanation would be to advance a questionable theory regarding the sectional distribution of the more admirable virtues. The charitable supposition would be that while patriotism was equitably distributed between Northern and Southern Democrats, the patriotic course of resisting violence and complying with the Electoral Commission law happened to coincide more nearly with the interests of the Southern than of the Northern Democrats—as they understood their interests." P. 183.

[78] For versions of the speech, see *Congressional Record*, 44th Cong., 2d sess., pp. 997-99; Mayes, *Lamar*, pp. 294-97.

[79] George F. Hoar, *Autobiography of Seventy Years* (2 vols.; London, 1904), II, 173.

from the earlier ones chiefly in the degree of preparation. As he grew older, he tended to prepare his speeches more carefully.

Lamar's first senatorial speaking was on the currency. In December, 1877, the Bland bill for the remonetization of silver was introduced. Lamar became involved as the debate continued in January. Significantly, Lamar had prevented his party in Mississippi from including a silver plank the previous summer. His speech opposing the Bland bill is significant for two reasons: it provided him with an opportunity to speak for the monetary policies he thought best for the national welfare; it likewise served to test his standing with his Mississippi constituency inasmuch as he violated specific instructions sent him by the Mississippi Legislature.

The action of the Mississippi Legislature in instructing Lamar to vote for the Bland bill was a test of his moral courage. Years earlier he had argued in the literary society at Emory that senators should not be instructed on how they should vote, and he now took the same position. Moreover, the agrarian South had close economic ties with the agrarian West. For Lamar to identify himself with the gold Democrats of the East presented an immediate hazard to his political future. Fortunately for him, he was just beginning a six-year term. If he ran counter to public opinion early in the term, later events might restore him in standing. Moreover, a position contrary to the one he assumed would not have placed him in such a favorable position to be selected for a Cabinet post when Cleveland, a gold Democrat, became President.

Lamar's basic position was that the monetization of silver was unnecessary, and that the obligation to pay bonded indebtedness in gold was paramount. Equally important was his corollary idea that the bill was dangerous to all elements in the American economic structure. He advanced the argument that free silver would bring hardships and undertook to refute the arguments of proponents of free silver. Whereas proponents of the bill said that there was not enough money in the United States, he quoted statistics to show that the countries which demonetized silver were the richest nations, per capita, in the world. To the arguments that free silver would bring more money into circulation, Lamar responded with causal reasoning to the effect that the country was filled with depreciated paper money, and that since the trade of the world followed coin, the coinage of silver would not remove the paper, and trade would not follow. The argument that silver would aid the laboring class Lamar countered by negative instances showing that labor's wages would not rise, that labor would have to pay higher prices but would receive less, and that farmers compelled to pay higher operating costs would not receive enough more than costs to make a profit. He viewed the consequences of free silver with skepticism:

206

It is something like what is seen in my State, when a crevasse, breaking through the banks, pours its water into a bay or harbor of the Gulf. It does not deepen the bay. Ships of no heavier draft than before can bring in their freight on account of it. It simply dilutes and displaces the strong salt quality of the water and destroys the oysters and other fish, of which there was a plentiful abundance before the influx of fresh water.[80]

This speech required moral courage. He had violated specific instructions from home and was in danger of repudiation. Moreover, he spoke less as a Southerner in this speech than in almost any effort of his life. Hence, as the debate drew to a close prior to final voting, he asked that the Mississippi resolutions be read before declaring to the Senate: "Mr. President, between these resolutions and my convictions there is a great gulf. I cannot pass it. Of my love to the State of Mississippi I will not speak; my life alone can tell it.... To-day I must be true or false, honest or cunning, faithful or unfaithful to my people." [81] The apprehension that his speech and vote would cost him his seat proved unfounded. More important, he added cubits to his stature in the acclaim he received. *Harper's Weekly,* devoting two columns to his stand, declared: "No Senator has shown himself more worthy of universal respect than Mr. Lamar, for none has stood more manfully by his principles in the face of the most authoritative remonstrances from his State." [82] *The Nation* lauded him: "At such a crisis...a man of Mr. Lamar's courage serves his State best by thinking only of the country. But how absurd and quixotic his performance must seem to Blaine or Conkling!" [83]

Early in 1880 Lamar became so ill he went home to recuperate. Upon returning to Washington he found the Senate in a heated debate on the so-called "exodus" of Negroes from the South. It had begun in 1879 with the exodus to Kansas and Indiana. A committee had been appointed to study the matter, and, on June 1, Senator Windom of Minnesota gave the majority report. His account was filled with references to Southern outrages. Three days later, Lamar, though ill, rose to speak, belabored Windom, calling his report a "diatribe," filled with "twaddle." Lamar's thesis was: the migration was not an "exodus" at all, but the result of a need for labor in the North, and he suggested that the migration might be a good thing for the Negro:

Sir, the exposure of these negroes to hunger and the rigors of a Northern climate, to the conflicts with the hostile forces of nature to which they are subjected for a bare subsistence, though painful and lamentable to contemplate, will develop a force

[80] For versions of the speech, see *Congressional Record,* 45th Cong., 2d sess., pp. 510-26; Mayes, *Lamar,* pp. 701-18.
[81] *Congressional Record,* 45th Cong., 2d sess., p. 1061.
[82] *Harper's Weekly* (March 9, 1878), p. 186.
[83] *The Nation* (February 21, 1878), p. 123.

of character, an energy of will, and a spirit of perseverance under difficulties and misfortunes—qualities which their easy life in the genial climate, bounteous soil, under indulgent employers, of the South, has suffered to lie dormant.

He devoted a considerable portion of the speech to a refutation of claims of Windom that conditions in the South were bad. Numerous quotations carefully gathered during three days of preparation from impartial Northern and foreign observers were given as evidence. The conclusion, typical of Lamar, was a plea for sympathetic fraternal action. Specifically, he asked that the South be freed from investigating committees that sought and found only what they cared to see and find. The good things of the South—its homes, schools, and churches—all had been ignored. Thus, he observed:

> And, sir, I say to-day with all the emphasis of truth that, if in the history of the last ten years the coming of peace has been delayed, . . . if the two races have not moved forward with the progress which was expectd toward a common prosperity, it is because the Senators and public men who wielded the powers of this great government and had the confidence of the mighty constituencies behind them have not risen to the level of their duty and opportunity to bring, as they could have done, rest and quiet and love and universal patriotism over this troubled land.[84]

During his term in the Senate three more subjects prompted Lamar to present major speeches. The first, on the election of officers for the Senate, or the "Republican Policy and the Solid South," was delivered on April 1, 1881. The second, on the tariff, came two years later, February 7, 1883. The third, on "National Aid to Education," was March 28, 1884.

Lamar's speech on the "Solid South" came during a bitter series of speeches early in 1881. He had been home most of the latter part of 1880 and returned to find that the Senate included thirty-seven Republicans and thirty-seven Democrats. The election of officers aroused animosities. As he began his speaking, Lamar called for the members of the Senate to forget sectionalism and recognize their duty to the nation. He replied to the Republican argument that the Democrats had committed treason in blocking the election of Republicans. He analyzed the causes which had kept the Republicans from allowing the Senate to get on with its business. His main argument was that the Republicans were trying to break up the solid South. Specifically, he showed how the Republicans had supported a faction in Virginia which had formerly been Democratic, and how they had offered to support any such group anywhere

---

[84] For versions of the speech, see *Congressional Record and Appendix*, 46th Cong., 2d sess., pp. 4527-34; Mayes, *Lamar*, pp. 723-39. In the version included in Mayes, the speech ends with the words: "Mr. President, I can pursue this subject no further, as my strength is entirely exhausted." Lamar was recovering from recurring attacks of vertigo and delivered this speech when he did not have the health to do so.

which would break from the national Democratic party. Lamar urged the Republicans to discontinue such practices, and replied at length to their arguments that the solid South was a detriment to the nation. Moreover, he showed that the South had no desire to control the nation through uniting with the minority party of the North, and demonstrated that the Northern Democrats themselves could control the government if they wished to do so. In addition, he pointed out that among Southerners in Congress there was actually no such thing as solidarity. They split their votes among themselves more often than not.

Lamar's speech was less conciliatory than was usual. He was direct and affirmative, with a touch of the defiant:

There is one point, and one only, upon which they [the Southern states] are solid, on which they will remain solid; and neither Federal bayonets nor Federal honors will dissolve that solidity. They are solid in defense of and for the protection of their own civilization, their own society, their own religion, against the rule of the incompetent, the servile, the ignorant, and the vicious.

Basically, however, the speech was another plea for understanding. Actually too ill to speak, saying, "I am too much exhausted to detain the Senate longer," Lamar made evident his ethical position as he closed:

I have said nothing to-day that was intended to stir up any feeling of animosity between individuals or sections. I belong to that class of public men who were secessionists. Every throb of my heart was for the disunion of these States. If that deducts from the force of the statements that I have made to-day, it is due to candor and to you to admit it. I confess that I believed in the right of secession and that I believed in the propriety of its exercise. I will say further that it was a cherished conception of my mind: that of two great free Republics on this continent, each pursuing its own destiny and the destiny of its people and their happiness according to its own will.

But, sir, that conception is gone; it is sunk for ever out of sight. Another one has come in its place; and, by the way, it is my first love. . . . May I tell you what it is, sir? It stands before me now, simple in its majesty and sublime in its beauty. It is that of one grand, mighty, indivisible Republic upon this continent, throwing its loving arms around all sections, omnipotent for protection, powerless for oppression, cursing none, blessing all! [85]

Two years later, after the severe illness of both himself and his wife, Lamar returned to Washington to deliver a speech on the matter of the tariff. To what was almost a joint session of Congress, since members of the House filled the galleries and sat in the aisles, Lamar spoke for nearly three

[85] For versions of the speech, see *Congressional Record*, 47th Cong., Special Senate sess., pp. 154-59; Mayes, *Lamar*, pp. 739-48.

hours. Demands had mounted in the early 1880's to reduce the tariff. Lamar had been instrumental in placing in the platform of the Democratic party the tariff-for-revenue-only plank in the 1880 campaign.[86] In 1883, as the issue was debated in the Senate, Lamar listened, prepared, and on February 7, made his extended address. First, he reviewed the other speeches which had been given in the series. He next defined the situation existing in the industries which were demanding high protective tariffs. Then he presented a comprehensive history of tariffs for the purpose of categorizing them into those designed for revenue and those for protection. He thus laid the foundation for disproving the contentions of the protectionists that American business prospered best when protected by a high tariff. His evidence, chiefly statistics, was next presented to prove the opposite.

The speech was a forceful call to the Senate to heed the demands of the people for reduced tariffs and to disregard the wails of the industrialists. The folly of industrialists and the protective interests in refusing to recognize the strength of the agricultural vote was placing the manufacturer in a position comparable to that of the Southern slave advocate in 1861:

I, sir, have seen something of this in my own experience. I saw a great institution, which was more firmly intrenched in statutes and organic law than the manufacturers are in this tariff law, become an object of popular uprising. I was among those, sir, who shared in the attempt to resist it; and I saw that institution go down—with all its vast capital, with all the political privileges which it conferred, with all the constitutional rights by which it was guaranteed—go down beneath the irreversible fiat of the American people. Sir, I warn the manufacturers of this country. The hand-writing is upon the wall of this protective system, and I trust that they will have the intelligence to comprehend its import.[87]

Tariff reductions were not possible as early as 1883. Lamar could do no more in his speech on the tariff than urge action not immediately possible.[88]

Before leaving the Senate, Lamar made one more brief but important speech. The Senate, in a Committee of the Whole, had under consideration a bill to aid in the establishment and temporary support of common schools. Long associated with education and a profound advocate of its support, Lamar

[86] Cate, *op. cit.*, p. 395.

[87] For versions of the speech, see *Congressional Record*, 47th Cong., 2d sess., pp. 4527-34; Mayes, *Lamar*, pp. 748-73.

[88] An interesting commentary from a protectionist newspaper regarding Lamar's speech is the following: "It is a misfortune for Mr. Lamar, and not for Mr. Lamar only, that his brilliant rhetoric and impressive oratory have not always been employed for the public welfare. When a man of such gifts makes a mistake, and gives his aid to the wrong side, the effect is sure to be remembered. Thereafter men may admire the oratory, but they distrust his reasoning, and do not dare to follow his leadership." *New York Tribune*, February 9, 1885.

was well equipped to participate in the discussion. He envisioned the national importance of the measure and saw very special benefits for the South. Specifically, he viewed the bill as a means of producing racial harmony, saying,

In my opinion, it is the first step, and the most important step, that this government has ever taken, in the direction of the solution of what is called the race problem; and I believe that it will tell more powerfully and decisively upon the future destinies of the colored race in America than any measure or ordinance that has yet been adopted in reference to it. . . .

He saw no dangerous precedent in federal aid to education: "I do not think that it is wise or just reasoning to say that a thing which is right in itself, beneficent in its objects, may be in the future perverted into a wrong; nor do I anticipate it." He reviewed the specific educational needs of the South and emphasized how rural and sparsely populated areas made costly the education of the citizenry. He found in the low salaries of teachers a reason for national aid: "You cannot command . . . teachers with the small salary that we are compelled to give them . . . from the State revenue that we raise by our taxation; and it is true of other States." Lamar stressed his ethical right to discuss the subject, saying, "I know something about this difficulty, for I have been connected with the education of the youth of the South. . . ." [89]

Thus Lamar brought to a close his speaking career in Congress. He had earnestly sought reconciliation. His speeches provide evidence that he sought it. Three ideas permeated all that he said: the war was unalterably over; the understanding of each other's problems would reunite the North and South; and what benefited the one was good for the other and for the Union as well.

The Calhoun Address: Lamar's Valedictory

In choosing his Cabinet, Grover Cleveland, the first Democratic President after the Civil War, turned to the South for two members and asked Lamar to be Secretary of the Interior. In response to the invitation, Lamar wrote Cleveland:

In accepting this important trust allow me to thank you personally for the honor you have done me and to express even more warmly my grateful sense of the obligation you have conferred upon the South in giving one of its representatives an opportunity of showing how loyally and faithfully it desires to serve the interests of a common country.[90]

[89] For versions of the speech, see *Congressional Record*, 48th Cong., 1st sess., pp. 2368-71; Mayes, *Lamar*, pp. 774-79.

[90] Lamar to President-elect Cleveland, February 21, 1885 (Cleveland MSS, Library of Congress, Washington, D. C.).

Thus Lamar prepared to assume the varied duties of the Cabinet post, which included the responsibilities of administering the pensions of the former federal soldiers.

His speaking career was over except for a limited number of occasional addresses. One speech, "John C. Calhoun—His Life, Character, and Public Services," delivered at the unveiling of a monument in honor of the South Carolinian, at Charleston, April 26, 1887, was among the most important of his life. Although the address, lengthy and philosophical in nature, has been largely relegated to oblivion in the days since its delivery, its importance cannot be overlooked. As Frederick Jackson Turner evolved and expressed in subsequent years his frontier theory of American history, he referred to Lamar's speech for support and evidence:

> But the purchase of Louisiana was called out by frontier needs and demands. As frontier States accrued to the Union the national power grew. In a speech on the dedication of the Calhoun monument Mr. Lamar explained: "In 1789 the States were the creator of the Federal Government, and 1861 the Federal Government was the creator of a large majority of the States." [91]

Whether Lamar's influence on Turner was great or small, Turner's citation is noteworthy for his appreciation of the manner in which Lamar demonstrated and expressed broad evolutionary concepts of American history in the Calhoun address. "Moreover," as Cate observes, "this was to be, as he intended, his valedictory to the people of the South and the nation, and it was to be expected that he would renew his plea for the death of sectional animosities and for the fostering of the broadest nationalism." [92]

In the parlor of Mrs. W. A. Snowden of Charleston, eleven women of the state had met on January 23, 1854, to organize the Ladies Calhoun Monument Association. By 1858 the cornerstone was laid, but the Civil War put a stop to further progress. In 1871 the association began its efforts again, and by 1886 the monument was completed. The Gentlemen's Auxiliary Committee then placed before the association the names of various individuals who might deliver the address at the unveiling. Lamar was chosen and, in April, 1887, he spoke. Assembled on the occasion were special regiments of troops, military bands, civil societies of many sorts. There were church organizations, medical societies, high-school and college groups. Other distinguished visitors included leaders in such lodge organizations as Free Masons and Knights of

[91] Frederick Jackson Turner, *The Frontier in American History* (New York: Henry Holt & Co., 1921), p. 25. For a statement regarding the influence of Lamar on Turner, see Cate, *op. cit.*, p. 465. For contrary opinion, see Charles S. Sydnor, review of Cate's *Lucius Q. C. Lamar*, in *Journal of Southern History*, I (August, 1935), 406-7.

[92] Cate, *op. cit.*, p. 465.

Pythias. There were foreign consuls, members of Cleveland's Cabinet, and state and local officials.[93] It was estimated that 5,000 visitors were in the city for the occasion, and that 15,000 heard the address, 1,400 of whom were seated on an immense, stage behind the speaker. Following a prayer and the playing of "Dixie" by the bands, six children, descendants of Calhoun, pulled the cords unveiling the monument. A nineteen-gun salute sounded just before Lamar spoke in dedication. The monument had cost $44,000.[94]

Lamar knew well in advance that he was to deliver the address. As early as October, 1886, he wrote Carl Schurz: "I am meditating a speech on John C. Calhoun. This is a subject on which your thoughts and mine would hardly move on the same plane, and if they did they would perhaps conflict; nevertheless, I would like to talk with you about it." [95] The dedication ceremonies were originally scheduled for November,[96] but in September Lamar was pleading with the Charleston Committee on Arrangements that spring would be more ideal for the occasion, and was lamenting the fact that "pressure of official engagements...gives me but little time for continuous preparation of a speech." [97] Lamar was made happy by the choice of April, and wrote in February: "I have not yet made an attempt to construct the opening sentence. The adumbration of the speech as a whole, is upon my mind, and if I had you to talk it over and to put into the materialization of words the inarticulate ideas in my mind, I would feel some assurance of its taking shape." He did, however, indicate the degree of preparation by his further statement: "I would like—first, to speak of the fact that his statue is erected not in the center of political, nor in the emporium of commercial capital, but in his own native state where he lived all his life and was buried." He had actually outlined what was ultimately to be expressed.[98] Much meditation preceded actual

[93] Clarence Cunningham (ed.), *A History of the Calhoun Monument* (Charleston: Lucas, Richardson & Co., 1888), *passim*.

[94] *New York Times*, April 27, 1887.

[95] Lamar to Schurz, October 2, 1886 (Schurz MSS, Library of Congress, Washington, D. C.).

[96] Lamar to Col. H. E. Young, June 9, 1886 (Letter Press Books, Department of Archives and History, Jackson, Miss.).

[97] Lamar to Col. H. E. Young, September 24, 1886, *ibid*.

[98] Lamar to Donn Piatt, February 23, 1887, *ibid*. The contents of the speech were crystallizing. Lamar stated to Piatt that following the introductory remarks he desired as a second point to treat of Calhoun in three particulars: "The affection and love between the people and himself; his private character and his life as a planter, and the picture of his home life; the domestic influence of the Southern planter and the manner in which those influences shaped the character and policies of the Southern people. Second—that it is due to him for his intellectual contributions to the age, apart altogether from his imposing career as a statesman in the House of Representatives during the war of 1812, his services in the Cabinet under Monroe, his vice-Presidency, and his

composition. Lamar wrote George W. Curtis in appreciation of certain suggestions offered: "...if the speech were anywhere near completion, I would
submit the manuscript at once to you so that you could make for me 'an abstract
of it, bringing it into a condensed shape.' " [99] Because the address evolved as
a comprehensive and philosophical product of much reflection, one additional
statement of how he prepared it is significant:

As to the address on Calhoun, it was not the result of any immediate or continuous
preparation, but simply noting down, through my private secretary, the result of
long years of reflection upon politics generally, and as expounded by Calhoun especially. I tried to throw the whole doctrine into a consistent whole, very much as
Cousin, in his criticism upon Locke's philosophy, was enabled to develop his own
system of philosophical eclecticism. In other words, the speech was the result of years
of reflection. I do not think in the whole time I had one hour of continuous, un-
broken preparation.[100]

What did Lamar finally compose to say about Calhoun, and how did he,
once more, speak to both the North and the South? In certain respects Lamar
delivered ideas found nowhere else in all his speeches; in other respects the
speech is a synthesis of his best previous utterances, even to the adept phraseology employed. Although Lamar in no previous speeech ever attempted the
whole gamut of what was spoken at Charleston, one is reminded, nevertheless,
of his pre-Civil War portrayal of Southern life: "The Southern planter pene-
trated the dense forests, the tangled brake, the gloomy wilderness of our river
swamps, where pestilence had its abode; and there, day by day and year by
year, amid exposure, hardship, and sickness, his foresight, his prudence, his
self-reliance, his adaptation of means to ends, were called into requisition."
    In the comprehensive pattern of the speech the name of Calhoun appears
in almost every paragraph. With the Carolinian the center of all the discussion,
Lamar treated, inevitably, a great segment of American historical develop-

---

unparalleled parliamentary exhibitions as Senator. . . . third—it is due to him for what
the people saw in their personal intercourse with the man; sterling integrity, stainless
purity of character, disinterestedness and honor, so that a monument to him will be a
monument to the majesty of moral rectitude." In a final section of the speech, Lamar
wished to deal with other matters: "I then wish to take up his political career, and I
believe that if I had the time, or could get your help, I could present him as a national
man to the American people, and his life as one consecrated to the greatness and glory
of the American Republic. I believe I could account for his alleged inconsistencies on
the tariff, bank &c. and show that there was underlying his actions on these subjects a
perfect consistency of subjects, and motive, and principle."
    [99] Lamar to George W. Curtis, April 4, 1887, *ibid.*
    [100] Lamar to H. S. Van Eaton, May 11, 1887, quoted in Mayes, *Lamar,* pp. 511-12.

ment. He drew upon European backgrounds for such names as Thucydides, Tacitus, Livy, Montesquieu, Guizot, Gibbon, Hume, Burke, and Macaulay. He ranged beyond political theories into the realms of philosophy and theology. It was the address of a scholar who, with historical and philosophical perspective, interpreted Calhoun as the expounder of the doctrine of nullification, yet presented him as being no less devoted to the Union than Webster or Clay.

The traits of Calhoun as a Southerner at Fort Hill, personifying the agricultural life of the planter, caused Lamar to rejoice that the monument was to be in South Carolina rather than in the National Capital "or in the emporium of American material civilization." Communities of the South that produced Washington, Jackson, Jefferson, Marshall, Clay, and Taney produced Calhoun. To his people of South Carolina, Calhoun belonged. His intellectual qualities and "stainless purity of life, his sterling virtue and integrity of character" constituted reasons enough for the erection of the monument.

This in essence, was Lamar's exordium, and he stated it in transition to other materials in the speech: "And now, fellow-citizens, I must take him away from your hearts, where he is enshrined in choicest affection and reverence, and bear him before those stern, ultimate judges: history, posterity, country, and God." Lamar traced events of American history before Calhoun's day— in the Colonial era, in the period of the Revolution, the making of the Constitution, and the Louisiana Purchase. Later events—those from the War of 1812 to the Civil War with which Calhoun was identified—involving conflict in ideologies, the tragedy of secession, and the darker days of Reconstruction—were placed early in the speech:

I have prefaced what I have to say of Mr. Calhoun with this brief sketch of the controversy in which he bore a part, because I believe if he were here to-day and could see his own South Carolina . . . he would say to her . . . she sacrifices no principle and falsifies no sentiment in accepting the verdict, determined, henceforth, to seek the happiness of her people, their greatness and glory, in the greatness and glory of the American Republic.

He would have told her, if such counsel were necessary, that a people who in form surrender and profess to submit, yet continue to secretly nurse old resentments and past animosities and cherish delusive schemes of reaction and revenge, will sooner or later degenerate into baseness and treachery and treason.

The specific services of Calhoun were treated in detail. His positions on all issues from 1809 to 1850—the War of 1812, the tariff, nullification, the National Bank, the Mexican War—and his relations with Presidents and senatorial colleagues were delineated as a "conflict between his love for the Union and his love for the Southern people." Describing differences among statesmen, Lamar observed:

The only difference between Mr. Calhoun, on the one hand, Webster and Clay and such statesmen, on the other, was that the measures hostile to slavery which they sometimes countenanced, and at other times advocated, he saw and predicted were in conflict with these guarantees in the constitution, and that their direct tendency and inevitable effect, and, in many cases, avowed motive, was the destruction of slavery in the States.

Lamar made clear that Calhoun loved the Union no less than his contemporaries. Insistence on the constitutional guarantees of slavery as an essential to the preservation of the Union, in a day when the course of history was moving in the opposite direction, was Calhoun's tragic sorrow: "Vain the forms of law! vain the barriers of the constitution! vain the considerations of State policy! vain the eloquence and the compromises of statesmen! ... They were all swept away before the irresistible force of the civilization of the nineteenth century, whose moral sentiment demanded the extinction of slavery."

Did Lamar dare to be critical of Calhoun? Could he do more than show that the greatness and the tragedy of Calhoun was that the current of American history was running against him? He could not declare that Calhoun was in error as to the historical constitutional guarantees protecting slavery. Rather, Calhoun's mistake was that of the great majority of Southerners. He noted this error of Calhoun and spoke words fittingly selected for Southern and Northern hearers and readers in 1887:

> Every benefit which slavery conferred upon those subject to it, all the ameliorating and humanizing tendencies which it introduced into the life of the African, all the elevating agencies which lifted him higher in the scale of rational and moral being, were the elements of the future and inevitable destruction of the system. The mistake that was made by the Southern defenders of slavery was in regarding it as a permanent form of society instead of a process of emergence and transition from barbarism to freedom. If at this very day the North or the American Union were to propose to reestablish the institution, it would be impracticable; the South could not and would not accept it as a boon. Slavery as it existed then could not exist under the present commercial and industrial systems of Europe and America. The existing industrial relations of capital and labor, had there been no secession, no war, would of themselves have brought about the death of slavery.[101]

---

[101] For a version of the speech revised by Lamar, see Mayes, *Lamar*, pp. 779-801. The Calhoun address was perhaps the longest speech Lamar ever delivered. Chauncey M. Depew tells of a conversation with Grover Cleveland following his presidency in which Cleveland paid tribute to the services of Lamar and referred to the Calhoun address which Lamar submitted to him before delivery. In reply to Cleveland who thought the speech very long and would require at "least three hours to deliver," and that he should "cut it down," because "A Northern audience would never submit to over an hour," Lamar said, " 'No, Mr. President; a Southern audience expects three hours, and would be better satisfied with five.' " Depew, *op. cit.*, pp. 387-88.

More of significance was said in this address than was comprehended by those who heard it. He included all that was due Calhoun. Over and beyond, he spoke to the South and to the North—in language partially new, but in sentiments reflected over the years. As to its reception and impact, the *New York Times*, calling it "worthy of the orator," declared: "There could be no more striking and conclusive proof of the completeness of the establishment of the Union than the manner in which Mr. Lamar, himself a former secessionist of the extreme type, disposed of the causes of secession and of its absolute, final, and perpetual defeat." The *Times* called it "a speech for the present and the future," and added that it "put aside, in a eulogy of the greatest of State sovereignty leaders and before an audience of his devoted admirers, the chief aims of that leader's career, the chief of his avowed principles, as something buried and the tomb sealed, and turned with hopeful spirit toward the lesson of the leader's life for his countrymen to-day." [102]

Conclusion

Among Lamar's lifelong sources of happiness was his membership at the University of Mississippi in the Sigma Alpha Epsilon fraternity. If one wishes for a tangible manifestation of the recognition and influence of speaking, one may today view the Peace Window in the Sigma Alpha Epsilon Temple at Evanston, Illinois, which was inspired by Lamar's eulogy on Sumner. The window, which pictures Christ in the center and a Union and Confederate soldier on each side, is a forceful reminder of the philosopher, dreamer, and statesman whose career ran concurrently with the expansion of the Deep South, the civil struggle for the essential features of its genteel agrarianism, and the convulsive aftermath of the war—reconstruction and reconciliation.

Born and reared in Georgia, tested and trusted in Mississippi, Lamar served the entire South. In so doing, he was never voluble or profuse; in his entire political career Lamar scarcely averaged more than one major speech a year in Congress. Nevertheless, when the defense of Southern institutions called for a clear, logical explanation, Lamar spoke. When the grievous wrongs of the postwar South needed clarification, Lamar spoke again. When the place of the South in the national scene needed definition, Lamar defined the position.

The immediate effect of Lamar's speeches was favorable. Opponents, including congressional contemporaries, such as Blaine and Hoar, were moved to admiration. Newspapers from coast to coast reprinted his speeches either in part or in their entirety, with complimentary editorial comment. The audiences

[102] *New York Times*, April 27, 1887.

present were often large and responsive. He received more requests for public speeches than he was able to fill. He delivered outstanding public addresses to the New York Chamber of Commerce, and at the unveiling of the statue of Calhoun. From time to time he spoke also at commencement exercises at some educational institution, notably Emory University.

The death of Lamar in 1893 occasioned many comments and appraisals. His life and services were reviewed, his positions before and after the war were analyzed, his personal traits of character and temperament were universally portrayed, and his speeches and speaking were observed as the essential medium through which his greatest influences were exerted. The *New York Times* which entitled its account "Few Men Who Had Won Such General Respect," declared: "Justice Lamar was interesting in being unlike the average man. He was a student, a thoughtful man, a man of sentiment, a delightful talker, strangely enough a man also of great force, with a reserved manner in public, and with a great horror of being called upon to speak when there was nothing to be said but common places."[103] The *New York Herald* viewed Lamar's eulogy on Sumner as his most significant contribution. It said: "He had been known ever since the ... war as one of the most eminent statesmen from the South, and his speech on the death of Charles Sumner, breathing a broad spirit of sincerity, as it did, and coming from one who had been the statesman's bitterest opponent, created a sensation. It was the great topic of the day...."[104] Another paper declared: "In sterling integrity, fidelity to conviction, and courageous stand for his convictions, in spite even of the demands of his constituents, Justice Lamar was one of the notable figures in American politics.... American politics would profit by a greater display of the Old Roman virtues practiced by Justice Lamar."[105]

While Northern papers printed many fine tributes, Southern papers printed even more devoted ones. Of the hundreds of appraisals, that published in the *Atlanta Constitution* may be viewed as among the best:

> The typical American has been the subject of much discussion. Some have found him in Lincoln, and others point to Lee. Perhaps it will not be amiss to take up another branch of the question—the typical Southerner. We believe that there will be no dissenting voice when we name Lucius Q. C. Lamar. Chivalric and yet conservative, imaginative and yet practical, scholarly and yet a man of affairs, 'loving a nation into peace,' and yet devoted to his native South—Lamar was all this and more.[106]

[103] *Ibid.,* January 25, 1893.
[104] *New York Herald,* January 24, 1893.
[105] *Public Opinion* (Washington), XIV (February 4, 1893), 421.
[106] *Constitution* (Atlanta), January 27, 1893.

The tributes of political opponents may be viewed as additionally significant in revealing the traits and influences of Lamar. George F. Hoar, like James G. Blaine, was an opponent of Lamar through years of congressional association. Nevertheless, few men earned Hoar's admiration as did Lamar. Hoar described Lamar's speaking as follows: "Lamar was one of the most delightful of men. His English style, both in conversation and in public speaking, was fresh and original, well adapted to keep his hearers expectant and alert, and to express the delicate and subtle shades of meaning that were required for the service of his delicate and subtle thought." [107] The Sumner eulogy remained in Hoar's memory. He recalled particularly Lamar's statement to the effect that he had "regretted that he had restrained the impulse... to go to Mr. Sumner and offer him his hand and his heart with it." [108] Hoar stated the central purpose of Lamar's postwar life when he wrote: "Yet Mr. Lamar desired most sincerely the reconciliation of the sections, that the age-long strife should come to an end and be forgotten, and that the whole South should share the prosperity and wealth and refinement and contentment, which submission to the new order of things would bring." [109] Hoar could not easily dispose of his memories and associations with Lamar. He recalled his traits of character, abilities in debate and public address, his devotions to duty and conviction, and his specific contributions in the House and Senate. Hoar's greatest tribute may be found in the reflection: "Afterward Mr. Lamar was made an Associate Justice of the Supreme Court of the United States. I voted against him—in which I made a mistake." [110]

The years of the world have been filled with philosophers who have tried to quiet the human prejudices of their fellows. The problems to which Lamar lent his abilities have not been, nor perhaps ever will be, settled. His efforts must be judged in terms of the effectiveness with which he asserted his sincere convictions.

SELECTED BIBLIOGRAPHY

Collections

Clement C. Clay, Jr. Papers. Duke University Library, Durham, North Carolina.
Grover Cleveland Papers. Library of Congress, Washington, D. C.
Jefferson Davis Papers. Mississippi Department of Archives and History, Jackson, Mississippi.
Lucius Q. Lamar Papers. Mississippi Department of Archives and History, Jackson, Mississippi.

[107] Hoar, *op. cit.*, II, 175.
[108] *Ibid.*, p. 176.
[109] *Ibid.*, p. 176.
[110] *Ibid.*, p. 177.

American Public Address

L. Q. C. Lamar—Robert Harper Papers, Georgia Department of Archives and History, Atlanta, Georgia.
Carl Schurz Papers. Library of Congress, Washington, D. C.

Books and Periodicals

ADAMS, HENRY. *The Education of Henry Adams: An Autobiography.* Boston: Houghton Mifflin Co., 1918.

BLAINE, JAMES G. *Twenty Years of Congress: From Lincoln to Garfield.* 2 vols. Norwich, Conn.: Henry Bill, 1886.

BUCK, PAUL H. *The Road to Reunion, 1865-1900.* Boston: Little, Brown & Co., 1937.

BULLOCK, HENRY MORTON. *A History of Emory University.* Nashville, Tenn.: Parthenon Press, 1936.

BURNHAM, PHILIP. "L. Q. C. Lamar," *North American Review,* 240 (December, 1935).

CATE, WIRT ARMISTEAD. *Lucius Q. C. Lamar: Secession and Reunion.* Chapel Hill: University of North Carolina Press, 1935.

CUNNINGHAM, CLARENCE (ed.), *A History of the Calhoun Monument.* Charleston, S. C.: Lucas, Richardson & Co., 1888.

COULTER, E. MERTON. *The Confederate States of America, 1861-1865.* Baton Rouge: Louisiana State University Press, 1950.

———. *The South during Reconstruction, 1865-1877.* Baton Rouge: Louisiana State University Press, 1947.

DEPEW, CHAUNCEY M. *My Memories of Eighty Years.* New York: Charles Scribner's Sons, 1924.

HALSELL, WILLIE D. "Prelude to a Career: L. Q. C. Lamar Tries Politics," *Journal of Mississippi History,* VII (April, 1945).

HOAR, GEORGE F. *Autobiography of Seventy Years.* 2 vols. New York: Charles Scribner's Sons, 1903.

LAMAR, CLARINDA PENDLETON. *Joseph Rucker Lamar.* New York: Knickerbocker Press, 1926.

MAYES, EDWARD. *Lucius Q. C. Lamar: His Life, Times, and Speeches.* Nashville, Tenn.: Publishing House of The Methodist Episcopal Church, South, 1896.

NEVINS, ALLAN. *The Emergence of Lincoln.* 2 vols. New York: Charles Scribner's Sons, 1950.

OWSLEY, FRANK L. "Lucius Quintus Cincinnatus Lamar," *American Review,* V (September, 1935).

PHILLIPS, U. B. (ed.) "The Correspondence of Robert Toombs, Alexander Stephens, and Howell Cobb," *American Historical Association Annual Report for 1911.*

RAINWATER, PERCY LEE. *Mississippi: Storm Center of Secession.* Baton Rouge: Louisiana State University Press, 1938.

STREETER, DONALD C. "The Major Public Addresses of Lucius Q. C. Lamar during the Period 1874-1890," *Speech Monographs,* XVI (August, 1949).

TURNER, FREDERICK JACKSON. *The Frontier in American History.* New York: Henry Holt & Co., 1921.

WADE, JOHN DONALD. *Augustus Baldwin Longstreet: A Study of the Development of Culture in the South.* New York: The Macmillan Co., 1924.

WILLIAMS, BEN AMES (ed.) *A Diary from Dixie,* by Mary Boykin Chesnut. Boston: Houghton Mifflin Co., 1949.

WOODWARD, C. VANN. *Origins of the New South, 1877-1913.* Baton Rouge: Louisiana State University Press, 1951.

Lucius Q. C. Lamar

WOODWARD, C. VANN. *Reunion and Reaction, The Compromise of 1877 and the End of Reconstruction.* Boston: Little, Brown & Co., 1951.

Newspapers

Clarion Ledger (Jackson, Miss.), January 25, 1893.
Constitution (Atlanta, Ga.), January 27, 1893.
National Republican (Washington, D. C.), April 28, 1874.
New York Herald, January 24, 1893.
New York Times, December 26, 1859; April 28, 1874; April 27, 1887; January 25, 1893.
New York Tribune, June 13, February 9, 1885.
Richmond Examiner, June 3, 1861.

Government Documents

Congressional Globe and Appendix. 35th Cong., 1st sess.; 36th Cong., 1st sess.
Congressional Record and Appendix. 43d Cong., 1st sess.; 44th Cong., 1st and 2d sess. 45th Cong., 2d and 3d sess.; 46th Cong., 2d sess.; 47th Cong., 2d and spec. Senate sess.

7

Dwight L. Moody

by ROBERT B. HUBER

Dwight L. Moody was born in Northfield, Massachusetts, on February 5, 1837. The death of his father, when Moody was only four, left the family in dire financial straits, and, as a result, Dwight received only the equivalent of a fifth-grade education. From 1854 to 1860 he worked as a shoe salesman in Boston and Chicago. Although he was quite successful in business, having accumulated $5,000 by the time he was twenty-one, he gave up salesmanship for religious work. From 1860 to 1873 he engaged in a variety of religious endeavors; he continued to build the Sunday school he had established in the slums of Chicago; he served in the capacity of a chaplain to the Civil War soldiers; although unordained, he founded and became the minister for a church; and he took a leading role in Sunday school work and conventions throughout the nation. The huge revivals, held first in the British Isles and later in America from 1873 to 1877, established him as the outstanding evangelist of his day. Throughout the remainder of his life Moody continued his evangelistic tours. A second tour of the British Isles was made during the years of 1881 through 1884; while a third was conducted during 1891 and 1892. Realizing his own lack of education and believing that poor youths should have such opportunities, he established the Northfield Seminary for girls in 1879 and the Mount Hermon School for boys in 1881. In 1880 he began the Northfield Summer Bible Conferences; one outgrowth of these conferences was the formation of the Student Volunteer Movement in 1886. In order to train young people in evangelistic and missionary work, he founded the Bible Institute for Home and Foreign Missions in 1886 in Chicago; since his death it has become known as the Moody Bible Institute. In order to make religious music and literature more readily available, he also became a publisher; the first edition of *Sacred Songs and Solos* for the people of the British Isles came from the press in 1873; *Gospel Hymns* was first published in America in 1875; in 1895 was begun the Colportage Library Publications of religious books and tracts. Moody's evangelistic tour of 1899 was interrupted by his death on December 22.

An Evangelist Speaks to Huge Crowds

A young medical student was on his way home from treating a patient in the slums of London. Walking along he came to a tabernacle where religious revival services were being held. Curiosity led him to the door, where he observed an old gentleman delivering a long-winded prayer. Suddenly, and much to the young man's astonishment, a stockily-built, energetic figure moved to the front of the platform and announced, "While our brother is finishing his prayer, let us sing hymn number...." Attracted by this unusual evangelist, the young man stayed for the sermon. So moved was he by the whole experience that it became the turning point in his life. He abandoned his plans for practising medicine in London and became a medical missionary to the Labrador Coast. That young medical student was William T. Grenfell.[1]

The student of public speaking and persuasion would be interested in the evangelist, in a speaker who could break through decades of tradition in order that the meeting might be conducted to produce the greatest possible results. That evangelist was Dwight L. Moody. Today, people may know about him through the Moody Bible Institute in Chicago. Others may know of the preparatory schools of Mount Hermon for boys and Northfield Seminary for girls in Massachusetts. Many in America have sung from his *Gospel Hymns,* numbers one to seven, hymnbooks that were published as a result of his services. People of Great Britain have purchased seventy million copies of his *Sacred Songs and Solos.*

Others have been influenced by him more indirectly, perhaps. Under his leadership the Student Volunteer Movement was started; it still continues in various denominational colleges. He was a pioneer spirit in the Young Men's Christian Association in America, and numerous other associations owe much to him for financial assistance. Summer Bible Conferences and summer religious camps and conferences received their early impetus from him.

Moody was distinguished for drawing large crowds. At the peak of his greatest meetings, he was able to draw 20,000 persons daily through the week and from 35,000 to 40,000 on Sundays to hear him preach. He was able to make noon prayer meetings on weekdays attractive enough to draw six to seven thousand persons. Four months of meetings in one city drew audiences totaling two and a half million, and during his career he spoke to nearly 100,000,000 persons. He seldom took up collections at his meetings except to aid some religious institution, yet at Philadelphia on January 19, 1876, in one collection, $100,226 was received.[2]

The modern student of rhetoric is anxious to discover the sources of persuasive power of the great speakers of the past. This study endeavors to uncover those sources under the following formula: the stimuli of Moody as a speech personality plus the stimuli of the content of the speeches plus the

---

[1] William T. Grenfell, *Congregationalist and Christian World,* November 12, 1914, p. 633.
[2] *Philadelphia Public Ledger,* January 22, 1876.

stimuli of the techniques in managing the crowds plus the psychological factors peculiar to the people of the time equal the results or reactions that the revivals produced.

Moody as a Speech Personality

The "ethos" of the speaker is a well-recognized force in persuasion, but modern writers often use the term "speech personality." Modern psychologists tell us that if we are to understand the personality of a man, we must discover "his persistent tendencies to make certain kinds and qualities of adjustment." [3] Let us observe those persistent tendencies of adjustment in Moody. His ancestors were English who had migrated to America and aided in the establishment of the colonies in New England. They possessed no superior family traits, no literary genius, no special prominence in politics, no superiority in the professional world. Their educational desires did not exceed those of the average citizen of the communities in which they lived. In the main, they were weavers, brickmasons, carpenters, and farmers. Moody got from them an above-average intelligence, a strong physique, and a physiological organism that abounded with energy.

There were several factors in the first seventeen years of Moody's life that left their imprint upon the mature man. His father died when he was only four years of age and the family was left in poverty. Along with the rest of the children of the family, Moody had to work in order to help the family. As a result, early in life he established habits of hard work. The austerity of the Puritan background of Northfield added a strong religious influence to his life. The Puritan concepts of resourcefulness, self-reliance, industry, thrift, simplicity, and honesty were ideals that were universally taught. In the home, the Puritan traditions of religion were observed. The Sabbath lasted from sundown on Saturday night to sundown on Sunday. The children returned home on Saturday night from their work with the neighbors and the whole family attended church and Sunday school the next day. Church services were held both in the morning and in the afternoon, with Sunday school coming in between. Evidently church and Sunday school attendance was more of a rigid discipline and duty than an inspiration to the young Moody, for he remarked in later life that he often slept through the sermons and that he never attended a prayer meeting until he was seventeen years of age.[4] The hard work, the strict discipline of the Puritan philosophy, and the lack of inspiration from his religion evidently depressed the young lad, for he some-

[3] L. F. Shaffer, *The Psychology of Adjustment* (Boston: Houghton Mifflin Co., 1936), p. 282.

[4] D. L. Moody, *To All People* (New York: E. B. Treat, 1877), p. 184; see also, his *The Great Redemption* (New York: National Library Association, 1888), p. 481.

times rebelled. These were, perhaps, some of the causes for the aggressiveness that dominated his personality throughout his life.

Opportunities for cultural development in the "finer things of life" were infrequent for young Moody. The town itself offered very little except home-talent programs, itinerant entertainers, home debates, and a lyceum program. In general, the town's entertainment was limited to the social gatherings of the various families. Playing cards was thought to be a device of the devil, and many thought dancing to be worse.[5] Moody, required to work because of the poverty of the family, had little opportunity to participate in the social gatherings that did occur. As a result, throughout his life and particularly early in his evangelistic career, he was often characterized as being crude.

Moody was often described as being uneducated. Altogether, he probably received not more than a fifth-grade education. The public schools of his day were rather poor, and not much more than the three R's was taught. Attendance was optional and usually irregular. Moody, being required to help in the busy farm seasons, attended irregularly, and he quit altogether at the age of thirteen. His speaking was marred by faulty pronunciation and errors in grammar, his writing was almost illegible, and his spelling was atrocious. He realized his deficiencies in his later life and worked diligently to overcome them. Thus, Moody's early life started the persisting tendencies of hard work and aggressiveness, and left him deficient in social finesse and formal education.

Business and Conversion

Throughout Moody's boyhood, the establishment and growth of factories in the larger cities brought an exodus of the young people from the villages. Moody became discontented with the prospects of farm life and the few opportunities it offered; he disliked the dullness of the life of the small town. In consequence, in the early months of 1854, shortly after his seventeenth birthday, with five dollars as his only capital, he arrived in Boston.[6] But finding work wasn't so simple; he was quite young and the work on the farm in Northfield was poor training for a business career. His youthful enthusiasm to build a fortune for himself was checked by the discouragement of walking the streets for days without success. He soon ran short of money, and this increased his despair. In later years, he sometimes credited this experience with having directed him to religion.[7]

[5] H. C. Parsons, *A Puritan Outpost, A History of the Town and People of Northfield, Massachusetts* (New York: The Macmillan Co., 1937).

[6] W. R. Moody, *D. L. Moody* (New York: The Macmillan Co., 1931), p. 24.

[7] Rev. Charles F. Goss, *Echoes from the Pulpit and Platform* (Hartford, Conn.: A. D. Worthington & Co., 1900), pp. 172, 173.

The work he finally got was that of a clerk in a shoe store of his uncle, S. S. Holton, located at 43 Court Street.[8] He set about his tasks of learning the shoe business and learning how to sell. He was ambitious and enthusiastic, and his abounding energy often took him out onto the sidewalks to attract customers into the store. He even persuaded his uncle to keep the store open on holidays so that he might share in the profits of sales made when other places of business were closed. Moody progressed rapidly in learning the retail shoe business, and he and his brother Luther were put in charge of a shoe store at 111 Court Street two years after Dwight's arrival in Boston.

The orbit of Moody's activities in Boston centered around his work, his boardinghouse, the Y.M.C.A., and the church and Sunday school he attended. Here Moody was stimulated to try to overcome his lack of education. He began to read more widely, to study arithmetic, and to attend lectures at the Y.M.C.A. The political events of the antislavery movement were so intense at this time as to affect most of the people of Boston. Moody lived and worked within two blocks of Faneuil Hall, and the reverberations of those exciting meetings reached him. William Lloyd Garrison, Theodore Parker, and Wendell Phillips were prominent among the speakers. Moody was a spectator at the Simms and Anthony Burns incidents. He attended Mount Vernon Church for services and Sunday school. This church was organized in 1842, chiefly to secure the services of Edward N. Kirk, D.D., as pastor.[9]

Dr. Kirk had acquired a wide reputation as an evangelist, had conducted revival services in England, Germany, France, and Italy, as well as in the United States, and was still prominent in evangelical movements.[10] So it was an evangelical church with a noted evangelist as pastor that Moody attended in Boston. In his later life Moody paid tribute to Dr. Kirk as "one of the most eloquent men I ever heard." [11]

The experience of conversion was considered to be an important incident in the life of the individual. The convert presumably passed from "darkness into light"; his soul was "no longer lost, but saved." He had now become a member of that group called "Christians," and he was one of that select number who would enjoy the pleasures of heaven after life on earth was finished. Judged from the standpoint of immediate increase in religious activity, conversion may not seem so important, but judged from the standpoint of the individual's own attitude toward it, the experience may be seen to be an

[8] *Boston City Directory*, 1854; W. R. Moody, *D. L. Moody*, p. 26.

[9] Moses King, *King's Handbook of Boston* (Cambridge, Mass.: Moses King, 1878), p. 176.

[10] Justin Windsor (ed.), *Memorial History of Boston* (Boston: James R. Osgood & Co., 1881), III, 412.

[11] See *Great Joy, Sermons and Prayer-Meeting Talks Delivered at the Chicago Tabernacle* (Chicago: E. B. Treat, 1877), p. 236.

extremely important influence in the participant's life. Such was the case with Moody. Edward Kimball taught the class to which Moody had been assigned and it was through him that Moody was converted. Shortly after his conversion and after the usual trial period he became a member of the Mount Vernon Church. That there was a great change in Moody immediately in Boston is unknown, for on September 18, 1856, he arrived in Chicago to seek his fortune there.

Giving Up Business for Religion

Moody's career as a shoe salesman left its stamp upon him as an evangelist selling salvation. This career as a businessman, begun in Boston, was continued in Chicago until 1860. Whereas progress had been slow in Boston, success was rapid in the Midwestern city. His first job, again as a shoe salesman, was with C. E. Wiswall. The pay of thirty dollars a week was good pay for a nineteen-year-old boy in those days. Nor was he to lack promotion long. Before his first year was finished he was transferred from the retail department to become a traveling salesman and credit man.[12] Moody soon found that he could make more money than just enough to live on. There were many opportunities for speculation and investment, and he followed the spirit of the times. A letter to his brother George reveals not only that he was speculating in real estate, but lending money as well. The young Moody wrote:

I can lend money here for two percent a month and get good security. I lent one hundred dollars the other day for seventeen per cent a day! I tell you here is the place to make money. I can make more here in one week than I could in Boston in a month.[13]

After two years with Wiswall, he received an even better position with the firm of C. N. Henderson, wholesale boot and shoe dealers. Evidently he rapidly won the respect of his new employer, for upon the latter's death and, after only one year of service, Moody was made administrator for the estate. Upon the completion of this task, he joined a third shoe firm and worked one more year as a salesman. At the age of twenty-two, and after six years in business, he was earning an annual income of $5,000 and had accumulated from $5,000 to $7,000.[14]

[12] W. R. Moody, *D. L. Moody*, p. 37.
[13] *Ibid.*, p. 39.
[14] Alex Patterson letter to A. P. Fitt (A. P. Fitt Collection, Northfield, Mass.); also, D. L. Moody, in a sermon given in July, 1893, at the Northfield Student Conference, A. P. Fitt Collection.

These six years in the business world left a strong impact upon Moody, the revivalist. Not only did he appear to be a salesman, selling salvation in the pulpit, but he was a superior administrator as well. His training in business management became the foundation for successful administration of the huge revivals and of the various institutions and enterprises he founded or initiated in his later years.

One might well wonder why a young man of twenty-two, having such success in the business world, would give up that work for religious endeavor. The factors involved in Moody's change of vocation reveal much about his personality. The Puritan influence on his early life and his conversion in Boston have already been noted. Immediately upon arriving in Chicago, he sought companionship among the young people of a variety of denominations. The Mission Band, a group of young men from the First Methodist Church, was engaged in distributing religious tracts and invitations to attend church and Sunday school; its members visited the hotels, saloons, billiard parlors, docks, and handed tracts to street pedestrians, as well. Moody participated in the work of this organization. He also rented pews in the Plymouth Congregational Church and, as he himself said, "I went out on the streets button-holing every man that came along to get him into the church. I filled one pew and then I got another, and I filled three pews." [15]

The business collapse of 1857 and the revival which followed became important influences in the life of Moody. With banks and well-established business firms failing, with personal fortunes being lost, with economic security gone, the people of the nation turned to the assurances within their religion. This religious revival in 1857 differed from all previous revivals in the spontaneous outburst of daily noon prayer meetings. In each of the various principal cities of the land, businessmen, professional workers, and laborers paused in the middle of the day to attend prayer services in some large hall. Spurred by this religious fervor, the churches of Chicago began to hold revival services in the evenings. Moody wrote home at the time: "I go to meeting every night. Oh, How I do enjoy it! It seems as if God was here himself. Oh, mother, pray for us. Pray that this work may go on until every knee is bowed. I wish there could be a revival in Northfield, that many might be brought in the field of Christ." [16] It is significant to note that the daily noon prayer services became an integral part of all his revivals in later years.

The Chicago Y.M.C.A. was organized as a result of the revival of 1857, with Moody as one of its most active members. The principal feature of its work during the early years was the daily prayer meeting, and the religious

[15] *The Great Redemption*, pp. 475-76.

[16] W. R. Moody, *The Life of Dwight L. Moody* (Chicago: Fleming H. Revell Company, 1900), p. 48.

efforts growing out of it. Moody could be seen outside, inviting and urging the passing pedestrians to attend the services, with the enthusiasm and energy of the well-known high-pressure salesman of today. He was made chairman of the committee to visit the poor and the sick; and the report of his first year's work showed that he visited 554 families, and bestowed in charity $2,350, raised by the association for that purpose.[17] In the years that were to come, he made the Y.M.C.A. the headquarters for his religious revivals.

Stimulated by the revival, Moody started to recruit scholars for the afternoon Sunday schools. Finding that he had a faculty of getting children to follow him, he started a mission of his own in 1858, just north of the Chicago River. It was in a slum area and the students were recruited from among poor families. The growth of the Sunday school was rapid and, by 1860, the average attendance was more than a thousand. It attracted wide attention and brought many observers and helpers. Among the helpers were Isaac H. Burch, president of one of the banks, and John V. Farwell, a prominent merchant. President-elect Abraham Lincoln came as an observer. In going from home to home, Moody found that opportunities for church attendance were just as scarce for the parents as for the children; therefore, he began the evening Gospel services which later developed into an organized church.

Thus, while Moody was having success in the business world, his success in the field of religious endeavors was even greater. While he was earning the approval of his business associates as a shoe salesman, he was attracting the attention, help, and approval of many important persons for his religious work. The serious illness of one of his Sunday school teachers provided the occasion for Moody to give up selling shoes and to devote all of his time to religion. The teacher felt that, before he died, he must convert every member of the class. Moody accompanied him on the mission. The last efforts of this dying man and his success in converting every member of the class made such a strong impression on Moody that he decided to give all his time to "saving souls."[18]

An Evangelist Evolves

The years of 1860 to 1873 were filled by Moody with energetic religious activities, and became the years of training for evangelism. During these years he learned to speak and to preach; he learned the techniques of getting

---

[17] A. T. Andreas, *History of Chicago* (Chicago: A. T. Andreas Co., 1885), II, 511, 512.

[18] Moody often told this story in detail in his revival meetings. See D. L. Moody, *Great Joy, Sermons and Prayer-meeting Talks Delivered at the Chicago Tabernacle,* pp. 154-55.

people to work in religious activity; he learned the best methods for conducting meetings; he matured as an administrator; he conducted his first revivals. Although he gained in stature and prominence and became known nationally in Sunday school and Y.M.C.A. conventions, no one would have predicted in 1873 that by 1876 he would have become the outstanding evangelist of his time; no one would have predicted that he would speak to as many as 40,000 to 50,000 people in one day, or that in his lifetime his total audience as an evangelist would approximate 100,000,000. The key to his later success lay in these years.

Hardly had Moody retired from business when the Civil War broke out. The Y.M.C.A. in various areas inaugurated a program of distributing religious literature, holding religious services, and furnishing other reading material and articles necessary for health and recreation. Moody's part in all this was that of both administrator and participant. He visited the hospitals, camps, and battlefields, distributing supplies, aiding chaplains, and holding special prayer meetings. He visited the sick and wounded both on the battlefield and in the hospitals, often writing letters home for the soldiers, or even writing the parents of soldiers who had died on the field of battle. Throughout all these visitations, Moody was concerned with the "saving of souls." He used a personal type of evangelism, often talking to an audience of one. Throughout his life, this direct personal method of speaking predominated even though his audience numbered 10,000. These talks with wounded or dying soldiers on the battlefields brought to Moody a broader understanding of the problems, troubles, and conflicts of mankind. Many of the stories he used as illustrations in later years were drawn from these experiences among the soldiers. Periodically, he would return to Chicago, where Camp Douglas was located. Under the leadership of Moody, Jacobs, and John B. Farwell, a chapel was built, and Moody held religious meetings for both the Union soldiers and Confederate prisoners.[19] This work in the Civil War brought Moody some of his earliest experiences and training in speaking and in conducting religious services.

A second step in Moody's training for evangelism lay in the establishment of a church in connection with the Sunday school. By 1864, mothers and fathers of children attending the Sunday school had gained sufficient strength to construct a building and organize as a nondenominational church. Regular pastors were hired until 1870, after which time Moody served, although he frequently called on others to help him conduct services or preach. The evangelistic Moody believed in putting converts and church members to work

[19] For detailed accounts, see Rev. Lemuel Moss, *Annals of the United States Christian Commission* (Philadelphia: J. B. Lippincott & Co., 1868), pp. 72-77, 83-87, ff.; Rev. E. B. Tuttle, *History of Camp Douglas* (Chicago: J. R. Walsh & Co., 1865).

and the result was that annually 800 meetings were held. By 1873, the church was a strong, active, religious organization of 300 members.

A third part of Moody's training for leadership and management of institutions and public meetings was achieved through his capacity as an officer and, later, president of the Chicago Y.M.C.A. Despite all his efforts in other fields, Moody spent more time with this work than any other. He was the agent for the City Relief Society to take care of the poor. He had from 500 to 800 people dependent upon him for their daily food. Because the noon prayer meetings had diminished in size through the war years, Moody went to work to build their attendance. In 1866, the daily attendance was 50 to 100 and, by 1869, the daily attendance ranged from 100 to 500 persons. The personal visitations of Moody and his recruits to saloons and to business firms, and their appeals to pedestrians brought the increased attendance. In the earlier years, ministers and church leaders directed meetings, but by 1867 Moody was the most frequent leader. He assisted the Mission Committee of the Y.M.C.A., canvassing the city to get the families to attend church and distributing tracts, Bibles, and religious literature. The committee responsible for planning open-air meetings held over 200 services annually, with congregations ranging from 50 to 1,000 persons. Moody was a frequent speaker at these meetings. Two publications were inaugurated under his direction: *Heavenly Tidings* and *Everybody's Paper*. Throughout all the activities, evangelistic efforts were dominant. Conversion which brought church membership and religious activity was the objective. Moody gained valuable experience in raising money for the building program. Four hundred thousand dollars was raised for the first building, dedicated in September, 1867. Four months later, it burned. A second Y.M.C.A. building was constructed during the presidency of Moody.[20] Through this experience, he learned to work with the financiers of the city.

The fourth step in his training was received in the state and county Sunday school conventions in Illinois and other states, from 1864 to 1873; he served as presiding officer, speaker, member of the executive councils, and president. Moody was one of three leaders who proceeded to organize the state on the county basis. In a period of two years, every county in the state was organized, and he became one of the frequent leaders of county conventions. His critics, although praising his ability to organize religious activities, often deplored his turning a convention into a revival. Throughout this work, his role was that of a promoter and organizer, not that of an ideational

[20] For detailed accounts, see Edwin Smith, John Grant, and Horace Starkey, *Historical Sketch of the Young Men's Christian Association of Chicago* (Chicago: Published by Y.M.C.A., 1898), pp. 64-84; Richard C. Morse, *History of North American Y.M.C.A.* (New York: Association Press, 1900), pp. 62-124.

reformer, yet he shared in instituting uniform Sunday school lessons. Having gained success and prestige in Illinois, Moody got calls from other states to participate in similar state conventions. He played a similar role in the state and international Y.M.C.A.

A fifth phase of his training was the conducting of revival services. It is difficult to mark the beginning of pulpit evangelism by Moody, nor is it easy to determine the time and place of his first revival experience. Reports in *The Advance* indicate that he conducted revival meetings as early as 1867. Moody probably conducted revival services at various churches before 1873, but not frequently.

The sixth type of training came through three trips to Great Britain for study under religious leaders in that country, and for establishing relationships with the Plymouth Brethren. The first trip was in 1867. For four months he visited England, Ireland, Scotland, and Paris. A second trip was taken in 1870 and a third in 1872. During these trips, he not only studied the habits, customs, and attitudes of the people of Great Britain but he participated in some of their religious conventions. As often as he could, he went to hear Charles H. Spurgeon speak. In 1884, Moody spoke at the Spurgeon Jubilee celebration and attested to the great influence of Spurgeon on his life. The Plymouth Brethren was a religious sect, evangelistic in nature, having only lay preachers, and on each trip he spent time attending their conventions. He attended these and other meetings in the role of a listener, taking notes or asking questions of the leaders. Moody learned to know leaders and laid the groundwork for the revivals which he began in 1873.

Thus, the years from 1860 to 1873 were years of training for Moody to become a revivalist. A detailed study of all his activities reveals a slow but certain progress. Moody improved steadily in speaking to larger and larger crowds; he grew to maturity as an administrator; he gained skill in organizing and conducting meetings.

Moody's religious attitudes were derived from various sources. The Puritan influence in his youth led to a conservative view of religion and life. The early Unitarian theology made little impression on him. His was an orthodox theology common to the Baptists, Methodists, Presbyterians, and Congregationalists of his day. His emphasis upon a personal gospel was derived from the prevailing trends of the day and from his acquaintance with the lives of many people through home visitations. The concept of a God of love instead of a God of revenge was becoming more common to the evangelical preaching of the day. The experience of hearing Harry Moorhouse preach seven sermons on successive nights on this theme gave impetus to Moody's belief in a God of love. The prevalent use of concordances gave impetus to Moody's practice of searching the Bible for ideas upon a particular subject. During this period he read biographies and the sermons of other preachers, but his chief reading was the Bible.

The Speaker and His Speeches

I. DELIVERY

Moody had a dynamic speech personality. His gestures were unplanned and seemed to result from the intensity of his feelings concerning the ideas he expressed. He was direct, personal, almost hypnotic. His voice was not particularly rich in quality, but he was adept at varying it to reveal meaning; it carried well throughout auditoriums and had unusual reserves of power. Moody spoke at a rate of more than two hundred words a minute, but the progress of the thought was slow. He varied the pitch as in conversation, avoiding the "cant" of many of the preachers of his day. The various practices in his delivery were unstudied; if the pause was used, it was to let the thought sink in. Although his enunciation and pronunciation were poor, audiences readily understood him; his speech was filled with the elisions common to the language of the streets. Provincial New England language habits remained, and he made frequent mistakes in grammar. Moody had uneducated diction but this did not reduce his persuasiveness for most of his audiences. His unsophisticated language gave rustic charm to the Bible stories he narrated, and made them appear more real. Only the very well-educated sometimes objected to his crude language, believing that it detracted from the sacredness of Bible stories hallowed by time.

He sometimes used special techniques in delivering his sermons. His entry upon the platform at the general services was quite dramatic; he appeared promptly at the scheduled time, one-half hour after the song services had begun, and bowed his head in silent prayer in full veiw of the singing congregation. When he made a humorous remark, he did not tarry for the responding laugh but plunged right on. He dominated the scene completely. If interrupted by outspoken auditors, faintings, or other disturbances, he instantly quelled them or utilized such events to support the theme of his sermon. Directions from the pulpit for needed ventilation were given at any time in the services, even during the sermon. He sometimes asked for affirmation from the pastors seated upon the platform or directed a question to some member of the audience, expecting a verbal answer. However, he never allowed any unique emotionalism to break forth. He preached with the air of "divine commission," holding the Bible in one hand and quoting from it at intervals.

He was characterized by the writers of the day as a businessman selling salvation. He seemed to have come forth from his place of business to set the auditors right on matters of the soul. Earnest, sincere, and genial in manner, he seemed to have an intense personal love and regard for each member of his audience. He seemed to be totally unconscious of self.

2. METHODS OF PREPARATION

Moody never wrote out his speeches. Numerous volumes of his sermons have been published. Other volumes of writing on religious subjects have been attributed to his authorship. Some of these volumes were ghostwritten; others consisted of stenographic reports of speeches published in newspapers. Most of the sermons published after 1880 were ghostwritten either by his son, William R. Moody, or his secretary and son-in-law, A. P. Fitt. As the latter said to the writer, "We tried to capture his style."[21] Probably the most authentic texts of Moody's sermons were those that appeared in the daily newspapers. These were stenographic reports of the sermons delivered from 1875-77 in New York, Chicago, Boston, and Cleveland, and published later in book form.

In choosing the subjects for his sermons, Moody was a pragmatist. He picked a subject, tried it out on an audience, and if it brought the desired results, he used it repeatedly. His main object was to convert his hearers and then get them to go out and convert others. His material for sermons was pragmatically tested. That which was effective in personal conversation, in the inquiry room, or in the prayer meetings was utilized in sermons. His sermons were always in the process of revision; each time he spoke he added new material to replace material found to be ineffective.

For every sermon subject, Moody had a blue linen envelope into which he put the outline of the speech, clippings of thoughts on the subject by outstanding men, clippings from concordances and pamphlets, and pertinent thoughts of his own. Anytime he found anything pertaining to the subject, he added it to the envelope. The envelope containing the sermon notes on "Faith," for example, had seventy-eight pieces of material in addition to the outline. On the outside, he wrote the date and place he had delivered the sermon. For instance, the envelope containing the sermon notes on "The New Birth" reveals that it was delivered 193 times from 1881 to 1899. He did not start recording this data until 1875. Thus, the number after 1875 was quite definite; however, the number of times and places he delivered a particular sermon during his lifetime is difficult to determine.[22]

Moody's most frequent speech purpose was that of securing action in the form of conversion. He sought to get the listeners to go to the inquiry room

[21] A. P. Fitt, in a personal conference with the writer, summer, 1939.

[22] The author examined the contents of 264 of these envelopes contained in the A. P. Fitt and W. R. Moody collections. Altogether, there were slightly more than four hundred of these envelopes at the time of Moody's death.

for personal conferences with the evangelist, ministers, or church members. A second purpose was to get Christian workers and new converts to go out and convert others to Christianity. The third purpose was to give information on how to study the Bible, how to conduct inquiry room meetings, prayer meetings and revival services, and how to bring about conversion.

Moody analyzed his audiences carefully. His background of experience had brought him personal knowledge of all the types and classes of people who constituted his audiences. When speaking to a general audience, he adapted his appeals to all these types. When he spoke to special audiences of young men only, young women only, women only, parents only, businessmen only, or "fallen" women, he adapted his illustrative material to the particular group. When speaking to businessmen, for instance, he drew from his own experiences in business and spoke in terms of stocks, bonds, sales, and keeping accounts.

Moody's two chief sources of sermon material were the Bible and his own personal experiences. He had a wide and thorough knowledge of the Bible, although many suggested that it was not a critical knowledge. To help him study his Bible more thoroughly, he used a concordance and a Scripture-text book. As the years passed, Moody drew more and more upon his ever-expanding experiences with people; each new series of revival meetings brought many experiences to relate, and his daily mail brought letters from various converts and Christian workers. He sometimes quoted from letters in his sermons. Three lesser sources were biographies, particularly of great religious leaders, such as Wesley, Knox, Whitefield; conferences and conventions; and the daily newspaper.

Moody spoke from an outline. He did not indicate the usual three divisions, introduction, discussion, and conclusion, nor did he use digits or letters to indicate main or sub-headings. On the contrary, he used a key-word or short-phrase outline. The outlines were written on sheets of paper 8½ by 11 inches. These sheets were folded crosswise in the middle; the notes were made on the front and back pages, with the inner portion left blank. His frequent biblical quotations were aided by cutting the verses from a Bible and pasting them on these notes at the proper place.

Earlier in life, Moody practiced delivery of his speeches rather infrequently. Much of the material of a new sermon had been used in personal conversation or with converts in the inquiry room; he got practice in this fashion. Later, however, as his son reveals, "It was his custom to preach a new sermon in a hay loft to familiarize himself with the subject matter." [23]

In this way, and with these methods, Moody prepared his sermons.

[23] W. R. Moody, *D. L. Moody*, p. 437.

3. Religious Message

As we have previously indicated, Moody's theology was chiefly that of the evangelical faiths of his day. This was modified by his own unique personal religious experiences, by his study and reading, and by contact with certain religious sects and religious leaders.

Moody's evangelism was more personal than that of many others. His most frequent audience throughout the years was the single individual. He visited the homes of many; he conversed with many; he observed many conversions and noted what changes they did or did not bring; he wrought changes in many by putting them to work in religious activity.

To Moody, religion was a way of life. The means to a successful, happy life was conversion, followed by participation in religious activities. The content of his speeches was not a kind that would develop critical evaluation, study, and investigation, but a kind that would produce action immediately. The "Blood of Atonement" was the chief doctrine that permeated most of his speeches. He preached a literal belief in the Bible, the divinely inspired word of God. His emphasis was not on hell-fire and damnation; God was pictured as all-powerful, all-seeing, all-knowing, yet loving. Probably the most dominant theme underlying Moody's preaching was that God was a God of love. So pronounced was this theme, and so prominent was Moody in the evangelistic field, that both Grover C. Loud and Frederick Morgan Davenport point to Moody as the man who freed revivalism of its irrational fears resulting from the preaching of a vengeful God.[24] Christ was pictured as the Son of God who died that man might be saved. Moody stressed the love and compassion of Christ. He believed that the Holy Spirit filled men as a result of conversion; that the Holy Spirit put men to work for Christianity and brought goodness to the world. Again and again Moody proclaimed that not he, but the Holy Spirit, drew the huge crowds to the tabernacle and produced the conversions. He described Heaven as an actual place, as much so as Boston or Chicago, a destination, a locality. He preached that conversion did not depend upon good deeds, nor righteousness, nor having lived a good life; it depended upon belief and acceptance. He did not emphasize repentance. It was necessary only that an individual should believe in Christ and accept a loving Father. Conversions, he believed, might be sudden or they might be gradual. Conversion gave the new convert the power and the will to overcome the world. Daily habits would be improved, chances of success increased, greater happiness attained, fear of death and the grave removed and, most

[24] Grover C. Loud, *Evangelized America* (New York: Longmans, Green & Co., 1928), p. 234; Frederick Morgan Davenport, *Primitive Traits of Religious Revivals* (New York: The Macmillan Co., 1905), pp. 204-5.

important of all, the new convert would take a great interest in religious activities.

4. RHETORICAL DEVICES

Moody's effectiveness as a speaker came from the excellent use of various rhetorical devices and psychological appeals. A suggestion that his speeches contained powerful psychological appeals and rhetorical devices wc ald have brought little response from Moody. Speaking, to him, was simply a matter of what to say to get results. He paid little attention to artistic excellence. This is why one seldom sees one of his sermons included in collections of great speeches.

To analyze the organization and arrangement of Moody's sermons is difficult, for he may have had ideas of arranging the material not discernible in the written speech. Elements of delivery may have produced a cumulative effect that escapes the reader. In general, his speeches may be characterized as formless. There was no distinct division into introduction, body, and conclusion. There was no calculated device for gaining attention, or gradual introduction of the subject, nor was there often a summary in the conclusion. Professor William C. Wilkinson, D.D., of the University of Chicago, who often heard Moody speak, has commented on the formlessness of the sermons:

It is partly to fullness of matter in the preacher's mind, but still more it is to his truly remarkable disregard of form, that we must charge the absence of crises, of culminating effects, of climaxes, in Mr. Moody's preaching. Unless the very lack of art itself is the consummation of art with Mr. Moody, then Mr. Moody is incomparably the most artless preacher in the world. Few, indeed, of the ordinary, conventional, mere rhetorical or oratorical artifices are practiced in his preaching. There is scarcely even the beginning, middle, and end of a discourse. The particular sermon is apt to be like so much preaching cut off from an endless reel of such. The piece cut off might be longer, or it might be shorter, and in either case the unity and the completeness would remain unaffected. The conclusion is where the preacher stops, not where the treatment has reached a goal. This does not mean that the conclusion is ineffective. On the contrary, it is thoroughly adapted to the practical end in view, and that practical end is the right practical end for all preaching, namely, the subduing of the individual will to the obedience of Christ. . . . The conclusion is only not led up to as to a goal not reached before. The goal has been as much in sight all the way as it is when the sermon stops.[25]

There were exceptions, however, to this general lack of organization and arrangement. In a few cases, he used an introduction, a discussion, and a summary conclusion. In certain cases his sermons were divided into parts. They

[25] William C. Wilkinson, "Dwight L. Moody as a Preacher," *Homiletic Review*, 36 (August, 1898), 114.

were partitioned on the basis of audience attitudes, or on a chronological basis, or according to a topical plan. Sermons dealing with biblical characters were usually arranged on a chronological basis.

Moody began most of his sermons with a scriptural text; the others were begun with the announcement of the subject. The rest of the speech which followed was the body; there seemed to be no formal conclusion. One of his favorite ways of ending was to use an illustration; another, was a general plea for conversion. A possible reason for the lack of formal conclusions was his practice of closing with a prayer. There were elements of recapitulation in some of these prayers, and they tended to serve as conclusions.

Although Moody did not structuralize his sermons carefully, he was careful in his over-all planning of the purposes of the sermons successively given during a series of meetings. The purposes of the first speeches were to instill greater belief and enthusiasm among the professed Christians of the city. The second group of speeches had for their purposes to get professed Christians to go out and help bring about conversions. The third group, and by far the greatest number, were those aimed at bringing about the conversion of the hearers. The fourth, were aimed at getting the converts to participate in Christian activities of all kinds, particularly to help convert others.

Moody was particularly effective in his use of supporting material in the form of illustrations, biblical narration, comparison and contrast, repetition, and direct discourse. If an illustration is a "window in the argument letting in light," he seldom left his listeners in the dark. In "How to Conduct Inquiry Meetings," a speech to inform, he used sixteen extended illustrations and thirty-four specific examples; this constituted most of the speech. Ten long illustrations composed 62 per cent of the sermon, "Where Art Thou?" Most of these illustrations were drawn from Moody's experiences. So extensive was his use of biblical narration that it deserves special attention. The sermons on the lives of such biblical characters as Abraham, Ahab, Naaman, and Lot, couched in language related to the experiences of a nineteenth-century audience, were really chronological narrations, with applications to the members of the audience interspersed. Comparison and contrast were used effectively and extensively. The theme of all his teachings lay in the comparison and contrast of the "saved" and the "unsaved"; illustrations and examples of the great success, happiness, and assurance of the former were contrasted with the failure, misery, and despair of the latter. One may find sermons with seventeen, twenty-five, or twenty-eight comparisons and contrasts used to develop the main theme.[26] The main theme or text of the sermon was dinned into the minds of the hearers by repetition and restatement. Moody was so

[26] These sermons are: "Where Art Thou?", "Sowing and Reaping," and "There Is No Difference," respectively.

anxious that his audience should remember his basic theme that he repeated or restated it after each bit of supporting material. Although he did this more sparingly in some sermons, in others, "Tekel" and "Charity," he restated as many as fifty-four and sixty-four times. He used dialogue, rhetorical and direct questions, and direct address to get the main theme accepted. Particularly in the longer illustrations, he made the stories more vivid by direct discourse or dialogue. Whenever he wished to climax an idea or to make a particularly strong plea, Moody made frequent use of the rhetorical or even the direct question. Stories were told in a style that one would use with a friend; questions were asked as though expecting an answer; the language was replete with such words as "I," "you," "us," "we," and "our." All of Moody's sermons seemed quite conversational, in that the content was of the same nature as that in a discussion by two individuals on a street corner, or in the salestalk of a clerk selling to a customer in a store.

Moody was probably unaware that his speeches contained strong motive appeals, numerous stereotypes and other emotionally-loaded words, and strong emotional appeals that owed their effectiveness to an appearance of logic. He used four general areas of motive appeals. The first was relief from the misery and sorrows of life; the second was centered around love, friendship, and loyalty to parents and friends; the third was the fear of death and the grave; and the fourth was the security of belief in a way of life. The infantile behavior patterns of security in the arms of parents were easily transferred to the figures of God and Christ, who were pictured as idealized parents. Moody's language was replete with those stereotypes and emotionally-loaded words common to the evangelical faiths of today. One may conclude that Moody was not ignorant of the power of words.

An appearance of logicality and reasonableness in his arguments constituted another psychological appeal. The Bible was always near at hand as he preached, and he turned to it as the authority for the principles he uttered. The illustrations and examples used were factual in nature, most of them being drawn from his own experiences. To make them more authentic, he sometimes quoted a letter he had received from the chief personage in the illustration. In addition, he used the short example as a basis for inductive proof of a statement. Figurative analogy added weight to this impression of "reasonableness." Taking truths of nature, such as, "Whatsoever a man soweth that shall he also reap," basic truths that would be accepted by his audience, Moody applied them to spiritual matters. This device gave a reasonableness to statements that might otherwise have failed to produce a response or to gain acceptance. Still another device was to use statistics to enhance the emotional response. To suggest that the average life span was only thirty-three years served to strengthen his appeal to become converted before it was too late. Moody used techniques of logic as a framework for material that was emotional in nature; he had neither the desire nor the time to develop an argument.

Moody's style was simple. Approximately 79 per cent of his words were of one syllable; 16 per cent were of two syllables, while 4 per cent were of three syllables. Affixed words were infrequent. His sentences were simple and short, averaging from sixteen to eighteen words in length. His language was highly figurative and often epigrammatic; short, concise, nicely turned phrases appeared frequently. He had been a shoe salesman, and his speaking style was much the same as that of any salesman, except that the stereotyped, highly figurative language of the Bible and religious leaders was adopted. His talk was always direct and conversational.

The Techniques Which Stimulated the Crowds

So far, we have noted the stimuli of Moody as a speech personality and the stimuli of the content of the speeches. Let us now turn our attention to the factors of audience psychology he utilized. Probably his greatest skills lay in his preparation, administration, and execution of those techniques which polarized the people of London, Chicago, Cleveland, and New York into psychological crowds. He stood out as a dynamic leader, director and commander. His greatest use of these techniques was during the revival campaigns of 1873 to 1877.

1. Preparation for the Meetings

Moody began to prepare for a revival in a particular urban area from three to nine months before the opening meetings. He would meet with the ministers and laymen who were interested in holding evangelistic services. Usually two general committees were formed, one, of ministers to handle those problems relating to religion and to secure the cooperation of the churches; the other, of businessmen to serve as an executive committee to build the building, raise the finances, and publicize the services. Prominent ministers such as Brooks, Spurgeon, Talmage, Beecher, and Cuyler served on the executive committees of ministers, while the names of Morgan, Vanderbilt, Jessup, Dodge, and Wanamaker were prominent among the businessmen.[27]

Finances to build the tabernacle and support the services were raised through guaranty funds, and the list of donors was published, with daily requests for more. Explanations were frequently made that neither Moody nor Sankey, his singer, received anything for their services. In New York,

[27] Taken from circulars put out by the committees: Mount Hermon Library Collection; A. P. Fitt Collection.

$40,000 was raised for the first series of services, for those in Philadelphia, $30,000, for the Chicago Tabernacle alone, $22,000, and for the four meeting areas and the two tabernacles constructed in London, $140,000. Such great amounts of money and the activities of the many people involved served to heighten expectations and polarize the community toward Moody.

The tabernacles, especially built for the services, were constructed to produce the maximum in polarization, suggestion, and social facilitation. Their size was determined by the expected crowds, large enough to create the feeling of universality, yet small enough to produce the greatest possible degree of social facilitation. The average size in the large cities was usually 8,000, with room for 2,000 more to stand. In London, Agricultural Hall accommodated 13,700, but overflow crowds there and elsewhere were accommodated in nearby auditoriums. The seats were placed close together; the platforms were built five or six feet above the floor; space on the platform was provided for prominent dignitaries. President Grant and other federal officials were conducted to the platform in Philadelphia in 1875.

Another large task in preparation for the services was publicity and distribution of tickets for admission. Posters were printed and distributed among the stores, pasted on billboards, and apportioned among the streetcars. Daily advertisements appeared in the newspapers, and handbills were printed and distributed. Day-by-day accounts of the meetings were printed in the news columns of the papers, while some even published stenographic reports of the sermons. Admission to the platform for the choir, ministers, and dignitaries and to the tables just in front of the platform, for newspapermen, was by ticket only. Tickets were also given to businessmen, laborers, and visitors from outside communities, who might otherwise have difficulty in gaining admission. The attitudes of value surrounding other programs to which admission was gained by ticket were transferred to the Moody services, thus enhancing the prestige of the services and the evangelist.

The selection and training of the choir, the ushers, and the inquiry room workers enhanced the process of polarizing the particular community. The choir was recruited about four weeks in advance of the meetings and was trained by a local choirmaster to sing the songs required for the revival. Even the ushers were recruited three weeks in advance and given training and instruction; efficiency in handling the press of the crowds and the emergencies demanded it. Moody had his own special method of handling converts in the inquiry rooms, located to the rear and under the platform of the tabernacle; during the closing hymn or after the benediction, converts went to those rooms. Ministers of the evangelical churches and members they recommended were given three weeks of training to conduct the person-to-person conferences with the new converts. The training and preparation of all these groups was thorough and exact. Selection of the members from all the evangelical churches tended to break down the in-group feelings of denominationalism; it constituted anticipatory behavior that produced a unity of purpose toward the goal of "saving souls"; it was another link in the chain of events that heightened the prestige of the coming evangelist.

There were various auxiliary groups engaged in activities preparatory to the revival. Special corps of policemen were delegated to the tabernacle area to direct traffic, to manage the gathering throng, and to protect the adjacent property. Special streetcars were run and sometimes special car tracks had to be constructed in order to provide closer access to the tabernacle. All available cabs were put into use, and numerous special trains were scheduled from the suburbs to the city. Eleven different railroad lines established special excursion rates to the Chicago meetings in 1876, and special trains were run from as far as Dayton and Cleveland, Ohio.[28]

Moody did not ignore the churches; the ministers were asked to prepare their groups for the approaching services. This was done in part by sermons that were aimed at building attitudes of participation and expectations of huge results. *The Brooklyn Eagle* of October 11, 1875, gives brief accounts of such sermons by Talmage, Cuyler, and Beecher. Prayer meetings, first small and local in nature, then building to large union prayer services, were held for a series of weeks prior to the revival. Then, just two or three days before Moody and his song leader, Sankey, arrived, a union service would be conducted in the tabernacle, with the choir, inquiry room workers, ushers, and others attending. All these services were another bombardment of repeated stimuli producing polarization and crowd facilitation.

Moody always pressed great numbers of people into preparatory activity. For Moody's first series of meetings in Philadelphia, 600 voices were trained for the choir, 300 were chosen to serve as ushers, while 300 more were trained to confer with the converts; it took 100 policemen to handle the crowds. Chicago required similar numbers, while New York needed even more: 1200 for the choir, 500 for ushers, 300 as inquiry room workers, and 150 policemen. Added to these, were the members of the various committees, those engaged in building or equipping the tabernacle, those publicizing the meetings, those transporting the people, and those participating in the preparatory services. The sum total of the persons affected by the revival before it began was very large. When interpreted in terms of families affected, one can readily understand the projected universality of feelings within the urban community. As a result, vast crowds attended opening services, and often thousands had to be turned away.

[28] *Chicago Inter-Ocean,* November 17, 1876.

2. THE SERVICES

When one of the main services began, there existed a high degree of polarization due to the preparatory activities. Social facilitation operated to heighten the expectations due to the crush of the crowds seeking admittance. The auditors sat close together or stood shoulder-to-shoulder around the walls. Promptly upon the hour scheduled, the services began, unless the auditorium had been packed early; in such cases they were begun even earlier. The first one-half hour was spent in congregational singing under the leadership of a local director. Exactly one-half hour after the service had opened, Moody and his song leader entered, the former going to the pulpit, the latter to his organ. Both bowed their heads in a moment of silent prayer; then Moody announced the next hymn. The hymns selected were related to the sermon subject. Interspersed with the hymns selected was a prayer by a prominent local minister and Scripture reading by Moody. The sermon closed with a prayer, and the congregation sang a hymn, during which some of the inquirers moved to the designated rooms.

Although this program at first glance may seem to be similar to those in most evangelical churches of today, Moody used methods that were especially helpful in heightening the suggestibility of the audience. Congregational singing is universally used as a method of polarizing a crowd, but Moody knew how to capitalize on this aspect of the service. He himself had no particular musical abilities; in fact, he couldn't even carry a tune.[29] However, he knew what kind of songs people liked to sing and what songs were effective in producing the desired results. Typical of Moody, when he didn't have the ability to perform a needed task, he turned to someone who could. His choice was Ira D. Sankey.

Religion and music had played prominent roles in Sankey's early life. Before he met Moody, he had sung in choirs, had directed them, and had taken a prominent role in music for the church. By the time he was fifteen years of age, although he had had no instruction other than that of the home, Sunday school, or church, he began to compose tunes for his own amusement. Like Moody, he learned what he knew through experience. That he had other qualities of leadership is signified by the fact that at nineteen years of age he was elected superintendent of a Sunday school; during the Civil War he had organized a choir for religious services in camp; he had also served as president of the Y.M.C.A. in his home town of Newcastle, Pennsylvania. Moody met Sankey in 1870 at a convention in Indianapolis. He was vastly impressed by Sankey's ability to lead songs in the services at the convention, and asked

[29] Goss, *op. cit.*, pp. 52-53. This fact is verified by W. R. Moody.

Sankey to become his song leader.[30] Sankey was married, had two children, and held a good job as collector of internal revenue. It took him six months to decide. Thus, in the early months of 1871, Sankey started off on his career as a singing evangelist. The following two years were spent in working out a system of song services for the revival meetings. The appearance and personality of Sankey were quite a contrast to Moody's. Sankey was about six feet tall, relatively dark in complexion, wore side whiskers and a mustache, but no beard. He was graceful in bearing, and his manner was unobtrusive. While Moody was brusque, dynamic, commanding, Sankey was quiet, friendly, easygoing.

Moody found that the old stately church hymns were poorly adapted to his methods; so in 1868 he had compiled a songbook under the title, "Northwestern Hymn Book." Since the hymns of this collection were not available in Great Britain, he published "Sacred Songs and Solos"; later, in America, he published "Gospel Hymns." The sale of these songbooks threatened to bring criticism upon the evangelist; so, the royalties were set up as a trust fund for religious activities. At first, these songs were viewed with distrust, particularly in England; the people had been accustomed to the old stately hymns, and the introduction of songs that were suggestive of the more popular secular tunes naturally aroused some opposition. The editor of *The Nation* described the contrast effectively by saying, "Musically speaking, the time of the old tunes is slow and regular and the expression in singing is of the simplest, but the Moody and Sankey hymns were written to religious words and made attractive by many secular contrivances. The time is now slow, now rapid, constantly changing, the notes of every variety of length, and the general effect of the whole designed to give pronounced meaning to the words." [31] Schoolboys whistled the tunes on the streets and the crowds gathering for the services sang them while waiting for the doors to open. The hymns chosen had words which motivated the singers to worship, to believe certain doctrines, or to live Christian lives.

Sankey was an effective "singer of the gospel." He both sang solos and directed the singing. These solos chosen for the "message" they conveyed were interspersed through the opening song service and were used again at the close of the service. Although the editor of *The Saturday Review* did not like this singing and characterized it as making one "think of a melodious costermonger crying his cabbages," he had to admit "whether it is pure art or not, it appears

[30] Ira D. Sankey, *My Life and the Story of the Gospel Hymns* (New York: Harper & Brothers, 1906), pp. 19-20.
[31] "Moody and Sankey in New York," *The Nation*, XXII (March 9, 1876), 156.

to be agreeable to the majority of the audience." [32] A second description from the editor of *The Nation* is probably more significant: "He is a trained ballad singer and dramatizes the sinner's and the believer's situation as he sings." [33]

The song service in the Moody revival produced three psychological effects: it built a psychological crowd; it built motor attitudes favorable to conversion and Christian work; and it augmented the release of these attitudes through the closing hymns. The process of following the directions of the song leader was a means of polarizing the attention toward the platform and the pulpit. Furthermore, the overt activity of singing songs that the individuals liked brought pleasant emotional exhilaration, and the rising together and sitting together brought social facilitation for these acts. The words of the hymns constituted autosuggestion to each individual singing. The repetition of the main theme common to these hymns enhanced the autosuggestion. Many observers and participants commented upon the impressiveness of the singing. Rev. J. T. Sunderland, a Unitarian minister, thoroughly opposed to these revivals and the beliefs preached, observed:

I insist that the greatest power of the music of the great meetings held has not lain in Mr. Sankey's singing. It has lain in the sweeping, surging, irresistible, overwhelming, singing of the congregations. . . . And you, too, though you have only gone in as an indifferent and critical spectator, before you know it you too are drawn into the enchanted current, and are being borne with strange intoxication on the bosom of the wild but wondrous song. . . . A theology which in sober thought a man would cast away with loathing, he would find himself before he knew it joining in the singing of, with the multitude; and finally, through the singing, he would be drawn actually to embrace it. Only he knows that who has himself stood in the midst of the great multitude, and that day after day and night after night, and felt himself thrilled and awed and borne away by the strange power of its mighty choruses.[34]

The delayed entrance of Moody and Sankey was dramatic, particularly to those who had not heard them before. With everyone seated on the platform during the one-half hour of preliminary singing, and with the expectation of the audience increasing during the song service, a strong polarization of attention upon the evangelist and the singer occurred. The moment of silent prayer had the effect of building among the observers an attitude of submission to a higher power.

Other factors producing strong social facilitations and polarization were the

[32] "Messrs. Moody and Sankey," *The Saturday Review*, XXXIX (March 13, 1875), 344.

[33] "Moody and Sankey in New York," *op. cit.*, p. 156.

[34] Rev. J. T. Sunderland, *Orthodoxy and Revivalism* (New York: James Miller, 1876), pp. 111-14.

rising together for the opening prayer and the sight of such ministers as Spurgeon, Beecher, Brooks, such laymen as W. E. Dodge, Marshall Field, and John Wanamaker, along with governors, senators, and members of the House of Lords on the platform. Moody seldom sought early overt manifestations to produce social facilitation, although once in a while he would ask for a show of hands. Overt manifestations for the release of attitudes, however, were frequent in the closing portion of the sermon and the closing phase of the service. These responses were in the form of verbal assent, raising hands, standing, and going to the inquiry room. Sometimes he asked a direct question which would bring as many as from three thousand to five thousand of the audience to their feet. On occasions, when asked how many wanted special prayer, whether saved or unsaved, the whole congregation of eight to ten thousand would gradually rise to their feet. However, Moody was careful that the release of attitudes did not stop there. He developed a framework of activities of response to the revival in the form of numerous types of additional meetings.

3. Inquiry Room Meetings

The inquiry room served to release and augment the motor attitudes of the "unsaved"; to Moody it constituted the means of "drawing the nets" after the sermon. The term, "inquirer," was used because those coming to the room were not necessarily converted. Conversion meant participation in religious activities, and the inquirers needed added stimulation. Professor William C. Wilkinson, D.D., of the University of Chicago, observed these meetings on several occasions and gave this description:

Doors closed against further ingress after the room was suitably filled; the appointed helpers disposed about the room with particular directions given in an undertone to each, a short familiar talk from Mr. Moody addrest collectively to all the persons present; then singing started at his instance by a select number of trained voices— with 'Just as I am', etc., for the first hymn—to be continued in a very soft and gentle tone and volume of sound throughout the entire inquiry-season—the idea being to supply a kind of medium, sympathetic in its nature and conducive to a religious frame of feeling, in which conversations of one with another could be conducted, with a certain sense of privacy secured to each, though carried on in the imminent presence of many, who but for the accompaniment of music might be supposed able to overhear. Without actual observation and experience of such a scene, one would hardly conceive what a help to the general effect, and to the particular effects as well, was contributed by that interfused and circumfused medium of half-silent sound in which all was transacted.

While those who would do so engaged in quiet conversation one with another, Mr. Moody, beginning at one corner, moved in somewhat regular circuit from seat to seat about the room, talking very briefly with each inquirer as he judged fit and requisite. Mr. Moody is nowhere else more successfully the man of affairs than in the inquiry room. This can not too strongly be said; but the guardian statement should always be added that also he is nowhere else further removed from vulgar egoism and from the trickery of such as make of revivalism a trade.[35]

The ministers and laymen trained as inquiry room workers held personal conversations with the inquirers. They had three duties: to talk with the inquirers, to pray with them, and to fill out blanks. The names and addresses were kept along with any church preference on one-half of the blank, while on the other half, given to the inquirer, were suggested Scripture readings and other aids to help in conversion; the greatest emphasis was placed upon Scripture reading. In this way, Moody sought to release and augment the attitudes of the "unsaved"; in this manner, he directed conversions.

4. Auxiliary Meetings

Accounts of the revival meetings of Moody indicate the great number of activities going on. Many auxiliary meetings in addition to the regular services were held in order to provide additional stimuli for conversion, and for widespread participation of church workers as well as for the new converts. The noon prayer meetings held in connection with the revivals drew large crowds. As many as six to seven thousand persons gathered during a lunch hour on weekdays. Many factors of crowd psychology were at work. A typical plan of the meeting was to have hymns, prayers, and Scripture reading interspersed with the reading of letters requesting prayer. Requests of individuals to have the congregation pray for them were so numerous that they had to be classified: for example, twelve brothers request prayer for the conversion of sisters; fourteen sisters, for brothers; nine children, for parents, and so on.[36] In larger cities, there were frequently more than a hundred in each class. Moody's drawing power at the noon prayer meetings lay not so much in the program of events as in the methods used in conducting the meetings. His speech on how to conduct prayer meetings reveals how Moody sought to gain his ends. He gave a total of seventeen specific directions, including such things as get the people close together, let the meeting-place be well ventilated, have good singing, don't let the presiding leader speak too long, have the meeting short, avoid discussion, and be punctual.[37]

Other auxiliary meetings included all-day Christian conventions similar to the conferences of earlier years, meetings for women, for men, for young

---

[35] William C. Wilkinson, "Dwight L. Moody as Man of Affairs," *Homiletic Review*, 36 (September, 1898), 204-5.

[36] *The Christian*, January 1, 1874, p. 9.

[37] A complete copy of this address was printed in *The Christian*, (December 8, 1898).

men, and for parents, and temperance meetings. These latter meetings were held at 1 o'clock, just following the noon prayer service, at 4:30 P.M. just following the afternoon Bible reading, or at 9 P.M., while the inquiry room conferences were being held. Although these programs were similar to the main services of prayer meetings, variety was an important factor. With all these meetings going on, the day of revival services was full. A typical day of meetings included a noon prayer service, a meeting for men only, and another for women only at 1 o'clock; afternoon Bible reading at 3:00 P.M.; inquiry room meetings for this service at 4:30 P.M.; evening services at 7:30 P.M., with one or two overflow meetings of the same kind; inquiry room meetings in two, three, or four different rooms, after-meeting prayer service in the main part of the tabernacle for those who remained, young men's meeting, inebriates' meetings, and boys' meeting all at 9 o'clock.[38] Moody furnished a bombardment of stimuli to those in attendance at the revival. He realized that repetition was needed if attitudes were to be molded permanently. This widespread social facilitation arising from the variety of meetings produced a psychological crowd within the community rather than just a psychological audience for a particular service.

5. CHRISTIAN WORK FOR ALL

Moody differed from most revivalists who preceded him, and even from those who followed, in his great desire to set converts to work in religious activities. He believed there would be no permanence to the conversion unless it brought action. Thus, he paid unusual attention to the development of programs in which the new converts could go to work. It was not enough for them merely to walk to the inquiry room; they must inaugurate habits of Christian work.

Moody's suggestions were reminiscent of his own earlier life; the activities in which he had engaged were recommended to his auditors. They were put to work distributing handbills on the streets, in their clubs, and in their boardinghouses. They were directed to go out and try to convert others. By the very force of numbers providing social facilitation, they were carried along in the building of habits of Christian work. Some of the converts who gave sufficient promise were allowed to work in the inquiry room in some of the later sessions. The various prayer meetings and auxiliary services provided them with a chance to verbalize their attitudes. House to house visitations of the whole city was planned, not only for the purpose of inviting the people of the city to attend the services, but also to give the converts a chance to develop habits of Christian endeavor. In ways such as these, Moody attempted

[38] Taken from daily reports and announcements of the meetings in the newspapers of the various cities where the revivals were held.

to release the attitudes of the converts and to augment them by social facilitation into new habits of Christian work.

Moody did not neglect the professed Christians and ministers. The same instructions and the same activities were open to professed Christians as were open to the new converts. Frequently, professed Christians were given positions of greater responsibility, particularly at the beginning of the revival series. However, much of Moody's effort was directed toward getting this group to participate more energetically in their own Sunday schools and church services. He tried to imbue the ministers of the city with the importance of saving souls. Ministers worked in the inquiry room, took prominent roles in the prayer meetings, and became the leaders of the auxiliary meetings.

Moody was so imbued with the importance of putting all people to work that he sought, wherever possible, to get evangelists to go out to nearby cities to conduct revival services of the same type. Reports of the success of these revivals were sent back to the noon prayer meetings and accounts of them were given in the newspapers of the city in which Moody was working. The reports contained in one of the leading newspapers, *Inter-Ocean*, of the 1875-76 revivals created the impression that revivalism was spreading in ever-enlarging waves from Chicago.

Another means of releasing and augmenting the attitudes for Christian work, and probably the greatest goal for which Moody strove, was to have the revivals continued after he left. He remarked again and again that he was only preparing the army for the real work that was to follow. The meetings started in Sunderland, England, in July, 1873, were still continuing in April, 1874. The work at Carlisle continued for more than five months.

From the foregoing, one can see that Moody used many techniques to develop a community into a psychological crowd. He was the commander-in-chief, instructing, directing, and guiding an army of people from all walks of life to carry on the revival. He was a great administrator.

The Cultural Context

Thus far we have analyzed the three parts of our formula, Moody as a speech personality, the speeches which stirred the crowds, and the psychological-crowd phenomena. We propose now to analyze the cultural forces operating during the periods of the revivals. To make a definitive and detailed study of the cultures and the variations within each, covering the years of 1873 to 1899 for both Great Britain and the United States, would require far too much space. Moody's audiences were drawn from all classes of society; therefore, any history of the peoples of those countries would reveal many characteristics of the people within his audiences. His audiences were specialized only through the common denominator that they were chiefly Protestant.

Religious revivalism has its own peculiar psychology. Such writers on the psychology of religion as Starbuck, Coe, Leuba, Martin, and Pratt have not chosen to relate their studies in a definitive way to existing social, economic, and political events and conditions. This must be done in order to get the motivation and compulsion for religious revivalism.

During the years of Moody's revivals there was a reservoir of emotion developed through reactions to social, economic, and political events and conditions that served to motivate religious activity once attention was focused in that direction. Throughout the history of the United States, when mass insecurities have been high, particularly in times of depression, revivalism has flourished. However, even in more normal times, life conditions in every culture give rise to anxieties, which frequently find their outlet in religious revivalism. These arise from traditional fears of demons, of violation of taboos, of the supernatural, of death. Furthermore, they arise strongly in cultures emphasizing rugged individual competition and in those filled with contradictions. This was the case in the latter part of the nineteenth century. In a strongly competitive society, the fear of failure is a realistic one because, in general, the chances of failure are greater than those of succeeding, and because failure in a competitive society entails a realistic frustration of basic wants. Loss of self-esteem from failure makes any person feel worthless. Cultural contradictions in the form of competition and success, on the one hand, and brotherly love and humility, on the other, between the stimulation of our wants and our factual limitations in satisfying them, between the alleged freedom of the individual and all his factual limitations, are a constant source of fears and anxieties. Insecurities, anxieties, and fears create a reservoir of emotion that can be changed by a revivalist into compulsive motivation for religious activity. The frequency and extent of this can be observed in the studies of F. M. Davenport and Grover C. Loud.[39]

Space permits only a brief summary of the conditions from 1873 to 1899 which gave rise to strong cultural contradictions leading to mass insecurities, anxieties, and hostilities. The period was one of growing industrialism, with increasing emphasis upon personal initiative. The ruthless methods of competition brought estrangement from society, resulting in a feeling of "aloneness." The threat of reprisals for pitiless destruction of rivals, or for fraud perpetrated on the public in the form of watered stocks created anxieties. The squeezing out of those unable to match the aggressive spirit of the growing corporations produced feelings of insecurity. Wages were being increased but living costs were rising faster. Work was plentiful, but a rising tide of immi-

[39] *Op. cit.*

gration furnishing cheaper labor threatened the security of many. The shift of the demand for labor to the growing industrial centers resulted in the abandonment of village homes and migration to the large cities. Desertion of the villages led to insecurities and feelings of isolation and aloneness within the new environment. Since nearly 70 per cent of Moody's potential audience consisted of immigrants or migrants, the father-symbol recalling infantile behavior mechanisms was a strong suggestive appeal. Insecurities and anxieties of the working classes resulted in increased unionism, strikes, and riots. The unrest of the farmer made possible one of the strongest movements for unity among that class in the history of the country. The miserable living conditions in rapidly growing tenement areas, the anxieties from the constant threat of epidemics of disease, and the insecurities of a crowded labor market gave rise to vice, drinking, and crime. The cultural contradiction between the mansions of the rich and the degradation of the alms and poorhouses gave rise to several movements of reform. Although the dominant attitude of the nation was one of growing optimism, the insecurity and anxiety level was high.

The year of 1873 brought a serious recession followed by several years of depression. Prominent banking houses and business firms closed their doors; the New York Stock Exchange was forced to close for ten days. From 2,915 business failures in a more normal year of 1871, there was an increase to 5,830 in 1874, followed by 7,740 and 9,092 in successive years. Unemployment steadily rose; the number of tramps increased from a negligible number to 3,000,000, out of a population of 40,000,000; riots and outbreaks were frequent. Hostile verbal thrusts were directed toward the grafting politicians, the corrupt financiers, and the greedy industrialists.[40] The revivals of Moody during this depression seemed to be nation-wide in character, but with the decrease of mass insecurities in the years that followed, they appeared to be more local in character. Moody's revivals always reached greater proportions in such depressions as those of 1873-77 and 1892-95.

Conditions in the religious field were calm in contrast to social and economic conditions; this provided a sanctuary. About six and one-half million persons were members of churches, with the evangelical denominations constituting the vast majority. The theology of the day was what we would now call fundamentalism and the Puritan characteristics of thrift, sobriety, and self-

[40] Allan Nevins, *The Emergence of America, 1865-1878* (New York: The Macmillan Co., 1927), pp. 295-305; H. M. Hyndman, *Commercial Crises of the Nineteenth Century* (2nd ed.; London: George Allen & Unwin, Ltd., 1932), pp. 116-20; William Archibald Dunning, *Reconstruction, Political and Economic, 1865-1877* (*The American Nation: A History*, Vol. XXII [New York: Harper & Brothers, 1907]), pp. 235-37.

denial persisted in the culture. Religion played a dominant role in the lives of professional men, mercantile and clerical workers, and farmers, and the role of the minister was one of prominence in the moral and intellectual life of the community. Religious revivalism was a part of the religious culture, with the churches having their one- or two-week annual winter revivals. The growing optimism of a progressing nation had changed the emphasis in preaching from the austere Calvinistic belief in a God of vengeance to an emphasis upon a God of love. Industrialism with its personal-initiative ideology had brought an even greater emphasis upon a personal gospel. However, the social needs giving rise to reform movements were providing fertile soil for the seeds of a social gospel. The threat of Darwinism was causing anxieties among religious leaders, but the masses only heard rumors of the looming struggle. Further anxieties were aroused among religious leaders over the growth of science and ideologies of higher criticism, but here again the masses heard only rumblings. "Freethinker," "infidel," "agnostic," and "atheist" were epithets of strong reproach. Thus, the church, and particularly religious revivalism, offered a means for discharging the insecurities and anxieties arising from the economic and social conditions of the time.

The Results

Having observed the variety of stimuli Moody used in his revivals and noted the psychological factors peculiar to his audiences, we may now ask: What were the results, the reactions to the revivals?

The number of people attracted to attend the revival meetings furnishes our first clue. So great was the attendance that the meetings attracted the attention of the newspapers and religious magazines of the day. Their estimates furnish the evidence of Moody's power to draw crowds to hear him preach. The attendance at the series of revivals in Great Britain and America from 1873 to 1877 was the largest. The average attendance at the first meetings, held in York, was small; the largest single audience numbered only about one thousand. But they grew larger as time elapsed and as he visited larger cities. The peak attendance at Sunderland was 3,000; at Glasgow, the evening services often drew 10,000, and overflow meetings were held for those unable to gain admittance.[41] Dublin, Manchester, and Liverpool produced even larger crowds. More meetings were held each day. London was the climax of the British tour. The first series of meetings was held in the northern part in Agricultural Hall, which was equipped to seat 13,700. Frequently, it was full, and the average daily attendance for the first few

41 *The Christian*, July 10, 1873, p. 392; September 4, 1873, p. 487; May 28, 1874, p. 346.

weeks was 20,000. On Sunday, April 4, 1875, Moody spoke to 40,000 persons.[42] After the London series was over the committee in charge reported the size of the crowds and the number of meetings in this fashion: "In Camberwell, sixty meetings attended by 480,000 people; in Victoria, forty-five meetings, attended by 400,000; in the Opera House, sixty meetings attended by 330,000; in Bow, sixty meetings attended by 600,000; and in Agricultural Hall, sixty meetings, attended by 720,000."[43] In other words, during the four months in London, Moody's revivals attracted 2,530,000 persons.

The size of the audiences attending the Moody revival meetings in the United States equaled those in Great Britain. The Brooklyn Rink, where the first American series of meetings was held, was not large enough to accommodate the crowds. Nightly, 7,000 persons crowded into the building, and overflow meetings were held. In Philadelphia, the old freight depot of the Pennsylvania Railroad, with a seating capacity of 10,200, was filled for most of the meetings. Upon one occasion President Grant, along with other federal government officials, attended and sat on the platform. The total estimated summary of all the meetings, except for the last three days, as reported by the secretary of the executive committee, Thomas K. Cree, was:

18	Sunday meetings	225,000
40	weekly evening meetings	320,000
56	Noonday meetings	200,000
14	Bible Readings	70,000
48	Young Men's meetings	24,000
36	Young Women's meetings	10,000
36	Men's and Women's afternoon meetings	20,000

The New York meetings were held in the Hippodrome, and the weekday attendance at the various services averaged 20,000, while on Sunday from 30,000 to 35,000 gathered to hear the evangelist. A special tabernacle was built for Moody in Chicago and the crowds continued, 13,000 during weekdays and 22,000 on Sundays. Boston, also, constructed a special tabernacle for the revival, accommodating 7,000 persons, but it was too small; numerous overflow meetings were required. On weekdays, 15,000 persons gathered to hear the evangelist, while each Sunday brought forth about 19,000.[44]

[42] *London Times*, April 3, 1875; *The Christian*, April 17, 1875, p. 246.

[43] W. R. Moody, *D. L. Moody*, p. 230.

[44] *Brooklyn Eagle*, October 11 to November 20, 1875; *Philadelphia Inquirer*, January 18, 1876; *New York Tribune*, February 8 to April 20, 1876; *Chicago Inter-Ocean*, September 23, 1876, to January 17, 1877; *Boston Daily Globe*, January 26 to May 30, 1877.

Beginning in 1878, Moody changed his tactics. He felt that too often in the large centers the interest aroused was dissociated from the church. For the next twenty-one years his revival services most frequently were held in the larger churches of each city visited. This limited the size of his audiences to the capacity of the churches. However, his techniques for polarizing a community remained the same. Periodically, he would return to the large tabernacle services. The reports of Moody's revivals from 1881 to 1899 in *The Evangelistic Record* (later called *The Record of Christian Work*) reveal audiences that ranged from 3,000 to 12,000 persons. In Washington, in 1894, 8,000 persons crowded to hear him speak, and overflow meetings were required; in Atlanta, in 1896, a building accommodating 6,000 would not hold all who wished to hear him.[45] His last revival services, held in the large Convention Hall in Kansas City, were a repetition of those in 1873-77. Nightly, the hall was packed and overflow services were numerous.

Our second clue to the results of the revivals of the evangelist should be found in the number of converts. With Moody, however, the only evidence for the number of converts may be found in the reports of the early years. He was very careful to avoid the publication of these results. In fact, he insisted that whether a man was converted or not was between the man and his God. He sought constantly to check those who might try to count the number of converts. There were clues, however, in the attendance at meetings for converts only, where admission was by ticket. There were 400 converts at Sunderland, 3,500 present at the last converts' meeting in Glasgow, and 3,000 at a similar meeting in Dublin. The ministers of London estimated that 7,000 had been converted during the four months of revival services there. The last meeting for converts in New York was attended by 4,000, and the same number attended a similar meeting in Chicago.[46]

Records of the numbers of converts in the revival services for later years are virtually nonexistent. Neither is it possible to discover evidence of the number of persons who were stimulated to go to the inquiry rooms. Newspaper reporters of the day would describe the number of inquirers as "many" or "a large number." Sometimes the word, "overflowing," would appear in the accounts of the meetings for inquirers.

The third clue to the results or reactions to the revivals can be found in the number of persons participating in the activities. To get people to engage

---

[45] *The Evangelistic Record,* later *The Record of Christian Work* (Chicago: Fleming H. Revell, 1881-99). The issues of this magazine carried news accounts of all of Moody's revivals as well as those of other evangelists.

[46] *The Christian,* September 4, 1873, p. 487; May 21, 1874, pp. 328; December 3, 1874, p. 774; July 22, 1875, p. 505. See also *London Times,* July 16, 1875; *New York Tribune,* April 19, 1876; *Chicago Inter-Ocean,* January 17, 1877.

actively in religious work was Moody's dominant aim. That many persons took part has already been observed in earlier portions of this study. A single example should serve our purpose here. The number of persons taking part in the New York services in 1876 is indicative. Fifty persons were on the committee in charge of the meetings; 1,200 were trained for the choir; 500 were trained to serve as ushers; 225 were specially trained to handle the converts at the end of each meeting.[47] Added to these were the people distributing the thousands of tickets to special meetings, holding various auxiliary meetings, handling advertising, passing out handbills, visiting saloons and billiard parlors to invite all to come to the meetings, and engaging in the systematized house-to-house canvass. With all this going on, it was no wonder that an observer, coming into the city where Moody was holding revivals, said: "There, certainly, everyone was on fire. Everyone I met had each his or her own tale of interest and share in the work, direct or indirect."[48] Evidence of how many of those participating were new converts is difficult to obtain.

The fourth clue to the results of the revivals can be found in the expressions of doubt by many people that church membership had been increased. Henry Ward Beecher said:

> Mr. Moody's work in Brooklyn was undoubtedly of some benefit—more to the members of churches than to the outside people. His stay here was too short for a full development of his methods. He should work for at least three months, as he has done in Chicago. It is noticeable that at Chicago, where he has hitherto spent years, and been best known, his preaching for the last four months has been most acceptable and fruitful over any at other places. . . .
>
> [Signed] Henry Ward Beecher

Brooklyn, N. Y. January 20, 1877 [49]

T. De Witt Talmage wrote:

> The best work of Messrs. Moody and Sankey was done among non-church goers. Multitudes of people, who are so prejudiced against ministers and churches that they will not attend regular places of worship, went to hear these evangelists. A great many of that class, no doubt, were converted, and, though they may have joined no church at all, may belong to the invisible kingdom of God. Only the last day can tell what work was done. The roll of the Lord's army cannot be read by the natural eye like the roll of an earthly army. Messrs. Moody and Sankey were in Brooklyn but one month. Of course the results of such a brief ministration could

---

[47] *New York Tribune*, February 5, 1876.

[48] Mrs. Peter MacKinnon, *Recollections of D. L. Moody* (Printed for Private Circulation, 1905), p. 11.

[49] A letter written to the editor of the *Boston Globe* in reply to the question of the permanence of the work of Moody and Sankey, published in that paper January 22, 1877.

not be expected to be equal to the more protracted stay in other cities. . . . I am in full sympathy with this revival movement. . . .

> Yours, etc.
>
> [Signed] T. De Witt Talmage

Brooklyn, N. Y., January 22 [50]

John T. Dexter writing in the *Boston Congregationalist* said:

The return of Messrs. Moody and Sankey to their native country has been followed on this side by an entire cessation of the movement they so vigorously conducted, and which it was resolved by the leave-taking conference of London ministers to be of the highest moment to continue. . . . The revival has, in the metropolis, altogether passed from sight and memory, in the brief interval elapsing since the departure of the revivalists. . . . I have serious doubts whether all ordinary Christian efforts will not be crippled by the withholding of funds by those who have subscribed (or will say they have) toward the cost of the revival.[51]

Rev. J. T. Sunderland went to some length to point out the lack of permanence of the revivals:

Some time after the departure of Moody and Sankey, a meeting of preachers was held in London, to discuss the question, "What has the revival left us?" . . . .The first speaker said: "By going the whole round of the churches we should find that there is an expectation that has not yet come." . . . The second speaker declared boldly that the revival had not reached the outside masses of people. The third speaker affirmed that the masses were left today just where they were before the evangelists came to England. Not only was there a disappointment at the failure to reach the masses, but "Where," asked the speaker, "are the conversions we expected and talked about?" His church was situated about midway between the Agricultural Hall and the Bow Road Hall, and they expected a large increase of church membership. They had only five applications for admission to the church, and three out of the five regularly attended his own services in Shoreditch Hall.

Reverend Sunderland then proceeded to point out similar evidence within the United States. From this he concluded:

From such testimonies as these it is not hard to draw an answer to our first inquiry: How great has the success of the evangelists, whose names have been on everybody's lips, really been? If by success we mean notoriety, or the attracting of great crowds, then extraordinary success they have certainly achieved. But if by success we mean accomplishment of a work whose results are at all permanent . . . the results attained are more than doubtful.[52]

[50] *Ibid.*

[51] *Boston Congregationalist*, (October 7, 1876). The article was headed "September, 1876, London England."

[52] Sunderland, *op. cit.*, pp. 103-5.

Other comments upon the permanence of the work were much more enthusiastic, suggesting that "multitudes were converted." W. E. Dodge, chairman of the committee for New York, stated that there were large additions to several of the churches, and cited the example of one church that had received nearly 400 new members.[53] A pastor in the north of England stated that 700 new church members were added as a result of the meetings, and that only a few had "back slidden." [54]

Moody also doubted the permanence of the results in the large, centrally located tabernacles. That was why, from 1878 until his death in 1899, he centered his revivals most frequently in the churches. Often, he would spend longer periods of time in a particular city, holding revivals in several different churches. In this way he hoped to add to the church membership.

There are additional factors in Moody's life, however, which reveal a desire to bring greater permanence to the work he was doing. Although he believed that it was essential to get people "stirred up," and though he spent the winter months in revival services, more and more of his energies were directed toward other activities. These were the founding and development of the Northfield Seminary for girls, the Mount Hermon School for boys, the Northfield Summer Bible Conferences, the Bible Institute for Home and Foreign Missions, and the Colportage Library Publications. In a sense, these institutions were testaments to Moody's ability to persuade.

Such are the clues that we have concerning the results of the revival meetings. Our picture of Moody as an evangelist, however, would not be complete without certain observations about his impact upon the course of revivalism.

Moody was responsible for two important changes in the course of revivalism. The first of these changes arose from his main theme, that God was a God of love. Prior to Moody, the great emphasis of evangelists was on a wrathful God and the awfulness of hell. Revivalists before Moody had preached the compassion and love of God, but they had not emphasized it. Davenport, in tracing the primitive traits in religious revivals, concludes: "With Moody, religious evangelism is emancipated from the horrid spectres of irrational fear." He suggests that this was due to Moody's emphasis upon "the love of the heavenly Father." [55] Grover C. Loud in his history of revivals also believes that Moody was responsible for this change.[56]

[53] Contained in a letter written to the editor of the *Boston Globe* and published January 22, 1877.

[54] Letter written by Rev. William R. Skerry to *The Christian*, February 25, 1875, pp. 129-30.

[55] Davenport, *op. cit.*, pp. 204-5.

[56] Loud, *op. cit.*, p. 234.

The second change that Moody wrought was the introduction of methods of organization and administration that were deliberately aimed toward developing an urban community into a psychological crowd in order to facilitate conversions and active participation in religious endeavors. Prior to this time many revival audiences had been transformed into psychological crowds, but never before had methods of business been introduced; never had tabernacles been built in successive cities; never had there been such deliberate and widespread planning. Isolated examples might be cited, but none on the scale of the Moody revivals beginning in 1873. In the twentieth century, Billy Sunday merely imitated the methods of Moody, making some variations. This connection can readily be traced, for Sunday learned from Chapman, and Chapman learned from Moody. William Adams Brown suggests, "Mr. Moody set the standard for all later, American evangelists, and has had many imitators, from W. J. Chapman to Billy Sunday."[57]

Moody believed that religion should be the dominant factor in men's lives. Conversion, church attendance, and practice of the principles of religion in business and professional life were not enough. He believed that each man, woman, and child, once converted, should establish allegiance with some religious organization; then each, working with such an organization, should spend time converting others and getting them to participate in religious endeavors. To Moody, this was the key to a happy life. Furthermore, he believed that the problems of the world could be solved better by people of this type. His life was devoted to the work of arousing religious sentiment and activity. That he achieved success in his time cannot be doubted.

However, the big problem was one of motivation; someone must get the people of the world "stirred up" to carry on this work. This was the role that Moody chose for himself. His personal philosophy was that he would rather "put ten men to work than do the work of ten men." Thus, he turned to the religious revival as a means to accomplish this. First, he would turn to church members and stimulate enthusiasm for getting new converts. Then, for a few weeks, he would join in their efforts, leading the way and showing them how. Before leaving a particular community, he would develop a program by which the work would continue, carried on by former church members and the new converts.

As the years passed, he saw that this was not enough; the period of a revival was too short to train strong leadership. Thus, he established two schools at Northfield, the Bible Institute in Chicago, and Summer Conferences as means for providing this training. Others were given this task, while Moody continued to work with the masses through his religious revivals.

[57] William Adams Brown, *Church and State in Contemporary America* (New York: Charles Scribner's Sons, 1936), p. 214.

With these methods, Moody hoped to make religion the dominant factor in men's lives.

SELECTED BIBLIOGRAPHY

Collections

A. P. Fitt Collection. Northfield, Massachusetts. This collection includes clippings of many newspaper and magazine articles, official publications of the institutions founded by Moody, two hundred and thirty-three sermon envelopes, petitions requesting revival campaigns, letters containing reminiscences of Moody, correspondence of A. P. Fitt to verify various of the data, letters of tribute, letters written to Moody and over four hundred letters written by Moody.

Moody Bible Institute Collection. Moody Bible Institute, Chicago, Illinois. This collection includes several collections of Moody's official correspondence relating to the management of the Institute, one set of sermon notes, one of Moody's marked Bibles, and a letter describing Moody's conversion, by his Sunday school teacher.

Paul D. Moody Collection. Northfield, Massachusetts. This collection includes a set of *The Christian* for those years during which Moody was conducting evangelistic tours of Great Britain, the Moody Genealogy Chart, and private publications on Moody.

W. R. Moody Collection. Northfield, Massachusetts. This collection includes thirty-one envelopes of sermon notes, correspondence of the Moody family, Mrs. D. L. Moody's Diary, letters of reminiscences of Moody, and correspondence concerning the Northfield schools.

Mount Hermon Library Collection. Mount Hermon Academy, Mount Hermon, Massachusetts. This collection includes tickets for admission to the Moody revivals, posters, executive committee announcements, and other miscellaneous material used in connection with the revival campaigns.

Northfield Schools Administrative Officers Collection. Northfield, Massachusetts. This collection includes some of the correspondence of Moody concerning the two schools and newspaper articles and pamphlets on the Moody Centennial.

Elmer Powell Collection. Chester, Pennsylvania. This collection includes virtually all the books published on and by Moody and manuscripts of the findings of Powell in his studies of Moody's life. (Elmer Powell is a retired Baptist minister who made a hobby of this study; the collection is now in the possession of the Crozer Theological Seminary Library.)

Washburne Collection. Racine, Wisconsin. This collection includes Moody family pictures, correspondence of Moody, particularly of his early life, mortgages, deeds, and the family Bible which records Moody's date of birth. The collection is the possession of Miriam Elim Washburne.

Books and Magazines

ANDREAS, A. T. *History of Chicago*. 3 vols. Chicago: A. T. Andreas Co., 1885.

BROWN, MARIANNA C. *Sunday School Movements in America*. Chicago: Fleming H. Revell Co., 1901.

BROWN, WILLIAM ADAMS. *Church and State in Contemporary America*. New York: Charles Scribner's Sons, 1936.

COPE, HENRY FREDERICK. *The Evolution of the Sunday School*. Boston: Pilgrim Press, 1911.

DANIELS, REV. W. H. *D. L. Moody and His Work*. Hartford, Conn.: American Publishing Co., 1876.

DAVENPORT, FREDERICK MORGAN. *Primitive Traits in Religious Revivals*. New York: The Macmillan Co., 1905.

DAY, RICHARD ELLSWORTH. *Bush Aglow*. Philadelphia: The Judson Press, 1936.

DUNNING, WILLIAM ARCHIBALD. *Reconstruction Political and Economic, 1865-1877*. (*The American Nation: A History*, ed. A. B. HART, Vol. XXII.) New York: Harper & Brothers, 1907.

FARWELL, JOHN V. *Early Recollections of Dwight L. Moody*. Chicago: Bible Institute Colportage Association.

FITT, A. P. *Moody Still Lives*. Chicago: Fleming H. Revell Co., 1936.

GOSS, REV. CHARLES F. *Echoes for the Pulpit and Platform*. Hartford, Conn.: A. D. Worthington & Co., 1900.

HYNDMAN, H. M. *Commercial Crises of the Nineteenth Century* (2nd ed.). London: George Allen & Unwin, Ltd., 1932.

LOUD, GROVER C. *Evangelized America*. New York: Longmans, Green & Co., 1928.

MacKINNON, MRS. PETER. *Recollections of D. L. Moody*. Printed for Private Circulation, 1905.

MILLS, A. H. *A Hundred Years of Sunday School History in Illinois* (Publications of the Illinois State Historical Library, No. 24.) Springfield, Illinois, 1918.

MOODY, D. L. *Anecdotes, Incidents and Illustrations*. Chicago: Bible Institute Colportage Association, 1898.

———. *The Great Redemption*. New York: Loomis National Library Association, 1888.

———. *Great Joy, Sermons and Prayer-meeting Talks Delivered at the Chicago Tabernacle*. New York: E. B. Treat, 1877.

———. *To All People*. New York: E. B. Treat, 1877.

MOODY, PAUL D. *My Father*. Boston: Little, Brown & Co., 1938.

MOODY, WILLIAM R. *D. L. Moody*. New York: The Macmillian Co., 1931.

———. *The Life of Dwight L. Moody*. Chicago: Fleming H. Revell Co., 1900.

MORSE, RICHARD C. *History of the North American Y. M. C. A.* New York: Association Press, 1913.

———. *My Life with Young Men*. New York: Association Press, 1918.

MOSS, REV. LEMUEL. *Annals of the United States Christian Commission*. Philadelphia: J. B. Lippincott & Co., 1868.

MOTT, JOHN R. "The Greatness of Dwight L. Moody," *Association Men* (February, 1915).

NASON, REV. ELIAS. *Lives of Moody, Sankey and Bliss*. Boston: B. B. Russell, 1877.

———, AND BEALE, J. FRANK, JR. *Lives and Labors of Eminent Divines*. Philadelphia: John E. Potter & Co., 1895.

NEVINS, ALLAN. *The Emergence of America, 1865-1878*. New York: The Macmillan Co., 1927.

Northfield Echoes. 6 vols. Northfield, Mass.: The Northfield Press, 1894-99.

PARSONS, H. C. *A Puritan Outpost: A History of the Town and People of Northfield, Massachusetts*. New York: The Macmillan Co., 1937.

Proceedings of the 9th Annual Convention of the Illinois State Sabbath School Association. 1867.

Proceedings of the 22nd Illinois State Sunday School Convention. 1880.

SANKEY, IRA. D. *My Life and the Story of the Gospel Hymns*. New York: Harper & Brothers, 1906.

SMITH, REV. EDWARD P. *Incidents of the United States Christian Commission.* Philadelphia: J. B. Lippincott & Co., 1869.

SMITH, EDWIN; GRANT, JOHN; AND STARKEY, HORACE. *Historical Sketch of the Young Men's Christian Association of Chicago.* Chicago: Y. M. C. A. of Chicago, 1898.

SUNDERLAND, REV. J. T. *Orthodoxy and Revivalism.* New York: James Miller, 1876.

TEMPLE, J. H., and SHELDON, GEORGE. *A History of the Town of Northfield.* Albany, N. Y.: Joel Munsell, 1875.

TUTTLE, REV. E. B. *History of Camp Douglas.* Chicago: J. R. Walsh & Co., 1865.

United States Christian Commission for the Army and Navy, Annual Reports. Philadelphia, February, 1863.

WILKINSON, WILLIAM C. "Dwight L. Moody as Preacher," *Homiletic Review*, 36, (August, 1898), 110-19,

———. "Dwight L. Moody as Man of Affairs," *ibid.* (September, 1898), 201-8.

Bible Institute Monthly [later*The Moody Monthly*]. Chicago, Illinois.

The Christian. London: Morgan & Scott, 1873-75; 1881-84; 1891-92.

The Evangelistic Record [later *The Record of Christian Work*]. Chicago: Fleming H. Revell Co., 1881-99.

Clarence Darrow

by MARTIN MALONEY

Clarence Seward Darrow was born in Kinsman, Ohio, April 18, 1857. He was educated at the Kinsman district school and academy, at Allegheny College (Meadville, Pennsylvania), and the University of Michigan law school. After his admission to the bar, he practised law in Ohio for a time, then moved to Chicago. Here he received an appointment to the legal staff of the city of Chicago, and eventually became head of the city's law department. He resigned this position to become general attorney for the Chicago and Northwestern Railway. When Eugene V. Debs was indicted on charges of conspiracy in 1895, following the American Railway Union strike, Darrow resigned in order to accept Debs' defense. From 1895 to 1913 he tried labor cases principally, representing the United Mine Workers in 1902, William D. Haywood in 1907, and the McNamara brothers in 1910-11. The last case led to Darrow's indictment on a charge of bribing a juror; and after his acquittal he turned to a more general practice which lasted until the early 1930's. Among his more celebrated cases in these years were the defenses of Richard Loeb and Nathan Leopold on a charge of murder, and of John Scopes on a charge of violating the Tennessee "anti-evolution" law. Darrow served on the National Recovery Review Board in the early thirties. He debated and lectured widely, especially during his later years. His written works would include autobiographies, lectures, debates, legal pleas, essays on religion, philosophy, and literature, a text on criminology, and a novel. His last few years were spent in retirement in Chicago. He died March 13, 1938.

This is a study of Clarence Darrow, a nonconformist by habit, a devil's advocate by profession. Such a man does not fit easily into any roster of "great orators," or even into a conventional history of American public address. If we go by the common verdicts of historians and critics, our "great orator" should bear some resemblance to a Webster, a Clay, a Roosevelt. He should be a man whose chief interest was in politics, who, by placing his talents as a speaker at the service of commonly debated national issues, contrived to play a part in the schoolbook history of his country. There are, of course, a few men who achieved their positions in the canon of orators largely because of the fruitfulness and originality of their thought. In this class we must place chiefly ecclesiastics and philosophers, speculators on religion and ethics like

Channing, Parker, or Emerson. But it is surely part of the American tradition, which has seemingly carried over into rhetorical criticism, to conceive of the lawyer-turned-politician as the "typical" orator of mark.[1]

Clarence Darrow was not a politician; and although he brought a very considerable talent as a pleader to the discussion of issues of great national importance, the point of view he represented was, at the time, that of an infinitesimal minority, and so was unlikely to prevail in national councils. He was concerned, for example, with various topics relating to capital and labor economics, but the arguments that he advanced on this subject between 1890 and 1914 were not seriously discussed in the American Congress until the 1930's. His concepts of criminology, of the administration of justice, of religion, philosophy, and ethics have scarcely been discussed systematically in any national forum to the present day. Nor was Darrow in any sense an original thinker, or even a thorough critic of the philosophies of others. His philosophic system was a patchwork: Nietzsche, Lombroso, Tolstoy, Darwin, and a host of others contributed to it.

How, then, are we to place Darrow in the ranks of orators great and not-so-great? It would seem unwise, indeed, to "place" him at all, to rate him according to the magnitude of the issues with which he was involved, to cite the gross facts of his career, noting that he defended some two thousand cases in court and won most of them, that he attracted great audiences to his lectures and debates, that he published a half-dozen books and perhaps fifty pamphlets and magazine articles, that he reached directly or indirectly an audience of millions. Darrow's status in American life from about 1895 to the time of his death in 1938 is not to be so simply detailed. It is true that, when he died, some thousands of persons still living had heard him speak. More remarkable, millions knew of him and felt for him that close bond of intimacy that is reserved for strangers whose lives seem to hold some special significance for us. As Irving Stone puts it, "He had become a myth during his own time. Few people in America did not know his name and his face. No one of his day was more discussed, more loved and more hated. . . ."[2] Stone uses the term "myth" casually; it is worth a closer examination. Many persons, it appears, achieve a special kind of status in public life; they are possessed of an indescribable charm which seems to lend their least action a disproportionate significance. They may be "heroes" or "villains" by label, but their fascination for great numbers of people is undeniable. In our society, the function of

[1] See, for example, W. N. Brigance's preface to *A History and Criticism of American Public Address* (New York: McGraw-Hill Book Co., 1943), I, vii-xi, for a discussion of the problem of "rating" speakers for inclusion in a history.

[2] Irving Stone, *Clarence Darrow for the Defense* (Garden City, New York: Doubleday, Doran, 1941), p. 497.

such individuals would seem to be a dramatic one. At least, actors, public entertainers, and persons with a marked dramatic flair appear to achieve the status of "living myth" very frequently.

It is possible to test the status of any public person, in this respect, by observing the general response to the last scene of his human performance: death. In the cases of individuals who have become "myths during their own time," this response is describable only as a general shock, a sort of public trauma. It may be observed in behavior as the news of death spreads, in behavior during the post-mortem rituals, and in editorials and obituaries in the press. Examples of this sort of response might be multiplied almost endlessly, even in the history of the present century; one need only recollect the public reaction to the deaths of such diverse individuals as Mohandas K. Ghandi, Franklin D. Roosevelt, Will Rogers, and Rudolph Valentino, to perceive the pattern. Darrow's death evoked a similar response. Irving Stone remarks that, after Darrow died, the funeral parlor in which his body lay was unable to close its doors for forty-eight hours because of the great throngs of people who came to see him for the last time. There were countless newspaper obituaries, public tributes and sermons, all of which eulogized Darrow and stressed the great public loss occasioned by his death.[3] This "public loss" was not a mere convention of the press; my own experience in interviewing and corresponding with persons who had known Darrow or heard him speak would suggest that, in his death, they had lost something meaningful and even necessary to their lives.

For purposes of criticism, then, we shall say that Darrow, in the most literal and technical sense of the term, had become a myth by the time of his death.

The functions of myth-patterns in a society need scarcely be described in detail here, but perhaps a brief summary is in order.[4] In any sort of society, at any time, certain attitudes, beliefs, and practices seem necessary to insure the survival of the society, or of individuals living within the society, or of both. These attitudes, beliefs, and practices must be learned and relearned as long as survival value attaches to them, and sometimes they continue to be learned long after they have become anachronisms. One of the mechanisms in the learning process is the myth-pattern. That is to say, where a philosophy or a system of ethics may provide a society with beliefs and attitudes at a very abstract level, it is the function of myth to translate these abstractions

[3] Stone, *op. cit.*, pp. 516-18. The nature and extent of the obituaries and eulogies on Darrow may be judged by the selection reprinted in *Unity*, May 16, 1938.

[4] For a careful treatment of this subject from an anthropological point of view, see Melville J. Herskovits, *Man and His Works* (New York: Alfred A. Knopf, 1948), especially chaps. 24 and 25.

into the specifics of everyday behavior. This has traditionally been accomplished through the arts and particularly through folklore, drama, painting, dance, and poetry. As Lawrence K. Frank points out,

Art is socially significant because it provides the patterns and the aesthetic experiences that rule human conduct, above and beyond all factors in man or in life. Whatever we are or may become we derive from the artist, however he be named or labeled, and in his creations we find our ideals, our hopes, our values and meanings which set our goals and dictate our conduct. The artist gives the form or pattern for human activity and invests our otherwise dull and shabby lives with significance and purpose.[5]

We may add to this that myths are not always consciously created by "the artist," however broadly defined; for sometimes a people will find their dramatized living-patterns in a spontaneous distortion of history or biography; and sometimes they clothe living persons with the luminous robes of myth. When this last thing happens, the person so selected achieves a special sort of influence over the lives of people to whom the myth has meaning.[6]

The general dramatic pattern of which Clarence Darrow's life provides a specific example is well known to folklorists and to students of cultural history in general. Herskovits, for example, writes,

Another manifestation of how, so to speak, folklore creates a world where vindications that the world of reality denies, are granted, is to be found in the

[5] Lawrence K. Frank, "Art and Living," in *Society as the Patient* (New Brunswick, New Jersey: Rutgers University Press, 1948), p. 269.

[6] An admirable example of this phenomenon is discussed in Thurman Arnold's *The Folklore of Capitalism* (New Haven: Yale University Press, 1937), pp. 390-91: "Roosevelt . . . has become a symbol for a political attitude which cannot yet be put into words. The fact that Roosevelt has become the symbol of a new attitude is shown by the fact that so many of those who support him are hostile or else indifferent to the particular measures he advocates.

"Hostile editors, observing the failure of some Roosevelt policy, are puzzled over the continuing Roosevelt support. They attribute it to his charming smile, his radio voice, and whatnot. The answer . . . has little to do with his personal characteristics. Institutions which express in concrete form the vague aspirations of any group always arouse that kind of allegiance. Never has this been expressed in a more striking way than by the parade of intellectuals who testified against the Roosevelt Supreme Court Plan before the Senate Committee. These individuals stated that they disapproved of the majority decisions of the Court on national affairs, yet they considered it essential to the nation that the Court continue in power over national affairs. For these persons, composed of radicals and conservatives alike, the Court represented the supremacy of intellect and reason. Hence they were for it, no matter what it did. To attribute this to Hughes's charming manner or Sutherland's public personality is to make the same mistake about the influence of the Supreme Court which is being made about the present Roosevelt influence."

stories wherein the weak prevail over the strong, where evil meets an avenger, or where many other of the less pleasant conditions of life are resolved in ways that are not those of the workaday world. Here, in terms of a kind of socialized fantasy, men and women are comforted for the hardships, the inequalities, the injustices of the daily round. They achieve this by identifying themselves with characters who get the best of those stronger than themselves, or who right the wrongs of the oppressed, or defeat the hard realities of time and distance and even solve the ultimate riddle of restoring life to the dead. . . . By transporting men and women into a realm where the problems of life are solved as they rarely are disposed of in actual living, folklore thus affords a release, provides them with courage, and shows itself as a many-faceted vehicle of self-expression on both the conscious and unconscious levels.[7]

It is our present hypothesis that Darrow's life served as a kind of living dramatization of this sort of theme, that his status in American life can best be understood if we think of it as essentially "folkloristic" or "mythical."

We must now inquire briefly into the general structure of the Darrow myth. When Darrow, in defending himself against a charge of bribery before a Los Angeles jury in 1912, said, "I have stood for the weak and the poor. I have stood for the men who toil,"[8] he suggested the nature of the fable. It was as a defender of the underdog, a devil's advocate, a man who stood perpetually opposed to the great and powerful of the earth, that he became known. His role is not unfamiliar in Anglo-American mythology, although its significance in Darrow's day had altered somewhat. One might suppose, on the face of the matter, that the "defender of the weak" myth has survived because the protection of the weak is in some sense necessary to the survival of our society. Perhaps that is true; but we shall point out that, in Darrow's lifetime, the myth had significance because so many people in the United States recognized themselves as underdogs, as outcasts, either real or potential. The twin strands of aggressiveness and insecurity interweave in the pattern of American attitudes;[9] and it is the major function of the "underdog" myth to rationalize and reconcile the two. Thus, an alien, a workingman, a Negro, following Darrow's triumphs, could see himself, in Darrow, triumphant over the forces that pressed him in, saving the unjustly doomed victim from the hangman, speaking out for freedom and justice; and at the same time might know himself the innocent victim, saved against all expectation from his enemies.

[7] Herskovits, *op. cit.*, p. 421.

[8] *Plea of Clarence Darrow in His Own Defense* (Los Angeles, 1915), p. 6.

[9] See, for example, Margaret Mead's discussion of this aspect of the American character in *And Keep Your Powder Dry* (New York: William Morrow Co. 1942), p. 138ff; also Lawrence K. Frank's discussion of the aggression-insecurity motif as it relates to our "competitive" psychology, *op. cit.*, p. 29ff.

It is not our purpose here to establish, in any definite or final way, the validity of this hypothesis. Rather we would offer it tentatively as a possibly useful means of arranging and explaining some of the facts in the public career of Clarence Darrow.

Education of a Barbarian

In describing the social philosophy of competition, Lawrence Frank provides some illuminating insights into the motives of a man like Clarence Darrow. He writes,

> The individual who in early life is personally insecure, who feels a strong desire to "get even" for his childhood unhappiness, or who is goaded by an inner feeling of inadequacy or guilt or hostility finds in the competitive game a release for these tensions and a further stimulus to increased tension. Each step forward in the competitive striving brings both the confidence for further effort and the incentive in the form of the more demanding requirements of the position ahead. Thus is set up that circular response that spirals up in intensity of activity paralleled by an equal or greater intensity of need for larger effort. One of the significant aspects of competition is this inability to attain any security in terms of the competitive activity in which it is sought. The reasons for this are more or less clear since competition denies any status that can be considered terminal; hence the competitors, while always setting goals for themselves, are forced to a continual rejection of those goals when attained, in favor of a more remote goal.[10]

These observations would seem to have a dual significance for a study of the career of Clarence Darrow. While it is true that Darrow did not share the "competitive" orientation as such, he does exemplify a kind of parallel orientation. As a result of childhood experience, he did set up for himself certain unattainable goals and attempt to reach them; he never achieved anything resembling a "terminal status" in his lifework; and the pattern of his adult life might be accurately described in terms of the "circular response" of which Frank speaks. Second, but quite as important, we should remember that Darrow entered on adult life in an America which was just beginning to develop on a grand scale the patterns of competition which Frank so admirably describes. Thus, we may observe a striking similarity between the fundamental kinds of problems which affected Darrow, and which he tried to resolve symbolically in his pleading, and the problems which were common to many members of his audience. This similarity, we shall suggest, may account at least in part for Darrow's "mythical" status in public life. First, however, we need to investigate the details of Darrow's early life, and the development of his personal outlook.

[10] Frank, *op. cit.*, p. 33.

According to the standards of middle-class, nineteenth-century America, Clarence Darrow was respectably born. To many, his birth was the only respectable thing about him.

Darrow himself was a little contemptuous of this one stain of respectability on an otherwise unblemished character. He wrote in his autobiography,

I have been told that I came of a very old family. A considerable number of people say that it runs back to Adam and Eve, although this, of course, is only hearsay, and I should not like to guarantee the title. Anyhow, very few pedigrees really go back any farther than mine. With reasonable certainty, I could run it back to a little town in England that has the same name as mine, although the spelling is slightly altered. But this does not matter. I am sure that my forebears run a long, long way back of that, even—but what of it, anyhow? [11]

One of these English Darrows came to New England during the seventeenth century. "He was an undertaker, so we are told, which shows that he had some appreciation of a good business, and so chose a profession where the demand for his services would be fairly steady." [12] One of the descendants of this pioneering undertaker took up arms against King George III. Thus, as Darrow remarked, his ancestry at least qualified him for membership in the Daughters of the American Revolution.[13]

The Darrows remained in Connecticut, as did the family of Clarence Darrow's mother, until a few years before the beginning of the nineteenth century. Then they started west; and Amirus and Emily Darrow, at least, ended the family peregrinations in Kinsman, Ohio, where a son, Clarence Seward, was born to them in 1857.

Kinsman was a sleepy little village, typical enough of the country town of pre-Civil War days. It was neither very prosperous nor very poverty-stricken. "Squire Allen" [14] had a great white house on the hill, set back from the road in a grove of trees, a house with tall white pillars and a brass knocker on the door; but most people in Kinsman had much less to live on, and worked hard to get what they had.

[11] Clarence Darrow, *The Story of My Life* (New York: Charles Scribner's Sons, 1932), p. 1.

[12] *Ibid.*, p. 2.

[13] *Loc. cit.*

[14] This sketch of the economic, moral, and social geography of Kinsman is based wholly on Darrow's recollections, as reported in *Farmington* (New York: Boni and Liveright, 1925) and *The Story of My Life*. Mention of "Squire Allen" comes from *Farmington*, pp. 90-91. This book was published as fiction rather than autobiography, but so closely does the narrative adhere to ascertainable fact that we may be fairly certain that "Squire Allen" actually existed in Kinsman, though no doubt under another name.

Kinsman was pious on Sunday; men, women, and especially children were solemnly soaped and scrubbed, solemnly dressed in sober and uncomfortable Sunday clothes, and they solemnly listened to lengthy and dull sermons in the United Presbyterian Church. Kinsman was not noted for its weekday virtue, nevertheless; farmers and businessmen drove hard, shrewd bargains not always untinged with dishonesty. Perhaps this statement is a trifle unfair; for in Kinsman, one gathered cash and lands to the greater glory of the Lord.

Kinsman attended district school and perhaps the academy, played baseball with much gusto, loved Fourth of July speeches and political debates, worked hard, raised large families, lived and died and were buried in the local cemetery under great stones or small, all in a fairly regular, commonplace pattern.

Within this pattern the Darrows lived, but as aliens. In the ancient sense of the term, they were barbarians, outsiders. "The non-conformist Darrows," writes Irving Stone, "who served as the town agnostics and intellectuals, stumbled onto the one eccentric and non-conformist house in the countryside, an octagonal-shaped structure with a wide wooden pavilion running around seven of its eight sides." [15] In their own eyes, and perhaps in the eyes of the community, they were separated from the "respectable" in their living by invisible boundaries, the hard reality of which has only been described in late years by social scientists. As George K. Zipf writes,

The boundaries in question need not be territorial, for they may be boundaries of privilege, of occupation, of religion, caste, or of some other field of common sentiments. The distinguishing feature of the boundaries is not so much the barbarian's difficulty of transgressing them, as his feeling of restricted freedom of action, once he has done so. [16]

Kinsman was not, in many respects, the likeliest birthplace in the world for a barbarian among barbarians, a man who could not, in his later years, identify himself with even the most scantily supported and embattled political groups, [17] whose one form of personal alliance was with the condemned and the outcast. Indeed, if ever a man, by ancestry and birth and surroundings, was destined to conservatism, to a comfortable acceptance of the manners and morals of his age, that man was Clarence Darrow. He was white, of Anglo-Saxon ancestry, he was born to Protestant parents in a typical rural community. What force could conceivably have pushed him into the ranks of the

[15] Stone, *op. cit.*, p. 10.
[16] George K. Zipf, "transformation: systematic empiric social science and the principle of least effort," in *transformation* 1^1, 1950, p. 13. Although my characterization of Darrow as "barbarian" does not wholly follow Zipf's formulations, I have nevertheless used them freely wherever they seemed pertinent to my data.
[17] See Stone, *op. cit.*, p. 175.

barbarians, could possibly have led him to identify himself with Negroes, labor agitators, and godless biologists? We may note in Darrow's adult relations with the Kinsman of his boyhood an odd sort of ambivalence. In many ways he was a true son of the village. He presented to the world a slow, sober, countrified appearance (which he exploited to some advantage with juries). In many superficial ways he followed the behavior patterns of rural America; he, too, played baseball and loved Fourth of July celebrations and practised the easy friendliness of the American small town. Yet in his deepest convictions and his most characteristic performances he was de-classed. It is difficult to recall any major action of Darrow's life, an action based on principle, which might have had important consequences for him, which did not violate some tenet of the ethical or philosophical system of Kinsman.[18]

Darrow's relationship with the community of his boyhood, while unusual, is by no means unique. The simultaneous attraction and repulsion, the underlying hatred and the rather sentimental affection: these features characterize many intimate human relationships, and especially those within the family. As Kenneth Burke writes,

Santayana has somewhere defined piety as a loyalty to the deepest roots of our being. Such a notion should suggest that piety is not confined to the strictly religious sphere.... The connection between our pieties and our childhood should seem clear, since it is in our childhood that we develop our first patterns of judgment, while the experiences of maturity are probably mere revisions and amplifications of these childhood patterns. An adult, for instance, may turn his thoughts from a father to a father-government; yet even in later life, should he take an axe and fell a great tree, we need not be surprised to find a strange misgiving permeate him as the noble symbol of shelter comes crashing to the earth. For however neutral his act, though the tree had been felled to satisfy the simple utilitarian needs of firewood, there may also be lurking here a kind of symbolic parricide. Not only firewood, but the father-symbol, may be brought down in the crash.[19]

Darrow's deepest pieties, we may feel sure, centered about the figure of his father. But the father was himself a lifelong rebel, a smasher of paternal images. Thus we find created the central psychological fact of Darrow's life: out of the deepest piety and filial affection, he was led into a life which might be described as a series of symbolic parricides. It is scarcely surprising, then, that we find Darrow at once accepting and rejecting, at once loving and

[18] The only exception to this statement, so far as I am aware, was Darrow's espousal of the allied cause in World War I: an action which he later regretted bitterly.

[19] Kenneth Burke, *Permanence and Change: an Anatomy of Purpose* (New York: New Republic, 1936), pp. 95-96.

hating, not only the "father community" of Kinsman, but his true father, Amirus Darrow.

We can at least be certain that his relations with his father concerned him to the end of his life. As Stone notes,

The last words he was to write, which were found in his desk, scribbled in longhand on composition-book paper, were an epitome of his life. "The fact that my father was a heretic always put him on the defensive, and we children thought it was only right and loyal that we should defend his cause. Even in our little shop the neighbors learned that there was something going on and that my father was ever ready to meet all comers on the mysteries of life and death. During my youth I always listened, but my moral support was with my father. I cannot remember that I ever had any doubt that he was right. The fact that most of the community were on the other side made him so much surer of his cause." [20]

It is well, then, to know something of Amirus Darrow; for his intellectual and spiritual life was intimately bound up with that of his son.

Amirus Darrow was one of a family of seven. As a child, he moved with his family from New England to eastern Ohio, which was then almost frontier country. His troubles seem to have started when he began to think about religion. After his marriage to Emily Eddy, he went with his wife to Meadville, Pennsylvania, and there enrolled in Allegheny College, a Methodist school. At the time of his graduation, according to his son, "He was still religious. His religion was born from a sensitive nature that made him pity the sad and suffering, and which, first and last, tied him to every hopeless cause that came his way." [21] Yet his faith in formal dogma was surely shaken. Having been graduated from the Methodist college, Darrow moved to a nearby Unitarian seminary, where he studied for a theological degree. By the time it was granted him, Darrow discovered that he had completely lost his faith. Through the remainder of his life, he refused to preach in any church.

So Amirus Darrow became woodworker and undertaker to the little community of Kinsman. He was an honest workman, but not an enthusiastic one. The concerns of the Greeks, the Romans, and the Jews occupied far more of his attention than did the prosaic business of building beds and coffins. "But day after day and year after year he was compelled to walk the short and narrow path between the little house and the decaying mill, while his mind roved over scenes of great battles, decayed empires, dead languages, and the starry heavens above." [22]

[20] Stone, *op. cit.*, p. 515.
[21] *The Story of My Life*, p. 10.
[22] *Farmington*, p. 38. In this book, Darrow changes his father's trade to that of miller.

As for Amirus Darrow's son, Clarence, he attended the Kinsman district school where he proved to be a good baseball player and a fair scholar. He took an interest in debate and elocution, but was not especially successful at either pursuit. After he was graduated from the academy, he attended Allegheny College, in Meadville, for a year. He then returned to Kinsman, where he worked for a time in his father's carpentry shop. During the winters he taught in the district school.

While he was teaching, Darrow began to read law; and at the end of three years, with the financial aid of a sister and an older brother, he attended the University of Michigan law school for a year. He then read further in a law office in Youngstown, Ohio, was admitted to the bar, and set up practice in the little town of Andover, Ohio. After a short period of practice in Andover, and a somewhat longer one in Ashtabula, Darrow made up his mind to go to Chicago.

So brief an outline of a man's youth is only apparently meaningful. In a sense, it is meaningless precisely because it is factual. To compose such a statement as a portrait of a man is not enough; it is only a skeleton, on which we can hardly imagine the living flesh. The spiritual flesh which Clarence Darrow nourished through these early years was largely a direct heritage from his father, and we shall do well to examine briefly the process by which he acquired it.

The compulsive sympathy between Darrow and his father was deep and abiding, and usually affected Darrow in his larger and more consequential attitudes. Their differences, though sometimes bitter, were usually over relatively trivial matters—for instance, the matter of education. Darrow comments that he did not learn his letters as rapidly as his elder brother had:

It must be that my father gave me little chance to tarry long from one book to another, for I remember that at an early age I was told that John Stuart Mill began studying Greek when he was only three years old. I thought then, as I do today, that he must have had a cruel father, and that this unnatural parent not only made miserable the life of his little boy, but of thousands of other boys whose fathers could see no reason why their sons should be outdone by John Stuart Mill.[23]

This resentment against his father's educational efforts seems to have carried over into a resentment against the educational system in general. This, Darrow considered to be like all systems, in that it was irrational and sometimes brutal and always inflexible.[24] Fortunately, he did not rebel against learning; the indirect influence of his father's example prevented that.

In a positive way, Darrow acquired from his father a skill and a habit of

[23] *Ibid.*, p. 41.
[24] See *The Story of My Life*, especially chaps. 2 and 3, and *Farmington*, chaps. 5, 6, and 7.

response. The skill was that of speech; the habit, a characteristic sympathy for other barbarians. Amirus Darrow's debate training was comprehensive. He gave his son a set of opponents, a set of colleagues, a set of topics, and a set of arguments. They lasted Clarence Darrow all his life.

The elder Darrow's perpetual dissension from the opinions of his neighbors quite naturally branded him as "an odd one." The villagers, finding Darrow markedly different from themselves, saw in him a potential enemy, if not a real one. And this verdict was extended from Amirus Darrow to his whole family. On this point, his son wrote:

On religious and social questions, our family early learned to stand alone. My father was the village infidel, and gradually came to glory in his reputation. Within a radius of five miles were other 'infidels' as well, and these men formed a select group of their own. We were not denied association with the church members; the communicants of the smaller churches were our friends. For instance, there was a Catholic society that met at the home of one of its adherents once in two or three weeks, and between them and our family there grew up a sort of kinship. We were alike strangers in a more or less hostile land.[25]

In these few sentences is contained a brief but pointed explanation of why Clarence Darrow was what he was. The long years of social ostracism, of stinging gossip, of smug epithets and casual contempt, must have taught Darrow to stand perpetually in a fighting pose. The majority of men, he learned, were his enemies; as such, he observed them; he saw their petty dishonesties, their sly indecencies, their safe brutality, their righteous wickedness. A thousand times a year he must have rehearsed these matters to himself; nothing else could account for his later use of invective in slashing at the rich, the powerful, the respectable. He never forgot that they were, officially and as a group, the enemy.

He learned, by the same token, that the poor and the despised and the outcast were his friends, his companions in the ill-regard of the mob. He did not forget this lesson, either. To the end of his life he could never refuse help to one of them who needed it.

He was Amirus Darrow's son. The fascination of verbal battles never left him. Indeed, it was this fascination which led him to study law. He had long admired the prosperous appearance, the loud, eloquent voices and the rich invective of the country lawyers; and so, as he grew older, he decided to study for the profession.[26] "I was never fond of manual labor," he wrote. "I felt that I was made for better things."[27] And again, "The tinner was the

[25] *The Story of My Life*, pp. 14-15.
[26] *Ibid.*, p. 28.
[27] *Ibid.*, p. 27.

justice of the peace (in Kinsman), and I never missed a chance to go over to his shop when a case was on trial. I enjoyed the way the pettifoggers abused each other." [28] A life of ease and controversy: this was the goal which Darrow later avowed had led him to the law courts. At least half of it was a heritage from his father.

There is, in Darrow's writing and speaking, the ever-recurring theme of death. Generally he faces it with a certain bravado, a great gesture of death-must-come-and-after-that-nothing. But the bravado is forced and the gesture lacks conviction. As he grew older, Darrow's fear of death became more haunting and morbid. By common consent, his friends did not mention the topic, although he himself sometimes did. [29]

How much of this fear grew out of childhood experience, and how much of it was projected from old age or middle age into the accounts of his childhood, is difficult to say. But there are, in his writings, many references to death and to the dead; they are usually grim and extraordinarily vivid.

Amirus Darrow, it will be remembered, was not a maker of household furniture alone; he also made coffins. In one corner of his workshop they were piled, waiting for their occupants. His son feared and avoided that corner in the little workshop; yet "even when very young used to wonder in a cynical way whether he [Amirus Darrow] felt more pain or pleasure over the death of a neighbor or friend." [30]

In *Farmington,* Darrow tells of his first actual experience with death. [31] It happened during the Civil War, when he was no more than four or five years old. Playing under the maple trees in the front yard, he heard the drum and fife over the hill, and ran out to see the soldiers go by. They rode in a two-horse wagon, both men and boys, and he stood there, hoop in hand, and watched them. For some reason, he saw clearly a boy who stood in the middle of the wagon: his face, and his smile. Then, a few months later,

I recall a great throng of people, and among them all the boys and girls from the school, and we are gathered inside the burying ground where they are carrying the young soldier who rode past our house a few months before. I cannot remember what was said at the funeral, but this is the first impression that I can recall of the grim spectre Death. What it meant to my childish mind I cannot now conceive. I remember only the hushed awe and the deep dread that fell upon us all when we realized that they were putting this boy into the ground and that we should never see his face again. [32]

[28] *Ibid.,* p. 29.
[29] Norman Thomas, Interview.
[30] *The Story of My Life,* p. 15.
[31] Pp. 24-26.
[32] *Ibid.,* p. 25.

It should be remembered that Darrow was a man in early middle age when he wrote these lines: not young enough to recall his early childhood easily, nor old enough to fear the imminent approach of death.

There are other references which might be listed: the death of Emily Darrow, which he describes in such curious terms as "despair and grief," "shudder and horror"; [33] his meditations on the death of the village squire: "It is many years since the worms ate up the last morsel of the old man that even a worm could find fit to eat, but still even after death and decay he lies there solitary and exclusive, the most commanding and imposing of all the names that seek immortality in the carved letters of the granite stones"; [34] and his childish awe of the "uncanny presence" of the village sexton. [35]

All his life, Darrow spoke of the common pursuits of men as "dope": work and sleep, play and love, religion and politics. He himself admitted that his customary drive into one case after another, one book after another, his endless ramblings up and down the land, his endless conversations with everyone he met—these, too, in the last analysis were "dope." He never mentioned, though, precisely what pain he was trying to dull. One wonders whether he did not live in a constant effort to numb, for a little while, his morbid fear of death.

This, then, was Clarence Darrow, lawyer. Because he was his father's son, time and eternity were alike ranged against him. He knew he never had a chance: he might win all the skirmishes, all the battles, but never the war. In a way, and precisely because he was his father's son, he stood fatherless and unprotected in a world which was both alien and hostile to him. It is probable that, aside from his immediate family ties, his only genuine human relationships were with the outcast, the hated, the condemned. It was not so much that he liked or even sympathized with the individual Negro, or anarchist, or murderer; it was simply that they were like him in the most important of ways. And most important of all, in defending them he could attack his enemies at a level and in a way in which he might momentarily win. A verdict of acquittal was, for Darrow, a hard stroke at Kinsman, a storming of heaven, a triumph over death.

This was the man who, at the age of twenty-nine, with a wife and a four-year-old son, left the quiet country practice of Ohio for the battleground of Chicago.

[33] *Ibid.*, p. 35.
[34] *Ibid.*, p. 93.
[35] *Ibid.*, p. 118.

School for Barbarians: The Social Context of Darrow's Pleading

We have spoken of Clarence Darrow's early years as "the education of a barbarian." Of the age in which Darrow grew to young manhood, it might accurately be said that one of its principal industries was the training of barbarians. Before the Civil War, America was chiefly an agrarian nation, particularly in outlook and, to a large extent, in fact. It was a country of small towns and empty spaces, whose citizens tended to have the free-and-easy attitudes of the frontiersman, whether or not they actually lived on the frontier. America was to a large extent unified in respect to religion, politics, and culture, since its citizens were chiefly Protestant by religion, English or Anglo-French in their political heritage, and British (with some Teutonic admixture) in their cultural patterns.

With the end of the Civil War, this situation changed. The frontier rapidly diminished, and the frontier attitudes went with it. For the free-and-easy gambler's outlook of the frontiersman was substituted the new industrial philosophy of uninhibited competition, which has so gripped the nation in our own times. The general basis of agreement which most Americans enjoyed in religion, politics, and habits of living was smashed under successive waves of immigration. The enormous prestige which has attached to science and technology as a result of the industrialization of America proved destructive of many common attitudes, especially religious and ethical ones.

With this change, came conflict. In general, it might be said that the established groups—political, religious, racial—feeling their positions endangered, resenting change, and yet, paradoxically enough, subscribing to the principle of competition, fought the new elements in society with all the weapons at their disposal. Since these groups were established, they succeeded in creating scores of more-or-less artificial minorities, of "barbarian" groups. As a natural concomitant, a tremendous and pervasive insistence on conformity developed, a conformity which extended to manners, morals, politics, education, and indeed to most of the minutiae of living. Two great classes of society began to emerge: the in-group (the orthodox or native Americans), and an assortment of out-groups of various kinds.

It will, of course, be clear that the established groups fought a losing battle. For one thing, very little was required to keep an individual out of the established group; he might be orthodox in all respects save one—his religion, for example—and on that score alone be suspect. For another, no group has ever successfully resisted time and change, a fact which became clearer to the established groups as the years went by. As a result, the orthodox Americans had always to look forward to a day when they would eventually falter and be submerged, while the barbarians, after the manner of barbarians in all times, inherited the earth.

Any highly compressed portrait of an era is of necessity inaccurate; it leaves out too much. Yet the foregoing comments, brief as they are, will serve to suggest the nature of Darrow's relationship to the world of his lifetime. Why should this man be drawn irresistibly into almost every major battle of his time, while a thousand others, indistinguishable from him in intelligence, in learning, in skills, in background, moved gently through lives of comparative calm? What we have seen of Darrow's early years—his relationship with his father, his resulting self-identification with the out-group, his terror of death and the endless search for an anodyne against this fear—these things not only insured him a restless life of searching and activity, they made certain as well that he would be drawn surely and directly into the conflicts of his America; for at bottom, Darrow's private stresses and dilemmas and questionings were not at all unlike the very public problems that afflicted the United States in these years. In a special sense, Darrow was America in microcosm.

It seems desirable, then, to examine in somewhat greater detail than we have so far done the nature of some of the conflicts that characterized American society during the years of Darrow's metropolitan practice.

Behind the changes we have already noted there was a mushroom growth in the American population. Between 1870 and 1900, the population of the country doubled; between 1850 and 1900, it trebled. In the former case, this meant a rise from 38,558,000 persons to 75,994,000. Immigrants and the sons of immigrants swelled these ranks: Germans, Irish, Swedes, men of a half-hundred nations. They poured into the country in an endless stream. It has been estimated that between 1820 and 1900, twenty million persons came from abroad to this country. Perhaps two-thirds to three-fourths remained.[36]

Private industry aided and abetted by the federal government, encouraged this vast immigrant flow. The government, in 1864, established an Immigration Bureau in Washington; and Congress legalized the importation of contract laborers from Europe and the Orient. Industry, through its agents abroad, made irresistible the long journey from the rebellion and oppression and poverty of Europe to the freedom and prosperity of America.

During these years of expansion, America was industrially rootless, traditionless. There was no aristocracy of industry; there were no patterns of behavior for the new rich to follow; there were no castes. There was only the vast richness of America to be exploited; there was a rapidly developing system of transportation to provide the means of exploitation; there was the

[36] Louis J. Hacker and Benjamin B. Kendrick, *The United States since 1865* (New York: F. S. Crofts & Co., 1938), p. 186 and pp. 128-29.

stimulus of the Civil War; there was a loud, polyglot, heterogeneous, ambitious population to exploit and be exploited.

The picture was not wholly pleasant. As Walt Whitman wrote,

The depravity of the business classes of our country is not less than has been supposed, but infinitely greater. The official services of America, national, state, and municipal, in all their branches and departments, except the judiciary, are saturated in corruption, bribery, falsehood, mal-administration: and the judiciary is tainted. The great cities reek with respectable as much as non-respectable robbery and scoundrelism. In fashionable life, flippancy, tepid amours, weak infidelism, small aims, or no aims at all, only to kill time. In business (this all-devouring modern word, business), the one sole object is, by any means, pecuniary gain.[37]

Of course, Andrew Carnegie was to idealize America's boisterous pursuit of money and power in 1902:

The successful man of affairs soon rises above the mere desire to make money as the chief end of his labors; that is superseded by the thoughts of the uses he performs in the line which I have just mentioned. The merchant soon finds his strongest feeling to be that of pride in the extent of his internal operations; in his ships sailing every sea. The manufacturer finds in his employees, and in his works, in machinery, in improvements, in the perfection of his factories and methods his chief interest and reward.[38]

This indeed was the same Carnegie who, having read Confucius, Buddha, and Zoroaster, decided to base his own belief on the biblical text, "The Kingdom of Heaven is within you" and to conclude that "... now and here is Heaven within us. All our duties lie in this world and in the present."[39]

But this was also in 1902, when the exploitation of the continent was no longer a battle royal, but a system.

No matter what phase of American living one examines during this period, much the same stresses appear. There were controversies within the church, too, symptomatic of a conflict between a rather static religious faith and a changing world. Men such as Robert Ingersoll lumped organized religion with organized wealth, and condemned them both; other writers and speakers leveled all manner of attack at religion, its preachers and practitioners.

Ingersoll had undoubtedly touched a sore spot in the religion of his day. Expanding industry brought about social abuses which were, even in the non-

---

[37] Walt Whitman, "Democratic Vistas," in *The Complete Writings of Walt Whitman* (Book Lover's Camden Edition; New York: G. P. Putnam's Sons, 1902), II, 62.

[38] Andrew Carnegie, *The Empire of Business* (1902), as quoted in H. R. Warfel, R. H. Gabriel, and S. T. Williams, *The American Mind: Selections from the Literature of the United States* (New York: The American Book Co., 1937), p. 927.

[39] Andrew Carnegie, *The Autobiography of Andrew Carnegie* (New York: The Houghton Mifflin Co., 1920), p. 206.

social ethic of that day, criminal. Yet the Puritan theology had always held that the acquisition of wealth was a symbol of God's blessing on the good man.

One resolution of this dilemma Russell H. Conwell provided in his lecture, "Acres of Diamonds." Here Conwell reiterated loudly the old Puritan creed, that to pile up dividends was the only form of prayer. Later, however, came the social gospel movement, which attempted to readjust Protestant Christianity to the problems of an industrial civilization; later still, in 1908, the General Conference of the Methodist Episcopal church and the Federal Council of Churches adopted a social creed of the most liberal nature; and finally, progressivism was carried to its extreme when in 1935 Reinhold Niebuhr, of the Union Theological Seminary, declared that organized Christianity must now take cognizance of Marxist doctrine.

Yet another, and a more popular solution to the dilemma of Protestantism was formed. Conservative religionists were forced to extreme fundamentalism, forced to support an evangelical revival. During the years following the Civil War, evangelical Protestantism was kept alive and thriving chiefly by the preaching of Dwight L. Moody and his partner, Ira D. Sankey, by the establishment of the Y.M.C.A. and Y.W.C.A., and by the spread of the Salvation Army. Early in the twentieth century, the conservative platform was definitely stated when Lyman and Milton Stewart, in California, published a twelve-volume work called *The Fundamentals,* a collection of statements of belief by Protestant ministers, religious workers, and laymen in America and Europe. The publication of this work marks the emergence of the modern fundamentalist movement. This movement prospered by means of innumerable religious organizations, such as the Christian Fundamentals League. During World War I, its controversy with modernism was heightened; fundamentalism was considered orthodox Americanism by most of its adherents, and modernism was identified with German philosophy. The most widely-publicized skirmish of this conflict was the Scopes trial in 1927, in which Darrow took a leading part.

It is clear, then, that between the end of the Civil War and 1920, American evangelical Protestantism found itself ever more threatened in its struggle for existence. It was threatened from without by increasing numbers of Catholics, Jews, atheists, agnostics, skeptics; from within, by increasing numbers of modernists and liberals.

All things considered, it is not surprising that the fundamentalists were obliged to ally themselves with the native American group, in proclaiming the virtues of white, gentile, 100% Americanism. Edward Y. Clarke, that genius of pressure advertising, built the modern Ku Klux Klan and the Supreme Kingdom, a fundamentalist organization, along similar lines. Aside from slight, superficial differences, the societies seemed much alike.

279

When William Jennings Bryan died, following the Scopes trial, Klansmen of Dayton, Ohio, raised a cross which bore the inscription: "In memory of William Jennings Bryan, the greatest Klansman of our time, this cross is burned; he stood at Armageddon and battled for the Lord." [40] There was more truth than comfort for Bryan's friends in that epitaph. He was, in essentials, "the greatest Klansman of our time." He was also the undisputed head, the symbol, of the fundamentalist movement.

This, then, is something of the world into which Clarence Darrow came as a young lawyer. Even the briefest summary of his career shows how he fitted himself into this turbulent society. If the age was one which specialized in the training of barbarians, Darrow was a man who could not have survived without them. In the violent conflict between capitalists and workers, he was on the side of the worker. Where new racial and national minorities clashed with old, native American groups, he was on the side of the minorities. Where modernists or Catholics or agnostics fell out with fundamentalists, he was on the side of the smaller number. Where socialists or anarchists got into hospitals or law courts, he stood with them. When John Peter Altgeld pardoned the last of the Haymarket anarchists, Darrow was their chief apologist. Conversely, Darrow was a man doomed to fame. Perhaps no other man in public life during this period could have dramatized so admirably the fundamental conflicts of the times.

Yet opportunity of this sort is not enough. No more is motivation, which Darrow had in abundance. The man who would turn a motive and an opportunity into specific accomplishment must find some mechanism within the culture of which he is a part, which his peculiar skills and knowledge permit him to use fruitfully. In Darrow's case, this mechanism was a channel of communication which, partly by chance, he was able to tap at a time when the channel was of great social importance.

Exploitation of a Communication Channel

Darrow came to Chicago in 1888: a young man, long, lean, and serious. He joined the Single Tax Club, and made speeches. "In those days," he says, "I was rather oratorical. . . . I did the best, or worst, I could to cover up such ideas as I had in a cloud of sounding metrical phrases." [41] Apparently, he perceived the religiosity of the Single Taxers and the falseness of his own oratory at about the same time. He modified both the belief and the technique by degrees.

[40] M. R. Werner, *Bryan* (New York: Harcourt, Brace & Co., 1929), p. 358.
[41] *The Story of My Life*, p. 42.

Darrow took a small apartment and desk room in an office. His first year was hard and lonely, yet he held on. Professional ethics forbid the lawyer to advertise his services; Darrow tried to fill his time and put his name before the public by indulging a long-standing interest in politics. He spoke at the Single Tax Club, and as the elections of 1888 approached, he was invited to speak at various Democratic meetings. Most of these appearances were failures, in the sense that Darrow apparently never impressed his audiences on his own account.

But Darrow managed to find an audience at last, and he did it in competition with Henry George himself. A Free Trade convention was being held in Chicago, and at the last meeting George was to speak, and with him Darrow. The meeting was held in Central Music Hall, and this great auditorium was packed. George spoke magnificently, according to Darrow's account. "Everyone but me was carried away with his able address. I was disappointed. I was sorry that it was so good." [42] At last, Henry George sat down. The applause mounted, and then subsided. The audience began to leave. Darrow nervously plucked the chairman's sleeve, mumbled, "For goodness' sake before everyone leaves the house!" The chairman obediently introduced Darrow, and some of his friends in the audience paused to give him a good reception, and he started to speak. Recalling the event, Darrow wrote:

I had discovered enough about public speaking to sense that unless a speaker can interest his audience at once, his effort will be a failure. This was particularly true when following a speaker like Henry George, so I began with the most striking phrases that I could conjure from my harried, worried brain. The audience hesitated and began to sit down. They seemed willing to give me a chance. I had at least one advantage; nothing was expected of me; if I could get their attention it would be easier than if too much was expected. Not one in twenty of the audience knew much about me. As a matter of fact, I had taken great pains to prepare my speech. The subject was one that had interested me deeply for many years, one that I really understood. In a short time I had the attention of the entire audience, to my surprise. Then came the full self-confidence which only a speaker can understand; that confidence that is felt as one visits by the fireside, when he can say what he pleases and as he pleases; when the speaker can, in fact, visit with the audience as with an oldtime friend. I have no desire to elaborate on my talk, but I know that I had the people with me, and that I could sway those listeners as I wished. [43]

It was probably the first successful speech that Darrow ever made. For the first time, he had successfully reached an audience; he had found a way to attack his problems in a meaningful fashion, and a way which promised

[42] *Ibid.*, p. 46.
[43] *Ibid.*, pp. 46-47.

social approbation and perhaps financial success into the bargain. As he spoke that night, the newspapermen down in front sat up, listened, and began to write. The audience applauded. Henry George congratulated the young man. And next day, his name was on the front page of all the newspapers. He knew, because he went out and bought them all.

After that, Darrow lost his loneliness. He received more invitations to speak. A mayoralty campaign was then in progress, and Darrow received not only an invitation to speak, but the privilege of choosing the hall and his colleagues on the program. "I named my hall, but I took no chances, and said that I would speak alone. And I did." [44]

For once, a Darrow candidate was elected. DeWitt C. Cregier became mayor of Chicago. Darrow did not know Cregier, nor did he call on the new mayor to ask for political favors. Instead, Cregier wrote the young attorney, asking him to call—when he had time. "The latter part of the sentence sounded like a joke. I had time right then." [45] He went to see the mayor, and came away with an appointment as special assessment attorney for the city of Chicago, at a salary of three thousand dollars a year: a tremendous sum, to him. His luck was surprising. Within three months the assistant corporation counsel for the city was forced to resign; Darrow got his place. Ten months after that, the corporation counsel fell ill; Darrow became acting corporation counsel, and head of the law department of the city of Chicago. He stayed in that position for two years, and then became general attorney for the Chicago and Northwestern Railway.

Thus, a speech launched Darrow on a successful career—successful, that is to say, in terms of financial returns, prestige, and comparative security. Successful it was not, in terms of Darrow's previous experience and basic attitudes. That he was uncomfortable in his new position is clear from his suggestion that, with the connivance of the railroad's general claim agent, he was able to help many people who had personal damage claims against the road. [46] He was able to maintain his non-conformism as a kind of hobby by speaking to "radical" groups, by writing, and through his friendship with John Altgeld, [47] a man of notably liberal outlook. But it was not enough. The trial of Eugene V. Debs, in 1895, provided him with an admirable excuse

[44] *Ibid.*, p. 48.

[45] *Ibid.*, p. 49.

[46] *Ibid.*, p. 57. See also chaps. 6 and 7 for a discussion of Darrow's feelings on this point.

[47] Darrow had read Altgeld's remarkable work on criminology, *Our Penal Machinery and Its Victims*, while still practising law in Ashtabula. When he came to Chicago, he promptly called on Altgeld, and the two men became intimate friends. See Stone, *op. cit.*, p. 29 ff.

for abandoning his career as corporation lawyer; but the excuse was, in all probability, only that. Had Debs successfully defied the forces of government and railway management in the great strike of 1894, Darrow would almost surely have found some other outcast to rescue him from respectability. Nevertheless, the Debs trial is worth examination.

In the fall of 1892, Eugene V. Debs had resigned his post as secretary of the Brotherhood of Locomotive Firemen, to begin the work of organizing the "one big union" which he hoped would eventually bring all railroad workers into a position where they could successfully bargain with management. The result was the American Railway Union, A.R.U. By the spring of 1894, the A.R.U. had to its credit 150,000 members, 465 locals, and a successful strike against the Great Northern Railroad.[48]

In May, 1894, the employees of George M. Pullman, the sleeping car magnate, went on strike in Chicago. The Pullman strikers approached Debs and asked for the support of the A.R.U. Debs, fearful that his organization was not yet strong enough to act, asked the strikers to try arbitration. They did so, but failed.[49]

In June, the A.R.U. held a convention in Chicago, a meeting occupied largely with consideration of the Pullman strike. In the end, the delegates voted a boycott, over Debs' objection, on all railroads handling Pullman cars, and the great A.R.U. strike was on.

It lasted until mid-July, succumbing finally to a combination of injunctions, "special deputies," federal troops, and the careful neutrality of Samuel Gompers. Debs and the other strike leaders were cited for contempt of court in carrying on the strike in the face of an injunction. To this charge was later added one of conspiracy to obstruct the mails.

Because Darrow was a railroad attorney, the outbreak and progress of the A.R.U. strike caused him particular uneasiness. His personal opinions were recognized and respected by his employers, yet he could not reconcile his service with the railroad and his sympathy for the strikers. Shortly after the strike broke out, Darrow was put on a committee of all the railroads to assist in the control of the strike. He went at once to the president of the Chicago and Northwestern, told him that he could not serve on the committee, and offered to resign. The officials of the road agreed that he need not serve on the committee, and asked him simply to remain neutral and stay with them. Darrow remained, but uncomfortably.[50] When the injunctions against

---

[48] Matthew Josephson, *The Politicos: 1865-1896* (New York: Harcourt Brace & Co., 1938), p. 568.

[49] McAllister Coleman, *Eugene V. Debs: a Man Unafraid* (New York: Greenberg, 1930), pp. 125-26.

[50] *The Story of My Life*, pp. 58-59.

the strike were issued, Debs and a number of Darrow's friends requested him to take up the defense of the A.R.U. officials. Though Darrow himself later protested at great length that he went into the case unwillingly,[51] he resigned his position with the Chicago and Northwestern to accept Debs' defense.

Debs and his associates were finally brought to trial toward the end of January, 1895. They were charged with violation of the injunction, and with conspiracy to obstruct the mails, a criminal charge. The criminal case was tried first, before a jury. The presiding judge, Grosscup, was one of the two federal judges who had issued an injunction against the A.R.U. strike.[52] When the case was nearly over, it was reported that one juror had fallen ill. The government moved for dismissal of the jury and a mistrial. The defense offered to go on with eleven men, and suggested, as an alternative, that a new juror be sworn in and the evidence read to him. The mistrial was declared, and the case was never again tried. Darrow notes that, according to his information, the jury stood at eleven to one for acquittal at the time of its dismissal.[53]

Federal Judge Woods, the other judge who had granted an injunction against the strike, then heard the same case over again, this time on the injunction-violation charge. There was no jury. He sentenced Debs to six months in jail, and his associates to three months.[54] The case was appealed to the Supreme Court, but the decision was not reversed. "Apart from corruption," writes James Truslow Adams, "the courts, which were the last resort of the people, seemed to be wholly on the side of the capitalistic few.... In the case of Debs and the Chicago strike, the Supreme Court had stretched the Constitution beyond the dreams of Hamilton in order to keep Debs in jail."[55]

The defense of Eugene V. Debs completes a definitely marked stage in Clarence Darrow's career. As his life up to the beginnings of his legal practice set his basic attitudes and problems, so Darrow's defense of Debs determined, once and for all, what expression those attitudes and problems should have. His speech on free trade represents a false start, and yet is important. Its success brought him before the public, gave him financial security, made him a personage in Chicago who might well be asked to undertake the trial of a difficult and highly controversial case. Yet the free trade speech directed Darrow's energies into what, for him, must have been a dead end. If we consider that he spoke largely in order to gain fame, and in defense of a point

[51] *Ibid.*, chaps. 7 and 8.
[52] Stone, *op. cit.*, p. 57.
[53] *The Story of My Life*, p. 66.
[54] Stone, *op. cit.*, p. 55.
[55] *The Epic of America* (New York: Triangle Books, 1941), pp. 322-23.

of view which even then he must have doubted a little,[56] we need hardly be surprised that the success which it brought him proved uncomfortable to him. The coming of the A.R.U. strike was, on the whole, fortunate for Darrow. His situation was sharply dramatic: he was a railroad lawyer, his sympathies were unalterably with the railroad strikers, and he was forced to choose. He chose, and thereby set the pattern of his life permanently.

It is interesting to note, too, that something of Darrow's typical court-room personality began to emerge during the Debs trial. He had already developed that casual sloppiness of dress, the sprawling, countrified manner which was to distinguish him in later cases. Spectators who had come to court to see Debs, the anarchist, the agitator, were surprised:

They sat back in frank disappointment when Gene was pointed out to them. This was no long-haired fire-eater. On the contrary, Debs was nearly bald, mild-appearing, with candid blue eyes behind gold-rimmed spectacles. . . . When Gene conferred with the sprawling Clarence Darrow (who even in those days chose to sit on the back of his neck) it was the young lawyer in his first big case whom one would pick as the fiery "rabble-rouser" rather than his dignified client.[57]

Darrow's opening statement, too, suggests that he had already developed much of the rhetorical technique which he was later to perfect in other labor trials. The prosecuting attorney had said, "Men have a right to strike." To this Darrow replied,

If this so, it ends this case, for no one but the evil genius that directs this prosecution believes these men did anything else. There is a statute which makes the obstruction of a mail car punishable by a fine of $100, yet no one had heard of the men who actually obstructed the mail during that strike being indicted under that statute. In order to make felons of honest men, who never had a criminal thought, they passed by that statute to seize on one that makes conspiracy to obstruct the mails a crime punishable by imprisonment in the penitentiary. To hound these men into the penitentiary is their purpose, yet they call this respect for law. Conspiracy from the days of tyranny in England down to the day the General Managers' Association used it as a club has been the favorite weapon of every tyrant. It is an effort to punish the crime of thought. . . . These defendants published to all the world what they were doing, and in the midst of a wide-spread strike they were never so busy but that they found time to counsel against violence. For this they are brought into a court by an organization which uses the government as a cloak to conceal its infamous purposes.[58]

---

[56] See *The Story of My Life*, p. 43 ff, and Stone, *op. cit.*, pp. 175-76.

[57] Coleman, *op. cit.*, p. 157.

[58] *Debs: His Life, Writings, and Speeches* (Girard, Kansas: The Appeal to Reason, 1908), pp. 23-24.

Even in this brief passage from an early plea, we may note some characteristics of Darrow's persuasive method: the attempt to present the facts in a case against a broad backdrop of history, and so to alter their significance; the suggestion that the prosecution is the tool of some blackly evil force, in this case the General Managers' Association; the use of invective against the prosecution and especially against agencies associated with the prosecution; the insistence upon the honesty, kindliness, and in general the ordinary qualities of the client. All of these elements, as we shall see later, are essential parts of Darrow's rhetorical system. In the trial of Debs, they appear on the record for the first time.

After Darrow accepted the Debs brief, he opened an office and went into private practice. "Neither then nor for any considerable time thereafter," he says, "did I need to worry over business prospects. For many years my practice covered almost all sorts of litigation." [59] Like most lawyers, he had intended to avoid criminal practice. But "by no effort of mine, more and more of the distressed and harassed and pursued came fleeing to my office door. What could I do to change the situation? ... Strange as it may seem, I grew to like to defend men and women charged with crime." [60]

Career of a Pleader

Darrow's private practice may have started with civil cases in the years 1894-95; if so, its character rapidly changed. As we may guess from our examination of his early history, Darrow was naturally drawn, almost compulsively so, to the trial of criminal cases. Only in these trials could he take any real satisfaction, for here the issue was essentially human, and the elements of the situation arranged themselves into the pattern most familiar and most necessary to him: the defendant as outcast, as barbarian, as animal at bay, hounded into court, into prison, to the hangman's gallows, by all the forces of organized society.

Of all types of criminal cases, probably those which resulted from the endless war between labor and management were most meaningful to him. Here the dramatic situation in which he played his part so often occurred in its purest form; in the acts of these trials, he could see the essence of injustice; in the persons of the defendants, the most genuine honesty and courage; in the prosecution, the blackest and most wanton malice. Thus, it is not surprising that over a period of nearly twenty years, between 1895 and 1913, Darrow's most celebrated cases were labor trials.

In 1898, he undertook a defense which was almost a literal repetition of

[59] *The Story of My Life*, p. 74.
[60] *Ibid.*, p. 75.

the Debs case. The employees of the Paine Lumber Company, of Oshkosh, Wisconsin, had gone on strike in May of that year. During the strike, warrants were issued for the arrest of Thomas I. Kidd, general secretary of the Woodworkers' International, George Zentner, who had acted as captain of pickets during the strike, and Michael Troiber, a local union member, charging them with conspiracy to injure the business of the Paine Lumber Company. The trial ended November 2, 1898, with the acquittal of the three defendants.[61]

Darrow's next case of major importance came as one result of the rise of the United Mine Workers. Between 1897 and 1902, this union had grown rapidly in power, membership, and influence. In May, 1902, the U.M.W. demanded of the anthracite operators union recognition, a nine-hour day, a wage increase of 20 per cent, and payment for coal by weight rather than by the carload.[62] These demands were refused, and the men went out on strike.

In October, 1902, President Roosevelt interfered. He ordered that both the operators and the union submit their differences to a commission, which he would appoint. After some debate, the commission was appointed, and the men returned to work.

Darrow represented the miners during the hearing that followed. Despite a very brief preparation, his conduct of the case was forceful, and his summation, which lasted five and one-half hours, is very much in the pattern of his earlier labor pleas.[63] As a result of the hearings, the commission granted a 10 per cent wage increase and a nine-hour day, and set up machinery for future arbitration of labor disputes.

On December 20, 1905, Frank Steunenberg, former governor of Idaho, was blown to bits by a bomb attached to the front gate of his Caldwell home. Steunenberg, while governor, had been a bitter enemy of the Western Federation of Miners, and had invoked martial law during a strike. At this time, Charles Moyer was president of the Western Federation of Miners, and William Haywood was secretary-treasurer. These two men, together with George Pettibone, a friend and sympathizer of the Federation, were in Denver when Steunenberg was killed. Nevertheless, Idaho authorities believed that they engineered the murder. When the Denver authorities did not consent to extradition, the three men were kidnapped and brought to Idaho.[64] Although

[61] See Stone, *op. cit.*, pp. 103-12, for a detailed account of this trial.

[62] Carroll D. Wright, *The Battles of Labor* (Philadelphia: George W. Jacobs & Co., 1906), p. 146.

[63] Charles Yale Harrison, *Clarence Darrow* (New York: Jonathan Cape and Harrison Smith, 1931), pp. 101-4.

[64] See Morris Friedman, *The Pinkerton Labor Spy* (New York: Wilshire Book Co., 1907), p. 206, and William D. Haywood, *Bill Haywood's Book* (New York: International Publishers, 1929), p. 191 ff.

Haywood was arrested in February, 1906, he was not brought to trial until May, 1907. Meanwhile, he was confined to jail, the Supreme Court having denied him a writ of habeas corpus.

Darrow entered the case toward the end of 1906, at the request of the Defense Committee of the Western Federation of Miners. Over a period of approximately two years he conducted four major trials. His record: two disagreements, two acquittals. After the second trial, that of Haywood, he fell ill, but continued with the other two cases to the point of complete collapse. Except for his self-defense some years later, this sequence of related cases represents the height of Darrow's career as a labor pleader. His summation in the defense of Haywood (again excepting the summation in his own defense) is perhaps his greatest forensic speech. Of it, Haywood writes,

When Darrow arose to address the jury he stood big and broad-shouldered, dressed in a slouchy gray suit, a wisp of hair down his forehead, his glasses in his hand, clasped by the nose-piece. . . . When he spoke he was sometimes intense, his great voice rumbling, his left hand shoved deep in his coat pocket, his right arm uplifted. Again he would take a pleading attitude, his voice would become gentle and very quiet. At times he would approach the jury almost on tiptoe. This speech was, I think, one of Clarence Darrow's greatest.[65]

The final series of events in Darrow's career as a labor lawyer began, like the Haywood case, with a bomb blast. On October 1, 1910, the offices of the *Los Angeles Times* exploded in a gush of flames.[66] Several lesser explosions followed the first, great one. The place was a trap for the few employees who were still working in the building; twenty of them were killed. Again, as in the Haywood affair, after some lapse of time, three union men were arrested: J. J. McNamara, head of the Iron Workers Union, J. B. McNamara, his brother, and Ortie McManigal. McManigal at once confessed; he had been the agent of the McNamaras in a series of bombings, although J. B. McNamara had bombed the *Times*.[67]

The A.F. of L., under the wily Sam Gompers, interested itself at once in the defense of the McNamaras. Gompers and several other members of the executive board went to Darrow at once, to ask him to undertake the defense of the two men.[68] Darrow refused at first. It had been a very short time since he had encountered, in the Moyer-Haywood-Pettibone affair, an almost paral-

[65] Haywood, *op. cit.*, pp. 215-16.

[66] *The Los Angeles Herald*, October 2, 1910.

[67] The gist of this confession may be found in Ortie McManigal, *The National Dynamite Plot* (Los Angeles: The Neale Co., 1913.)

[68] Gompers later protested that he had known nothing of the McNamaras prior to the trial. See *Seventy Years of Life and Labor* (New York: E. P. Dutton & Co., 1925), II, 185.

Clarence Darrow

lel case which had cost him two years of his life and had nearly killed him. But the labor men were persistent, and in the end, he did not refuse.[69]

The date of the trial was set for October 11, 1911. Long before the trial commenced, Darrow became convinced that his clients were guilty, and that probably the prosecution would be able to uncover sufficient evidence to prove them so and hang them. His only chance was to have the two men plead guilty. This course the situation made very difficult. A plea of guilty would destroy organized labor in Los Angeles, would alienate the A.F. of L., and would seem a betrayal of the entire American labor movement, for labor unions everywhere had taken the attitude that the McNamaras were innocent, and that Darrow would save them.

By the time the trial had begun, and a jury had been partially selected, the prosecution had turned up quantities of unshakable evidence that the Mc-Namaras were guilty. At this point, around November 15, a journalist from the *New York Globe*, Lincoln Steffens, arrived in Los Angeles. Steffens was a man who believed in Christianity. Mercy is scientific, he proclaimed.[70] It would be so much easier, when all was said and done, for prosecutors and defense counsel to get together and settle their differences without resorting to the pitched battle of the law courts. The McNamaras could at least be saved from the hangman, and the prosecutors would nevertheless satisfy the law. Darrow finally agreed, without much hope, that Steffens should approach the businessmen of Los Angeles, and through them the prosecution. His motivation is clear; he was afraid that his clients would be hanged, a motive which Steffens explains in a passage in his *Autobiography*:

One day when we were walking from court along the street to his [Darrow's] office he was expressing a winning sureness of his case. A passerby halted, and drawing him aside, whispered a few words and went on. When Darrow rejoined us his face was ashen, and he could hardly walk; he was scared weak, and he did not recover for an hour. "I can't stand to have a man I am defending hanged. I can't stand it." [71]

Darrow now faced what was, to him, the ultimate catastrophe: his clients, with whom he had as usual closely identified himself, were to die, and to die the sort of violent death which was a particular obsession with him. They were to be hanged. For Darrow this prospect was, symbolically, the prospect of his own death. The noose tightened about his neck. It is probable that he would have done almost anything, at this point, to keep the McNamaras alive.

[69] *The Story of My Life*, pp. 173-75.
[70] Lincoln Steffens, *The Autobiography of Lincoln Steffens* (New York: Harcourt Brace & Co., 1931), p. 666 ff.
[71] *Ibid.*, p. 665.

Steffens' original proposal was that the charges against the McNamaras be dropped, and that Los Angeles labor and management then negotiate their differences. When this suggestion was rejected, he managed to work out a tentative compromise: J. B. McNamara, who was directly guilty of the bombing of the *Times*, was to plead guilty and receive a life sentence, while J. J. McNamara, who had been at worst indirectly connected with the bombing, was to maintain his plea of not guilty and have the charges against him dropped. Although this compromise suggestion was rather favorably received, at the crucial moment the prosecution demanded that both men plead guilty, and enforced this demand by the arrest of Bert Franklin, a detective whom Darrow had employed to investigate jurors, on a charge of jury bribing. The suggestion was made that unless both of the McNamaras plead guilty, further steps would be taken to embarrass the defense.[72] Under this pressure, both of the McNamara brothers entered pleas of guilty. J. J. McNamara was sentenced to serve fifteen years in San Quentin; J. B. McNamara, to serve a life term.

Darrow now stood entirely alone. He had no friends, either among those who sympathized with the McNamaras, or among their enemies. The McNamaras had been sentenced on December 8, 1911. On May 12, 1912, Darrow was brought to trial on a charge of bribing a juror named George Lockwood, using Bert Franklin as his agent. Darrow had retained Earl Rogers, one of the great criminal lawyers of the time, as his chief of staff; and the conduct of the case fell heavily on Rogers' capable shoulders.[73] The trial was a spectacular one, involving the examination of such witnesses as Lincoln Steffens and William J. Burns, head of the Burns Detective Agency.

Darrow's final plea in his own defense was by no means anti-climactic. On almost every count, it was the greatest address he ever delivered. He was at the height of his power as a courtroom orator, and he had the greatest stimulus imaginable to eloquence: he was pleading for his own life. The biographers of Earl Rogers describe the speech in terms which at times approach the grotesque:

Darrow, who had made many eloquent pleas in the years that had gone, surpassed himself. He was pleading for his own liberty now. The tremor in his voice was not simulated; the tears in his eyes were genuine. It is quite likely that no such moving argument was ever before delivered to a jury. Wiping his streaming eyes with a handkerchief until it was a sodden ball, he finally flung it on the floor before the listening jurors. From then until he had finished he used the sleeves of his coat to mop the undiminished flow of his grief. Several of the jurymen were in tears. When

[72] Alfred Cohn and Joe Chisholm, *Take the Witness!* (Garden City: Garden City Publishing Co., 1934), p. 204.
[73] *Ibid.*, p. 211.

Darrow reached his peroration, Ben Smith, the hard-boiled official reporter, was crying as though his heart would break, the tears falling thick and fast into his notebook as he took down the speech. Darrow himself was almost at the point of exhaustion as he took his chair. He was trembling as though with ague.[74]

The jury was out for half an hour. The verdict was not guilty.

Darrow was then indicted for a second time, on a charge of bribing another juror, Robert Bain, and, after about three months, was tried. On March 7, 1913, the second Darrow jury came out, stayed out for several days, and finally reported a disagreement. The case was never resumed.

The McNamara trial, and its aftermath, is another of the turning points in Darrow's career. His own trial marked the virtual end of his career as a labor lawyer. Whether this happened because he was now in ill-repute with organized labor, or because of his own distaste for such cases, one cannot be sure; but he tried no more major cases of this sort. The pattern of Darrow's public life, which had been set by the Debs case, was now disrupted; but as events proved, it was not destroyed. He could no longer defend organized labor in its struggles; but there were other kinds of barbarians available. In their defense, he rapidly reconstructed his life along the old lines.

The plea which he made at Los Angeles probably represents the very height of Darrow's forensic speaking. He had, of course, command of a remarkable pleading method which he had developed in a half-dozen cases, and found successful in the trial of William Haywood. But more important, in this trial the elements of the typical Darrow situation were reversed. Where previously he had attacked his basic problems symbolically, identifying himself with his client, fighting the client's enemies as if they were his own, here his own liberty was at stake. Here, for the first time, Darrow faced the actualities of his life, made concrete in the courtroom situation he knew so well. While he was convinced that in this situation he symbolized "the weak and the poor . . . the men who toil," still there was the instant necessity for keeping himself out of prison, a necessity which almost broke him at first, but which finally spurred him into delivering his most eloquent plea.

The months which he spent in Los Angeles left on Darrow a deep and lasting mark, which may well account for some of his later bitterness and pessimism. Hervey White, an old friend of Darrow, recalls that his trial for bribery was one subject about which he would never joke.[75] Twenty years later, when Judge Michael Musmanno asked Darrow how he felt about his own trial, "the wrinkles in his face fairly rippled with indignation—not at me, but at those who were responsible for making him a defendant. 'The

[74] *Ibid.*, p. 223.
[75] Letter, dated May 1, 1941.

sons of bitches,' he muttered. 'They knew damn well I was innocent, but they also knew damn well that if they accused me there would be somebody to believe the accusation.' " [76]

Darrow now entered a period of general criminal practice, which is interesting chiefly because his pleas represent the final fruition of his legal career. During the twenties, particularly, he began to enjoy national and even international celebrity. In 1920 and 1921, he defended Arthur Person, a workingman of Rockford, Illinois, and a group of Chicago communists on indictments which charged these defendants with conspiracy to overthrow the government by force. In 1924, he tried the case of Richard Loeb and Nathan Leopold, two wealthy young men of Chicago who had confessed to the murder of fourteen-year-old Robert Franks. He went to Tennessee in 1925 to appear in behalf of John Scopes, in a test-case involving the recently-passed anti-evolution bill. In 1927, he defended Dr. Ossian Sweet and others of Sweet's family, all Negroes, for the murder of a white man during a Detroit race riot. In 1929, he defended Calogero Greco and Donato Carrillo, Italian anti-fascists of New York City, for the murder of two members of a fascist group.

Of these defenses, the Loeb-Leopold case and the Scopes case probably had the greatest significance for Darrow. The pleas in defense of Person and of the Chicago communists seem to represent a sort of conscience payment which Darrow felt that he had to make because he had supported America's entry into World War I. In the latter plea, he says, "If I had believed that after one autocracy had been overthrown, that here in America, where we cherish individual liberty; here in America, twenty states would pass a statute like this, which we had got along without one hundred and fifty years, so that great interests might silence every human voice while they were robbing the people ... perhaps I would not have believed we should have entered this War." [77] This feeling on Darrow's part was probably the reason why the speeches are not among his greatest. No pleader is at his best when he feels he must justify himself. The summation which he delivered in the Sweet case, though excellent in many ways, was probably rendered somewhat less effective by the fact that Darrow had never, in his early career, had any direct concern with the problems of Negroes. While the basic pattern of his life and the rhetorical technique he had developed made it possible for him to conduct the case successfully, he was certainly more effective in those trials which touched immediately on his specific interests. As for the Greco-Carrillo affair, it repre-

---

[76] From a manuscript article, unpublished, by Judge Musmanno.

[77] *Argument of Clarence Darrow in the Case of the Communist Labor Party in the Criminal Court, Chicago* (Chicago: Charles H. Kerr & Co., 1920), p. 13.

sents the beginning of Darrow's period of decline; he was then seventy-two years old.

The Loeb-Leopold and Scopes cases, however, gave Darrow a stage with the world for audience, on which he could enact the drama of his own special myth, dealing with characters and situations familiar to him through years of study and work. On May 31, 1924, the Chicago newspapers informed the public that Nathan Leopold and Richard Loeb had confessed to the murder of Robert Franks. Darrow was at once engaged for the defense. He did not attempt an acquittal. The defendants had already confessed, and there was more than enough evidence to support their confessions. They could only plead guilty, and hope that the judge who sentenced them would not exact the death penalty. There was one sound legal reason why the two should not have been put to death. As Judge Caverly phrased the matter in his decision, "In choosing imprisonment instead of death, the court is moved chiefly by the consideration of the age of the defendants, boys of 18 and 19 years.... The records of Illinois show only two cases of minors who were put to death by legal process... to which number the court does not feel inclined to make an addition." [78] Victor Yarros suggests that Judge Caverly was sympathetic with Darrow's criminological views, and would have sentenced the defendants to life imprisonment in any case. The only real issue, the youth of the boys, could have been stated in half an hour. While Darrow's three-day argument no doubt gave the presiding judge some excuse for his decision, to Darrow the Loeb-Leopold trial must have seemed an enormous megaphone, through which he could broadcast truth about the criminal law to a tremendous public. [79]

Darrow's plea in the Loeb-Leopold case, then, while it had relatively little to do with the fate of Loeb and Leopold, had real significance. Darrow's first acquaintance with modern criminology came when, as a young lawyer, he read John Altgeld's *Our Penal Machinery and Its Victims*. [80] From about 1900 on, he lectured and wrote extensively about the problems of crime and punishment. [81] Now, in 1924, he was retained in a case which gave him an opportunity to employ these years of philosophizing, a case so sensational that it provided him with an international audience for his theories. The plea which resulted is certainly one of his finest; it can be ranked only after his own defense in Los Angeles in 1912 and his speech in defense of Haywood. In the

[78] Maureen McKernan, *The Amazing Crime of Leopold and Loeb* (Chicago: The Plymouth Court Press, 1924), p. 375.

[79] Victor Yarros, one of Darrow's law partners, in an interview.

[80] Stone, *op. cit.*, p. 29 ff.

[81] See especially his *Crime and Criminals* (Chicago: Charles H. Kerr & Co., 1919), *Crime, Its Cause and Treatment* (New York: Thomas Y. Crowell & Co., 1922), and the chapters on criminology in *Resist Not Evil* (Chicago: Charles H. Kerr & Co., 1903).

Loeb-Leopold trial, the issue was limited almost to the vanishing point; the question was not one of guilt or innocence, which did not concern Darrow greatly, but of life or death, which concerned him to the point of obsession. Although the defendants had confessed to a particularly brutal and pointless murder, Darrow was still able to defend them honestly and eloquently; for he conceived the deliberate execution of two boys by hanging to be far more horrifying than any crime they might possibly have committed. In this plea, then, the dramatic situation was exceedingly strong. The defendants become children, sick and confused, their own lives stained and corrupted by the blood they have shed. They sit in a courtroom, ringed by the vicious and bloodthirsty representatives of society. Their only hope is in an appeal to the humanity and understanding of the judge who is to sentence them. In this situation, Darrow himself appeared as a spokesman, not simply for Loeb and Leopold, but for all unhappy, tormented children who must be judged by an adult world they do not understand.

As for the Scopes trial, it did not produce a great plea. The only speech Darrow made was on a motion to quash the indictment against Scopes, and it cannot be considered one of his best efforts. Yet the case had a special significance, both for Darrow personally and in terms of his public career. It gave Darrow a remarkable opportunity to attack one of the bogies of his boyhood, organized religion, before the eyes of the world. It gave him the perfect opponent in the person of William Jennings Bryan. As a result, the conduct of this trial was one of the greatest satisfactions of his life.[82]

The routine of criminal procedure usually provided Darrow with a framework of dramatic conventions, which he used much as a playwright uses the structure of a stage, to limit and define his performance. Thus, in most of his trials, the drama began with the examination of jurors, continued through the taking of evidence, and reached its climax in the final summation of the case before the jury. This sequence of events was not followed in the Scopes case. Considered as a kind of play, the trial was chaotic and pointless; the content of the trial was not appropriate to a court. These deficiencies were made up, however, by one feature of the Scopes affair: the recurrent clashes between Darrow and Bryan, which reached their climax and were resolved in Darrow's examination of Bryan as an "expert witness" on the Bible. This was, for the public, the high point of the Scopes trial; although Scopes was convicted, and his conviction upheld on appeal, Darrow won his case. In an afternoon of merciless verbal dissection, Darrow so discredited Bryan and his fundamentalism that the trial may be said almost to end with Bryan's cross-examination. It was even suggested that Bryan's death, two days later, was occasioned by "a broken heart" resulting from Darrow's grilling.

[82] See *The Story of My Life,* chap. 31.

294

The years which remained to Darrow after his conduct of the Greco-Carrillo case, 1930 to 1938, were years of repetition and decline. In 1932, he was chief of defense counsel in the notorious Massie case in Honolulu, which saw Lieutenant Massie, an American naval officer, and others charged with the murder of a Hawaiian who was supposed to have raped Mrs. Massie. By this time, Darrow was well past his professional prime, and only the habit of many years brought him into the case and through it. He also appeared from time to time in minor trials, and in addition, lectured and debated widely. His debates, during these years, were repetitive patchworks of argument drawn from earlier and greater speeches; his lectures were the same that he had delivered on crime and punishment, on philosophy and philosophers, during his earliest years of practice. Even these activities he was forced to give up around 1935-36; and from that time until the spring of 1938, when he died, he lived in virtual retirement.

Darrow's Use of Persuasive Technique

It should by now be clear that Darrow's effectiveness as a pleader was not wholly a matter of rhetorical skill. The influences of his childhood, the nature of the world in which he found himself, the fact that the public platform in his day was an important means of communication: all of these factors circumscribed Darrow's life and tended to turn him to the career which he pursued so successfully. Nevertheless, working within the limitations of his peculiar environment, he developed an interesting persuasive technique, which is well worth examination.

One of Darrow's main forensic techniques was his skill in selecting juries. One of the few situations in which it is possible for a persuasive speaker to select the audience whom he is to address is a trial by jury. Consequently, the selection of the twelve jurors is made an important part of the criminal law. Prosecution and defense counsel are permitted to question each prospective juror, with the idea of discovering whether or not he is too prejudiced to give fair judgment in the case. If they show that he is, he may be challenged for cause and excused. In addition, both sides are allowed a certain number of peremptory challenges, which are used to dispose of undesirable jurors who cannot otherwise be challenged.

Darrow was an expert in selecting and influencing juries. He knew, almost instinctively, how to select men to whom his habitual appeals would be effective. While defending a Negro charged with rape, Darrow peremptorily challenged one juror because he lived in Evanston, Illinois. No one who lived in Evanston, Darrow explained, was possessed of either human sympathy or emotional understanding of his client.[83] During the Greco-Carrillo case, he challenged another individual because he had been a banker for seventeen years.

In order to use peremptory challenges as sparingly as possible, Darrow gradually built up an excellent method, Socratic in nature, for discrediting jurors he did not want. He would begin with easy discussion of the juror's opinions on the trial, until the man betrayed himself; and then he would snap, "Challenge for cause!" and the juror would be excused. As Haywood said of Darrow's examination in the Idaho case, "It was like killing snakes." [84] Reporters who watched Darrow's courtroom methods almost always commented on these simple, innocent questions, the casual approach.

Darrow habitually proceeded on the theory that a man's intellectual and emotional habits carry over from his everyday life to his period of jury service. He was quite frank in describing the basis on which he selected a jury. At a dinner of the Quadrangle Club, in Chicago, 1933, he said:

Jurymen seldom convict a person they like, or acquit one they dislike. The main work of a trial lawyer is to make a jury like his client, or at least, to feel sympathy for him; facts regarding the crime are relatively unimportant. I try to get a jury with little education but with much human sympathy. The Irish are always the best jurymen for the defense. I don't want a Scotchman, for he has too little human feeling; I don't want a Scandinavian, for he has too strong a respect for the law as law. In general I don't want a religious person, for he believes in sin and punishment. The defendant should avoid rich men who have a high regard for law, as they make and use it. The smug and ultra-respectable think they are the guardians of society, and they believe the law is for them. The man who is down on his luck, who has trouble, who is more or less a failure, is much kinder to the poor and unfortunate than are the rich and selfish.[85]

Having selected the sort of audience he wanted, or as near it as the prosecution would permit, Darrow became a brilliant manipulator of jurors' emotions. Arthur Garfield Hays, who was associated with Darrow in several cases, has summarized his method neatly:

Then Darrow would stand up, slouch his shoulders, talk quietly, and for an hour would hardly mention the facts of the case on trial. In homely language and with a great wealth of illustrations, he would talk about human beings, the difficulties of life, the futility of human plans, the misfortunes of the defendant, the strange workings of fate and chance that had landed him in his trouble. Darrow would try to make the jury understand, not so much the case, as the defendant.... Even his statement of the facts of the case will have to do with the defendant himself as

[83] Victor Yarros, Interview.
[84] William Haywood, *op. cit.*, p. 209.
[85] Edwin H. Sutherland, *Principles of Criminology* (Philadelphia: J. B. Lippincott Co., 1939), p. 290.

a human being, rather than with the legal significance of the evidence. In the ordinary labor case, where the defendant is charged with crime, Darrow will show that his client was not moved by greed or personal interest; he was fighting for his fellows. He will travel far beyond the immediate issue of guilt or innocence, leaving with the jury a desire to do what they can for the defendant, even if guilty; to acquit him if innocent. The whole background of a case takes on a different coloring from this deeply sympathetic manner of presentation.[86]

Darrow himself was sometimes cynical about his approach to defending a client. Hervey White tells how "once I had spoken of reasoning with a jury. He [Darrow] turned on me with good-natured, even affectionate contempt. 'You don't reason with a jury. You make the jury want to free the prisoner, and they will find the reason!'"[87]

The selection of an audience was almost the only rhetorical technique about which Darrow had worked out a detailed theory. His comments on other aspects of persuasion are so generalized that the reader comes to feel that he spoke more by instinct than by conscious plan. Probably this was the case. Darrow refused to prepare his addresses;[88] his dilatoriness in looking up legal precedent for his cases was the despair of his partners.[89] When notes for his pleas were prepared for him by his assistants, he refused to use them.[90] The same thing cropped out again in connection with his debates. According to George Whitehead, Darrow's debate manager during two debate tours, Darrow would sometimes ask for some blank paper and a pencil just before he debated, with the comment that he "had to fix up a speech." But usually he did not write on the paper; or at best, jotted down brief reminders for his rebuttals.[91] Norman Thomas confirms this opinion of Darrow's haphazard direct preparation; he tells how Darrow was to debate on one occasion, on the topic of the World Court. He wandered into the anteroom where Thomas, the chairman of the debate, and his opponent were waiting. "Either of you boys got a copy of the protocols of the Court?" he demanded. "I never read them."[92]

In short, as far as any available evidence goes, Darrow never prepared a jury plea or a debate in his entire career, and refused to use notes which others had prepared. Our earlier observations of Darrow's general outlook

[86] Arthur Garfield Hays, *Trial by Prejudice* (New York: Covici-Friede, 1935), pp. 356-57.

[87] Hervey White, letter dated June, 1941.

[88] Irving Stone, Interview.

[89] Victor Yarros, Interview.

[90] This was true, for example, of his conduct of the anthracite coal hearings in 1902.

[91] George Whitehead, *Clarence Darrow—the Big Minority Man* (Girard, Kansas: Haldeman-Julius Publications, 1929), p. 6.

[92] Norman Thomas, Interview.

and of his motives in pleading make this fact understandable. Darrow's finest legal arguments came in the course of or at the end of long periods of study and thought and discussion on the specific topics they concerned. His labor pleas and the Loeb-Leopold summation are especially good examples. As for his debates, they were for the most part extensions of his legal argument in which he tried to popularize his beliefs with a larger audience than the court-room permitted. But even more important than this, Darrow's speeches were rather definitely determined in content, persuasive appeals, and techniques by the nature of the myth he enacted. So deeply rooted were they in the most intimate experience of his life that he could scarcely have done otherwise than say what he did, and as he did. It was not simple laziness that caused Darrow to debate on the World Court, for example, without having read the protocols of the Court. The truth is that the specific topic under discussion, the specific evidence developed in a trial, did not matter much to Darrow. Some subjects lent themselves better to what he had to say; but that was all. Almost regard-less of topic, regardless of evidence, regardless of situation, he always made the same basic speech. The dramatic elements in his play were always the same. Defendants and causes came and went, but the myth remained.

It would be difficult, in limited space, to present a complete rhetorical profile of Darrow in action. However, we can sketch some of the more impor-tant aspects of his forensic technic; to do so, we must look at the formal structure of his speaking, and the dramatic characterization which he created for himself.

The characteristic pattern of logical proof in Darrow's legal arguments is dual. In almost every instance he either adopts two major lines of argument, differing in form, or he uses two types of argument to establish a single major contention.

The first and most important of these lines of argument is causal. Either Darrow attempts to justify his clients by an inquiry into the motives behind their acts, or he delves into the historical, causative factors of the act itself. In the Loeb-Leopold case, much of Darrow's plea dealt with the psychological factors behind his clients' crime; his argument ran that Loeb and Leopold had murdered Robert Franks because of certain physical and psychological defects for which they could not be held responsible. In the Massie case, he used essentially the same line of argument, claiming that Massie was nearly insane as a result of his personal misfortunes when he shot Joseph Kahahawai. In most of his labor cases, Darrow dealt with the historical causes of the acts in question. Thus, in the woodworkers' case he pointed out throughout his speech that the strike of the woodworkers was not an isolated occurrence but rather an incident in "the great battle of human liberty"; and in doing this, he placed the case in an entirely new context, very favorable to his clients.

298

When Darrow defended Haywood, he used his client as a symbol for the whole labor cause, and so related the trial to all the struggles of the poor.

These statements of causation were extremely important in Darrow's method. When he discussed motives, he was trying to get sympathy for his client, and this was the essential element in his entire method. When he dealt with the social and economic philosophy and history implied especially in many of his early cases, he was doing something almost as important. He was educating his jurors to see the entire case in a long perspective of events. In effect, he was recoloring and reshaping the whole case for them.

The second of Darrow's characteristic lines of argument is argument from sign. Having assigned the causes of a given act in terms of motive or social forces, he turns to the specific evidence in the case to establish the conclusions thus drawn. From his rehearsal of this evidence he draws numerous inferences regarding what precisely has happened in a specific case. Thus, in the Loeb-Leopold case, Darrow tries first of all to establish the causes of his clients' irresponsibility. He does this mainly through the reports and testimony of defense psychiatrists. But then, having done this, he analyzes the story of their crime, in all its grotesque detail. Were these two boys sane when they killed Robert Franks? Were they responsible? These are his constant questions.

Darrow's pleas typically start with the argument from cause, and generally this argument takes the form of a discussion of the status of the case. Then he discusses evidence, and draws his inferences from the signs thus uncovered. Afterwards, he alternates these two types of argument throughout the speech, ending always with the causal argument.

The pattern of Darrow's pathetic proof seems to be determined in quantity, kind, and position in the speech by his line of logical argument. Especially where he deals in argument from sign, he attempts, from time to time, to point out the perfidy of the prosecution scapegoat whom he always selects, thus inspiring in his listeners disgust, anger, or contempt for the opposition. An example is his treatment of Dr. Krohn, one of the prosecution psychiatrists in the Loeb-Leopold case:

Krohn told the story of this interview [with the defendant]. . . . And how he told it! When he testified my mind carried me back to the time when I was a kid, years ago, and we used to eat watermelons. I have seen little boys take a rind of watermelon and cover their whole faces with water, eat it, devour it, and have the time of their lives, up to their ears in watermelon. And when I heard Dr. Krohn testify in this case, to take the blood of those two boys, I could see his mouth water with the joy it gave him, and he showed all the delight and pleasure of myself and my young companions when we ate watermelon.[93]

[93] From a typed manuscript of the plea.

On the other hand, when he deals in causations, he is usually trying to justify his client; and so, through the narratives and descriptions which make up his causal arguments, he tries to inspire in the jury sympathy or pity or affection for his clients.

This pattern of argument occurs in all of his forensic speeches, and is reproduced rather faithfully in his debates and occasional lectures. Its weakness and its strength lay in its casualness and apparent spontaneity, a characteristic which suited admirably the kind of courtroom character which Darrow had developed for himself.

In court, Darrow appeared to be a simple, unsophisticated, countrified sort of person, in no way intrinsically superior to the average juror, except that he had read a bit more and could speak his mind more eloquently. The keynote of this character was tenderness and pity for the suffering. His was a Lincolnesque personality; curiously enough, when Darrow is compared, by those who heard him speak, to any other individual in history, it is almost always to Lincoln or, more rarely, to Christ.

Darrow's dress in court was always extremely casual. He wore old tweed suits when he could, and they usually looked as if they had been slept in since they had left the tailor's hands. He never wore a coat in warm weather if he could avoid it, and the lack of this garment generally revealed to the jurors broad blue galluses of an antique cut. His tie was always badly tied, and normally the knot rested about halfway around his neck, under one ear. One lock of his hair always dangled on his forehead.

His behavior in court, too, was free in the extreme. He slouched in his seat, resting generally on the middle of his back. Occasionally, it is said—though no written evidence supports this story—he would nurse, with a great appearance of discomfort, a large bunion on one of his feet.

Yet when he spoke, his listeners at once understood that here was a man whose opinions were worthy of respect. He was spokesman for no group, he spoke his own mind. If he was wrong, he was honestly wrong.

Besides, it was perfectly easy to see that his beliefs grew out of a great love of men and women. Nor was this a saccharine sentiment, for Darrow was honestly cynical about the performances of men. He believed only in their good intentions. More than this, he loved them and felt sorry for them.

Thus, the expression of his biases, the affection he showed for many of his clients, the scathing anger which he directed at prosecutors—all these, because they were based upon emotions that the average juror could understand and admire, added greatly to his prestige with them.

The Structure of Darrow's Philosophy

We have now reached a point in our analysis of Clarence Darrow's career as a pleader where we must consider the basic attitudes he expressed, the structure of his philosophy, the content of the Darrow myth. Darrow spoke and wrote chiefly about three subjects: capital and labor economics, criminology, and philosophy and religion. From his statements on these subjects it is possible to outline the main features of his personal philosophy, and perhaps to suggest why audiences responded to him as they did.

Darrow's ideas on philosophy and religion were deeply rooted in his childhood experience. Amirus Darrow, it will be remembered, had come by tortuous and tortured paths from Methodism to agnosticism; and as a result, he and his family were shut off from the more pious society of Kinsman. We need not re-examine the mechanisms by which the torture of Amirus Darrow's doubts and the stinging pain of social ostracism were transferred to his son.

Young Darrow's earliest memories were those of philosophical dispute; perhaps the earliest scholastic training which interested him was that of debate.[94] In Kinsman, he listened to the debates of the academy's literary society, and later became an enthusiastic member.

Debate was forever identified for Darrow with religion. "My interest in these exercises," he wrote, "was stimulated by my father. The fact that he was a heretic always put him on the defensive, and we children felt that it was only right and natural and loyal to echo and champion his cause. Even in our little shop the neighbors heard vigorous discussions and found my father willing to meet all comers on the mysteries of life and death."[95]

Curiously important were these same discussions, for out of them Darrow apparently derived almost all of the attitudes and many of the arguments which were to provide his philosophical stock-in-trade in later life. In 1925 at Dayton, in 1932 when he wrote his autobiography, even to the day of his death in 1938, he was echoing arguments that had originally been propounded in Amirus Darrow's little workshop in the 1850's and 1860's.[96]

It is true that Darrow's debates and incidental speeches on religion and philosophy are filled with echoes and quotations from Nietzsche, Schopenhauer, Tolstoy, Darwin; but their doctrines seem to have expanded the details of his

---

[94] *The Story of My Life*, p. 11.

[95] *Ibid.*, p. 376.

[96] One is tempted to pose such questions as these: When, in debate after debate, he used the same arguments to blast the same ancient theological work (Paley's *Natural Theology*, then nearly a hundred years old), and when time and again he used the example of the Lisbon earthquake (which had provoked Voltaire's cynicism in *Candide*), was he harking back to these well-remembered disputes?

301

philosophical structure, rather than to have contributed much to its real foundation. One suspects that he read Schopenhauer, for example, because the reading gave him support for what he already believed.

Harry Elmer Barnes says, "It would seem that his antipathy to authority and tyranny grew primarily out of his childhood impressions with respect to the arrogance, harshness and intolerance of conventional religion and traditional morality. His youthful rebellion against all this was amplified by his more mature experiences and studies."[97] An editorial in the *Christian Century* at the time of his death made a similar comment: "He seemed to be opposing conceptions that are no longer current among competent Christian thinkers and to be fighting over the battles of half a century ago."[98] Darrow's contact with the Christian world stopped short at about 1875.

Nearly as basic to Darrow's outlook as his ideas on philosophy and religion were his attitudes on capital and labor. These, too, came from Amirus Darrow; at least, the fundamental, emotional biases did, and these were his chief stock-in-trade when he dealt with labor problems. It may be, too, that the elder Darrow provided his son with materials and arguments a little more specific than these. Amirus Darrow certainly followed radical theory in his day; and his son once wrote that, after the triumph of abolition, his father had begun to "fight the same stubborn, threatening, public opinion for a new and yet more doubtful cause."[99] One is led to believe, from the context of the remark, that this cause was the cause of labor. This conclusion is also supported, to some extent, by Darrow's claim that "my father had directed my reading and insisted that I study political economy."[100]

But whether or not Amirus Darrow provided his son with anything other than the emotional convictions which he carried through life is not especially important; for these convictions, applied to the circumstances of each particular case, make up the bulk of his early pleas.

Darrow's philosophy of criminology was not so early established. In essence, it can easily be summarized. From Altgeld,[101] Darrow took a belief in the inflexibility of the penal system, in its harshness and inefficiency. From his reading of Tolstoy he took a belief in non-violence. From his own experience and from his associations with radical groups, he derived the belief that poverty and disease and ignorance are causative factors in crime. All of these derivations and beliefs, one should remember, were possible only because of

[97] "Clarence Darrow—the Man and the Philosopher," *Unity*, May 16, 1938, p. 93.
[98] Reprinted in *Unity*, May 16, 1938, p. 94.
[99] *Farmington*, pp. 247-48.
[100] *The Story of My Life*, p. 43.
[101] Both from his early reading of Altgeld's *Our Penal Machinery and Its Victims* and from their long friendship.

his characteristic sympathy for the outcast, a heritage from his father. Thus, he came to the conclusion that crime is a kind of social disease, which the legal system as it existed then could not heal. Crime should be prevented by social reform, and treated, when it did occur, as any other disease would be treated, without hatred or anger, but with compassion and human sympathy.

These ideas Darrow did not change very much in the course of his lifetime. He only acquired and discarded evidence that tended to support them.

With this brief sketch of the genesis of Darrow's philosophy, we may now be prepared to consider its specific nature. To simplify this inquiry, we shall discuss his attitudes under three headings: the universe, the backdrop against which the human drama is played; humanity, the actors; and violence, the specific act with which he was most concerned.

The nature of the world. In Darrow's cosmogony, the universe was not merely a neutral backdrop for human activity. It was at best a chaotic battlefield, at worst an active enemy. To the old argument that the natural universe exhibits design, which must lead one to infer a designer, he replied time and again,

To discover that certain forms and formations are adjusted for certain action has nothing to do with design. None of these developments are perfect, or anywhere near so. All of them, including the eye, are botchwork that any good mechanic would be ashamed to make. All of them need constant readjustment, are always out of order, and are entirely too complicated for dependable work. They are not made for any purpose; they simply grew out of needs and adaptations; in other words, they happened. Just as God must have happened, if he exists at all.[102]

More revealing is Darrow's conception of the cruelty of nature. To him the natural world was one endless panorama of death and destruction, in which the beasts (of whom man is a slightly more efficient example) engaged in a constant and bloody struggle for existence. He observes:

We speak of the seemingly peaceful woods, but we need only look beneath the surface to be horrified by the misery of that underworld. Hidden in the grass and watching for its prey is the crawling snake which swiftly darts upon the toad or mouse and gradually swallows it alive; the hapless animal is crushed by the jaws and covered with slime, to be slowly digested in furnishing a meal. . . . The spider carefully weaves his web to catch the unwary fly, winds him into the fatal net until paralyzed and helpless, then drinks his blood and leaves him an empty shell. The hawk swoops down and snatches a chicken. . . . The wolf pounces on the lamb and tears it to shreds.[103]

[102] *The Story of My Life*, p. 413.
[103] *Ibid.*, p. 392.

Nor does man escape Darrow's tongue in this respect. Being simply a specialized animal, he behaves in harmony with the rest of creation:

He seems to add treachery and deceit that the other animals in the main do not practice, to all the other cruelties that move his life. Man has made himself master of the animal world and he uses his power to serve only his own ends. Man, at least, kills helpless animals for the pleasure of killing alone.[104]

In this world there is no hope for charity or kindness:

Nature knows nothing about right and wrong, good and evil, pleasure and pain; she simply acts. She creates a beautiful woman, and places a cancer on her cheek. She may create an idealist, and kill him with a germm.... She knows no mercy nor goodness. Nothing is so cruel and abandoned as Nature. To call her tender or charitable is a travesty upon words and a stultification of the intellect.[105]

The horrors of this universe he thought unbearable; hence, his claim that religion is a mere narcotic agent, designed to protect the individual from the terrible vision of things as they are. Thus, he wrote,

All kinds of things have been invented to take away the sting of life—religions, philosophies, creeds, whiskey, cocaine, morphine, chloroform, mental and physical anodynes, anything to take away the reality, so life will be one long succession of pipe-dreams; and that is all right if you don't wake up, and if the awakening is not more horrible than the dream. No man can look at the truth and live; we must live by our emotions and illusions. We must live by such visions as the brain can conjure up.[106]

The nature of man. Through this horrifying universe stalks man, a soulless machine:

All of these plants and all of these animals have the same basis of life as man. My friend says that a human being can grow, and a machine can't grow. A mechanistic organism can grow. Every plant grows; all animal life grows and decays. It is born and it dies. It lives its time and goes its way. Now what is the difference? If a man is made differently from a machine, then a tree is.[107]

Naturally, the machine has no freedom of action. A mature man may do what he pleases; but he has very little control over *what* he pleases. "I very

[104] *Ibid.*, p. 393.

[105] *Ibid.*, p. 394. Darrow repeated these arguments almost word for word in many debates. E.g., in his debate with Robert MacGowan (*Is Religion Necessary?* Girard, Kansas: Haldeman-Julius Publications, 1931), he used the "beautiful woman with a cancer on her cheek" idea almost as it is here.

[106] "Schopenhauer," *The Liberal Review*, March, 1917, p. 22.

[107] Clarence Darrow and Will Durant, *Are We Machines?* (Girard, Kansas: Haldeman-Julius Publications, 1928), p. 41.

seldom do anything that I do not want to, because I have found out pretty well that there are a lot of things I can not do, and so I do not want to do them."[108]

This grim interpretation of the universe convinced Darrow that life, after all, is not worth living, and certainly not worth prolonging.[109] The only anodyne to the cruelty of life, for him, was lack of self-consciousness, which might be achieved in constant, engrossing activity, in sleep, and ultimately in death.

In his attitudes toward other human beings, Darrow might be described as pro-human. If Amirus Darrow taught his son one thing, it was a belief in the sanctity of human life. Darrow's bias against religion is due in part to this belief. His criminological theories are based on it. Every action of his life, and particularly his decision to defend Debs in the A.R.U. case, is a manifestation of it.

In his speeches, this attitude is expressed in an indirect way. It makes possible his tender and persuasive portraits of his clients. Thus, he describes Thomas I. Kidd as a good man, self-sacrificing and heroic and rigorously honest. Arthur Person is a man ignorant in the world's wisdom, but nevertheless a real human being: hard-working, affectionate, sacrificing his life to the well-being of his community. Bill Haywood is a hard-bitten, rough individual, true; but he has dedicated himself, like Person and Kidd, to the selfless service of others. Always Darrow makes his labor clients seem to possess these qualities, which are most admirable to him: courage and unselfishness. When he himself stood on trial in Los Angeles, and was forced to defend his own way of life, he did it in the same way: "I have stood for the weak and the poor. I have stood for the men who toil."

When Darrow considered the great masses of working people, his attitude toward them was one of pity for their conditions and admiration for their courage. An excerpt from his plea in defense of Kidd, Zentner, and Troiber will illustrate:

Sixteen hundred men and boys of Oshkosh, the brawn and sinew of your city, the men who take their dinner-pails in the morning and go to work in these prisons for a small pittance, and go home at night tired and weary and worn for the life that has gone out of them for the benefit of George M. Paine. Sixteen hundred criminals, all of whom are your citizens and your neighbors, and yet this District Attorney assures you that they are criminals, whom you should send to jail.[110]

---

[108] *Loc. cit.*

[109] "I fancy that if I really went dead, if anybody would awaken me and tell me to begin living again, I would kill him. I can say that and still not want to die. For the desire to live goes with living." *Pessimism, a Lecture* (Chicago: Rationalist Education Society, 1920), p. 6.

[110] From a typed manuscript of the speech.

Precisely this feeling of admiration and pity becomes bitterness and anger in Darrow's vicious diatribes against prosecutors and detectives and, occasionally, employers. In his defense of Kidd, Zentner, and Troiber, again, he uses this attitude with great skill when he describes George M. Paine looking at the children who work for him and parodies the biblical words: "Suffer the little children to come unto me, and forbid them not, for of such is the prison pen of George M. Paine!" Normally, however, Darrow reserved his most violent attacks for prosecutors such as Hawley in the Haywood case, and for witnesses whom he regarded as venal or as turncoats, such as Dr. Krohn in the Loeb-Leopold trial or Harry Orchard in the Haywood affair. He could understand the crimes of industrialists—the industrial system made them difficult to avoid—but the prosecutors and witnesses he regarded as traitors against common humanity, and so doubly contemptible.

The truth is, that Darrow was unalterably opposed to all institutions, organizations, and other non-human "persons." This was no doubt the real basis of his anti-religious bias. While he would almost certainly have defended Christ before Pilate, Darrow despised all Christian churches, simply because they were organized. Himself a lawyer, he despised legal institutions, and especially those of the criminal law. Pessimistic concerning the larger results of his pleading, he nevertheless felt and said that he had accomplished much in saving as many men as he did from the law. Victor Yarros reports that Darrow, while trying a minor case before a jury, was interrupted by the prosecutor, who urged that the defense was trying to cheat the law of a dangerous criminal. Almost without taking a breath, Darrow shouted, "The law? To hell with the law! My business is to save this defendant from the law!" Oddly enough, he was not cited for contempt.[111]

The act of violence. In the world of Darrow's philosophy, violence was a natural concomitant of its structure. Here was a cosmos chaotic, meaningless, and cruel, in which human beings were pitted against mechanized and powerful organizations in a hopeless struggle for existence, in which human traitors often went over to the side of the machine. How could anything but violence result? Darrow's attitude toward this act was somewhat contradictory. In principle, he did not believe in violence; he had found Tolstoy too much to his taste for that. Yet every so often a situation arose in which violence was or could be directed at the enemy; and what then? The answer we may find in a passage from Darrow's speech in defense of William Haywood: "But you can't tell me, gentlemen, that the great mass of the men who go down into the earth with their lives in their hands to dig up gold for other men are criminals. If for any reason a thousand men deliberately determined to go and blow up the Bunker Hill mill, then it needed blowing up. It needed it,

[111] Victor Yarros, Interview.

just as much as if you go into a town and persuade everyone to join in the civil war to liberate the slaves. You can't get great masses of men to act from evil purposes." [112] Clearly, Darrow's belief in non-violence could be stretched a good deal. One must conclude, from reading Darrow's speeches and writings, that he deprecated violence in the abstract. He could not condone it as a general proposition. His handling of the concrete example relates closely to the structure of argument in his forensic speeches. When violence was committed by organizations against human beings, he found it, of course, malicious and horrifying; he was given to examining the signs of the available data to establish the degree of malignity of the act. When violence was committed by human beings against organizations, he immediately saw and used all the extenuating circumstances that appeared in the situation, using his typical causal argument to do so.

From this analysis we can readily reconstruct the nature of the Darrow myth as audiences came to know it. In a world increasingly hag-ridden with machines, bedevilled with super-organizations, all of which did and do in fact hem in, stifle, and pulverize human individuality, Darrow's personal and public battle had the luminous significance of a great epic. Its meaning, in relation to the facts of history and of social structure, we need not discuss. Darrow's drama may have been merely a fiction which re-echoed the life of an earlier and easier world; it may have been a valid prophecy for the future. In any case, to millions of people in the United States and abroad, Clarence Darrow provided a myth in which "men and women are comforted for the hardships, the inequalities, the injustices of the daily round ... a release that provides them with courage" and a hope for the future.

Conclusion

This analysis of the speaking of Clarence Darrow began with the observation that he, like many other speakers and other public persons, seemed to exert an influence on the public which could not be accounted for by the ordinary standards of rhetorical critics. We then advanced the hypothesis that Darrow's public career might best be understood if we looked on him as a "myth-maker," or even as the living personification of a myth which supplied some vital need in the lives of many persons of his day. In the course of testing this hypothesis, we attempted to find a meaningful parallel between the structure of Darrow's life and the structure of American society, especially in the years 1895-1938. Through an examination of Darrow's behavior, and of his speeches in particular, we attempted to discover something of the nature

[112] From a typed manuscript of the speech.

of the myth involved, and of the techniques which he used to develop and dramatize it.

From this study, the following observations seem to emerge:

1. The main feature of Clarence Darrow's boyhood was his intimate relationship with his father. As a result of this relationship, Darrow learned that organized groups of human beings (in this case, the community of Kinsman, with its smaller churchly, economic, and other in-groups), must always be regarded as the enemy, and that only individuals, most especially those out of favor with the organized groups, could be regarded as friends. This philosophy not only ran counter to Darrow's family heritage, it also forced Darrow, whose ties with his father were very strong, into the position of attacking and rebelling against nearly all the paternal symbols available in his society. He thus developed a distinctly ambivalent attitude both toward his father and toward the community of his boyhood. This deep confusion in his outlook may have caused him to suffer feelings of guilt, and may even relate to his undeniably morbid fear of death.

2. As a result of many factors, including the closing of the frontier, the development of rail transportation, the rise of industry, and the great waves of immigration, the psychological unity of American society was weakened if not destroyed during the decades following the Civil War. The older, established groups organized to protect themselves against the many new groups which appeared to be rising in power. The result was the fragmentation of society, and the creation of a greater variety of out-groups, the members of which we labeled "barbarians." In short, the basic conflict of Clarence Darrow's life was very similar to one of the major conflicts in society in general during the years of his public career.

3. Part of Darrow's heritage from his father was his propensity for attacking problems verbally, and especially within the framework of oratory and debate. This habit made possible the development of Darrow's career as we have studied it, for in the utterances of speakers and writers, many "levels of meaning" may legitimately be discussed. Thus, a speaker's words may be taken "literally" as a statement about the objective realities he is presumably discussing. Or his words may be taken "figuratively," in the sense that, although they may seem to apply to one set of realities, they are intended to apply to some other situation which may be superficially quite different. Or, most important of all, a speaker's words may be intended to convey a literal or figurative meaning, in the above senses, and may also, perhaps without the speaker's conscious intent, represent a symbolic attack upon problems which the speaker is not able to deal with in a more direct way. Thus, Darrow's speeches and writings may be considered as an attempt, regardless of changes in

their obvious subject matter, to resolve the basic conflicts of his life, which derive from his earliest years.

4. A corollary to this observation is that many types of moral, ethical, and other problems can be and are in practice generalized, so that the resemblance between two specific cases in which the same general problem occurs can be seen, even though the circumstances in the two cases may differ considerably. This is an observation which has most frequently been made in connection with dramatic literature. Thus, a speaker like Clarence Darrow who expresses, dramatizes, or otherwise deals with conflicts common to many members of his audience may achieve a special sort of popular success and public status. Such a person is, in effect, a true myth-maker, and tends to become identified with the myth he has created.

5. Darrow's arrival in Chicago in 1888, his first successful speech in Chicago, and his defense of Eugene V. Debs, may be taken together to represent a major turning point in his career. His speech at the Chicago Free Trade convention solved a mechanical problem, but one of the first importance, for him; it provided him with access to an important channel of communication, gave him the stimulus of success, and established a functional relationship between him as a speaker and an audience. The decision to defend Debs, and the comparative success of his defense, established the pattern of his public career for the remainder of his life. It would appear, from an examination of Darrow's case at least, that once the speaker-audience relationship has been set, it tends to be self-perpetuating.

6. From the time of the Debs case to the time of his own trial for bribery, Darrow's career represents a development of the basic elements already set. Even the disaster which overtook him as a result of the McNamara trial did not destroy the pattern of his life, but simply altered the context of his activity.

7. While we cannot expect to describe satisfactorily the "causes" of Darrow's success as a pleader in terms of speech technique, an examination of his consciously used rhetorical skills is interesting. Perhaps the main observation to make is that Darrow seems to have spoken "by ear"; his technical skill in speech was largely habitual, almost instinctive. He did work out a method for selecting juries, and for disqualifying those jurors he did not want. His direct preparation was almost non-existent, a fact which might suggest that Darrow's chief concern in speaking was the re-enactment of a basic pattern of attack and defense, almost without regard to specific subject matter. This pattern we have identified as a "myth." The main features of Darrow's speaking are his distinctive use of causal argument and argument from sign, with their related emotional appeals, and his development of a convincing courtroom and platform "character."

8. The structure of Darrow's philosophy, the content of the Darrow

myth, comes directly from Amirus Darrow's influence. We may summarize it briefly here: (1) the universe in which we live is cruel, chaotic, and merciless; (2) we human beings are alone, friendless, and outcast, constantly forced to defend ourselves against the terrors of nature and the menace of human social inventions; (3) all organizations and institutions are anti-human, evil, and always to be attacked; (4) the significant aspect of human life is the act of violence, which in general must be condemned, but which is excusable if directed against organizations.

This is a sketch of Darrow's life and public career, and of his significance for the people of his day. Irving stone phrased his epitaph very well when he wrote, "He was a propagandist for humanity." [113]

SELECTED BIBLIOGRAPHY

ALLEN, LESLIE H. *Bryan and Darrow at Dayton*. New York: Arthur Lee & Co., 1925.

ALTGELD, JOHN. *Live Questions, Including Our Penal Machinery and Its Victims*. New York: The Humboldt Publishing Co., n.d.

ANTHRACITE STRIKE COMMISSION. *Report to the President on the Anthracite Coal Strike of May-October 1902*. Washington, D. C.: The Government Printing Office, 1903.

Argument of George F. Baer, Esq., before the Anthracite Coal Strike Commission. Privately printed, 1913.

BANCROFT, EDGAR A. *The Chicago Strike of 1894*. Chicago: The Gunthrop-Warren Printing Co., 1895.

BURNS, WILLIAM J. *The Masked War*. New York: George H. Doran & Co., 1913.

Category of Crimes of the Mine Owners' Association Compiled by the Western Federation of Miners. Denver: Miners' Magazine Print, 1904.

CLEVELAND, GROVER. *The Government in the Chicago Strike of 1894*. Princeton: The Princeton University Press, 1913.

COHN, ALFRED, AND CHISHOLM, JOE. *Take the Witness!* Garden City, N. Y.: The Garden City Publishing Co., 1934.

COLEMAN, MCALLISTER. *Eugene V. Debs: A Man Unafraid*. New York: Greenberg, 1930.

CRANDALL, ALLEN. *The Man from Kinsman*. Sterling, Colorado: Privately printed, 1913.

Criminal Record of the Western Federation of Miners from Coeur d'Alenes to Cripple Creek, 1894-1904. Colorado Springs: Privately printed, 1904.

CULIN, STEWART. *A Trooper's Narrative of Service in the Anthracite Coal Strike*, 1902. Philadelphia: George W. Jacobs & Co., 1903.

DARROW, CLARENCE. *Argument of Clarence Darrow in the Case of the Communist Labor Party in the Criminal Court, Chicago*. Chicago: Charles H. Kerr & Co., 1920.

———. "Argument in Defense of William Haywood." Typed ms.

———. "Argument in Defense of Loeb and Leopold." Typed ms.

———. "Argument in the Case of Arthur Person." Typed ms.

[113] Stone, *op. cit.*, p. 519.

DARROW, CLARENCE. *Argument of Clarence Darrow in the Case of Henry Sweet.* New York: National Association for the Advancement of Colored People, 1927.

——. "Argument in the Woodworkers Case." Typed ms.

——. *Crime and Criminals.* Chicago: Charles H. Kerr & Co., 1919.

——. *Crime, Its Cause and Treatment.* New York: Thomas Y. Crowell, 1922.

——. *An Eye for an Eye.* New York: Fox, Duffield & Co., 1905.

——. *Facing Life Fearlessly.* Girard, Kansas: Haldeman-Julius Publications, 1929.

——. *Farmington.* New York: Boni & Liveright, 1925.

——. *Insects and Men: Instinct and Reason.* Girard, Kansas: Haldeman-Julius Publications, n.d.

——. *The Myth of the Soul.* Girard, Kansas: Haldeman-Julius Publications, 1929.

——. *The Open Shop.* Chicago: Charles H. Kerr & Co., 1909.

——. *The Ordeal of Prohibition.* Girard, Kansas: Haldeman-Julius Publications, 1925.

——. *A Persian Pearl and Other Essays.* Chicago: C. L. Ricketts, 1902.

——. *Pessimism, a Lecture.* Chicago: Rationalist Education Society, 1920.

——. *Plea of Clarence Darrow in His Own Defense to the Jury at Los Angeles.* Los Angeles: The Golden Press, 1912.

——. *Resist Not Evil.* Chicago: Charles H. Kerr & Co., 1903.

——. *Response of Clarence Darrow to Birthday Greetings, April 18, 1918.* Chicago: Walden Book Shop, 1918.

——. *The Story of My Life.* New York: Charles Scribner's Sons, 1932.

——. *Voltaire.* Chicago: John F. Higgins, 1918.

——. *War Prisoners.* Chicago: Maclaskey & Maclaskey, Court Reporters, 1919.

——, and DURANT, WILL. *Are We Machines? A Debate.* Girard, Kansas: Haldeman-Julius Publications, 1928.

——, and FOSTER, GEORGE B. *Do Human Beings Have Free Will?* Girard, Kansas: Haldeman-Julius Publications, 1928.

——, and HOLMES, JOHN H. *Debate on Prohibition.* Girard, Kansas: Haldeman-Julius Publishing Co., 1924.

——, and KENNEDY, JOHN C. *Is the Human Race Permanently Progressing toward a Better Civilization?* Chicago, John F. Higgins, 1919.

——, and MACGOWAN, ROBERT. *Is Religion Necessary?* Girard, Kansas: Haldeman-Julius Publications, 1931.

——, and MUSMANNO, M. A. *Does Man Live Again?* (The Reviewers Library No. 5.) Girard, Kansas: Haldeman-Julius Publications, 1936.

——, and ЯICE, WALLACE. *Infidels and Heretics: an Atheist's Anthology.* Boston: The Stratford Co., 1929.

——, and SMITH, T. V. *Can the Individual Control His Conduct?* Girard, Kansas: Haldeman-Julius Publications, 1928.

——, and STARR, FREDERICK. *Is Civilization a Failure?* Chicago: Privately printed, 1920.

——, and STARR, FREDERICK. *Is the Human Race Getting Anywhere?* Girard, Kansas: Haldeman-Julius Publications, 1925.

——, and STARR, FREDERICK. *Is Life Worth Living?* Girard, Kansas: Haldeman-Julius Publications, 1925.

——, and STODDARD, LOTHROP. *Is the U. S. Immigration Law Beneficial?* Girard, Kansas: Haldeman-Julius Publications, 1929.

311

DARROW, CLARENCE, and TALLEY, ALFRED J. *Resolved, That Capital Punishment Is a Public Policy.* New York: The League for Public Discussion, 1924.

———, and YARROS, VICTOR S. *The Prohibition Mania: a Reply to Professor Irving Fisher and Others.* New York: Boni and Liveright, 1927.

———, and WHEELER, WAYNE B. *Dry-Law Debate.* Girard, Kansas: Haldeman-Julius Publications, 1927.

———, and WILSON, CLARENCE T. *Should the 18th Amendment Be Repealed?* Girard, Kansas. Haldeman-Julius Publications, 1931.

Debs: His Life, Writing and Speeches. Girard, Kansas: The Appeal to Reason, 1908.

DEBS, EUGENE V. *Speeches of Eugene V. Debs.* New York: International Publishers, 1928.

Ex parte Eugene V. Debs et al. Privately printed, 1894.

GOMPERS, SAMUEL. *Seventy Years of Life and Labor: an Autobiography.* New York: E. P. Dutton, 1925.

HALDEMAN-JULIUS, MARCET. *Clarence Darrow's Two Great Trials.* Girard, Kansas: The Haldeman-Julius Press, 1925.

HARRISON, CHARLES Y. *Clarence Darrow.* New York: Jonathan Cape & Harrison Smith, 1931.

HAYS, ARTHUR GARFIELD. *Trial by Prejudice.* New York: Covici-Friede, 1935.

HAYWOOD, WILLIAM D. *Bill Haywood's Book, the Autobiography of William D. Haywood.* New York: International Publishers, 1929.

MCKERNAN, MAUREEN. *The Amazing Crime of Leopold and Loeb.* Chicago: The Plymouth Court Press, 1924.

MCMANIGAL, ORTIE. *The National Dynamite Plot.* Los Angeles: The Neale Co., 1913.

NATIONAL RECOVERY REVIEW BOARD. *First Report to the President of the United States; Second Report; Third Report.* All volumes issued and bound by Jesse L. Ward, Official Reporter, Washington, D. C., 1934.

Sixteenth Report of the National Association for the Advancement of Colored People. New York: NAACP, 1925.

STONE, IRVING. *Clarence Darrow for the Defense.* Garden City, N.Y.: Doubleday, Doran & Co., 1941.

WERNER, MORRIS. *Bryan.* New York: Harcourt Brace & Co., 1929.

The World's Most Famous Court Trial, Tennessee Evolution Case. Cincinnati: National Book Co., 1925.

WRIGHT, CARROLL D. *The Battles of Labor.* Philadelphia: George W. Jacobs & Co., 1906.

9

Theodore Roosevelt

by RICHARD MURPHY

Theodore Roosevelt, naturalist, author, rancher, public servant and public speaker, twenty-fifth Vice-President of the United States, and twenty-sixth President, was born at 28 East Twentieth Street, New York City, October 27, 1858. He was in the seventh generation of the Roosevelt line established by Klaes Martensen van Roosevelt, Dutch burgher, who settled in Manhattan in 1650. His father, Theodore, was a prosperous merchant. His mother, Martha Bulloch of Roswell, Georgia, was descended from Scotch-Irish, Huguenot-French, and Palatinate-German ancestry. In 1880, he was married to Alice Hathaway Lee of Boston, who died in 1884. One child, Alice Lee (Alice Roosevelt Longworth), was born. In 1886, he was married to Edith Kermit Carow of New York City. There were five children to this union: Theodore, jr., Kermit, Ethel Carow (Mrs. Richard Derby), Archibald Bulloch, and Quentin.

In 1880, Roosevelt was graduated from Harvard College. He served three terms in the New York State Assembly, 1882-84. From 1884 to 1886, he was a rancher in the Badlands of South Dakota. In 1886, he was defeated as candidate for mayor of New York City. He was United States Civil Service Commissioner, 1889-95, and president of the Police Commission of the City of New York, 1895-97. From 1897 to May 1898, he was Assistant Secretary of the Navy, a position he resigned to become lieutenant-colonel of the First United States Volunteer Cavalry (the Rough Riders) in the Spanish-American War. In November, he was elected governor of New York and served one term. He was inaugurated Vice-President on March 4, 1901, and upon McKinley's death on September 14, became President. In 1904, he was elected President. Upon retiring from the presidency in 1909, he hunted in Africa and toured Europe. As Progressive party (Bull Moose) candidate for President in 1912, he was defeated by Woodrow Wilson. In 1913 and 1914, he explored the Brazilian wilderness. The rest of his days were given to speaking, writing, and public service. He was contributing editor of *The Outlook* from 1909 to 1914, editorial writer for the *Metropolitan* from 1914, and of the *Kansas City Star* from 1917. His offer to raise and equip a division of volunteers for service in France in 1917 was rejected by President Wilson. Theodore Roosevelt died of a blood clot in the heart as he slept in his home at Oyster Bay, January 6, 1919.

313

$\mathcal{N}$ature and Extent of Speaking

Roosevelt's career in public speaking began in the New York Assembly and extended until the end of his days. In his thirty-seven years on the platform he campaigned in his district and his state, toured the country at large, gave lectures on subjects from history to the good life, dedicated buildings and felicitated graduates, addressed juries in libel suits as plaintiff and as defendant, and gave speeches of inspiration to patriotic, religious, and welfare groups. With a vigor undiminished to the end, he exhorted millions of people on four continents.

Indeed, the nature of his speaking in the larger sense was so varied that this single study in public address cannot encompass it. He issued a stream of statements to the press, as President sent more than four hundred messages to Congress, and issued almost a thousand executive orders and proclamations. He was active as conciliator and arbitrator; the first use of voluntary arbitration on a large scale at government insistence occurred in the anthracite strike of 1902 when Roosevelt called to the White House [1] representatives of labor and capital. In 1905, he served as conciliator in the war between Russia and Japan, effected the Peace of Portsmouth, and received the Nobel Prize. In the Civil Service Commission at Washington, on the New York City Police Board, with his presidential Cabinet, in countless party caucuses and political sessions, Roosevelt worked in conference and group discussion.

When the one hundred-fifth session of the New York Assembly convened in January, 1882, the representative from the twenty-first district was the youngest member. Before the session had adopted its rules, he had made a speech [2] widely reported in the state. And before it adjourned, the fledgling had demonstrated his courage and audacity by calling for an investigation of Supreme Court Justice T. R. Westbrook,[3] against the wishes of leaders of both parties. At the end of his third and last term in the legislature he went as delegate to the Republican Convention in Chicago, in June, 1884. He was pleased with his short speech seconding the nomination of John R. Lynch, a Negro from Mississippi, as chairman of the convention: "It was the first time I had ever had the chance of speaking to ten thousand people assembled together." [4] The convention over, Roosevelt retired to his ranch in Dakota.

[1] October 3, 1902. Roosevelt was then living at the temporary White House, 22 Lafayette Place.

[2] Hermann Hagedorn (ed.), *The Works of Theodore Roosevelt* (20 vols.; National ed.; New York: Charles Scribner's Sons, 1926), XIV, 3. (Hereinafter referred to as *Works*.)

[3] *Ibid.*, pp. 7-11.

[4] *Letters from Theodore Roosevelt to Anna Roosevelt Cowles* (New York: Charles Scribner's Sons, 1924), pp. 55-56. (Hereinafter referred to as *Cowles*.)

He had much to think about. The February before, his mother and his wife had died within the same twenty-four hours. He had to decide whether to bolt the party or stay with it and support Blaine. He was determined to continue his writing, but it looked as though his political days were at an end. But that fall he was back in Massachusetts campaigning against the Mugwumps and for Henry Cabot Lodge.[5] In the fall of 1885, he campaigned for the Republican ticket in New York.[6] In 1886, he left the ranch to run for mayor of New York against Abram S. Hewitt, Democrat, and Henry George, Independent. As he was speaking at Cooper Union a voice called out, "You will be elected!" It was a gratifying interruption. "I think so myself,"[7] replied the candidate in a bold front, for his main concern was that he should not be defeated too badly.[8] He ran third. The month of his defeat he took respite from national affairs, sailed for England, and was married in London.

The next two years were relatively quiet ones so far as speaking was concerned. He was a "kind of stop-gap orator"[9] in this period, he thought. In the fall of 1888, he made a short campaign tour as far west as Minneapolis. From 1889 to 1895, while Civil Service commissioner in Washington, Roosevelt emerged as a speaker of national prominence. Chautauqua, Baltimore, and Deadwood, South Dakota, received him on matters of good government or current elections. Often he spoke on historical subjects; in 1893, he addressed the State Historical Society of Wisconsin at Madison.[10] By 1895, he was in the whirl of reform as police commissioner of New York City. "We war against all criminals,"[11] he told the New York Preachers Meeting. Badgered and heckled on such matters as his attempts to enforce Sunday closing laws, he spoke "in packed halls...with the temperature at boiling point, both as regards the weather and the audience."[12] In his speaking he was on his own: "The party leaders...have come as near casting me off as they dared."[13] In October, 1896, he journeyed to Chicago and Detroit to denounce Bryan, Debs, Governor Altgeld of Illinois, and soft money.[14] In

[5] Specimen speeches are given in *Selections from the Correspondence of Theodore Roosevelt and Henry Cabot Lodge* (2 vols.; New York: Charles Scribner's Sons, 1925), I, 12-25. (Hereinafter referred to as *Lodge.*)

[6] A specimen speech, before the Young Republican Club of Brooklyn, is given in *Works*, XIV, 58-67.

[7] *Ibid.*, p. 73.

[8] See *Lodge*, I, 47 ff.

[9] Letter of October 19, 1888. *Ibid.*, p. 72.

[10] *Works*, IX, 544-49.

[11] *Ibid.*, XIV, 216.

[12] Letter of August 27, 1895. *Lodge*, I, 167.

[13] Letter of October 13, 1895. *Cowles*, p. 161.

[14] The speeches are in *Works*, XIV, 258-79.

1897, Roosevelt became assistant secretary of the Navy, a position that inhibited his public speaking. "Of course I cannot speak in public," he wrote to his brother-in-law, a captain in the Navy, "but I have advised the President... to settle this matter instantly by armed intervention."[15] The matter became the Spanish-American War. But before he resigned his position to become lieutenant colonel of the First Volunteer Cavalry, he found occasion to speak on matters other than intervention, to campaign for Hanna in Ohio, and to admonish the Naval War College that "peace is a goddess only when she comes with sword girt on thigh."[16] Five months after he left the Navy office, Roosevelt had been through what John Hay described to him as "a splendid little war,"[17] and had said farewell to his men at Montauk, Long Island, exhorting them that "the hero-business is over for good and all."[18]

But a month later Roosevelt was campaigning for governor, with full standing in the party, and a personal appeal that brought the crowds with cries of "We want Teddy!" Over the state he toured in a special train, with Rough Riders in uniform as attendants. At the stops a bugler sounded assembly and the hero of San Juan doffed his black felt campaign hat as the crowd gathered. Between October 5 and November 7, 1898, he made three hundred speeches. The year 1899, begun with a short inaugural address as governor, was a strenuous one in speech-making. To the universities he traveled, to Michigan and Cornell. Into Maryland, Ohio, and Massachusetts he went to help the Republican cause. In Chicago was delivered one of his most famous speeches, "The Strenuous Life." He visited New York county fairs and made speeches, and found time to address firemen's conventions and chambers of commerce. In June, 1900, Roosevelt interrupted his usual program of speech-making to Republican clubs, the Friendly Sons of St. Patrick, and a reunion of Rough Riders, to second the renomination of William McKinley at the Philadelphia convention. In turn he was nominated for Vice-President to fill the vacancy on the ticket created by the death of the incumbent, Garrett A. Hobart. "I am as strong as a bull moose and you can use me up to the limit, taking heed of but one thing and that is my throat,"[19] he wrote to Mark Hanna, who, as Republican chairman was managing the campaign.

[15] Joseph Bucklin Bishop, *Theodore Roosevelt and His Time* (2 vols.; New York: Charles Scribner's Sons, 1920), I, 89. (Hereinafter referred to as Bishop.) Letter of March 30, 1898, to W. S. Cowles.

[16] *Works*, XIII, 183.

[17] William Roscoe Thayer (ed.), *The Life and Letters of John Hay* (2 vols.; Boston and New York: Houghton Mifflin Co., 1915), II, 337. (Hereinafter referred to as *John Hay*.)

[18] *Works*, XI, 154.

[19] June 27, 1900. Theodore Roosevelt Papers, Library of Congress. (Hereinafter referred to as LC.)

McKinley was to maintain his presidential dignity and do little more than make a few speeches from his porch in Canton. Roosevelt was to do the campaigning, singing praises of McKinley and the full dinner pail, warning the country of Bryan, and minimizing his own genius as much as possible. Whereas, in the gubernatorial campaign, party leaders had tried to restrain the candidate lest he talk himself out of being elected, in 1900 they almost worked him to death. He opened the campaign in July at St. Paul. In September, he began a grand tour, working his way west to Idaho and Montana on a special train. The usual daily program was eight scheduled stops, with talks from the rear platform of the train, and a mass meeting in a city each evening. A specimen day can be seen in a schedule in the Rocky Mountain area, September 25:

Cheyenne, Wyoming	9:10	LV.
Eaton, Colorado	10:40	5″
Greeley	11:05	40″
Ft. Collins	12:30	30″
Loveland	1.23	10″
Berthoud	1:45	5″
Longmont	2:09	30″
Niwot	2:50	5″
Boulder	3:15	40″
Denver	5:00	AR.

On the following two days Roosevelt and entourage, which included Henry Cabot Lodge and Curtis Guild, had their most strenuous campaigning, through the silver mining area of Colorado. Everywhere they were met with cries of "16 to 1," and "Bryan, Bryan!" The most troublesome meeting was at Victor, in the Pikes Peak region. The 2,500 persons in the hall were an excited audience. Roosevelt was heckled about bimetallism, Republican rotten beef in the Spanish-American War, and policy toward the Philippines. A reporter wrote, "Infrequently through the noise could be heard Roosevelt shouting: 'I appeal to you for the sake of your material prosperity and for the sake of the flag.'"[20] The party hurried to the train which pulled out quickly while boys threw stones at the retreating campaign special. Three weeks later, Roosevelt had talked his way back through Baltimore to New York. What he had hoped would be a quiet, dignified campaign of limited speaking had turned into a tour through 24 states, with stops at 567 towns, and with 673 speeches delivered to 3,000,000 persons on an itinerary of 21,209 miles.[21] After victory was achieved, Roosevelt reflected with pride that he

[20] Details are from the Denver *Daily News*, September 27, 1900.
[21] *New York Times*, November 3, 1900.

had not said anything he had to take back nor in any way had been unwise.[22]

In March, 1901, Roosevelt as Vice-President gave a short inaugural address to the Senate and presided for the five days of a special session. He began what he dreaded as a chore, with resolve to preserve dignity and decorum; when there was applause from spectators he threatened to have the sergeant-at-arms clear the galleries.[23] In May, he formally opened the Pan-American Exposition in Buffalo. On September 6, he was making a speech near Burlington, Vermont, when word came that McKinley had been shot at the Exposition.

The presidential years were filled with speechmaking, not only in Washington but in all parts of the country. In 1902 he toured New England, the Midwest, and the South. In 1903, he spoke through the Midwest and on to the Coast, in preparation for the campaign of 1904; he thought a President should not openly stump for re-election. He had many strenuous days. On March 17, 1905, he reviewed the St. Patrick's Day Parade in New York, addressed the Friendly Sons of St. Patrick, and the Sons of the American Revolution, and gave away his niece, Eleanor, in marriage to Franklin Delano Roosevelt. In 1906, he visited Panama and Puerto Rico. Early in 1909 there was a round of farewell speeches.

In the spring of 1909, Roosevelt left the White House, public affairs, and the public platform to hunt in Africa and to write of his adventures. Six months before, he had received an invitation to deliver the Romanes Lecture at Oxford University in 1910. He accepted with delight. "This puts the matter right," [24] he wrote to Lodge. He wanted to visit England, and this would give him a reason. Other invitations came in, and what was planned as a short trip through a few European countries became a speaking tour through a dozen. On March 16, 1910, Roosevelt spoke at Khartum on the White Nile in British Sudan. He went on to Cairo, Rome, Budapest, Paris, Amsterdam, Copenhagen, Stockholm, Christiania, Berlin, London, and Cambridge. On June 7, he gave his Oxford lecture, which had been postponed three weeks because of the death of Edward VII.

Roosevelt returned from hobnobbing with the princes and populace of Europe with no plans for speaking. But within two months two thousand invitations to speak had been received.[25] With the Frontier Celebration at Cheyenne as focal point, Roosevelt set out August 23 and returned to New York September 11, 1910. In that time he spoke to a third of a million people in 14 states and traveled 5,500 miles. In many ways it was his most triumphal

[22] Letter to E. S. Martin, November 22, 1900. LC.

[23] *Congressional Record,* 57th Cong., Spec. Sen. sess., March 8, 1901, p. 31.

[24] Bishop, II, 121-22.

[25] Bishop, II, 300.

speaking tour; the crowds showed an interest and affection greater than in the presidential years. In Fargo, North Dakota, an outdoor audience of 10,000 persons waited through a rainstorm to hear him.[26] In 1911, he dedicated the Roosevelt Dam in Arizona, extemporized a series of lectures at the Pacific Theological Seminary in Berkeley, and made speeches coming and going on the trip. During the summer and autumn he took one of his few respites from speaking. The following year, 1912, was a strenuous one. By February, he was active in the preconvention campaign to be selected Republican nominee for President. In June came the convention in Chicago. On the eve of the first session Roosevelt addressed his followers in a preconvention rally in the Auditorium.[27] Three days later, when it became clear that Taft, although lacking popular support of a majority, would be able to manage renomination through parliamentary maneuvering of disputed delegations, Roosevelt bolted. A temporary organization was set up and at the end of the Republican Convention a rally of Progressives was held in Orchestra Hall with Roosevelt addressing them. In August, the Progressive Party Convention was held in Chicago. Roosevelt's "Confession of Faith" was delivered, and 3,000,000 copies were printed for distribution in the Bull Moose campaign. With little state organization, tours were mapped for Roosevelt and the vice-presidential candidate, Hiram Johnson of California. Roosevelt's first tour, in August and September, was through Iowa, Minnesota, to Oregon, Utah, California, and back to New York. In October, a second tour was planned. From Duluth to Oshkosh to Chicago to Milwaukee Roosevelt worked his way. On October 14, as he was standing in an automobile to be driven to the Auditorium to make a speech, he was shot by John Flammang Schrank. The bullet tore under the right nipple and into the fifth rib, but was deflected by a glasses case and the manuscript of the speech to be delivered. There were fifty glazed pages, folded once. Through the line, "Mr. Wilson has suffered many [bullet hole] changes of heart..."[28] went the shot. He was sufficiently recovered by October 30 to give a speech to 15,000 persons in Madison Square Garden. And at the end of the year he gave a presidential address in Boston, but it was as president of the American Historical Association that he spoke.

After the defeat of the Progressives in 1912, Roosevelt was a spokesman for a minority, and frequently was on the defensive. With World War I, he plunged into the last phase of his speechmaking. In 1915, he made

---

[26] Oscar King Davis, *Released for Publication* (Boston: Houghton Mifflin Co., 1925), pp. 216-18. (Hereinafter referred to as Davis.)

[27] *Works*, XVII, 204-31.

[28] This page is on display at Theodore Roosevelt House. Davis, p. 382, has a photostat of another page showing the bullet hole.

patriotic speeches to California and back. In 1916, although willing to be nominated for President on the Republican ticket, he made no campaign, and refused the nomination made by the Progressive party. He continued his talks on preparedness and made a furious ten-day tour for Hughes to Phoenix, Albuquerque, and Denver. In 1917, he toured the Midwest on several trips for the Red Cross, the YMCA, and in the cause of Liberty Loans. The touring continued in 1918, although on the last trip, to Montana, he was ill much of the time. His last speech was made November 2, in Carnegie Hall, under auspices of the Circle for Negro War Relief.[29] On Sunday evening, January 5, 1919, there was a mass meeting in the Hippodrome sponsored by the American Defense Society. Roosevelt was too ill to attend, but he prepared a statement and it was read. The papers of January 6 carried the statement and notice of his death.

The Man They Came to Hear

"It made but slight difference what Roosevelt said," observed Vice-President Thomas R. Marshall in his memoirs; "it was Roosevelt, the man, that people followed."[30] It is certainly true that the crowds came not so much to hear a speech as to see and hear Roosevelt. He himself traced the development of his personality.[31] At an early period, he testifies, he acted so independently of others that he could accomplish little. Later, able to work with groups but beset by ambition, he so calculated each move that he became fettered. At last he "found himself"; he learned to do with dispatch the particular jobs before him, and to work in the philosophy of "practical idealism," with anyone who was traveling his general way. Through his letters, and frequently in conversation with friends, ran moods of doubt and introspection but the public before him saw only the man of confidence and decision.

Roosevelt's character was not transparent; behind the straight lines of his speech and action was a configuration of conditioning and motives. But the public saw in him, and responded to, several dominant traits. One was his capacity for leadership. Asked by a friend whether he had genius, Roosevelt replied, "Most certainly I have not." To reinforce his statement he made a quick inventory of his talents. He was "no orator," he decided, and writing he found difficult. But at the end he wavered enough to reveal: "If I have anything at all resembling genius it is the gift for leadership."[32] The gift

[29] William Griffith (ed.), *Newer Roosevelt Messages* (New York: Current Literature Publishing Co., 1919), pp. 1028-37. (Hereinafter referred to as *Newer Messages.*)

[30] *Recollections of Thomas R. Marshall* (Indianapolis: Bobbs-Merrill Co., 1925), p. 51.

[31] *Autobiography, Works,* XX, 88.

[32] Statement to Julian Street. *Works,* X, 357.

was displayed early in his public career. A few years out of college he was a spokesman in the legislature and had around him a group of sufficient size to exert minority influence. As a rancher in Dakota he called the organization meeting of the Little Missouri Stockmen's Association, presided and kept the minutes, and was elected chairman of the group.[33] From the days when as a colonel on horseback he led his men at Santiago, he was the leader, always the center of whatever movement he was engaged in. Roosevelt was regarded by many as an opportunist, an astute politician with ability to hold divergent groups together, and with a keen sense of how far he could go without losing public support. This concept he vigorously denied: "I did not 'divine' how the people were going to think; I simply made up my mind what they *ought* to think, and then did my best to get them to think it." [34]

Roosevelt was a man of many interests and many talents, and it is doubtful if he ever came across a person in his audiences with whom he did not have much in common to talk about. While in college he projected *The Naval War of 1812* and published it two years after graduation. His writings reveal the breadth of his interests: literature, history, geography, zoology—most of the humane subjects and many sciences. As President he found time to discuss relatively unknown poems called to his attention by his son Kermit,[35] to review them favorably,[36] and to procure a government job for their author, Edwin Arlington Robinson. In packing for the expedition to Africa he looked not merely to the guns but to the books to be taken in "The Pigskin Library." It was probably on the Dakota frontier that Roosevelt learned to take people for what they were worth, to treasure the bonds of friendship, and to show a warmth for people that made him magnetic to the crowd. At the Progressive Convention in 1912 he proudly posed [37] with four delegates from the West with whom he had played seven-up his first night on the Little Missouri. Roosevelt's interests were reflected in his social companions at the White House, loosely affiliated as the "Tennis Cabinet." A regular member was the scholarly French Ambassador, Jules Jusserand, and an honorary member was John Abernathy of Oklahoma, who specialized in capturing wolves alive by thrusting a gloved hand into the victim's mouth. But the impulsive sincerity, the strong feeling, had their negative side. Often his opinions were expressed in blunt or intemperate remarks. "He saw things

[33] See Ray H. Mattison, *Roosevelt and the Stockmen's Association* (Bismarck: State Historical Society of North Dakota, 1950). The minutes in Roosevelt's handwriting are preserved at Theodore Roosevelt House.

[34] Letter to E. A. Van Valkenberg, September 5, 1916. Bishop, II, 414.

[35] Will Irwin (ed.), *Letters to Kermit from Theodore Roosevelt* (New York and London: Charles Scribner's Sons, 1946), p. 83. Letter of November 3, 1904.

[36] *Works*, XII, 296-99.

[37] The picture is given in the Macmillan 1913 edition of *An Autobiography*, p. 104.

as either black or white," wrote the historian Albert Bushnell Hart. The "intensity of his convictions," Roosevelt's Harvard classmate thought, "sometimes blinded him to the sincerity and even to the justice of other points of view."[38]

Roosevelt always associated himself with good causes. Indeed so worthy were the movements he originated or joined that he could hardly help being impressed with the worthiness of himself. As a young naturalist he stored a litter of white mice in the family ice chest. When his mother threw out the specimens, young Theodore's thoughts were not for himself, but for the movement: "The loss to Science! The loss to Science!"[39] he remonstrated. When campaigning for Vice-President in 1900, he made clear to his sister that the fate of the country and not his own destiny was at stake: "If we are beaten, my own disappointment will not be a drop in the ocean to my bitter regret and alarm for the Nation."[40] When Roosevelt was wounded in Milwaukee, both Taft and Wilson offered to refrain from campaigning. In a statement issued from the Chicago hospital, Roosevelt declined the offer: "This is not a contest about any man; it is a contest concerning principles."[41] Roosevelt's association with righteousness reached its peak in the Chicago Coliseum when he concluded his address to the Progressive Convention with "We stand at Armageddon, and we battle for the Lord."[42]

Roosevelt was not one to let his worthiness go unannounced or undefended. Through his speeches he reviewed the merit of his appointments, how Catholic, Jew or Protestant, white or black, old stock or first generation immigrant, received from him reward determined only by merit. He would do anything in his power for labor, anything for business, anything, that is, "except anything that was wrong."[43] Scrupulously Roosevelt protected his honor in things financial. The volumes of his *Presidential Addresses and State Papers* carried notice that the author "retains no pecuniary interest in the sale of the volumes"; they were "dedicated to the public." In the same spirit the Nobel Prize was turned over to establish a foundation to promote industrial peace.[44] Critics pointed out, especially in the 1904 campaign, that

---

[38] *Encyclopaedia Britannica*, 12th ed., *s.v.* Roosevelt.

[39] William Roscoe Thayer, *Theodore Roosevelt* (Boston and New York: Houghton Mifflin Co., 1919), p. 8.

[40] *Cowles*, p. 246. Letter of June 25, 1900.

[41] Bishop, II, 340.

[42] *Works*, XVII, 299.

[43] *Presidential Addresses and State Papers* (Homeward Bound Edition; 8 vols; New York: Review of Reviews Co., 1910), VI, 1377. (Hereinafter referred to as *PA&SP*).

[44] See HR 25606, 59th Cong., 2nd sess., February 12, 1907: "A Bill to Establish the Foundation for the Promotion of Industrial Peace." In 1918 the money, then $45,482.83, was returned to Roosevelt and he distributed it to various war charities.

the interests he fought were heavy backers of himself and his party. But he had letters to prove that he directed the Republican National Committee not to accept pressure money, and was assured it had been returned.[45]

The enthusiasm with which Roosevelt pursued his interests led even many of his friends to describe him as a perpetual boy. Whether from youthful exuberance or adult joy of life, his vigor was colossal. When the English author and statesman, John Morley, was a guest of Roosevelt at the White House he exclaimed that the two most extraordinary things in the United States were "Niagara Falls and the President... both great wonders of nature."[46] Presidential burdens seemed but to add to his energy. At the New Year's reception in the White House in 1909, he received 6,665 persons, and shook hands with everyone.[47] While waiting for the Russians and the Japanese to come to agreement on the Peace of Portsmouth, he went down in a submarine, the *Plunger*, and stayed an hour.[48] With his visit to Panama he became the first President to leave the country. Nor was there any letdown in vacations. His refusal to shoot a bear cub in Mississippi led to a famous cartoon and the vogue of the Teddy Bear.[49] John Burroughs, worn down by following Roosevelt through Yellowstone, pondered that their nature study had been an interlude in a tour of two months and nearly three hundred speeches and exclaimed: "He is doubtless the most vital man on the continent, if not on the planet." On Roosevelt's vigor of life, both friend and foe could agree. "Every now and then," he declared, "I like to drink the wine of life with brandy in it."[50]

For his public, there was no strain Roosevelt would not impose upon himself. At the close of his presidency he set off for Africa to face the lions, with his left eye useless from a blow received in boxing at the White House,[51] the right eye never strong, and nine pairs of eyeglasses.[52] On location in Africa, after the day's hunt, he wrote *African Game Trails* for his *Scribner's Magazine* audience, with a mosquito netting over his head and wearing

---

The dispositions are listed in *The Great Adventure* (New York: Charles Scribner's Sons, 1918), Appendix B.

[45] See Bishop, I, 329; II, 97 ff.

[46] *Ibid.*, I, 338.

[47] Lawrence F. Abbott (ed.), *The Letters of Archie Butt* (Garden City: Doubleday, Page & Co., 1924), p. 265.

[48] *Works*, XIX, 490.

[49] The cartoon in the Washington *Post* is reproduced in Mark Sullivan, *Our Times* (New York and London: Charles Scribner's Sons, 1926-35), II, 446.

[50] John Burroughs, *Camping and Tramping with Roosevelt* (Boston: Houghton Mifflin Co., 1907), pp. 60-61; Lodge, I, 36. October 30, 1885.

[51] *Autobiography, Works*, XX, 44. The fact was not revealed at the time.

[52] L. F. Abbott (ed.), *Letters of Archie Butt*, p. 346.

gauntlet gloves.[53] For the same audience he wrote *Through the Brazilian Wilderness,* noting on one page of the manuscript, "not written very clearly; my temperature is 105."[54] During his last speaking tour he suffered from inflammatory rheumatism, and in the last major speech, in Carnegie Hall,[55] he endured great pain from sciatica in the legs. But he spoke vigorously for two hours and a quarter. The Milwaukee bullet, Roosevelt took with him to the grave. He did not mind it more, he once explained, than if it had been "in his waistcoat pocket."[56]

The man they came to hear carried with him an aura of leadership, of vigor, of devotion to causes. He was known to be willing to pay with his body for the soul's desire.[57] But the personality he so developed was unique in American history. As Stuart P. Sherman wrote: "Mr. Roosevelt's great and fascinating personality is part of the national wealth, and it should, so far as possible, be preserved undiminished."[58]

Roosevelt's Basic Ideas

Roosevelt drew the topics for his speeches from the events and movements of his time and his particular relation to them. But how he fused his material and gave it purpose was determined by his basic philosophy. Whatever else may be said of this philosophy, it was consistent. Through his speeches runs a thread of unity on all subjects he considered. Hermann Hagedorn, who edited Roosevelt's works and has studied him from all angles, schematized Roosevelt's thinking:

All his moral, social, political and economic ideas may be grouped about five fundamental conceptions . . . :
I. The elemental virtues—the basis of good citizenship;
II. Good citizenship—the basis of just government;
III. Just government—the basis of national unity;
IV. National unity—the basis of national strength;
V. National strength—the basis of international peace.[59]

[53] Bishop, II, 361.
[54] Corinne Roosevelt Robinson, *My Brother Theodore Roosevelt* (New York: Charles Scribner's Sons, 1921), p. 278. (Hereinafter referred to as Robinson.)
[55] October 28, 1918. *Works,* XIX, 389-95.
[56] Bishop, II, 345.
[57] In 1918, Roosevelt dedicated *The Great Adventure* "To all who in this war have paid with their bodies for their souls' desire."
[58] "Roosevelt and the National Psychology," *The Nation,* CIX (1919), 599.
[59] Hermann Hagedorn, *The Americanism of Theodore Roosevelt* (Boston: Houghton Mifflin Co., 1923), p. v.

The elemental virtues included clean living, hard work, decency and honesty, and a willingness to support one's faith by force. The radiating source of the virtues was woman, the patient wife, mother of large families, and repository of the finer things of life. In this scheme of individual virtue there was no place for Horatio Alger's philosophy of rewards. Virtue, to Roosevelt, was its own reward, and there was no relation between it and remuneration or recognition. "The great prizes come more or less by accident," he told an audience, and to clinch the point added, "no human being knows that better than the man who has won any of them." [60]

The good citizen was one "willing to pull his weight," and not "a mere passenger." [61] The primary duty of citizenship consisted of being a good person, a good husband or mother, a good neighbor. "The foundation-stone of national life," declared Roosevelt aptly in laying a cornerstone of a public building, "ever must be the high individual character of the average citizen." [62] Beyond that the good citizen took an interest in public affairs, worked to get good men in his party to run for office, and if convinced that the party was wrong, bolted it. Unless he wished to be ruled by muckers, he himself had to be active in ruling.

It was to the role of government in human affairs that Roosevelt devoted his greatest energies and made his greatest contributions. As the Beards have pointed out, Roosevelt was the first President to propose using political forces to effect the distribution of wealth.[63] But, they add, he never clearly explained how this was to be brought about in a system where wealth was so entrenched. Theoretical economics never quite came within the sphere of Roosevelt's many interests. "I know nothing of currency myself," [64] he wrote to his sister. He found it easier to answer Bryan by comparing him and his followers with Shakespeare's Jack Cade [65] and rabble, than by making an analysis of economic fallacies. Around the "Square Deal" centered Roosevelt's philosophy of economic reform. It was not the concept of the welfare state. The government's job was not "to give every man the best hand. If the cards do not come to any man ... that is his affair." But there must be "no crookedness in the dealing." [66] So to government was assigned the role of seeing that the competitive game of life, with all its hazards, was played according to rules.

[60] *PA&SP*, III, 240.
[61] *Ibid.*, I, 200.
[62] *Works*, XVI, 424.
[63] Charles A. and Mary R. Beard, *The Rise of American Civilization* (New York: The Macmillan Co., 1940), II, 596.
[64] May 6, 1894. *Cowles*, p. 142.
[65] *Works*, XIV, 275.
[66] *PA&SP*, III, 321.

He entered the presidency, he confided, without "any deliberately planned and far-reaching scheme of social betterment."[67] But he had "certain strong convictions." His specific ideas varied according to the platform he supported. In 1900, it was good roads, reclamation of arid lands, high tariff, and sound money. By 1912, it had become child labor legislation, workmen's compensation, the income tax, the eight-hour day, social insurance against sickness, unemployment, and old age, and equal suffrage. It was Theodore, not Franklin, Roosevelt who conceived of big government to combat big business. "All very big business, even though honestly conducted, is fraught with such potentiality of menace that there should be thoroughgoing government control over it,"[68] he declared in 1912. Theodore Roosevelt sought to make government strong, but to keep it the creature of the people. There was no wisdom in governmental procedures which transcended the common sense of the electors. In one of his most severely attacked speeches, that to the Ohio Constitutional Convention in 1912, he declared:

I do not say that the people are infallible. But I do say that our whole history shows that the American people are more often sound in their decisions than is the case with any of the governmental bodies to whom, for their convenience, they have delegated portions of their power.[69]

Bitterly criticized for advocating the recall of judges, he put the matter bluntly: if the people are competent to elect judges, they are also "competent to un-elect them."[70]

Roosevelt had a passion for national unity. To understand this one has to look into his early years. His mother was a Bulloch of Georgia, an unreconstructed rebel. His father was a strong Lincoln Republican. His mother's mother and his mother's sister lived with the Roosevelts. An uncle had helped to build the raider "Alabama," and another uncle was gunner on her when she was sunk off Cherbourg by the "Kearsarge"; both had retired to Liverpool at the end of the war. So through his tours and campaigns Roosevelt always had a word for the Blue and the Gray, and an expressed hope that from the horrors of civil strife would emerge the greater unity. Persistently he argued that Americans were pretty much alike wherever you found them. "What I have to say to you," he told a group in Kansas City, "is exactly what I should say to your fellows who dwell on the Atlantic Coast, on the Pacific Slope, or beside the Great Lakes, or on the shores of the Gulf of

[67] *Autobiography, Works*, XX, 376.
[68] *Works*, XVII, 282.
[69] *Ibid.*, 142.
[70] "A Short Political Creed," *The Outlook*, C (1912), 721.

Mexico." [71] Roosevelt never wavered in his intense nationalism. "I am an American from the crown of my head to the soles of my feet," [72] he declared in 1886. Accused of being a jingo, he accepted the label. In 1895, he described one of his speeches as "my jingo speech the other night." [73] Superpatriot, chauvinist, rabid nationalist—in such terms has Roosevelt been described. Certainly there is much in Roosevelt's utterances to justify his being called a supernationalist, with occasional racist propensities. He was born in the old aristocracy, grew up with some snobbishness, and despite his strenuous efforts to overcome cultural lag, never quite freed himself. He could justify a humane colonialism for the good of the people in the backward areas. He could speak of the higher races. He thought it humorous to refer to Negro soldiers as "sun-burned Yankees" [74] in a talk to the Circle for Negro War Relief. He compared the "Jew" to the "native American," intending to be flattering to the Jew. [75] But in fairness one must recall Roosevelt's official insistence on judging every man "on his merits as a man," [76] as he wrote to an official who protested Booker T. Washington's staying for dinner at the White House. Roosevelt judged men quickly and primitively; his first canon of judgment was whether a man would be good to camp out with.

Roosevelt's ideas on nationalism and internationalism were very simple. Patriotism is the feeling for one's country that corresponds in private life to love of family; internationalism compared to the feelings one has for his neighbors. The nation should be strong, under a system of universal military training. The nation should work in good faith with other nations, enter into agreements and form leagues to keep the peace. Not the treaty, but the fleet, was our greatest security. It was nonsense, he argued during World War I, to talk of making the world safe for democracy; our job was to "make the world safe for America." [77]

As a systematic thinker Roosevelt has lost rather than gained prominence in America. A critic of ideas today, Henry Steele Commager, writes of him:

Only by using the term in its broadest sense could Theodore Roosevelt be called a political philosopher.... Roosevelt was the instrument chosen by destiny for the

[71] *The Progressive Party; Its Record from January to July, 1916* (New York: Mail and Express, 1916), p. 53. (Referred to hereinafter as *Progressive Party*.)

[72] *Works*, XIV, 74.

[73] Letter of October 29, 1895. *Lodge*, I, 195.

[74] *Newer Messages*, p. 1031.

[75] *Works*, XIV, 233.

[76] To Albion W. Tourgee, U.S. Consul at Bordeaux, November 8, 1901. Bishop, I, 165.

[77] *Newer Messages*, p. 873.

327

implementation of a reform movement whose origins he scarcely knew, whose character he but dimly understood, whose objectives he failed to appreciate, and whose consequences he often deplored. Like Bryan, he carried on his education in public. . . .[78]

A student of progressivism, Russel B. Nye, has decided Roosevelt failed to emerge as "a real progressive leader" during the period of his power as President, because he "was all things to everybody," and compromised too frequently "in order to maintain his standing as an all-round political athlete."[79] Roosevelt never claimed for himself any striking inventiveness in ideas. As governor he wrote to his old friend of the 1884 convention, Andrew D. White, then ambassador to Germany:

Do you know, I have come to the conclusion that I have mighty little originality of my own. What I do is to try to get ideas from men whom I regard as experts along certain lines, and then to try to work out these ideas.[80]

He was less interested in the historical genesis of a good idea than in the practical concerns of getting it accepted. Late in life Roosevelt was asked about his originality. John Hay had noted in his diary that "The President spoke of his own speeches, saying he knew there was not much in them except a certain sincerity and kind of commonplace morality which put him *en rapport* with the people he talked with."[81] A friend wrote to check on the accuracy of the statement. By this time, Roosevelt had become irked at charges that he was platitudinous. He replied vigorously:

The average person who says I am commonplace and not original is almost always a nice little cultivated goose, who hasn't the remotest idea of what originality is. My remark to John Hay referred of course to what we were then discussing; the speeches in which I was endeavoring to get the people to take the right view of certain matters of policy and morality which were vital but commonplace.[82]

It would be an error to measure in terms of the history of ideas the thoughts Roosevelt brought to the millions. Some of the ideas were commonplace, some original, some conservative, some radical—but for all he assumed the burden of disseminating them to the people, and to all he brought the full impact of a man in action. To many commonplaces, such as the need for honesty and

[78] Henry Steele Commager, *The American Mind* (New Haven: Yale University Press, 1950), pp. 347-48.

[79] Russel B. Nye, *Midwestern Progressive Politics* (East Lansing: Michigan State College Press, 1951), pp. 250-51.

[80] Letter of December 26, 1899. LC.

[81] *John Hay*, II, 354-55.

[82] Charles G. Washburn, "Theodore Roosevelt," *Harvard Graduates' Magazine* (June, 1919), p. 474.

decency in politics, he gave new meaning in concrete service. Roosevelt's ideas will have to be weighed on a scale that registers not merely the weight of them, but also their total effect.

Preparation as a Speaker

Roosevelt never received any formal training in public speaking. He had, however, a basic desire to speak, general background to draw upon, and the willingness to practice on every possible occasion. "I had considerable difficulty in teaching myself to speak,"[83] he wrote in his *Autobiography*. The self-training did not begin until he found himself on the floor of the legislature.

Because of ill health Roosevelt did not attend grammar school but was tutored and encouraged to inquire for himself. He entered Harvard when almost eighteen. There was in his college studies much of later value to a man in public affairs. He had a course in Jevons' logic, a course in rhetoric, two courses in themes and two in forensics, all with emphasis on writing. In the forensics course in the senior year he had as instructor A. S. Hill, author of *Principles of Rhetoric* and the only one of his Harvard teachers (who included William James and George Palmer in their early teaching days) he acknowledged in his *Autobiography*: "I owed much to [him]."[84] His interests then were in natural history, and he confessed in later years that he did not gain as much as he might have in themes and forensics because he took so little interest in the subjects.[85] Preserved in his Harvard Scrapbook are examination papers in natural history, but no speciments of themes. He did, however, make a phenomenal 94 (50 was passing and grades were generally lower than today) in sophomore rhetoric, using as text Abbot's *How to Write Clearly*. When one considers that Roosevelt at Harvard lived the life of a gentleman, that he engaged in boxing and wrestling, belonged to the fashionable Dickey, Hasty Pudding, and Porcellian, at times kept a horse and cart, and fell in love his senior year with Alice Lee of Chestnut Hill, his academic career was superior. He finished twenty-first in a class of 158 and was a member of Phi Beta Kappa.[86]

Although Roosevelt's career as an undergraduate public speaker was inconspicuous, there exists sufficient record to show the degree of his proficiency. His Harvard friend William Roscoe Thayer reported his impres-

[83] *Works*, XX, 66.
[84] *Loc. cit.*, 24.
[85] *Ibid.*
[86] Grade reports are in the Harvard Scrapbook. A memorandum on Roosevelt's academic career at Harvard was prepared by J. M. Blum in 1949 and is available at Harvard College Theodore Roosevelt Collection (referred to hereinafter as HCTRC).

sions of Roosevelt's speaking in his junior year. The occasion was the annual dinner of the *Harvard Crimson* and Roosevelt was present to represent the *Harvard Advocate*:

On being called on to speak he seemed very shy and made, what I think he said, was his maiden speech. He still had difficulty in enunciating clearly or even in running off his words smoothly. At times he could hardly get them out at all, and then he would rush on for a few sentences, as skaters redouble their pace over thin ice. He told the story of two old gentlemen who stammered, the point of which was, that one of them, after distressing contortions and stoppages, recommended the other to go to Dr. X, adding, "He cured me." [87]

There is a record of what Roosevelt said in a speech made his senior year. The occasion was a dinner held by Alpha Delta Phi (which became the "Fly Club" in 1910) to celebrate the revival of the Harvard chapter. Delegates from Amherst, Cornell, Yale, and ten other colleges assembled in Young's Hotel in Boston. Grace was said by Phillips Brooks, who also spoke on "Alpha Delta Phi in the Pulpit." Edward Everett Hale talked, and George William Curtis sent his regrets. Representing the local chapter, Roosevelt made this speech, which is given complete:

Mr. President and Gentlemen: I thank you in behalf of the younger members of the society for your kind reception. We now number in Harvard about twenty members. We have chosen members from the Pudding, Pi Eta, and Signet. We have tried to choose men who will be able to sustain the reputation of the society, though it seems almost presumptuous for any of us to hope to do as much as has been done by our brethren, or to influence men from principle as has been done. Yet it is a great thing for us to feel, if in our lives we do but half as much as many of you have done, that we shall not have lived without doing something.[88]

The speech was received with applause, but there is little in the tortured composition to indicate that its author would become a speaker celebrated on four continents. Roosevelt's experience as a speaker in college was slight. He had some opportunity to talk in connection with the various clubs he belonged to. With Robert Bacon, later for a short term his Secretary of State, he prepared a paper on taxation which they presented to the Finance Club. He participated in a debate at the Harvard Union,[89] and taught a Sunday school

[87] Thayer, *op. cit.*, p. 20. See Donald Hall, *The Harvard Advocate Anthology* (New York: Twayne Publishers, Inc., 1950). *The Advocate* was in this period "an argumentative publication" (p. 13). Roosevelt was treasurer in his senior year.

[88] *Responses at Fifth Annual Dinner of New England Graduate Association* (Boston: Privately printed for Alpha Delta Phi, 1880), p. 18. The dinner was held January 22, 1880.

[89] Bradley Gilman, *Roosevelt the Happy Warrior* (Boston: Little, Brown & Co., 1921), p. 39.

class three and a half years of his college career. But there was nothing in his college experience comparable to consistent practice in a debate club.

Looking back on his college career, Roosevelt felt there had been a deficiency in his speech training. More than thirty years after graduation he reflected:

I am sorry I did not study elocution in college; but I am exceedingly glad that I did not take part in the type of debate in which stress is laid, not upon getting a speaker to think rightly, but on getting him to talk glibly on the side to which he is assigned, without regard either to what his convictions are or to what they ought to be.[90]

His explanation of why he did not debate is consistent and thoroughly developed. But why did he not study elocution? He gives the answer to that, too: "I had at the time no idea of going into public life, and I never studied elocution or practiced debating." [91] Public speaking in his mind was associated with public affairs, and in the college years Roosevelt felt no association with either. But once in public life he began to cultivate his speaking ability. It went slowly at first. His appeal for re-election to the legislature, made at the Lyric Hall Republican rally in 1882, was aloof and cold:

If you are satisfied with what I did last year, you may return me; if not, I will take my dismissal. The duties of an assemblyman are not of a very high nature.[92]

A year later he was able to report to his mother that a speech in the Assembly "went off very well; I did not forget a word, nor was I at all embarrassed." [93] A few years later, pondering in Dakota, he wrote, "I hate speech making." [94] But upon his return to public affairs he came to regard speaking as quite as normal and natural in working with people as riding a horse was in herding cattle. Although in his letters there are complaints of fatigue at having to work and work on speeches, having to talk to people when he had nothing to say, and having to sit through interminable banquets and exercises, he learned to love to speak and to have people mill around him. In his days in Washington as Civil Service Commissioner, in the rough-and-tumble period as New York City Police Commissioner, in the conferences and hearings and conversations, and in varied public speaking experiences, he worked out a style of speaking which was to serve him well when he attained state, national, and international prominence.

[90] *Autobiography, Works,* XX, 25.
[91] *Loc. cit.*
[92] *Works,* XIV, 12.
[93] February 20, 1883. *Cowles,* p. 52.
[94] April 20, 1887. *Lodge,* I, 54.

The Preparation of the Speeches

Statements concerning the extent to which Roosevelt prepared his speeches are conflicting. *The Pageant of America* [95] records that "Roosevelt's habit of making many speeches left him little time for preparation." Albert Shaw, who edited the volumes of Roosevelt's *Presidential Addresses and State Papers* explained in the preface that the "speeches have not been carefully prepared." They were "in the main the spontaneous utterances of a richly stored mind." [96] The editor meant, of course, that Roosevelt spent little time in invention, in looking for materials, and not that he failed to work out any speeches in advance. Professor William Norwood Brigance [97] grouped Roosevelt among the speakers who prepared with great care, and this would seem to be his proper classification. Roosevelt made more off-the-cuff impromptu or extemporaneous talks than manuscript speeches. But once he had agreed in advance to speak on an occasion, he set about to prepare his remarks. He usually pondered well what he released to the public, and, always one to work within the interests of the group he was representing, he sought the opinions of his co-workers. It was on the steamer *Alton* from St. Louis to Cairo, in connection with the Deepsea Water Convention, that he rose to respond to a toast. In the presence of seventeen governors he told the reporters: "I do not want you to take down and publish this speech, because it is necessarily of a tentative character." [98]

The first step in preparation was to think over ideas and talk them over as occasion arose. Sometimes when a speech was not to be reported he talked out an idea with a group and later prepared it for public presentation. Such was "The Man with the Muckrake," originally given without preparation to the Gridiron Club, March 17, 1906, and a month later in carefully prepared form used at the laying of the cornerstone of the House of Representatives office building. On another occasion when a message on Santo Domingo had to be prepared for the Senate, John Hay and Elihu Root had dinner at the White House, and then discussed the subject with Roosevelt for two hours. A stenographer was then called in and the President began to dictate. This is how Hay described the scene:

It was a curious sight. I have often seen it, and it never ceases to surprise me. He storms up and down the room, dictating in a loud and oratorical tone, often stopping, recasting a sentence, striking out and filling in, hospitable to every suggestion, not

[95] J. S. Bassett (ed), *The Pageant of America* (New Haven: Yale University Press, 1928), IX, 253.

[96] *PA&SP*, I, vi, vii.

[97] "In the Workshop of Great Speakers," *American Speech*, I (1926), 589.

[98] October 2, 1907. From stenographic notes of the speech. Addresses Scrapbooks, LC.

in the least disturbed by interruption, holding on stoutly to his purpose, and producing finally, out of these most unpromising conditions, a clear and logical statement, which he could not improve with solitude and leisure at his command.[99]

An important part of the early process was the stimulation he received from those around him. "I loathe speaking," he told the secretary of his Harvard class, "unless it is 'borne in on me to testify,' as our Methodist brethren say."[100] In the Progressive campaign of 1912, on the first long trip to the Coast, the speeches were stale, the party secretary thought, and lacking in news value, because Roosevelt was not sufficiently stimulated. On the second tour, through the Midwest, he was supplied with continuous reports on Wilson's activities and with a history of his thinking on various problems. The result was that Roosevelt would leave the table after a vigorous discussion and dictate speeches far in advance.[101]

Having prepared a draft of the speech, he next sought the views of others. Any speech involving matters of party policy had to be checked with the leaders of the party. In his second annual message to the legislature, given January 3, 1900, Senator T. C. Platt, as the controlling boss of the party in the state, had to be at least nominally consulted. "I send you a proof of my message," he wrote to Platt two weeks before the message was given. "All the important parts I had gone over by various experts."[102] He deliberately sought suggestions from people with no ax to grind. From the scholarly John Hay[103] and Henry Cabot Lodge he was willing to receive advice on matters of composition. "One verbal suggestion," wrote Lodge about the phrase "Judaslike." "Is it too rhetorical for a President's message?"[104] But in the main the suggestions he received dealt with accuracy or propriety, and not with matters of style. Gifford Pinchot[105] recalls how Roosevelt prepared a speech or state paper well in advance, put it in a drawer of his desk at the White House, and brought it out for discussion with callers whose opinions he desired on specific sections. Sometimes he submitted a whole speech for criticism. The Oxford lecture, which dealt with biology, was read by Henry Fairfield Osborn, president of the American Museum of Natural History. Speeches to be given in South America in 1913 were submitted to the countries' ambassadors in Washington, particularly for their views or state-

---

[99] *John Hay*, II, 362. The message was sent March 6, 1905.
[100] Letter to Frederic Almy, December 5, 1916. In F. S. Wood, *Roosevelt as We Knew Him* (Philadelphia: John C. Winston Co., 1927), p. 3.
[101] Davis, pp. 353 ff.
[102] December 19, 1899. LC.
[103] See a letter of July 13, 1904. *John Hay*, II, 379.
[104] October 17, 1901. *Lodge*, I, 507.
[105] *Works*, XV, xxvi.

ments about the Monroe Doctrine. "I've changed that sentence," [106] he told the ambassador from Brazil as the expedition set sail. In his later days Roosevelt became less amenable to suggestion. "His mind is getting to be mechanical," observed Lincoln Steffens in 1915; "that is to say, his mind goes on about its business, regardless of what you throw into it." [107] But he still conferred about his speeches. Hermann Hagedorn recalls luncheons at the Harvard Club during the war, at which "representatives of all shades of loyal German-American opinion" [108] were invited. After lunch was ordered, Roosevelt would read a speech, and then have it discussed section by section as he marked it up.

A good picture of Roosevelt at work on a manuscript after it had been commented upon by others is given by O. K. Davis. [109] After the Bull Moosers bolted the Republican Convention in June, 1912, Roosevelt returned to Sagamore Hill and began to consider what he should say at the Progressive Convention to be held in August. He consulted friends and workers in the party. He wrote the speech and had it put into proof with wide margins, and copies were distributed by party headquarters. When the proofs were returned from the advisers, Davis took the sets, about twenty in number, to Sagamore Hill. Together they went through the suggestions. Roosevelt worked steadily for two or three hours, marking up the sheets, then handed them to Davis and asked how soon they could be printed.

Some specific instances of how Roosevelt revised his speeches may help to reveal his method. Although he was never one to linger doubtfully over a paper when a deadline had to be met, he kept the speeches somewhat flexible, even making corrections on the final copy before delivery. After the Republican Convention in June, 1904, at which Roosevelt was nominated for a term in his own right, he set to work on a speech of response to the committee which was to notify him at Oyster Bay, July 27. Secretary William Loeb sent a copy to Senator Lodge on July 12, with a request that he "go over and comment upon very freely." [110] A week later the draft had been returned with suggestions, and Roosevelt had talked over the speech with Secretary of War Elihu Root and Attorney General Philander C. Knox. Roosevelt, reported his secretary, was trying "to strengthen the speech generally a little." [111] There are available for study three corrected drafts of the speech

[106] *Ibid.*, xv.

[107] Ella Winter and Granville Hicks (eds.), *The Letters of Lincoln Steffens* (New York: Harcourt, Brace & Co., 1938), I, 359.

[108] Hermann Hagedorn, *The Bugle That Woke America* (New York: John Day Co., 1940), pp. 151-52.

[109] Davis, pp. 320 ff.

[110] *Lodge*, II, 87.

[111] *Ibid.*, 90-91.

and the final copy.[112] The revision of a point dealing with one of the matters on which Roosevelt was least articulate, currency, shows his characteristic way of touching up rhetorical effect rather than supplying exposition. The first draft contains these sentences:

We have placed the finances of the nation upon a sound gold basis. We know what we mean when we speak of an honest and stable currency.

In correcting, the author inserted between the two sentences a reminder of the struggle against the dangerous bimetallists:

We have done this in spite of the violent opposition of most of our opponents, an opposition given strength by the silent acquiescence or support of the remainder.

On the next typed draft this sentence was marked over and revised until corrections were hardly legible. On the bottom of the sheet he made this revision, including acknowledgment of support from some members of the opposition:

We have done this with the hearty aid of many who were formerly our opponents, and in spite of the convinced and violent opposition of the mass of our present opponents—an opposition which was given strength by the unconvinced and silent acquiescence or support of the remainder.

In the final revision the word "hearty" was withdrawn from "aid" received from the friendly opposition, but their stout character was further revealed:

We have done this with the aid of many who were formerly our opponents, but who would neither openly support nor silently acquiesce in the heresy of unsound finance; and we have done it against the convinced and violent opposition of the mass of our present opponents, who still refuse to recant the unsound opinions which for the moment they think it inexpedient to assert.

In this belabored and not too clear version the inserted sentence went to the printer, where it rested between the original two simple and direct statements.

On another occasion, evidently because he felt the expression to be used before the Gloucester fisherman was undignified, that he did his "work on the hurricane deck of a broncho," he crossed it out and inserted the more prosaic "did my work on horseback among the men of the ranch and the round up."[113] Frequently he would insert a transition, such as "Let me give you an example," or make more particular application to an audience as he approached the scene. Instances of these practices can be seen in the Pittsburgh

[112] The drafts are in the New York Public Library; the speech is in *Works*, XVI, 363-71.
[113] Addresses Scrapbooks, LC.

speech of April 9, 1912. The speech also well illustrates his practice of deviations from the manuscript in actual wording but not in basic idea. The final draft of the speech had this introduction:

Men and Women of Pittsburgh: I feel a peculiar sense of appreciation to Pittsburgh. It was a body of three hundred from Pittsburgh who came down to the steamer to see me off to Africa. . . .

Before he spoke he corrected the introduction:

Men and Women of Pittsburgh: I feel a very real appreciation of all that Pittsburgh has done for me. It was a body of three hundred men from Pittsburgh who came down to the steamer to see me off to Africa. . . .

What he actually said, as taken down by a reporter was:

Mr. Chairman, and you, my friends and fellow citizens, men and women of Pittsburgh: Naturally I have a peculiar feeling toward Pittsburgh. Again and again you have received me with more than kindness in this great, typical American city. Three hundred of your citizens came down to say good-by to me when I went to Africa. . . .[114]

In preparing the speeches Roosevelt was eclectic in the sources he drew upon. From his wide and varied reading he made many citations. Ideas supplied him by confidential advisers, quite understandably, were used without public acknowledgment. Accused of plagiarizing a speech of one of his Cabinet members he cheerfully acknowledged his guilt in a letter to the original author, Elihu Root, and noted that he was planning to repeat the tribute.[115] In the speech to the Colorado legislature, August 29, 1910, he drew upon a statement prepared by Associate Justice of the Supreme Court William H. Moody, in denouncing the courts for blocking social legislation.[116] Two days later, at Osawatomie, Kansas, in what is generally regarded as the most radical speech Roosevelt ever made, human rights were extolled above property rights. The point was made with a quotation from Lincoln, and Roosevelt took pains to credit the idea, although he added that he himself probably would be "strongly denounced as a Communist agitator...anyhow."[117] When he received from his touchstone of respectability and pro-

---

[114] The MS is at LC. The report is in the Pittsburgh *Post*, April 10, 1912.

[115] Letter to Root, April 23, 1903. Cited in Pringle, p. 414.

[116] The text is in Theodore Roosevelt, *The New Nationalism*, introd. by Ernest Hamlin Abbott (New York: Outlook Co., 1910), p. 38 ff. (Hereinafter referred to as *The New Nationalism*.) O. K. Davis, p. 209, says the speech was not prepared and that Roosevelt had given Moody's statement to reporters when pressed in advance for what he would say.

[117] *Works*, XVII, 8.

priety, Henry Cabot Lodge of Massachusetts, a painful but mild remonstrance about what people were saying, Roosevelt replied it was curious that the most radical thing in one speech was a quotation from Lincoln, and that the strictures on the courts in the other speech had been suggested by a Massachusetts member of the Supreme Court and the exact text was supplied by Arthur Hill, a former District Attorney of Boston.[118]

Something of Roosevelt's schedule of preparation can be seen in the tour from Khartum in the Sudan, through Europe, following the expedition in Africa. Speeches for Oxford, the University of Berlin, and the Sorbonne were prepared while he was in the White House, more than a year before delivery. The speech to the Nobel Prize Committee was written in the field, in Africa, with an indelible pencil. Remarks at the University of Cairo were written out and submitted for local counsel because of a Nationalist uprising which had resulted in the assassination of the Egyptian prime minister. The Guildhall speech in London, also on the troublesome problem of Britain in Egypt, was carefully worked over. The rest of the dozens of replies and speeches at receptions and banquets were given without preparation. At least thirteen of these were of more than local significance, including talks at the University of Christiania, Cambridge University, and in Amsterdam. On his return to New York he was welcomed at the Battery by Mayor Gaynor ready to start the procession up Broadway. Roosevelt made a "spontaneous" reply which he read from a manuscript prepared on the boat. The tour was representative of Roosevelt's preparation. When he had the opportunity he prepared painstakingly. But when occasions suddenly arose, or when engagements got out of hand, he was able to draw upon his background of previous preparation and upon his extensive reading experience to produce a speech without much difficulty.

Roosevelt's Relations with His Audiences

When Roosevelt spoke, it was no soliloquy; he always had one audience in mind, and sometimes two audiences, the immediate and the general. Early in his career he learned the value of wide reporting. His brief maiden speech in the assembly [119] received wide attention in the press. "Sensible and well delivered remarks," reported the *Albany Evening Journal*. "A very favorable impression," said *The Evening Post* of New York; *The New York Times* inserted (laughter) in the humorous passages, and *The Criterion* of Albany thought the speech made "a record for honesty, judgment and a conception of statesmanship." Roosevelt saw in this experience the possibilities

[118] *Lodge*, II, 388 ff.
[119] *Works*, XIV, 3. The speech was given January 24, 1882.

of a larger audience, and henceforth he distinguished between what he called "the immediate audiences" and "the people at large."[120] Of a speech in 1885, made in Brooklyn, he noted that it had been criticized in New York, but "went well in the West."[121] He hoped, before the itinerary of the 1900 tour got out of hand, to make an appearance in as many states as possible, and to give one speech "which can be read throughout it."[122] In 1911, he avowed to his sister that he would make no more speeches unless the cause or occasion was such as to "render the speech one not really to the audience addressed, but to a National audience."[123] Frequently, Roosevelt used an occasion to release statements for the people at large. An audience at Quincy, Illinois,[124] heard a pronouncement on currency, with little local application or reference. O. K. Davis[125] describes a speech made to an outdoor audience at Oriskany on the first stop of the 1910 tour. Roosevelt used the occasion to read from a printed copy his advice on improving farms. The audience, expecting a rousing political speech, and feeling itself quite as competent as the speaker to deliberate on rural matters, grew restless. Some people started to leave. Immediately Roosevelt ad libbed to arouse their interest, and as soon as they had sat down on the grass, continued to read his prepared speech. It must have taken much self-discipline for Roosevelt to follow copy as closely a he did in the major speeches. But since he made a point of giving copies of his prepared speeches in advance to the press, he felt an obligation to follow the text. His relations with the working press—if not always with publishers, especially Pulitzer and Hearst—were always congenial. He established a press room[126] in the White House, and began the custom of regular presidential press conferences. As Archie Butt said, "Roosevelt was his own press agent, and he had a splendid comprehension of news."[127]

Roosevelt's interactions with his audiences were noteworthy. Everywhere he went he found things in common with his audience: some of his Rough Riders had come from the district, he had close friends in the area, he had read the history of the locality. He told an audience of Presbyterians that he often attended their services because they were so much like those of his own

---

[120] See, for example, a letter of October 1, 1907. *Letters to Kermit*, p. 218.

[121] Letter of October 25, 1885. *Lodge*, I, 34-35.

[122] Letter to Henry Clay Payne, August 18, 1900. LC.

[123] Letter of June 29, 1911, *Cowles*, p. 291.

[124] *PA&SP*, I, 335-36.

[125] Davis, pp. 197-98.

[126] James E. Pollard, *The Presidents and the Press* (New York: The Macmillan Co., 1947), p. 574.

[127] *Taft and Roosevelt; The Intimate Letters of Archie Butt, Military Aide* (Garden City: Doubleday, Doran & Co., 1930), I, 30.

church, the Dutch Reformed.[128] In high mood on his return from addressing what he thought at the time was his last audience in Washington as President, the African Diamond Jubilee of the Methodist Episcopal church,[129] he confided to his military aide: "I would rather address a Methodist audience than any other audience in America... everyone there is an American."[130] He reminded the legislature in Texas that he had been a legislator and a governor, and, seeking a common denominator between Republican and Democrat, asserted that 95 per cent of the work done by any public officer was nonpartisan in nature.[131] Always he sought to bring the women and children of the audience into the sphere of importance, by specially noting and acknowledging the honor they paid him by attending. He was quick to turn the presence of someone or some group to advantage. When a delegation of the Railway Employees' Orders visited him at the White House with a grievance, he emphasized the importance of business executive leadership by turning to an engineer wearing a G.A.R. button: "just as you, comrade of the Civil War, needed a general who knew his business."[132] In Rome, when Mayor Nathan welcomed him in French, Roosevelt started to reply in French, but soon broke off to talk English, insisting that it be translated sentence-by-sentence into Italian.[133] At the Sorbonne, he interjected extemporaneous sentences in French to make meanings clear.[134]

Roosevelt brought to his audiences a sense of dignity and respect for people. He observed the rigors of his speaking schedules with a discipline he would have shown in a military campaign, no matter what the condition of his health or of travel may have been. When he was shot in Milwaukee on his way to make a speech, he insisted on going to the Auditorium rather than to a hospital: "Let's go to the hospital," pleaded the man who was to introduce him. "You get me to that speech," Roosevelt replied. "It may be the last one I shall ever deliver, but I am going to deliver this one."[135] Particularly during the presidential years Roosevelt's graciousness to audiences was marked. It was no strain on his presidential dignity to address a meeting in Carnegie Hall and then rush to the Central Presbyterian Church to talk to an overflow meeting of the Board of Home Missions.[136] As President, he

---

[128] *PA&SP*, I, 45.
[129] *Ibid.*, VIII, 2071-89.
[130] *Letters of Archie Butt*, p. 298.
[131] *PA&SP*, III, 324-29.
[132] *Ibid.*, IV, 558.
[133] Lawrence F. Abbott (ed.), *African and European Addresses by Theodore Roosevelt* (New York and London: G. P. Putnam's Sons, 1910), p. xxi.
[134] *Ibid.*, p. xxiii.
[135] Davis, p. 378.
[136] *PA&SP*, I, 44-53.

could serve as minor functionary at a Y.M.C.A. meeting to introduce a clergyman, although his own remarks [137] ran on for five pages and directed little attention to the speaker; focusing a spotlight on another was not one of Roosevelt's talents. To the endless task of talking to audiences anxious to see the President, he frequently applied the language of a courtier. "I could not deny myself the privilege of saying a word of greeting to this noteworthy gathering," [138] he told the Tuberculosis Congress. "I needed no invitation to come before you today," he assured the Long Island Medical Society. "All I needed was permission." [139] On tour as President he would go charging back to the rear platform at the sight of a figure or a group along the tracks. "Good luck," he would yell as he waved, and then return to his seat with great satisfaction that interested citizens had seen a President in the flesh. On the tour to Hodgenville, Kentucky, in 1909, to give the Lincoln Centenary Address, his itinerary was not announced; he was in combat with Congress and at a low point of popularity. At Altoona a crowd of 5,000 persons had gathered to see him. Overjoyed, he got on a truck to address them. It was on this trip that he told Archie Butt of the time he dashed out to wave at a crowd, and discovered the crowd was a herd of cows.[140]

Although he sought good will, he enjoyed needling an audience. "Don't applaud what is a self-evident fact, gentlemen," [141] he chastised the City Club of New York. "I am even more anxious that you who hear what I say should think of it than that you should applaud it," [142] he teased a Massachusetts audience. Excoriating the "divorce colony" he taunted a Reno audience on a major industry: "It is one colony of which you want to rid yourselves." [143] After welcoming the Lumbermen's Association on a visit to the White House, and paying his especial respects to the women and children who accompanied the delegates, he rebuked them with the point that they should do something to make "the lumber industry a permanent industry." [144] Roosevelt's audacity reached a high point in his Guildhall Address in London when he vexed the British with a review of their rule in Africa. "Useful, even if not wholly palatable," commented *The Times*.[145]

[137] October 3, 1908. Addresses Scrapbooks, LC.

[138] October 3, 1908. Addresses Scrapbooks, LC.

[139] *PA&SP*, IV, 429.

[140] *Letters of Archie Butt*, pp. 336 ff.

[141] *Public Papers of Theodore Roosevelt, Governor*. (Albany: Brandow Printing Co., 1899), p. 322. (Referred to hereinafter as *Public Papers*).

[142] *PA&SP*, I, 139.

[143] Bishop, II, 310.

[144] March 4, 1908. Addresses Scrapbooks, LC.

[145] The speech is given in *African and European Addresses*, pp. 157-72. For press comment, see Abbott's preface.

Not content with correcting or shocking an audience, Roosevelt sometimes worked with his auditors until he got from them the response he wanted. In dedicating the McKinley Monument in Canton, he got loud applause for a denunciation of dishonest businessmen, but silence on a defense of "honest men who acquire wealth by honest means." If the audience wanted to applaud one part of the point, it should applaud the other, Roosevelt insisted. "I challenge the right to your support in one attitude just as much as in the other...I will read a little of it over again." And when he had the applause he wanted, he said, "Thank you. Now I'll go on." [146] In 1910, he addressed the Colorado legislature, met in joint session, with the House floor and gallery jammed with visitors. A denunciation of corrupt politics, made in general terms but with obvious applications to current local scandals, got scant response. A later denunciation of the venal press brought applause and quizzical looks toward the press table. Roosevelt deserted his outline:

> I trust that it is not because this is a legislative assembly that you have applauded this more than what I said about public officials. Now, I will go with you to the last point in condemning the man who in the public press writes an untruth, if you will go with me in condemning equally actively the legislator who acts corruptly. Now, I will resume my sentence where I left off. I speak of the man who writes in the public press. I speak of the man who writes in the magazines. I speak of the politician on the stump.

There was a pause, and silence. "Applaud," cried Roosevelt, and there was loud applause. "I knew I would get it when I pointed out the need of it." At the conclusion of the speech Roosevelt thanked the audience "for the patience with which you have listened to me, and I am very glad I finally got all the applause I wanted at the points I wanted it." [147] Equally pleased was an auditor at the press table, who reported in the Denver *Daily News*,[148] "Never did Colonel Roosevelt give a better demonstration of crowd psychology. These astute politicians were as children under his skillful manipulation."

When challenged, he replied sometimes in humor, sometimes in brutal repartee, but he always asserted his position of dominance over the crowd. In extemporizing to the Cambridge University Union, after having been made an honorary member, he referred to the time a Harvard crew had been beaten in England by Oxford. Calls came, "Cambridge." Roosevelt took the correction in good humor: "Well, I never took a great interest in defeats." [149]

---

[146] *PA&SP*, VI, 1370.
[147] The speech and proceedings are given in *The New Nationalism*, pp. 34-48.
[148] August 30, 1910.
[149] *Works*, XIII, 574.

Remonstrances from the audience in Milwaukee that he should stop talking because of his gunshot wound brought the reply: "You would find that if I was in battle now I would be leading my men just the same. Just the same way I am going to make this speech." [150] Two of the most famous replies to heckles occurred before he was President. One was at a fair in Hornellsville when Roosevelt as governor was heckled by a farmer who wanted to know more about the New York canal scandals. "Infamous lies and slanders," roared the governor, adding that the heckler was "not quite sober." [151] The following year, at the tumultuous rally in Victor, Colorado, a miner yelled, "What about the rotten beef?" Now the colonel of the Rough Riders had made his own denunciations of "embalmed beef" and various mismanagements in the Spanish-American War. But he was on a loyalty tour for President McKinley, and he shot to kill: "I ate it, and you'll never get near enough to be hit by a bullet or within five miles of it." [152]

Roosevelt's anxiety to have an audience see the whole truth as he saw it led him to convert many meetings into forensic occasions. At the Gridiron Dinner of 1907, he lectured the malefactors of great wealth, shook his fist in J. P. Morgan's face, and made a rebuttal to Senator J. B. Foraker's speech. [153] In 1917, at a public reception for the newly established Russian Republic, he catechized Samuel Gompers and shook his fist in his face. [154]

After the Progressive campaign of 1912, Roosevelt began to lose rapport with his audiences. He still drew thousands to hear him, as he talked on with heightened purpose. And his reading audience was maintained with frequent press releases, books, and editorials in the *Metropolitan* magazine and the *Kansas City Star*. In the declining years he tried to make up with his own energy for an apathy in audiences, stultified, he thought, by Woodrow Wilson's pacifism. In 1915, there occurred in Syracuse the trial of *Barnes* v. *Roosevelt*. During the 1914 Progressive campaign, quite intentionally Roosevelt had made a statement to the press about the major parties, denouncing the "invisible government of the party bosses working through the alliance be-

---

[150] *Ibid.*, XVII, 324.

[151] Henry F. Pringle, *Theodore Roosevelt* (New York: Harcourt, Brace & Co., 1931), p. 211. (Hereinafter referred to as Pringle.) Criticized for refusing to face an honest question on dishonest deals by members of his party, Roosevelt later regretted his statement. "Unquestionably a mistake," he wrote, because it was "open to misconstruction by men who desired to misconstrue it." (Letter to Josephine Shaw Lowell, February 20, 1900. LC.)

[152] Sullivan, *op. cit.*, I, 346.

[153] See Owen Wister, *Roosevelt—The Story of a Friendship*. (New York: The Macmillan Co., 1930), p. 212. The dinner was reported in the Washington *Post*, January 29, 1907.

[154] Bishop, II, 432-44.

tween crooked business and crooked politics." [155] William Barnes, Republican leader, was linked with Tammany in the unholy alliance. He brought action for libel. Roosevelt was on the stand ten days, six of them in cross-examination. The verdict was acquittal. In some ways it was a hollow victory. "The thing that to me was painfully evident was that at least nine-tenths of the men of light and leading, and a very marked majority of the people as a whole desired my defeat," [156] he wrote. The jury was for him. That was because "I could reach them personally." But to the millions he no longer could reach personally, he was "like an engine bucking a snowdrift. My progress was slower and slower; and finally I accumulated so much snow that I came to a halt and could not get through." In Chicago, where in abundance of hope and energy he had delivered "The Strenuous Life," and where he had achieved so many triumphs on the platform, he told the Bar Association in 1916 "My appeal may not be heeded," and perhaps the people would respond "to the appeal of some other man, able to speak more strongly and more convincingly." [157] To his sister he confided, "Mere outside [not in a party or movement] preaching and prophecy tend after a while to degenerate into a scream; after that point has been reached the preacher can do no good, and had better keep quiet; and I am within measurable distance of that point." [158] In the election of 1916, pressed for an answer as to whether he was a candidate for President on the Republican ticket, he replied: "It would be a mistake to nominate me unless the country has in its mood something of the heroic." [159] But as he later put it philosophically, "the country wasn't in heroic mood." [160]

Arrangement and Style

The pattern and texture of Roosevelt's discourse were highly individualistic; as well as any speaker he demonstrated Buffon's contention that style is the man. Into his rhetoric went the energy, the ego, and the assertiveness of a personality never quite disciplined by the forces around him. In the main, arrangement in his speeches is episodic. They are essayish in that they are spun around the mood that was upon him, whether of moral righteousness, patriotism, or preparedness. And he permitted himself many asides. But upon

[155] The statement was made July 22, 1914, at Oyster Bay. N.Y. Appellate Division— *Record in the Matter of William Barnes vs. Theodore Roosevelt* (Walton: Reporter Co., 1915), I, 5.
[156] Bishop, II, 381-82.
[157] *Progressive Party*, p. 16.
[158] Letter of April 27, 1916. *Cowles*, p. 308.
[159] *Works*, XVII, 410.
[160] Letter of June 16, 1916. *Cowles*, p. 308.

the desultory structure of his speeches were studded the balanced sentences, the striking phrases, the vivid words that made his style distinct.

He could design a unified speech. His first speech to attain national literary reputation, "The Strenuous Life,"[161] delivered to the Hamilton Club in Chicago when he was governor, has a consistent relevance of detail pertaining to the larger theme of striving by nation and self. His address to the Harvard Union,[162] made in 1907 when he was President, shows a nice progression from lesser to more important ideas on the theme of athletics, scholarship, and public service, and a dwelling at the end on fundamentals. A favorite plan was by arrangement of topics under some main head, a pattern used in his reports to Congress. The form can be seen in a speech on "Natural Resources"[163] made in St. Paul on the tour of 1910. Under the general head these subdivisions were discussed:

> Waterways
> Drainage
> National Forests
> Human Efficiency
> National Conservation Commission
> Pan-American Conservation
> State and Federal Control
> The Conservation Fight

These topics were prefaced with a general introduction on resources and concluded with admonitions to action. Sometimes his speeches were built around examples, as in the address at the Harvard Commencement Dinner[164] in 1902. After paying tribute to people present who had served the public with distinction, he discussed the public lives of Leonard Wood, William Taft, and Elihu Root as exemplary of public duty. He ended with a personal tribute to their work. Rare in his arrangement is any pattern of question and answer, although he did build one speech in the 1900 campaign, at Evansville, Indiana,[165] around questions Bryan asked the Republicans.

An early instance of Roosevelt's skeletal thoughts in a rather tight forensic form is preserved. The occasion was a dinner of the Civil Service Reform Association of Boston, in the days when Roosevelt was Civil Service Commissioner. As he talked he followed a two-page outline written in longhand. At the conclusion he tore the sheets lengthwise and discarded them. Charles Eliot Norton of Harvard, who was to speak later on the program, picked

[161] *Works*, XIII, 319-31.
[162] *Ibid.*, 559-70.
[163] *The New Nationalism*, pp. 77-105.
[164] *PA&SP*, I, 78-84.
[165] *Works*, XIV, 386-89.

up the pieces thinking he might garner an idea. Twelve years later, when Roosevelt was President, Norton pieced the notes together and presented them to the Harvard College Library. This was the outline, in shortened form:

(1). The fight still on hand . . . [four lines with additions scrawled across the top of the sheet.]
(2). Need of every effort on the part of friends of the reform . . . [two lines.]
(3). Need to make the people understand the truth . . . [three lines.]
(4). Classes of men against merit system; place mongering and place hunting politician; the men with low ideals . . . ; all cynics . . . ; honest men . . . misled by clamor . . . [five lines.]
(5). They generally propose other systems . . . [three lines.]
(6). Our system must be compared with the real, not an ideal system . . . [three lines.]
(7). Folly of thinking that system really one where officers do their own appointing.
(8). Our questions . . . [three lines.]
(9). Our system works well . . . [five lines.]

This is as tight a structure as Roosevelt ever achieved. In general the design of his speeches was one of interweaving experiences, observations, and maxims around a subject held in rather loose grasp. As he gained skill in public garrulity, and as manifold experiences and references became stored in his mind for ready use, he became more and more discursive. Near the end of his speaking career, in 1916, he set himself the task of a disciplined, scientific address in dedicating the New York State Museum. The general theme was "Productive Scientific Scholarship," [166] and illustrations were drawn from the fields of science in which he regarded himself most competent, ornithology and mammalogy. But try as he might, other themes intruded. Memories crowded in, of Rough Rider days, Indians in his regiment, the Iroquois League and modern leagues. Near the end he was recalling that not only the elephant once flourished in New York, but also the moose.

Imperfections in Roosevelt's arrangement came not from indifference, but rather from the volatile, excursionish nature of his thinking. "I do not like a certain lack of sequitur that I do not seem able to get rid of," [167] he wrote from Dakota when he was assembling his Life of Thomas Hart Benton. Attempts to achieve better structure can be found in the revisions of his speeches. But one does not discover in the marked-up manuscripts of Roosevelt's speeches much experimenting in rhetorical architecture. Nor does one discover in the final versions much consistent drift of thought, nor clearly

---

[166] *Opening of the State Museum* (University of the State of New York *Bulletin* No. 634, Albany, March 1, 1917).
[167] Letter to Lodge, March 27, 1886. *Lodge*, I, 38.

marked progressions to climaxes. The episodic nature of his speeches was relieved somewhat by transitions. Always his shifts in ideas took into account that the audience must go with him, and see some reason for it. A favorite transition was, "Now let me say a word about..." Talking to an Atlanta [168] audience about the merits of Uncle Remus, he shifted to the theme of reckless attacks on public men, with "Let me say a word about something entirely different." Telling a Denver [169] audience about the government program for breeding horses with stouter forelegs, he suddenly took up the powers of the Interstate Commerce Commission with "I want to say a word..." Transitions were not close knittings but rough splices.

Getting started in a speech, once he was on the ground, caused Roosevelt no concern. Frequently his opening salutations were specific: "Men and women of my Mother's State," [170] he addressed a Georgia audience; "Mrs. President, and members of the Society, and you, my comrades, and finally, officers and men of the Regular Army, whom we took as our models in the war four years ago," he saluted the Colonial Dames of America and an assorted audience at Arlington Cemetery. [171] Before setting forth on the main themes of a speech, Roosevelt usually acknowledged all honors due among the assembly, and cleared the ground by approving of what was good in what had gone before, or correcting what he thought was in error. He could agree with the sentiments of a college orator, [172] or reprove the Governor of Arkansas [173] for seeming to express approval of lynchings. Often it was a struggle to get to his theme, so many occasional matters loomed.

If getting started was no chore for Roosevelt, getting ended was an obstacle. At Mound Bayou, [174] a village in Mississippi in which he was particularly interested because it was entirely Negro in population, he was still lecturing in his best presidential manner on the joys of temperance and the evils of drink as the train pulled out of the station. Speaking to the men on the *U.S.S. Louisiana*, [175] half of his speech went "in closing." At Hampton Institute he required three pages of a nine-page address to get concluded after he announced "Now, in closing..." [176] But he could end dramatically, quickly, with a stirring phrase, such as "Remember...the simple and loyal motto,

[168] *PA&SP*, **IV**, 502.
[169] *Ibid.*, III, 354.
[170] *Ibid.*, IV, 488.
[171] *Ibid.*, I, 53.
[172] See the speech given at Gallaudet College, *ibid.*, V, 738.
[173] *Ibid.*, IV, 533.
[174] October 21, 1907. Addresses Scrapbooks, LC.
[175] *PA&SP*, V, 874 f.
[176] *Ibid.*, V, 760 ff.

America for Americans."[177] Over and over he broke off a talk to school and college audiences with a slogan from the football field, "Don't flinch, don't foul, and hit the line hard!"[178] And he could rise to a sustained peroration, as at Cooper Union in the close of the Hughes-Wilson 1916 campaign. Throwing down his manuscript, Roosevelt excoriated on a theme well rehearsed on the hustings, his contempt for President Wilson:

> Mr. Wilson now dwells at Shadow Lawn. There should be shadows enough at Shadow Lawn; the shadows of men, women, and children who have risen from the ooze of the ocean bottom and from graves in foreign lands; the shadows of the helpless whom Mr. Wilson did not dare protect lest he might have to face danger; the shadows of babies gasping pitifully as they sank under the waves; the shadows of women outraged and slain by bandits; the shadows of Boyd and Adair and their troopers who lay in the Mexican desert, the black blood crusted round their mouths, and their dim eyes looking upward, because President Wilson had sent them to do a task, and had then shamefully abandoned them to the mercy of foes who knew no mercy. Those are the shadows proper for Shadow Lawn; the shadows of deeds that were never done; the shadows of lofty words that were followed by no action; the shadows of the tortured dead.[179]

The tone of Roosevelt's speeches was consistently hortatory. He incessantly extolled some gospel, and in a manner distinctly homiletical. "Our whole movement," he declared, "is simply and solely to make the decalogue and the golden rule of some practical moment in both the business and the political life of the community."[180] Wits accused Roosevelt of thinking he had discovered the Ten Commandments. Irked at first by the jibes, he came to accept his role as evangelist. "You have let yourselves in for a sermon"[181] he told a delegation who called upon him at the White House. In reading to some friends the manuscript of a forthcoming speech he interrupted himself to say: "I suppose my critics will call that preaching. But I have such a bully pulpit."[182]

Contributing, too, to Roosevelt's reputation as preacher was his habit of drawing upon commonplaces and didactic anecdotes. The virtues of the good life, the sound body, the vigorous mind, the alert nation—through and through his speeches run strains of commonplaces drearily accepted by any audience in the abstract, but which, if one works from homiletic view, have to be redis-

[177] *Progressive Party*, p. 85.

[178] See, for example, the speech given at **Georgetown** College Commencement, *PA&SP*, V, 790.

[179] *Works*, XVIII, 442-52.

[180] *PA&SP*, VI, 1470.

[181] *Ibid.*, VII, 1674.

[182] Lyman Abbott, *Silhouettes of My Contemporaries* (New York: Doubleday, Page & Co., 1921), p. 310.

covered, freshened, applied, and lived. "Gentlemen," he could tell a Southern audience which needed the encouragement, "our nation has a wonderful future." [183] The country learned from Roosevelt's Inaugural address in 1905 that "Much has been given us, and much will rightfully be expected from us." Graduation classes from Columbia [184] to California [185] were charged with the same responsibility.

From a simple anecdote, Roosevelt could draw a large moral. Used over and over was the story of his opportunistic ranchhand. Once on the roundup one of his cowboys, thinking to impress the boss, started to put Roosevelt's brand on a neighbor's calf. "Go back to the ranch and get your time," roared the owner of the Elkhorn. The moral was clear; a man who will steal for you will steal from you, and the man who will wrong someone else to please you, will wrong you if it is to his advantage. Admirers at Lake Providence, Louisiana,[186] were exposed to the lesson, and the savants at the Sorbonne [187] found the setting if not the moral unique.

Although Roosevelt's style was one of didactic assertion, with little induction, always there was a tone of reasoning the matter through with an audience. Common sense, and the impulses found in any decent person were the bases of the appeal. How can sons of workers become officers in the army when the system is one of voluntary officer training paid for by the candidates themselves,[188] he would reason. How well would a football team do if it began training the day of the game,[189] he would ask a college audience. So in military training, we must be prepared long before the actual contest. And besides, if we are thoroughly prepared, the opponents will be so intimidated they will avoid conflict. In the reasoning process, Roosevelt made much use of the analogy, sometimes loosely figurative, at other times literally tight. Can a man be half loyal to his wife and half loyal to another woman? [190] The answer is the same in nationalism and internationalism. You can't be half loyal to your country and half loyal to other nations. In answering objections that his insistence on a standing army of a quarter of a million was militaristic, he could explain to a Chicago audience [191] that he was asking for no more on a national basis than the proportion of policemen to the city population.

In the reasoning process, there was much reliance on either-or choice. "If

[183] *PA&SP*, VI, 1456.
[184] *Ibid.*, I, 31.
[185] *Ibid.*, II, 405.
[186] Addresses Scrapbooks, LC.
[187] *Works*, XIII, 525.
[188] *Progressive Party*, p. 63.
[189] *Commencement at Trinity College* (Hartford, 1918), p. 11.
[190] *Ibid.*, p. 13.
[191] *Progressive Party*, p. 25.

you don't fill up the hours with something that is good, they will be filled up with something that is bad," he told a Y.M.C.A. audience. "Nature abhors a vacuum."[192] Look what happens when you discourage the fighting spirit and become pacifistic. Look at China, nonmilitant, backward, overrun by foreigners. If you don't want to become like China, encourage the fighting spirit.[193] The audience could take its choice between a supine, pacifistic China and an alert prepared America. There was no in-between.

In keeping with the general assertive tone of the speeches, there are few statistical bases for an audience to induce an inference on its own. Occasionally, Roosevelt did mass facts and figures. In a message to Congress[194] he sent a partial list of outbreaks in Panama in fifty-seven years, indicating that Colombia never had been able to establish a stable government on the Isthmus. To an audience at Howard University,[195] he cited figures on the material prosperity of Negroes. A Conservation congress learned that the National Forests were "used by 22,000 cattlemen, with their herds, 5000 sheepmen, with their flocks, 5000 timbermen with their crews...."[196] At the Deep Waterway Convention in Memphis[197] Roosevelt cited the alarming figure:

> One-fifth of a cubic mile in volume, or one billion tons in weight of the richest soil matter of the United States, is annually gathered in storm rivulets, washed into the rivers, and borne into the sea.

But even here, instead of gathering statistical matters into a reckoning, he made a general appeal, that the loss to the farmer was a tax greater than all other land taxes combined. The question has to be answered—why did Roosevelt, who so loved detail in story and event, bring so little fact and information to his audiences? The answer is to be found in a letter he wrote to Sir George Trevelyan[198] about historical method. Someone must "gather bricks and stones," he admitted. The ability to "marshal and weigh the facts" is important. But the "great master builder," someone like Macaulay, produces works which rise above mere detail. Roosevelt speaking was the master builder; he saw himself on the platform as no mere informer, expositor, or public entertainer; he tried to blaze the main trails of worthy human conduct.

Although he made little use of curiosity, he could use dramatic suspense on occasion. When he was criticized for attacking the courts' blocking of social legislation, he sometimes read a historical denunciation of Lincoln for

[192] *Public Papers*, p. 259.
[193] *Progressive Party*, p. 19.
[194] First Message, 58th Cong., 2d sess. *PA&SP*, II, 700.
[195] *Ibid.*, VII, 1484.
[196] *The New Nationalism*, p. 86.
[197] *Works*, XVI, 116.
[198] January 23, 1904. Bishop, II, 141.

making "war on the decision of the Supreme Court." [199] He substituted his own name for Lincoln's, and did not reveal until later that he was quoting Stephen A. Douglas.

Roosevelt's public address made relatively little use of humor. The absence is noteworthy in that he liked a good joke, even on himself. Little strains of humor ran through his associations with people. A favorite was the story of the Rough Rider who had trouble getting to a reunion because he had killed a man. When asked to explain how he could have done such a thing, he innocently replied, "with a .38 on a .45 frame, Colonel." After the shooting in Milwaukee the colonel telegraphed his old friend Seth Bullock in Dakota to assure him nothing serious had happened because the gun was merely a .38 on a .45 frame. [200] But in his formal speeches Roosevelt seldom indulged his sense of fun. Sometimes he inserted little flashes, such as denying as "gross exaggeration . . . that all the Rough Riders who were not in the penitentiary were in office." [201] In unveiling a statue of General McClellan, he noted that it did not, like some modern statuary, add "a new terror to death." [202] A sarcastic twist appeared at times; he spoke of "pacifists of both sexes, as far as you can predicate sex of a pacifist." [203] The early speeches relied heavily upon irony. The theme of his maiden speech in the New York Assembly [204] was that the longer the legislature remained unorganized and inactive, the better off would be the people of the state. On the stump as a young politician speaking against Governor Cleveland for President, he covered his brashness by remarking, "I have not been in politics a long time, but Grover Cleveland's public career is still shorter." [205] But as Roosevelt more and more preached the gospel, he had less and less humor, more and more straightforward sermonizing. His rather serious verbal style was relieved, of course, by platform antics, grimaces, and humorous falsetto emphases in his voice.

Roosevelt had a reputation as a writer before he attained distinction as a speaker. No man of his time had an audience comparable to his in both the written and the spoken word. To understand him as a speaker, it is necessary to put the question: How did his oral and his written style compare? In the main they are similar. Many of his letters and his shorter articles were dictated, and hence were recordings of his oral moods. The purpose in each was the same, to get at the reader or listener as simply, as forcibly, as directly

---

[199] For example see a speech at Syracuse. *The New Nationalism*, pp. 235-36.
[200] *Autobiography, Works*, XX, 129.
[201] *Opening of the State Museum*, p. 32.
[202] *PA&SP*, VI, 1229.
[203] *Commencement at Trinity College*, p. 12.
[204] *Works*, XIV, 3.
[205] *Ibid.*, p. 47.

as possible. To a writer having stylistic difficulties he advised reading the "manuscript aloud and striving to make his sentences shorter and more simple." [206] In neither oral nor written style was Roosevelt consciously artistic and he sought no schemes of indirection. The substance of his writing and his speaking differed in that he seldom spoke on anything specialized; he gave no minutiae of bird classification. But the chief difference was the infrequent use in his speeches of description and narration—qualities which made him distinctive as a writer. He could paint a vivid picture and could tell a story with suspense. Some of his descriptions of the Western country—"All the land is like granite; the great rivers stand still in their beds, as if turned to frosted steel" [207]—are as powerful as Willa Cather's. His stories of the African trail are finely told—"Rearing, the lion struck the man, bearing down the shield, his back arched; and for a moment he slaked his fury with fang and talon." [208] But in the speeches, picture and tale are seldom used, and then are drawn from previous writing. [209]

On a number of occasions Roosevelt observed that the average voter does not "regard the political picture as an etching and follow out the delicate tracery. He treats it as a circus poster," with colors vivid and "laid on with a broad brush." [210] So in his literary writings, Roosevelt worked for finesse, but in his political pronouncements, whether speech, statement, or broadside, he often sought the gross effect with primary colors. It was not the literal form that mattered, but the nature of the audiences. In high persuasive mood, Roosevelt's style whether written or oral took on a florid, oratorical roll, marked by high imagery and increasing cadence. In the *Metropolitan* magazine he wrote on an old theme, sadly revivified by the death of his son Quentin in France:

> Only those are fit to live who do not fear to die; and none are fit to die who have shrunk from the joy of life and the duty of life. Both life and death are parts of the same Great Adventure. [211]

With variations, in his last speeches and articles, he wrote and spoke on loyalty to flag and language:

> We have room in this country for but one flag, the Stars and Stripes, and we should tolerate no allegiance to any other flag, whether a foreign flag or the red flag

[206] *Ibid.*, XII, 260.
[207] *Ibid.*, I, 341.
[208] *Ibid.*, IV, 296-97.
[209] *Cf.* descriptions in a talk (*Works*, XI, 283) with those previously done in a letter (*Letters to Kermit*, p. 202). Gladys L. Borchers, "A Study of Oral Style" (unpublished Ph.D. dissertation, Wisconsin, 1927), in a detailed study of mechanical stylistic aspects, could find no distinctive difference between Roosevelt's speaking and writing.
[210] See, for example, *Works*, XII, 238.
[211] *Ibid.*, XIX, 243.

or black flag. We have room for but one loyalty, loyalty to the United States. We have room for but one language, the language of Washington and Lincoln, the language of the Declaration of Independence and the Gettysburg speech; the English language.[212]

Not in structure or disposition of particular points, but in the smaller units of composition Roosevelt's speeches were most distinctive. Let us examine his use of the sentence, the phrase, and the word. He was a master of what Mark Sullivan [213] called "the balanced and cushioned" sentence, the use of which Sullivan considered an "intellectual habit with him." The pattern consisted of a bold assertion, later so conditioned that the first force was curtailed or redirected. Here are specimens:

Message to the New York Legislature: "Much of the outcry against wealth, against the men who acquire wealth, and against the means by which it is acquired, is blind, unreasoning, and unjust; but in too many cases it has a basis in real abuses."

The Sorbonne, Paris: "War is a dreadful thing, and unjust war is a crime against humanity. But it is such a crime because it is unjust, not because it is war."

Chamber of Commerce in New Haven: "I am a radical who most earnestly desires to see the radical programme carried out by conservatives."

"I see our President has been making another 'Yes, I guess not' speech on business, corporations, etc.," [214] observed Grover Cleveland during one of Roosevelt's speaking tours. But it was Mr. Dooley who really took off Roosevelt's balanced sentence, in a monologue:

'Th' thrusts,' says he to himself, 'are heejous monsthers built up be th' inlightened intherprise iv th' men that have done so much to advance progress in our beloved counthry,' he says. 'On wan hand I wud stamp thim undher fut; on th' other hand not so fast.' [215]

The balanced structure was commonly regarded as a skillful device for advocating both sides at the same time. Stuart P. Sherman [216] thought that Roosevelt with his "rhetorical balance" was "the greatest concocter of 'weasel' paragraphs." But the designer of the form had his own explanation, which he once made to Lincoln Steffens:

[212] *Ibid.*, p. 301.
[213] Sullivan, *op. cit.*, II, 408-9.
[214] Allan Nevins (ed.), *Letters of Grover Cleveland* (Boston and New York: Houghton Mifflin Co., 1933), p. 616.
[215] Elmer Ellis (ed.), *Finley Peter Dunne—Mr. Dooley at His Best* (New York: Charles Scribner's Sons, 1938), pp. 104-5.
[216] Sherman, *op. cit.*, p. 605.

I try to put the whole truth in each sentence; that is, if I propound a proposition I back hard against it all that conditions it. And the reason for this habit is that I've found out how one sentence quoted without context can be made to stab back and hurt me.[217]

In using the striking phrase Roosevelt was a master. His personal philosophy became famous as "The Strenuous Life" (although he later preferred "The Vigor of Life"). His political philosophy was the "Square Deal." In general, the tried and true phrases were used over and over. Less than 100% Americans were denounced as "fifty-fifty Americans," or "hyphenated-Americans." Those who went beyond his idea of progressivism were "parlor socialists," "pink tea parlor bolsheviks," on "the lunatic fringe," "outpatients of Bedlam." Those who conditioned their words were accused of using "weasel words." It was an old Maine expression he learned in his early hunting days, but he put it into the dictionary.

The vigor of life shone through his expressions. "My hat is in the ring," he announced before the conventions in 1912. In the Spanish-American War Roosevelt began to feel "as strong as a bull moose,"[218] a phrase which became a trademark. As governor he expressed in a letter his fondness for "the West African proverb: 'Speak softly and carry a big stick!' "[219] Soon he was advocating the policy from the platform, and he never abandoned the phrase. In 1916, he accused an opponent: "Instead of speaking softly and carrying a big stick, President Wilson spoke bombastically and carried a dishrag."[220] Of all Roosevelt's phrases, none has been so consistent a subject for caricature and cartoon.

Roosevelt had a keen sense of the graphic word. "Rough-riders" he used a dozen years before the word became popular in the Spanish-American War. "Bully" described the perfection of things; "mollycoddle" the low point in spiritual and physical non-vigor. Those who saw supernatural camouflage in the coloration of animals and the plumage of birds were "Nature-Fakers." Parents who willfully restricted the size of families were guilty of "race-suicide." Spoiled army beef was "embalmed beef." The writer who exposed dirt for its own sake was a "muckraker." The petty party functionary in public office was a "bureaucrat." A Roosevelt audience which did not hear at least a few characteristic expressions hissed at them would have felt that they had not seen and heard the original production.

Roosevelt's style was energetic, at times to the point of violence. "I'll

---

[217] Winter and Hicks (eds.), *op. cit.*, I, 152.
[218] Letter of July 10, 1898. *Lodge*, I, 322.
[219] To Henry L. Sprague, January 26, 1900. LC.
[220] *Newer Messages*, p. 1073.

cut for blood," [221] he said of a speech made when he was Civil Service Commissioner. "I hit him as I never hit anyone before in a debate, and he literally broke down and sobbed," [222] he proudly reported of a performance when he was New York City Police Commissioner. He thought he "drew blood in a little speech," [223] made when he returned from Africa. "Make your points as clear as possible; and thrust the steel well home. It is foolish to show mercy," [224] he advised a friend about to make a speech.

It was as a young legislator that Roosevelt rose in the Assembly and charged:

The *New York World*, a local stock-jobbing sheet of limited circulation, of voluble scurrility and versatile mendacity—owned by the arch-thief of Wall Street [Jay Gould] [225]

He asked a friend, in this period, to convey to Godkin and his associates on *The Nation* the message that "they were suffering . . . from a species of moral myopia, complicated with intellectual strabismus." [226] In 1916, in the Cooper Union speech, made on request of twenty-five distinguished citizens, he castigated the President of the United States:

He has made our statesmanship a thing of empty elocution. He has covered his fear of standing for the right behind a veil of rhetorical phrases. He has wrapped the true heart of the nation in a spangled shroud of rhetoric. [227]

Roosevelt's penchant for invective was habitual. Indeed it has been the subject of a dissertation. [228] In conversation and letters, even in public statements, the impulse was more freely released than in speeches. Asked on one occasion whether he would reply to an attack, he declared:

To that miserable creature? I doubt if it's worth while. He reminds me of a cockroach creeping over a marble floor. It is just a question whether it is better to crush the cockroach or to refrain from staining the marble. [229]

Probably his most famous invective in a press release was his denunciation of a charge by Judge Alton B. Parker in the 1904 election, as "Monstrous . . .

[221] *Lodge*, I, 126.
[222] *Ibid.*, p. 161.
[223] *Ibid.*, II, 392.
[224] *Ibid.*, I, 95.
[225] Sullivan, *op. cit.*, II, 230.
[226] *Lodge*, I, 5.
[227] *Works*, XVIII, 447.
[228] Gordon W. Winks, "A Study of Theodore Roosevelt's Use of Invective in His Public Speeches" (M. A. thesis, Northwestern University, 1933).
[229] H. J. Whigham, "The Colonel As We Saw Him," *Metropolitan*, XLIX (March, 1919), 7.

Wicked falsehood . . . unqualifiedly and atrociously false." [230] The Ananias Club was reserved for those Roosevelt had publicly called "liar."

Roosevelt's arrangement and style are not models to be imitated by a student of public address; they are expressions of a unique personality. His composition had the episodic nature of a well-experienced, restless man, a balance of treatment characteristic of a thoughtful man, the vivid phrasing of an imaginative man striving to communicate, the invective of a fighting man. Was he an orator? Neither he nor his friends thought so. O. K. Davis gave the answer:

Colonel Roosevelt was not often eloquent. He had a style that did not lend itself to moving oratory. He always felt it necessary to balance his statements in a way to make his meaning perfectly explicit, and, although he was a master at coining phrases that would stick in the memory, he rarely built up oratorical periods. [231]

Roosevelt on the Platform—Voice and Manner

Roosevelt's voice and manner of speaking were untrained, and showed little artistry, but were consistent with the rough-and-ready vigor of his personality. The characteristics of his speaking voice are described in an opinion questionnaire made by William Behl, [232] in which forty-six colleagues and contemporaries of Roosevelt—such as William Allen White, Gifford Pinchot, Harold Ickes, and Hermann Hagedorn—described twenty years after his death what they recalled in his voice. A synthesis of their answers would indicate that Roosevelt spoke in a rather high-pitched, forceful voice at a moderately fast rate with a tendency toward clipped, staccato, falsetto tones. On whether the pattern was conversational or oratorical the auditors were equally divided, but on a choice of whether timidity or confidence was revealed in the voice, timidity got not a vote.

Phonograph recordings reveal a strong, direct voice, slightly strained and rasping but not unpleasant in quality. There is little change in tempo, little variation in pitch except for falsetto. The falsetto was used for emphasis, often in humor. Replying to charges that he had persecuted the Standard Oil Company, [233] Roosevelt rose to falsetto on *Standard Oil,* imparting to the phrase a suggestion of *poor, set-upon, abused, defenseless corporation.* Except for falsetto quality there is little emphasis by inflectional pattern, but a consistent use of force. As to general pitch, when Jerome Fisher [234] analyzed parts

[230] Statement released November 4.

[231] Davis, p. 213.

[232] William Behl, "The Speaking and Speeches of Theodore Roosevelt" (Ph.D. dissertation, Northwestern University, 1942), pp. 416-18.

[233] "The 'Abyssinian Treatment' of Standard Oil." Victor Record 35249-B.

[234] See Behl, *op. cit.,* pp. 367, 387.

of the recording, "The Liberty of the People," he found the median pitch to be 178.67 cycles per second, rather high in comparison with the average man's pitch of 128 c.p.s.

Roosevelt's words were frequently described as being bitten out or hissed out, and parodies of his speaking often were separated word by word or letter by letter. The New York *Sun,* in covering the first speech in the legislature, spoke of a "quaint drawl," and recorded one phrase thus: "r-a-w-t-h-e-r r-e-l-i-e-v-e-d."[235] Technical explanation of his staccato quality is not hard to find if one studies the phonograph records. The plosions are percussive, the sibilants strong: "no*t t*rue"; "men of thi*s s*tamp."[236] Frequently words are given with tendency to equal syllabic stress, as in his famous rejoinder upon meeting somebody, "dee-lighted." *Cooperative* was spoken ['koʊ'ɑp•'reɪ'tɪv].[237] There is a kind of word-for-word phrasing as though he were dictating carefully to a stenographer: [ðə 'mæsɪz 'ʔʌv 'ɑʊwə 'pipl̩].[238] Although early caricatures of Roosevelt often imparted to his speech a foppish character suggestive of Oscar Wilde—indeed, he was often likened to the dainty Englishman—by the time the recordings were made in 1912 there is strong General American characteristic in his speech, with suggestions of his early Southern and Eastern influences in pronunciations. When Behl[239] played Roosevelt recordings to several hundred faculty and student members of Brooklyn College, and asked them whether their born and bred Manhattan neighbor was "decidedly Eastern," a majority disclaimed him and said no. In general, Roosevelt's voice, by testimony of his contemporaries and by evidence of the recordings, was distinctive but not distinguished. Despite his peculiarities, he spoke in high conversational quality, with a keen sense of what he was saying and a strenuous desire to communicate. His voice had little of the calm and deliberateness of William Howard Taft's, less of the pedagogical periods of Woodrow Wilson's cultured tones, and nothing in common with William Jennings Bryan's orotundity.

Roosevelt's voice was not always equal to the tasks he set upon it, and was a constant cause of concern. At fourteen, from Germany, he wrote to his father that he had a "slight attack of asthma," and could not "speak without blowing like an abridged hippopotamus."[240] When in the Assembly, he wrote

[235] January 25, 1882.
[236] "The Liberty of the People." Victor Record 31872.
[237] *Ibid.*
[238] *Ibid.* An observer in Holland, M. J. Brusse, noted in his *With Roosevelt Through Holland* (Rotterdam: Holland-America-Line, 1911): "Roosevelt's American-English is difficult for Dutch ears, especially when he raps out every word like a blow from a sledge hammer." (P. 42).
[239] Behl, *op. cit.,* p. 421.
[240] Robinson, pp. 78-79.

to his mother: "I do not speak enough from the chest, so my voice is not as powerful as it ought to be."[241] He felt that in the 1898 campaign for governor he had so strained his voice that it "never recovered from the effects."[242] Through the campaign of 1900 his throat was a constant trouble, and occasionally Curtis Guild[243] spoke for him. Near the end of the campaign, in late October, he wired his sister to have a throat specialist at her house upon his return to New York. Treated and advised to remain quiet through the evening, he talked till dawn about his experiences on the stump.[244]

Through the presidential years his voice held up fairly well. "My voice has held out astonishingly,"[245] he wrote during the long 1903 tour. About the Inaugural of 1905, John Hay noted in his diary: "The high wind made speaking difficult, but his voice lasted well."[246]

Roosevelt's throat was one of the main concerns in the Progressive campaign of 1912. In Chicago he spoke in a tent on the lake front. To give the overflow audience a chance to see the proceedings the flaps were raised, and a raw October wind blew through. That night in the Coliseum, Roosevelt's voice broke, and he was unable to finish his speech. On the way to Milwaukee, two days later, at the station stops Congressman Henry A. Cooper of Wisconsin spoke to the crowds explaining why Roosevelt could not talk. The candidate himself appeared, and shook hands, but said nothing. In Milwaukee he could speak only in a whisper. That evening he resolutely tucked his manuscript in his inside coat pocket, determined to give as much of the speech as he could. In the general confusion of the shooting, nobody remembered that the speaker of the evening had no voice. The speech that was given had its variations from the manuscript, but the voice was not only restored but lasted for the hour and a half.[247] In the campaign of 1914, Roosevelt, weakened by jungle fever, was warned to avoid speaking lest he suffer permanent injury to his throat.[248] But he spoke.

From that time on, concerns of general health took precedence over worries about his voice. The tight throat, the contortions of the neck muscles, the sounds forced rather than flowing—it is remarkable his voice held out as well as it did. It is an irony that the instrument of his orality should have been below rather than above normal proficiency, and that he should have taken so little interest in cultivating it.

[241] February 20, 1883. *Cowles*, p. 52.
[242] Letter to Henry Clay Payne, August 18, 1900. LC.
[243] Thayer, *Theodore Roosevelt*, p. 152.
[244] Robinson, p. 199.
[245] *Lodge*, II, 13. May 11, 1903.
[246] *John Hay*, II, 364.
[247] Details of this episode are from Davis, pp. 366-86.
[248] Robinson, p. 280.

From photographs and films, and from descriptions by those who heard him, we have a clear picture of Roosevelt on the platform. A typical posture would be that of the man on the flag-draped temporary platform, standing at the edge nearest the audience, the weight on the ball of the left foot, frock-coat tails blowing in the outdoor breeze, the left hand extended palm open to receive the right as it came down in smacking emphasis of a point. Another typical pose would be the man leaning over the rail of the platform, or of the rear coach of a train, pointing a finger with arm full length to the crowd. At times he pantomimed. At Cambridge University he held up a water tumbler from the stand to illustrate the size target a hunter aims at in shooting a lion in the heart or brain. In more casual mood, he might stand straight, with the left hand resting on his trousers pocket, or perhaps lightly touching the heavy gold watch chain across his vest, or the black silk fob from which dangled two Phi Beta Kappa keys, while he shaped the point with the right hand at eye level. When he used a manuscript, frequently the papers were taken along in gesture, and upon completion of a page he liked to crumble and drop it to the floor. Concerning his physical movements, those replying to Behl's questionnaire had these opinions:

Movement	Much	0
	Moderate	20
	Little	19
Gesture	Frequent	37
	Infrequent	9
	Excessive	0
	Graceful	1
	Abrupt	36

Most expressive was the face. The snapping, extended jaw, the flashing teeth, the full moustache gyrating as he exaggerated his diction for full clarity to the crowd, the eyes narrowing in intensity behind the nose glasses—all were trademark features drawn upon by the cartoonists. His whole manner was vigorous, suggestive of his moods. He did little prancing about. He shook his fist, but it was at a real or a hypothetical enemy. The movement was not graceful, not Delsartian, but it was excellently coordinated with the thought. Mannerisms which would have seemed burlesque in another, were genuinely expressive of his personality. There is no doubt that a Roosevelt speech gained in its delivery. As the Archbishop of York said of the Oxford lecture, referring not so much to voice and gesture as to the platform presence of the man: "We agreed to mark the lecture 'Beta Minus,' but the lecturer 'Alpha Plus.' " [249]

[249] Quoted in Pringle, p. 520.

Conclusion

Two questions may be raised, and answers ventured, in conclusion. One question is: Which of Roosevelt's speeches are most significant? The answer depends upon what aspect one examines. His own opinion of his speaking has been indicated. The Romanes lecture at Oxford was the kind of speech he best liked to give, a speech thoroughly prepared and seasoned, founded on personally experienced technical knowledge, with implications extending to all human affairs, and given on a noteworthy occasion. The speech most closely identified with his personality, and the one which gave him greatest impetus as a speaker of national importance is "The Strenuous Life." As most attuned to the times, and having the greatest impact on the culture of the period, the speech selected would have to be "The Man with the Muckrake." As artistic and well-rounded as any of the speeches is the Abraham Lincoln Centenary Address at Hodgenville, in 1909. The most radical speeches were those before the Colorado legislature and at Osawatomie. His mature personal political philosophy was probably nowhere better expressed than in the Madison Square Garden speech at the end of the 1912 campaign. Most disastrous in its effect was the address to the Ohio Constitutional Convention in Columbus, in the preconvention campaign of 1912, a speech which so frightened Republican leaders that nomination became impossible. Speeches at which he received the greatest audience ovations would have to include the address to the Progressive Convention—the convention gave him a fifty-five minute demonstration at the beginning, and interrupted the speech with cheers and applause one hundred and forty-five times [250] and the Cooper Union address of 1916, at the conclusion of which the audience rose and stormed the platform.

The other question to be answered is: How did Roosevelt compare with his contemporaries as a speaker? If one were to judge by some academic checklist of technical speech standards, Roosevelt would rank low. As a contemporary critic [251] noted, Roosevelt lacked Bryan's vocal power, the dramatic artistry of Robert LaFollette, the intellectual clarity of Woodrow Wilson, and the all-round oratorical ability of Senator Beveridge. It might be added that he lacked, also, the penetrating boldness of Debs. But the critic explained that it was Roosevelt who got the crowds, and that he was "One of the most effective of speakers." His reputation suffered because he did not have the cultivated, polished oratorical manner so much admired in the period in which

[250] William Draper Lewis, *The Life of Theodore Roosevelt* (The United Publishers, 1919), p. 372.
[251] William Bayard Hale, " 'Friends and Fellow-Citizens'—Our Political Orators of All Parties, and the Ways They Use to Win Us," *World's Work* (April, 1912), pp. 673-83.

he spoke. In addition, too many recall only the shouting and the ranting of the later years when he no longer was attuned to his audiences. Woodrow Wilson, giving a private judgment on his severest critic, took him to be in "insane distemper of egotism"; [252] but in calmer mood he reflected that Roosevelt was "a real, vivid person, whom they [the people] have seen and shouted themselves hoarse over and voted for, millions strong." [253]

Time has not yet supplied perspective. A generation ago critics found in Roosevelt's speaking much that was political commonplace or superpatriotism. Edgar Lee Masters thought Roosevelt had corrupted the noble art of oratory with his "demagoguery." "As an orator Mr. Roosevelt has nothing to say and says it as poorly as possible." [254] What to friends of Roosevelt seemed to be vigor or manliness, his critics denounced as brutalizing. Eugene Debs thought Roosevelt was "morally...still in the jungle." [255] But since Roosevelt has passed on, America has passed through periods of domestic political corruption and economic despair and severe international crises. His words on integrity in office and unity of defense, his statements of moral principles, civil rights, and faith in the future are now quoted in the best American tradition. In a limited listing of American orators in the classical tradition, he may not belong. But he is among the dozen most effective speakers in American history. In the variety and extensiveness of his speaking, in the vigor of his ideas and the communication of them, in the success he achieved in rallying supporters for causes he represented, in the degree to which he used the public platform to bring about political and social reforms and to assert humanitarian principles, Theodore Roosevelt belongs among the elect.

SELECTED BIBLIOGRAPHY

Books, Pamphlets, Unpublished Theses, Speeches

BIBLIOGRAPHY:

HART, ALBERT BUSHNELL, and FERLEGER, HERBERT RONALD. *Theodore Roosevelt Cyclopedia.* New York: Roosevelt Memorial Association, 1941.

WHEELOCK, JOHN HALL. *A Bibliography of Theodore Roosevelt.* New York: Charles Scribner's Sons, 1920.

SOURCES OF SPEECHES (arranged chronologically):

HAGEDORN, HERMANN (ed.). *The Works of Theodore Roosevelt, National Edition.* 20 vols. New York: Charles Scribner's Sons, 1926. About 160 speeches are given through the entire period of speaking.

[252] Letter to Edith G. Reid, May 26, 1912. Ray Stannard Baker, *Woodrow Wilson— Life and Letters* (Garden City: Doubleday, Doran & Co., 1931), III, 316.

[253] *Ibid.,* p. 390. Letter to Mary Hulbert, August 25, 1912.

[254] *The New Star Chamber and Other Essays* (Chicago: Hammersmark Publishing Co., 1904), p. 34.

[255] *The International Socialist Review,* XII (January, 1912), 399.

HAGEDORN, HERMANN (ed.). *The Americanism of Theodore Roosevelt; Selections from His Writings and Speeches.* Boston and New York: Houghton Mifflin Co., 1921.

State of New York. *Public Papers of Theodore Roosevelt, Governor, 1899 [1900].* 2 vols. Albany: Brandow Printing Co., 1899 [1900].

LINCOLN, CHARLES Z. (ed.). *Messages from the Governors, 1683-1906.* Albany: J. B. Lyon Co., for the State of New York, 1909. Vol. X, 1899-1906.

LODGE, HENRY CABOT (ed.). *Addresses and Presidential Messages of Theodore Roosevelt.* New York and London: G. P. Putnam's Sons, 1904.

JOHNSON, WILLIS FLETCHER. *Theodore Roosevelt Addresses and Papers.* New York: Sun Dial Classics Co., 1908.

Presidential Addresses and State Papers [and European Addresses]. 8 vols. New York: Review of Reviews Co., 1910. Vols. 13-20 of the Homeward Bound edition of Roosevelt's works.

RICHARDSON, JAMES D. *A Compilation of the Messages and Papers of the Presidents.* New York: Bureau of National Literature, 1911. Vols. IX and X pertain to Roosevelt.

ABBOTT, LAWRENCE F. (ed.). *African and European Addresses by Theodore Roosevelt.* New York and London: G. P. Putnam's Sons, 1910.

ROOSEVELT, THEODORE. *The New Nationalism.* New York: Outlook Co., 1910. Introduction by Ernest Hamlin Abbott.

YOUNGMAN, ELMER H. (ed.) *Progressive Principles: Selections from Addresses Made during the Presidential Campaign of 1912.* New York: Progressive National Service, 1913.

The Progressive Party—Its Record from January to July, 1916, Including Statements and Speeches of Theodore Roosevelt. New York: Mail and Express, 1916.

Record in the Matter of William Barnes vs. Theodore Roosevelt. 4 vols. Walton, New York: Reporter Co., 1916.

Americanism and Preparedness—Speeches of Theodore Roosevelt July to November, 1916. New York: Mail and Express, 1917.

GRIFFITH, WILLIAM. *Newer Roosevelt Messages.* New York: Current Literature Publishing Co., 1919. This is vol. III of *The Roosevelt Policy—Speeches, Letters and State Papers Relating to Corporate Wealth and Closely Allied Topics.*

The number of separate speeches published is beyond record. Many were issued by the Government Printing Office. Others are more rare, and include: *Sayings of Social Wisdom, Together with an Address to the Dutch, His Kinsfolk, Delivered in Amsterdam on the 29th of April, 1910,* The Hague, W. P. van Stockum and Zoon, 1910; *Le Citoyen D'Une République,* Paris, Hachette et Cie, 1910. For details of separate speeches, including the very rare reprint of a speech at Nairobi, Africa, see Nora E. Cordingley, "Extreme Rarities in the Published Works of Theodore Roosevelt," *Papers of the Bibliographical Society of America,* XXXIX (1945), 20-50.

LETTERS:

MORISON, ELTING E. (ed.). *The Letters of Theodore Roosevelt.* 8 vols. Cambridge: Harvard University Press, 1951-54. It is much regretted that this collection had not yet appeared when this study was made.

BISHOP, JOSEPH BUCKLIN. *Theodore Roosevelt and His Time Shown in His own Letters.* 2 vols. New York: Charles Scribner's Sons, 1920.

Letters from Theodore Roosevelt to Anna Roosevelt Cowles, 1870-1918. New York: Charles Scribner's Sons, 1924.

IRWIN, WILL (ed.). *Letters to Kermit from Theodore Roosevelt.* New York: and London: Charles Scribner's Sons, 1946.

Selections from the Correspondence of Theodore Roosevelt and Henry Cabot Lodge, 1884-1918. 2 vols. New York and London: Charles Scribner's Sons, 1925.

ROBINSON, CORINNE ROOSEVELT. *My Brother Theodore Roosevelt.* New York: Charles Scribner's Sons, 1921.

THAYER, WILLIAM ROSCOE. *The Life and Letters of John Hay.* 2 vols. Boston and New York: Houghton Mifflin Co., 1915.

BIOGRAPHICAL:

ABBOTT, LAWRENCE F. *The Letters of Archie Butt, Personal Aide to President Roosevelt.* Garden City: Doubleday, Page and Co., 1924.

BUTT, ARCHIE. *Taft and Roosevelt; The Intimate Letters of Archie Butt, Military Aide.* 2 vols. Garden City: Doubleday, Doran and Co., 1930.

DAVIS, OSCAR KING. *Released for Publication—Some Inside Political History of Theodore Roosevelt and His Times.* Boston and New York: Houghton Mifflin Co., 1925.

HAGEDORN, HERMANN. *The Bugle That Woke America—the Saga of Theodore Roosevelt's Last Battle for His Country.* New York: John Day Co., 1940.

———. *Roosevelt in the Bad Lands.* Boston and New York: Houghton Mifflin Co., 1921.

———. *The Roosevelt Family of Sagamore Hill.* New York: The Macmillan Co., 1954.

LONGWORTH, ALICE ROOSEVELT. *Crowded Hours.* New York and London: Charles Scribner's Sons, 1935.

PRINGLE, HENRY F. *Theodore Roosevelt.* New York: Harcourt, Brace and Co., 1931.

RIIS, JACOB. *Theodore Roosevelt the Citizen.* New York: Outlook Co., 1904.

THAYER, WILLIAM ROSCOE. *Theodore Roosevelt.* Boston and New York: Houghton Mifflin Co., 1919.

WISTER, OWEN. *Roosevelt—The Story of a Friendship.* New York: The Macmillan Co., 1930.

WOOD, FREDERICK S. *Roosevelt As We Knew Him—the Personal Recollections of One Hundred Fifty of His Friends and Associates.* Philadelphia and New York: John C. Winston Co., 1927.

UNPUBLISHED THESES:

BEHL, WILLIAM A. "The Speaking and Speeches of Theodore Roosevelt," Ph.D. dissertation, Northwestern University, 1942.

CAIRNS, PAUL. "Theodore Roosevelt, the Speaker," M.A. thesis, University of Michigan, 1941.

CHERNEY, SHELDON. "An Analysis of the Modes of Persuasion in Theodore Roosevelt's Speeches Concerning Corporate Wealth, 1902-1904," M.A. thesis, Wayne University, 1951.

PROSS, EDWARD L. "A Critical Analysis of Four Representative Speeches of Theodore Roosevelt, the Progressive," M.A. thesis, State University of Iowa, 1940.

WINKS, GORDON W. "A Study of Theodore Roosevelt's Use of Invective in His Public Speeches," M.A. thesis, Northwestern University, 1933.

GENERAL REFERENCES:

BEHL, WILLIAM A. "Theodore Roosevelt's Principles of Invention," *Speech Monographs,* XIV (1947), 93-110.

Theodore Roosevelt

BEHL, WILLIAM A. "Theodore Roosevelt's Principles of Speech Preparation and Delivery," *Speech Monographs* XII (1945), 112-22.

Democratic National Committee. *Democratic Campaign Book.* 1900; 1904; 1912.

KOHLSAAT, H. H. *From McKinley to Harding.* New York and London: Charles Scribner's Sons, 1923.

MOWRY, GEORGE E. *Theodore Roosevelt and the Progressive Movement.* Madison: University of Wisconsin Press, 1946.

NYE, RUSSEL B. *Midwestern Progressive Politics.* East Lansing: Michigan State College Press, 1951.

Republican National Committee. *Official Proceedings of the Republican Conventions.* 1900; 1904; 1912.

———. *Republican Campaign Text-Book.* 1884; 1900; 1904; 1912.

REGIER, C. C. *The Era of the Muckrakers.* Chapel Hill: University of North Carolina Press, 1932.

SULLIVAN, MARK. *Our Times.* 6 vols. New York and London: Charles Scribner's Sons, 1926-35.

STEFFENS, LINCOLN. *The Autobiography of Lincoln Steffens.* New York: Harcourt, Brace and Co., 1931.

TWEEDY, JOHN. *A History of the Republican National Conventions from 1856-1908.* Danbury, Conn.: Tweedy, 1910.

Films and Recordings

Theodore Roosevelt House has a series of films which are available for loan. "T. R. Himself" (400 feet) shows Roosevelt in various speaking situations.

There are at least ten recordings of Roosevelt's speaking. In print is a selection of a speech made to the Boys' Progressive League in 1913, part of "Voices of Freedom" (long playing 33 1/3 r.p.m. disc and on tape at 3¾ in. and 7½ in. speeds) issued by Educational Services, 1702 K Street, N.W., Washington 6, D.C.

Edison recordings, made in 1912, are: "The Right of the People to Rule," 3707; "The Farmer and Business Man," 3708; "Social and Industrial Justice," 3709; "Progressive Covenant with the People," 3710?.

Victor recordings, made in 1912, are: "The Liberty of the People," 31872; "Mr. Roosevelt Pays His Respects to Penrose and Archbold," 35249-A; "The 'Abyssinian Treatment' of Standard Oil," 35249-B; "Why the Trusts and Bosses Oppose the Progressive Party," 35250-A; "The Farmer and the Business Man," 35250-B. "The Liberty of the People," originally an acoustical recording was reissued as an electrical recording in 1940, Victor Album PS-1, *Cavalcade of United States Presidents.*

Papers, Manuscripts, Documents, Repositories

The bulk of the Roosevelt papers are in the Library of Congress. The series of "Addresses Scrapbooks" includes revisions of speeches and stenographic reports of speeches not fully reported. There is a catalogue of speeches (not complete).

Theodore Roosevelt House, 28 East 20th Street, New York, N. Y., has papers, films, recordings, and many curios. In the twenties the Theodore Roosevelt Collection was assembled here, in an attempt to get everything that had been written by Roosevelt and about him and his contemporaries. In 1943, the collection was moved to Harvard College, with Miss Nora E. Cordingley in charge.

The Harvard College Theodore Roosevelt Collection includes many original papers, and photostats and microfilms of important holdings in the Library of Congress and

363

other libraries. There are 150 scrapbooks of newspaper clippings Roosevelt had collected. The Public Catalogue of the Collection, under "Addresses, messages, etc.," has a listing of speeches available. Originally compiled by R. W. G. Vail at Theodore Roosevelt House, this is the most nearly complete bibliography of Roosevelt's speeches.

The Roosevelt Cabin, maintained by the State Historical Society of North Dakota, on the Capitol Grounds at Bismarck, contains books and mementos but no manuscripts.

The American Museum of Natural History, New York, N. Y., has a permanent exhibit of papers, photographs, curios, and mementos, in Roosevelt Memorial Hall. The exhibit was opened in 1953.

Sagamore Hill, Oyster Bay, N. Y., Roosevelt's home, was opened to the public in 1953. It is virtually as he left it at death, and contains his books, souvenirs, mementos, and authentic atmosphere of his time. It is maintained by the Theodore Roosevelt Association.

William E. Borah

by A. E. WHITEHEAD

William E. Borah was born on June 29, 1865, in Jasper Township, Fairfield, Illinois. After a somewhat interrupted education in public school, in a Cumberland Presbyterian academy at Enfield, Illinois, and at the University of Kansas, where he enrolled as a freshman on September 11, 1885, he was admitted to the bar in 1889. In the fall of 1890, he moved to Boise, Idaho, where he set up a law practice. By 1892, he became active in politics and was chosen chairman of the State Central Committee by the Republicans. He first attracted national attention in 1899, with his summation for the people in the Coeur d'Alene mining riots. He was elected to the United States Senate in 1907. The following year, on April 20, he gave his first major Senate speech in connection with the Brownsville, Texas, case. His service to the nation as United States senator was continuous—and, to say the least, conspicuous—for the rest of his life. Sometimes alone, sometimes as the spearhead of the opposition, he stood out against many of the major issues that concerned Congress during his years in the Senate. Many times he denounced the World Court and he strongly opposed the entrance of the United States into the League of Nations. He was largely instrumental in bringing about the World Disarmament Conference of 1920-21. In 1922, he became chairman of the Senate Committee on Education and Labor. Two years later, he was made chairman of the Senate Committee on Foreign Relations, an office he held until 1933. His last, and seventh, election to the Senate was in 1936. He gave his last major Senate address in defense of the arms embargo, on October 2, 1939. He died in office on January 11, 1940.

The Making of an Independent Republican

William E. Borah was frequently called the great American enigma. He was called the maverick and bad boy of the Republican party. He was called the most self-contradictory man in American politics. He was called the Republican who never kept step with his party and never left the ranks. He was called an individualist, a dreamer, an isolationist, a prima donna, a false alarm, a blue pencil, a rogue elephant, an obstructionist, an implacable, an irreconcilable, a lone wolf, a negationist, a daily challenge, a Progressive, a third-party man, and a trimmer. He had, it was said, too great a liking for the sound of his own voice and for the sight of his own name in newspaper headlines. He

365

did not, some said, achieve his potentialities. Some groups in American life turned to him, they felt, only to be disillusioned. It was charged that he would embark upon a course only too often to draw back just before the final step. Various reasons were offered in explanation: he was so individualistic he could not cooperate; he was erratic; he had lost his power to fight to the end; he was incapable of sustained loyalty; he did not have a well-thought-out program.

Borah was the man who opposed a woman suffrage amendment and advocated a prohibition amendment both on the grounds of States' rights. He was the man who was against all bonus legislation until 1934 but supported the plan of direct federal grants for the relief of the unemployed. He was the man who was against child labor but opposed a child labor amendment. The liberals liked his labor legislation but were disappointed with his opposition to the woman suffrage and child labor amendments. The States' rights men applauded his opposition to these amendments but were not pleased when he voted for the Eighteenth Amendment. The drys were displeased when he fought the search-and-seizure provisions of the Volstead Act. Those who cheered his stand in opposing the League of Nations disapproved his recognition of Russia.

Borah stated in June, 1938:

I am not one of those who think we are going to get into war. Whatever may be our sympathies, we are not going to back them up with force. We ought to have our own foreign policy and realize once and for all that there are no friendships in international affairs.[1]

By January of 1940, Borah, the voice of protest in American politics for twenty years, was dead, and the European struggle that he believed would be over by spring was just beginning.

Borah's early background offers some clue to the understanding of this baffling and contradictory man. His only biographer, C. O. Johnson, observes:

It is not possible to estimate the influence of this background. . . . All agree that it was tremendous. A few might say we need go no further to understand Borah. At any rate, some of his characteristics and attitudes seem very definitely to have their roots in that background.[2]

As a youth, he was impressed with the gentleness and kindness of his mother, traits that he displayed in personal relationships. His father was stern and austere; he expected and received obedience. Between him and his son, however, existed a bond of mutual respect and confidence. Although disci-

---

[1] *Portland Oregonian,* June 10, 1938.
[2] C. O. Johnson, *Borah* (New York: Longmans, Green & Co., 1936), p. 490.

plined in an exacting manner, Borah admitted that there was justice and reasonableness in his father's demands upon his children.

Possibly the most important influence exerted by Borah's father was religious. He was a leader in the Presbyterian church and a constant reader of the Bible. Borah did not accept his father's fundamentalist view, but he was impressed by his father's charity and tolerance, and they seemingly served as a basis for his philosophy in such matters as race prejudice, persecution of war prisoners, and religious intolerance. To an Idaho friend, Borah wrote:

I am a believer in the fundamental principles of religious liberty. It was instilled into me by my father's earliest teachings. . . . If the time ever comes when I shall have to sacrifice my office for these principles, I shall unhesitatingly do so.

Borah's concern for and his advocacy of those in the lower economic strata, his advocacy of free speech for minority groups, his advocacy of justice and tolerance for Soviet Russia and Mexico, and his advocacy of the plain people in the League of Nations and the World Court disputes may well be attributed to the moral teachings of his father. Although Borah did not practice law after his election to the Senate in 1907, one may truthfully say that he continued to be a lawyer. His clients were the people. He was proud to be the champion of the inarticulate masses.

Besides influencing his son in an ethical and moral way, the father personally encouraged his education. Looking back on his childhood, Borah remarked:

My father was a student of politics. . . . He often discussed public affairs with me, and I perceived that the mistakes of the great men of the Civil War period came from their blind partisanship.[3]

An important factor in Borah's development as a speaker was his prolific reading begun as a youth and continued throughout life. While his law practice was expanding, he studied history, government, and law. He read the speeches of Cicero, Demosthenes, Sheridan, Fox, Pitt, Burke, Lincoln, Douglas, and Phillips.

In addition to this reading, he still had time for novels and poetry. In commenting on his reading, he said:

At the risk of being called an old fogy, I still follow Carlyle's example and each time a new book is published I read an old one. And right now I may as well confess that I am vitally interested in novels. . . . When I tell you that one of my favorite novelists is Hawthorne you will see that I do not shrink from morbidity. . . . My other favorite novelist is Balzac. I like Dickens and Thackeray. . . . Balzac's characters are real. I feel their humanity rather than their nationality.

[3] J. Mitchell, "Borah Knows Best," *New Republic*, XXCV (January 29, 1936), 333-34.

The three poets whom I most admire and whose works I read and re-read so often that I can quote pages from them are Shakespeare, Milton, and Dante. . . .

As for Emerson, nobody knows the amount of inspirational comfort that I have received from his essays. Many a night after a terribly trying day in the Senate when everything has seemed to go wrong, when I have doubted even my own convictions, I have taken up a copy of Emerson and turned to his essay on self-reliance. It has put new life into me . . . and often when I have been on the point of giving up, that work has kept me sticking to my guns.[4]

In a revealing radio interview with Norman Hapgood and Sherman Mittell over NBC, Borah reiterated that books had played an important part in his life and added that the keenest observation that Emerson had ever made, one that he had often been tempted to quote to his colleagues on the floor of the Senate when he felt they were stubbornly refusing to be convinced, was this:

"Beware when the great God lets loose a thinker on this planet. Then all things are at risk. It is as when a conflagration has broken out in a great city, and no man knows what is safe, or where it will end. There is not a piece of science but its flank may be turned tomorrow. The very hopes of man, the thoughts of his heart, the religion of nations, the manners and morals of mankind, are all at the mercy of a new generalization. Generalization is always a new influx of the divinity into the mind. Hence, the thrill that attends it." [5]

In this same interview, he stated that he always had a volume of Burke close at hand because Burke could be read for information, pleasure, and style. He was "fond of Bagehot" and was particularly impressed by his description of a constitutional statesman as "one who most felicitously expresses the creed of the moment, who administers it, who embodies it in laws and institutions, who gives it the highest life it is capable of, and who induces the average man to think, 'I could not have done it any better if I had had time myself!' "

Borah believed that anyone taking part in American public affairs ought to make himself familiar with the writings of Hamilton, Jefferson, Madison, Washington, and others who determined the nature of the Constitution. These men he quoted with ease.

This independent and individualistic man who became the spokesman for political isolationism was born in Lincoln's state. The Borah family shared the common feeling of many who tended toward deifying both Lincoln and Washington. Washington's injunctions against interweaving our destiny with that of any part of Europe became Borah's thesis in his anti-League of Nations

---

[4] *Boise* (Idaho) *Capital News*, January 25, 1936.
[5] Radio Broadcast, *An American Fireside*, NBC, January 13, 1935.

speech given in the Senate on February 21, 1919. He referred to Washington as a man with "as wide a vision and...as far-seeing a vision as ever accompanied a human mind upon this mundane sphere." And again, "the work of Washington is still the most potent influence for the advancement of civilization and the freedom of the race."

Finally, Borah's early training in the frontier civilization of Idaho became an important factor in determining his political philosophy. Borah represented the independence of a pioneer region in which individualism was a dominant culture-pattern. His attitude toward world affairs was linked with the mental aloofness of a state which nurtured his independence. The essence of Borah was self-sufficiency and independence, and he never went through the transition of a desire to conform.

When Borah opened his law office in 1890 in the frontier village of Boise, law, as law, had little authority. Such frontier settlements had but recently been unincorporated territories. They had been "lawless," in the sense that they had no organized law. They had dealt justice in their own way. In such communities the lawyer had to be able to make the frontiersmen see the reason for the law. Mark Sullivan in commenting on the frontier discipline stated:

> The late Senator Walsh of Montana once told me with humor that took all egotism from his words that the three best constitutional lawyers in the United States were himself, Justice Sutherland, and Senator Borah. He said the reason they were the best lay in the scenes of their early practice. All three began in little Rocky Mountain towns.[6]

These, then, are the main factors which influenced the "inscrutable" Borah: the ethical and moral influence of his father; the influence of a home where reverence for Washington, Lincoln, and the Union was great; an early love of good reading; and the maturity of self-reliance developed on the democratic frontier.

The Voice of Protest

Borah's principal function in the Senate was that of exercising the power of protest and veto. In his exercise of this function, he believed himself to be more constructive than destructive. He believed that his vote opposing the League of Nations was the most important he ever cast. Borah testified that it was his role of opposer of which he was most proud:

> My critics say that I have no program, that I am not constructive. They say that I have been a man without a party. I should not be blamed for not doing what

[6] *Star* (Washington, D. C.), April 5, 1936.

only a man with a party, or something tantamount, behind him might do. I have had no organization through which to put forward a program of affirmation, no machine with which to construct. Nevertheless, I will say this about my record: the votes which I am proudest of were "no" votes. If as a Senator I have rendered any service that is of merit, the best of that service has been in opposition. My highest claim for credit is for what I may have helped to prevent.[7]

Again, in 1936, he observed:

I have been in an extreme minority ever since I came to the Senate. It is difficult for a minority to be constructive—the best it can do, usually, is to take advantage of situations as they arise. In spite of this, I have been able to help with work which I think unquestionably constructive: the eight-hour day, the creation of the Department of Labor, the creation of the Children's Bureau, the election of senators by popular vote, the outlawry of war.[8]

On his seventieth birthday, Borah said that the biggest thrill of his twenty-eight years in the Senate was the deathblow to American participation in the League of Nations. This vote was part of the dramatic rejection of the Versailles Treaty with its mandatory League membership. Borah stated in June, 1935, "The defeat of the Treaty and the League climaxed the tensest day I've ever spent in the Senate."

In the struggle with President Wilson over the League, Borah was one of the leaders of the "Irreconcilables." He played as important a part as anyone in keeping the United States out of the League. Borah demonstrated that there was enough public feeling against the League to justify and make possible congressional opposition to it.

In his first major speech against the League on February 21, 1919, he maintained that the League represented a radical departure from policies which had prevailed since the government was established. It was clear to Borah that if the United States was to join the League, a change in the Constitution of the United States would be necessary. Consequently, the proposal of United States' adherence to the League should be submitted to the people and the Constitution amended in the proper manner.

Borah contended that European wars had always spread and that Washington set about to separate the European system from the American system in order to divorce America from European quarrels. The Monroe Doctrine was designed to support the policy of Washington. These two policies were mutually dependent. The great question now was whether those doctrines were to be maintained. Would America enter Europe permanently and invite Europe with her systems of government to come to America? In

[7] *New York Times*, February 13, 1927.
[8] *Boise Capital News*, January 28, 1936.

Borah's view, the League would abrogate the policy of both Washington and Monroe.

Article X of the League Constitution read: "The high contracting parties shall undertake to respect and preserve as against external aggression the territorial existence and existing political independence of all states members of the League." Borah interpreted this to mean that the United States would have to protect the territorial integrity of the British Empire. The constitution of the League was the "greatest triumph for English diplomacy in three centuries."

Finally, the League was a step toward internationalism and a start toward sterilizing nationalism, the nationalism of Washington and Lincoln. Internationalism would mean the loss of Americanism as exemplified by Theodore Roosevelt, a "free, untrammeled nation, imbued anew and inspired with the national spirit...the unentangled freedom of a great nation to determine for itself where duty lies...."

Borah launched another argument in March, 1919. The League to Enforce Peace had been organized in 1918; Borah felt that it rested upon the principle of force. It was likely that this principle would be incorporated into the League of Nations and, if it were, not only would the United States have conscription in time of war but in time of peace.

Any scheme to establish peace by force Borah regarded as more destructive to human justice and liberty than Prussianism. Since the whole scheme appeared to him to tend toward military force and toward one ultimate power, he felt the United States would be yielding the principles of American government to two evil forces from the Old World—Prussianism and internationalism.

The Versailles Treaty which contained the Covenant of the League was officially given to the Senate on July 10, 1919. Borah studied the treaty and pronounced it iniquitous. He expressed the hope that President Wilson accepted the treaty only because the League was attached. He did not see how the President could have been induced to accept a treaty "so at variance with every principle he had advocated and all things for which he had stood" unless he thought the League would eventually humanize the treaty's terms.

One of the reasons Borah loathed the Versailles Treaty was the manner in which it had been negotiated. He had always contended against secret treaty-making, and he believed that secret diplomacy led an ignorant public to war. Secrecy should never reach the point where the policy of a nation would be determined before a full, open discussion.

On November 19, 1919, Borah gave an address that caused Henry Cabot Lodge to say, "When I find myself with tears in my eyes I know I am hearing a great speech." And Vice-President Marshall observed, "May a mummy say that you almost galvanized him to life." Borah contended that there could be no compromise; his objections to the League had not been met by Wilson's fourteen reservations. If the United States had any honor, she would be completely bound to the League even with reservations. With or without reservations the United States surrendered the policy of freedom from entangling alliances. Once having entered European affairs, Europe would enter the affairs of the United States.

The Senate was divided into three groups on the issue: first, the Borah and Johnson group who wanted no treaty regardless of amendments and reservations; second, a group led by Senator Lodge who wanted important reservations attached; and third, the group led by Senators Kellogg and Walsh who were satisfied with mild reservations. The treaty came up for a final vote on March 19, 1920, and the original reservations were practically the same as they had been on November 19, 1919. The treaty was defeated by a margin of seven votes; 49 voted for it and 35 against it.

During the League debates Borah lost patience with Republican leaders for their failure to seize upon the League as an important issue. In response to a query as to whether he was taking a big risk in differing with his party on public questions, the Senator made a reply that explains in part why he was able to follow his honest convictions and still be returned to the Senate term after term:

A man who has political ambitions or whose success is inseparably bound up with politics thinks of how his words or acts will affect his future chances. But I have the fortune to come from a part of the country which, so far as the liability of infection by certain political germs is concerned is generally regarded as immune, and there is no great risk in speaking out when one is immune.[9]

Borah was attacked for clinging too firmly to tradition, for ancestor worship, for political antiquarianism, for setting up straw men, and for offering nothing constructive. He was never criticized, however, for lack of sincerity. Even President Wilson realized that Borah was absolutely honest in his opposition to the League, and said that he had high regard for Borah's integrity.

The League was Borah's supreme abomination because of his ardent nationalism. This nationalism was not jingoistic but rather was based upon his reverence for the "Founding Fathers" and upon his belief in American democracy and freedom. For Borah, nationalism was devotion to country, the "noblest passion outside of those which spring from man's relation to his God."

Inevitably, Borah opposed adherence to the World Court. He maintained he recognized the worth of an international judicial tribunal and that

[9] *Boise Statesman*, November 23, 1922.

he would like to be helpful in its creation. But he was interested in it only as an institution for peace. If an international court of justice could be built on a thorough plan; if it could be given independent judicial power; if it could be divorced from the control of international politics and instead made a strong voice of law and order in international affairs, Borah believed it could command respect. Because the World Court which President Harding proposed to join did not meet these requirements in Borah's opinion, he opposed participation.

His first objection was that while the Court was designed to administer international law, this law had never been organized or codified. To endow it with the attributes of a court without a body of laws to govern its action, to define its jurisdiction and circumscribe its powers was to create an "intolerable and despotic institution." Because international law was confused and unclassified the Court would be trying to administer justice without any established basis for its decisions, and Borah thought this just as bizarre as establishing a Supreme Court in the United States and not writing a constitution.

Borah believed that by joining the Court the United States joined the League. He argued that the members of the Court were elected by the League; that the vacancies in the Court were filled by the League; that the Court had no existence and could have no existence except upon the initiative of the League; that the Court was paid by the League; that the League called upon it for counsel and the Court was bound to give that counsel; that all expenses connected with the Court were paid by the League; that the Court was open only to members of the League and no nation could use the Court without the authority of the League; and that the League fixed the conditions on which the Court was open to other states. Consequently, when the League broke down, the Court broke down.

Two articles submitted by the League displeased Borah: (1) "The jurisdiction of the Court compromises all cases which the parties refer to it and all matters specially provided for in treaties and conventions in force"; and (2) "The decision of the Court has no binding force except by the parties and in respect to that particular case."

Borah could interpret the articles to mean only that the Court was reduced to the level of a mere court of arbitration, a tribunal with no jurisdiction except that conferred on it by consent of the parties involved and with no power to establish precedents. Its decisions would have no binding force except regarding the particular case at hand. The League, by denying the Court compulsory jurisdiction, had made the Court "nothing more than the plaything of the foreign offices of different governments." There was a "lurid element" of despotism in the power of the Court to ignore international law, precedents, and treaties.

Another contention was that the Court's decisions would have to be carried out through force. Force was still the "law" among European powers. The sanctions of the League and the Court were the same: both might use navies and armies to enforce decisions. Rather, the power of public opinion, as in the instance of the Supreme Court, should be the enforcing agency. In Borah's opinion force used against a nation would practically constitute a declaration of war.

Borah's position was attacked by many individuals and groups. For example, John Greer Hibben, president of Princeton University, urged him to discontinue his opposition. In a letter to him, Borah rationalized his position:

I belong to a small group of irreconcilables who voted a 7,000,000 majority strong to stay out of the League in 1920 and repeated the instructions in 1924. I myself have been elected twice by a very satisfactory majority on a pledge to do everything within my power to keep this country out of the League. The party of which I am a member is pledged to that policy. It seems clear to me, therefore, that those who voted against our joining the League have a right to expect that we shall not go into the League through a Court. That would be sheer trickery and a betrayal of the confidence of the pledge to the great majority of the American people. There seems to me only one honorable thing for me to do and that is to keep this country out of the League. . . .

From 1923 to 1935, Borah reiterated his arguments. In 1935, President Roosevelt asked the Senate to ratify the Court Protocols. The Senate defeated the proposal by a vote of 52 to 36. Borah regarded this action as one of the "most important actions since the conclusion of the World War."

Borah was opposed to relaxing our neutrality in the years preceding World War II. As early as December, 1936, he called for a tightening of the neutrality law which expired the following May. On December 23, 1936, Borah pointed out that the Supreme Court had sustained the principle of a broad discretionary power for the President concerning neutrality. While problems pertaining to general trade could be left to the discretion of the President, Borah asserted that the shipment of arms and the lending of money or credits and travel on ships of belligerents should come under a mandatory principle. The main thing for the United States was to keep free from all political commitments in order to be free as a government to deal with any exigency that arose. In no way should anything be done to indicate partiality.

In March, 1937, Borah opposed the Senator Pittman "cash and carry" provision. He objected to the doctrine of transferred risk. His arguments centered around Section 2 of the Pittman resolution which would provide that in time of war American vessels could not carry commodities embargoed by the President and would prohibit shipping any goods to belligerents except where all right, interest, and title in them had been transferred from American nationals to foreigners. Borah painted a picture of the ports of the United States suffering aerial bombardment from a belligerent even though this country attempted to preserve its neutrality. He objected to the cash-and-carry provision because it would, in effect, make this country the ally of the nation having the greatest navy—Great Britain. The United States, as one of the great powers, might be willing to carry goods on conditions other than those Great Britain would admit.

By November, 1937, he felt that American diplomacy had bungled the Chinese-Japanese conflict. America either should have invoked the Nine-Power Treaty against Japan at the start of the invasion or else have had nothing to do with that instrument of peace. It was a diplomatic error for the United States to have remained silent about the pact until an "impotent League of Nations" invoked it and then to have followed this "internationally anonymous leadership." He was aroused, too, by the action of the State Department in indorsing the League's denunciation of Japan as the aggressor in China and as a violator of both the Nine-Power Treaty and Kellogg-Briand anti-war treaty. This policy placed the United States in the position of being afraid to speak for itself while resorting merely to being a "me too" recipient of information of the League's activities.

Borah believed that all hope of the ability of the Brussels Conference to restore peace in the Far East was lost when the United States first denounced Japan as an aggressor and treaty violator before joining in the League's invitation to the Japanese to attend a peace conference. This American diplomacy may have cost the American people the friendship of Japan while booming British prestige in the Far East. He believed that British diplomats had maneuvered the United States into taking the initiative against Japan in an effort to halt the Chinese-Japanese conflict while Great Britain remained in the background. The statement of British Foreign Secretary Anthony Eden placing the initiative on the United States for holding the Nine-Power Conference in Brussels and asserting England would only follow the pace set by America, Borah interpreted as a sign on Great Britain's part to inform Japan that she would do nothing to halt her invasion of China unless forced to do so by the United States.

His first major speech on American policy was a radio address over NBC on March 28, 1938. The Versailles Treaty which "affronted every principle of justice and challenged the deepest passion of the human heart, that of nationality," had brought Europe to a state of bitter unrest.

Borah repudiated the idea that nations were drawn together because of similar philosophies of government. The theory that a democracy could be saved through an alliance with another democracy was misleading; such an alliance would only bring dangers. A nation acted from the law of self-interest as Great Britain did when it took its stand with the arbitrary governments during the invasion of China in violation of the Pact of Paris and the Covenant of the League. Imperative tasks were closer home. The danger to democracy lay in the army of unemployed, in the five million boys and girls who left school unable to find a reward for their talents, in the fifty million people living on the margin of poverty.

Even cooperation did not seem feasible. There were those who would have had the United States cooperate with Great Britain when she seemed ready to engage in war with Japan, but what would a policy of cooperation be if Britain again recognized Japan's authority over North China and became her ally? If the United States cooperated with France against Germany, would she cooperate with France's ally, Russia? Cooperation would plunge the United States into a maelstrom where a "few men play with human lives as pawns."

Throughout the summer of 1938, Borah kept hammering at his themes emphasizing that whatever European nations saw fit to do in their efforts to secure peace was a matter upon which they alone would have to pass judgment, for the people of the United States were not interested in European boundary disputes. When Leon Blum proposed American intervention to establish peace in Europe, Borah said:

> What such suggestion really means is that the United States furnish the money and men which may be necessary in case of war. It would have been more in harmony with that national honor so often exemplified in French history had Mr. Blum given his attention to the fact that France has a solemn treaty with Czechoslovakia to come to her rescue and instead of advising the United States as to her duty had advised his own people to stand by their treaty.[10]

When the Munich agreement became known, Borah felt that his arguments had been reinforced and that his opinion that wars were started by a handful of men in the chancelleries of Europe had been validated. "The Munich pact," he said, "makes the violation of treaties a cardinal tenet of modern diplomacy. The Munich pact makes the mere name of 'treaty' a byword and a hissing."

Borah's last year as a senator was spent almost exclusively in pleading for a type of neutrality that would keep the United States out of Europe and out of war. As 1939 opened, he said he was opposed to economic sanctions. The United States could not impose them without becoming involved in war; such an action was war. The same rule should be applied to dictators that was applied to all governments. So long as dictators respected the rights

[10] *Washington* (D. C.) *Post*, October 30, 1938.

of the people, the United States could have no quarrel with their form of government. It was what governments did and not what kind they were that should concern the United States.

In February, President Roosevelt presented a plan to expand the Army Air Corps. Borah opposed this on the ground that it was "jitterism." He defended himself, saying: "I have testimony from experts that it is not in the interests of security. Ultimately it would cost billions...and you will have a proposition that would bankrupt the nation."

By March, he stated he would like to vote for a bill which would prohibit the sale directly and indirectly of all instruments of war to any nation engaged in armed conflict. The fact that nations might have the ships to come and get arms should make no difference. He advised no alliances, reliance on the Monroe Doctrine, and the shunning of the power politics of the Old World as the way to avoid war. He blamed Prime Minister Chamberlain for permitting Hitler to reach a position in which Germany could violate the rights of men and nations.

As debate on the neutrality issue dragged, President Roosevelt said that the Senate would have to accept responsibility for failure to act. Borah retorted:

Of course the responsibility must rest on the Senate, Mr. President. We are a co-ordinate branch of the legislative department and we have not yet acted. We are not under Hitler yet and until we are the Senate will continue to fulfill its responsibility.[11]

President Roosevelt countered that if the Senate did not take action on neutrality, he would take the matter to the country and see what the people had to say. Borah replied that the Senate would carry its side to the country, too.

The impasse led to the famous White House Conference of July 19, 1939. Senator Barkley brought Republican leaders to the White House when the President said he wanted a first-hand opinion on the minority's attitude. Borah agreed to attend as a member of the Senate and not as a spokesman for the minority. President Roosevelt and Secretary of State Hull painted a somber scene of war preparations in Europe. Borah observed that he, too, received advice from abroad and that war was not as imminent as they let themselves think. Secretary Hull demurred that Borah's sources were not comparable with the State Department's sources. President Roosevelt got the senators to agree that full responsibility for failure to change the neutrality law now should rest with them and that neutrality would be the first order of business on their calendar during the next session. Borah objected, however, to confining the special session to consideration of the Neutrality Act revisions. He thought Congress should inquire into all developments and policies and

[11] *Congressional Record*, July 6, 1939, 76th Cong., 1st. sess., p. 8675.

that Congress should remain in session until January to meet important questions. He served notice that he would not tolerate any effort to obtain cloture.

Borah's last major speech was given in the Senate on October 2, 1939, in defense of the embargo on arms. He believed that the government had the right, without invasion of the principles of international law, to pass a law providing for an embargo on arms; that there were precedents for such laws; that the leading authorities on international law sustained this principle; that the law met with support from the government and the people when it was passed; that to repeal the law in the present circumstances would be an affirmative act of intervention; that repeal was urged with the purpose of favoring the Allies. He stated:

I look upon the present war in Europe as nothing more than another chapter in the bloody volume of European power politics. . . . Was it anything but power politics when the Premier of Great Britain, holding aloft an agreement of settlement between the Premier of Great Britain and the Premier of Germany, told the people that there was peace, and peace with honor, that the master of Germany could be trusted?

I am not a pacifist. If any nation attacks this nation I am ready again to vote for a declaration of war. . . . I am seeking now to do that which I think will prevent war.[12]

On October 27, the cash-and-carry provisions passed the Senate by a vote of 63-30. Of the three schools of neutrality which sought to control the peace policies, the sanctionist school, led by Mr. Stimson, which aimed to penalize aggressor nations by depriving them of United States credits; the school that adhered to the 1914 international law which gave a neutral certain rights in trading with belligerents; and the isolationist school that believed the United States could best keep out of war by having nothing to do with a nation that became involved in war, Borah, of course, belonged to the isolationist group.

It is difficult to reconcile Borah's isolationism and nationalism with the world after 1920. While Borah gladly confessed his nationalism, he refuted charges of isolationism. He declared that his foreign policy of peace with all nations, trade with all nations, honest friendship with all nations, but political commitments to none was not isolationist. On the contrary, it was freedom of action; it was independence of judgment; it was free government. In all those matters in which a "free and enlightened" people could have a part—trade, finance, and the relief of suffering—Borah denied isolation. But in all political matters which encroached on the free action of the people or which circumscribed their judgment, he wanted isolation. He liked to

[12] *Congressional Record*, October 2, 1939, 76th Cong., 2d sess., p. 6667.

think of himself as a political nationalist and an economic internationalist.

Borah remained an implacable opponent of British diplomacy because he believed Britain's purpose was to involve this country in military alliances for the purpose of preserving her empire. British diplomats from 1812, he said, had sought to destroy Washington's warning against entangling alliances. He sometimes suspected President Roosevelt of favoring an alliance with Great Britain and thought he was deterred only by the pressure of the American people "for minding our own business." Borah believed that Britain supported Hitler in seizing Czechoslovakia because she wanted Hitler dominant in Central Europe. Germany would thus constitute a barrier to the spread of communism. Britain, he asserted, would give Hitler a free hand so long as he made no move that could be interpreted as a threat to the British life line.

Borah died expecting that peace would be restored in Europe in the spring of 1940. Several weeks before his death he declared: "This is no real war. This is only window dressing for a general revision of the Versailles Treaty. It has to come."

There were no considerations of political expediency influencing Borah's position. But his attitude was an incredibly optimistic refusal to look at realities. It did not occur to him that the United States could have been taking sides by following his proposals—Hitler's side. Under any circumstances, it was unnecessary, as Walter Lippmann suggested, to create a false dilemma by inflating the arms-embargo question into the greater question of participation in the war. If history is primarily concerned with what is done rather than what is not done, the "Great Negator" of American politics on the issues of the League, World Court, and neutrality could well be only a footnote.

Minor Protests of an Independent Republican

While Borah's major protests were concerned with foreign policy, he also opposed domestic policies and frequently those policies advocated by his party.

President Coolidge gave his first address to Congress on December 6, 1923. He presented five major proposals, only one of which Borah supported. He agreed with President Coolidge in opposing the bonus, but on support of the World Court, the Mellon plan, restraint toward Russia, and the tariff he disagreed. On December 3, 1924, President Coolidge again addressed the Congress. His main proposals included those of non-intervention with respect to the tariff, support of the World Court, rejection of the farm bloc, and economy. Borah agreed with the economy issue. A year later on December 2, 1925, Coolidge spoke again in favor of the World Court, debt settlement with Belgium and Italy, and disarmament. Borah favored disarmament.

Borah was a leading campaign speaker for Herbert Hoover. He opened the campaign of 1928 with a speech in Detroit on September 20, praising Hoover as an "executive genius" with a broad view and firm grasp of the "essential tenets of humanity." The Minneapolis *Tribune* for October 2, 1928, wrote:

> Before the biggest political gathering in the history of Presidential campaigns in Minneapolis, Borah ignited the tinder and inflamed 25,000 persons into a spontaneous frenzy of enthusiasm as he tore from the tomes of Tammany records of indictment against the Democratic candidate on the issues of prohibition, farm relief, and inland water development.

After Hoover's election, however, Borah felt compelled to disagree with him on such important issues as prohibition, tariff, farm relief, appointments to the Supreme Court, silver and currency expansion, and government economy.

Soldier's Bonus. In opposing the bonus to veterans, Borah stood alone in his indifference to public opinion. His main argument was based on the premise that the country was facing bankruptcy and that the already over-taxed people could not stand the extra strain of a billion dollars in cash bonuses. He said:

> This debt which now rests like a mortgage in process of everlasting foreclosure upon the brain and energy of the human family staggers computation and in its demoralizing and deadening effect beggars description.... I think public debt a curse. It eats the substance of the people, kills initiative, corrupts society, breeds discontent, and often destroys government itself.[13]

Furthermore, the veteran was interested in the welfare of the nation, and his patriotism would guide him to the wise conclusion that the solution for this "Dantean hell of misery" was the restoration of the prosperity of a people. The soldier would resent putting his patriotism on a dollar-and-cents basis. It was an insult to those who had fought for democracy to place them on the "sordid level of money consideration" by offering them a "tip" according to the scale of the journeyman laborer. A more substantial benefit would be a policy of land settlement or educational reconstructive measures that would advance the welfare of the entire country. In solving this problem, Borah believed, as he did on practically every problem, that the intelligence of the masses was being underestimated.

Prohibition. While Borah opposed the repeal of the Eighteenth Amendment because the liquor traffic was a "curse to humanity," the crux of his argument was that since prohibition had been written into the Constitution, violation of the amendment meant violation of that document. He had no

[13] *Congressional Record,* February 17, 1921, 66th Cong., 3d sess., p. 3316.

objection to the orderly repeal of the amendment by the people, but to disregard the Constitution while still refusing to change it was nullification. It was "treason, disloyalty to the first principle of a Federal union, and violation of the oath which every Federal officer takes when he takes office." The federal government should not abandon the interpretation and enforcement of its own Constitution and "through sheer, cowardly, contemptible expediency" leave it to forty-eight states with forty-eight standards to enforce it.

One reason Borah did not support Hoover in 1932 was the Republican plank on prohibition. This plank permitted the voters to pass on a proposed amendment to allow the states to deal with the liquor problem individually with federal protection for dry states. Borah thought it was impossible to discover just where the Republican party stood on the Eighteenth Amendment. It was a "singular document, wholly inadequate and unresponsive to the demands of the people."

Tariff. The Hawley-Smoot tariff measure elicited Borah's opposition. Further increases in industrial rates, in his judgment, were unnecessary. He agreed that the farmers got all they asked in the Fordney-McCumber Tariff Act of 1922, but those persons representing them made the mistake of acquiescing, at the same time, in increases in industrial levies. The disparity between agricultural and industrial interests resulting from that bill would be continued by the Hawley-Smoot measure.

President Hoover sent a special message to the Senate urging the retention of the authority given him in the existing law to increase or decrease a tariff rate by 50 per cent if recommended by the Tariff Commission or to reject the Commission's recommendations.

Borah opposed this flexible tariff provision in a speech on September 26, 1929. The President already enjoyed more power "than any living sovereign." No further power should be given. Again, the consumer did not secure any relief from the flexible tariff provision of 1922; practically no reductions had occurred over a period of seven years. Neither was there any authority in the Constitution for such a transfer of power; or if Congress did want to transfer power, it would first have to get authority from the people.

A farm bloc was formed and led by Borah to defeat Hoover's flexible tariff provision. The coalition was strong enough to place six or seven items on the free list, much to the exasperation of the regular Republicans. Borah was attacked for leading the fight against Hoover. He and his followers were called "sons of wild jack¿..es," "obstructionists," "demagogues," and "insurgents."

Although several hundred economists signed a petition and sent it to President Hoover asking him not to sign the Hawley-Smoot Bill, he did sign it after it had passed the Senate on June 13, 1930, by a vote of 44 to 42. Borah was bitterly disappointed, feeling that the Republican party had broken its pledge to the farmer so far as the establishment of economic equality with industry was concerned.

Borah also opposed the reciprocal tariff proposal of 1934. This was to him another step away from constitutional democracy. It was a delegation to the President of the taxing power entrusted to Congress by the framers of the Constitution. The precedent established by President Roosevelt would be claimed and enlarged on by all his successors; and precedents established by capable hands for desirable purposes were still precedents for incapable hands and undesirable purposes. He admitted that the Supreme Court had held that Congress could delegate the power to make tariff agreements if Congress, at the same time, set up a fixed principle which the President could use as a guide in exercising his authority; but Borah denied that any such guiding principle had been set up. He contended the President had a free hand in working out tariff agreements.

Relief. When the depression began in 1929, Borah started a campaign for relief. In a speech on February 2, 1931, he denounced the Administration forces in the House for opposing the $25,000,000 relief appropriation passed by the Senate. He proclaimed himself willing to help in forcing an extra session by holding up supply bills unless the government agreed to aid the hungry.

One year later on February 10, 1932, Borah and Senator Fess battled for three hours over government aid for the unemployed. Fess attacked the LaFollette-Costigan measure which would allocate $375,000,000 to the states for use in relieving distress. He said that this was the first step toward a dole system.

Borah, "his hair disheveled and face unusually pale," shouted at the Republican chairman that "the flag of any government which will not protect its people is a dirty rag that contaminates the air in which it flies." Indisputable facts had been given the Senate of the need for federal assistance. The precedent for such help was established by the Reconstruction Finance Corporation Bill taking $500,000,000 out of the Treasury to save frozen banks and railroads. It had been demonstrated that local communities were not providing adequate relief. Federal aid bore no resemblance to a dole, but even if it were a dole it would be no different from the funds being paid out by the states of Pennsylvania and Illinois for direct relief. The bill, however, was defeated, 48 to 35.

National Recovery Act. Borah declared that the National Recovery Act was a first step toward complete repeal of the antitrust laws and a step toward the ultimate concentration of wealth. Trusts, combines, conspiracies, and restraint of trade prevailed "not only without restraint but rather under the shelter of the government." Furthermore, the NRA was destroying local and state rights and creating a vast federal bureaucracy that could easily be turned to dictatorial ends. It was a "planless revolution," a mass of hastily conceived recovery expediencies.

In May of 1935, Borah advised his constituents to ignore NRA codes and conduct their intrastate business in their own way, to disregard fees and fines, and to advise him if the government attempted to interfere.

He advocated a five-point program against the NRA: (1) appeal to the entire nation's interests to come forward fearlessly with complaints of injustices in NRA codes; (2) make clear to the nation that the onslaught on NRA was not directed against the President and that he had the full support of the Progressives in his general recovery program; (3) continue to demand that the small-businessman be enabled to lodge complaints against oppressive monopolies with some punitive government agency entirely outside the influence of NRA; (4) concentrate attack against NRA administration but refuse to enter into an epithet-throwing contest with General Hugh Johnson; and (5) fully restore the antitrust laws.

When the Supreme Court killed the NRA, Borah said, "The Constitution has been re-established." The Court's decision affirmed three of his beliefs. First, the theory was false that when an emergency existed, principles of constitutional government could be abandoned. Second, Congress alone could make laws for the people, and it could not surrender this power to the Executive. Third, Congress could not regulate the internal affairs of the states.

Borah venerated the Constitution, but he could still make this observation:

I do not wish to be understood as contending that the Constitution is a sacred document never to undergo amendment. Neither do I wish it to be inferred that the decisions of the Supreme Court are above the criticism of the people.

But I do wish to be understood as contending that the great underlying principles of the American Constitution are indispensable to a republican form of government, that to strike at those principles is to strike at the life of a representative democracy.[14]

Agricultural Adjustment Act. Borah opposed the program of the Agricultural Adjustment Act. In theory, he believed the act was wrong. Instead of pursuing a defeatist policy of production curtailment, the United States should be expanding foreign markets, rehabilitating monetary and banking systems, and restoring the antitrust laws. The United States could restore purchasing power in the Orient by the remonetization of silver and at home by attacking those monopolies that fixed prices. But, as it was, the philosophy of crop reduction was "driving the country to national suicide."

[14] W. E. Borah, "Supreme Court Decision," *Vital Speeches of the Day*, VI, (June 17, 1935), 587.

Anti-Lynching Bill. In April, 1935, Borah was asked to take the chairmanship of a sub-committee which was to pass on the constitutionality of the Costigan-Wagner Anti-Lynching Bill. Even though the committee thought the bill was unconstitutional, it was reported out for discussion.

On May 1, Borah addressed the Senate in opposition to the anti-lynching measure. He was convinced that it was an unsound policy to remove responsibility from the local governments in the matter of law enforcement. Eventually this would result in breaking down all sense of duty on the part of the citizen.

There was a perfect precedent for the Costigan-Wagner Bill in the NRA and the AAA. If the government could go into Idaho and direct business and agriculture, it could go into Alabama and make the sheriff abide by the rules Congress laid down. States' rights would be annihilated. The anti-lynching measure was in conflict with the most fundamental principles upon which the republic rested since it violated the spirit and purpose of the dual system of government.

The bill was a sectional one, an attempt on the part of the North to "sit in harsh judgment" upon its sister states. The Southern states had met the race problem with patience, tolerance, and success, and it was not in the interest of national unity to "stir old embers, to arouse old fears, to lacerate old wounds, to again brand the Southern people as incapable to deal with the question of human life."

Supreme Court. When President Roosevelt suggested in the early part of 1937 that the United States Supreme Court be enlarged by one new appointee for every justice who declined to retire on full pay after his seventieth birthday, he suggested a change that was contrary to one of Borah's basic political tenets. Borah rose at once to defend the unfettered function of the Supreme Court to interpret the Constitution. While the decisions of the Court were not above criticism, while it was not "a divine institution," nevertheless, Borah contended, without the power of the Court to declare acts of Congress, in contravention to the Constitution, void, the Constitution as the supreme law would disappear and the United States would pass from a constitutional government to a dictatorial one. The Court was not always exempt from the influence of politics, but "it is the most nearly perfect human institution yet devised by the wit of man for the dispensation of justice and the preservation of liberty."

Borah contended that the Court was not blind to economic developments. However unwise economically an act might be that was passed by Congress, if there was authority for it in the Constitution, the Court would uphold it; and if there were no authority, regardless of how wise the law, the Court would reject it.

Admittedly, the decisions of the Court had frequently been a blow to centralized government, but that was because the Constitution did not provide for a centralized government; it did provide for the protection of States' rights. If a greater authority was desired in the solution of economic problems or if States' rights were to be eliminated, the people would have to decide through the power of amendment. Because the adoption of amendments to the Constitution was the "most vital exertion of political power in which a people can engage," Borah urged deliberation; however, he believed the people should not be afraid to consider amendments. The amendment process might be slow, but it was not too slow. There could hardly be too much debate on the matter of amendments to the Constitution.

The framers of the Constitution took care to create an independent judiciary because they were mindful of the lessons of history and the long struggle for unpurchasable judges. One did not need to go beyond his own history to find that the executive and Congress had at times disregarded practically every guarantee in the Bill of Rights.

Borah raised the question whether modern conditions made imperative greater federal control over the internal affairs of the states. That the Court had felt compelled to hold that Congress had at times transgressed the plain terms of the Constitution was no surprise to those who still believed in the dual system of government. Regarding the NRA, the decision of the Court was unanimous. Borah said he would be a bold liberal who would declare that Justice Brandeis was not a liberal. "I take the liberty," Borah stated, "of mentioning him because of the general charge that the Court while honest and capable is suffering from a case of arrested development and plagued with the views of ancient days."

On February 24, 1937, Borah offered a resolution as a compromise measure to effect some of the aims of the judiciary reorganization proposal. His compromise was directed at the Fourteenth Amendment. He wanted to redraft this amendment in order to give to the states full power to treat their social and economic problems within each state. In effect, the provision would prevent the Supreme Court from invalidating state laws under the due-process clause of the Fourteenth Amendment. The application of the due-process clause under which much state legislation had been declared unconstitutional would have been limited. Borah's amendment provided that "due process of law as herein used shall have reference only to the procedure of executive, administrative, or judicial bodies charged with the execution and enforcement of the law."

Presidential Appointments. Borah opposed President Harding's appointment of Charles Evans Hughes to the post of Secretary of State; he wanted Senator Knox. He objected to the appointment of William Howard Taft as Chief Justice because he believed Taft had been too intimately connected with politics. He led the attack on the confirmation of Charles B. Warren to be Attorney General because of Warren's business connections and his speculations. He led the fight against the seating of Truman H. Newberry of Michigan who had been elected to the Senate after spending over $200,000 for the seat. "Newberryism" demonstrated that a coterie of wealthy men could combine to control an election by use of money. He was active in trying to secure the removal of Attorney General Daugherty after the Teapot Dome oil scandal. He thought it reprehensible for the Republican party to cover up any corruption. Hushing exposés, closing one's eyes to the demands of privilege, and apologizing for class legislation which happened within one's own party did not represent true partisanship. These things were a betrayal of the party and the people.

President Hoover nominated Charles Evans Hughes for the chief-justiceship of the Supreme Court when Mr. Taft resigned. Borah at once threw all his influence into an attempt to defeat Hughes's confirmation.

Borah looked upon Hughes as a protagonist of property rights as against human rights. His accession to the chief-justiceship meant to Borah the addition of another judge to that element on the bench whose final interpretation of the laws was constantly rendered to the accompaniment of "Justice Holmes and Justice Brandeis dissenting." He felt that Hughes's economic philosophy was such that he would place no restraint on corporations. Borah remarked:

In an era when the greatest question before us is determining the relationship of these vast corporate interests to the millions of people who must pay them toll year after year, could there be any more profound question touching the interest of every person than the question of how much the oil people, the transportation people and all others dealing with those questions shall charge.[15]

Foreign Relations. As chairman of the Senate Foreign Relations Committee from 1924 until 1933, Borah was in a strategic position to apply his political philosophy, especially his insistence on open diplomacy. His political security in Idaho gave him a unique independence.

The two main problems confronting the committee when Borah assumed its leadership were the World Court and the French debt. He did not regard the latter problem as a "delicate" one, as did some of his colleagues. On all questions, he favored open discussion. He stated that France was in better condition to meet her obligations than any country in Europe, and if she adopted a sound fiscal policy and stopped spending money to carry on war, she could pay her debt to the United States.

He denounced the effort to show that the United States was playing the

---

[15] *Congressional Record*, February 11, 1930, 71st Cong., 2d sess., p. 3448.

role of Shylock. Instead of acting the exacting creditor, the United States had been the most generous creditor in the history of international affairs. If there had been disregard anywhere, it had been disregard of the American taxpayer and not of our associates in the war.

France, he accused, was yielding to the same practices which brought on the World War: exploitation, seizure of territory occupied by foreign peoples, secret understandings, armaments.

The French occupation of the Ruhr was exasperating to Borah. Of French policy, he said:

> France holds the key to the restoration of economic health throughout Europe. . . . With a liberal live and let live policy on the part of France, a policy which would fix a definite sum which Germany could pay and which could abandon the occupation of the Ruhr so fruitless to France . . . it would re-animate with energy an entire continent and give hope to an entire world.[16]

Six years later Borah told French newspapermen who had accompanied Pierre Laval to the United States that the European nations must consent to a peaceful revision of the Versailles Treaty and the St. Germain Treaty under which Germany and Austria were held in economic subjection. He said he had in mind cancellation of reparations in their entirety and also the cancellation of international debts. The time for moratoriums was past. He announced that he was opposed to any security pact with France; that he opposed American intervention in Europe under any circumstances; that the Polish Corridor would have to be changed.

This interview stole the spotlight from the Laval-Hoover conversations. Pierre Laval said: "I have not come to Washington to engage in polemics with Senator Borah or to discuss the revision of the Versailles Treaty. Tell the journalists not to be disturbed by the words of a Senator which represent only his personal opinion."

In December of 1925, the Mexican government issued a set of land and petroleum laws that alarmed American entrepreneurs because they said the effect of these laws was to confiscate their property. As the relationship between the United States and Mexico became more strained, Borah took the position that Mexico had the right to regulate her internal affairs. American property and persons should be protected by judicial processes, by the courts of Mexico if possible and, if that was impossible, by an arbitration tribunal. He was opposed to substituting American troops for judicial processes.

Borah stressed that the Monroe Doctrine was not a cloak for imperialism. As this doctrine had been construed by the Administration, it constituted a menace to the Mexican government. According to Borah's interpretation,

[16] *Washington* (D. C.) *Herald,* May 1, 1925.

there was no right, expressed or implied, to interfere with the sovereignty of any Latin American government. And because the Monroe Doctrine could be misunderstood, he felt that America should be scrupulously careful in respecting the national integrity of other countries. The Monroe Doctrine was not a "stepmother's creed." It was called into existence because the United States felt that the European maneuvers threatened security and not in any sense because the United States wished to dominate the states of the Western Hemisphere.

In his judgment, the United States government interfered much further in Nicaragua than was necessary to protect American lives and property. The Nicaraguan government was seized by force and was being held by force. The resources were being exploited in shameless fashion while the Nicaraguan people were helpless under the presence of United States Marines. Occupation of the country did not have the sanction of international law and the troops should be withdrawn immediately. Borah could see no application of the Monroe Doctrine to Nicaragua since there was no European power seeking to acquire territory and no foreign power was trying to overthrow the government.

Borah expressed his desire for the abolition of extra-territorial rights in China. He stated that he did not wish to be understood as criticizing the government, but "I do wish to say that the nation which invokes brutal force in China will be the deliberate assassin of justice in the Orient for decades." We should recognize and deal with the Chinese as a great people upon terms of equality.

Just as Borah thought the "red" menace was being used as a blind by business interests in the Mexican difficulties, so he thought it was being used to prevent China's liberation from foreign domination. China was in need of aid and advice from friendly nations, and because Russia was wise enough to offer assistance, the other powers saw the spread of communism.

Borah opposed the Platt Amendment under which the United States undertook to preserve Cuban independence. He felt that the amendment really was designed to sustain the government of Cuba no matter how tyrannical it might be. It paralyzed initiative because of the fear that American troops would enter Cuba against the revolutionists. In September of 1933, Borah supported Grau San Martin for the presidency of Cuba but opposed any intervention on our part.

His attitude toward the Philippines was that they should have independence as soon as possible. The Hawes-Cutting Act of 1932 granted the Philippines independence in ten years and provided for a naval base. Borah voted against the bill because of the naval base clause and because it did not grant independence soon enough. Borah supported Roosevelt's proposal of 1934 on Philippine independence.

As chairman of the Foreign Relations Committee, Borah emerged as a kind of governmental entity in himself. The importance of his office was no deterrent to his independence of speech and action. Walter Lippmann observed:

> He is not concerned apparently about the difficulty which foreigners experience because they do not know whether they are being lectured by William E. Borah of Idaho or by the Senate of the United States as a co-ordinate part of the treaty-making power. He feels himself privileged to use the prestige of his office to promote the influence of his opinions. The ensuing troubles of the Executive do not break his heart, and the demands ... that men suppress themselves and conform mean very little to him.[17]

Because of his hatred of secret diplomacy, Borah took the attitude that the President and the State Department were agencies to be checked and restrained. His technique of exposing evil was through publicity. He was determined to make the Senate a full partner in diplomacy. His determination was inspired by his faith in the appeal to the people. He even disapproved of informal collaborative sittings with the State Department because he feared that too much confidential information would be given to the committee and a "gag of confidence" would prevent any critic on the committee from appealing to public opinion. Borah thought it was the duty of the Senate to compel the President to consult the people and thus convert the treaty-making powers of the Senate into a medium of open diplomacy.

Borah believed that the Senate had the right to negotiate independently with a foreign power. He negotiated independently during the Mexican oil disputes when he wrote to President Calles for information. In his defense, he stated:

> I felt justified in attempting to gather facts on this subject from all proper sources. ... I have a right to get my information from any source I wish. This I propose to do, and I know of no power that can stop me. We have not yet got Mussolini in the United States.[18]

Why did Borah protest so much? He was not an uninformed or an arrogant man. He was not a man lacking in knowledge or excessive in vain opinions. Yet in many of his foreign policies, history reveals that he was disastrously wrong.

Part of Borah's recalcitrance can be attributed, of course, to his belief

[17] Walter Lippmann, *Men of Destiny* (New York: The Macmillan Co., 1928), pp. 148-49.
[18] *New York Times,* March 21, 1927.

that his main function in the Senate was to exercise the voice of protest and veto; that his "no" votes were more constructive than his affirmative votes.

Actually, Borah never escaped from the limitations of an isolationist Middle West where he was born and an isolated Far West where he lived. Intellectually, he lived in the Snake River Valley of Idaho. He never doubted that his country was impregnably protected by the Pacific and Atlantic oceans. He could not sense that these barriers were as futile in the twentieth century as the Bitteroot Mountains and the Grand Tetons. The frontier state of Idaho fostered and nurtured the individualism, the aloofness, the independence of a man who never learned to conform.

Another explanation for Borah's protests lies in his observation that he had no organization behind him to put forward a program of affirmation. Borah was frequently at odds with the Republican organization, both state and national.

Although a member of the Republican party, Borah was often opposed to Republican measures. Shortly after President Harding's election, he observed that "with the utmost respect let me say that I shall not abdicate my judgment in the next four years any more than in the last four."

In his judgment, republicanism during the Harding and Coolidge administrations "reached an all-time low." The party could be saved only if the Republicans based their foreign policy on humanitarianism and justice instead of exploitation, property rights, and militarism. There would have to be more democracy and less bureaucracy in government. The game of politics played below the level of the intelligence and patriotism of the electorate of America would have to stop. There would have to be a return to a belief in the Constitution. The gag rule in Congress would have to go. The Treasury could no longer be used as a depository for campaign funds to be tapped every time it was necessary to buy votes. The moral courage and idealism of Lincoln would have to be followed and the fight for justice carried on regardless of political expediency. The Republican party could not continue to rely on patronage unless it wanted to go down to defeat.

The Republican party asked Borah to declare himself for Hoover, but Hoover never took a position in his campaign that Borah felt he could support. In opposing Hoover, he said he was following a course which he had pursued since he had been in the Senate—the advocacy of those principles in which he believed. He could not compromise his views just because they were not pleasing to the Administration; he could not act as an "intellectual prostitute" for a party organization.

The platforms for both parties in 1932 failed to meet what he regarded as the most important issue before the people—the depression. In a speech in Burley, Idaho, on October 2, 1932, he commented:

What I shall have to say in this campaign will not be in harmony with either the Republican or Democratic platforms. Both candidates for the Presidency have disregarded their platforms. For this they are entitled to high commendation. It is the most encouraging event in the campaign.

The Republicans in Idaho were not pleased with Borah's recalcitrancy. The *Boise Statesman,* a paper that usually supported the Senator, stated on June 25, 1932:

It was typical of Senator Borah that as soon as he learned he could not have his way in the shaping of the prohibition amendment he refused to attend the convention. Borah never would play unless he could be the absolute boss. Because the prohibition plank displeases him, he uses this as an excuse he has been looking for on which to base his refusal to support his party's candidate for re-election. Borah's following has not been the President's following and so it seems logical to conclude that the declaration will not greatly harm the President's candidacy.

In 1922, Borah had annoyed Idaho Republicans with his insistence on the enactment of a new primary election law for that state. After an absence of three years, Borah came back to campaign in a homecoming that was not in the traditional style. Instead of swearing fealty to the state platform, he denounced it as a "painted glass affair." Feeling ran so high that regular candidates objected to Borah's appearance as a party spokesman in their districts.

Borah stumped the state defying the Republican machine. He challenged Charles Moore, the Republican candidate for governor, to reject the Republican platform and make one of his own. Borah said:

I defy the whole outfit.... I don't propose to go back to the Senate at the suggestion of the organization. I don't even ask their consent to go back to the Senate.... I want the Republican party, but I want it right.... The next two years belong to me and nobody but God Almighty can take them away from me, and during that period I am going to say precisely what I think, and advocate policies in which I believe regardless of the political consequences to the Republican party.[19]

As usual Borah was under attack for recreancy to the Republican party. In defense, he emphasized his allegiance to the doctrine of Edmund Burke that a Republican should not yield his views to those even of his constituency when the two were in conflict. To contend otherwise would be to assert that political allegiance was above allegiance to the principles of republican government. Party domination which went to the point of demanding the surrender of convictions was indefensible.

In his campaign for re-election in 1924, which he won by a wide margin, he said:

[19] *Boise Capital News,* October 10, 1922.

I have followed my convictions in the past. I am sure you will expect me to do so in the future. I strive by all means within my power to meet public questions in the light of public interest. I claim the right as your Senator to oppose any measure by whomsoever proposed which I believe to be injurious to the public interest or unwise in government. I claim the right to support any measure by whomsoever proposed which I believe to be in the public good. . . . This states the whole thing. I would rather have the people of my state believe that I have the courage to vote as I think I ought to vote, regardless of passion or party, than to have any office they can give me.[20]

And in 1936 he remarked:

In the thirty years in which I have been in the Senate, I can truthfully say that I never supported an issue or a measure simply because it was a Republican measure and never voted against a Democratic measure simply because it was a Democratic measure.[21]

Though he often broke with the Republican party on matters of principle, he never identified himself with a third-party movement. New parties, he thought, could not be successfully organized by a few men however able and sincere they might be. New parties had to come up from the grass roots. Hence, he stayed with the Republican party because, he said, he had been able to render as efficient service in it as he could have in any other party. On the whole, he thought that the things he advocated were good Republicanism. He once remarked, "Question my Republicanism if you will and I am relatively numb, but question my loyalty to the Constitution and then you play on a raw nerve."

And again, he observed:

I believe in parties, have always belonged to one and have supported it in what seemed to me its proper sphere. They say I have been a Republican only during campaigns. Well, in campaigns parties are proper and desirable. I have gone with my party on such matters as organization of the Senate and patronage. But I have not felt that I should go with it against my own convictions on questions of fundamental policy. A prime objection to going blindly with a party is that you never know whether the party's position will be the same at the end as at the beginning of a discussion. Rigid party government inevitably makes for corruption.[22]

Borah thought the charge of insincerity brought against public men sprang largely from a vicious conception of the function of political parties and from an unreal theory about the relation of the individual to his political party.

[20] *Boise Statesman*, October 10, 1924.
[21] *Portland Oregonian*, March 23, 1936.
[22] *Boise Statesman*, October 25, 1925.

There was a constant conflict between the public interests and party expediency. Often it was not politically expedient to deal with a public question in a candid fashion. Hence, unwilling wholly to disregard the public welfare and hopeful of serving party expediency, one chose a middle course; sophistry took the place of logic, and plausibility the place of reality.

Another aspect of Borah's political philosophy was his belief that the Senate should not accept automatically the President's nominations for office but should exercise its duty of scrutinizing the nominee's fitness. He insisted on the right of the Senate to exercise coordinate power with the President. He served with and not under Presidents, seven of whom were chafed by his dissents.

Another reason Borah opposed so many things was because he was passionately for a few things. He defended the Constitution and democracy. The story of the writing of the Constitution, its submission and its adoption, Borah believed, was one that needed constantly to be reread and retold. The boldness of that enterprise, the unselfish devotion of the leaders to the cause of human liberty, and the blessings which this plan of government gave to the average man lifted the story into the realm of "sacred history." The Constitution should be read as one would read the prose-poems of Milton on liberty: "lift yourselves from its technical and legal worth into that spiritual realm where you hear the Cathedral music of great deeds." He believed that before human liberty could perish, the Constitution would first have to perish. The terms of the document made one great design, and that was to guarantee human liberty; it embodied a new scheme of life and lifted the average man from a state of serfdom to that of a sovereign.

Concurrent with this concept of the Constitution was a faith in plain people. Indeed, he placed more reliance on the people's judgment than on that of Congress. "The people are not always right," he said, "but in this country they are seldom wrong after they have heard the facts and the discussion and have had time to reflect." There was no one with so much at stake in the preservation of a representative democracy as the people. Their earnings, the security of their homes, depended upon established law and applied constitutional principles. There was, therefore, no crime against the people equal in magnitude to the crime of taking from them the real sources of political power—that of amending the Constitution and freedom of speech and press.

Borah believed in a decentralized political power. He was fond of saying that he regarded it almost as a divine happening that Hamilton and Jefferson both lived in the same period. Hamilton would have given a government of too great a centralization of powers. Jefferson would have weakened the general government but, in each working for his plan, there resulted a

393

"magnificent combination," a national government for national affairs and state government for state affairs. Because of the conflict between Hamilton and Jefferson, the United States had the nearest to a perfect system of government the world had ever known. Borah conceded that changes should be made to meet new conditions, but there was no reason why the fundamentals of the system, the dual sovereignty between the state and the nation, the checks and balances of the three independent departments of the federal government, should be disturbed. He believed the people did not want them disturbed.

He recoiled from the concentration of power in Washington and the growing number of bureaus. The people would have to be taught that in encouraging the centralization of their affairs in Washington they were endangering their government. Bureaus and commissions had been allowed to usurp executive and judicial functions with the resulting danger of the absence of responsibility. Both the executive and legislative branches of government, he declared, had been devitalized by the setting up of agencies of government which did not belong to any of the three main departments and yet they exercised powers belonging to all. Unless a halt was made to find a legislative cure for all private and public ills, there would be an officer for every ten persons; every activity of "mind and body" would be under the direction of a bureau; inspectors would spy on citizens and accompany them in their daily vocations; 40 per cent of the national income would be demanded for the public expenses. This tinkering with the government, he warned, must cease.

Borah, of course, did not oppose all measures. He could be an advocate, particularly if the issue concerned the welfare of the people. Thus, in the New Deal he favored the Tennessee Valley project, the inflation amendment, stock exchange control, the silver purchase act, social security legislation, holding company acts, the work relief act, and the gold reserve act. His affirmative position on these problems was determined by his sympathy for his fellow men during the depression.

In 1909, he gave three speeches in the Senate in support of the income tax. He believed that the income tax issue should be resubmitted to the Supreme Court first, because history revealed the intents and purposes of the framers of the Constitution regarding taxes. The framers did not intend that all the taxes should be placed on those who toil and on consumption. And second, it should be resubmitted in the light of the decisions which had been rendered by the Court since the income tax had been first declared unconstitutional. He contended that Congress had the power to levy an income tax under the Constitution. The sole question was whether it should be apportioned, and the sole purpose and the only effect of the amendment was relief from the necessity of apportionment. There was no necessity for any extension of power, but there was a necessity from a practical standpoint for changing the rule for the exercise of a conceded and unlimited power.

He advocated the election of senators by direct vote. One of the things the people should do was to select their political servants. Congress should be in direct touch with the people. Give the people responsibility and they would not abuse it. Only under such a system could men grow to the full stature of citizenship.

Borah supported legislation that would help homesteaders. He urged aid for the "brave, home-loving, empire-building" people who were settling in the West. He insisted that the Interior Department classify those lands which were agricultural and turn them over for use; he denounced the "monopoly of non-use." He believed that the five years' residence provision of the homestead law was excessive and that two or three years would test the good faith of the settler, whose mere presence under harsh conditions indicated his good faith. The West, he said, was not opposed to conservation, but it was opposed to reservation. Thus the President should not have the power to withdraw public lands. Any conservation policy must have as its fundamental principle that of economic use and development. To the Easterners he said that, if they would join the West on that proposition, the West would join them in formulating a policy of regulation and control to avoid waste and monopoly.

Borah urged recognition of Soviet Russia from early in 1920 until President Roosevelt granted it in 1933. He maintained that the suffering people of Russia were entitled to sympathy and counsel and deserved any outside help they could receive; that 180,000,000 persons could not be outlawed physically or spiritually without jeopardizing the peace and prosperity of the world; that the revolution was justified; that the Russian revolution was comparable to the French Revolution, after which the United States received a minister from the French Republic and extended recognition; that the present Russian government had demonstrated its stability and the people had demonstrated their support; that the United States was forfeiting trade and commerce with Russia to other countries; that the propaganda menace could be dealt with more effectively if the United States were on a friendly basis with Russia; and that reasons for unfriendly acts would no longer exist if amicable relations were established.

Borah was a consistent advocate of disarmament and was instrumental in forcing the Harding administration to call the Washington Disarmament Conference in 1921. He argued that, in addition to placing tremendous tax burdens on the public, armaments were also prime incentives to war. "An armed world is a fighting world," he proclaimed. The competition between Great Britain and Germany from 1903 on was one of the great contributing causes of World War I. Given twenty years of naval building, the world would again be in such fear, suspicion, and jealousy that the slightest misunderstanding could flame into war. He did not believe that the United States should disarm alone, but neither could the United States expect other nations to disarm unless there were evidence of united faith in such a cause. The first line of defense of every nation was neither the Navy nor the Army, but the well-being and contentment of citizens.

From 1918 through 1931, Borah spoke for the Samuel O. Levinson plan for the outlawry of war. Borah introduced a resolution in the Senate in 1923 which provided that war between nations should be outlawed as an institution or as a means of settling international disputes. He meant to give war the same status in international law that murder has in domestic law. He meant to place the judgment of mankind against war as an institution and to substitute law and judicial tribunals. "I maintain," he said, "that the first step in the abolition of war is the changing of the attitudes of the public mind toward war and to give war its proper place in the public opinion of mankind."

Borah consistently advocated a program to cure economic ills during the depression. First, the question of reparations would have to be settled. The German debt should be reduced from twenty-six billion dollars to twelve or fifteen. Second, if Europe would agree to reduce the cost of armaments, and if the debts were canceled, Europe's purchasing power would be increased sufficiently to help the world economic situation. But he was adamant that there should be no reduction of debts without reduction of arms. Third, silver would have to be restored to the place it occupied before foreign demonetization in 1925. This would furnish a large part of the human family the means by which they had transacted business for years. It would relieve the drain on gold. It would help restore the purchasing power of the people of the United States and of the Orient. The attempt to force a gold standard on silver-using countries was a "fearful mistake." Until the United States restored "the money of the Constitution," until the country gave the people of the world a metallic basis for their currency, the United States could not expect commerce from that part of the world which had no metallic money. Fourth, the unequal distribution of the gold supply would have to be changed. With the United States and France holding 71 per cent of the supply, the price of commodities was being affected. Fifth, the currency would have to be expanded by five billion dollars. Sixth, waste in government expenditure would have to be eliminated and taxes reduced.

These, then, are the main principles which Borah opposed and supported. While he did, from time to time, vote and speak with the majority, his reputation will be based upon his opposition to issues. This was a fact Borah proudly admitted.

Borah's Theory and Technique of Persuasion

Borah had a philosophy of persuasion. The speaker should seek economy of expression and integrity of thought. The speaker should make no appeal to prejudice, nor indulge in efforts to mislead. The people should be spoken to in the language of reason. Exaggeration, impugning, shrieking and other "cheap and common arts of public speaking" were never necessary; they were an insult to the intelligence of the audience and the speaker.

Borah believed in extemporaneous speaking, saying that if the speaker used a manuscript, he would try to recall his manuscript instead of thinking of his subject. "If you don't get any new thought while on your feet, you'd better sit down." He also felt that a manuscript gave him a sense of restriction and rigidity. When he did use notes, he scrawled them in large letters on big cards and kept them on his desk. He could glance at them quickly and inconspicuously.

Sarcasm, Borah admitted, was a familiar and sometimes an honorable intellectual weapon. It was ordinarily used, however, in defense of stale and worn-out institutions. He remarked:

> That which the conscience can not well support, the intellect will sometimes slavishly defend, and when it does, it generally indulges in taunt and sarcasm, because it is an easy method by which to "get by" and it is generally quite pleasing to the speaker himself.[23]

Borah's appearance was a persuasive asset. His firm chin with its well-defined cleft in the center, his thick, brown hair parted in the middle and allowed to grow long in the back, his dark eyebrows almost meeting above his short nose, his penetrating eyes, his determined mouth—this was unmistakably Borah.

His complexion was ruddy, betokening health and strength. His round face, full but not bulging lips, pugnacious nose, and expression of candor created a rather boyish impression. His face was strong without being harsh. His Western habit of wearing long hair added to the leonine face. He was rugged-looking; there was something formidable in his massive features.

The most frequent assessment of Borah by analysts, friendly and unfriendly, was that he was completely sincere. Claude G. Bowers, not exactly

[23] Borah Scrap Books (University of Idaho Library, Moscow, Idaho), X, 121. This collection of scrapbooks consists of fifty-five volumes. The scrapbooks contain newspaper clippings, some speech manuscripts, and letters.

a friendly critic, said of Borah at the time of the League of Nations controversy:

The Senator from Idaho ranks easily as one of the half dozen men who rises to the dignity of statesmanship. Earnest, honest, free from the taint of demagogy and subserviency to plutocracy, he is one of the few members of the Senate to whom all parties give ear. His speeches on the League are among the few that champions of the League can read with patience. This is due to their manifest sincerity, the absence of cant, of misrepresentation. No one can read the Borah speeches against the League without the conviction that he would rather be for it but that his convictions make it impossible.[24]

A section of Borah's League address of February 19, 1919, illustrates his sincerity:

But I offer in justification of my course nothing of my own save the deep and abiding reverence I have for those whose policies I humbly but most ardently support. I claim no merit save fidelity to American principles and devotion to American ideals as they were wrought out from time to time by those who built the Republic. . . . In opposing this treaty I do nothing more than decline to renounce and tear out of my life the sacred traditions which through fifty years have been translated into my whole intellectual and moral being. I will not, I can not, give up my belief that America must, not alone for the happiness of her own people, but for the moral guidance and greater contentment of the world, be permitted to live her own life. . . . Since the debate opened months ago those of us who have stood against this proposition have been taunted many times with being little Americans. Leave us the word American, keep that in your presumptuous impeachment, and no taunt can disturb us, no gibe discompose our purposes. . . . If we have erred, we have erred out of too much love for those things which from childhood you and we together have been taught to revere—yes, to defend even at the cost of limb and life. . . . If we have erred it is because we have placed too high an estimate upon the wisdom of Washington and Jefferson, too exalted an opinion upon the patriotism of the sainted Lincoln. And blame us not therefore if we have, in our limited vision, seemed sometimes bitter and at all times uncompromising, for the things for which we have spoken, feebly spoken; the things which we have endeavored to defend have been the things for which your fathers and our fathers were willing to die.[25]

After the League debates, Woodrow Wilson said of Borah, "There is one Irreconcilable that I can respect." This reluctant testimony was elicited because he admired Borah's sincerity and because Borah had kept the debate impersonal.

A second conspicuous quality was courage. In his opposition to the payment

[24] *Boise Statesman,* February 24, 1919.
[25] *League of Nations* (Washington, D. C.: Government Printing Office, May 2, 1919), p. 21.

of the bonus and in his advocacy of the recognition of Russia, Borah stood almost alone in his indifference to public opinion. When Senator Penrose moved to send the Bonus Bill back to the Finance Committee, Borah was about the only senator who frankly announced that he favored the motion because he opposed the bill. He could have voted and let it go at that without revealing his attitude, but this was not Borah's way.

On April 3, 1922, the American Legion Post of Pocatello, Idaho, telegraphed Borah:

> Your absurdly fallacious speech opposing bonus unanimously condemned by Pocatello Legion. You opposed the war. You opposed foreign loans. You opposed sending troops. You opposed espionage law. You apparently are opposed to everything but Borah. We can hire an obstructionist for less money.

Borah's courageous reply was that if he had wanted to stay in the Senate at the price of his convictions, he could have made the bonus one of the first bids for political power. He said:

> It would have been most agreeable personally to have voted for the bonus and it would have been advantageous politically. It is your privilege to condemn my course. But I beg you to know that it was taken with much personal regret. . . . I felt I could not do otherwise and discharge my obligation to the people as a whole and to the country.
>
> I observe the threat which you impliedly make as to future political punishment. It was wholly unnecessary for you to make this threat. It reflected upon you and it has had no effect whatever upon me. . . . I haven't much respect for the man who buys office, even though he pays for it with his own money. But the most slimy creature which disgraces American politics is the man who buys office by paying for it with appropriations out of the public treasury and charges his venal political obligations to the taxpayers.[26]

In Mark Sullivan's opinion the final credit for defeating the Bonus Bill should go to Borah because "it was largely the outspoken courage of his speeches that crystallized enough feeling throughout the country."

Borah summed up this aspect of his philosophy in a letter to E. A. Burrell who had criticized him for not supporting the woman suffrage amendment. Burrell had written, "As our representative, you have no moral or legal right to set up your individual views against the collective judgment of the people." Borah replied:

> Yes, I have, and then the people have the greater right to retire me. But, Burrell, to say that because a man is a Senator he is to have no views of his own, no convictions, no conscience, is to advocate a doctrine which upon reflection you will

[26] *New York Times,* April 23, 1922.

be ashamed of and which you yourself as a Senator would never accept. If I go before the people and pledge myself to certain policies, I am bound to carry them out, but if questions arise here, as this question does, I have a right and am in honor bound, to respect my convictions and then submit my case to the people, and if they approve they will keep me here and if they disapprove they will retire me. . . . You said in your conclusion that if I should change my attitude the people would applaud my actions. They would denounce me in their hearts if not in words, as they should, as a miserable, cringing coward who changed a life-long conviction in order to get an office. I should have their contempt, and what is even worse for me, my own.

Borah was courteous in debate. He always managed to keep discussion on a high level of impersonality; always he was debating the issue. In the hundreds of instances when he was interrupted with the question: "Will the Senator from Idaho yield?" almost invariably his reply was "Certainly." He acknowledged the ability and wisdom of his colleagues—frequently when he knew more about the question than they did. An excellent example of his courtesy and tact is the introduction to his speech dealing with the riots in Brownsville, Texas, in 1908. He was a freshman senator at the time. He began:

I shall not likely add any considerable amount of new material to this discussion. Probably I shall add none. But during the somewhat uneventful and leisurely days which a new member has at his disposal it has occurred to me to go carefully through the evidence . . . and it has occurred to me also that I might be able in a limited way to assist in epitomizing and placing the evidence before the busier members of this body. Not much more than this is it my ambition upon this occasion to do. . . . I think I ought to say, in order to remove a handicap . . . that I have no ambition to appear in any respect as answering the argument of the Senator from Ohio [Foraker]. It is a task entirely beyond my power to answer the Senator from Ohio. So I shall confine myself to the smaller task.[27]

Borah seldom had more than one or two main assertions in an address, assertions which he supported by pyramiding evidence. His favorite authorities were the Constitution, Supreme Court decisions, the "Founding Fathers," writers in the field of history, economics, and political science, but he also made liberal use of newspaper editorials, periodicals, and modern and classical literature. His address on the power of the President to withdraw public lands given in the Senate on May 11, 1910, is representative. His thesis was that from the time Congress began to discuss the question of the power of the Executive to withdraw public lands, Congress had assumed, the Executive had assumed, and the courts had assumed that, without authority from Congress, the Executive could not act. He supported this thesis with eight quotations from

[27] *Congressional Record*, April 20, 1908, 60th Cong., 1st sess., p. 4970.

the Constitution, eleven statutes dating from 1792, five decisions of former Secretaries of the Interior, fifteen Supreme Court decisions, and five writers on constitutional law.

Again, in an address on June 20, 1910, on the conservation of natural resources, his assertion that the state alone can deal properly with control of water resources was supported by thirty-four Supreme Court decisions.

In his address on the recall of judges, August 7, 1911, in which he argued for an independent judiciary, he quoted the Bible, "the Father of our Country," John Adams, Alexander Hamilton, Daniel Webster, President Harrison, Wendell Phillips, Woodrow Wilson, Colonel Roosevelt, Chief Justice Marshall, and Edmund Burke. Invariably, Borah justified his authorities, explaining why they were qualified to offer evidence. Before quoting Burke in this speech, for example, he prefaced the quotation with Burke's qualifications:

We think of him [Burke] as only a great orator, but he was a master of the science of politics, using that term in its highest and best sense. Among the multitude of brilliant men from that unhappy isle he stands out distinct and impressive in not only his brilliancy, but his profound insight into government.

He made conspicuous use of the inductive method and of analogy. For instance, in his speech for a strong Navy, July 17, 1916, he argued that weakness is a source of war. His first illustration was developed in these words:

When Demosthenes entered public life in Greece he found unpreparedness of Athens both in army and navy to meet those who were aggressors. . . . It is startlingly interesting even at this hour to see the applicability, the pertinency of the argument of Demosthenes. He pleaded with the people of Athens to give him a navy . . . not for conquest but for defense. But they saw no enemy in sight. . . . They were not interested and we all know the results. The aggressors easily took possession.

His generalization was supported by several other instances: the story of the fall of Venice after she refused to believe that Turkey would attack her; the success of William the Silent against aggressor countries because he insisted on a strong navy; unpreparedness in 1812, when the United States was saved only by England's engagement with Napoleon; and the failure of England to follow Lord Salisbury's advice in 1900 to prepare for war. Borah's generalizations were remarkable for the number of instances he cited in support of them and his ready admission of exceptions.

In general his speeches were incisive, clear, and logical. The reporting, for example, of C. E. Davis in the *New York Times* for July 26, 1907, after Borah's final speech in the Haywood case, though extravagant, was consistent with other press comments:

With wonderful lucidity . . . he gathered up the vital facts of the whole case, and brushing away all the mass of sophistry and immateriality presented a vivid living picture of the conspiracy.

It was not a personal arraignment of Haywood. There was nothing of invective or vituperation in it. It was simply an over-powering marshalling of the evidence presented by the prosecution.

His speeches were replete with colorful and dynamic phrases: "warning voice of wisdom," "good offices," "faithless recreants," "kenneled in some foreign clime," "inscrutable and tantalizing fact," "uglier passions," "consecration of other days," "braced by the traditions," "re-baptism of national spirit," "blighting mildew," "economic cannibals," "saturnalia of expenditure," "whelps of the same kennel," "machinations of imperialism," "broken sobs of nations," "mad hosts of disorder," "intolerable presumption," "cruel absurdity," "horrid spell," "transcendent moment," "mad propensity," "lurid element," "imperious intellects."

His speeches often contained phrases that endured, as did his remark in regard to Mexico: "God has made us neighbors—let justice make us friends." This caught the public imagination and lingered in public memory.

Borah used direct address, refrain, and variety in sentence structure. These were conspicuous characteristics of his method. A single illustration from one of his League speeches may serve to indicate these aspects of his style:

The whole scheme is founded on force. These advocates of this particular league can find no amelioration, save that based on force. "Kill them off!" cries the League's most distinguished exponent. Are all conflagrations to be put out save those which meet with their approval? The Fathers started a conflagration in 1776. India, with her countless millions, may in future years express a desire for independence and for freedom. What will be the doctrine of the League? They have announced it— "Kill them off!"

The people have been told of the halcyon days that were to come with the League. Men would no longer make war. The crushing burdens of stupendous armaments were to be lifted. But not so. We are to have a larger standing army than ever. Why? In order to support the league of peace. We are to compose all the troubles and put out all the conflagrations started to destroy kingship or bureaucracy. And how are we to stop the troubles? Why, in the same old way; nothing new about it at all. Precisely the same way and in the same method of the Holy Alliance— "Kill them off!"

If the people are to be taxed and taxed, and if they rebel against the burden are to be killed off, I do not see the virtue of the scheme. I confess that my vision may be somewhat blurred and I know my fancy is somewhat troubled when I see these vast equipments of war, this vast array of force, standing armies, conscription, great navies, and taxes without stint or limit, with no answer to give the people when they cry out in resistance save the cry coming down through the centuries from the lips of tyrants and despots, "Kill them off!"

The interrogation was a favorite construction. Frequently, entire paragraphs consisted of interrogation only. In his address opposing the repeal of the embargo on munitions, he queried:

Why are we asked to repeal this law? Why are we asked to repeal a law which forever prohibits furnishing of these instrumentalities of human destruction and furnishing them for gain, and thus again to identify ourselves with the war business of Europe? Why are we here in special session and in apparent haste asking for repeal? Did the cry for repeal originate or does it spring from the people of this country? Did the voice of labor initiate the agitation for repeal? Did it come from the young men who are just now hoping to enter business or a chosen profession? Where did the call come from? It came from the war hounds of Europe! [28]

Borah was fond of parallel structure which permitted a cumulative use of detail. Such examples as the following are frequent:

If you think you can seek out and do justice to all nations, great and small; if you think you can found an organization based upon the principles of human progress and whose decrees are enforced by public opinion; if you think you can prescribe reasonable rules for change and growth; if you think you can look into the hearts of a particular people and interpret that inexplicable passion which when the appointed hour comes melts away all obstacles, rejects all restraints, and forces its way from a small to a great nation; if you think you can look upon a French revolution cursed with apparent stupidity and steeped in blood and foretell that in a hundred years those same people, disenthralled and free, will stand between civilization and organized barbarism as the French stood at the Marne; if you think you can now look upon a broken and dismembered and bleeding Russia and foretell her future; if you think you can do what the living God has not been able to do— standardize the human family; if you feel you can undo what He in His inscrutable wisdom did when He planted race prejudice in the hearts and stamped color upon the faces of men—then give us your prospectus. We will be glad to look it over. . . .[29]

More than most men in public life, Borah discussed principles, abstractions, and institutions. He rarely fought men but rather sought to avoid wounding them. Partly, this was expediency. He knew that someday he might need the vote of a senator who was his adversary at the moment. But to a greater extent, it was a matter of principle. He disagreed in a way that left his opponent feeling that he understood and respected his position and in return

[28] *Congressional Record*, March 10, 1938, 75th Cong., 3d sess., p. 4728.
[29] William E. Borah, *American Problems* (New York: Duffield and Co., 1924), p. 76.

asked an understanding and respect of his own. Although he was more often in the fighting opposition than any other man in the Senate, there was probably no senator who hated Borah or wanted to see him retired. Attacking any subject, he built his case slowly and logically, objectively presenting his arguments. He did not pander to the sympathy of crowds, yet his fairness and objectivity won their sympathy. He did not seek to arouse mere passion nor to arouse prejudice; he aimed at securing understanding.

He had a good sense of timing. Sometimes for months he would not speak, holding a speech until he could give it with greatest effect. In February, 1927, Colonel Robins and Mr. S. O. Levinson wrote Borah repeated letters urging a speech in the Senate on the outlawry of war. Borah replied: "Intuitively I arrive at conclusions with reference to speaking on these subjects, and intuitively I feel that this would not get across at this time." Not until May did Borah think the time for speaking had arrived. In the same way, Borah's speech of January 17, 1911, to unseat Lorimer, and his speech of March 16, 1925, opposing the confirmation of Charles Warren as attorney general were both impromptu because the ideal moment for each could not be foreseen. When it came unexpectedly, Borah, who preferred long and careful preparation, did not hesitate to take the floor impromptu.

The main qualities in Borah's speaking, then, were his personal qualities of sincerity and courage; his logic and use of evidence; his impersonal and objective attack; and the psychological timing of the speech.

Borah's Effectiveness

It is difficult to determine objectively what effect Borah's speaking had on the course of legislation. But the reaction of the press and of Borah's colleagues to his important speeches tends to show that Borah had influence. In his first important speech on April 19, 1908, in regard to the Negro riots at Brownsville, Texas, Borah was credited by the press with changing the views of senators. Representative was the observation of the Salt Lake City *Tribune* of April 20, 1908: "So thorough was his grasp of the subject . . . that Senators heretofore in doubt confessed that they were satisfied after the speech that Borah's contention was the correct one."

On January 17, 1912, Borah made a speech that, according to the *Portland Oregonian* News Bureau, "actually changed votes." This address was on the Borah-Jones Three Year Homestead Bill. Whereas there had been opposition to the measure, when Borah called it up before the Senate it was passed without a dissenting vote. The *Boise Statesman* for March 12, 1912, said: "Passage of Homestead Bill makes Idaho say, 'Thanks to Borah.'"

William E. Borah

The *New York Times* for February 17, 1911, stated after Borah's speech on February 16 in favor of direct election of senators that "the effect of Borah's great speech was immediately evident on both sides of the chamber. Senators of three political camps united in pressing about him and congratulating him on the masterful effort." The resolution came within four votes of passing when it came to a vote on February 28, 1911. Borah said he "was pleased with the progress the measure had made." On May 1, 1911, the measure passed the Senate by a vote of 64 to 24. As a testimonial to Borah's effort in securing its adoption, he received one of the four pens used in signing the amendment.

Charles Merz, writing in the *New Republic* for June 3, 1925, stated:

There is no doubt that it was Borah's influence beyond that of any other member of the Senate which counted on the side of what small liberalism survived in war days. . . . His stand on war issues won him a wide and respectful audience of those who never did agree with him but found themselves impressed as time after time—in the matter of war aims, espionage laws, effects of profiteering—the logic of events went on to prove that Borah's judgment had been right.

It is reasonable to assume that Borah played as important a part as anyone in keeping the United States out of the League of Nations. After his first speech against the League on February 21, 1919, Borah received such an ovation that Senate business was suspended while he received congratulations from the Republicans and from fifteen Democrats. Borah went to the public with the League issue in March, 1919. His speeches were widely applauded. They made the Republicans realize that the League was a real political issue and that there was more public sentiment against the League than Republican leaders had thought. With Hiram Johnson, Borah again went to the people to counteract the influence of President Wilson's tour of the fall of 1919. Lodge called Borah's speech of November 19, 1919, "a great speech." Beveridge said it was "clear, simple, convincing, and exalted." On this date, the ratification of the League was defeated by a vote of 49 to 35. *The Nation*, July 21, 1921, commented in regard to Borah's leadership in the League struggle:

When the history of that remarkable struggle which seemed so hopeless at the beginning is written, it will show that for steady driving ahead, resoluteness of purpose, remarkable strategy and absolute determination to succeed, the palm belongs to Senator Borah.

On the final defeat of the Bonus Bill in 1922, Mark Sullivan said:

Final credit for defeating it should go to Borah because it was largely his aggressive energy that built up a following in the Senate from almost nothing and

405

it was chiefly the outspoken courage of his speeches that crystallized enough feeling through the country to bring about the present result.[30]

With each address that Borah gave for the recognition of Russia, he felt that he had "reduced the opposition to some extent." When recognition was extended in 1933, Mr. Litvinoff wrote to Borah that "the present occasion is in large measure the result of your vision and persistent efforts."

The press acknowledged Borah's influence in the calling of the Washington Disarmament Conference in the fall of 1921. The Philadelphia *Public Ledger* termed it "an indisputable triumph for Senator Borah." The *Washington Post* said it was "a matter of remarkable leadership on the part of Senator Borah."

After Borah's address of December 18, 1925, against the World Court, the *Washington Post* wrote: "Though preceded by Senator Lenroot and Senator Walsh both of whom argued for the Court, Senator Borah dominated the day's proceedings and his speech was the outstanding feature." And the *New York Times* of January 12, 1926, stated that there was "a feeling that if debate on the Court continued, Borah might have swung enough votes to defeat the resolution, but cloture was invoked."

In 1935, when President Roosevelt asked the Senate to ratify the Court Protocols, it appeared that the Senate easily had enough votes to comply with the President's wish. Borah and Johnson spoke against the measure. Otherwise, opposition was negligible. The Court proposal was defeated by a vote of 52 to 36. Borah believed that few senators changed their vote because of the deluge of telegrams that resulted from Father Coughlin's radio address against the Court.

At the Republican Convention in Kansas City in 1938, Borah's influence was such that the *Kansas City Star* commented: "Senator Borah is the only one of them with a vivid, commanding personality that can lay a spell on delegates and make them listen whether they wish to or not."

After Borah's campaign for Hoover in 1928, Will Hayes, chairman of the Republican National Committee, wrote to him: "I congratulate you upon the manifest influence of your speeches on public opinion."

On the defeat of President Roosevelt's Supreme Court proposal of 1937, James Truslow Adams wrote to Borah: "As an American citizen I wish to express to you my very deep appreciation of the stand you have taken. In one of the great crises of history . . . you have played an heroic part."

On January 7, 1938, Borah gave a speech in the Senate in opposition to the Wagner-VanNuys anti-lynching measure. The *Washington Post* of January 23, 1938, said: "They say a speech never changes opinions and votes in

[30] *New York World*, September 22, 1922.

Congress, but Borah's did. It showed the southern Senators they had an issue and taught them how to use it." The *Chicago Tribune* of January 8, 1938, wrote: "This speech was believed by many to have marked the turning of the tide against the Wagner-VanNuys Bill."

There is evidence that Borah exerted an influence in regard to presidential appointments. When President Coolidge appointed Charles B. Warren attorney general, Borah gave a speech in opposition. Frederic Wile, writing in the *New York Times* for March 27, 1925, said of this speech:

> Borah dominated when he was on his feet as if he had hypnotized the crowded galleries and floor. Borah bestrode the Senate on the last day of the Warren debate like a colossus of Rhodes.

The Senate rejected the confirmation of Warren by a vote of 46 to 39. Again when President Hoover appointed Charles E. Hughes to the chief justiceship of the Supreme Court, Borah opposed his appointment. When Borah had concluded his address on February 11, 1930, the *Washington Post* for February 12 declared: "It was obvious that Hughes faced serious opposition. Senators who had pledged themselves to vote for Hughes joined the opposition." At one time thirty-five senators were against the Administration. Joe Robinson, abroad at the time, was asked to notify the Southern Democrats to support Hughes. Twenty-six finally voted with Borah and fifty-two for the Administration.

Borah led the successful fight in the Senate against the confirmation of J. J. Parker for the Supreme Court. He spoke on April 28, 1930, and again on May 7, on which date the Senate by a vote of 41 to 39 refused to confirm his appointment. William Green of the American Federation of Labor wrote to Borah: "The logic, force, and the truth of your masterful addresses delivered in connection with the consideration of the appointment of Judge Parker proved to be unanswerable and irresistible."

All of Borah's persuasive powers were used to get President Hoover to appoint Cardozo to the Supreme Court. Paul Y. Anderson, newspaperman, wrote: "For the finest and most popular act of his Administration, President Hoover can thank Borah. It was Borah who virtually dragooned him into naming Justice Cardozo to the Court." [31]

Conclusion

Borah was not inscrutable. He loved the common man. This accounted for much of a political philosophy that seemed to baffle many. He believed that governments were instituted for men and that, in the interests of

[31] *Lewiston* (Idaho) *Tribune*, September 18, 1932.

humanity, the masses should have a controlling voice in government. It accounted for his veneration of the Constitution and of the Supreme Court. Borah yielded to no one in his respect for civil rights.

His nationalism annoyed the internationalists. He opposed foreign political commitments of the type that permitted diplomats of other countries to determine the obligations of the United States. But commitments of an economic nature he encouraged, and he frequently urged international economic conferences. His nationalism was not imperialistic; it embraced the national aspirations of other countries—Russia, China, India, and Latin America. Borah's nationalism was his faith in American democracy.

Borah's conception of representative democracy paralleled Burke's, Madison's, and Webster's. The elected representatives of the people were not messenger boys, and the constituents should not attempt to dictate to their representatives. This philosophy frequently placed Borah in a delicate situation with the national Republican party and Republicans in his own state. However, Borah always reported to the electorate, explaining his position. If they disagreed, he reminded them of the coming election. Principles were more important to him than parties, and issues more important than men.

Borah was well-liked in the Senate. Senators of both parties gave him respectful attention when he spoke, because his was not only the Voice of Protest but also the Voice of Conscience. And in his own state he had no machine, no organization, but he was able to persuade the people of Idaho to send him to the Senate for seven terms in spite of the frequent opposition of the Republican party.

To many, Borah steered a devious course because he seemed to be the only one that knew the shallows and the snags. But through all his vagaries and his wanderings and his loneliness, he kept his stability and dignity.

SELECTED BIBLIOGRAPHY

Manuscripts

Borah Manuscripts. University of Idaho Library. These are reprints of all of Borah's major speeches.
Borah Scrap Books. University of Idaho Library. These fifty-five volumes contain newspaper clippings, some speech manuscripts, and letters.

Books

BORAH, WILLIAM E. *American Problems,* ed. Horace Green. New York: Duffield & Co., 1924.
HAWLEY, J. H. *History of Idaho.* Nampa. Idaho, 1920.
HICKS, FREDERICK C. *Famous American Jury Speeches.* St. Paul: West Publishing Co., 1925.

William E. Borah

JOHNSON, CLAUDIUS O. *Borah of Idaho.* New York: Longmans, Green & Co., Inc., 1936.
LIPPMANN, WALTER. *Men of Destiny.* New York: The Macmillan Co., 1927.

Newspapers

Boise Statesman, June 21, 1891; May 6, 1892; August 9, 1892; August 20, 1892; September 27, 1896; July 16, 1906; January 4, 1907; January 16, 1907; July 29, 1907; October 3, 1907; February 20, 1908; April 22, 1908; July 5, 1910; April 6, 1912; September 15, 1912; January 13, 1915; May 9, 1915; May 1, 1917; September 8, 1919; April 16, 1924; July 19, 1926; February 18, 1929; September 27, 1929; January 24, 1932; June 25, 1932; November 6, 1932; May 10, 1933; November 4, 1935; November 28, 1935; June 12, 1936; February 15, 1938; May 21, 1939.

Boise Capital News, October 2, 1902; January 16, 1907; October 2, 1907; July 15, 1915; June 9, 1916; December 17, 1917; October 10, 1922; October 8, 1924; September 10, 1935; August 12, 1936; November 4, 1936.

Boston Transcript, October 23, 1906; January 3, 1915.

Lewiston (Idaho) *Tribune,* May 20, 1896; October 8, 1904.

New York Sun, August 8, 1911; April 22, 1915; April 12, 1929.

New York Times, July 26, 1907; October 4, 1907; August 2, 1910; December 23, 1916; April 5, 1917; April 23, 1922; May 9, 1922; December 30, 1923; November 16, 1924; March 27, 1925; August 15, 1926; March 21, 1927; March 15, 1927; November 10, 1934; September 15, 1935; June 8, 1936; August 13, 1936; December 3, 1936.

New York World, September 1, 1921; April 7, 1924; May 15, 1933.

Portland Oregonian, August 1, 1905; August 2, 1905; August 10, 1906; March 9, 1907; August 1, 1907; February 19, 1908; April 20, 1908; April 22, 1908; February 8, 1911; January 20, 1913; April 27, 1917; February 11, 1920; June 1, 1926; June 16, 1928; December 30, 1929; September 15, 1932; February 23, 1936; May 12. 1936; May 7, 1937; September 18, 1939.

Washington (D. C.) *Herald,* April 17, 1910; June 22, 1910; November 15, 1924; December 5, 1924; May 12, 1925; May 23, 1925; October 5, 1925; May 25, 1934; June 5, 1935; December 22, 1935; April 27, 1938.

Washington (D. C.) *Post,* December 28, 1922; April 11, 1923; March 26, 1927; April 9, 1927; January 5, 1929; February 19, 1929; September 22, 1929; February 12, 1930; May 10, 1934; January 24, 1936; April 7, 1936; June 8, 1936; June 30, 1938; May 20, 1939.

Periodicals

BORAH, WILLIAM E. "A Bond Issue for Reclamation," *The Independent,* LXVII (November 11, 1909).

———. "Income Tax Amendment," *North American Review,* CXCI (June, 1910).

———. "State and Nation in Child Labor Regulations," *Annals of the American Academy,* XXXVIII (July, 1911).

———. "War with Monopoly," *The Independent,* LXIV (March 6, 1913).

———. "Will Humanity Be Heard at Washington?" *Sunset,* XLVII (December, 1917).

———. "American Liberty's Crucial Hour," *Current History Magazine of the New York Times* (May, 1918).

———. "Perils of Secret Treaty Making," *Forum,* LX (December, 1918).

———. "The Threat of Bolshevism," *Current Opinion,* LXVI (March, 1919).

BORAH, WILLIAM E. "Ghost of Versailles at the Conference," *The Nation*, CXIII (November 9, 1921).

――――. "Why the Conference Must Act." *Sunset*, XLVIII (January, 1922).

――――. "Results of Secrecy," *Sunset*, XLVIII (February, 1922).

――――. "Toward the Outlawry of War," *New Republic*, XXXIX (July 9, 1924).

――――. "Public Opinion Outlaws War," *The Independent*, CXIII (September 13, 1924).

――――. "The Fetish of Force," *Forum*, LXXIV (August, 1925).

――――. "Freedom of the Seas," *Current History*, XXIX (March, 1929).

――――. "Where Would the Money Go?" *Colliers*, LXXXVIII (July 18, 1931).

HARD, W. "Borah the Individual," *Review of Reviews*, LXXI (February, 1925).

MERZ, C. "Borah's One Man Party," *New Republic*, XLIII (June 10, 1925).

――――. "The Idaho Minority of One," *ibid.*, (June 3, 1925).

NEVINS, ALLAN. "Borah and World Politics," *Current History*, XXXVII (February, 1933).

SIMONDS, F. "Making the G. O. P. Safe for Borah," *New Republic*, XXXVII (February 6, 1924).

WHITE, W. A. "Lone Lion of Idaho," *Colliers*, LXXVI (September 12, 1925).

11

Harry Emerson Fosdick

by ROBERT D. CLARK

Harry Emerson Fosdick was born in Buffalo, New York, May 24, 1878. He received his formal education from the Buffalo Public Schools, from Colgate University (A.B., 1900), Union Theological Seminary (B.S., 1904), and Columbia University (A.M., 1908). Ordained to the ministry of the Baptist Church in 1903, he served as pastor of the First Baptist Church, Montclair, N. J., 1904-15, as associate minister of the First Presbyterian Church, New York, 1918-25, as pastor of the Park Avenue Baptist Church (known as the Riverside Church after 1930) from 1926 to 1946. From 1908 to 1915 he was instructor in homiletics at Union Theological Seminary, and from 1915 to 1946, professor of practical theology. He has received numerous honorary degrees, among them the D.D. from Colgate University, 1914, from Yale University, 1923, Glasgow (Scotland) University, 1924, Harvard University, 1933. His more than twenty published books include several volumes of sermons (beginning in 1933, with *The Hope of the World*), and the popularly received devotional guides, *The Meaning of Prayer*, 1915, *The Meaning of Faith*, 1917, and *The Meaning of Service*, 1920. Since his retirement in 1946 Dr. Fosdick has been pastor emeritus of the Riverside Church and professor emeritus of Union Theological Seminary.

I

Late in December of 1918, the pastoral relations committee of the First Presbyterian Church of New York announced that Harry Emerson Fosdick, Professor of Practical Theology at the Union Theological Seminary, had accepted a call as associate minister and permanent preacher.

No one thought at the time of comparing him to Henry Ward Beecher or Phillips Brooks; no one anticipated that he would soon become the center of the nation's most spectacular quarrel on religious doctrine, nor did any guess that he was about to take his place as America's most prominent radio preacher, or that John D. Rockefeller would build a million-dollar skyscraper church for him, or that his slender volumes on prayer and faith and service, written for Y.M.C.A. study groups, would sell over a million copies.

But even in 1918 people recognized that Harry Emerson Fosdick was a great preacher. As supply minister at the First Presbyterian Church in the fall of 1918, he had attracted attention and prompted the pulpit committee

411

to extend a unanimous call to him. When he was announced to preach, the people crowded the church, and when he stepped to the pulpit they listened eagerly. A small, wiry man, quick in his movements, he impressed them with his energy and his earnestness. With his hands tightly gripping the collar of his gown, he spoke with scarcely a gesture, save for the vigorous and emphatic bobbing of his dark, bushy head.[1]

But he spoke directly and urgently, with his black eyes searching the faces of the people. He spoke sharply and critically, and yet hopefully, and the recurring upward inflection in his voice, the persistent suggestion of a ministerial tone served only to temper the occasional asperity of his criticism and the imperative challenge in his voice.

Fosdick was forty years old in 1918. Born in 1878 in Buffalo, New York, he had been reared in a Baptist home. His father was a school teacher, for twenty-five years the principal of a public high school. Young Harry and his brother and sister were steeped in the traditions of religion and learning.

Although the elder Fosdick was a liberal in theology, the tenets which he had come to accept had not yet filtered down to the Sunday school and the children's books through which his son secured most of his religious instruction. Young Harry was nurtured on three volumes of Bible stories, written especially for the young. *Line upon Line* and *Precept upon Precept* told the stories of the Old Testament, *The Peep of Day* recounted those of the New. They were pictures of violence and death as well as of courage and sacrifice, of a vengeful more than a loving God, of a jealous, watchful tyrant who sat on his great white throne, marking down all the wrongdoings and even naughty thoughts of men and women, and of little boys and girls. On that final day of judgment he would open his great book, seek out those who did not love him, bind them in chains, and throw them into a lake of fire. There they might gnash their teeth and weep and wail forever, but they should not have one drop of water to cool their burning tongues.[2]

When he was seven, young Fosdick cried himself to sleep in dread of hell, and when he was nine he was ill from "panic terror" lest he had committed the unpardonable sin. Years afterward the Reverend Dr. Fosdick remembered with "resurrected wrath," the long Sunday evening sermon which had persuaded him and a few others to sign a pledge never to drink sweet cider, and the time he had missed his only opportunity to hear Edwin Booth in *Hamlet* because some pious brethren had stirred up his sensitive conscience on the evils of the theater, and the many times when, with

---

[1] Helena Huntington Smith, "Respectable Heretic," *Outlook and Independent*, CLIII (October 9, 1929), 209.

[2] Harry Emerson Fosdick, "Morals Secede from the Union," *Harper's Magazine*, CLXIV (May, 1932), 682-83.

agonizing scruples, he had refused to dance the Virginia Reel or to read George Eliot's novels.[3]

If his religion were solemn, his play at least was "right." The family lived for a number of years in a small rural community several miles from Buffalo. Harry roamed the woods, fished in Plumb Bottom and Cayuga Creek, made mud dams, and joined his gang in building a shanty. His father now and then took him fishing on the Niagara, and he learned to love the falls with a fearful and awesome love—the rush of the river as it split and whitened on the jutting rocks, the roar of the cataract, the fateful plunge over the cliff, the boiling water in the stream below. He loved the quieter aspects of nature, too, the delicate flowers of the woods which contrasted so strangely with the garish floral patterns in the parlors of the homes he knew. And he thought the calm radiance of a summer dawn not unlike the quiet way his mother moved through her simple, household tasks.[4]

While he was thus engrossed with church and outdoor sports, he also found much time to read—biography and history, the novels of Dickens and Thackeray, and the dime-novel adventure stories written by his father's younger brother. When he was ready for high school, the family moved back to Buffalo. He attended the school where his father was principal and studied Latin and Greek under his direction. But his most influential teacher was a young instructor who introduced him to literature—Browning, Wordsworth, Whitman, and read aloud with him the whole of Lecky's *History of European Morals*. Under this young man's critical eye he learned to make Cicero's orations, when translated, sound like "real orations," and Vergil's *Aeneid* sound like poetry.[5]

He was a shy, embarrassed youngster in high school, "petrified with stage-fright," when he was first called upon to participate in the activities of his debating society. But like it or not, he was expected to stand up and talk. Before long, despite persistent fear before an audience, he discovered that once in a while he "got something across and liked it." He was graduated in 1895 as valedictorian of the class, and delivered an oration on the Armenian massacres.[6]

Fosdick was eighteen years old when he entered Colgate University at

[3] Fosdick, "Are Religious People Fooling Themselves?" *ibid.*, CLXI (June, 1930), 62; Fosdick, "The Trenches and the Church at Home," *Atlantic Monthly*, CXXIII (January, 1919), 30-31.

[4] Autobiography (Typescript, cited by permission of the author), pp. 11, 14, 26, 27; "Living for the Fun of It," *American Magazine*, CIX (April, 1930), 56; *The Hope of the World* (New York: Harper & Brothers, 1933), p. 105; *Successful Christian Living* (New York: Harper & Brothers, 1937), p. 215.

[5] Autobiography, pp. 25, 26.

[6] *Ibid.*, pp. 26, 28.

Hamilton, New York. Colgate was a denominational institution, under the control of the Baptists. The president of the college was a Baptist minister, as were several of the professors, including Albert Brigham, the professor of geology and the college's lecturer on such subjects as "Science and the First Chapter of Genesis." [7] Young Fosdick at once found himself at home in the religious activities of the campus.

The professors were generally conservative, religiously, but not unfriendly to critical thinking. Eager and keen-minded, Harry found college a great experience, an intellectual-emotional revolution. For the first time he explored the doctrines of Charles Darwin, and in them he found a new universe. He had had no thought of ever relinquishing the tenets of his religious faith, but before his freshman year was over, he had become an avowed evolutionist. Impressed by his own boldness, he prepared a letter, a bomb to drop into the peaceful circle of his family. With some interest and anxiety he awaited the explosion. His father wrote to him simply and directly: "Dear Harry: I believed in evolution before you were born." [8]

His course at Colgate, although considerably removed from the traditional language-centered program of an earlier period, consisted of first-year classes in Greek, Latin, and French, as well as mathematics, rhetoric, and public speaking. In the sophomore year Harry substituted German for French, took two more terms of rhetoric, elected English literature for two terms, and continued his courses in Latin, Greek, mathematics, and public speaking. As a lower classman he must take "systematic exercise" in the new and modern gymnasium which was "thoroughly equipped with the most approved apparatus."

In his junior and senior years he elected a great variety of courses: logic, ethics, history of philosophy, psychology, Anglo-Saxon, history of art, history of education, biology, zoology, geology, history of evolution and, every term, one to three courses in public speaking.[9]

Almost at once he impressed his classmates with his studiousness and his intellectual superiority. Quiet and serious, he seemed from the very beginning of his college career to be destined for the Phi Beta Kappa and *summa cum laude* which he eventually earned. Systematic in his study habits, he sat at his "big wide desk" in his fraternity room, "two unabridged dictionaries in their racks—one on each side of him," and pored over his books or composed his English projects and his speeches. He wrote his first drafts in a cheap,

[7] *Madisonensis*, XXVIII (February 17, 1896), 139.

[8] Fosdick, "Evolution and Religion," *Ladies' Home Journal*, XLII (September, 1925), 12. Cf. Autobiography, p. 30.

[9] Colgate University *Annual Catalogue* (Hamilton, New York, 1895), pp. 14, 15, 26, 44; Records of the Registrar, Colgate University, 1895-1900.

lined notebook on lines 1, 4, 8, etc., reserving the spaces between for revisions, new words plucked from the dictionaries, new sentences conjured up out of his thought.

Better mannered and better dressed than most of the "rather raw set" of Colgate students, and "by no means a bookworm," despite his studious habits, he was rushed by three fraternities and pledged by Delta Upsilon. His attractive appearance, erect stature and good bearing gave him more dignity than freshmen were supposed to have and led a few students to regard him as one who was not unaware of his superior abilities. But most of his fellows thought him modest, cordial, and "genial enough." [10]

At the end of his first few weeks in school he earned his first honors when *Madisonensis,* the students' biweekly magazine, published his poem, "The Sirens," twenty-eight lines of iambic pentameter, a fable, in the Grecian mood, of the transformation of lovely sirens into the rocky islands off the coast of Sicily. He did not take part in sports, but he was an enthusiastic spectator, and regular enough to write his class yell. He was regular enough, too—in a day when nicknames were a symbol of familiarity which contrasted with the formal address of the classroom and chapel—to be dubbed "Fuzzy" Fosdick, not simply because of his shock of dark, kinky hair, but also because he and his fellows knew and loved Kipling's poem, "Fuzzy-Wuzzy." In his junior year he was editor-in-chief of the school annual, *The Salmagundi,* and in his senior year he was associate editor of *Madisonensis,* as well as class poet, and president of the student association. [11]

The dominant activity in Fosdick's life at Colgate, in classroom and out, was public speaking. He had weekly exercises in declamation during his freshman and sophomore years. As a sophomore he also studied elocution and voice culture—breathing, "diaphragmatic action," articulation, pronunciation, and "vocal expression." In this third year he took up the principles of speech composition, writing and delivering orations which were "freely criticized" prior to the required public presentation. He also elected courses in argumentation and debate, with parliamentary practice, legislative procedure, and debates on public questions.

His instructor in rhetoric and public speaking was Ralph Thomas, "a somewhat pompous and thick-set litle fellow," who later resigned from his teaching position to practice law and to take his place as a member of the

---

[10] Letters to the writer from H. D. Gray, January 29, 1954; John M. Sayles, February 2, 1954, and others of Fosdick's classmates at Colgate, a few of whom prefer to remain anonymous.

[11] *Madisonensis,* XXVIII (November 11, 1895); letters to the writer from Norman F. S. Russell, February 1, 1954; John M. Sayles, February 2, 1954; Frank S. Squyer, February 10, 1954.

New York State Legislature. Fosdick remembers him as an elocutionist; he was "all for the old-time oratory," says a classmate: "right hand gesture here, two steps to the left there." To some of his students he was "as empty of original ideas as a bass drum," but others recall that he emphasized organization and style more than gesture and vocal exercise. He taught his students "how to formulate a plan for debate," how to gather materials, weigh facts, search out and refute the opposing arguments. He put "much emphasis on writing speeches," and then insisted that the student "get the substance inside till it obsessed him." Whatever else may be said, he used Genung's *Practical Elements of Rhetoric,* with its emphasis on style and invention, as the textbook in his writing courses.[12]

Toward the end of his freshman year, Fosdick was chosen as one of six men in his Greek class to appear in a public debate in the Academy chapel on the question, "Resolved, that the *Iliad* and *Odyssey* represent distinct periods of Greek civilization, and cannot, therefore, be the composition of one author." In the same year, coached by a senior member of his fraternity, he took first prize in the Kingsford Declamation Contest. As a sophomore he won first prizes in Latin, Greek, and English essay contests. By the time he was a junior, he was eligible to compete in one of the numerous prize contests in public speaking and, with an oration on "The Battle of Omdurman," won first place and $60.[13] A picture in *Madisonensis* showed him an eager, youngish-looking student, his chin held high above the stiff, straight collar, and his dark, curly hair parted precisely down the middle.[14]

His senior year was a regular campaign of speeches, debates, and orations. As student-body president, in the fall of 1899, he took the chapel platform, along with the college president and dean, to make one of the addresses celebrating Dewey Day, in honor of Admiral George Dewey's victory over the Spanish at Manila Bay. The reporter for the *Madisonensis* thought that Mr. Fosdick "illustrated and amply sustained" his points in a "clear, forceful and polished manner." Speaking on "College Students and American Life," he carefully partitioned his subject, marking out the points in parallel con-

[12] Colgate University *Annual Catalogue,* 1897. Letters to the writer from Charles W. Briggs, February 1, 1954; H. Loren Fassett, February 8, 1954; H. D. Gray, January 29, 1954; Burt G. Grenell, February 6, 1954; James H. Howlett, February 3, 1954; Charles M. Newton, February 1, 1954; William M. Parke, February 3, 1954; Norman F. S. Russell, February 1, 1954; John M. Sayles, February 2, 1954; Frank S. Squyer, February 10, 1954; Stuart R. Treat, February 4, 1954, and others of Fosdick's classmates. See also Roy C. McCall, "Harry Emerson Fosdick, Paradox or Paragon," *Quarterly Journal of Speech,* XXXVIII (October, 1953), 284, 285. Cf. f. n. 19.

[13] *Madisonensis,* XXXI (May 31, 1899), 251; H. D. Gray to the writer, January 29, 1954.

[14] *Ibid.,* XXXII (March 12, 1900), 153.

struction. The man whom the American people "long inexpressibly to be," he said, "is fired with the spirit which should inspire America—*devotion to duty;* he is trained with the discipline which should control America—*self-control;* he is crowned with the victory which is America's destiny—*victorious ability.*" [15]

A few weeks later, he was the major hope of the seniors in the inter-class debate with the juniors. The debate, planned weeks in advance, and preceded by eliminations and long hours of study and practice, was one of the out-standing events of the fall term. The chapel was packed for the occasion. Each class had its cheering section; many townspeople, even ministerial can-didates from the seminary were present; and students from the Academy, unable to find seats, lined the walls. The question was, "Resolved: that indus-trial trusts are economically sound." Fosdick spoke first for the affirmative and gave the one rebuttal allotted to his team. His voice was pitched a little too high, the reporter thought, and he spoke at a "nervously rapid rate." But his argument was coherent, and he did not have "those hitches and halts in delivery which are sometimes—and wrongly—thought to be the invariable accompaniment of extemporaneous debate." The juniors put up a stiff battle, but the seniors, at the conclusion of the debate, were confident of victory, a confidence sustained a half-hour later when, after an intentionally torturous review of the issues, the chairman announced the decision.[16]

It was in oratory, however, that Fosdick particularly excelled. The formal composition, written and memorized, gave him opportunity to mold his thought into figurative language, to polish his phrases, and to smooth out the rhythm of his periods until the whole sounded like a peroration. Early in the spring of 1900 at the Sheldon Opera House, he won first prize in the Rowland Oratorical Contest with a speech on "The Rough Riders." He used a dramatic incident, Roosevelt's charge on San Juan Hill, to symbolize his concept of American democracy. Some there were who thought America hopelessly divided—the South against the North, labor against capital, the poor against the rich—some who thought patriotism itself was dead. But America had made reply "in the crowning representative of her life and character." The men at San Juan Hill were made of "that stuff that makes America." A cosmo-politan lot, they were rich, poor, ignorant and learned; they represented every race, occupation, and religion; in their number were Negroes, Indians, and Irishmen, and yet, "trained with the discipline that shall preserve America," they charged when the command came to charge, and intrepid in their courage, glorious in their self-sacrifice, they were at last "laureled with the victory which

[15] *Ibid.*, XXXII (October 9, 1899), 7.
[16] *Ibid.*, XXXII (December 18, 1899), 84-86.

is America's destiny." [17] And so he learned the arts of oratory, but he learned also to confuse sentiment and insight, to stir the people, and to win prizes.

As commencement season approached he made a clean sweep of the honors, winning, in addition to the Rowland Contest, the first-place award of $40 in the annual senior class debate, and the first prize of $60 in the Lewis Oratorical Contest.[18] In the years after he had become one of the nation's most famous platform men, he remembered his college training in oratory as "one of the most useful disciplines" of his educational experience. "I cannot overestimate the value," he said, "[or] the time it saved me in developing technique as a public speaker. . . ." [19]

But while he grew more facile in speech, he became increasingly perplexed about what to say. The simple faith of his freshman days did not return. Darwin would not down, nor did Fosdick, once having accepted survival of the fittest, find it easy to harmonize the principles of natural selection with supernatural creation and the God of the Baptists.

For some two years he enjoyed a delightful rebellion. Friends who had known him as a devout Christian were astonished at the change in him. He could not be dragged into church, he scorned the prayer meeting, he taunted the young saints for their simple beliefs, and he noted with pride that a pious group at the Y.M.C.A. was praying for him.[20] He eagerly devoured Andrew D. White's two-volume *History of the Warfare of Science with Theology in Christendom*. White's relentless uncovering of the superstitions of the Bible and the church, his documentation of the consistent triumph of science against the opposition of the theologians finally "smashed" the whole idea of biblical inerrancy for Fosdick. "I shall have to clear God out of my universe," he told his mother as he left home to begin his junior year at Colgate.[21]

However, his rebellion soon ran full circle and he began to doubt his doubts. White's history, despite its criticism, was essentially sympathetic to the Christian faith; the professors at Colgate were religious men long accustomed to the rebellions of students. Chief among them, in Fosdick's mind, was William Newton Clarke, a professor in the theological seminary who, despite the fact that he was under fire for his liberal views, remained loyal to the church. Fosdick sought out the professor and found sympathy for his

[17] *Ibid.*, XXXII (March 12, 1900), 153-55.
[18] *Ibid.*, XXXII (June 21, 1900), 251-52.
[19] Lionel Crocker, "The Rhetorical Theory of Harry Emerson Fosdick," *Quarterly Journal of Speech*, XXII (April, 1936), 207.
[20] Autobiography, p. 33.
[21] *Loc. cit.*

own critical thinking, but the older man chided him, too, for his naïve rebellion.[22]

In his senior year, in a course in philosophy, he fell under the influence of Royce's concept of loyalty and Borden Parker Bowne's insistence on the primacy and ultimacy of personality. These he tempered with the earthy, optimistic pragmatism of William James. Before he had completed the course, he had come to believe that "there really is a God."[23] He put God back into his thinking, but not, as he said, back into his life. His was an intellectual God, the kind about whom a man might speculate, but not the kind on whom he could depend, emotionally. Nonetheless, he elected to attend a theological seminary—to prepare himself to teach religion.

The chief obstacle to Fosdick's continued study was financial. One year he had interrupted his course at Colgate to work and help out with the family income. When he was graduated he took the teacher's examinations in Buffalo and was offered a position teaching Latin in the high school. His younger brother and sister were in college and his family needed the additional financial support. But his father urged him to go on to seminary. "Harry, you know that you will never be satisfied outside the Christian ministry," his father had told him even before he had finished his undergraduate studies.[24]

He had a scholarship to cover his tuition at Hamilton Theological Seminary at Colgate and needed only money enough to meet his board and room and other expenses. Calling upon the skills he had learned in college, he entered an essay contest on the evils of vivisection. His argument was specious, but persuasive. He won third prize of $250, enough to launch him on his ministerial career.[25]

At seminary he took all of the courses offered by William Newton Clarke, some of them intended only for advanced students. But he was not satisfied to remain at Hamilton. The scholarship of Clarke and of visiting lecturers whetted his appetite for study with great teachers. He transferred, therefore, to Union Theological Seminary in New York, across the street from Columbia University.

Union offered him the kind of intellectual liberty and spiritual leadership that he had dreamed of at Colgate and Hamilton.[26] There were strong men on the staff: Charles Cuthbert Hall, president and professor of pastoral

[22] *Ibid.*, p. 36.
[23] *Ibid.*, pp. 39, 179.
[24] *Ibid.*, p. 38.
[25] *Ibid.* Years later, in his retirement, Fosdick was to write: "I have always felt guilty about my specious arguments against vivisection . . . but at least I believed them when I wrote them. . . ."
[26] *Ibid.*, p. 53.

theology; Arthur Cushman McGiffert, who taught church history; Francis Browne, Hebrew and cognate languages; William Knox, ethics and philosophy of religion; and Charles A. Briggs. Briggs was past his prime but his influence in the institution was marked. In 1892, he had been tried for heresy because he did not accept the ultimate authority of the Scriptures. The Presbyterian Church suspended him from the ministry, but lost control of the seminary. Briggs remained at the seminary but was transferred to the Chair of Biblical Theology, and the liberal tradition which he had tested at Union grew stronger with the years.[27]

Fosdick went down to New York in the summer of 1901 to work in the Vacation Daily Bible Schools. Admitted to Union on a scholarship, he was given a winter's job helping to run a mission in the Bowery. He was greatly keyed up by the prospect of at last entering a great university. Moreover, he had fallen in love and was beside himself with joy and wonder.[28]

At the opening of school his excitement reached a new pitch when he passed a special examination for advanced standing in Greek. He enrolled in classes in philosophy at Columbia, theology at the seminary, and assisted at the mission in the Bowery. He learned much, especially in the Bowery, where he helped to conduct as many as nine meetings on a single Sunday. Panhandlers, naïve as children in religious matters, clever as Wall Street merchants in driving a shrewd bargain for assistance, taught him lessons he could not learn in his textbooks.

Had it not been for his financial troubles, he might have handled his rigorous schedule and disciplined his nervous excitement. But his resources were so slender that he abused his body with overwork and improper diet. His most expensive meal of the week was a twenty-five cent dinner on Sunday.[29]

In November he broke down completely from nervous strain, overwork, and undernourishment. It was, he wrote later, "the most hideous experience of my life."[30] He went home, a victim of melancholia. After months of purposelessness and disintegration, he went to a sanitarium where, by tutoring his physician's son, he gained a modicum of self-confidence. His fiancée's father sent him to Europe, and slowly through the months he regained his health. But his spirit did not revive. His religion was an intellectual exercise, not a faith. "I was in hell," he said afterwards, "and had to get a vital faith

[27] George L. Prentiss, *The Union Theological Seminary in the City of New York: Its Design and Another Decade of Its History* (Asbury Park, N.J.: J. M., W. & C. Pennypacker, 1899), pp. 311-35.

[28] Autobiography, p. 47.

[29] *Ibid.*, pp. 48-49.

[30] *Ibid.*, p. 49.

to climb out."[31] The faith came gradually, and with it, the lifting of the clouds. When he returned to the seminary the next fall, struggling yet to find his way, he had learned a lesson of vital significance to his ministry, a lesson of faith that Union, with its splendid staff of professors, could not teach him.

At the end of his second year in the seminary, he took over his first pastoral charge, a tiny church in the Adirondacks where he preached during the summer months. In the fall, following an unusually successful speech which he gave at the Colgate banquet in New York, and which attracted the attention of George C. Lorimer, minister of the Madison Avenue Baptist Church, Fosdick was appointed student assistant at the church. Upon his graduation from Union in 1904, he was called to the pastorate of the Montclair, New Jersey, Baptist Church.[32]

Fosdick served the Montclair church until 1915, a period of eleven years. A somewhat conventional preacher, he did not give much evidence of the intellectual struggle he had gone through, nor of the extent to which he had abandoned the faith of his fathers, nor yet of the shock which he was about to inflict upon all Protestant America.

He published his first book in 1908, *The Second Mile,* a slender volume which grew out of a sermon he had preached one Sunday morning. He followed it with *The Manhood of the Master,* in 1913, and *The Meaning of Prayer* in 1915. All were exceptionally well received and *The Meaning of Prayer,* subsequently republished, sold nearly a half-million copies of the American edition.[33]

By the time he was ready to leave Montclair, he had already arrived at the fundamental tenets of his later preaching: that personality is the supreme value; that religion is an experience, not an intellectual exercise, an intuitive knowledge of God, not an argument about Him; that its consequence is to be measured in conduct, not in rules, or creeds, or theologies; and that authority is to be found, not in the written word, even of the Bible, but in the experiences of men.

But if he was inclined to be conventional in his ministry, he was nonetheless effective. The skill in speaking he had learned at college gave a resonance to his message, an amplifying depth and intensity that excited the interest and commanded the respect of his people. He was already master of the point concisely stated and vividly illustrated, and he could look into the eyes of his congregation and speak directly, in an impassioned manner if need

[31] Edward Clary Root, "The Power of Faith," *The American Magazine,* CI (May, 1926), 156.

[32] Autobiography, p. 53.

[33] *Ibid.,* p. 66.

be, without the crippling aid of manuscript or notes. The membership of his church trebled in the eleven years he was at Montclair.[34]

Two things he learned, particularly, in these early years: he learned first to study: to set aside the morning hours, to read, reflect, and prepare his sermons; to maintain his schedule against all hazards; he learned the advantage of an office away from his home and his church, the greatly increased efficiency in having a secretary copy and file the passages he had marked and classified; he learned the discipline of writing, of reducing his thoughts to paper and of studying what he had written in the light of questions or objections which particular members of his congregation might raise.[35]

He learned, secondly, to take his sermons from the personal problems of men and women, to regard all preaching as problem-solving, to make each problem so real that every man could recognize it as his own, to argue the alternative courses of action, and to plead the advantages of the way of Jesus.

In the fall of 1908, Fosdick began to lecture at Union Theological Seminary on Baptist principles and polity. Three years later he became an instructor in homiletics. In 1915, he resigned his pastorate at Montclair to accept an appointment at Union as the Morris K. Jesup Professor of Practical Theology. His task, he said in his inaugural address, was to teach the young ministers to use the Bible in their preachings. In recent years scholars had revealed the historic Bible, with all of its primitive concepts of science, ethics, and theology, and in consequence had shattered many a layman's faith in the present values of the Scriptures. His business was to teach the "real nature of God's revelation in the Bible"—that men must see meanings of the universe "in terms of personality and the meanings of personality in terms of Christ. . . ."[36]

II

Fosdick was finally dislodged from his essentially conservative preaching not by critical studies nor by liberal influences but by an event of world-shaking significance, the great war which broke out in Europe in 1914.

His analysis of the war was essentially rhetorical. He saw it in the stereotyped pattern of his preaching—a problem to be dramatized and resolved. He hated war because of its "persistent debauching and brutalizing of men's souls"; he hated it because it took hold of the finest qualities in human life—courage, devotion, sacrifice—and utilized them to kill and lay

---

[34] *Current Biography* (New York, 1940), p. 309.

[35] Autobiography, p. 64.

[36] Fosdick, *A Modern Preacher's Problem in His Use of the Scriptures*, An Inaugural Address, as Morris K. Jesup Professor of Practical Theology, Union Theological Seminary, September 13, 1915, pp. 18, 20-21, 27, 32.

waste; he hated it because of the injustice it worked, and the succeeding wars it spawned, until men came to believe that war itself was an integral part of the system of international relations.[37]

But while he hated war, and preached his hatred, he saw in this one war the possibility, remote perhaps, that international anarchy would yield to law, that the resort to arms as a means of settling disputes would give way to the courts of world government. Indeed, the Christian, and only the Christian (who was first of all a citizen of the Kingdom of God on earth), could translate patriotism into world-wide loyalty.[38] For the moment war was terrifying and horrible, a barrier to human progress, but in the long perspective of history wars were but jutting rocks around which the advancing stream of humanity swirled and moved on.

For the present, action was necessary. He saw that clearly in alliterative terms—"the horrors of Verdun, the mutilated bodies of Belgian boys, the bleaching bones of countless children...and after sixty generations of Christian opportunity, some five million wounded men in the hospitals of Europe." How could America keep heart and stand aloof? [39]

The basic dilemma of his faith—how a Christian, believing in the absolute value of personality, could go to war and kill—he resolved, oddly enough, in the manner of his evangelical fathers. *"Personality and physical existence,"* he said, *"are not identical."* A man's personality was one thing, his physical existence another. If a bayonet reached a man's body, the problem of personality passed "far beyond an earthy battlefield." [40]

As the war progressed he grew "increasingly anxious" that the United States should get into it. He was impatient with Wilson, indignant when the President announced that he was "too proud to fight." In 1916, he condemned Charles Evans Hughes for not pledging to take America into the war. He wrote a volume on *The Challenge of the Present Crisis,* conservative and anti-militaristic in some respects, but on the whole strongly in support of the war. He preached pro-war sermons at Stanford and at Harvard (the latter one of the "most moving" addresses he had ever delivered), and he stumped New York State with a team of speakers in a campaign for war and world federation.[41]

When at last war came, a crusade to make the world safe for democracy,

---

[37] Fosdick, *The Challenge of the Present Crisis* (New York: Association Press, 1918), p. 63.

[38] *Ibid.,* p. 77.

[39] *Ibid.,* p. 31.

[40] Fosdick, *Challenge,* p. 39.

[41] Autobiography, pp. 81-83. He later repudiated these activities and said that *The Challenge* was the only one of his books he regretted having written.

nationalism and Christianity joined forces in one great religious impulse. While President Wilson demanded a peace without victory on the political front, the president of the Federal Council of Churches of Christ in America was declaring that "The war for righteousness will be won! Let the Church do her part." [42]

In the spring of 1918, Fosdick visited the war front. He talked to the boys of courage and sacrifice, of home and democracy, of victory and peace, of the use of force for moral ends. He praised them for their unstinted dedication, for their self-denial, for their faith which now and then flamed out like a flare in No-Man's Land, for the magnificent ways in which they were fundamentally religious.

But all the while he despised the pettiness of the Church—his brethren of the ministry who denounced the dance, the theater, cards, drink, smoke, and Sabbathbreaking, or solemnly warned the boys that more important than the work in France was "the preparation of your souls to meet the Lord who speedily will return!" [43] He was disgusted with the pettiness of the sectarian appeal. While the Church busied itself with denominational creeds, the Army preached a crusade. "I used to wonder at the Cross," a soldier said to him; "not now! I think that Jesus was a lucky man to have a chance to die for a great cause." Let the Church proclaim social aims worth fighting for, and her day of unprecedented opportunity was at hand; let her make "ethical negations only the shadows cast by the great light of positive ideals"; let her practice as well as preach fraternity, and she need not fear for her contribution, nor for her place in the lives of the men, either when they were in the army, or after they were out of it. [44]

Never before had he seen quite so clearly that the old creed, with its shackling customs and dogmas, and its sectarian exclusiveness, must be shattered before the minister of God could preach the essential elements of a liberal faith.

III

Critical as he was of the Church's petty negativism, Fosdick did not regard himself as an iconoclast called of God to shatter the idols of orthodoxy. The pulpit of the First Presbyterian Church, offered to him in the fall of 1918, was a liberal pulpit, open to the liberal preachers of the New York Presbytery

[42] Ray H. Abrams, *Preachers Present Arms: A Study of the War-time Attitudes and Activities of the Churches and the Clergy in the United States, 1914-1918* (New York: Round Table Press, Inc., 1933), p. 58, citing *Federal Council Bulletin* Vol. I, No. 3 (March, 1918), 12. Frank Mason North was then president of the Council.

[43] Fosdick, "The Trenches and the Church at Home," *Atlantic Monthly*, CXXIII (January, 1919), 26.

[44] *Ibid.*, pp. 26, 33.

and the learned doctors of the Union Theological Seminary. The laymen who sat in the pews had already accommodated their Calvinistic doctrines to the higher criticism and the evolutionary hypothesis. They were no more shocked, therefore, when Fosdick challenged a docile acceptance of creeds than they were when he attacked a blind faith in progress.

For three and a half years Fosdick preached to the congregations of Old First Church without unusual incident. Sunday after Sunday the people crowded to hear him. On one occasion he caught the brief attention of the press when his congregation, for the first time in the history of the Old Presbyterian Church, openly applauded the remarks of a preacher—for his denunciation of the "narrow nationalism" of George Harvey, American ambassador to the Court of St. James. He was cited again for attacking the war spirit, and for demanding that the United States end the warlike tension in the Far East.[45]

No unusual circumstance attended his preaching on Sunday morning, May 21, 1922. He had announced his sermon title, "Shall the Fundamentalists Win?" in advance, but no one, least of all Fosdick himself, anticipated that he was about to preach the most sensational and widely-publicized sermon of his generation.

Only a few Sundays earlier, Dr. Clarence E. Macartney of Philadelphia had visited the First Presbyterian Church and heard Fosdick preach. An arch-conservative and a leader in the Philadelphia Presbytery, Macartney was soon to become Fosdick's major antagonist. But on the morning of his visit he was only an interested observer. Arriving at the church some twenty minutes before eleven o'clock, he was surprised to find long queues of people standing in front of the doors, such crowds as he had not seen since he had worshipped in the popular churches of Edinburgh.[46]

Escorted to a pew at eleven o'clock, he noted that in a short time the entire church was filled and "not a few" people were seated on chairs in the aisles and in the adjoining chapel. He found the church large and beautiful, the platform approached by long marble steps. At the left was the lectern for the reading of the Bible, in the center the conducting desk, and on a pillar at the right, the pulpit.

The three ministers of the church made their appearance, the young assistant, Mr. Speers, in the lead, followed by the venerable pastor, Dr. Alexander, and at last Dr. Fosdick, "an earnest-looking man with a heavy shock of black hair, and from a distance with an Oriental cast of countenance." Mr. Speers made the announcements, Dr. Alexander prayed a "beautiful

[45] *New York Times,* June 6, November 9, 1921.

[46] "Sermons Here and There, II. Hunting for Christianity in New York," *The Presbyterian,* XCII (June 8, 1922), 8, 26.

prayer," and Dr. Fosdick read the Scriptures. The stragglers who came in during the singing of the hymn were placed on the marble steps in front of the pulpit. When the venerable and distinguished-looking General Charles King (a writer of Civil War tales and the clerk at Plymouth Church in Brooklyn) was about to join the "bleacherites," Fosdick stepped down "graciously" and invited him to sit on the platform.

Although, as Macartney observed from his place in the pew, Fosdick did not take a text, he did base his sermon upon a biblical incident. He spoke in a pleasing voice, without gesticulation, but he made a "ringing and powerful appeal to men and women . . . to be true to the sanctity of life." "No one," he said, "could have mistaken it for anything but a notable discourse." There was, however, an ominous note in Macartney's reaction. The sermon could not have been improved upon, he thought, for "the territory which it covered." But something was missing: the great preacher did not touch upon the "hopes and warnings of the gospel." He spoke of the vain sacrifices of parents for a wayward boy, but he did not "tell his great congregation that Christ had died on the cross for them. . . ."

No Macartney sat in the congregation on May 21 to record his impressions for the press. Again, as on the earlier occasion, Dr. Fosdick took no text. He announced abruptly that he and the audience would think together on the fundamentalist controversy which threatened to divide the American churches, "as though already they were not sufficiently split and riven." [47] The fundamentalists, he said, were intent upon driving men and women of liberal views out of the evangelical churches, and no denominations were more affected than the Baptist and the Presbyterian.

He was concerned with the necessity for Christians to adjust their faith to the new knowledge, especially that derived from the critical studies of the Scriptures (the higher criticism) and the scientific findings of the biologists. Among the items of faith which needed re-examination, he singled out three: the literal transcription of the Scriptures, the virgin birth, and the second coming of Jesus.

He did not attack the doctrines directly but condemned, rather, the intolerant fanaticism with which the fundamentalists clung to them. They not only rejected the new knowledge but, in the spirit of intolerance, were determined to shut the door of Christian fellowship against all moderns who sought to reconcile science and religion. There were great tasks before the

[47] Fosdick, *Shall the Fundamentalists Win?* A sermon preached at the First Presbyterian Church, New York City, May 21, 1922, stenographically reported by Margaret Renton, p. 1. See also *The New Knowledge and the Christian Faith*, ed. Ivy Lee, reprinted from a sermon by Dr. Fosdick, preached at the First Presbyterian Church, New York, May 21, 1922.

church—men and women were on the rocks spiritually, crying for help; the world had not yet found a means to solve the problem of war; and the Turks were massacring Christians in Armenia. In the face of these colossal issues the Church could not afford to quarrel over creedal matters, to "play with the tiddledywinks and peccadilloes of religion." It was almost unforgivable that men "should tithe mint and anise and cummin, and quarrel over them" when the world was perishing "for the lack of the weightier matters of the law, justice, and mercy, and faith."

Fosdick's blunt sympathies with modernism were apparent, but his sermon was in some measure conciliatory. He recognized that there were many "beautiful and gracious souls" who clung to a belief in the virgin birth and the infallibility of the Scriptures. So he appealed to tolerance, he pleaded for a church broad enough to contain both groups.

The sermon might have passed unnoticed had not one of his parishioners, the head of a nationally known publicity agency, undertaken to distribute it. With a publicist's eye for easy reading, he cut the sermon into short paragraphs, used captions which brought the controversial sections into sharp focus, and deleted parts of it, including, unhappily, the conciliatory introduction and conclusion. He then inserted a small printed slip saying that Mr. Fosdick was preaching to the largest congregation in New York and, without indicating who was responsible for the printing of the sermon, mailed it to hundreds of preachers across the continent.[48]

The reaction among the fundamentalists was widespread, and vocal. Macartney, who was soon to be elected moderator of the General Assembly of his church, was amazed to think that Fosdick, who was not a Presbyterian, should stand in a Presbyterian pulpit and take his bread from a Presbyterian congregation while he openly defied the Presbyterian creed. He was shocked by the "almost unpardonable flippancy" in Fosdick's comparison of the virgin birth, the inspiration of the Bible, and the second coming of Christ to mint, anise, and cummin. William Jennings Bryan, characterizing Fosdick as the "most altitudinous higher critic" of his acquaintance, denounced Darwinism and atheism to 5,000 persons in the Moody church in New York.[49]

The warfare thus opened raged for more than three years, with the fundamentalists determined to drive the modernists from their strongholds within the Church. In the meantime, with the newspapers giving full play to the attack of the fundamentalists, Fosdick was preaching regularly to overflow

[48] *The Presbyterian,* XCII (September 7, 1922), 24; Fosdick, Autobiography, p. 113.
[49] Clarence E. Macartney, "Shall Unbelief Win? An Answer to Dr. Fosdick," *The Presbyterian,* XCII (July 13, 1922), 26; *ibid.* (July 20, 1922), 8-10; *New York Times,* January 9, 1923.

congregations. But in the end, despite the warm support of his own congregation and of the New York Presbytery, he felt compelled to resign. His resignation, tendered in the fall of 1924, was to take effect the following spring.

Invitations for him to preach poured in from all over the country; he was offered a pulpit in Edinburgh for the summer of 1925; and he was invited to preach at the opening of the League of Nations—to occupy the pulpit of John Calvin, the great Geneva reformer and the founder of the Presbyterian faith. The conflict had proved but a sounding board for his preaching: where he had been heard by a few hundred in New York, he was now known across the continent, and his name had appeared in headlines from Christiania, Norway, to Istanbul, Turkey.[50]

IV

Aside from the internecine battles on fundamentalism, the major problem facing the Church in the 1920's was that of its relation to war. Not long after the signing of the armistice, Sir Philip Gibbs exposed the fraud of the Belgian atrocity stories and scholars began to challenge the thesis that Germany was responsible for the war. The treaty at Versailles, despite the pledges of Woodrow Wilson, had handed about subject peoples to meet the demands of the victors, and the League of Nations, for all its merit, guaranteed the new boundaries by armed force and the blood of the youth. It was the best that we could do, the President had said, and acceptable only because the terms of the League made possible a future peaceable adjustment of inequities. But his high-flung banner, "Make the World Safe for Democracy"—a cloud by day and a pillar of fire by night to the Great Crusade—was soon to become a mockery on men's lips. The Church, particularly, was deeply penitent over its recent equating of God and patriotism.

Fosdick, taunted by the pacifists for having "prostituted Christ," and condemned by his own conscience for his participation in the war, sought expiation in energetic support of the League of Nations, the World Court, and other modes of international cooperation. The "most important single social problem" confronting humanity, he said, "is the provision of international substitutes for war."[51] In his opening sermon for the League of Nations in the Protestant Cathedral of St. Peter in Geneva, he warned: "If mankind does not end war, war will end mankind." His voice rang out, reaching every corner of the great edifice, in words both "courageous and

[50] Autobiography, p. 150.

[51] *New York Times*, March 12, 1923. For the most thoroughgoing attack on Fosdick, see Henry W. Pinkham, *Collective Homicide, Letters to Harry Emerson Fosdick* (Brookline, Mass.: Association to Abolish War, 1923). The letters are dated 1919.

brilliant."[52] He condemned not war alone, but nationalism. Christians, he said, believing in God as the Father of all mankind, must learn that narrow nationalism is "the most explicit and thoroughgoing denial of Christianity, its thought of God and its love of man that there is on earth." Only the year before, in London, his faith swept away in the high idealism of his rhetoric, he had prophesied that he would live to see the United States join the League of Nations.[53]

Not all of the peace groups concurred with Fosdick in his endorsement of the League of Nations, nor did all of them agree with him in eschewing nationalism, at least American nationalism. Confused as to their aims, the seekers after peace were by the mid-1920's marked out by their critics as prophets of Babel, a multitude of voices, with no common tongue. The banner under which the diverse groups were finally able to unite was the outlawry of war. The idea, suggested by an American, was espoused by Charles Clayton Morrison, editor of the *Christian Century*, John Dewey, William E. Borah, and others. In 1926, Aristide Briand proposed it as the basis of a bilateral treaty between the United States and France; Secretary of State Frank B. Kellogg responded by suggesting that the treaty be extended to include other major powers. After some months of negotiation, the great powers of the world met in Paris in August, 1928, and signed a pact which solemnly condemned "recourse to war for the solution of international controversies," and renounced war as "an instrument of national policy in their relations with one another."[54]

Fosdick approved of the renunciation of war, but he did not easily lose his perspective. He greeted the pact with the question: "magnificent or mad"? It would be magnificent, he said, if it were implemented by adequate substitutes for war, mad if people relied on the stroke of a pen to solve their international tensions.[55]

To the American people, however, and to the churches especially, and eventually to Fosdick himself, the appeal of renunciation of war (buttressed, paradoxically, by a sense of security derived from the apparent fact of geographical isolationism) was irresistible. The farther removed they were from

[52] Fosdick, *A Christian Conscience about War:* A Sermon delivered at the League of Nations Assembly Service at the Cathedral at Geneva, September 13, 1925 (New York, 1925); *New York Times*, September 14, 1925.

[53] *New York Times*, May 15, 1924.

[54] Selig Adler, "The War-Guilt Question and American Disillusionment, 1918-1928," *Journal of Modern History*, XXIII (March, 1951), 1-28; Charles Clayton Morrison, *The Outlawry of War; A Constructive Policy for World Peace* (Chicago: Willett, Clark & Colby, 1927); Allan Nevins, *The United States in a Chaotic World* ("The Chronicles of America Series," Vol. 55 [New Haven, 1950]), Chap. iv.

[55] *New York Times*, April 16, November 12, 1928.

the war, the more they knew of its origins, and the more they reflected on its deceits and its brutality, the keener their sense of guilt and the greater their feeling of revlusion. Historically, pacifism had been only a tiny stream in American life, the confluence of a few devout and courageous Quakers, Mennonites, and Brethren, men who denounced war in times of war as well as in times of peace. Now a romanticized, peacetime pacifism, preached in the classroom, advocated by student groups, made the subject of youth gatherings and church conferences, quickly swelled into a great flood. In increasing numbers men avowed their determination to go to jail rather than participate in war. There were waiting lines for martyrdom.

In 1934, in the second of two nation-wide polls of Protestant ministers on the question of war, 67 per cent of the 20,000 ministers who replied said that they would refuse to sanction any future war.[56] At this point Fosdick, in the most dramatic speech of his career, was thrust into the leadership of the Protestant peace crusade. The results of the poll were announced and discussed at a mass meeting in New York on May 7, 1934, at the Broadway Tabernacle, in the presence of some of the most prominent clergymen of the nation, and with Fosdick as the principal speaker. The meeting had been well-publicized and reporters of both the religious and the secular press were present. Fosdick's subject was announced as "My Account with the Unknown Soldier." He had preached the same sermon to his own congregation six months earlier, on the Sunday preceding Armistice Day, but on that occasion important elements of the drama—the gathering of prominent clergymen, the mass meeting, the results of the poll, and the reporters—all were missing.

Dr. Fosdick spoke, said the *New York Times*, "as if he were making a confession to the Unknown Soldier."[57] His sermon was extraordinarily personal. It was a penance for past sins, a catharsis for the years of self-condemnation.

He tried to picture the Unknown Soldier, a conscript, no doubt, coerced to fight. He had no doubt that he knew the Unknown Soldier, that he had met him somewhere on the battle front. He recalled the night in a ruined barn behind the trenches when he spoke to a company of hand-grenaders detailed to raid the German trenches. They said that on the average no more than half a company ever came back from such a raid. And he, "a minister of

---

[56] "What 20,000 Clergymen Think," *The Nation*, CXXXVIII (May 9, 1934), 524; Dixon Wecter, *The Age of the Great Depression, 1929-1941* (New York, 1948), pp. 306-7.

[57] May 8, 1934. The sermon is published in Fosdick's *The Secret of Victorious Living; Sermons on Christianity Today* (New York: Harper & Brothers, 1934), pp. 88-98.

Christ, tried to nerve them for their suicidal and murderous endeavor." A "gullible fool," he had thought that modern wars could make the world safe for democracy. Was the Unknown Soldier in that barn that night?

Some there were who thought war a thrilling experience, the "most exciting episode of our time," but they were the ones who had never seen a battle. Some were thrilled to stand at Arlington before the tomb of the Unknown Soldier, where he lay in the full panoply of military glory, knowing that he was the symbol of the highest idealism and courage of America. No doubt about it. But it was these thoughts that made war "a blistering fury" on his lips and "a deep self-condemnation" in his heart, for war laid its hands on the "strongest, loveliest things" in men and used the "noblest attributes of the human spirit" for the ungodliest of deeds! Only war could recount with glee the tale of an infantryman, his ammunition exhausted, arming himself with a spade and splitting the skulls of enemy soldiers as one by one they rounded a traverse, and only war could produce in countless numbers the pictures painted by an officer, of "a pair of hands (nationality unknown) which protruded from the soaked ashen soil like the roots of a tree turned upside down...."

Did they wonder that he, who had been sent into the camps to awaken idealism, had an account to settle between his soul and the Unknown Soldier?

As for himself, he would settle the war problem, not sentimentally, but hard-headedly. He would plead with his country to stay out of war, to cooperate with every movement that had any hope for peace: to enter the World Court, to support the League of Nations, to demand disarmament, but above all to stay out of war. "We can have...this monstrous thing or we can have Christ, but we cannot have both."

As for his own account, he would settle that, too, by the renunciation of war. "I renounce war," he said, in a final dramatic pledge, "I renounce war and never again, directly or indirectly, will I sanction or support another! O Unknown Soldier, in penitent reparation I make you that pledge."

The newspapers of the city caught up the story, featured it on the front page, and the wire services dispersed it across the country. *Christian Century* reprinted the sermon in full, *Scholastic* and *Scribner's Commentator* published extensive excerpts, and other magazines quoted the most dramatic passages. When he preached it again in substance at Yale University, he was startled for the first time in thirty years of speaking in college chapels, to have the students break into the sermon with applause. Letters and telegrams poured in from all over the country.[58]

[58] *Christian Century*, LI (June 6, 1934), 754-56; *Scholastic*, XXVII (November 9, 1935), 9-10; *Scribner's Commentator*, XI (November 4, 1941), 97-100; Fosdick, *Secret*, p. 102.

With his instinct for the dramatic, Fosdick had placed himself at the head of the pacifists and, unwittingly, in the vanguard of the isolationists. He had excited a dream for a world of peace which the people who heard him could never forget, but it was a dream which took little account of the realities of the international scene.

V

Fosdick had scarcely resigned from the First Presbyterian Church in 1925 before he was offered the pulpit of the Park Avenue Baptist Church where John D. Rockefeller and his son were prominent members. After some hesitation, he accepted the call, first having stipulated that his annual salary should not exceed $5,000, and that baptism by immersion should not be required of new members. The church accepted the conditions and agreed further, in anticipation of the large crowds he would attract, to replace its newly-constructed but small building with a much larger edifice which they would erect uptown, in the vicinity of Columbia University. Rockefeller, in order to reduce Fosdick's embarrassment as pastor of the "richest man in America," established and placed under control of the church a trust fund, the interest of which was to constitute his annual contributions.[59]

Fosdick was installed on May 31, 1925, only two months after he had preached his farewell sermon at the First Presbyterian Church. He had, however, already arranged with the Union Theological Seminary for a sabbatical year in Europe and Palestine, and therefore did not begin his active ministry until the fall of 1926. In the meantime, Rockefeller purchased a site on Riverside Drive and 122nd Street and, with Fosdick's approval, began the construction of a mammoth edifice, popularly referred to as the "skyscraper" church.[60]

Ready for occupancy in 1930, the new building was a large neo-Gothic church, unmatched in American Protestantism, save by the Cathedral of St. John the Divine, which was but a few blocks distant. Its gigantic tower, reaching 400 feet above the level of the street, looked out over the Hudson River and housed the offices, educational plant, the smaller assembly rooms, and the recreational facilities. The nave, with seating for 2,400 people, was lined on the side walls with ten stained-glass windows which depicted the progress of man in learning, religion, and the arts. The pulpit was on the right of the chancel, the reading desk on the left, and between them a great stonework screen embellished with figures of Christ and the apostles.

[59] "Open-Shop Parson," *Time Magazine*, XLI (March 15, 1943), 54; *New York Times*, May 29, 1925; Autobiography, p. 147.

[60] *New York Times*, May 26, July 12, 25, August 8, 1925; January 29, 1926.

Some were impressed with the great beauty of the new structure, others only with its vastness and its cost.[61]

From the day Dr. Fosdick had accepted the call to the Park Avenue Baptist Church, all American Protestantism had experienced a feeling of tension over his new adventure. The fundamentalists were disturbed that such a master of "brilliant sophistries" and "graces of oratory" should have so prominent a pulpit from which to proclaim his heresies. Of one thing they were certain, however: the power of God would not be in the pile of cold stones erected by Mr. Rockefeller. The radicals were concerned lest Fosdick, failing to accept his responsibilities of leadership, should give way to the forces of conservatism. Even his friends were not yet ready to say that he could escape the onus of wealth reflected in the very elegance and beauty of the new church. Was it possible for the pastor of such a church to avoid trimming his gospel or "suppressing an inconvenient segment of it?" [62]

Whatever the doubts of others, the people who heard him approved. Thirty-two hundred crowded into the nave and one of the assembly rooms on the opening Sunday, and hundreds were unable to find seats. On the following Sabbath the authorities placed loud-speakers in three assembly rooms and the small chapel. A line, four abreast, which began to form about nine o'clock, had by 10:30 A.M. reached down Riverside Drive to the south end of the church grounds; by the time the services began, 4,000 persons had pressed their way into the nave and the assembly rooms. Week after week, and year after year at periodical intervals, the press carried reports of such overflow crowds.[63]

If Fosdick preached to thousands in his congregation on Sunday morning, he preached to hundreds of thousands in his radio audience on Sunday afternoon. He had begun his radio preaching while he was still at the First Presbyterian Church, and at Park Avenue had broadcast his Sunday morning services. In 1927, he initiated the nation-wide broadcast of the National Vespers, a half-hour program sponsored by the National Broadcasting Company and devoted chiefly to his sermon. Always an attractive Sunday feature, the Vespers, at its interest peak, was rebroadcast by 125 stations, and was heard by an estimated two-to-three million listeners. Fosdick received over 100,000 letters a year from members of his radio audience.[64]

[61] John Hyde Preston, "Dr. Fosdick's New Church," *World's Work*, LVIII (July, 1929), 56-58; "Dr. Fosdick Accepts the Challenge," *Christian Century*, XLVII (October 15, 1930), 1239.

[62] John Roach Straton in *New York Times*, May 20, 1925; "Dr. Fosdick Accepts the Challenge," *Christian Century*, XLVII (October 15, 1930), 1240.

[63] *New York Times*, October 6, 13, 1930.

[64] *Ibid.*, December 21, 1924; Autobiography, pp. 171-73.

His popularity in the pulpit and on the radio was reflected in his publications. When he accepted the call to the Park Avenue Church he had already published nine volumes, including the Lyman Beecher lectures at Yale, the Cole lectures at Vanderbilt, and his popular little devotional books on *The Meaning of Prayer*, *The Meaning of Faith*, and *The Meaning of Service*. He continued to write: two volumes on the modernists' religion, a book-length report on his pilgrimage to Palestine, a scholarly guide to the understanding of the Bible, and, beginning in 1934, a half-dozen volumes of his sermons. In 1942, his three volumes on prayer, faith, and service, having sold an aggregate of over one-half million copies, were reissued as a single volume; one of his last books to be published was issued with an original printing of 50,000 copies, their largest original print order for a religious book.[65]

What did this man preach, that he should command so large an audience, that he should become a prophet to the nation, that he should be heralded by his colleagues as the "greatest preacher in the English tongue"? [66]

He believed God to be an objective reality, revealed not in tablets of stone or in authoritarian Scriptures, but in the progressive insights of men. He found the highest intuition of God in Jesus, the essential superiority of Christianity in its ethical code, the basis of which was its reverence for personality. In the tradition of Wesley and Schleiermacher he regarded the emotional state as the essential datum. Religious experience he defined as containing two attributes: (1) self-commitment, devotion to something greater than one's own personal interests—to truth, to beauty, or to goodness, not in the abstract, but as embodied in particular causes; and (2) a transforming inward sense of peace and unity, of power and confidence, of harmonious relations with the vital forces of the universe.[67]

In a sense, his emphasis was not unlike that of the fundamentalists. Where the latter dramatized sin and its effect and called for repentance, Fosdick dwelt upon personal problems—tensions, maladjustments, purposelessness—and pointed the way to relief and power through the experience of religion. He not only recognized these identities in fundamentalism and modernism, but

[65] Charles W. Ferguson, "Who Reads Religious Books?" *Saturday Review of Literature*, XVI (July 10, 1937), 14; "Open-Shop Parson," *Time Magazine*, XLI (March 15, 1943) 54.

[66] E. W. Powell in *New York Times*, June 12, 1925; Charles W. Gilkey, "Dr. Fosdick Preaches: Review of *The Hope of the World*," *Christian Century*, LI (April 4, 1934), 459-60; Dr. Stephen S. Wise in *New York Times*, February 4, 1930. On his retirement the *Christian Century* characterized him, along with Henry Ward Beecher and Phillips Brooks as one of the three greatest names of the American pulpit. See "Dr. Fosdick Will Retire Next May," *Christian Century*, LXII (June 20, 1945), 725.

[67] Fosdick, *As I See Religion* (New York: Harper & Brothers, 1932), pp. 10-20.

on this basis justified his adherence to the Church even though he had sloughed off many of the traditional doctrines. He attacked the fundamentalists not simply on the basis that they denied the findings of science, but that, in an effort to defend an outworn creed, they had, like the Pharisees of Jesus' time, neglected the experience.

To Fosdick, religious experience, since it was not circumscribed by creed and doctrine, was not limited to the church or the synagogue. Sometimes a "downright unbelieving scientist," he said, who gave himself to his science and stood by it "through thick and thin" seemed "closer to New Testament Christianity than many of us in the churches." [68] "You who are carried out of yourselves by something greater than yourselves, like the Fifth symphony of Beethoven," he said to the students of Columbia University, "are religious for me, no matter what terrible opinion you may have of yourselves." [69] Men and women who felt an inner sense of strength, of serenity and power in time of trouble, a power not "self-generated" but appropriated from some source beyond themselves, these people were religious whatever their creed.

In thus attacking doctrine and eulogizing experience, Fosdick faced a dilemma which his critics were quick to point out: if emphasis upon creeds made religion formal and barren, emphasis upon experience might well make it anarchistic. What excesses of emotion, what bizarre and irrational conduct had mankind indulged in, in the name of religion! Recognizing the dilemma, he sought to delimit the experience of religion on empirical, pragmatic, not a priori grounds. Through generations of trial and error, progress and retreat, through the insights of the poets and prophets, mankind had learned the utility of belief in God, of faith, of devotion to social ideals, of placing the highest value on personality.

Although a man might find religious experience in music, or science, or social work, he would not realize its full significance, Fosdick preached, save through belief in God. Having said as much, he found it difficult to define God, who, as he put it, "had never sat for his photograph." [70] In a sense, God was a work of art, an objectifying of man's finest thoughts and highest ideals. Each man, having something of the artist within himself, created in his mind's eye his own image of God, but he was vastly aided by the great artists, the men of greater sensibilities and keener insights, the poets and the prophets. These were dependent, in turn, upon one another, the greater upon the lesser, the latter upon the crude imaginings and graven images of their pred-

[68] Fosdick, *The Power to See It Through; Sermons on Christianity Today* (New York: Harper & Brothers, 1935), p. 7.

[69] *New York Times*, December 10, 1929.

[70] Fosdick, *The Secret*, p. 155.

435

ecessors, until Jesus himself had swept aside the clouds and revealed the very face of God.

Thus faith in God had come to mean a faith in "an eternal moral purpose," which gave a man "wide horizons, long outlooks, steady hopes." [71] In their efforts to understand their experiences of such a God and to communicate to others, men had resorted to symbols. They thought of God as father, or mother; they recalled or intensified their religious emotions with a crucifix, a cross, candles and an altar, a hymn, or a prayer. The highest symbol of God was Jesus, who was neither omnipotent nor omnipresent, but who, more than any other man, partook of the essence of God. He was as the tiny inlet is to the ocean. A man might view the inlet, taste its waters, launch his boat upon it, and know that, tiny as it was, it was yet of the essence of the mighty ocean—the near view of it. [72]

Fosdick was not satisfied in his mind, however, with this empirical, genetic approach to God. He was a theistic evolutionist. He could not think of the wonders of the universe, of a "cosmos infinite and infinitesimal, and as unified as it is vast," and of personality, the most amazing miracle of all, without seeking explanation in "the law of adequate causation." [73] So in concert with many of the modernists, he posited the God of the philosophical idealists, the God who is the necessary cause for the otherwise inexplicable phenomena of the universe. Drawing freely upon the discoveries of science, from Copernicus and Newton to Darwin and Einstein and Freud, he preached the wonders of the universe and the marvel and sacredness of personality, and eulogized the God of creative force.

He had no formula for getting religion or taking hold of God, but he believed that there was one indispensable element in the apprehension of Him: faith. Faith was a doctrine not easy to preach to the disillusioned, skeptical, debunking twenties. Fosdick, himself, in his attack on fundamentalism, was a part of the revolt against formalism and creeds, and thus far did he and his congregation both yield to the spirit of the times. But he would not yield the essential tenets, the reliance on God as the cosmic force, as the intellect and will which gave order and purpose to the universe. Attacking the skeptics of the twenties, he reaffirmed the wonders of the universe, the greatest of which was man himself. He ridiculed the believers in chance, the fortuitous falling-together of the stellar universe, the worshippers of dynamic dirt, the "little men," the mechanistic philosophers on college campuses who whipped out

[71] Fosdick, *Power*, p. 9.

[72] Fosdick, *Secret*, pp. 166-67.

[73] Fosdick, "Religion's Debt to Science," *Good Housekeeping*, LXXXVI (March, 1928), 21; *Secret*, p. 135.

"final solutions of the eternal mysteries" with the same confidence that western Kentucky Baptists affirmed the superiority of their faith.[74]

His ultimate appeal, however, was not to the God of causation, but to the pragmatic test. Forget your prayers, he said to his congregation, and in their stead some morning say to yourself, "I am an accident, a fortuitous by-product of the dust." And at night salute yourself with the same thoroughgoing honesty of the irreligious, as for example: "I am 'a parasite infesting the epidermis of a midge among the planets.' " "Do you really think," he asked, "that such words help to keep men on their feet?" [75]

So he preached faith, a quality which he did not so much define as illustrate. He praised the courage of Helen Keller who "out of the limitations of defeat... rose up to win one of the shining successes of human history"; he cited the determination of the Wright brothers, who, despite the cynicism of their neighbors ("nobody's ever going to fly; and if anybody ever did fly it wouldn't be anybody from Dayton"), persisted in their attempts to fly. He told of Phillips Brooks and the bitterness of his despair when he failed at teaching, of the greatness of his success when he turned to the ministry. "Blessed be biography," he said, as he searched the pages of history for incidents of triumphant faith.[76]

When the fundamentalists attacked Fosdick on the grounds that, in rejecting the Bible as divinely inspired, he had no moral code to preach, he replied that the accumulated experience and wisdom of man, particularly as revealed in Jesus, was sufficient sanction. He based his preaching on social issues, on the proposition, which he credited to Jesus, that personality is the supreme value. That which is degrading to personality, therefore, is unchristian, and conversely, that which is uplifting to personality is of the very essence of Christianity. On these grounds he condemned war for its destruction of human life, its debasing of conquered and conqueror alike; he lashed out against the corruption in Harding's Cabinet, demanded the removal of Mayor "Jimmy" Walker and the repudiation at the polls of that "highly organized plunderbund," Tammany Hall. If in 1927 he eulogized business for its "morality" in having shared the products of industry "more widely than has ever been done in modern times before," he at the same time warned against the swaggering arrogance of a prosperous nation.[77]

Those who feared that he had yielded to the charm of Rockefeller's wealth were somewhat reassured by his vigorous demands, following the crash of 1929, for fundamental reforms in the economic structure, for

[74] Fosdick, *Secret*, p. 132.
[75] Fosdick, *Hope*, p. 81.
[76] *Ibid.*, p. 83; *Secret*, p. 5.
[77] *New York Times*, November 22, 1926; April 25, 1927; July 4, 1932.

abandonment of the "crazy idea" that "competition is the life of the trade," for socialization of the basic industries. With some reservations politically, he even praised the New Deal for its efforts to codify competitive practices. He warned that capitalism was on trial with communism, that millions living under the shadow of economic insecurity were easy prey to the enemy. "Starvation does not call out devotion," he said. He joined 18,000 other Protestant ministers in a declaration against the "rugged individualism" of the capitalistic system, and he won for himself the distinction of a listing in Elizabeth Dilling's *The Red Network*. He lashed out at Lathrop Stoddard and the "cynical gospel" of the superiority of the Nordic race, and denounced Hitler's anti-Semitic campaign. He was equally forthright in his condemnation of racial prejudice at work in America.[78]

He discussed issues of conduct, too: condemned the "lawlessness," and the devotion to "self-expression" of the twenties, the "freedom of flapperism and the hip flask"; he deplored the laxity in sex standards, the increasing divorce rate, and Judge Ben Lindsay's companionate marriage. He rebuked the novelists for their low tastes and censured the people themselves, the "wicked consumers," for their patronage of the New York theater. Conversely, he supported Margaret Sanger in her campaign for the dissemination of information on birth control. "God pity the children that come when they are not wanted," he said.[79]

When all of this is said, it must be admitted, however, that Fosdick was not primarily, nor even fundamentally, concerned with social issues. Aside from the subject of war, he rarely devoted an entire sermon to a social or economic question. He did not resort to the direct assault, the searching and withering fire of a prophet, but favored rather the incidental denunciation of the social problem as an illustration of the moral lack in individuals. Social and personal problems, he said, are like the two ends of the Holland tunnel: "if starting with personal religion we are constrained to go through to the problems of society, so starting with the problems of society, we are constrained to go through to personal religion."[80] "There is no social sin whose central responsibility is not inside individuals." The world ought to be transformed, he asserted, but in the meantime, while it is not transformed, "...we must transcend it, rise above it, be superior to it, and carry off a spiritual victory in the face of it."[81]

[78] *Ibid.*, November 9, 1930; October 2, 1931; April 25, 1932; October 16, 1933; April 25, 1927; "What 20,000 Clergymen Think," *op. cit.*, p. 524.

[79] *New York Times*, June 15, 1925; January 16, 1928; December 17, 1928; Fosdick, "What Is Happening to the American Family," *American Magazine*, CVI (October, 1928), 96.

[80] Fosdick, *Hope*, p. 30.

[81] *New York Times*, August 8, 1929.

In view of the collapse of American prosperity and the rise in Europe of a new nationalism with the accompanying specter of war, Fosdick's emphasis on personal problems seemed to some Christians a retreat from the social and ethical issues of the day. For several years the modernists, and by reason of his pre-eminence, Dr. Fosdick in particular, had been under severe attack from the "New Realists," those "disenchanted liberals" of Marxian or Barthian influence, the neo-Orthodox.[82]

The neo-Orthodox charged that the modernists did not understand sin whether expressed in the individual or in society. Nor did the modernist understand the nature of man, his strange perversity, his inevitable sinfulness; the modernist could not comprehend the absolute distance between God and man, and the necessity for a revelation which would simultaneously charge man with the tension of condemnation and forgiveness.

When, therefore, Fosdick preached a sermon in 1935 calling upon his congregation to go "Beyond Modernism," he produced a sensation. Long before the American followers of Kierkegaard and Barth had arisen to criticize the easy optimism of the modernists, Fosdick had warned, in his Yale lectures of 1922, against the "perils and delusions of progress." But in 1935, he had been sick and out of the pulpit for nine months; the press expected a story, of perhaps sensational proportions, and played it with the suggestion that the leader of the modernist forces, the great heretic himself, finding his liberal religion inadequate, was returning to the God of the fundamentalists. Even the reliable *Christian Century* saw great significance in the fact that the "most important, popular figure in the Protestant pulpit for two decades" was about to lead his people out of the barren wilderness of modernism.[83]

Those who read the sermon, or heard it, knew full well that Fosdick gave small comfort to the fundamentalists, however much capital they made of his remarks. He appropriated rather than repudiated the gains of biblical criticism and the efforts to reconcile religion and science; these, he said, were the necessary starting point beyond which modernism must go.

Nor did he ally himself with the neo-Orthodox. He agreed with them that "inevitable progress" was a delusion, a sentimental softness induced by the rise of democracy, the improvement in economic conditions, the increase in humanitarianism, all sanctified by the doctrine of evolution. He insisted, in the manner of the neo-Orthodox, upon the reality of sin which "leads men

---

[82] "Dr. Fosdick Shifts the Emphasis," *Christian Century*, LII (November 20, 1935), 1480.

[83] *Loc. cit.*; Fosdick, *Successful Christian Living; Sermons on Christianity Today* (New York: Harper & Brothers, 1937), pp. 153-64; Fosdick, *The Modern Use of the Bible* (New York: The Macmillan Co., 1924), pp. 169-206; E. H. Abbot, "Dr. Fosdick's Religion," *Outlook*, CXXXIX (March 11, 1925), 364.

and nations to damnation" and upon the reality of God as the "central message and distinctive truth of religion." He admitted, also, that modernism had too often lost its "ethical standing-ground and its power of moral attack." In its efforts to harmonize doctrines and science, it had too frequently accommodated religion to culture, adapted Christianity to nationalism, imperialism, and racism. The function of the Church, he said, was not to adjust itself to the prevailing culture, but to "Stand out from it and challenge it!"

But he did not go along with the neo-Orthodox. He had appropriated their criticism but not their theology. "Beyond modernism" meant to him to go beyond biblical criticism, beyond the reconciling of religion and science to the fundamental religious experience. What application of his new modernism he would make was soon to be apparent in his dealing with the problem of World War II.

VI

The social revolution of the 1920's brought temporary disaster to a good many American churches. Although membership remained more or less constant, attendance figures skidded to new lows. Short skirts, bobbed hair, bathtub gin, and Freud seemed quite out of accord with the teachings of Sunday morning. The New Freedom mocked traditions of religion as blithely as it laughed at fashions of dress and codes of social conduct. Cartoonists standardized the caricature of the Protestant clergy: an elongated stern-faced puritan who saw and smelled evil in every pleasurable activity of his fellows. Sinclair Lewis, having with microscopic care uncovered the secrets of Main Street and Babbittry, put the clergy under his lens and revealed the ankle-gazing, pious-mouthed Elmer Gantry.

But Harry Emerson Fosdick was not easily mocked. Others might preach to empty pews but he had overflow crowds and waiting lines. Out-of-town visitors were advised to write in advance for special admission tickets. The First Presbyterian Church had ordered plush cushions so that late-comers might sit more comfortably on the marble steps leading to the platform. And even the new edifice on Riverside Drive, with its provisions for overflow crowds, was not able to accommodate the people who wanted to hear him.[84]

Some thought it was the gospel he preached and the publicity he received that attracted the crowds. But he was preaching to overflow congregations at the First Presbyterian Church long before he made the headlines with the quarrel over his sermon, "Shall the Fundamentalists Win?" And he continued to attract the crowds despite his refusal to carry the quarrel into his pulpit.

Others thought that the source of his appeal lay not only in his modernist

[84] *New York Times*, October 1, 1923; February 16, 1924; October 4, 1926; October 27, 1930.

gospel but in the manner of his sermonizing. Fosdick thought so himself. The trouble with most preaching, he said, was that it was "uninteresting." It did not matter. "It could as well be left unsaid." [85] He condemned the expository approach. Who would seriously suppose that one-in-a-hundred in the average congregation was deeply concerned over the meaning of words which Moses, Isaiah, Paul, or John had spoken two thousand years ago? Within a moment or two after the preacher had begun to speak, wide areas of the congregation ought to recognize that he was "tackling something of vital concern to them." To prove his point, he appealed to the advertisers: Whether they sought to sell a five-foot shelf of books or an insurance policy, they plunged as directly as possible after contemporary wants, felt needs, actual interests and concerns. It should be the same with a sermon. The essential element of sermonizing, he said, was "the solving of some problem—a vital, important problem, puzzling minds, burdening consciences, distracting lives...."

A good divine, Fosdick practiced his own preaching. His whole process, not only of preaching but of sermon preparation was geared to the problem-solving approach. He was primarily interested in persons, not in texts. He could never feel that a sermon was really under way, he said, until he had clearly in mind some difficulty that people were facing, some question that they were asking. The people had caught on to Darwin and his attractive doctrine that an organism, irritated by its environment, seeks constantly for a more satisfactory adjustment. They had embraced Spencer with his infinite hope for the progress of mankind. They had heard of Dewey and approved of his reduction of the thinking process to the solving of problems. They knew something of Freud, too, and his playing upon the eternal restlessness of man, his dipping down into the subconscious to find and conjure up the great disturber of man's peace.

Small wonder, then, that Fosdick should sermonize by problem-solving. The greater wonder is that more preachers of his era did not consciously use the same technique, that so few of them were able to throw off the homiletic tradition, the argument and exposition of the learned seminaries, the tradition of doctrinal preaching, the terminology, the incantations of an earlier century so completely divorced and yet so oddly present in the "scientific age."

The approach was admirably designed to persuade. Once a preacher had wrought his congregation into a sufficiently high state of tension over a problem, he had rendered them suggestible and readily amenable to the solution he had to offer. The technique was familiar to generations of evangelical preachers who, having vividly portrayed the wrath to come, pointed to the mourner's bench or the sawdust-trail as the sure way of salvation. Fosdick

[85] Fosdick, "What Is the Matter with Preaching?" *Harper's Magazine*, CLVII (July, 1928), 134.

was thus in the evangelical tradition in his basic method of sermonizing as well as in his emphasis on experience, and he knew it. His approach was scarcely so exploitative, however. His problem-solving was closer to the classroom lecture than to the advertiser's poster or Billy Sunday's call to repentance.

He liked to think that the solutions he offered were reasoned discourses into which he introduced opposing personalities, conflicting hypotheses, arguments he must answer before his own solution could prevail. He thought this "Hegelian" approach not only more interesting to the audience but more useful in helping them to reach a logical conclusion.[86] Had his sermons fitted the pattern which he thus laid out they would have, indeed, been remarkably parallel to Dewey's formula for scientific investigation. But Fosdick was a rhetorician, not a scientist. While it is true that in the years of his argumentative attacks on fundamentalism he sometimes introduced argument and refutation into his solution, he rarely treated the disparate views as hypotheses. As a matter of fact, he rarely formalized and presented opposing views. More often (and especially so in the later years of his affirmative emphasis on experience) he resorted to concession, or even to the taking over of his opponent's views. Did a critic attack the church? Fosdick not only conceded the point, but appropriated the argument and directed it against the peccadilloes of fundamentalism or the negativism of the modernist-liberal tradition. Did a church member protest that events were overwhelming, that life was essentially disillusioning? Fosdick conceded the burden of his complaint, perhaps enlarged upon it, only to bring into sharper relief the magnificence of the Christian faith. When he set forth an opposing view, he did not always represent it in a favorable light. He could on occasion lay down a withering barrage against the faith of the skeptics in "dynamic dust" or the devotion of the fundamentalist to "Biblical literalisms." But whether he argued, or conceded, or attacked, he left no doubt with the audience where his sympathies lay. His business was persuasion.

With all of his emphasis upon problems and solutions, Fosdick did not fall into any simple rhetorical approach built upon the Dewey problem-solution pattern. Quite unconscious of the "motivated sequence" speech of the modern-day psychological rhetoricians, he constructed his sermons on the simple classical model which he had studied at college. Far from restricting the problem to the introduction, he sometimes used it like a minor chord, its disturbing melody rising again and again to heighten the effect of the triumphant major. If he opened his sermon psychologically with a problem, he treated it rhetorically as an introduction. He regularly focused all of his opening remarks upon a single question or proposition which he then proceeded to answer or develop

[86] *Ibid.*, pp. 134-37.

442

in three or sometimes four and occasionally five or six topics, the "body" of his speech.[87]

What ingenuity he put into the phrasing of that central question or those topical divisions! With what verbal dexterity he could clothe the same recurring ideas or from what provoking and intriguing angles he could exhibit an old thought! His technique was exciting to the auditor. It was like the trick of the psychological perception test—one might look at a dull series of light and dark lines drawn at sharp angles and then blink his eyes, and, behold! a staircase. So one might look at the old ideas he held up and suddenly see them with a new insight.

Ordinarily, he clearly marked out the major steps of his sermons. Sometimes like a guide he stepped aside from the trail, the people gathered about him, for a moment's backward glance over the ground they had traversed, and a quick view of the road which lay ahead of them. More often he simply numbered his points: "let us say first"; "This first step alone, however, does not carry us out of our difficulty...So we must now face the fact..."; and "Finally and logically, then...." Occasionally, without enumeration, he made his direction clear by a simple transitional phrase and the repetition of the key words of his central thought, as, for example, when he made "an excursion into remembrance, an endeavor to recall some of the old words which century after century, through stormy days, have kept men on their feet." "One such word," he said, "is that *life is an entrustment*"; "Here is another word that might help, that the *supreme successes of the world have been defeats....*"[88]

Now and then he drew upon some striking line from an illustration, a brief quotation perhaps, as a refrain which like a melodic theme recurred again and again and bound the whole together much more tightly than could any logical relation of main points. Consider, for example, his sermon on "Facing the Challenge of Change." In the introduction he told the story of Jeremiah who, distraught with the misfortunes of Israel, looked across the Jordan at placid Moab. Unlike Israel, Jeremiah cried out, "Moab hath been at ease from his youth...and hath not been emptied from vessel to vessel." Picking up the figure, Fosdick applied it conversely, praising the man who "never surrenders to sluggishness or stagnation—poured from vessel to vessel he makes change his friend." He praised the Christian ideal of the "maladjusted life," maladjusted to the war system, to economic injustice, race prejudice, and taunted his fellow-churchmen who would complacently permit

[87] Gilbert S. MacVaugh, "Structural Analysis of the Sermons of Harry Emerson Fosdick," *Quarterly Journal of Speech*, XVIII (November, 1932), 531-46. The analysis made by MacVaugh—showing that Fosdick's points are, from first to last, successively shorter in treatment—is not borne out with any degree of consistency in the sermons of the printed volumes.

[88] *Hope*, pp. 78-82.

non-Christians to beat them at what ought to be their own game, "pouring mankind from vessel to vessel." [89]

He could utilize for his refrain, not only a verse of Scripture, but such a commonplace phrase as Br'er Rabbit's taunt, "Bred and bawn in a brier-patch," or a phrase from a contemporary incident, "they have sold something valuable very cheap." [90]

In structure, then, his sermons, in whatever manner they were bound together, were essentially arguments—"too intellectual," said one of his friendly critics, to constitute the best of sermonizing.[91] But while he argued in the framework, he was not argumentative in the details. He did not so much prove his points as illustrate them. Rather than pile up fact on fact or biblical citation upon biblical citation to buttress a theological dogma, he seized upon an illustration and used it like a lens to bring his proposition into sharp, clear focus, to magnify it, if need be, a hundredfold. Or, swinging an analogy into place like a floodlamp, he suddenly illumined his whole point with a full, bright light. Not infrequently he employed montage (a technique older to rhetoric than to the movies): the Wright brothers fighting derision and defeat in their own community of Dayton, Ohio; Helen Keller rising to victory against tremendous odds; *Cyrano de Bergerac*, crushed and dying but able to say, "One thing without stain...my white plume"; Socrates taking the cup; Jesus on Calvary; the supreme successes of history springing from defeats— all compressed into a single paragraph.[92]

The illustration—insight, argument from example rather than legal evidence—was especially suited to Fosdick because his propositions were drawn from experience rather than from dogma; they were psychological rather than theological. Yet he did not, on occasion, hesitate to argue like a lawyer to prove his psychological premises. He used the Bible for its poetic insights, but he turned to the psychologists and scientists for authoritative proof.

He ranged widely in his search for illustrative material and was unusually resourceful and imaginative in seeing relationships, or in looking at an old event from a new angle. He drew freely and without apology from his personal experience. He remembered with vivid detail the bucket of raspberries his mother made him pick, the pool of water he and other boys made by damming a little stream. He remembered with equal vividness events of his adult life: the late afternoon, at sunset, in a ruined barn behind the trenches, when he spoke to a company of hand grenaders who were about to raid the Ger-

---

[89] *Ibid.*, pp. 107-16.

[90] *Ibid.*, pp. 11-20, 79.

[91] Joseph Fort Newton (ed.), *If I Had Only One Sermon to Prepare* (New York: Harper & Brothers, 1932), p. 108.

[92] *Hope*, pp. 83-84.

man lines; the engineer, a friend of his, who vainly sought to explain relativity to him by comparing it to a shuffleboard game on a ship's deck.[93]

He pored over the biographies which crowded the booksellers' shelves of the twenties and thirties: the life stories of Phillips Brooks, Voltaire, Daniel Webster, Thomas Jefferson, George Arliss, Gladstone, Elizabeth Fry, Clarence Darrow, Henry Ward Beecher, and scores of others. He drew upon the novels he had read in his youth, Dickens, Eliot, Thackeray, and cited (more often to condemn than to praise) the despairing and cynical voices of his contemporaries, Lewis, Dreiser, Fitzgerald. He cited the professors of his day: MacIver, Beard, Whitehead, Fairchild, James, Royce, Haldane, and upon rare occasions, John Dewey.

Now and then he picked up a dramatic incident from the newspapers: the strange duality in human nature exhibited by two boys at a salacious show, giving their lives to rescue others when fire caused a panic; the leading and successful artist who killed himself, and of whom the New York *Herald Tribune* said, "he was a successful artist, with editors eager to snatch the paper from beneath his pencil, but he found life emptier than do the hungry men on the breadlines"; the woman, who, in housecleaning, disposed of her old books to a ragman, only to remember, too late, that one of them contained four thousand dollars—she had "sold something very valuable very cheap." [94]

Of poetry, he knew the familiar passages from the standard poets, and knew them well: Shakespeare in his many guises from Macbeth (a tale told by an idiot), to Polonius (to thine own self be true), and Romeo; Wordsworth, "I have felt a presence that disturbs me," Browning, Tennyson, Keats, Lanier. He knew Markham's "He drew a circle that shut me out," Kipling's "Something hidden. Go and find it," and the hymns of the church. He seemed not, however, to be a lover of poetry, a venturer among the muses, but a rhetorician who quoted it for the moral rather than for the beauty. Hence, he could cite Shelley's magnificent lines,

> Life, like a dome of many-coloured glass,
> Stains the white radiance of Eternity [95]

and in the next paragraph, save one, the uninspired doggerel,

> I am battered and broken and weary and out of heart,
> I will not listen to talk of heroic things, . . .
> But be content to play some simple part,
> Freed from preposterous, wild imaginings. . . .

[93] *Secret*, pp. 2, 89, 164.
[94] *Ibid.*, pp. 4, 218-19; *Hope*, p. 79.
[95] *Secret*, pp. 174-75.

He loved music and drew upon it as he did upon poetry, for illustrative purposes. He was not a musician, nor a critic, nor even a technically skilled listener, but a worshipper. He turned to music, therefore, for those indescribable emotional experiences which were akin to his religion: Toscanini and the Ninth Symphony, so conducted "that we came down from hearing it as from a Transfiguration mountain, trailing glory into the common street." Not infrequently he was as interested in the musician as in the music—Kreisler's early failure but ultimate triumph at the violin, Beethoven's struggle with the "darkening shadow of his inevitable deafness," and the divine afflatus of their music encompassing both of them.[96]

He was fond of odd facts, verbal twists, unexpected views of familiar scenes, sharp contrasts. There are a million notes in Wagner's opera, *Die Walküre*, he reported, "but what makes the opera great is the way the artist combined these isolated items into a community and cried, 'Say our!'" He was pleased with a cryptic remark of Whistler who, having failed at West Point, and succeeded in art, exclaimed, "If silicon had been a gas I should have been a major-general." He could even seize upon a bit of grammar and with a few deft twists have a finely wrought filigree to illustrate his point: we have learned in this nation, he said, as no other nation ever has how to conjugate the verb *to have* in all its moods and tenses, but "Progress consists in learning how to conjugate another verb altogether, *to be*." [97]

Only rarely did his cleverness betray him into the analogical trick of the evangelicals—the figurative language and the double-talk of the dramatic incident with an obvious religious application. Such was his story of the man in the Welsh mountains, lost for two nights and a day in the fog, when suddenly, out of the unseen he heard a voice say, " 'I wonder if by any chance he could have come this way?'" So, said Fosdick, "May some such word come to some one here who thinks himself lost in the fog! May he hear a word out of the invisible that will put him on his feet!" [98] The illustration undoubtedly gained force through the suddenness of insight with which the audience perceived the point, but it lacked the Hallelujahs which would have given it resonance in an audience of fundamentalists.

The ability to look at a familiar incident from a different angle was of greatest value to Fosdick in his frequent use of biblical illustration. He could take a case like that of Demas, for example, mentioned only three times in the New Testament, unknown to most Christians, and read into it an instance of

---

[96] *Successful Christian Living*, p. 76, *Secret*, pp. 7, 221; *Living under Tension; Sermons on Christianity Today* (New York: Harper & Brothers, 1941), p. 205.

[97] *Living*, pp. 83-84; *Hope*, p. 69; *Secret*, p. 44.

[98] *Hope*, p. 86.

tragedy, the familiar story of a well-intentioned person who "lacked the power to see it through." Paul mentioned him first in a letter of Philemon: "Demas, Luke, my fellow-workers," and secondly to the Colossians, in inverted order, "Luke, the beloved physician, and Demas," and finally in one of the last letters Paul ever wrote, "Demas forsook me, having loved this present age." [99]

Fosdick's illustrations were nearly always short, occasionally a brief dramatic narrative, more often a quick setting forth, a summarization of difficult circumstances, and nearly always, whether incident or summary, brought to a climax by a well-selected quotation. It required infinite pains and untold industry to be specific instead of general, to cite an exact line from biography or history rather than to paraphrase vaguely, but it paid off in audience interest, and it made possible the repeated use of familiar incidents from popular figures: Lincoln, Helen Keller, Emerson, Beethoven.

He heightened interest in his illustrations not only by the use of the specific but by the use of contrast. He liked to throw into juxtaposition the atheist and the man of faith, the pretentiousness of a man like Sir John Bowring who could write "In the cross of Christ I glory" even while he was forcing the opium trade upon China; Paul, lying in prison on Nero's order, but towering above the tyrant in the course of history; Gutenberg, printing his Bible and revolutionizing Western civilization at the very time that the now-forgotten Tamerlane, the Tartar, was terrorizing Central Europe.[100]

Although he was not master of Emerson's incandescent phrase, Fosdick knew the economy of a metaphor or simile. His more vivid figures were products of his own imagination, sudden intuitive flashes that fused the experiences of his everyday world and the reflections of his study. He thought the conventionalized Jesus of the churches "as unlike the real one as the floral patterns on wall paper are unlike the flowers of the field"; he thought modern industrial society a "good deal like the subway—it throws men together in physical proximity without uniting them in spiritual sympathy." He insisted upon restraint in human affairs—the result of letting everything go helter-skelter "would be like the corner of Broadway and Forty-Second Street without traffic regulations." Sobered by the catastrophes of war and depression, he was amused by his earlier confidence in progress, the temptation of his generation "to relegate God to an advisory capacity, as a kind of chairman of the board of sponsors of our highly successful human enterprise." [101]

His favorite source of figurative language was water—the streams and pools of his childhood, the turbulent Niagara, the restless seacoast in Maine

[99] *Power*, p. 1.
[100] *Hope*, p. 99; *Power*, pp. 11-12; *Secret*, p. 221.
[101] *Hope*, pp. 36, 105, 205; *Successful*, p. 160.

where he had his summer cottage. He saw purpose in life as "an ever increasing central current, on which float the back eddies of our lesser loyalties," and he knew from the common emotion he had experienced in prayer and in looking out along the shoreline from his cottage that "Communion with God is a great sea fitting every bend in the shore of human need." He thought nothing more futile in religious history than the "outward forms from which the life has fled, like dry irrigation ditches with no water in them." [102]

Now and then he compressed his thought into a cryptic epigram: "You never can cleanse the water of a well by painting the pump," or "Calvary is only six miles from Bethlehem." More often, he adapted the familiar rhythms and antitheses of the Bible: "unless we manage well in handling change, change will manage ill in handling us." [103] On rare occasions, when the tide of emotion was full, resorting to the ancient rhetorical device of apostrophe, he turned from his congregation to speak directly to the Herod of his sermon, the Christ Child, or the Unknown Soldier.

Whatever the details of his sermon, Fosdick always preached to persuade. Aside from his basic pattern of organization which was itself persuasive, his chief technique was to set forth the Christian ideals in a manner which would create a favorable climate of public opinion, and effect a change in personal lives. He thought the imagination stronger than the will. "If we hang beautiful pictures on the walls of our souls," he said, "mental images that establish us in the habitual companionship of the highest we know, and live with them long enough, we cannot will evil." [104]

He was not, however, a sentimentalist. The readiness with which he admitted the shortcomings of the great men, the vigor with which he exposed the impostors, the men who intoned pious creeds to cover sharp practices, lent a sense of realism to the ideals he praised. Even at the height of his attack on fundamentalism he was more evangelical than iconoclastic. He preached to fulfill the law, not to destroy it.

Another of his persuasive techniques was the use of the ancient language of the church to mean something quite different from what it meant to the fundamentalists. The intellectuals who sat in his congregation, who for all their rational approach to religion and science still found it difficult to sever the emotional ties of an old evangelicalism, responded most favorably to this pouring of the new wine into old bottles. Fosdick justified this tactic on the basis that the essential identity in the religion of Jesus and that of the twentieth century was in the psychological experience and not in the creed, and that modernism, therefore, was the heir and bearer of the Christian tradition.

[102] *Successful*, pp. 4, 59, 245.
[103] *Hope*, pp. 107, 138, 144.
[104] *Ibid.*, p. 208.

Jesus, he said, *"did his best to adapt his new truth to the understanding of his people and to make it easy for them to accept it,"* and moreover, he "scrupulously worked within the boundaries of their synagogues," "used ancient and honored terms," and when he took a new position tried to mediate it "by arguments that the Jews could understand."[105] Even though he repeatedly pointed out the new significance which he gave to the old language, Fosdick's critics upbraided him sharply for his "subtle use of orthodox phrases." He is, said the Rev. I. M. Haldeman, the "most dangerous teacher in the professing Church...."[106] However ungenerous the critics were on the matter of integrity, they were assuredly right on the question of persuasion.

Quite as important as a technique of persuasion was Fosdick's use of concession. He rarely condemned without praising, he rarely eulogized without having first stated his reservation. He understood the temptation of a preacher to seek only the "sympathetic response," to give the people "what they want,"[107] but he also understood the effectiveness of his persuasive technique. He could damn flagrant patriotism, even of the American variety, after he had first conceded the incalculable value of nationalism in enlarging the human community; once he had praised the sacrifice, the courage, and the heroism of men in war, he could condemn war itself for its depredations, damn it for its prostitution of the noblest attributes of men; he could praise capitalism for the free play it gives to individual initiative and daring, but arraign capitalists who made the country's economic life a "mere sordid, competitive struggle for wealth"; and he could disclaim his intention as a minister to speak for "special economic theories" but assert his responsibility to weigh business in the pulpit as "a matter of human relationships," and to condemn "every sordid and selfish policy which registers itself in broken homes, ruined childhood and blasted opportunities."[108]

That he was in some degree equivocal on these issues is not to be denied; but he was also bold and persuasive. His apparent equivocation was intimately bound to his theory of salvation: he preached not to society, but to men and women within society; he sought social reform through the reformation of individuals; he was more evangelical than prophetic.

Critics of public addresses commonly analyze the "motive appeals" of the speaker under categories borrowed from the psychologist: self-preservation, property, power, reputation, sentiments, and so forth. If the speaker throws the right switch, so the theory runs, he will close the circuit, deliver the charge,

[105] *Manhood of the Master* (New York: Association Press, 1913), pp. 110-11.
[106] I. M. Haldeman, *Dr. Harry Emerson Fosdick's Book: "The Modern Use of the Bible,"* A Review (Philadelphia: The Sunday School Times Co., 1925), pp. 84, 86.
[107] *New York Times*, June 4, 1923.
[108] *Ibid.,* January 4, October 5, 1931; *Secret*, p. 47.

and activate the auditor. Certainly these appeals, regarded as value concepts, are motivating, but rarely, save in advertising and the crassest rabble-rousing, do they appear in undisguised forms. The analysis of motive appeals errs in its simple one-to-one, speaker-to-auditor relation. Aside from elementary physiological drives, values are motives only as they inhere in the structure of society; and even the physiological drives are conditioned by the group. The speaker appeals not simply to motives abstractly stated but to the self-consciousness of the group, and the standards by which group acceptance or rejection of the individual are determined. The more highly self-conscious the group, the more effectively can the speaker appeal to group norms and so actuate individuals.

Persuasion, then, calls not simply for the apotheosis of one or more of universally recognized values, the pressing of buttons to release springs of action, but the speaker's ability to intensify and utilize the group's self-consciousness. The agitator or the rabble-rouser knows his business well: stimulate discontent, malign the opponent, exalt the movement, deify the leader. A speaker of Fosdick's integrity, while disdaining any simple psychological formula for motivating men, while disdaining the techniques of the agitator, is nonetheless bound by the same laws of persuasion. The difference lies in the relative absence of distortion and the presence of the rational factor. Fosdick heightened group consciousness by criticizing the fundamentalists on the one hand and the materialists on the other; he charged the fundamentalists with ignorance, the skeptics with hopelessness; he condemned the fundamentalists for their worship of creeds, the materialists for bowing down to "agglutinated dust," and both of them for failing to solve the personal and social problems of men. In the growing intellectualism of his day, his appeal was tremendous. People were anxious to break the shackles with which fundamentalism bound their reason, but they were equally desirous of clinging to the emotional values attached to their old religion. So Fosdick and his colleagues in the liberal faith were able, between the extremes of fundamentalism and materialism, to wall off a somewhat self-conscious group, the modernists. These people, in part as a product of their times, in part as a result of the preaching of men like Fosdick, were committed to intellectualism and to the cardinal values of the liberal Christian faith: the worth of personality, the coming of the kingdom of God (social progress), the validity of the religious experience. These, then, were the values, the "motives" to which Fosdick appealed, and his rhetorical theory was admirably designed to induce persuasion, for in his problem-solution approach, he first exploited the discontent of his auditors, gently upbraided them for failure to achieve the social justice or inner peace to which their group subscribed, and then exalted the values of their group faith as the chief means of solving the discontent. His persuasion lay not simply in appeal to motives, but in the adaptation of his appeals to the complex social structure of his group.

VII

The entire period of Fosdick's preaching was characterized by intellectual ferment and social upheaval. He began his ministry at a time when the recalcitrant American church was just beginning to feel the impact of Darwin and the higher critics, and, although he himself was nearly as conservative as the people to whom he preached, he was moved by circumstances to lead the fight of the modernists against the fundamentalists. He was reared in a martial age, schooled in patriotism and the glamour of war; he "conscripted Christ" for the glorious crusade of 1917, but when the war was over, repenting of his militarism, he campaigned for the League of Nations, the World Court, and the Kellogg-Briand pact; and then, as his personal remorse deepened and his hope for peace burned more brightly, he sought penance in the self-abnegating pacifism of the thirties. He was swept into national prominence in the prosperous twenties, called to the pulpit of a skyscraper church especially erected for him by the richest man in America, but he achieved his highest eminence in the age of the great depression, preaching his ablest sermons to men and women who, harassed by fear and financial disaster, sought comfort and faith and hope in his psychological gospel.

It was altogether fitting that such a ministry should encompass the final and most catastrophic event of the first half of the twentieth century, World War II. He had dreaded the coming of the war, he said, as "one might dread perdition."[109] In the last years of the decade he had repeatedly denounced the rising nationalistic spirit of Europe, and particularly the racism of the Nazis. He had been denounced in Hitler's papers for his "disgraceful agitation" in the pulpit, and for his cooperation with the "notorious cabaret performer, Erika Mann." He had sharpened his understanding of democracy, had come to think of it as the political embodiment of the Christian values, the essence of which was "not the rule of the majority, but the rights of the minorities." But he preached not simply to eulogize the American people but to judge and call them to repentance. "Stalin is not alone in making an economic class his god," he said. "A capitalist can do that as thoroughly as a Communist."[110]

When war broke out in Europe, he pleaded for neutrality and was vastly relieved to find that the overwhelming majority of Americans wished to stay out of the conflict. He warned his people against the siren call of the propa-

[109] *A Great Time to Be Alive* (New York: Harper & Brothers, 1944), p. 3.
[110] *New York Times*, April 14, 1937; May 29, 1939.

gandists. "Only a delusive sense of mission," he said, "would betray America into fighting Europe's war." He took the stump for neutrality, testified before a congressional committee against peacetime conscription, and opposed the measure in public rallies at Cleveland and Detroit.[111]

He hated the war with his whole being, not only for the killing and the bombing, the laying waste of cities and the mass murders of civilians, the savagery of the concentration camp, and the paralyzing suddenness of the blitzkrieg, but for the way it laid hold of and exploited the virtues of men, and most of all, perhaps, for what it had done to the churches, for what it had done to him in 1917 when he had gone all-out for the war, and had been proud after a speech when an officer told him he was "worth a battalion." "God damn the wars," he said, quoting Whitman and insisting he was not cursing but praying, "God damn every war: God damn 'em! God damn 'em."[112] If the United States were swept into war, he warned, he would remain true to his pacifist principles, he would become a conscientious objector.

When war finally came, he was surprised to learn that, even with the shock of Pearl Harbor, the attitude of the people was vastly different from that of 1917. He was strongly sympathetic with the American cause, but he held it the responsibility of the church to stand aloof from the conflict, that it might hold to the "eternal verities" and that it might better minister to the victims. His gospel and his ethic were strongly individualistic. When he preached world organization, he insisted upon its spiritual foundation. It cannot, he said, be built upon pride and complacency, nor upon vindictiveness and ill will, nor upon skepticism and cynicism, but it must be laid upon the solid foundation of humility and penitence, good will and magnanimity, faith and courage; he denounced the American sins of nationalism, Jim Crow segregation, and anti-Semitism, but he called for penitence, a change of heart, more than for new laws or group action. Righteousness, even among nations, he said, "is always, at bottom, a personal affair." He preached encouragement in the face of despair, faith in times of disillusionment, the inner calm of religious experience for those who suffered from personal strain. Difficult times, he said, call out the best in man. Confronted by disaster, some men merely endure, others are intellectually and spiritually stimulated, some are emotionally affected by the passions of bitterness and hatred, others become world-minded citizens, patriots for humanity. He held up to them the great men who had faced desperate times, Jefferson and the Revolutionary fathers, Whittier and the abolitionists, Jeremiah and the prophets of Israel, Jesus and his followers. These, he felt, were the greatest sermons of his career. Certainly they were

[111] *Ibid.*, October 16, 1939; August 3, 1940; May 25, 1941.
[112] *Living*, pp. 28, 29.

preached to men and women at the time of their greatest need, and preached without a selling-out to the passions of war.[113]

Fosdick was, by contractual arrangement with his church, to have retired in 1943 when he had reached the age of sixty-five. Because of the war, however, his congregation prevailed upon him to continue. In the last years he frequently took stock of his ministry, looking back down the years to evaluate the issues for which he had stood.[114] He was still opposed to fundamentalism, although he had long since ceased to make it the focal point of his preaching. He was an avowed pacifist, and an ardent champion of world order, but these, along with his pleas for social justice, he subordinated to the personal religious experience. Throughout his ministry he had preached the God of the first cause, the premise of the philosophical idealist to explain the wonders of the universe, but to the congregations of his latter years the argument scarcely seemed necessary. It was enough that men and women, troubled and tense and disillusioned, could find satisfaction, and peace, and faith in the religious experience that he preached. Or almost enough. In his last years one new note crept in. He preached not only the God of causation and the God of personal experience, but the God of history. The catastrophic events of his times had lessened his faith in progress. He had come to believe that there was not only Christ but Anti-Christ. The God of history, he believed, "sitteth above the circle of the earth, and the nations are accounted as a drop in the bucket."[115] He was a God to judge men and nations. And yet, for all of his warnings, Fosdick did not go the way of pessimism marked out by Karl Barth and Reinhold Niebuhr. Underlying his warning was a residuum of optimism, an assurance that the democracies were the chosen people, and that God's word to the dictators had not "lost its power." Although somewhat more conservative, the faith of his latter days was strangely akin to that of his youth when he believed,

> . . . somehow good
> Will be the final goal of ill.

He was retired from the Riverside Church, as well as from Union Theological Seminary and the National Vespers radio program, in 1946,

[113] Elnora M. Drafahl, "An Analysis of the Figures of Speech Used to Promote Clearness in the War Sermons of Dr. Fosdick" (Master's thesis, University of South Dakota, 1946). Dr. Fosdick expressed his estimate of these sermons in a letter to Miss Drafahl. See pp. 2-3.

[114] *A Great Time to Be Alive; Sermons on Christianity in Wartime* (New York: Harper & Brothers, 1944), p. 201; *On Being Fit to Live With, Sermons on Post-war Christianity* (New York: Harper & Brothers, 1946), p. 14.

[115] *Living*, p. 115.

shortly after his sixty-eighth birthday. To the last, the crowds poured into Riverside Church or tuned their radio dials on Sunday afternoons to hear him. His voice still vibrant, his message still alive to the needs of his people, he was to thousands of men and women a symbol of their emancipation from worn-out creeds and the revitalization of their religious experience. Even in his retirement the people, demanding of him sermons, books, active participation in public affairs, could not let him rest.

SELECTED BIBLIOGRAPHY

Books and Sermons

ABRAMS, RAY H. *Preachers Present Arms; A Study of the War-time Attitudes and Activities of the Churches and the Clergy in the United States, 1914-1918.* New York: Round Table Press, Inc., 1933.

ATKINS, GAIUS GLENN. *The Making of the Christian Mind.* Garden City, New York: Doubleday, Doran & Co., Inc., 1928.

BAINTON, ROLAND H. *The Churches and War: Historical Attitudes toward Christian Participation, A Survey from Biblical Times to the Present Day.* Reprinted from *Social Action Magazine* (January 15, 1945).

BURTT, EDWIN A. *Types of Religious Philosophy.* New York: Harper & Brothers, 1939.

Colgate University Annual Catalogue. Hamilton, New York, 1895, 1896, 1897, 1898, 1899.

DRAFAHL, ELNORA M. "An Analysis of the Figures of Speech Used to Promote Clearness in the War Sermons of Dr. Harry Emerson Fosdick." Unpublished Master's thesis, University of South Dakota, August, 1946.

FAY, SIDNEY B. *The Origins of the World War.* (2nd ed.). 2 vols in 1. New York: The Macmillan Co., 1930.

GORDON, ERNEST. *An Ecclesiastical Octopus: A Factual Report on the Federal Council of the Churches of Christ in America.* Boston: Fellowship Press, 1948.

HALDEMAN, ISAAC M. *Dr. Harry Emerson Fosdick's Book: 'The Modern Use of the Bible,' A Review.* Philadelphia: The Sunday School Times Co., 1925.

HOFSTADTER, RICHARD. *Social Darwinism in American Thought, 1860-1915.* (American Historical Association: Albert J. Beveridge Memorial Fund) Philadelphia: University of Pennsylvania Press, 1945.

FOSDICK, HARRY EMERSON. *Adventurous Religion, and Other Essays.* New York: Harper & Brothers, 1926.

———. *A Great Time to Be Alive; Sermons on Christianity in Wartime.* New York: Harper & Brothers, 1944.

———. *As I see Religion.* New York: Harper & Brothers, 1932.

———. *The Assurance of Immortality.* New York: The Macmillan Co., 1913.

———. *A Christian Conscience about War.* A Sermon delivered at the League of Nations Assembly Service at the Cathedral at Geneva, September 13, 1935. New York.

———. *The Challenge of the Present Crisis.* New York: Association Press, 1917.

———. *Christianity and Progress.* New York and Chicago: Fleming H. Revell Co., 1922.

Harry Emerson Fosdick

FOSDICK, HARRY EMERSON. *A Guide to Understanding the Bible; the Development of Ideas within the Old and New Testaments.* New York: Harper & Brothers, 1938.

——. *The Hope of the World: Twenty-five Sermons on Christianity Today.* New York: Harper & Brothers, 1933.

——. *Living under Tension; Sermons on Christianity Today.* New York: Harper & Brothers, 1941.

——. *The Manhood of the Master.* New York: Association Press, 1913.

——. *The Meaning of Faith.* New York: Association Press, 1917.

——. *The Meaning of Prayer.* New York: Association Press, 1915.

——. *The Meaning of Service.* New York: Association Press, 1920.

——. *The Modern Use of the Bible.* New York: The Macmillan Co., 1924.

——. *A Modern Preacher's Problem in His Use of the Scriptures.* Inaugural address as Morris K. Jesup Professor of Practical Theology, Union Theological Seminary, September 13, 1915.

——. *The New Knowledge and the Christian Faith.* Reprinted from a sermon preached at the First Presbyterian Church, New York, May 21, 1922.

——. *On Being Fit to Live With, Sermons on Post-war Christianity.* New York: Harper & Brothers, 1946.

——. *The Power to See it Through; Sermons on Christianity Today.* New York: Harper & Brothers, 1935.

——. *The Second Mile.* New York: Young Men's Christian Association Press, 1908.

——. *The Secret of Victorious Living; Sermons on Christianity Today.* New York: Harper & Brothers, 1934.

——. *Shall the Fundamentalists Win?* A sermon preached at the First Presbyterian Church, May 21, 1922. Stenographically reported by Margaret Renton.

——. *Successful Christian Living; Sermons on Christianity Today.* New York: Harper & Brothers, 1937.

——. *The Value of a Great Heritage.* A sermon preached before the Washington Association of New Jersey, Morristown, N. J., February 22, 1921.

MACHEN, J. GRESHAM. *Christianity and Liberalism.* New York: The Macmillan Co., 1923.

MCPHERSON, G. W. *Radicalism Unmasked.* A sermon preached July 3, 1922, Old Tent Evangel, Yonkers, New York.

MORRISON, CHARLES CLAYTON. *The Outlawry of War; A Constructive Policy for World Peace.* Chicago: Willett, Clark & Colby, 1927.

NEWTON, JOSEPH FORT (ed.). *If I Had Only One Sermon to Prepare.* New York: Harper & Brothers, 1932.

NIEBUHR, REINHOLD. *Moral Man and Immoral Society, A Study in Ethics and Politics.* New York: Charles Scribner's Sons, 1932.

PINKHAM, HENRY WINN. *Collective Homicide: Letters to Harry Emerson Fosdick.* Brookline, Mass.: Association to Abolish War, 1923.

PRENTISS, GEORGE L. *The Union Theological Seminary in the City of New York: Its Design and Another Decade of Its History.* Asbury Park, N. J.: J. M., W. & C. Pennypacker, 1899.

RIAN, EDWIN H. *The Presbyterian Conflict.* Grand Rapids, Mich.: William B. Eerdmans Publishing Co., 1940.

SCHNEIDER, HERBERT WALLACE. *Religion in 20th Century America.* Cambridge, Mass.: Harvard University Press, 1952.

The Courses of Study . . . New York: Union Theological Seminary, 1901, 1902.

Periodicals

"The Correspondence between Dr. Fosdick and Dr. Macartney anent the Philadelphia Overture," *The Presbyterian*, XCII (December 7, 1922), 6-8.

CRAIG, S. G. "Christianity according to Dr. Fosdick," *ibid.*, XCIII (February 22, 1923), 7-10; *ibid.*, (March 1, 1923), 7-10.

CROCKER, LIONEL. "The Rhetorical Theory of Harry Emerson Fosdick," *The Quarterly Journal of Speech*, XXII (April, 1936), 207-13.

DIEFFENBACH, ALBERT C. "Religious Liberty—The Great American Illusion; the Fundamentalists Possess the Land," *The Independent*, 118 (January 15, 1927), 64-66.

———. "Lost Leaders of Protestantism," *ibid.*, 119 (September 17, 1927), 207-72 ff.

"Dr. Fosdick Accepts the Challenge," *The Christian Century*, XLVII (October 15, 1930), 1239-41.

"Dr. Fosdick at Geneva," *The Review of Reviews*, 72 (November, 1925), 538.

"Dr. Fosdick Shifts the Emphasis; Modernism not Enough," *The Christian Century*, LII (November 20, 1935), 1480-82.

"Dr. Fosdick Will Retire Next May," *ibid.*, LXII (June 20, 1945), 725.

"Epoch-Making Pact or Futile Gesture?" *The World Tomorrow*, 11 (September, 1928), 357.

FOSDICK, HARRY EMERSON. "Are Religious People Fooling Themselves?" *Harper's Magazine*, CLXI (June, 1930), 59-70.

———. "Blessed Be Biography," *The Ladies' Home Journal*, XLI (April, 1924), 18.

———. "Heckling the Church," *The Atlantic Monthly*, CVIII (December, 1911), 735-42.

———. "Putting Christ into Uniform," *The Christian Century*, LVI (December 13, 1939), 1539-42.

———. "Science and Mystery," *The Atlantic Monthly*, CXII (October, 1913), 520-30.

———. "Then Our Men Came!" *The American Magazine*, LXXXVI (December, 1918), 30-31.

———. "The Trenches and the Church at Home," *The Atlantic Monthly*, CXXIII (January, 1919), 22-33.

———. "What Christian Liberals Are Driving At," *The Ladies' Home Journal*, XLII (January, 1925), 18.

———. "What Is the Matter with Preaching?" *Harper's Magazine*, CLVII (July, 1928), 133-41.

———. "What the War Did to My Mind," *The Christian Century*, XLV (January 5, 1928), 10-11.

"The Fundamentalist Controversy," *The Christian Work*, 115 (October 27, 1923), 487-88.

GILKEY, CHARLES W. "Dr. Fosdick Preaches," Review of *The Hope of the World*. *The Christian Century*, LI (April 4, 1934), 459-60.

MACARTNEY, CLARENCE E. "Sermons Here and There, II. Hunting for Christianity in New York," *The Presbyterian*, XCII (June 8, 1922), 8, 26.

———. "Shall Unbelief Win? An Answer to Dr. Fosdick," *ibid.*, (July 13, 1922), 8-10; *ibid.*, (July 20, 1922), 8-10.

MACVAUGH, GILBERT STILLMAN. "Structural Analysis of the Sermons of Harry Emerson Fosdick," *The Quarterly Journal of Speech*, XVIII (November, 1932), 531-46.

Madisonensis, 1895-1896; 1897-1900.

"Modernism in Confusion," *The New Republic*, 48 (September 1, 1926), 33-34.

MORRISON, CHARLES CLAYTON. "The Treaty Is Signed," *The Christian Century*, XLV (September 6, 1928), 1070-71.

"The New Reformation," *ibid.*, XL (February 15, 1923), 198-99.

NIEBUHR, REINHOLD. "What the War Did to My Mind," *ibid.*, XLV (September 27, 1928), 1161-62.

"Open-shop Parson," *Time Magazine*, XLI (March 15, 1943), 54.

ROOT, EDWARD CLARY. "Power of Faith: An Interview with Dr. Harry Emerson Fosdick," *The American Magazine*, CI (May, 1926), 18-19.

SMITH, HELENA HUNTINGTON. "Respectable Heretic," *Outlook and Independent*, CLIII (October 9, 1929), 208-10.

VAN DUSEN, HENRY P. "The Sickness of Liberal Religion," *The World Tomorrow*, 14 (August, 1931), 256-58.

VILLARD, O. G. "Dr. Fosdick Renounces War," *The Nation*, CXXXVIII (May 23, 1934), 581.

"What 20,000 Clergymen Think," *The Nation*, CXXXVIII (May 9, 1934), 524.

Newspapers

The Indianapolis News, May 15, 16, 21, 23, 24, 1923.
The Indianapolis Sun, May 18, 1923.
The New York Sun, April 10, 1923.
The New York World, March 2, 1925.
The New York Times, 1919-1950.
The Philadelphia Evening Bulletin, May 25, 1923.

Manuscripts

FOSDICK, HARRY EMERSON. Autobiography (in typescript).

457

Franklin Delano Roosevelt

by EARNEST BRANDENBURG *and* WALDO W. BRADEN

Franklin D. Roosevelt, thirty-second President of the United States, was born at Hyde Park, New York, January 30, 1882. He received his elementary education largely from his mother, private tutors, and travel abroad. At fourteen he entered Groton, a private academy for boys in Massachusetts, where he spent four years. From 1900 to 1904 he attended Harvard, graduating with an A. B. degree. He studied law at Columbia University from 1904 to 1907. Upon gaining admission to the bar of New York State, he left school without graduating and entered the law firm of Carter, Ledyard, and Milburn. In March, 1905, he married Anna Eleanor *nee* Roosevelt, a sixth cousin, who was the niece of Theodore Roosevelt. From 1911 to 1913 Franklin Roosevelt served in the New York Senate, representing his home district which included Putnam and Columbia, as well as Dutchess, counties. In 1913, Roosevelt was appointed Assistant Secretary of the Navy. He held this post for seven years. In 1920, he was the Democratic nominee for the vice-presidency. In August, 1921, he was stricken with poliomyelitis, suffering a complete paralysis of both legs. After a partial recovery, he was able to walk with the aid of braces and crutches or with the support of another person. In 1928, Roosevelt was elected governor of New York. After serving two terms as governor, he was nominated for the presidency by the Democratic Convention of 1932. He became the first President in history to be elected four times to the highest office of the land. His presidential years encompassed the period of the development of a new domestic policy, the New Deal, the period of World War II, and the period of planning the United Nations. After an unprecedented twelve years in office, Roosevelt unexpectedly died April 12, 1945.

At the time of his death in 1945, in the thirteenth year of his presidency of the United States, millions of Americans could echo the words that Roosevelt himself had cabled to his great English contemporary, Winston Churchill, "It is fun to be in the same decade with you," so keenly aware had they become of his enormous personality. Although other millions of his critics may have doubted the privilege of coexistence, they, too, were keenly aware of his presence. Americans believed they knew Roosevelt, intimately and well. They had heard him in ball parks, in convention halls, from the rear platform of railway trains, on sound tracks in the movies, and chiefly over the radio. Indeed, millions of people throughout the world believed they knew him as well as Americans knew him. No previous American President placed so much faith and importance in the spoken word as did Roosevelt. And it was by this means chiefly that he taught Americans to know him.

Historians and biographers have now written copiously on Roosevelt. His speeches and papers have been searched for evidences of his growth and development in economic philosophy, political philosophy, social philosophy. Indeed, every aspect of the life of this many-sided contemporary has been examined and minutely narrated. It is not the purpose of this study to recall an already well-told story. We are concerned specifically and only with Roosevelt's ability to communicate his thoughts and his feelings to the millions of people whose attention he captured and held, partisans as well as political opponents.

We shall attempt to answer such questions as: What was his specific training in the art of communication? What methods or qualities characterized this successful practitioner of the art of communication?

Education and Experience of the Speaker

Roosevelt got an appreciation for many tongues early in life. Child of an internationally-minded family, he was only three when his parents first took him to Europe; after that, the family went abroad practically every year. Young Roosevelt had French and German governesses who taught him their languages. He also learned some Spanish and Italian. At the age of twelve, he attended school for several weeks at Nauheim, Germany. Twice with a tutor he toured Germany and Switzerland by bicycle.[1]

When young Roosevelt went to Groton, he was two years older than most boys who entered there. Because of tutoring, travel, and reading, he was enrolled in the "third form" with those his own age. The program of study at Groton at the time was essentially classical:

> The curriculum was in the classical vein, with Latin, Greek, English Literature and Composition, and Mathematics dominant, plus the modern languages of German and French, . . . courses. The Rector taught Sacred Studies.[2]

[1] See, Emil Ludwig, *Roosevelt, A Study in Fortune and Power* (New York: The Viking Press, 1938), p. 9; Alden Hatch, *Franklin D. Roosevelt* (New York: Henry Holt & Co., 1947), pp. 16-17; Karl Schriftgiesser, *The Amazing Roosevelt Family, 1613-1942* (New York: Funk & Wagnalls Co., 1942), p. 307; Eric Brandeis, *Franklin D. Roosevelt The Man* (New York: American Offset Corp., 1936), p. 11; Gerald W. Johnson, *Roosevelt: Dictator or Democrat* (New York: Harper & Brothers, 1941), p. 49; Archibald Campbell Knowles, *Franklin Delano Roosevelt, The Great Liberal* (Burlington, New Jersey; Enterprise Publishing Co., 1936), p. 10.

[2] *F. D. R., His Personal Letters*, ed. Elliott Roosevelt (New York: Duell, Sloan & Pearce, 1947), I, 31.

During Franklin's first year at Groton, each of his grade reports gave his relative position in the class, which was never poorer than fifth in a group of seventeen, nor better than second of nineteen students. Letter grades without relative standings during his last three years show that his best grades were in German, French, Latin, and geometry. Upon graduation, he was awarded the school Latin prize, a forty-volume edition of the Temple *Shakespeare*. English composition was consistently his poorest subject; almost always he received C's, although occasionally the grade rose to B or dropped to D. His general average was B.[3]

Roosevelt did not particularly distinguish himself as a student or as a leader. According to the headmaster, "He was a quiet, satisfactory boy of more than ordinary intelligence, taking a good position in his Form but not brilliant."[4] Of the approximately one thousand who took tests for entrance to Harvard University the year he did, Franklin received "sixteen points"—the highest rating anyone earned, and above any of the other Groton students.[5]

Groton and its headmaster, the Reverend Endicott Peabody, made strong impressions upon young Roosevelt. He later explained, "As long as I live his [Dr. Peabody's] influence will mean more to me than that of any other people next to my father and mother."[6] That influence was deeply spiritual.

Groton, an Episcopal preparatory school, required its students to attend religious services twice a day each weekday, and three times each Sunday. In addition, daily Bible study was planned so that the student read the entire Old Testament and New Testament in a two-year period. Consequently, Roosevelt studied through the Bible twice during the four years he spent at Groton. Eleanor Roosevelt attributes Franklin's extensive use of biblical quotation in his speeches more to the headmaster of Groton than to any other influence.[7]

At Groton each boy was required to belong to either the Junior or Senior Debating Society, each of which held monthly debates during the winter term on subjects selected by the boys. Franklin participated in these activities with enthusiasm, sometimes enlisting the aid of his parents in sending him articles on his subjects.[8] He achieved no great distinction, but did a creditable job.[9]

[3] Based upon scattered references found in *Personal Letters*, I.

[4] Frank D. Ashburn, *Peabody of Groton* (New York: Coward-McCann, Inc., 1944), p. 341.

[5] Mrs. James Roosevelt, *My Boy Franklin* (New York: Ray Long and Richard H. Smith, Inc., 1933), pp. 48-49.

[6] "Notes and News," *School and Society*, LX (1944), 346.

[7] Interview with Mrs. Eleanor Roosevelt, Hyde Park, August 17, 1947.

[8] *Personal Letters*, I, 156, 274.

[9] The school's monthly publication wrote reports of six debates in which he partici-

Students at Groton frequently heard great literature read aloud; Franklin's letters home reveal that those experiences were highly enjoyable and made significant impressions upon him.[10] In addition to professional actors and actresses who read periodically to the students, Dr. Peabody read every evening, usually from the Bible, and before each Christmas, the rector's father, Samuel Endicott Peabody, took several evenings to read Dickens' *Christmas Carol*. As an adult Franklin Roosevelt enjoyed reading aloud. Each Christmas Eve, he read the *Christmas Carol* to his family. He once explained to Frances Perkins, "You know, I like to read aloud—I would almost rather read to somebody than read to myself."[11]

It seems apparent that Groton contributed to Roosevelt's understanding not only of his own but of foreign tongues, gave him a touch of experience in debate, an appreciation for the oral reading of literature, and helped to establish his ethical ideals. In 1940, he wrote his old teacher:

> More than forty years ago you said, in a sermon in the old Chapel, something about not losing boyhood ideals in later life. Those were Groton ideals—taught by you—I try not to forget—and your words are still with me with hundreds of others of "us boys."[12]

In the fall of 1900, Roosevelt went to Harvard University. He had a varied program there. His study of classical subjects included a course labeled "Latin Literature: Livy (Book 1); Horace (Odes and Epodes); Terence (Andria and Phormio)." He had one semester of "English Literature (Bacon)," a year of "French Prose and Poetry. Corneille, Racine, Molière, Victor Hugo, George Sand, Alfred de Musset, Sainte-Beuve."

His primary academic interests were in history and government. His professors included such well-known scholars as A. Lawrence Lowell in "Constitutional Government," Frederick Jackson Turner in "The Development of the West," and Edward Channing for "American History to 1783."

During his Sophomore year at Harvard, he took a one-semester course, entitled English 10hf, "Public Speaking." Throughout the year 1902-3 he studied the "Forms of Public Address" under George P. Baker, the most famous teacher of speech in the country at that time. In 1904, Professor

---

pated. Three of these he won; three, he lost. See, *The Grotonian* (Groton, Massachusetts), 13 (February, 1897), 79; 14 (February, 1898), 91; 14 (March, 1898), 112; 15 (February, 1899), 97; 15 (March, 1899), 115; 16 (February, 1900), 93.

[10] *Personal Letters*, I, 40, 56, 247, 338, 340.

[11] Frances Perkins, *The Roosevelt I Knew* (New York: The Viking Press, 1946), p. 32.

[12] Letter of April 25, 1940, written from Warm Springs, Georgia, Ashburn, *op. cit.*, p. 347.

Baker published a text for the course. It indicates that students in the course studied models and preparation of a variety of types of speeches. The introduction of the text explained the purpose of the course as follows:

I wish . . . most to emphasize: that the public address which not only produces results at the moment but has permanent value rests primarily on the thought; commanding and holding attention, not for external graces given it by the speaker's manner or phrasing, but because it has something new to say, or, more often, because, though it says nothing absolutely new, it shows the reaction of an individual mind on the material. . . .

Ideal public address means, then, significant thought presented with all the clearness that perfect structure can give, all the force that skillful sifting of the material can produce, all the persuasiveness that perfect understanding of the relation of the audience to speaker and subject can give, with vivid narration and description, a graceful style, and an attractive personality.[13]

The class met three times a week throughout the college year. "Besides the classroom work, each student . . . [drew] at least two briefs and . . . [wrote] five manuscripts of 1,000 to 1,500 words."[14]

Roosevelt's interest in hearing literature read aloud continued at Harvard. There the great Charles Townsend Copeland, teacher of English composition and literature, affectionately known as "Copey," delighted the undergraduates. Roosevelt became one of "Copey's" many friends and often spoke in later years of the enthusiasm with which he and his classmates gathered to hear this stimulating teacher read from the Bible and from eminent English and American authors.[15]

As an undergraduate, Roosevelt showed an active interest in journalism. According to his mother, his "major activity, beginning with his sophomore year was the *Crimson*,"[16] the university newspaper. He advanced on the staff from the rank of reporter to that of editor, managing editor, and finally to the presidency. Biographers comment that he was responsible for making the "formerly lifeless" college paper "as vital in its field as any outside daily in its larger sphere."[17]

Through the columns of the *Crimson*, Roosevelt tried to stimulate interest in debating at Harvard. He wrote:

[13] George P. Baker, *The Forms of Public Address* (New York: Harcourt, Brace & Co., 1904), p. xix.

[14] *Ibid.*, p. xxii.

[15] Interview with Mrs. Roosevelt, August 17, 1947.

[16] Mrs. James Roosevelt, *op. cit.*, p. 57.

[17] Leland M. Ross and Allen W. Grobin, *This Democratic Roosevelt* (New York: E. P. Dutton & Co., 1932), p. 49. Also, Hatch, *op. cit.*, p. 34. Roosevelt's mother's praise is no less extravagant, Mrs. James Roosevelt, *op. cit.*, p. 58.

It is surprising that more men do not engage in our debating. . . . The unique training which debating affords in thinking clearly and quickly and in speaking with precision and conviction gives it peculiar value. In no wise can these powers of thought and speech be more surely gained than in debating: this is the reiterated opinion of teachers, lawyers and professional men. It is therefore regrettable if men from all sides of our college life—athletes as well as students—do not take an active part in the debating clubs. The time taken by the work of the clubs will be missed by few—the training few can spare.[18]

Roosevelt was a member of a great number of clubs, the Institute of 1770, Hasty Pudding Club, St. Paul's Society, the Memorial Society, Signet Society, and the Fly Club. He also helped to found a Political Club, "to give a practical idea of the workings of a political system—of the machinery of a primary, caucus, convention, election, and legislature."

Roosevelt could have taken his degree in three years, because of certain college-credit courses he had completed at Groton, but his election to the presidency of the *Crimson* and his general enjoyment of life at Harvard influenced him to remain the full four years. His academic record at Harvard was only average.[19] However, his journalistic, political, and social activity indicated considerable alertness of mind.

The remainder of Roosevelt's formal education consisted in the study of law at Columbia University. Although he studied under some of the great legal minds of the day, including Harlan Fiske Stone, William C. Dennis, and Charles Thaddeus Terry, he showed little enthusiasm, nor was he an outstanding student at Columbia. Admitted to the New York bar in 1907, he left Columbia without completing work for his law degree, and joined the well-established legal firm, Carter, Ledyard, and Milburn. His career as a lawyer has been properly labeled "more or less casual." By 1910 it was over.

From 1910 to 1933, when Roosevelt emerged as the promise of the nation to lead it out of the financial depression, the play of life forces had schooled him for the position to which he was elected. He had been tried on the hustings in 1910 in a colorful campaign for the New York Senate; in 1914 and 1920, he had suffered defeat in his trial for the United States Senate and the vice-presidency; he had seven years of experience as Assistant Secretary of the Navy during the troublous times of World War I; he had triumphed spiritually over the crippling effects of poliomyelitis after seven years

[18] *The Harvard Crimson*, October 24, 1903, p. 2. See also issues of December 5, 1903, p. 2, and December 22, 1903, p. 2.

[19] During the three years he was an undergraduate student, Franklin Roosevelt received twenty final course grades: sixteen of those were C's; three, B's; and one, E (failure). *Transcript* of the "Record of Franklin D. Roosevelt," dated March 31, 1950, from the Office of the Registrar, Harvard College, Cambridge, Massachusetts.

of retirement from public life; he had served the people of New York successfully as governor for four years. Life had indeed been many-sided.

Out of the play of all life upon him had come the four themes that he persistently developed: social justice, internationalism, hemispheric solidarity; and the interdependence of all people. Through the years of the depression, the Nazi rise to power, the tragedy of war, the architectural stage of the United Nations, he came to the people on scores of occasions to inform, to advise, to seek re-election, to banish fear, to rally the nation, to activate its latent energies, to articulate and unify its courage. That the people responded to him is recorded in the destruction of time-honored precedents of two-term presidencies. To demonstrate his success is unnecessary; to describe him in his success may be worthy endeavor.

The Preparation of Speeches

I. GENERAL METHODS

By the time he had completed his first term as President, Roosevelt's methods of speech preparation had elicited much comment. He has explained in his own words his method of preparing "campaign speeches as well as speeches on other occasions":

> ...I have called on many different people for advice and assistance.... On various subjects I have received drafts and memoranda from different people, varying from short suggestions as to a sentence here and there to a long memoranda of factual material, and in some cases complete addresses.

> In addition to such suggestions, I make it a practice to keep a "speech material file...." [for] anything [which] catches my eye, either in the course of reading articles, memoranda, or books, which I think will be of value in the preparation of a speech.

> In preparing a speech I usually take the various office drafts and suggestions which have been submitted to me and also the material which has been accumulated in the speech file on various subjects, read them carefully, lay them aside, and then dictate my own draft, usually to Miss Tully. Naturally, the final speech will contain some of the thoughts and even some of the sentences which appeared in some of the drafts or suggestions submitted.

> On some of my speeches I have prepared as many as five or six successive drafts myself after reading drafts and suggestions submitted by other people; and I have changed drafts from time to time after consulting with other people either personally or by telephone.[20]

[20] *The Public Papers and Addresses of Franklin D. Roosevelt* (New York: Random House, 1938), V, 391-92.

During the remainder of his life he continued to follow the same procedure; in his later presidential years he applied the formula more rigorously, insisting that more drafts be made before the final speech. He received far more unsolicited comments as the public became aware of his methods, and he also sought advice from a greater number of people after his first term.

In 1936, Roosevelt wrote, "I have prepared as many as five or six successive drafts myself...." For none of his speeches before that time has the Hyde Park Library more than five drafts saved and available to the public. For the State of the Union address of 1938, there are eight drafts; for that of 1941, eight drafts; for the address of May 27, 1941, ten drafts. Important speeches after 1941 typically have from eight to twelve drafts.

Samuel Rosenman played a greater part than any other Roosevelt adviser in helping prepare his speeches through the years. Rosenman declares: "The speeches as finally delivered were his [Roosevelt's]—and his alone—no matter who the collaborators were. He had gone over every point, every word, time and again. He had studied, reviewed, and read aloud each draft, and had changed it again and again, either in his own handwriting, by dictating inserts, or making deletions. Because of the many hours he spent in its preparation, by the time he delivered a speech he knew it almost by heart." [21]

Frances Perkins, who served in Roosevelt's Cabinet during the entire time he was President, relates that his advisers and associates were eager to do their best in helping the President, and that Roosevelt, in turn, was happy to receive suggestions.[22] Robert Sherwood explained:

> When he wanted to give a speech for some important purpose ... he would discuss it first at length with Hopkins, Rosenman, and me, telling us what particular points he wanted to make, what sort of audience he wished primarily to reach and what the maximum word limit was to be. He would dictate pages and pages, approaching his main topic, sometimes hitting it squarely on the nose with terrific impact, sometimes rambling so far away from it that he couldn't get back....[23]

Eleanor Roosevelt has emphasized the "regular routine" aspect of her husband's speech preparation:

> First of all he decided on the subject with which he was going to deal, then he called in the Government officials charged with the responsibility for the work on this particular subject: for instance, if it was to be a fiscal speech, the Treasury Department and the Federal Reserve Board were consulted; if agriculture, the Department of Agriculture and allied agencies, and so on.

[21] Samuel I. Rosenman, *Working with Roosevelt* (New York: Harper & Brothers, 1952), p. 11.
[22] Perkins, *op. cit.*, p. 113.
[23] Robert Sherwood, *Roosevelt and Hopkins* (New York: Harper & Brothers, 1949), p. 213.

After he had all the facts, he usually sat down with two or three people and explained his ideas of what he wished said. They made a first draft and brought it back to him. He then went over it, and sometimes there were as many as six or eight or ten drafts of the same speech. . . . In between each rewriting my husband went over it again. . . .

When a speech was finally written, my husband always practically knew every word that was in it by heart, as he had gone over it so often. It was the final expression of his original thoughts.[24]

Those who worked with Roosevelt insisted that it was he who made the final decisions. He often obtained ideas and supporting material from many persons, but the final thought and the final form of expression were his own. Even after discontinuing work on the President's speeches and maintaining some bitterness toward Roosevelt, Raymond Moley agreed that the President was the one whose ideas and phraseology were predominant in his addresses. Moley advised a friend:

He and I have argued endlessly over what the substance of a speech should be. But once he reached a decision, I've never slipped anything over on him. . . . Remember, when you get to work on speeches, that you're a clerk, not a statesman.[25]

Attempts to determine the exact origin of specific concepts within a Roosevelt speech are understandably difficult. The "quarantine" expression in Roosevelt's address of October 5, 1937, which was headlined throughout the world, was first suggested by Secretary of the Interior, Harold L. Ickes:

I [Secretary Ickes] remarked [October 3, 1937] that the international situation was just like a case of contagious disease in a community. . . . I suggested that householders in a neighborhood had a right to *quarantine* themselves against a threatened infection. The President interrupted, "That is a good word; I will write it down and some day I will use it." Drawing one of his little scratch pads to him, he did write it down.

Two days later the President used the term and it "became a sensation." [26]

Raymond Moley has volunteered the origins of several of the striking phrases of the address delivered at Topeka, Kansas, September 14, 1932. He declares that Adolph Berle, Jr., was the author of the phrase "political skywriting"; M. L. Wilson inserted the "shadow of peasantry"; Moley confesses

[24] Eleanor Roosevelt, "If You Ask Me," *Ladies' Home Journal*, LXV (October, 1948), 45.

[25] Raymond Moley, *After Seven Years* (New York: Harper & Brothers, 1939), p. 343.

[26] Harold L. Ickes, "My Twelve Years With FDR," *Saturday Evening Post*, 221 (July 17, 1948), 97.

that he personally borrowed the phrase "seamless web" from Maitland's *History of the English Law*.[27] Since so many people offered suggestions, since passages were constantly being reworked and rewritten by a number of experts, including the President, several people might "recognize" in any finished product their own suggestions.

Those who were close to the President during an extended period have been extremely reluctant to identify those passages authored by someone other than Roosevelt. "There was no pride of authorship; there was no carping criticism of each other."[28] Although Judge Rosenman prefers not to talk about the authorship of specific passages, he has, however, identified certain items from various addresses.[29] Robert Sherwood, who joined Roosevelt's inner circle of speech advisers and collaborators during the campaign of 1940, has explained that he is able to identify a few passages:

... [There are] specific passages or ideas that were suggested by Hopkins, Rosenman, or me or by others outside the White House, but the collaboration between the three of us and the President was so close and so constant that we generally ended up unable to say specifically who had been primarily responsible for any given sentence or phrase.[30]

When asked about a specific passage which Grace Tully, Roosevelt's personal stenographer from 1928 through 1945, thought might have been written by him, Mr. Sherwood explained:

I worked throughout the long preparation of that speech [delivered May 27, 1941]—in fact, I was living in the White House at the time—but I can quite honestly say that I have no idea who made the major contribution to the paragraph you quote. I should guess that it represented a composite of the various minds then at work, but the final sentence about "our children ... goose-stepping in search of new gods," sounds to me as if it had been written entirely by President Roosevelt himself.[31]

How Roosevelt drew upon available sources can be illustrated by his well-known Quarantine address delivered at Chicago, October 5, 1937. The Roosevelt Library has preserved a note, dated September 18, 1937:

Dear Mr. President:—
    Enclosed you will find two additional drafts for possible use.
Norman H. Davis

---

[27] Moley, *op. cit.*, p. 44.
[28] Rosenman, *op. cit.*, p. 6.
[29] *Infra*, "Preparation of Selected Speeches."
[30] Letter, dated October 1, 1948.
[31] *Ibid.*

Attached to that note are two and one-half pages of suggestions, which include the paragraphs given below in the column on the left. Certain of Roosevelt's statements (given on the right) when delivering the speech corresponded closely with the suggestions of Mr. Davis.

An overwhelming majority of the peoples and nations of the world today want to be left alone to live in peace. Nevertheless, the peace, the freedom, and the security of these peoples and nations are jeopardized by the remaining ten per cent, who are threatening a breakdown of all international order and law. Surely the ninety per cent who want to live in peace under law and according to moral standards that have received almost universal acceptance can and must find some way to make their will prevail.

War is a contagion. It can engulf states and peoples remote from the original scene of hostilities. However determined we may be to keep out of war and entrench ourselves against the disastrous effects of war and the dangers of involvement . . .

The overwhelming majority of the peoples and nations of the world today want to live in peace. . . .

The peace, the freedom and the security of ninety per cent of the population of the world is being jeopardized by the remaining ten per cent who are threatening a breakdown of all international order and law. Surely the ninety per cent who want to live in peace under law and in accordance with moral standards that have received almost universal acceptance through the centuries, can and must find some way to make their will prevail.

War is a contagion, whether it be declared or undeclared. It can engulf states and peoples remote from the original scene of hostilities. We are determined to keep out of war, yet we cannot insure ourselves against the disastrous effects of war and the dangers of involvement. We are adopting such measures as will minimize our risk of involvement, but we cannot have complete protection in a world of disorder in which confidence and security have broken down.

On September 18, 1937, Frank William Sterrett, Episcopal bishop of Bethlehem, Pennsylvania, wrote a letter to the President. In his address of October 5, Roosevelt, after inserting the statement, "A bishop wrote me the other day," quoted the exact words of Bishop Sterrett, except for the minor additions indicated by brackets:

. . . It seems to me [that something] greatly needs to be said in behalf of ordinary humanity against the present practice of carrying the horrors of war . . . to helpless civilians, especially women and children.

. . . It may be that such a protest might be regarded by many who claim to be realists as futile . . . but may it not be that the heart of mankind is so filled with

468

horror at the [present] needless suffering . . . that that force could be mobilized . . . in sufficient volume to lessen such cruelty in the days ahead. . . .

Even [though] it may take twenty years (which God forbid) for civilization to make [effective] its corporate protest against this barbarism, surely strong voice [s] . . . may hasten the day.

Evidence that he did at times have others prepare the first draft of a speech is supplied by a Postal Telegraph message, dated October 5, 1936:

To Colonel Marvin H. McIntyre
Secretary to the President

The President requested me on September twelfth to prepare suggested draft on speech for him on electric power and outlined general ideas stop have just completed suggested draft stop please advise where I should mail this in order to avoid loss of time

David E. Lilienthal

According to Raymond Moley, Charles Michelson prepared the first draft of Roosevelt's Fireside Chat, March 12, 1933.[32]

A study of seventeen addresses on international affairs delivered between September 3, 1939, and December 7, 1941,[33] showed that in those addresses the President himself normally dictated the first draft to Miss Tully, from his general knowledge or from materials which he had requested concerning certain issues. Frequently, some of his close advisers, such as Rosenman, Hopkins, or Sherwood, who were present, would intersperse comments or make suggestions.

After a first draft had been completed, copies of it were circulated to those designated by Roosevelt. For example, Secretary Hull read the speeches having to do with foreign policy. After Henry L. Stimson became a member of the Cabinet, June 20, 1940, he was sometimes called upon for suggestions concerning foreign policy. If material concerning national defense was to be included, General Marshall and perhaps Admirals Leahy and King were asked for opinions. The various comments and suggestions were then reviewed by Roosevelt or his immediate speech assistants after which the President would dictate another draft. Or, one or more of the President's advisers, working from marginal notes written by Mr. Roosevelt, might prepare a new draft. The next draft would again be circulated.

With the receipt of comments and suggestions, and usually in the presence

[32] Moley, *op. cit.*, p. 155.
[33] Earnest Brandenburg, "An Analysis and Criticism of Franklin D. Roosevelt's Speeches on International Affairs Delivered between September 3, 1939, and December 7, 1941" (Ph. D. dissertation, State University of Iowa, 1950).

of one or more of his close advisers, Roosevelt dictated a new version of the address. He dictated (holding before him the previous draft which he had marked up in considerable detail) by striking out and substituting words, sentences, or entire sections. Each speech had from three to ten complete revisions.[34]

The role of such people as Cordell Hull, Sumner Welles, and George Marshall, whose advice was frequently sought, but who were not within the inner circle of those most active in speech preparation, is indicated by the fact that copies of important speeches were shown them and they did make suggestions.[35] For example, the study of Roosevelt's speeches on international

---

[34] Available at the Roosevelt Library at Hyde Park, New York, are drafts which have been numbered for each of those seventeen addresses as follows:

September 3, 1939: Drafts 1, 2, and the Original Reading Copy
September 21, 1939: Draft 2 and the Original Reading Copy
January 3, 1940: Drafts 1, 2, and the Original Reading Copy
April 15, 1940: One draft, unnumbered, and the Original Reading Copy
May 10, 1940: No available drafts
May 16, 1940: Drafts 1, 2, and the Original Reading Copy
May 26, 1940: Drafts 1, 2, and the Original Reading Copy
June 10, 1940: No available drafts
July 19, 1940: Drafts 1, 2, 3, and the Original Reading Copy
September 2, 1940: Drafts 1, 2, and the Original Reading Copy
December 29, 1940: Drafts 1, 4, 5, 6, 7, and the Original Reading Copy
January 6, 1941: Drafts 1, 2, 3, 4, 5, 6, 7, and the Original Reading Copy
January 20, 1941: Drafts 1, 2, 3, 4, 5, 6, and the Original Reading Copy
May 15, 1941: Drafts 1, 2, 4, 5, and the Original Reading Copy
May 27, 1941: Drafts 1, 2, 3, 4, 5, 6, 8, 9, and the Original Reading Copy
September 11, 1941: Drafts 1, 2, 3, and the Original Reading Copy
October 27, 1941: Drafts 1, 2, 3, 6, and the Original Reading Copy
Original Reading Copy is the designation the President gave to the *final copy*— the actual manuscript from which he spoke. The term is employed here to maintain the identifications of manuscripts available at the Roosevelt Library, Hyde Park, New York.

[35] Note, for example, the following two letters to Hopkins concerning the President's address of January 7, 1943:

January 6, 1943

MEMORANDUM FOR MR. HARRY HOPKINS:
Subject: President's Address to Congress
1. The statistics included in the message, because of their evident accuracy, will give valuable information to the enemy on matters regarding which we are compelled to speculate as to his numbers. However, I think there is more to be gained by the use of the statistics than we hazard in releasing the information.
2. Another point: it seems to me that the President should make pointed reference to the highly satisfying fact that at last American and French are again fighting side by side and shedding their blood in the same cause.

relations between 1939 and 1941 revealed that most Cabinet members saw some draft of each major address before it was finally delivered. Cordell Hull, or the Acting Secretary of State, usually saw one or more of the drafts of every one of the foreign policy speeches during World War II.

Both solicited and unsolicited contributions were thus used. The opinions of experts were sought and followed, but the final decisions as to ideas and the language in which they were to be couched were inevitably made by Roosevelt himself.[36]

2. SPEECH MATERIAL FILE

Roosevelt used a Speech Material File. According to him, "Whenever anything catches my eye [either in the course of reading articles, memoranda, or books] which I think will be of value in the preparation of a speech, I ask her [his personal secretary] to put it away in the speech material file." Personal letters, excerpts from speeches, solicited and unsolicited suggestions,

---

3. On page 8 there is a reference to *ten different fronts*. I do not know just how this number was arrived at.

4. First sentence of page 7 might include the clause "very limited communications."

G. Marshall
Chief of Staff

January 6, 1943

Dear Harry:

I am returning herewith the copies of the draft which you sent to Secretary Hull and to myself last night.

Secretary Hull asked me to let you know that he has no suggestions to make.

I myself would like very earnestly to suggest that the sentence at the bottom of page 19 which runs to the top of the page 20 be changed so as to read: "They know, and we know, that it would be inconceivable—it would be, indeed, sacrilegious—if this nation and the world did not attain some real, lasting basis for the world peace out of all these efforts and sufferings and bloodshed and death."

In its present form, I think the sentence is a very great understatement of what the objective should be, and since the sentence is in the nature of a key sentence, I believe it would be so regarded by the public generally.

I also suggest that the sentence on the top of page 21 be revised so that the last clause reads, "and that after the last war their fathers did not gain that right." It is not the young men of today who fought in the last war but their fathers.

With regard to everything else in the draft, I am enthusiastically in favor of it.

Believe me

Yours very sincerely,
S. Welles

[36] In the words of Grace Tully, "It should be known that the President was always the Commander-in-Chief. ... By the time a speech was delivered it was his creation, not merely an assembly line production of a corps of ghost writers." Grace Tully, *F.D.R. My Boss* (New York: Charles Scribner's Sons, 1949), p. 87.

with ideas which might later be helpful, were collected and edited for this file by the two or three advisers most active at the time, as well as by Mr. Roosevelt. The file also included material carefully prepared for possible future use. For example, an undated forwarding note from John Franklin Carter (who uses the pen name, Jay Franklin), stated, "The President asked me to do some research on the Civil War 'Copperheads.'" That research consisted of fifty-five pages, including: a seven-page general memorandum on the Copperheads; a three-page memorandum phrased as a speech on the subject; forty pages, identified as "general but extensive data"; a bibliography; and an index.

The collection which the Roosevelt Library has labeled "President's Personal File—1820—Speech Material" obviously contains more than the President had in mind in referring to his "speech material file." [37] Within that collection is a "Subject File," consisting now of twenty-four file boxes, each four inches thick. Sixty-three separate Manila folders within these boxes are arranged alphabetically under such headings as: 1. Accomplishments, 2. Advice, 3. Agriculture, 4. Apt Phrases..., 61. Unemployment, 62. Veterans, and 63. W.P.A.[38] These folders, kept in filing cabinets, were maintained for

[37] It has four sections: I. Official Transcripts of Roosevelt's Speeches; II. Correspondence relating to speeches; III. Subject File; IV. Shorthand notebooks containing stenographers' drafts of speeches.

[38] Cowperthwaite's analysis of the contents of these folders states that they "are filled with a variety of materials which may be roughly classified as follows: 1. memoranda from numerous persons and sources (both solicited and unsolicited); 2. private and open letters from friends, representatives of special interest groups, political associates, and heads of government departments; 3. newspaper and periodical clippings of articles, speeches and editorials; 4. printed copies of speeches of praise and blame by politicians, business men and others; 5. press releases and presidential press conference reports from the White House; 6. presidential messages; 7. graphs, charts and statistical reports on general economic conditions; 8. excerpts from the *Congressional Record*; 9. printed copies of Supreme Court decisions; 10. reports of meetings of various national groups; 11. extracts from speeches and statements of political opponents—accompanied wherever feasible by later statements of same persons designed to show inconsistencies and self-contradiction; 12. stories and anecdotes—sent in letters, clippings, extracts from books, e. g., Mark Twain; 13. "apt phrases"—composed of excerpts from speeches and writings from historical and contemporary personages of note, i. e., St. Thomas Aquinas, Erasmus, Francis Bacon, Bensoni (Italian historian, 1572), Gouverneur Morris, George Washington, Alexander Hamilton, Thomas Jefferson, T. B. Macaulay, Washington Irving, Abraham Lincoln, Mark Twain, Robert Southey, Woodrow Wilson, V. L. Parrington, T. R. Roosevelt, J. P. Morgan, William James, Robert F. Wagner, Harold Ickes, Harold J. Laski, James B. Conant, A. M. Landon, Herbert Lehman, Marriner S. Eccles, Heywood Broun, Robert H. Jackson, Glen Frank, George S. Brady, Arthur Krock, John T. Flynn, George N. Peek, Raymond Clapper, Walter Lippmann. Of these the most frequently quoted were Thomas Jefferson, Abraham Lincoln, V. L. Parrington, and Mark Twain." Lowery Leroy Cowperthwaite, "A Criticism of the Speaking of Franklin

general use. Before and during work on a specific address, materials were temporarily transferred to a single folder containing data for that occasion only. For example, a note on White House stationery, dated December 19, 1940, has written across the top in pencil, "Annual Message 1941"; the following is typewritten:

GRACE:
Will you start a "message file" for me to take up Saturday or Sunday of this week.

F. D. R.

Franklin Roosevelt's Speech Material File consisted, then, of both solicited and unsolicited contributions from a wide range of sources. These materials went into the file only at the direction of the President or one of his very close advisers. In addition to the general file, organized according to subject matter, a special folder was typically started a week or more in advance to contain materials for possible use in a specific address. During political campaigns and before important speeches known to be forthcoming, hundreds of unsolicited speech suggestions poured into the White House.

3. Preparation of Selected Speeches

Since Roosevelt delivered thousands of speeches, since he was surrounded by highly energetic, capable people, and since speech preparation was always an item of much importance to him and his advisers, one can find examples of many modes of preparation. Although his most common methods have been described in general, illustrations of what was done in the preparation of specific addresses further clarify his methods.

Address of December 8, 1941. Grace Tully has explained that the address, coming immediately after the Japanese attack upon Pearl Harbor, was delivered in almost the identical form it was originally dictated to her by the President.[39] Even this speech went through three drafts, however, before it was typed into a final reading copy. Apparently because of the historic signifi-

---

D. Roosevelt in the Presidential Campaign of 1932" (Ph. D. dissertation, State University of Iowa, 1950), pp. 175-76.

[39] ". . . The Boss called me to his study. He was alone, seated before his desk on which were two or three neat piles of notes containing the information of the past two hours. . . . He addressed me calmly:
" 'Sit down, Grace. I'm going before Congress tomorrow. I'd like to dictate my message. It will be short.'
" . . . He began in the same calm tone in which he dictated his mail. Only his diction was a little different as he spoke each word incisively and slowly, carefully specifying each punctuation mark and paragraph. . . .

473

cance of the address, Harry Hopkins later attached the following to the first draft which is now preserved at the Roosevelt Library:

December 15, 1941

MEMORANDUM:

This is the first draft of the message dictated by the President to Congress. The pencilled notes are mine.

HARRY L. HOPKINS

Hopkins had written a sentence to be inserted before the final paragraph: "With confidence in our armed forces—with faith in our people—we will gain the inevitable triumph—so help us God." That suggestion was accepted; Roosevelt changed only the second phrase. Roosevelt actually said, "With confidence in our armed forces—with the unbounding determination of our people—we will gain the inevitable triumph—so help us God."

One other change occurred between Roosevelt's original dictation and his final address. Hopkins had penciled a question on the first draft above the word *mincing*, near the end.[40] *Mincing* remained in draft two, but in draft three the sentence became, "There is no *blinking at* the fact...."

Third Inaugural Address, January 20, 1941. Available at the Roosevelt Library are three sheets of yellow paper upon which Franklin Roosevelt had written in pencil what was obviously the first draft of his Third Inaugural address, delivered January 20, 1941. Seven successive drafts, which have been preserved, indicate that it went through at least that many stages. Yet the first half of the final speech followed closely the pattern of ideas found in the President's original draft, and many striking phrases remain almost exactly the same. In the President's handwriting, for example, appeared the paragraphs in the left column below. In the right column are excerpts from the address as actually delivered by Roosevelt:

Always it is worth while in the midst of swift happenings to pause for a moment to take stock of our thoughts. If	To us there has come a time, in the midst of swift happenings to pause for a moment and take stock—to recall what

---

"As soon as I transcribed it, the President called Hull back to the White House and went over the draft. The Secretary brought with him an alternative message drafted by Sumner Welles, longer and more comprehensive in its review of the circumstances leading to the state of war. It was rejected by the Boss and hardly a word of his own historic declaration was altered. Harry Hopkins added the next to the last sentence." Tully, *op. cit.*, p. 256.

[40] "Hostilities exist. There is no mincing the fact that our people, our territory and our interests are in grave danger."

we do not we risk a pitfall or a wrong turning.

Eight years ago a danger hung over our land; we were in the midst of it; we knew its shock and its actual immediate bearing upon our daily lives as individuals and as a nation. We sensed its causes, and we were in agreement that quick action, unwanted action, bold action, was not merely desirable but urgently requisite.

our place in history has been, and to rediscover what we are and what we may be. If we do not, we risk the real peril of isolation, the real peril of inaction. . . .

Eight years ago, when the life of this Republic seemed frozen by a fatalistic terror, we proved that this is not true. We were in the midst of shock, but we acted, we acted quickly, boldly, decisively.

Address of September 11, 1941, on "Freedom of the Seas." Almost all the specific facts that Roosevelt used in his speech were included in a five and a half page memo from Cordell Hull.[41] Robert Sherwood, however, quotes at some length from Harry Hopkins' notes to show that Roosevelt requested and used Hull's ideas, but only to the extent that he agreed with them. Hopkins recorded:

The President liked the statement Hull was making verbally [at a conference on Sept. 5th of Roosevelt with Hopkins to discuss the address of Sept. 11, 1941] and asked him to dictate what he had just said and send it to the White House late that afternoon.

The draft from Hull arrived and instead of being the vigorous, determined memorandum that had been represented in his verbal talk with the President, it was a pretty weak document, although it built up a fairly strong case for the necessity for some action. But there was no recommendation of any action.

The President, of course, said at once that Hull's draft was totally inadequate. . . . We made another draft. . . .

I later learned from the President that Hull made a very strong argument, urging the President to take out of the speech the real guts in it [reference to shooting first]. The speech itself indicates that this was not done.[42]

Further reports of his preparation for this address have been publicly recorded:

On his way from Hyde Park his train stopped at the 138th Street station in New York and picked up Harry L. Hopkins, who brought him a report from all government departments and, it was understood, from Prime Minister Churchill on recent developments.

[41] Dated September 6, 1941, the memorandum was in the form of a telegram signed by "Hull." In Roosevelt Library.

[42] Sherwood, *op. cit.*, pp. 371-72.

The two, together with Judge Samuel I. Rosenman, who assists the Chief Executive with some speeches and is regarded as a defense organization expert, were closeted together all the way from New York to Washington.

The President was greeted at the Union Station here by Secretary Hull, who went aboard the Executive's car for a brief chat before they drove to the White House, where they were joined by Secretaries Stimson and Knox.[43]

Before actually giving the speech, the President called in congressional leaders to get their reactions:

Present at the [hour and a half] meeting, in which the Executive took the Representatives of Congress into his confidence, were Vice President Wallace; Senator Barkley, majority leader; Senator McNary, minority leader; Senator Connally, Chairman of the Foreign Relations Committee; Acting Speaker Woodrum; Representative Cochran, acting majority leader; Representative Martin, minority leader; and Representative Bloom, chairman of the Foreign Affairs Committee.[44]

Address of January 6, 1941, "State of the Union." On December 19, 1940, almost three weeks before the speech was to be delivered, Roosevelt started gathering material for his coming annual message. The first draft, preserved by the Roosevelt Library, is only five pages long. In a memorandum to Harry Hopkins, Adolph A. Berle, Jr., referred to a draft which is not now available for this address, but which seems to have been one of the first efforts at a definite manuscript.[45] From later drafts of the address which have been preserved, additional facts concerning the preparation can be learned. Although the second draft keeps all the ideas and most of the phraseology of the first, it is almost three times as long. It consists of:

a) ten typed pages which provide the basic structure of the speech. Into the ten typed pages are inserted at various places five yellow pages written in pencil. The handwriting is that of Judge Rosenman.

---

[43] Frank L. Kluckhohn, "Roosevelt Likely to Announce Navy Will Protect U. S. Shipments on Seas," *New York Times*, September 11, 1941.

[44] "Congress Leaders See President for Advance View of his Speech," *New York Times*, September 12, 1941.

[45]   December 31, 1940
MEMORANDUM TO THE HONORABLE HARRY HOPKINS,
THE WHITE HOUSE
Attached is a sighting shot at a draft of the message. I intend to go on working at it. It can be both shortened and tightened. I am not satisfied with it, but sent it along for speed's sake.

The explosive matter is on pages 12 and 13. I have not yet discussed this with Secretary Hull.

A. A. B., Jr.

b) pages marked eleven and twelve are also in Rosenman's handwriting on the same type of yellow paper.

c) page thirteen is typed, but half the type is elite, the other half, pica.

d) page fourteen concludes in two lines the thought of page thirteen but is handwritten on yellow paper.

The third draft has many corrections in F.D.R.'s handwriting. Inserted into this draft immediately after the first paragraph on page nine are two typed pages apparently submitted by the Department of War.[46] The inserts deal with expenditures for Army and Air Corps, numbers of men and plans for the future. One and a half pages submitted by the Navy are also inserted here; they are headed NAVAL ACCOMPLISHMENT—1940. Page "14 A" contains two-thirds of a page in shorthand, at the top of which appears in parentheses, "Grace." Two typed pages follow "14 A"; the order of these two pages had been reversed; a forwarding note is attached:

> Dear Sam
> This is very rough.
> Ben V C [47]

At the end of the third draft is a penciled statement of the "four freedoms," with "Peroration" written across the top in pencil.

The fourth draft has many changes in pencil, almost all in Rosenman's handwriting. Several brief, typed inserts on White House stationery were apparently dictated by the President; one of these inserts consists of three pages (also on "short" White House stationery) headed:

> MEMO FOR S.I.R.
> On the Army and Navy I would do this:

The fifth draft has many penciled changes, most of which seem to have been made by Rosenman, but there is a yellow sheet to insert into page five which was written by someone other than the President or Rosenman.

The sixth draft has many penciled changes—all in Roosevelt's handwriting. It has also many brief inserts written in Mr. Roosevelt's hand on slips of paper.

The seventh draft has many penciled changes by Roosevelt, Rosenman, and at least one other person.

Indicative of the vast quantities of materials consulted and of the many people called upon for help are the materials preserved by the Roosevelt

---

[46] Across the top of the first of these two pages "War" is written in pencil.

[47] In January, 1941, Benjamin V. Cohen was General Counsel to the National Power Policy Committee. At various times, from 1936 to 1945, he assisted in the preparation of the President's addresses.

Library in connection with this address. A memorandum for the President, dated December 2, 1940, sent by Lauchlin Currie contained, "Some language for the Message on the youth, job, and security program." The second paragraph begins, "But as men do not live by bread alone, men do not fight with armaments alone. Not only those who man our defenses, but those who build our defenses must have grit and courage and a passionate belief in the way of life which they are helping to defend." This statement found its way into Roosevelt's address of January 6, 1941.

Just before Roosevelt speaks of the "four freedoms" in this address, several statements appear which were apparently inspired by a memorandum, dated December 23, 1940, from A. J. Altmeyer, Chairman of the Social Security Board. The subject was given as "An Expanded Social Security Program," and in pencil across the letter of transmittal was written, "Annual Message, 1941." (See paragraphs on left.) Roosevelt actually delivered these thoughts as they appear in sentences on the right.

. . . The Board recommends: A. Liberalizing the present Federal old-age and survivors insurance system and broadening this system to include temporary disability, permanent disability and medical care. . . . C. Extension of social insurance protection to all gainfully occupied persons including not only all wage earners, but farmers, businessmen and other self-employed persons. . . .	Many subjects connected with our social economy call for immediate improvement. As examples: We should bring more citizens under the coverage of old-age pensions and unemployment insurance. We should widen the opportunities for adequate medical care. We should plan a better system by which persons deserving or needing gainful employment may obtain it.

Many additional items were obviously carefully consulted by the speech writers for this address and are available at the Roosevelt Library, but no actual transfers of thought or language can be positively stated.[48]

[48] A memorandum from Mr. Altmeyer to the President, dated January 2, 1941, began, "In compliance with your instructions at our conference on Tuesday, I am attaching the following:"

A letter, dated January 3, 1941, from Paul V. McNutt, then Federal Security Administrator:

My dear Mr. President:

In a recent conversation with the Chairman of the Social Security Board, you requested the submittal of suggested paragraphs dealing with Social Security for inclusion in your Message to Congress on the State of the Union.

I am pleased to attach herewith the suggested material which you requested.

Lauchlin Currie sent a memorandum, "Re: Old Age Pensions," dated November 27, 1940: "Following our discussion at Warm Springs I worked up a national old age

A study of the preparation of specific addresses reaffirms the general concept that Roosevelt sought and received help from many people in the preparation of his addresses.[49]

Different methods were used with different speeches. The final manuscript from which he spoke was in some instances very close in substance and in form to his first plans. In other cases most of the ideas and work did not come from the President. Frequently his advisers devoted much attention to certain drafts. For example, in a given speech, draft three and draft four might be entirely revised by one or more of his advisers. But in all instances, the President gave much personal attention to the final manuscript in order to make it conform to what he wanted to say.

4. PLATFORM REVISIONS

While he was speaking, Franklin D. Roosevelt made many changes from his prepared manuscript. On the last page of the typed copy from which he delivered his address of July 19, 1940, appear these words in his own handwriting, "I put in a number of extemporaneous interpolations." Similarly, on the last page of the Original Reading Copy of the March 15, 1941, address, Roosevelt wrote under his signature "Original Reading Copy, but there was much ad libbing!" Those comments were not exaggerations; they might well have been made for almost any of his addresses.

According to Robert Sherwood, "Those who worked with him on speeches were all too well aware that he was no slave to his prepared text. He

---

pension scheme along the lines you then had in mind. In addition to a technical memorandum, I tried my hand at presenting the scheme in a more or less popular speech, so that you could be in a better position to assess its political potentialities."

A letter to the President from Aubrey Williams, Administrator of the National Youth Administration, was dated December 3, 1940. "On Saturday last I submitted to you an over-all measure for unemployed youth. I should like now to indicate how this expansion should be accomplished:"

Leland B. Morris, counselor of the embassy in Berlin, sent a six-page telegram, dated December 27, 1940, to the Secretary of State, in which he carefully reviewed the situation in Germany.

A forwarding note, dated December 27, 1940, from "SKH" (Stanley K. Hornbeck) Department of State Advisor on Political Relations, to "Mr. Secretary" consisted of two typed pages, written as a speech.

A "PENSION MEMO" from Bob Allen consisted of two pages. A memorandum, dated December 3, 1940, was sent to the President from Frederick A. Delano, Chairman of the National Resources Planning Board.

[49] For additional insight into the preparation of a particular address, see Samuel Rosenman's detailed descriptions of the various stages in preparing Roosevelt's address of February 23, 1942. Rosenman, *op. cit.*, pp. 3-8.

could and did ad lib at will, and that was something which always amused him greatly." Sherwood goes on to explain:

Hopkins, Rosenman and I would sometimes unite in opposition to some line, usually of a jocose nature, which the President wanted to include. It was our duty to make every effort to avoid being yes men and so we kept at him until we had persuaded him that the line should be cut out; but, if he really liked it well enough, he would keep it in mind and then ad-lib it, and later would be full of apologies to us for his "unfortunate slip of the tongue." [50]

When Roosevelt addressed the Foreign Policy Association, October 21, 1944, Grace Tully noted that he "ad libbed" at "some length":

...I began to wonder when and if he would ever get to his prepared text. Bob Sherwood and Sam Rosenman, who had assisted in preparing the speech and were listening by radio, told me they had the same doubts.[51]

On the other hand, Robert King's comparison of what Roosevelt actually said in his Second Inaugural address with the final text released to the press revealed "that the President in this address followed his text closely—but not exactly." [52]

The first two or three minutes of his address of September 2, 1940, illustrate Roosevelt's typical *platform* revisions. The italicized portions were added to the text during delivery; the sections in parentheses were omitted by the President from his prepared manuscript:

Secretary Ickes, Governor Hoey, Governor Cooper and our neighbor, Governor Maybank of South Carolina, and my friends from all the states:
I have listened with attention and great interest to the thousands of varieties of plants and trees and fishes and animals that Governor Cooper told us about, but he failed to mention the hundreds of thousands of species of human animals that come to the park.

Here in the Great Smokies, we (meet today) *have come together* to dedicate these mountains, and streams and forests, *the thousands of them,* to the service of the *Millions of* American people. We are living under governments (which) *that* are proving their devotion to national parks. The Governors of North Carolina and of Tennessee have greatly helped us, and the Secretary of the Interior is so active

[50] Sherwood, *op. cit.*, p. 218.
[51] Tully, *op. cit.*, p. 282.
[52] "The original White House copy of the address contained 1798 words. During the course of the address the President inserted 25 words, omitted 10 and substituted 6. . . . Counting each word omitted and each word substituted as one change each, the President thus made 41 alterations or slightly more than 2%. . . . However, many of the changes [were] minor and did not distort the original meaning." Robert D. King, "Franklin D. Roosevelt's Second Inaugural Address," *Quarterly Journal of Speech,* XXIII (October, 1937), 439-44.

that he has today ready for dedication *a number of other great National* (two more) parks—*like* Kings Canyon in California and the Olympic National Park in the State of Washington, *the Isle Park up in Michigan and, over here, the Great Cavern of Tennessee*, and soon, I hope, *he will have another one for us to dedicate* (a third,) the Big Bend Park, *away down* in Texas, *close to the Mexican line.*

Roosevelt showed his ability to adapt his phrasing and thoughts with instant facility. In delivering his address of September 21, 1939, the President, instead of saying as he planned, "When and if repeal of the embargo is accomplished," introduced, following the word *if*, the additional sentence, "I do not like even to mention the word *if*, I would rather say when—when . . ."

In his address of May 26, 1940, the President followed a rhetorical question with some unpremeditated explanation. After the sentence, "What did we get for this money?" he added, "Money, incidentally, not included in the new defense appropriations, only money hitherto appropriated."

Besides deliberately introducing ideas and comments as he was speaking, he also adapted his words to fit the unexpected. In his address of January 20, 1941, for example, he had planned the sentence, "If we do not, we risk the real peril of inaction." Instead of saying *inaction*, he misread the word as *isolation*, but then immediately followed with the words, "the real peril of inaction." The sentence as actually delivered was: "If we do not, we risk the real peril of isolation, the real peril of inaction." Roosevelt's own pride in his ability to do this sort of thing is indicated by the note in his handwriting on the Original Reading Copy of this address. He underlined the word *inaction* and wrote, "I misread this word as 'isolation'—then added 'and inaction.' All of which improved it! FDR."

Mr. Roosevelt frequently placed long dashes in his manuscript, apparently where applause was expected. When applause from his immediate audience unexpectedly interrupted his train of words, the President skillfully adapted to the situation by introducing some additional bit of explanation. In the State of the Union address of January, 1940, the President had stated: "The only important increase in any part of the budget is the estimate for national defense. Practically all other important items show a reduction." Applause broke out. Roosevelt had intended to express then his request for additional taxes "to meet the emergency spending for national defense." He met the unexpected applause, however, with the rejoinder: "But you know you can't eat your cake and have it, too." The applause which followed this impromptu remark lasted more than twice as long as that which preceded it, and Roosevelt then continued as he had intended.

In his "defense message" of May 16, 1940, the President planned to say: "I ask for immediate appropriation of $896,000,000 divided approximately

481

as follows:"; but as he stated the amount of money, Congress, to whom he was speaking at a joint session, broke into applause. He then made the comment: "And may I say that I hope there will be speed in giving the appropriations," which drew even greater applause. After that, Roosevelt continued: "That sum of $896,000,000 of appropriations I would divide approximately as follows..."

Roosevelt followed common practice in releasing copies of his speeches to the press before they were actually delivered. Before delivering a particular address, he frequently wrote into his own copy some deviations from the text released to the press. Sometimes the President wrote in a change, but preferred in delivery the presentation he had previously approved, or changed the wording in still another way.

Method of Developing a Speech

Frances Perkins has commented: "Proceeding 'from the book' no matter how logical, never seemed solid to him. His vivid imagination and sympathy helped him to 'see' from a word picture." [53] Indeed, this observation seems true. Roosevelt seldom gave the impression of attempting to prove an argument in the strict logical sense. His characteristic method more often was to assume the correctness of his position and then to give the impression of explaining or clarifying his argument for his listeners. He apparently thought that if the people understood a proposition they would accept it without a logical demonstration.

As is commonly known, speeches gain credibility in the minds of listeners not only through logical demonstration, but through the touching off of attitudes and feelings of listeners, and from the power that resides in the character of the speaker himself. These conventional modes of appeal do not operate separately; they integrate and give the appearance of unitary force. Such was obviously the case with Roosevelt's speaking. We may, with profit, however, observe these modes separately.

I. The Appeal to Reason

Roosevelt was essentially inductive in logical procedure. He demonstrated both an aptness in and a fondness for the use of the example, the comparison, the analogy. He disdained vague formulas and generalities. One may demonstrate Roosevelt's tendency to be specific by taking a group of his speeches at random and subjecting them to quantitative analysis. Such an analysis yields the following results:

[53] Perkins, *op. cit.*, p. 97.

Franklin Delano Roosevelt

FORM OF SUPPORT	SPEECH							TOTAL FOR 7 SPEECHES
	1	2	3	4	5	6	7	
General Example	15	7	10	3	15	9	4	63
Detailed General Example	1	1	2	1	2	2		9
Specific Example		7	20	5	4	3		39
Detailed Specific Example		4	1	7			2	14
Hypothetical Example	1						1	2
TOTAL EXAMPLES	16	20	33	16	21	14	7	127
Illustration-Analogy		2	8	1	1	1	1	14
Illustration-Simile, Metaphor	6	4	2	3	1	5	6	27
TOTAL ILLUSTRATIONS	6	6	10	4	2	6	7	41
Testimony		4	2	5	1		4	16
Statistics				2	4	6	2	14
TOTAL FORMS [54]	22	30	45	27	28	26	20	198

In the President's Fireside Chat following this nation's declaration of war against the Axis powers, he listed specific instances and dates to prove in a most effective manner "actual collaboration so well calculated that all the continents of the world, and all the oceans, are now considered by the Axis strategists as one gigantic battlefield":

In 1931, ten years ago, Japan invaded Manchukuo—without warning.
In 1935, Italy invaded Ethiopia—without warning.
In 1938, Hitler occupied Austria—without warning.
In 1939, Hitler invaded Czechoslovakia—without warning.
Later, in 1939, Hitler invaded Poland—without warning.
In 1940, Hitler invaded Norway, Denmark, the Netherlands, Belgium, and Luxembourg—without warning.
And this year, in 1941, the Axis powers attacked Yugoslavia and Greece and they dominated the Balkans—without warning.
And now Japan has attacked Malaya and Thailand—and the United States—without warning.
It is all of one pattern.

Even with the Fascist powers at the pinnacle of their "success," Roosevelt bitterly rejected the concept that they represented a "new" and vigorous philosophy. In attempting to make clear their motives, he compared their

[54] Robert T. Oliver, Dallas C. Dickey, and Harold P. Zelko, *Essentials of Communicative Speech* (New York: Dryden Press, 1949), pp. 102-3. The seven speeches considered were, in order: First Inaugural, March 4, 1933; Democratic Victory Dinner, March 4, 1937; 150th Anniversary of Constitution, September 17, 1937; Jackson Day Dinner, January 8, 1938; Fireside Chat, May 7, 1933; Forbes Field, Pittsburgh (Campaign), October 1, 1936; and, Second Inaugural, January 20, 1937.

methods to the "tyranny" and the "security" of the Egyptian Pharaohs, the rulers of Rome, the feudal system, and a "conquering Napoleon." [55] His historical illustrations were well chosen to prove his point. A sufficient number of his listeners were acquainted with those familiar figures or periods and in agreement with his interpretation to make the specific instances effective support for his general principle that Nazi Germany represented an undesirable form of government.

In his 1936 State of the Union address, the President asked a series of rhetorical questions which were actually illustrations to convince his listeners that "positive action" should be continued:

> Shall we say that because national income has grown with rising prosperity, we shall repeal existing taxes and thereby put off the day of approaching a balanced budget and of starting to reduce the national debt? Shall we abandon the reasonable support and regulation of banking? Shall we restore the dollar to its former gold content?

> Shall we say to the farmer, "The prices for your products are in part restored. Now go and hoe your own row?"

> Shall we say to the home owners, "We have reduced your rates of interest. We have no further concern with how you keep your home or what you pay for your money. That is your affair?"

> Shall we say to the several millions of unemployed citizens who face the very problem of existence, of getting enough to eat, "We will withdraw from giving you work. We will turn you back to the charity of your communities and those men of selfish power who tell you that perhaps they will employ you if the Government leaves them strictly alone?"

Throughout his address dedicating the Boulder Dam, September 30, 1935, Roosevelt used many statistics to reaffirm his thesis sentence, "The transformation wrought here in these years is a twentieth century marvel." [56]

---

[55] Address of July 19, 1940.

[56] "We are here to celebrate the completion of the greatest dam in the world, rising 726 feet above the bed-rock of the river and altering the geography of a whole region; we are here to see the creation of the largest artificial lake in the world—115 miles long, holding enough water, for example, to cover the State of Connecticut to a depth of ten feet; and we are here to see nearing completion a power house which will contain the largest generators and turbines yet installed in this country, machinery that can continuously supply nearly two million horsepower of electric energy. . . .

"Last year a drought of unprecedented severity was visited upon the West. The watershed of this Colorado River did not escape. In July the canals of the Imperial Valley went dry. Crop losses in that Valley alone totaled $10,000,000 that summer. Had Boulder Dam been completed one year earlier, this loss would have been prevented, because the spring flood would have been stored to furnish a steady water supply for the long dry summer and fall."

Mr. Roosevelt was highly effective when relating an extended illustration to support a proposition. November 17, 1942, he told the *New York Herald-Tribune* Forum that the "one all-important job is fighting and working to win." He selected the story of one naval vessel to show that the armed forces were doing their part:

> The SAN FRANCISCO sailed right into the enemy fleet—right through the whole enemy fleet—her guns blazing. She engaged and hit three enemy vessels, sinking one of them. At point-blank range, she engaged an enemy battleship—heavily her superior in size and fire power. She silenced this battleship's big guns and so disabled her that she could be sunk by torpedoes from our destroyers and aircraft.

> The SAN FRANCISCO herself was hit many times. Admiral Callaghan, my close personal friend, and many of his gallant officers and men gave their lives in this battle. But the SAN FRANCISCO was brought safely back to port by a Lieutenant Commander, and she will fight again for her country.

Apt comparisons and cryptic analogies enabled Roosevelt to clarify his views, to hold the attention of his listeners, and to strengthen his proofs.[57] Early in 1933, he explained his willingness to experiment in order to bring economic recovery; his warning to the people not to expect too much was expressed in terms of the "national pastime": "I have no expectation of making a hit every time I come to bat. What I seek is the highest possible batting average, not only for myself, but for the team."[58] His campaign address of October 1, 1936, was delivered in the National League baseball park at Pittsburgh. Throughout the speech he compared the government's financial records with the box score of a baseball game. References to the "management of your team," the "national scoreboard," "shut-outs," and "second base" both clarified and supported his arguments.

Cryptic analogies were common through all of Roosevelt's speeches. The following are typical examples:

> I am waging a war in this campaign [1932]—a frontal attack—an onset—against the "four Horsemen" of the present Republican leadership: The Horsemen of Destruction, Delay, Deceit, Despair. And the time has come for us to marshal this "Black Horse Cavalry"!

> We changed a gold standard that had become, not the assurance of a sound economic life, but a strait-jacket which pressed upon and paralyzed the nerve centers of our economic system.

[57] See, Laura Crowell, "An Analysis of Audience Persuasion in the Major Campaign Addresses of Franklin D. Roosevelt in the Presidential Campaign of 1936" (Ph. D. dissertation, State University of Iowa, 1948), p. 61.
[58] Second Fireside Chat, May 7, 1933.

The experience of the past two years has proven beyond doubt that no nation can appease the Nazis. No man can tame a tiger into a kitten by stroking it.

Is it a negotiated peace if a gang of outlaws surrounds your community and on threat of extermination makes you pay tribute to save your own skins?

We must especially beware of that small group of selfish men who would clip the wings of the American eagle in order to feather their own nests.

Franklin Roosevelt made less use of the testimony of others in his addresses than do many capable speakers. Yet he had available to him greater resources for the gathering of apt quotations than perhaps any other speaker in history. Whenever he did employ authority, he was highly effective. In his Fireside Chat of December 29, 1940, the President quoted Hitler, himself, to support the contention that peace for America was dependent upon world peace.[59] In this same address, Roosevelt also gave the exact words of an unnamed "leader of a conquered nation," to show that the Germans had attacked without warning.[60] He referred to a telegram he had received which "expressed the attitude of the small minority who want to see no evil and hear no evil, even though they know in their hearts that evil exists."

His Fireside Chat on the reorganization of the judiciary made extensive use of testimony. Since the situation demanded authoritative proof, Roosevelt quoted three different times from the Preamble of the Constitution, and he cited statements of five Supreme Court justices, ranging in date from the early 1800's to the present.[61]

Roosevelt occasionally employed causal argument. During the thirties, particularly in the campaigns of 1932 and 1936, he frequently used causal reasoning in discussing the depression and his New Deal policies. In his first campaign he argued that the country faced difficulties (effect) because of the inaction of the Republican administration. At Columbus, Ohio, August 20, 1932, he expressed these sentiments in the following words:

I propose to show that this leadership misunderstood the forces which were involved in the economic life of the country, that it encouraged a vast speculative boom, and that when the reckoning came, the Administration was not frank, not honest, with the people, and by blundering statements and actions postponed necessary readjustments.

Conversely, Roosevelt argued that economic progress accomplished after 1933 was the effect of his administration. In the 1936 campaign he used this argument before a Boston audience, October 21:

[59] Text of Hitler's Address, *New York Times*, December 11, 1940.

[60] "As an exiled leader of one of these nations said to me the other day—'The notice was a minus quantity. It was given to my Government two hours after German troops had poured into my country in a hundred places.'"

[61] Address of March 9, 1937.

The full fruit of these Republican policies of twelve years is found in the record of what happened to New England's industries under those policies. New England was engulfed by the depression five years before the rest of the country. That is New England's debt to the Republican leadership of the boom era.

What has this Administration done?

We have raised wages and living standards in other sections of the country. They are being brought up toward the standards of New England. That kind of unfair competition is being destroyed. Most of us are in favor of that.

These causal arguments appeared in many different forms throughout Roosevelt's speeches during his first two terms. In using such reasoning, he fell into errors characteristic of politicians seeking to impress voters. He was guilty of oversimplifying complex causal relationships in these instances, for he failed to point out that the depression was the result of many causes and that the upswing after 1932 was the result of many other causes.

Roosevelt's methods and his successes with causal reasoning are illustrated by his attack upon the embargo provisions which restricted American shipping at the outbreak of World War II. The President asked for repeal of the embargo provisions, September 21, 1939, because "they are, in my opinion, most vitally dangerous to American neutrality." He argued that America's traditional policy proved that the Neutrality Acts were ill-advised. The only time, he contended, that the United States had ever tried completely to shut off products from going to belligerent nations had been the Embargo and Non-Intercourse Acts of the Napoleonic Wars. None of his three reasons concerning the "disastrous failure" of that policy was sound. True, it had caused great economic losses to American shipping interests, but Roosevelt's first argument that "it brought our own nation close to ruin" was aside from the issue of neutrality which he purported to be discussing at the time.

His second reason, "that it was the major cause of bringing us into active participation in . . . the War of 1812," was faulty causal reasoning. The acts did precede the war, but instead of the Embargo Acts causing the war, a more accurate evaluation was that failure to abide by their provisions resulted in American ships being on the high seas with goods which one belligerent would not allow to go to the other. Hence, ships were intercepted by both the British and French and unpleasant incidents occurred. When the War of 1812 came, "It was the men of the agricultural frontier who cherished ambitions [for expanding frontiers] and at last brought about the declaration of hostilities against England." [62] To say, as Roosevelt did, that "one of the results of the policy of embargo and non-intercourse was the burning in

---

[62] Charles A. Beard and Mary R. Beard, *The Rise of American Civilization* (New York: The Macmillan Co., 1931), I, 406.

1814 of the [national] capitol," was to err in causal reasoning. Historians do not lay the blame of the war upon those Acts.[63]

Roosevelt's opposition on the question of the repeal of the Embargo Acts did not, however, criticize his references to American history, but rather charged that repeal would be the first of a series of steps which would lead the United States into war. Led by Senators Borah of Idaho, La Follette of Wisconsin, Johnson of California, and Vandenberg of Michigan, an active group of legislators began immediately after the President's message to Congress on September 21, 1939, to plan for the defeat of his proposals to repeal the embargo on arms.[64] Outside Congress, the President's most effective opposition came from the Rev. Charles E. Coughlin and Colonel Charles A. Lindbergh. The Detroit radio priest, in his regular Sunday broadcasts, repeatedly charged the enactment of the "cash and carry" provisions would lead the United States into war and make the President a dictator. Lindbergh's theme was that the war between Germany and England and France was simply another of Europe's "internal struggles" and that America should remain completely aloof and disinterested.

Both Roosevelt and those who disagreed with him advanced a number of other arguments of significance to this issue,[65] which, of course, complicates the rhetorician's judgment of the effectiveness of any one line of argument. The fact must not be ignored, however, that the President's recommendations were far more successful with both Congress and the American people than were those of his opposition, even though his arguments regarding neutrality and his pleas for abandonment of the embargoes were neither historically accurate nor logically sound.

A study of Roosevelt's speches on international relations prior to America's entrance into World War II reveals the evolution of his contentions as he led the American people through the steps from sympathy for the Allied cause (but a determination to give no help that might lead to war itself) to a position unequivocally on the side of the opponents of the Axis. It also reveals his characteristic acceptance of "bold experimentation" and willingness to be inconsistent in immediate arguments in order to attain ultimate goals. The following chart illustrates these matters for some of Roosevelt's arguments between September 3, 1939, and December 7, 1941:

[63] "On 18 June 1812 Congress declared war against Great Britain. But the fundamental reason for this act had little or nothing to do with maritime affairs. . . . Frontiersmen wanted free land, which could be obtained only at the expense of the Indians and the British Empire." Samuel Eliot Morison and Henry Steele Commager, *The Growth of the American Republic* (New York: Oxford University Press, 1930), p. 295.

[64] Turner Catledge, "Roosevelt Asks Congress to Repeal Arms Embargo; Hard Fight Indicated as 24 Senators Map Resistance," *New York Times*, September 22, 1939.

[65] Fireside Chat of September 3, 1939.

The Evolution of Some of Roosevelt's Lines of Argument

"NEUTRALITY" Sept., 1939—May, 1940	"NON-BELLIGERENCY" May, 1940—May, 1941	"ACTIVE DEFENSE" May, 1941—Dec., 1941
Peace	*Peace*	*Peace*
The best method of maintaining peace is to subscribe to my policies for I am determined that the United States not go to war.	Peace for the United States is significant only in terms of world peace.	There are other matters we desire which are more important than peace.
Neutrality	*Neutrality*	*Neutrality*
The United States should remain a neutral nation (in action if not in thought), because that will best maintain "the safety and integrity of our country."	Whether or not the United States attempts to maintain neutrality makes little difference as to its getting into the war.	(no mention)
Aid to the Allies	*Aid to the Allies*	*Aid to the Allies*
Making supplies available to belligerents is not unneutral if they are required to receive and pay for the materials within our boundaries. (American vessels should be restricted from danger zones.)	The United States must provide aid to the Allies because such aid is essential to the defense of the United States. The Allies must not be made to surrender because of inability to pay for needed materials.	Providing needed supplies to the Allies is more important to the United States than peace. American vessels are on "legitimate business" in carrying such supplies. ("American merchant ships must be free to carry goods into the harbors of our friends.")

Roosevelt occasionally stated his arguments in a framework of deductive reasoning. In late 1940 and early 1941, he urged that the United States should aid the Allies because the Axis was "being held away from our shores" by the Allies.[66] At least three syllogisms were involved in the President's arguments. A categorical syllogism was as follows:

[66] Address of December 29, 1940.

Major premise: The Axis plans to conquer and dominate the entire earth.
Minor premise: The United States is a part of the earth.[67]

Conclusion: The Axis plans to conquer and dominate the United States.

From this syllogistic reasoning, Roosevelt moved directly to a hypothetical syllogism:

Major premise: If the United States is to be kept from attack by the Axis, the British fleet must remain in the Atlantic.
Minor premise: The United States is to be kept from attack.
Conclusion: The British fleet must be maintained in the Atlantic.

Or, a broader application of the same reasoning was often used with the hypothetical syllogism:

If we do not want the Allies to suffer defeat, we must give them aid.
We do not want the Allies to suffer defeat.
We must give the Allies aid.

In January, 1941, this conclusion was the basis used for the President's argument that the Allies should not be made to surrender because they could not pay for the materials they needed:

We cannot, and will not, tell them that they must surrender merely because of present inability to pay for the weapons which we know they must have.

And so the speaker argued that the United States "must integrate the war needs of Britain and the other free nations resisting aggression"; that "our most useful and immediate role is to act as an arsenal for them as well as ourselves." Those syllogistic arguments underlay his proclamations of aid to the Allies on the basis of their needs, for whatever they needed, he seemed to assume, the United States would want to provide:

The British people and their Grecian Allies need ships. From America, they will get ships.
They need planes. From America, they will get planes.
They need tanks and guns and ammunition and supplies of all kinds. From America, they will get tanks and guns and ammunition and supplies of all kinds.

Many of the numerous epigrams which Roosevelt included in almost every speech are enthymematic in form. In his Fireside Chat of June 28, 1934, he summarized a portion of his argument with this terse epigrammatic statement: "Our new structure is a part of and a fulfillment of the old." Within this statement there is the following implied categorical syllogism:

[67] Since the minor premise was not stated by Roosevelt this might also be called an enthymeme of the second order.

A part of and a fulfillment of the old is desirable.
Our new structure is a part of and a fulfillment of the old.
Therefore, our new structure is desirable.

Roosevelt was fond of these statements which epitomized his thought. He believed that given a suggestive statement his auditors would supply the missing premises.

Although Roosevelt employed deductive reasoning in comparatively few instances, those uses were skillfully framed in terms of audience reactions.

2. The Appeal to Ethical Values

When Roosevelt spoke, he was keenly aware of the significance of the ethical judgments to be made by his listeners. He frequently identified himself and his audience with religious ideals, with respect for human rights, and with virtues of honesty and consistency.

Roosevelt's appeals to religious beliefs commonly involved some statement indicating that he was in the habit of praying or that his decisions had been reached only as a result of much prayer.[68] He frequently condemned the doctrines of the Axis powers because they violated "spiritual values."

From his first political campaign until his death, Roosevelt placed great emphasis on the importance to the politician of visiting his constituency personally. His many trips provided him with excellent material to strengthen his ethical appeal. Often in the opening sentences of his speeches he impressed his listeners with the fact that he was well informed because he had recently made a "look-see trip." In one Fireside Chat, for example, he told his radio listeners: "I have been on a journey of husbandry. I went to see first hand conditions. . . . I saw the drought. . . . I talked with families who had lost their wheat crops. . . . I saw cattle. . . . I shall never forget the fields of wheat so blasted by heat. . . ."[69]

During the war he made repeated references to his trips abroad and his conferences with important people. For example, on August 21, 1941, he said: "Over a week ago I held several important conferences at sea with the British Prime Minister." The impact of these and similar remarks was to stimulate confidence in Roosevelt and his ability to deal with difficult problems.

Roosevelt's speech efforts designed to add to opinions of his high intelli-

[68] "I pray God . . ." Address of April 15, 1940.
"I, too, pray for peace." Address of May 16, 1940.
"I am certain that out of the hearts of every man, woman, and child in this land, in every waking minute, a supplication goes up to Almighty God; . . . your prayers join with mine—that God will heal the wounds and the hearts of humanity." Address of May 26, 1940.
[69] Speech of September 6, 1936.

gence included his statements of the accuracy of his previous predictions. He reminded his listeners at the outbreak of World War II that he had spoken of the possibility of wars becoming more and more probable. As other predictions were substantiated by events, the President called attention to these facts and to his previous warnings. His frequent recollection in 1939 of the domestic emergency when he first took office significantly aided Roosevelt's ethical proof, for it refreshed people's minds concerning his decisive actions. The wisdom of those actions was widely enough accepted for such references to enhance the speaker's intelligence and ability in the minds of his listeners.[70]

The President's constant reiteration of his philosophy of social justice provided effective ethical proof, for it called attention to the speaker's good will. Roosevelt contended that the lack of such social and economic rights as adequate wages and standards of living was one of the causes of Europe's troubles. He blamed World War II upon the use of or the threat of the use of force in preference to such "fundamental moralities" as "humanity," "justice," "truth," and "sincerity." The vast majority of his listeners believed that the President's New Deal had provided substantial aid to the less fortunate in the United States. Hence, his fears that the fascists endangered social and economic rights recalled to his audiences the President's past accomplishments, and encouraged them to support him as the individual most likely to safeguard their social rights while carrying out his other duties.

Franklin Roosevelt's proclamation of "four essential human freedoms" upon which the world of the future should be founded served primarily as ethical proof. These principles placed the Nazis in an unfavorable light, and strengthened favorable opinions of the Allies. Public reaction to the "four freedoms" and to the President for having voiced them was overwhelmingly complimentary.

The very nature of his Fireside Chats also enhanced Roosevelt's ethical appeal. He often referred to these speeches as "reports" to the people. Frequently, he remarked, "You know and I know..." Directly and indirectly he implied that he had nothing to conceal and that he had great faith in the people's judgment. In his speech accepting the Democratic nomination in 1932, he explained his precedent-breaking appearance as a "symbol of my intention to

---

[70] A *Fortune* poll of November, 1939, recorded more than twice as many people approving as disapproving his "record as President." Items receiving the highest percentages of votes favoring his policies included: the C.C.C., banking legislation, stock-exchange legislation, foreign policy, relief program, farm aid, and his personality as a President. "Gallup and Fortune Polls," *Public Opinion Quarterly*, IV (March, 1940), 86.

The American Institute of Public Opinion found, in February, 1940, that 63% approved of Roosevelt as President while only 37% disapproved. *Ibid.*, IV (June, 1940), 341.

be honest and to avoid all hypocrisy or sham...." This theme appeared again and again in his speeches.

In addition to understanding Franklin Roosevelt's ethical proof by which he sought to build up his own character, one must note his success in disparaging his opponents. He was particularly effective at finding emotionally loaded words to refer to those who disagreed with his policies. He spoke of his oppositions as "Tories," "Copperheads," "chiselers," "professional skeptics," "cynical men," "bankrupt Republican leadership," and "those men of little faith." In 1932, for example, he bitterly condemned the "shallow thinkers" who took no effective action to aid the "seven million or ten million people who are out of work." In 1936, when he urged Americans to fight for economic liberty as they had fought in 1776 for political liberty, his primary target was the "economic royalists." His 1937 condemnations of a "horse and buggy" judiciary, which met with less popular approval, were equally vigorous indictments of his political enemies.

After the outbreak of World War II, Roosevelt sought frequently to destroy the position of the Axis by labeling their so-called "new order" as "tyranny." Similarly, he referred to the firing of German submarines upon merchant vessels as "piracy." When Roosevelt said, "Although Prussian autocracy was bad enough in the first war, Naziism is far worse in this," he was obviously seeking to arouse the disgust and hatred of his listeners.

After the United States embarked upon a policy of "non-belligerency" and "active defense," the President intensified his attacks on the Axis powers and openly aligned himself with the forces opposing those powers. He used ethical persuasion in order to discredit persons who could see no danger to the United States. He ridiculed the isolationists by likening them to "ostriches" and suggesting that it was "not good for the ultimate health of ostriches to bury their heads in the sand." He said, "Only an ostrich would look upon these wars through the eyes of cynicism or ridicule." [71] In aroused indignation he became bitter with the "appeasers." He disparaged those who did not share his opinion by contending that they were saying the same things as the "Axis bureau of propaganda," that they were guilty of "loose talking and loose thinking," and that they showed a "lack of interest or a lack of knowledge." He spoke of the "mean and petty spirit that mocks at ideals, sneers at sacrifice." He did not hesitate to exert the power of his position as Chief Executive to make it seem that those who opposed his ideas were actually opposing their own government in a time of crisis.[72]

[71] Address of January 3, 1940.
[72] "A free nation has the right to expect full cooperation from all groups. A free nation has the right to look to the leaders of business, of labor and of agriculture to

The conclusion is inescapable that Franklin Roosevelt used ethical proof frequently and skillfully throughout his addresses. The occasions and the audiences he faced frequently demanded such proof.[73] Usually the President was highly successful not only in meeting the demands of the situation, but also in furthering the acceptance of his ideas. He fulfilled the rhetorician's requirement of ethical proof, for his character was made a cause of persuasion in his speeches.

3. THE APPEAL TO FEELING

No responsible critic has ever denied Roosevelt's consummate skill in stimulating the emotions of his listeners. According to Adolph A. Berle, Jr., who assisted in the preparation of some of the President's addresses, Roosevelt deliberately planned his radio addresses "to make some definite appeal to every class or group of people," and he also appreciated the value of using "varied motivations." [74]

Probably his most effective method of gaining emotional support was his timely presentation of impressive facts; he relied on the conditions of the moment to give these factual statements emotional emphasis. For example, when the President appeared before Congress, May 16, 1940, with a special defense message, the German *blitzkrieg* against Western Europe, launched only a few days before, was overriding all opposition. Under those circumstances, the Chief Executive's statements of the following type were emotional as well as logical in their effect:

Motorized armies can now sweep through enemy territories at the rate of 200 miles a day. . . .

Let me analyze for a moment.

The Atlantic and Pacific Oceans were reasonably adequate defensive barriers when fleets under sail could move at an average speed of five miles an hour. Even in those days by a sudden foray it was possible for an opponent actually to burn our National Capitol. . . .

But the new element—air navigation—steps up the speed of possible attack to 200 to 300 miles an hour. . . .

---

take the lead in stimulating effort, not among other groups but within their own groups.

"The best way of dealing with the few slackers or troublemakers in our midst is, first, to shame them by patriotic example, and if that fails, to use the sovereignty of government to save government." Address of January 6, 1941.

[73] See Fireside Chat, September 3, 1939.

[74] See Paul L. Soper, *Basic Public Speaking* (New York: Oxford University Press, 1949), p. 319. Also, personal letter from Mr. Berle, dated July 10, 1951.

The Azores are only 2,000 miles from parts of our Eastern seaboard, and if Bermuda fell into hostile hands it is a matter of less than three hours for modern bombers to reach our shores.

From a base in the outer West Indies the coast of Florida could be reached in 200 minutes.

The statements about flying times and distances appealed to the motive of self-preservation. The President accomplished the same effect by enumerating specific events in his address of May 27, 1941:

... The night spread over Poland, Denmark, Norway, Holland, Belgium, Luxembourg, and France. . . .

Today the Nazis have taken military possession of the greater part of Europe. . . . The war is approaching the brink of the Western Hemisphere itself. It is coming very close to home. . . .

The blunt truth of this seems to be this—and I reveal this with the full knowledge of the British government: the present rate of Nazi sinkings of merchant ships is more than three times as high as the capacity of British shipyards to replace them; it is more than twice the combined British and American output of merchant ships today.

The seriousness of these situations provided a tremendous emotional impact.

In sixteen of seventeen speeches on the international situation delivered before the attack on Pearl Harbor, Roosevelt appealed to the motive of self-preservation. This appeal frequently involved statements intended to arouse his listeners' emotions by convincing them that they were actually in danger. As the war progressed, he made this danger seem more vivid. Such statements as the following were made primarily as emotoinal appeals:

Never before since Jamestown and Plymouth Rock has our American civilization been in such danger as now.[75]

I use the word "unprecedented" because at no previous time has American security been as seriously threatened from without as it is today.[76]

The speaker also emphasized certain specific fears, such as the danger of fifth-column activities, the danger of isolationism, and the danger of lack of unity.

The depression which gripped the nation when Roosevelt campaigned and won the presidency provided obvious opportunities for appeals to the profit motive, and Roosevelt made full use of them. He sought to show a

[75] Address of December 29, 1940.
[76] Address of January 6, 1941.

causal relationship between the Republican policies of the 1920's and the financial collapse which followed by quoting from Mr. Hoover's 1928 campaign statements: "Without the wise policies which the Republican Party has made effective through the past seven and a half years, the great prosperity we now enjoy would not have been possible." As one critic has explained, "The emotional impact of this type of argument... [upon Americans who] already believed that the Republicans were responsible for their financial plight... doubtless far outweighed any logical force it may have had."[77] "Through the use of humorous satire, dialogue, and such rhetorical devices as simile and metaphor," Roosevelt painted a vivid picture of Republican policies that had led to financial ruin:[78]

The poorhouse was to vanish like the Cheshire cat. A mad hatter invited everyone to "have some more profits." There were no profits, except on paper. A cynical Father William in the lower district of Manhattan balanced the sinuous evil of a pool-ridden stock market on the end of his nose. A puzzled, somewhat skeptical Alice asked the Republican Leadership some simple questions:

"Will not the printing and selling of more stocks and bonds, the building of new plants and the increase of efficiency produce more goods than we can buy?"

"No," shouted Humpty Dumpty. "The more we produce the more we can buy."
"What if we produce a surplus?"
"Oh, we can sell it to foreign consumers."
"How can the foreigners pay for it?"
"Why, we will lend them the money."
"I see," said Alice, "they will buy our surplus with our money. Of course, these foreigners will pay us back by selling us their goods?"
"Oh, not at all," said Humpty Dumpty. "We set up a high wall called the tariff."
"And," said Alice at last, "how will the foreigners pay off these loans?"
"That is easy," said Humpty Dumpty, "did you ever hear of a moratorium?"[79]

Although economic conditions had much improved by 1937, Roosevelt made clear in his Second Inaugural address that the recovery of the preceding four years had not, in his opinion, solved the nation's basic economic problems. His theme, which he repeated over and over in subsequent addresses,[80] was, "I see one-third of a nation ill-housed, ill-clad, ill-nourished."

In the maintenance of his basic premise of social justice, Roosevelt stressed the necessity of correcting certain social problems. These difficulties were

[77] Cowperthwaite, *op. cit.*, p. 335.
[78] *Ibid.*, p. 337.
[79] Address of August 20, 1932.
[80] In 1937, for example, on March 4, at a Democratic Victory Dinner; March 9, Fireside Chat; May 24, to Congress; June 15, Press Conference.

primarily matters of economic opportunities; an appeal to the profit motive was made with demands for:

Jobs for those who can work.
Security for those who need it.
.... The enjoyment of the fruits of scientific progress in a wider and constantly rising standard of living.

Another motive utilized by Franklin Roosevelt was the appeal to basic human affections. He expressed ideas that would produce favorable responses from listeners who had a kindly concern for the welfare of others, who resented selfishness and believed in altruism. He talked of "the happiness, the life of all the boys and girls of the United States." Late in 1941 he appealed directly to feelings of parental love:

There has now come a time when you and I must see the cold inexorable necessity of saying to these inhuman, unrestrained seekers of world conquest and permanent world domination by the sword—"You seek to throw our children and our children's children into your form of terrorism and slavery. You have now attacked our own safety. You shall go no further." [81]

Particularly effective was his recounting of the home states of the dead and wounded from a United States ship torpedoed by a German submarine, for he brought the matter just as close to all his listeners' own experiences and interests as he could.[82] The President deplored the tragedies of warfare because of the hardships it wrought upon innocent people; on one occasion he began a Fireside Chat with a plea "in the name of our common humanity" for contributions to aid the Red Cross "in rushing food and clothing and medical supplies to destitute civilian millions."

The sentiments of Roosevelt's audiences, their desires to believe and to do what was fair and honorable, were appealed to in several different ways. Religious beliefs were expressed, or referred to, in a manner calculated to show profound respect for those ideals. From the early argument that a Nazi victory would threaten the right of freedom of worship, the speaker finally contended that Hitler planned "to abolish all existing religions." [83]

Frequent allusions to the Bible and many direct quotations from it appeared in Roosevelt's speeches. His campaign address of October 2, 1932, concluded with language inspired by the final verse in the thirteenth chapter of St. Paul's first letter to the Corinthians:

[81] Address of September 11, 1941.
[82] Address of October 27, 1941.
[83] Address of October 27, 1941.

And so, in these days of difficulty, we Americans everywhere must and shall choose the path of social justice—the only path that will lead us to a permanent bettering of our civilization, the path that our children must tread and their children must tread, the path of faith, the path of hope and the path of love toward our fellow men.

In his analysis of Roosevelt's speaking in 1932, Cowperthwaite [84] concludes that "doubtless the language of the following passage from the campaign address on unemployment [October 31, 1932] was inspired by the familiar words of the General Confession in the *Episcopal Book of Common Prayer*":

He [President Hoover] did not do what in his 1923 report he said ought to be done. Instead of that, and on top of that, he did what he said ought not to be done.[85]

Praise of the Americans' spirit of patriotism served to encourage that spirit; on other occasions Roosevelt felt compelled to appeal to the necessity of maintaining that patriotism. But a more common appeal in this connection was to duty. He spoke of American citizens' "first obligation," of their "high duty." These appeals to duty were clearly emotional pleas to gain acceptance of his ideas concerning unity and cooperation. In other appeals to the sentiments, Roosevelt stressed such factors as justice, truth, sincerity, and humanity; he talked of "conquering disease and poverty." Such considerations affected the emotions of those desirous of fulfilling their moral obligations. When he spoke of the need for the world of the future to be "founded upon four essential freedoms," he again appealed to the impelling motive of sentiment.

Roosevelt also touched the emotions of his listeners by frequent references to American traditions. Memories of the early pioneers, of their struggles to gain certain ideals, served to rouse his auditors' desires to preserve the traditions so hard won.

Pathetic proof frequently and skillfully won his listeners' support, and Roosevelt's emotional appeals were all the more effective because they typically appeared within the framework of his logical proofs. Similarly, he "enhanced the emotional force of many of his arguments through the use of highly connotative and figurative language. His speeches abound in vivid metaphor, simile, imagery, and analogy,"[86] which added to their emotional impact.

Franklin Roosevelt relied more upon personal and emotional proofs than upon the logical mode; in fact, his logical arguments were occasionally fallacious. Rhetorical critics have not consistently praised Roosevelt's proofs, al-

---

[84] *Op. cit.*, pp. 223-24. The preceding illustration is also noted by Cowperthwaite.

[85] From the General Confession: ". . . We have left undone those things which we ought to have done; and we have done those things which we ought not to have done. . . ." *Book of Common Prayer*, p. 6.

[86] Cowperthwaite, *op. cit.*, p. 434.

though they have admired his invariable choice of specific examples and vivid comparisons in preference to vague generalities. Roosevelt's supporting arguments were frequently inconsistent. Yet, his four victorious campaigns for the presidency, his leadership of the American people through World War II, and his success with the vast majority of issues for which he spoke resulted in important measure from his characteristic methods of support and their effectiveness with his audiences. It is unquestionably true that his ethical stature and his capacity to appeal to the deepest wants of people rhetorically compensated for his deficiencies in logical consistency.

Structure of Speeches

The organization of Franklin D. Roosevelt's speeches was invariably clear, although the skeleton was seldom made obvious by signposts such as "one, two, three." Since his addresses were given careful attention both by him and by his advisers and were typically revised several times, they contained such essentials as effective transitions and an adherence to principles of relevancy and sequence. Critics who have carefully analyzed specific addresses generally agree that Roosevelt's speeches deserve neither praise nor blame for their organization and that no particular patterns of development occur frequently enough to be called characteristic.[87]

From the hundreds of Roosevelt speeches examined through various stages of their preparation, the authors of this study found only three instances[88] in which preliminary outlines appeared to have been used by Roosevelt and his collaborators. In each of these cases, the outline seems to have provided the structure for a preliminary draft or the working basis from which the final speech evolved. According to Grace Tully, the President ordinarily made no attempt to work out an over-all plan as the beginning step in preparation. Typically, he surrounded himself with pertinent data he had received from many sources, and dictated a "rough, first draft." Judge Samuel I. Rosenman has explained that the organization of Roosevelt's speeches evolved and changed from draft to draft, but at no time did the speech structure receive special attention from anyone preparing the addresses.[89]

Although he occasionally developed his ideas inductively without well-

---

[87] For example, Cowperthwaite's study of twenty addresses in the 1932 campaign led him to conclude: "Structurally, Roosevelt's speeches follow no consistent pattern. They ranged from a clearly logical type of arrangement to loosely constructed entities that seemed to unfold in a natural pattern dictated by the subject and its relation to the audience and occasion." *Ibid.*, p. 413.

[88] Outlines are available at the Roosevelt Library for the addresses of: May 7, 1933; February 5, 1937; March 4, 1937.

[89] Interview, December 29, 1950.

defined separation of his introductory remarks from the rest of the speech, more often Roosevelt began with obvious attempts to win a friendly and attentive hearing before launching into his main arguments. His introductions varied widely. From the hundreds of speeches he delivered, examples can be found of a great variety of attention-arresting devices.

On some occasions, Roosevelt presented his thesis as a part of his introduction. He followed this plan, for example, in the speech which he delivered at the dedication of Great Smoky National Park on September 2, 1940, at Newfound Gap, Tennessee. He began with a bit of impromptu humor about the wide variety of "human animals" who would come to the park to join the many "varieties of plants and trees and fishes and animals that Governor Cooper told us about." He mentioned other parks soon to be opened to the public and then spoke with praise of the old frontier spirit which "lives and will live in these untamed mountains to give to the future generations a sense of the land from which their forefathers hewed their homes." He moved from his introduction to the main part of the speech with a clear statement of his basic idea for the address: "If we are to survive, we cannot be soft in a world in which there are dangers that threaten Americans—dangers far more deadly than were those the frontiersmen had to face."

Roosevelt sometimes withheld a statement of his thesis until later in his speech. More than four-fifths of the address of September 11, 1941, was completed before Roosevelt stated the proposition that henceforth American ships and planes would "shoot first" at Axis vessels in American patrol areas. Before this drastic announcement, the President had related the attacks made by Germans on American ships; he discussed German designs "to acquire absolute control and domination of the seas for themselves." He thus attempted to soften his opposition before presenting a thesis with which many of his listeners disagreed.

When Roosevelt accepted the Democratic nomination, July 19, 1940, he was obviously trying to justify his failure to clarify earlier his position on the third-term issue and to show that he could better handle the duties of the presidency than any other candidate. Since the necessity, or at least the desirability, of such an attempt was inherent in that speaking situation, a succinct statement of his position would have lessened his effectiveness. A terse statement of his thesis, moreover, might have been twisted by his opposition to mean, "I consider myself indispensable."

In his opening sentences Mr. Roosevelt often attempted to stimulate friendly interest and attention. Whether or not he stated his thesis in the introduction depended upon his analysis of probable audience reaction to his theme. If his listeners were likely to respond negatively, he withheld his main idea until he had elicited favorable reactions from them.

Franklin Roosevelt planned his speeches to end on a "high note." [90] The conclusion was intended to be "somewhat formal," to reach an emotional peak, to climax the "tempo and spirit" of the address. On several occasions, for example, Roosevelt said to Judge Rosenman, "Sam, try your hand at a peroration." On the other hand, Raymond Moley has disclaimed any part in preparing conclusions to Roosevelt's addresses. He explained, "It had been and remained customary for me to make no attempt to draft a peroration for any speech of Roosevelt's. He always preferred to do that part of a speech in longhand, by himself." [91] Rosenman and Moley agree that the concluding remarks were considered an extremely important part of the total speech preparation.

Some of Roosevelt's most well-known passages evolved from efforts to produce inspiring perorations. The final paragraph of his address accepting the Democratic nomination at Chicago, July 2, 1932, is an illustration of a peroration planned with great care,[92] and one which was highly successful in accomplishing the purposes desired:

I pledge you, I pledge myself, to a new deal for the American people. Let us all here assembled constitute ourselves prophets of a new order of competence and of courage. This is more than a political campaign; it is a call to arms. Give me your help, not to win votes alone, but to win in this crusade to restore America to its own people.[93]

The Roosevelt Library has preserved a sheet of yellow paper with the third draft of the address of January 6, 1941. In Judge Rosenman's handwriting is a statement of the "four freedoms"; across the top of the sheet in Secretary Dorothy Brady's handwriting is the word "Peroration." Roosevelt originally dictated this statement to Rosenman who copied it (in the immediate absence of any of the secretaries) and then made minor changes. Eventually this passage, inserted into the main body of the address, produced such effect that the speech today is commonly remembered as the Four Freedoms address.

Mr. Roosevelt seldom summarized or restated his main ideas or re-emphasized the thesis of a speech in his final sentences. Rather, his conclusions communicated the great emotion he felt. He identified himself and the audience with religious sincerity and patriotism. Almost always, he made an emotional appeal to a motive force such as self-preservation, property, patriotism, or love

[90] Interview with Samuel I. Rosenman, December 29, 1950.
[91] Moley, *op. cit.*, p. 28.
[92] Interview with Rosenman.
[93] Moley said of this address, "The peroration (i.e., the last five paragraphs) was new." *Op. cit.* Moley had played a significant role in the total preparation, although the peroration was "new" to him.

of family. Appeals to the uplifting sentiments of unselfishness, tolerance, and wisdom were also common. Roosevelt consistently identified himself with his listeners by using such expressions as "we," "us," "you and I," "our children," "our ideal—yours and mine," "I know you are praying with me." By this identification of himself with his audience, Roosevelt placed their mutual trust in divine guidance or implored such aid. The following was typical:

> I am certain that out of the hearts of every man, woman and child in this land, in every waking minute, a supplication goes up to Almighty God; that all of us beg that suffering and starving, that death and destruction may end—and that peace may return to the world. In common affection for all mankind, your prayers join with mine—that God will heal the wounds and the hearts of humanity.[94]

In the body of the speech, Roosevelt ordinarily considered three to twelve different topics. His addresses of more than ten or twelve minutes usually had at least seven or eight main divisions. In many instances no special reasons are discernible to explain the ordering of divisions. For example, Roosevelt's address at a dinner of White House correspondents, March 15, 1941, can best be outlined into the following ten main divisions:

    I. The American people are united.

    II. Nazi forces seek the destruction of all elective systems on every continent.

    III. Democracy can adjust to the reality of a world at war.

    IV. Arms are urgently needed and must be sent overseas.

    V. Sacrifices will be necessary for the good of our nation.

    VI. The output of industry and agriculture depends upon the national will to sacrifice and work.

    VII. The British (also the Greeks and Chinese) have demonstrated praiseworthy courage and morale.

    VIII. The United States will play its full part (as the arsenal of democracy).

    IX. No superior races exist on earth.

    X. Every nation can eventually "increase its happiness, banish the terrors of war, and abandon man's inhumanity to man."

When a particular point was being developed, Roosevelt completed his discussion of that aspect of the subject before moving to the next point. Although the explanation for the ordering of divisions was not always clear, ample evidence shows that the organization of some speeches was carefully adapted to his audiences. In addition to withholding the statement of his thesis at times when his listeners might respond negatively, Roosevelt ordinarily

[94] Fireside Chat, May 26, 1940.

dealt in the first portions of his speeches with those points upon which he and his listeners were most likely to agree.

When the President called a special session of Congress in September, 1939, after the outbreak of World War II, the foremost concern of more than nine out of ten Americans [95] was that the United States remain at peace. Consequently, he first developed the idea that "all loyal Americans want peace for the United States." After placing himself on common ground with his listeners, he reviewed the trends and events preceding the outbreak of the war. This led him to the consideration of what he called "traditional American policy towards belligerent nations." Under this general heading, he showed that in the only instance in which the United States had embargo provisions during a major conflict these provisions had proved a dismal failure. From this interpretation of American history, he moved to the contention that "embargo provisions are against American interests." That, in turn, was logically followed by the conclusion that the existing "embargo should be repealed."

Roosevelt showed his astuteness as a speaker by spending more time on the arguments about which disagreement was probable than upon those which his audience was likely to accept immediately. He devoted additional attention to those matters which his audience considered to be most vital. Some of his speeches depended "on the progressive unfolding of ideas." Regarding his address of September 29, 1936, at Syracuse, New York, for example, a critic observes:

Having repudiated the "false" issue of his Communistic leanings, Roosevelt proceeded to clarify the "real" issue of the development of Communism in America by discussing three logical steps—the conditions under which it would develop; the comparison of the action of the opposing parties on these conditions; the certainty of Republican return to neglect of such conditions—steps leading to the conclusion that democracy was safest in Democratic hands. [Thus] . . . the conclusion lay several steps from the opening position.[96]

By such methods, Roosevelt adapted his organization to the prevailing attitudes in his audiences.

[95] According to public opinion polls.

[96] Laura Crowell, "Franklin D. Roosevelt's Audience Persuasion in the 1936 Campaign," *Speech Monographs*, XVII (March, 1950), 53.

At Portland, Oregon, September 21, 1932: "In a loosely constructed, 'natural' unfolding of his subject, Roosevelt set forth the basic principles underlying the concept of a public utility, the place of the public utility in American life, the reasons why Americans were not utilizing electric power to the extent that was desirable, and, finally, his 'New Deal' for the consumers of electricity." Cowperthwaite, *op. cit.*, pp. 392-93.

The obvious climax to the President's speech of September 21, 1939, came with his request that the embargo on arms be repealed. During the remaining one-third of the address he listed "certain other phases of policy reinforcing American safety [which] should be considered." He argued that the nation's "acts must be guided by one single hard-headed thought—keeping America out of this war." He then concluded with a plea that "partisanship" be abandoned and that all join in "helping to maintain in the Western World a citadel wherein civilization may be kept alive." This unfolding of ideas took the President's audience from the one issue upon which they were overwhelmingly agreed through successive contentions progressively more controversial until he called for repeal of the embargo on arms.

Analysis of his State of the Union address in January, 1940, reveals that the order in which the different topics were presented was well adapted to the attitudes of the audience. Roosevelt first explained that "wars abroad justify discussion of foreign affairs." This led him to the idea that "lives of American citizens are affected by conditions on other continents." The President's audience was overwhelmingly convinced that the United States should remain at peace; hence, Roosevelt immediately followed his discussion of the effects upon Americans of the war with the reassurance that the United States would "not become involved in military participation." Having established that the war was of significance to this country, but that, in his opinion, the United States would not have to fight, the President then explained that this nation could "strive for a peace that will mean a better world." To have introduced this idea earlier might well have alarmed his audience and caused them to react negatively for fear that fighting would be involved.

Although Roosevelt did not carefully draft a plan of the organization as a first step in preparation, the constant redrafting and the meticulous rewriting produced addresses which were reasonably well arranged. The over-all organization was clear. From three to twelve topics were typically discussed. On some occasions, Roosevelt ordered these topics so that the ideas most likely to arouse disagreement appeared only after materials certain to arouse favorable response. He frequently withheld his thesis until late in the address when it was likely to engender hostile reactions at the outset.

Roosevelt and his advisers appreciated the value of good introductions and conclusions to speeches. Early drafts of his addresses occasionally had sections bearing such labels as "opening paragraphs," "Beginning," "End," and "Peroration"; these evolved into the introductions and conclusions actually delivered. He began his addresses by encouraging friendliness, interest, and attention before developing his main arguments. His conclusions were designed to inspire faith in his views.

Language and Style

Grace Tully has reported that Roosevelt "took a keen pleasure in the precise selection of words. It always delighted him to debate fine meanings with Sherwood or Rosenman, particularly if he could prove that his own choice of a word carried a more exact meaning than one they had substituted." [97]

Roosevelt was a conscious stylist. At the heart of his theory of style was an insistence upon clarity and simplicity. He wanted to be "clear enough for the layman to understand." [98] He believed he had a duty to keep his nation-wide audience informed and this necessitated talking in a language that people could understand. He insisted upon "simplification or even oversimplification," [99] observed Sherwood. Frances Perkins corroborates this by noting that he mastered his material by "simplifying it." "That was his technique and he was always good at it. He simplified every question I had prepared for him...." She goes on to illustrate how material she submitted to him was made to conform to his stylistic standards:

In one campaign he asked me to write a speech in which he wanted to stress what had been done in social security and why, and to sketch the future of this program. I summed up one section by saying, "We are trying to construct a more inclusive society." I heard that speech over the radio some weeks later, and this is how he, with his instinct for simplicity, wound up that section: "We are going to make a country in which no one is left out." [100]

Objective statistical studies indicate that Roosevelt's language conformed to the standards he advocated. One study of his First Inaugural address and of his radio address of October 22, 1933, reports that about 70 per cent of his words, as compared with 78 per cent of the words of Lincoln's Gettysburg address, fall within the limits of the five hundred most commonly used words of the *Thorndike Word List*. Within the first five-thousand word range fall 92 and 94 per cent of the words respectively, which compares favorably with the 98½ per cent of the words of the Gettysburg address. [101] A similar investigation of Roosevelt's Second Inaugural address, delivered January 20, 1937, reveals percentages almost identical to those of his First Inaugural. [102] In his famous message delivered to Congress December 8,

[97] Tully, *op. cit.*, p. 97.
[98] Eleanor Roosevelt, *This I Remember*, p. 73.
[99] Sherwood, *op. cit.*, pp. 212-13.
[100] Perkins, *op. cit.*, pp. 105, 113.
[101] Richard S. Schultz, "President Roosevelt's Vocabulary," *School and Society*, XXXIX (June 23, 1934), 813-14.
[102] Seventy per cent are among the five hundred most commonly used words; 94 per cent are among the first five thousand. Based upon an investigation made by Charlotte

1941, in which he asked for a declaration of war on Japan, his language was somewhat more difficult. About 60 per cent of the words fall within the first five hundred, 70 per cent in the first thousand, and 90 per cent in the first five thousand. Of course this speech was intended primarily for his congressional listeners although it was broadcast to the nation.[103]

Numerous investigators have found the Roosevelt sentence-length to vary from speech to speech, with average lengths running from sixteen to twenty-seven words.[104] The extent of this range seems to reflect attempts to adjust to different audiences and diverse occasions. When compared with other orators, past and present, the Roosevelt sentence-length compares favorably. According to one study, Woodrow Wilson's average sentence-length was over twenty-nine words. Wendell Phillips used sentences with an average length of about twenty-three words.[105] One estimate found the average Churchill sentence-length to be twenty-six words.[106] Since all of these speakers are known for their simple style, it is evident that Roosevelt conformed to elements involved in such a style.

Nevertheless, the frequent observation that short sentences completely predominate in his speeches is an exaggeration. His deliberate oral phrasing and his slow rate of utterance were partially responsible for this misconception.

Jaynes in a class of one of the authors. Text used, based upon a recording, is found in *Representative American Speeches, 1937-1938.*

[103] In making this study the authors used Thorndike's *Teacher's Word Book of 20,000 Words,* the same list that Schultz used.

[104] In a study of fifty speeches, Bach found the mean sentence-length to be 23.47 words. Earl Charles Bach, "An Objective Study of the Speech Style of Franklin Delano Roosevelt" (M.A. thesis, Marquette University, 1938).

Mostrom, in a study of two speeches, found the mean sentence-length to be 23.5 and 27.3 words respectively. Victor G. Mostrom, "A Critical Study of Franklin D. Roosevelt's Neutrality Speeches of September, 1939" (M.A. thesis, State University of Iowa, 1940).

Schrier found the mean sentence-length for four speeches to be 27, 16, 27, and 21 words. Charlotte Pfiffer Schrier, "A Comparative Study of the Oral Style of Franklin Roosevelt in Representative Occasional and Campaign Speeches" (M.A. thesis, State University of Iowa, 1939).

King found the mean sentence-length in the Second Inaugural address to be 19 words with a range from 6 to 49 words. Robert D. King, "Franklin D. Roosevelt's Second Inaugural Address," *Quarterly Journal of Speech,* XXIII (October, 1937), 439-44.

[105] Howard L. Runion, "An Objective Study of the Speech Style of Woodrow Wilson," *Speech Monographs,* III (1936), 75-94.

[106] Based upon a random sample of 145 sentences containing 3823 words taken from 7 speeches. Halbert Gulley, "A Study of Selected Speeches on Relations with Germany Delivered by Winston Spencer Churchill in The House of Commons, 1935-1938" (Ph.D. dissertation, State University of Iowa, 1948), II, 475.

Second, this impression may have arisen from his practice of stating in short sentences the ideas he wanted to stress. For example, when he addressed Congress September 21, 1939, he said, "It [his recommended legislation] is a positive program for giving safety." A few words later he emphasized, "There lies the road to peace." Often he included a pungent short statement to crystallize a point which he then further amplified in longer sentences.[107] Sometimes he achieved his purpose by a series of short statements. On May 26, 1940, he interjected,

I did not share those illusions. I do not share these fears. Today we are now more realistic. But let us not be calamity-howlers and discount our strength. Let us have done with both fears and illusions. On this Sabbath evening, in our homes in the midst of our American families, let us consider what we have done and what we must do.

On September 2, 1940, at the dedication of Great Smoky Mountains National Park he shot out in rapid succession these ideas:

We must prepare in a thousand ways. Men are not enough. They must have arms. They must learn how to use those arms. They must have skilled leaders—who in turn must be trained. New bases must be established and I think will be established to enable our fleet to defend our shores. Men and women must be taught to create the supplies that we need. And we must counter the agents of the dictators within our nation.

Such sentences used at the crux of his arguments served to create the illusion that all his sentences were short. The listener, hearing his deliberate delivery, remembered these striking rapierlike thoughts and overlooked the longer sentences, complex and compound, that were always present.

His syntax naturally involved all types of sentences, simple, compound, and complex. In his carefully prepared talks he used a slight preponderance of periodic sentences. On many occasions he made little use of interrogation, either direct or rhetorical.[108] In his seventeen important speeches on foreign policy, delivered between 1939 and 1941, only twice did he include a series of rhetorical questions.[109]

[107] "I have authorized the addition of a hundred and fifty persons to the Department of Justice to be used in the protection of the United States against subversive foreign activities within our borders. At this time I ask for no further authority from Congress. At this time I see no need for further executive action under the proclamation of limited national emergency. Therefore, I see no impelling reason for the consideration of other legislation at this extraordinary session of the Congress." Address of September 21, 1939.

[108] Notable exceptions include his campaign speeches delivered at Chicago, October 14, 1936, and at Boston, October 30, 1940.

[109] Brandenburg, *op. cit.*

Robert Sherwood stresses that Roosevelt "was happiest when he could express himself in the homeliest, even the tritest phrases, such as 'common or garden,' 'clear as crystal,' 'rule of thumb,' 'neither here nor there,' 'armchair strategists,' or 'simple as A B C.'"[110] Running throughout the Roosevelt speeches indeed are many evidences of his delight with the common idiom, colloquial and folk expressions, as well as occasional slang. Particularly in his campaign appearances and his Fireside Chats are such expressions as "the doubting Thomases," "Model T farming," "in the driver's seat," "running around in circles," "three square meals a day," "a cat and dog fight," "water over the dam," "in the bag," "half-baked promises," "down to earth talk," and "all over but the shouting."

Often in campaigning he coined such striking phrases as "the do-nothing-or-wait-and-see policy," "the well-upholstered, hindsight critic," and "an every-man-for-himself kind of society." At times he felt no embarrassment at using words such as "shenanigans," "botch," "razz," and "chisel," which many might have considered slang. Such language, prevalent in the popular vernacular, was well understood by his diverse listeners, and it also re-enforced the impression of directness and conviviality. In this manner he gave to his speeches the common touch that made him seem more human to millions of his fellow Americans.

When Roosevelt felt that his meaning might be misunderstood or obscure, he often inserted synonyms or phrases in apposition in order to clarify his thought. On one occasion he said, "I am sure that those ... who are devotees of outdoor life, whether fishermen, hunters, naturalists, campers, or hikers, will rejoice...."[111] At another time he clarified his meaning in the following manner: "Next they want peace in the community, the peace that springs from the ability to meet the needs of community life—schools, playgrounds, parks, sanitation, highways—those things which are expected of solvent local government."[112]

Eleanor Roosevelt reports "he often insisted on putting in simple stories drawn from conversation with visitors or friends in Warm Springs or Hyde Park...."[113] Commonplace examples and homely analogies were among his favorite forms of support. Informally, he might introduce an illustration by saying, "A prominent manufacturer told me ..." or "A very important businessman of New York came to see me." Upon the rare occasions when he used statistical evidence he usually put his figures into round numbers and then further amplified them by concrete examples.

[110] Sherwood, *op. cit.*, pp. 212-13.
[111] October 1, 1936.
[112] In a speech at Madison Square Garden, October 31, 1936.
[113] Eleanor Roosevelt, *This I Remember*, p. 73.

His speeches are packed with figurative analogies, drawn from experiences familiar to his audiences. For example, on one occasion he said, "But you people know what I mean when I say it is clear that if a train is to run smoothly again the cars will have to be loaded evenly."[114]

In presenting his side of the quarrel with the Supreme Court, he told the people in a Fireside Chat,

Last Thursday I described the American form of government as a three-horse team provided by the Constitution to the American people so that their field might be plowed. The three horses are, of course, the three branches of government—the Congress, the Executive, and the Courts.[115]

The three-horse-team comparison was one that the laborer and farmer were more likely to understand than if Roosevelt had couched his thoughts in legalistic terms. Perhaps more amusing but equally effecive was his reference to "the ninety-six inch dog being wagged by a four-inch tail." To emphasize his meaning, he added, "If you work that out in feet and inches, it is an amazing dog."[116] In the 1940 campaign he told a Boston audience that the Republicans "before every Election Day . . . always uncork the old bottle of soothing syrup and spread it thick."[117]

A marked preference of Roosevelt, therefore, was his desire to use simple words, folk expressions, simple illustrations, and homely analogies. These trademarks of his style are found in almost every speech. Naturally they are more prevalent in his popular efforts and extemporaneous remarks than they are in his more formal addresses to Congress and foreign diplomats.

A third important stylistic preference of Roosevelt was his desire to give his speeches an oral quality. Sherwood says, "Sometimes Roosevelt read the speech out loud, to see how it sounded, for every word was judged not by its appearance in print but by its effectiveness over the radio."[118]

Roosevelt attempted to aid his listeners in their efforts to follow his development. Frequently in presenting a plan or program he numbered the progressive steps. In addition, he included such typical expressions as the following: "now listen to that," "picture to yourself," "just a word or two on," "let me give you an example," "let me state a simple fact," "I'll give you a simple illustration," "one word more," "let me make it clear to you," and "finally I should like to say a personal word to you." As was shown earlier, he often indulged in what has been called "platform authorship" and inserted words and phrases to facilitate the listening process.

[114] Speech of October 14, 1936.
[115] March 9, 1937.
[116] Speech of January 8, 1938.
[117] Speech of October 30, 1940.
[118] Sherwood, *op. cit.*, p. 215.

Throughout his speeches Roosevelt profusely sprinkled pronouns in the first and second persons. His talks seemed more conversational because he spoke in terms of "I," "we," and "you," and the related pronominal adjectives. In his address of May 10, 1940, he used "we" twenty-five times, "our" eleven times, "us" six times; this adds up to forty-two uses of the first person plural in a speech containing a total of forty-nine sentences.[119] One critic believes that the use of personal pronouns was "one of the outstanding elements of his style." [120]

The opening sentences of his Fourth Inaugural address, delivered January 20, 1945, well exemplify the personal element which he included in so many of his speeches. He said,

You will understand and, I believe, agree with my wish that the form of this inaugural be simple and its words brief.

We Americans of today, together with our allies, are passing through a period of supreme test. It is a test of our courage—of our resolve—of our wisdom—of our essential decency.

If we meet that test—successfully and honorably—we shall perform a service of historic importance which men and women and children will honor throughout all time.

As I stand here today, having taken the solemn oath of office in the presence of my fellow countrymen—in the presence of our God—I know that it is America's purpose that we shall not fail.

In the days and in the years that are to come we shall work for a just and durable peace as today we work and fight for total victory in war.

We can and we will achieve such a peace.

Another significant oral characteristic of Roosevelt's style was his frequent use of repetition and parallel sentence structure. Sometimes he achieved the desired rhythms by repeating the same word several times within a sentence as in this series: "old customs, old language, old friends." [121] In the following sentence he heightened the emphasis by repeating the verb: "I believe, I have always believed, and I will always believe in private enterprise...." Often he introduced a series of sentences arranged in parallel form

[119] In his address of September 3, 1939, "there were seventy-two personal pronouns, or approximately 1.4 per sentence. . . . There were thirty-five first person singular pronouns and nineteen first person plural, for a total of fifty-four, as compared to thirteen second person pronouns and five third person."

The number of first and second person pronouns used [Sept. 21, 1939] were: I, forty-three; my, six; myself, one; we, twenty-one; us, eighteen; our, thirty-five; you, six; and your, one. Mostrom, *op. cit.*, pp. 64-65, 131.

[120] Schrier, *op. cit.*, p. 85.

[121] Speech of October 28, 1936.

with the same words. His lines frequently possessed a studied, regular, recurring beat, reminiscent perhaps of Whitman, Sandburg, or sometimes the Bible.[122] These lines naturally often fall into iambic, anapestic, spondaic meter. The Roosevelt prose rhythm built upon repetition, parallel structure, and regularity of beat is well illustrated in his famous passage which he included in his speech to the Democratic Victory Dinner, March 4, 1937. Roosevelt said:

Here is one-third of a Nation ill-nourished, ill-clad, ill-housed—NOW!

Here are thousands upon thousands of farmers wondering whether next year's prices will meet their mortgage interest—NOW!

Here are thousands upon thousands of men and women laboring for long hours in factories for inadequate pay—NOW!

Here are thousands upon thousands of children who should be at school, working in mines and mills—NOW!

Here are strikes more far-reaching than we have ever known, costing millions of dollars—NOW!

Here are Spring floods threatening to roll again down our river valleys—NOW! Here is the Dust Bowl beginning to blow again—NOW!

If we would keep faith with those who had faith in us, if we would make democracy succeed, I say we must act—NOW!

Each sentence is introduced by "Here" and closed by "NOW!" Within each sentence words such as "thousands upon thousands" add to the cadence.

Another excellent example of parallel structure is found in his stirring persuasive appeal delivered to Congress December 8, 1941. By his language he suggests the quickness of the Japanese attack. He said,

Yesterday the Japanese government also launched an attack against Malaya.
Last night Japanese forces attacked Hong Kong.
Last night Japanese forces attacked Guam.
Last night Japanese forces attacked the Philippine Islands.
Last night the Japanese attacked Wake Island.
This morning the Japanese attacked Midway Island.

One of Roosevelt's more stirring passages, delivered during the war, possesses effective parallel structure. With the war effort in this country well under way, Roosevelt made a fighting speech, designed to stimulate greater effort on the home front. He said,

From Berlin, Rome and Tokyo we have been described as a nation of weaklings—"playboys"—who would hire British soldiers, or Russian soldiers, or Chinese soldiers to do our fighting for us.

[122] Joseph Shiffman, "Observations on Roosevelt's Literary Style," *Quarterly Journal of Speech*, XXXV (April, 1949), 222-26.

Let them repeat that now!

Let them tell that to General MacArthur and his men.

Let them tell that to the sailors who today are hitting hard in the far waters of the Pacific.

Let them tell that to the boys in the Flying Fortresses.

Let them tell that to the Marines! [123]

These passages involving oral rhythms were not accidents, nor were they confined to any one period of the Roosevelt years. They occurred frequently in most of his carefully prepared speeches from 1933 until his death.

In 1936, at a dedication of the Theodore Roosevelt Memorial, Franklin Roosevelt eulogized his illustrious kinsman for his "fighting epithets" and his gift for "pungent" phrases.[124] Perhaps Theodore Roosevelt influenced his cousin's style, for F.D.R. also demonstrated a delight in including in his speeches epigrams, striking phrases, and witticisms. Members of his speech staff were constantly on the alert for clever sayings and pithy sentences that might be incorporated in his speeches; his private secretary maintained a special file for this type of material. But the pungent phrases were not always lifted out of material written by others. Charles Michelson, who acquired the reputation of a phrase-maker himself, says, "Franklin Roosevelt is a better phrase-maker than anybody he ever had around him." [125] Henry Steele Commager observes, "To fight the stereotypes of his critics he created stereotypes of his own, and not even the first Roosevelt had displayed a comparable talent for coining words and phrases that caught the public imagination. . . ." [126]

Regardless of where Roosevelt found a given phrase, it is important to note that seemingly he had a keen appreciation for what would appeal to his listeners. The phrase "the new deal," first uttered in his speech of acceptance before the Democratic National Convention, July 2, 1932, is perhaps his most famous example of a fortunate choice of language.[127] His speeches abound with similar expressions which became popular terminology in the conversation

[123] Delivered February 23, 1942.

[124] From an address delivered at the Dedication of the Theodore Roosevelt Memorial, January 19, 1936.

[125] Charles Michelson, *The Ghost Talks* (New York: G. P. Putnam & Sons, 1944), p. 13.

[126] Henry Steele Commager, *The American Mind* (New Haven: Yale University Press, 1950), p. 357.

[127] A debate has arisen over the origin of this phrase. Moley claims that he first used the expression in a memorandum. See Moley, *After Seven Years*, p. 23. Another source reports that F.D.R. admitted that he first read the phrase in the writings of Mark Twain. See Cyril Clemens, *The Literary Education of Franklin Delano Roosevelt* (Webster Groves, Missouri: Privately Printed, 1935), p. 35. The phrase is remarkably like "The Square Deal," which was coined by Theodore Roosevelt.

of his fellow countrymen. Some of his better-known expressions are "the hand that held the *dagger*," "good neighbor policy," "economic royalist," "freedom from fear," "freedom from want," "a date which will live in infamy," "arsenal of democracy," "prophets of calamity," "in the wastelands of want and fear," and "no blackout of peace."

Frequently he quoted or paraphrased some biblical expression in order to make his meaning more impressive. In his First Inaugural address he spoke as follows: "The money changers have fled from their high seats in the temple of our civilization." On January 8, 1940, he used the quotation, "By their motives may ye know them." On October 28, 1936, he said, "They came to us speaking many tongues." Often he used the expression, "Man cannot live by bread alone." He built one speech around two lines from the Twenty-third Psalm:

> "He maketh me to lie down in green pastures
> He leadeth me beside the still waters."

Throughout the speech he used the biblical illusions many times. In one paragraph he said:

Green pastures! Millions of our fellow Americans, with whom I have been associating in the past two weeks, out on the Great Plains of America, live with prayers and hopes for the fulfillment of what those words imply. Still waters! Millions of other Americans, with whom I also have been associated of late, live with prayers and hopes either that the floods may be stilled—floods that bring with them destruction and disaster to fields and flocks, to homesteads and cities—or else they look for the Heaven-sent rains that will fill their wells, their ponds and their peaceful streams.[128]

From his extensive knowledge of history, particularly of the American Colonial period, Roosevelt often summoned up historical allusions. He made repeated references to such great Americans as Thomas Paine, Jefferson, Jackson, Webster, Lincoln, Theodore Roosevelt, and Woodrow Wilson. Often he quoted choice passages from his favorite figures.

In political campaigns he often demonstrated his adeptness at using stinging ridicule and biting sarcasm. In the 1936 campaign he scored the Republicans before a New York audience with these words:

For twelve years our nation was afflicted with hear-nothing, see-nothing, do-nothing government. The Nation, the Nation looked to that Government, but that Government looked away. Nine mocking years with the golden calf and three long years of the scourge! Nine crazy years at the ticker and three long years in the breadline! Nine mad years of mirage and three long years of despair! And, my

[128] Speech delivered September 10, 1936, at Green Pastures Rally, Charlotte, N. C.

friends, powerful influences strive today to restore that kind of government with its doctrine that that Government is best which is most indifferent to mankind.[129]

The storm over Fala during World War II brought forth some of Roosevelt's most telling ridicule. In the presidential campaign he began his "partisan speaking" on September 23, 1944, before the Teamsters' Union with an address which his close advisers think was probably the greatest campaign speech of his career.[130] The "whispered stories" which were current in all of his campaigns included one in the fall of 1944 which got into print. Supposedly, the President's dog, Fala, had been left by mistake on an Aleutian Island after Roosevelt's visit there, and a United States destroyer had been sent back to find him.[131] Before a crowd of cheering teamsters, chauffeurs, and warehousemen, Roosevelt answered his critics as follows:

These Republican leaders have not been content with attacks on me, or my wife, or on my sons. No, not content with that, they now include my little dog, Fala. Well, of course, I don't resent attacks, and my family doesn't resent attacks, but Fala *does* resent them. You know, Fala is Scotch, and being a Scottie, as soon as he learned that the Republican fiction writers in Congress and out had concocted a story that I had left him behind on the Aleutian Islands and had sent a destroyer back to find him—at a cost to the taxpayers of two or three, or eight or twenty million dollars— his Scotch soul was furious. He has not been the same dog since. I am accustomed to hearing malicious falsehoods about myself—such as that old, worm-eaten chestnut that I have represented myself as indispensable. But I think I have a right to resent, to object to libelous statements about my dog.[132]

This passage is often referred to as an outstanding example of humor and sarcasm which not only won the argument over the immediate issue, but also contributed most significantly to the campaign.

Roosevelt was well aware that the success of his administration depended in large measure upon how well he presented his program to the people. In addition, he was aware that historians would evaluate his work by what he said and how well he said it. He was eager, therefore, to achieve an impressive style, one with sufficient emotional coloring to give force and energy to what he said. His speeches were invariably phrased in oral style. Concrete, simple language, vivid descriptions, striking phrases and epigrammatic statements, frequent allusions to the Bible, and occasional short, terse sentences contributed

[129] From the stenographically reported speech, delivered at Madison Square Garden, New York, October 31, 1936.

[130] Sherwood, *op. cit.*, p. 822.

[131] Because this was a radio speech to be paid for by the Democratic National Committee the exact number of words he could deliver in thirty minutes was carefully planned and counted, but the roars of laughter and applause were so frequent and prolonged that the speech ran fifteen minutes overtime. *Ibid.*, p. 217.

[132] Speech delivered in Washington, D.C., September 23, 1944.

impressiveness to what he said. His frequent use of historical allusions and striking quotations as well as inclusion of effective ridicule and sarcasm gave a memorable quality to his speaking.

Delivery[133]

Franklin D. Roosevelt's delivery—his pleasing voice quality, his highly expressive intonations and inflections, his mastery of the conversational mode, and his direct speaking manner—unquestionably contributed to his effectiveness. His detractors often asserted that his delivery was the sole source of his effectiveness. Though such claims are refuted by the presence in public life of many less successful persons with as good or better voices and vocal control, this reluctant testimony gives an important clue to Roosevelt the orator.

1. APPEARANCE AND PERSONALITY

Eleanor Roosevelt has agreed with countless others that Franklin's polio attack molded his character and personality most significantly. "Perhaps the experience, above all others, which shaped my husband's character along more definite lines and gave him a strength and depth that he did not have as a young man, was the long struggle with infantile paralysis." [134]

As Roosevelt fought back against the affliction which had struck him in August, 1921, there were many times when everyone else feared that he was doomed to almost complete invalidism. His major leg muscles became completely useless to him, and not until a year later could he hobble about even with the aid of crutches. His wife and Louis Howe above all others encouraged and fostered within him the determination not to retire to Hyde Park but to continue to take an active part in public affairs. Gradually, through the middle 1920's, there emerged a somewhat changed Roosevelt, who was able by 1928 to campaign vigorously for the New York governorship. The handsome features mellowed and matured; the large, full face acquired deep lines; youthful self-assurance gave way to humility of spirit, thoughtfulness, and determination.

It is impossible, of course, to assess the exact influence of his physical disability upon his personality, but it must necessarily have affected his outlook and attitudes. During the remainder of his life he could not stand unsupported. Frances Perkins describes a not uncommon situation in which she saw him during the 1920's:

I remember plainly the mixture of admiration and consternation I felt when I saw him speak in a small hall in New York City's Yorkville district. . . . The only

---

[133] The writers are much indebted to Professor C. M. Wise of Louisiana State University for his helpful and expert criticism of this section, especially of the material on Roosevelt's pronunciation.

[134] *Personal Letters*, II, xviii.

possible way for any candidate to enter the stage without being crushed by the throng was by the fire escape. . . . I realized with sudden horror that the only way he could ever get over that fire escape was in the arms of strong men. . . . Those of us who saw this incident, with our hands on our throats to hold down our emotion, realized that this man had accepted the ultimate humility which comes from being helped physically. . . . It was in those accommodations to necessity that Franklin Roosevelt began to approach the stature of humility and inner integrity which made him truly great.[135]

When Roosevelt spoke to an audience he had to use at least one arm constantly to grip some support, the speaker's stand, a friendly arm, or the iron railing of the observation platform. In many situations he used both hands and both arms to steady himself. Heavy steel braces supported his weight; consequently, his bodily movements were severely restricted. With his free hand he managed as best he could the pages of his manuscript or notes. Of necessity he used gestures sparingly. These physical limitations on his arms and hands perhaps account for the vigorous head movements and the eloquent facial expressions which came to characterize his speaking.

His broad, friendly smile and his highly expressive countenance were important assets to Franklin Roosevelt as a speaker. His mobile face could reflect a wide variety of reactions. It "changed expression with the quickness and sureness of a finished actor's. It was amused, solemn, sarcastic, interested, indignant. It was always strong and confident and it was never dull."[136] He took pride in his ability to reflect his changes of mood by his manner, and he liked to think of himself as an actor. Once he said to Orson Welles quite seriously, "You know, Orson, you and I are the two best actors in America."[137]

By countless hours of exercising Franklin Roosevelt developed a powerful torso. His weight became about a hundred and eighty pounds, and his slim, six-foot frame acquired new dimensions and strength. By 1934, he easily merited high praise for his physique, despite the limitations imposed upon it by his affliction:

From the waist up, the President is a magnificent figure. His shoulders are enormously broad, and his arms, wrists, and hands are very strong. He can propel himself almost the length of the White House swimming pool with a single thrust of his arms.[138]

[135] Perkins, *op. cit.*, pp. 44-45.
[136] "Americans Loved the Roosevelts," *Life*, XXI (November 25, 1946), 110.
[137] "After seeing himself in a newsreel once [Roosevelt] grinned, 'That was the Garbo in me.' " John Gunther, *Roosevelt in Retrospect* (New York: Harper & Brothers, 1950), p. 62.
[138] Henry F. Pringle, "The President," *Roosevelt Omnibus* (New York: Alfred A. Knopf, 1934), p. 68.

He was highly photogenic. This was a great advantage since as President he was constantly being photographed. But the innumerable pictures which the American people saw after 1932 were from the waist up.[139] Thus his physical handicap detracted little from his appearance and personality as judged by the vast majority of the listeners who comprised his radio and newsreel audiences; rather, he was thought of as a handsome, strong individual who had won a moral and physical victory over the dreaded infantile paralysis.

Franklin Roosevelt knew how to use his physical attributes so that immediate audiences would respond favorably to his appearance and his personality. His public appearances were tremendously successful:

When appearing in public, he was the champion, the colorful leader with his chin arched upward and his big hand in the air.

... He could thrill a crowded stadium by just this simple wave of a hand, or his brown felt hat. That was all it took to jerk a hundred thousand people to their feet in a screaming frenzy.[140]

Even his most severe critics agree that his appearance and personality prompted highly favorable responses:

Roosevelt, as the world saw him, was a man of unusual personal charm. He was large, broad-shouldered, handsome; he exuded physical vitality and there was a warm, genial, exuberant flow of spirits. There was the suggestion of personal force— a certain positive and resolute manner greatly enhanced by his physical appearance. People liked him quickly. The remote, somewhat lofty bearing of his earlier days had vanished. Amongst people he was easy, gracious, hearty and friendly.[141]

By his fine appearance and his responsive face, Roosevelt was able to inspire confidence, admiration, and good will among his listeners. Each auditor received the impression that Roosevelt was talking directly to him, as "a sympathetic, authoritative, and omniscient friend; as almost every American knows, you could practically feel him physically in the room."[142] By his conversational manner he stirred the emotions of his listeners and conveyed the impression of informality, spontaneity, and friendly interest. Claude G. Bowers' observation of one address in the 1932 campaign that Roosevelt's speech bore "the stamp of deep sincerity which the audience did not miss"[143] typically applied to all his addresses. The crowds which gathered to hear him

---

[139] See A. Merriman Smith, *Thank You, Mr. President* (New York: Harper & Brothers, 1946), p. 63.

[140] *Ibid.*, pp. 63-64.

[141] Flynn, *The Roosevelt Myth*, p. 281.

[142] Gunther, *op. cit.*, p. 38.

[143] *New York Journal*, November 9, 1932.

were fascinated by his speaking personality. The *New York Times* said in an editorial in 1932:

The great crowds who gather to see him or to hear him in the cities through which he has passed are undoubtedly more interested in his personality than in anything he says. . . . Moving pictures and newsreels and talkies had made his face and smile and even voice familiar to them. Yet it all evidently did not lessen their eagerness.[144]

His most notable personality trait, according to James A. Farley, was that "he always gave the air of being happy."[145] Roosevelt probably laughed "more times per day than any man in politics."[146]

Campaign audiences whether in huge auditoriums or at his rear-platform appearances inevitably were drawn by his warm, friendly attitude. According to one observer, Roosevelt's pleasing personality "always got over to the crowds," largely because of "his real feeling of good will toward men."[147]

Roosevelt had the ability to project his charming personality as a speaker to his radio listeners. Considering his campaign address delivered before the Teamsters' Union in 1944, Frances Perkins wrote:

When he told how Fala, his little dog, had been kicked around, he spoke with naturalness and simplicity. . . . The laughter of those gathered around radios of the country was a natural, sincere, and affectionate reaching out to this man.[148]

John Royal, director of programs for the National Broadcasting Company, explained when Roosevelt first became President that the unusual gift of making listeners feel, even though they might be hundreds of miles away, that he was talking with them instead of at them, was the key to Mr. Roosevelt's success on the air. "His voice carries a feeling of intimacy with his audience as well as with his subject."[149] His directness was unmistakable and the effects of that directness were equally unmistakable:

I have sat in those little parlors and on those porches myself [where people were gathered to hear Roosevelt speak] . . . and I have seen men and women . . . listening with a pleasant, happy feeling of association and friendship. The exchange between them and him through the medium of the radio was very real. I have seen tears come to their eyes as he told them of some tragic episode, of the sufferings of the persecuted people in Europe, of the poverty, during unemployment, of the sufferings of the homeless, of the sufferings of people whose sons had been killed in the war, and they were tears of sincerity and recognition and sympathy.[150]

[144] *New York Times*, September 26, 1932.
[145] Cowperthwaite, *op. cit.*, p. 264. Personal interview with James A. Farley.
[146] Lindley, *Franklin D. Roosevelt*, p. 39.
[147] Claude G. Bowers, *New York Journal*, November 9, 1932.
[148] Perkins, *op. cit.*, pp. 10-11.
[149] "When Roosevelt Goes on the Air," *New York Times*, June 18, 1933.
[150] Perkins, *op. cit.*, pp. 10-11.

The skillful delivery of his speeches resulted in part from Roosevelt's methods of speech preparation. Having shared so largely in the preparation, he was familiar both with the ideas and the language of his final draft. Ordinarily he did not spend a great amount of time rehearsing his delivery with his final manuscript. According to Robert Sherwood:

> When a speech was finally closed up . . . he chatted or worked on his correspondence or his stamp albums, without seeming to give much attention to the final reading copy of his speech which was typed on special limp paper, to avoid rustling noises as he turned the pages. . . . But when he started to broadcast he seemed to know it by heart. When he looked down at his manuscript, he was usually not looking at the words he was then speaking but at the next paragraph to determine where he would put his pauses and which of his large assortment of inflections he would employ.[151]

Invariably Roosevelt was excellently prepared to attain his optimum effectiveness in delivery. At the dinner preceding his address before the Foreign Policy Association in New York, October 21, 1944, he finished eating and then went to work on his speech text:

> Pencil in hand, wetting his big thumb from time to time as he turned the pages, he read the speech over to himself, speaking softly, gesturing slightly. . . . As he read he would jot down little interpolations, asides, and personal stage directions. This was an old experienced actor going through the final rehearsal. . . . Suddenly the floodlights came up; the President was his old broad-smiling self, waving gaily as diners applauded, smiling and joking with others at the head table.[152]

Frequent ad libbing and excellent adaptations to immediate situations characterized Roosevelt's speaking and obviously enhanced the effectiveness of his delivery. Sherwood observes:

> As one who has had considerable experience in the theater, I marveled at the unfailing precision with which he made his points, his grace in reconciling the sublime with the ridiculous, as though he had been rehearsing these lines for weeks and delivering them before audiences for months.[153]

Franklin Roosevelt's speaking personality, inextricably interwoven with his ideas and the language in which they were couched, proved tremendously successful with audiences. *Time* magazine in reporting a campaign speech delivered at Philadelphia in 1940, told how "the old campaigner" won his audience. "He was sarcastic, sly, arch, tough, ironic, intimate, confidential. He ad libbed, he laughed, rolled his eyes sidewise, lifted his eyes in mock

---

[151] Sherwood, *op. cit.*, pp. 217-18.
[152] "Dinner at the Waldorf," *Time*, XLIV (October 30, 1944), 12-13.
[153] Sherwood, *op. cit.*, p. 218.

horror."[154] The conservative *Christian Science Monitor* said that another address of the same campaign "showed his full, versatile, forensic repertoire, and he played on the multitude like a musician on an instrument. He seemed, at times, like the whole Barrymore family in one—not excluding Ethel."[155] The effectiveness commonly accorded Franklin D. Roosevelt's delivery in his speeches was unquestionably due in part to his appearance and personality.

2. VOICE

The President's voice quality was widely praised. Critics have observed: "The cues in Franklin D. Roosevelt's voice—the voice alone—inspired confidence [in his Inaugural address in 1933].... If Herbert Hoover had spoken the same words into the microphone...the stock market would have fallen another notch and public confidence with it."[156] Roosevelt's voice frequently was given such labels as "fresh," "brilliant," "pleasant," "rich," and "melodious." According to one critic Roosevelt had "the best modulated radio voice in public life."[157] John Carlile, production director of the Columbia Broadcasting System, called his voice "one of the finest on the radio."[158] The radio director of the University of Chicago characterized him as the "glamour boy of radio," with a voice "like honey syrup oozing through the steel filter that jackets the microphone."[159] Even his bitter critic, John T. Flynn, freely admits the "general verdict...that Roosevelt possessed a golden voice and a seductive and challenging radio technique."[160] Perhaps no other aspect of Roosevelt's speaking evoked such unanimity of opinion as the superior quality of his speaking voice.

Although it is obviously impossible to divorce one aspect of a speaker's delivery completely from all others (or to divorce his delivery from his language or from his proofs),[161] final judgments need to be based both upon general impressions and upon the careful analysis of specific elements. The

[154] *Time*, XXXVI (November 4, 1940), 1.
[155] *Christian Science Monitor*, October 24, 1940.
[156] Lew Sarett and William Trufant Foster, *Basic Principles of Speech* (New York: Houghton Mifflin Co., 1936), pp. 193-94.
[157] Robert T. Oliver, "The Speech That Established Roosevelt's Reputation," *Quarterly Journal of Speech*, XXXI (October, 1945), 274.
[158] "Personality on the Air," *New York Times*, March 20, 1932, Section 8, p. 14.
[159] Sherman H. Dryer, "Air Power," *Collier's*, 106 (September 14, 1940), 18.
[160] Flynn, *The Roosevelt Myth*, p. 283.
[161] According to Harold P. Zelko, for example, "rhythmic structure is not a random technique of Franklin Roosevelt's. It is . . . designed as a basis for a better style and [also] for helping to achieve a rhythm and cadence in delivery." Harold P. Zelko, "Franklin D. Roosevelt's Rhythm in Rhetorical Style," *Quarterly Journal of Speech*, XXVIII (April, 1942), 138.

study of Roosevelt's vocal pitch, speaking rate, and use of loudness as separate factors should contribute to the rhetorician's ultimate understanding of the speaker's voice.

Roosevelt's habitual pitch, that is, the pitch that he used most frequently, is difficult to ascertain; his voice quality is equally difficult to describe in exact terms. His voice was ordinarily described as tenor. As a youth he was a member of the tenor section of the Groton Glee Club. This tenor voice which proved to be "one of his greatest assets,"[162] radiated "friendliness, good will, reassurance." During most of his speaking, his voice was clear, resonant, and as one observer said, "vibrant with enthusiasm,"[163] but occasionally his sinus trouble gave him a slightly nasal quality.[164]

What was popularly regarded as Roosevelt's pronunciation was often much more than pronunciation, for it included the inseparable concomitant— intonation. When persons caricatured Roosevelt's speech they invariably repeated expressions such as, "My Friends," "I hate war," "My Fellow Americans," or perhaps the entire sentence, "I have said not once, but many times, that I have seen war and that I hate war. I say that again and again."[165] These expressions were hallmarks of his speech in the minds of millions. The characteristics imitated included his intonations and inflections as well as his pronunciations of certain words such as *war* [wɔə] and *again* [əgeɪn].

The tenor voice, never monotonous, was capable of either wide and startling or slight and subtle changes in pitch, but Roosevelt did not place extreme reliance on pitch changes. Occasionally, like many who do much public speaking, he ended a sentence with an upward inflection when a downward inflection would have been more meaningful. This effect seemed to occur at the ends of sentences for which he apparently expected and invited applause,[166] or where, although he had reached the end of a statement, his immediate, central idea was to be continued into the next sentence.[167]

---

[162] Cowperthwaite, *op. cit.*, p. 307.

[163] Orrin E. Dunlap, Jr., "A Study of Voices," *New York Times*, September 6, 1936, Sec. 9, p. 10.

[164] Ross J. McIntire, *White House Physician* (New York: G. P. Putnam's Sons, 1946), pp. 56-58.

[165] From the Fireside Chat delivered September 3, 1939.

[166] For example, the following sentence ended on an upward inflection and, quite obviously, Roosevelt expected and asked for applause by the inflection of his voice: "And the strength of the British fleet in the Atlantic has been a friendly strength; it is still a friendly strength." Address of January 6, 1941.

[167] For example: "I regret that the Congress passed that act. I regret equally that I signed the act.

". . . but that is not the issue. The step I recommend is to put this country back on a solid footing of real and traditional neutrality." Address of September 21, 1939.

His speaking rate was comparatively slow. Most studies report extremes for individual speeches between 95 and 125 words per minute, with a mean rate over several speeches of about 105 to 110 words per minute. Persons who assisted in the preparation of his speeches considered 100 words per minute [168] a normal rate for him—a rate which was unquestionably slower than that of most superior speakers. When addressing a large audience in his immediate presence, he followed the advice of authorities by speaking more slowly than before a small audience such as he had at the White House for his Fireside Chats.

He was able consciously to vary his speaking rate to meet the rigid requirements of radio schedules. He often marked off his final reading copies [169] into five-minute sections, and he seldom had trouble making his speaking rate conform to changes necessitated by applause or by his own impromptu insertions.

Roosevelt frequently divided his sentences into short phrases, four to six words in length, relieved by occasional long phrases or entire sentences with no pauses, introduced for variety. The cadence of his speech ofttimes was measured and deliberative, with words in important passages receiving equal stress and with pauses between words and sentences for dramatic emphasis.[170] His use of pauses has been frequently noted.[171] He was adept at pointing up parallel structure through the repetition of patterns of intonation and inflection.

In general, important passages were delivered more slowly and with more pauses than less important passages. Vowels in the stressed syllables of emphasized words and significant words were prolonged.[172] According to one critic, his slow speaking rate caused Roosevelt "to prolong slightly" his vowel and semivowel sounds which in turn made his speech more euphonious and more pleasant to the ear than it would otherwise have been.[173]

[168] Sherwood, *op cit.*, p. 217; Tully, *op. cit.*, p. 98.

[169] The addresses delivered on the following dates, for example, had five-minute time intervals marked in ink or pencil: May 26, 1940; May 27, 1941; September 11, 1941.

[170] Note, for example, the pauses he made where diagonal lines are inserted: "Our acts must be guided by one / single / hard-headed / thought /—keeping America /out / of this war." Address of September 21, 1939.

[171] See Lionel Crocker, *Public Speaking for College Students* (New York: American Book Co., 1950), p. 425; George W. Hibbitt, *How to Speak Effectively* (Garden City, New York: Garden City Publishing Co., 1947), p. 219.

[172] "No soporific lullabies that a wide ocean protects us from him—can long have any effect on the *hard*-headed, *far*-sighted, and *real*istic American People." Address of September 11, 1941.

[173] Joanna Givan, "A Consideration of the Qualities Which Contribute to the Effectiveness of the Speeches of Franklin Delano Roosevelt" (M.A. thesis, College of the Pacific, 1944), p. 68.

Although he has been praised for using wide variations in loudness,[174] seldom, if ever, was Roosevelt's speech staccato and never did he sound hurried. According to the reports of those handling radio control boards while he was speaking, Roosevelt did not reach the extremes of being very loud or very weak in volume.[175] Yet, he did frequently employ variations in loudness to emphasize important words and thoughts,[176] although he was rarely guilty of violent outbursts or conversely of periods of imperceptibility.[177] Syllables and words as well were emphasized by combining prolongation of the vowel sound with increased loudness.[178] Roosevelt's practice of underlining words in the final reading manuscript as a reminder to speak them more loudly when he delivered the address indicates that these variations in loudness were often consciously planned and produced.

Franklin Roosevelt had the faculty of adapting his conversational mode of delivery to a variety of circumstances. Grave passages became measured and deliberate. Sentences of less consequence were delivered more rapidly with less ponderousness. In a rear-platform appearance he could be extremely conversational and informal while he jokingly introduced his "little boy Jimmy," or replied to an impromptu question from a bystander. When the occasion demanded, he could resort to the sustained, uplifted tone of the great leader. At the political rally he became direct and informal, engaging in raillery, sarcasm, scorn, and earnest pleading—whatever the immediate moment demanded. Over the radio he gave his listeners the feeling of direct conversation and gracious familiarity. The analyst of one of his addresses explains, for example, "The voice came into their own homes from the familiar radio grill . . . in friendly, social tones—neighborly, yet with a patrician assurance

[174] "His tremolos, his staccatos, his crescendos and fortissimos are masterpieces." Brandeis, *op. cit.*, p. 6.

[175] Dryer, "Air Power," *op. cit.*

[176] "That is why every member of the executive branch of the government and every member of the Congress face *great responsibility—great accountability.*" Address of January 6, 1941.

[177] Professor Charles H. Voelker's "phonetic study" of Roosevelt's annual address to Congress on January 3, 1936, offers some contrary evidence. "His use of loudness emphasis sometimes causes words to become too staccato. It shortens his prolongation of vowels so as to be characteristic of a much younger speaker. This gives an impression of choppiness. This is especially evident in words starting with plosives, such as [p], [b], [g], etc. Final [l] is sometimes omitted. Final [s] is sometimes lowered in pitch so as to become a mere passing of breath. Polysyllabic words at times become monosyllabic." Charles H. Voelker, "A Phonetic Study of Roosevelt," *Quarterly Journal of Speech*, XXII (October, 1936), 366.

[178] For example: "Such aid is not an act of war, even if a dictator should *uni*laterally proclaim it so." Address of January 6, 1941.

of born leadership."[179] Another critic declared: "Whether you agree with what he says or not, to any discriminating ear his voice has projection, power, personality, and charm. Above all, it has a friendly tone."[180] Since he never resorted to bombast or to what might be referred to as old-time oratory, Roosevelt was able readily to adapt his speaking to the microphone. His power to extend his personality, to convince, and to win radio listeners was due in important measure to his ability to adapt his vocal control to a variety of occasions.

What conclusions can we reach concerning Franklin Roosevelt's voice? Its quality proved a significant advantage, for it was pleasant and distinctive. Skillful variations, although never extereme, in pitch, rate, and loudness helped communicate specific ideas and emotions. We note that he talked at an unusually slow rate and that his voice was typically identified as tenor. Unquestionably, Franklin Roosevelt's superior vocal control was one of his important assets as a speaker.

3. Pronunciation

In spite of the popular assertion that he had a "Groton-Harvard" accent, Franklin D. Roosevelt only spoke like other members of the educated class of New York city and its environs. Correctly speaking, he used what phoneticians call the Eastern dialect. James F. Bender points out that this observation needs qualification. "Like most people with good hearing capacity, the President's speech is influenced by his environment, and the Presidents' environment has been varied. That is why his speech includes a number of deviations from the Eastern dialect."[181]

An analysis of Roosevelt's pronunciation of the sounds *r, ju, m,* and *a* clearly indicates his general adherence to the Eastern dialect. A consideration of these more conspicuous elements is far short of a study of every sound in every combination; nevertheless it should be helpful here.

The most conspicuous characteristic of his Eastern dialect was his treatment of the preconsonantal, final (before a pause), and intervocalic *r*. With practically complete consistency, his *r* was silent after [a], [ɜ] and [ə] followed by a consonant. Thus *hard* [haɪd], *heard* [hɜd], *world* [wɜld], *fostered* [fɔstəd], *sisters* [sɪstəz]. With the same consistency, *r* was silent after [ɜ], [a], and [ə] finally before a pause. Thus, *star* [sta], *concur* [kən'kɜ], *father* [faðə]. After [ɔ], preconsonantally or finally before a

---

[179] Oliver, "The Speech That Established Roosevelt's Reputation," *op. cit.,* p. 274.

[180] Elizabeth Ferguson von Hesse, *So To Speak* (New York: J. B. Lippincott Co., 1941), p. 161.

[181] James F. Bender, "Two Men: A Radio Analysis," *New York Times,* September 17, 1944, Sec. 6, p. 36.

Franklin Delano Roosevelt

pause, *r* was either silent or pronounced [ə]. Thus, *world order* [wɜld'ɔdə], *armed force* [amd fɔəs], *war* [wɔ], *I hate war* [aɪ heɪt wɔə]. After all other vowels (including most diphthongs), preconsonantally or finally before a pause, *r* was pronounced [ə]. Thus *years* [jɪəz], *fear* [fɪə], *where* [ʍɛə], *to serve their country* [tə sɜv ðɜə 'kʌntrɪ], *fair weather* [fæə wɜðə], *care* [kæə], *more men* [moə mɛn], *door* [doə], *poor time* [puə taɪm], *sure* [ʃuə], *fire them* [faːə ðɛm], *tire* [taɪə], *our peace* [auə pis], *our* [auə].

All this runs true to the Eastern pattern. But Roosevelt's consistency wavered a little in the case of [au] in *our* and in possibly a few other words, where the *r* was occasionally lightly pronounced, suggesting the General American pattern. Thus, *our way* [aur weɪ], *our wisdom* [aur'wːzdəm], *our people* [aur pipl]. It was probably this inconsistency with the diphthong [au] that caused some commentators to speak of the General American characteristics in Roosevelt's speech. But this slight deviation is actually much less conspicuous than similar ones in the speech of many Easterners, who often stray momentarily from what is regarded as the strict regional pattern. Roosevelt's wide travel and his association with General American speech would make for some leaning toward this dialect.

In respect to the intervocalic *r*, Roosevelt held with nearly perfect consistency to the Eastern pattern. If the intervocalic *r* occurred within a single word, he never failed to pronounce it, saying *very* [vɛrɪ] and *carry* [kærɪ]. If the intervocalic *r* occurred at the end of a word which was immediately, i.e., without pause, followed by a word beginning with a vowel, he pronounced it. He said, for example, *war is* [wɔr ɪz], *their arms* [ðɛr amz].[182]

A pause will inhibit a linking *r* in Eastern speech as in *"we shall try next year* [jɪə]. *After that..."* Here the pause between "year" and "after" precludes the link. Roosevelt's pauses were sometimes very brief, so that the researcher, playing a recorded speech, sometimes expects a link which does not materialize. But a second playing will usually reveal that the pause, even if brief, is overt.

Roosevelt was inconsistent in his use of [ju] in words in which *u, eu,* and *ew* followed [t], [d], and [n]. He said [djutɪ] and [djurəbl], but he used both [ju] and [u] in the word *new;* sometimes it was [nju] and at other times it was [nu]. In his Lend Lease message of January 6, 1941, he spoke of a *new congress, new needs, new circumstances* [nju kaŋgrəs], [nju nidz], and [nju sɜkəmstænts]. On another occasion, he spoke of the [nu ɔdə]. The word *neutral* in the famous speech delivered at the outbreak

---

[182] This intervocalic *r*, or linking *r*, may have confused some hearers who did not recognize it for what it is, a standard feature of Eastern speech. The linking *r* should not suggest General American speech when found in context with preconsonantal and final *r*'s which are silent or pronounced [ə] as indicated earlier.

of World War II, September 3, 1939, gave the President some difficulty. In three sentences he used three pronunciations: [njutrəl], [nɪutrəl], and [nutrəl]. Nevertheless, apparently he leaned toward [ju], which is the choice of many Easterners.

Roosevelt used [ʍ], not [w], in such words as *where*, *whether*, and *when*. Furthermore, he did not use the so-called "broad" *a*. He might say *ask* [æsk] or *vast* [væst], or he might say [ask] or [last] or [pasɪŋ]. Both of the pronunciations, as well as [ɑ] are accepted in Eastern dialect. The tendency to use the [a] may have been developed during the period of Groton and Harvard, since [a] in "broad" *a* words is exceedingly common in New England, but seldom found in the New York area. In no sense was his pronunciation extremely broad Eastern dialect.

In general, Roosevelt's pronunciation was crisp and distinct. He consistently enunciated vigorously. He always sounded his final consonants, and he never substituted [n] for [ŋ] as in *writin'* [raɪtɪn] for *writing* [raɪtɪŋ]. Roosevelt brought to countless Americans their first, and unquestionably their most impressive, knowledge of how Easterners talk. The exact effect of his dialect in terms of winning or losing support is not a matter of general agreement. His dialect has been assumed by some to have been an advantage, by others to have been a handicap. Perhaps Roosevelt's "cultivated, Eastern" pronunciation actually inspired confidence from the "one-third ill-housed, ill-clothed and ill-fed" whom he constantly championed; perhaps the downtrodden were more inclined to accept his words because they identified him not only as a man highly sympathetic to their cause but also as one whose background and experiences were "superior" to their own and who, therefore, deserved their support.

Because Roosevelt almost invariably merited praise for clear and incisive articulation, because he seemed clear and natural, his pronunciation received acclaim, in spite of minor inconsistencies. Many American listeners were not prepared to analyze the President's dialect; consequently, they usually were so impressed by his friendly, direct manner that they forgot what seemed like idiosyncrasies. Furthermore, the frequency with which he spoke made his speech familiar.

Henry Steele Commager has aptly observed: "Nature gave him a personality that won crowds and enchanted individuals, an impressive physical presence, an infectious grin, and a reassuring voice, and the radio and the airplane made it easy for him to exploit these gifts." [183] No judgment concerning the effectiveness of his ideas or his language can ignore his superior speaking voice, his attractive appearance, or his captivating speaking personality. Super-

[183] Commager, *op. cit.*, p. 356.

lative delivery became so much a part of his speaking that when circumstances combined to prevent optimum use of his voice and speaking manner listeners were quick to sense the difference.

Conclusion

Few public men have demonstrated greater respect for the power of the English language, or worked harder to use it effectively in the achievement of what he conceived to be social good, than did Roosevelt. He was not more gifted intellectually, nor was his early education superior or greatly different from that of many men of his time. Groton and Harvard helped shape his ideals, and the latter, particularly, provided opportunity to gain a sense of being a participant in the work of the world. Having entered Harvard in an election year with McKinley and his cousin "Teddy" pitted against William Jennings Bryan, Roosevelt took delight in worming out of President Eliot his choice of candidates,[184] and in throwing his own weight against his cousin. The many clubs in which he had membership and his role in the management of the Harvard *Crimson* nourished gregariousness. Then, as throughout his life, he was fonder of life among men than he was of books. Both at Groton and at Harvard he displayed considerable interest in oral discourse. It is not unlikely that he learned to recognize the vitality of ideas when supported by the resources of the human personality from men like Peabody, Kittredge, and Copeland, to whose oral presentation of the Bible and other literary works he responded enthusiastically and from whom he undoubtedly caught the enthusiasm to practice the art himself. But, in general, it was probably not chiefly from early training or books that Roosevelt learned to communicate effectively. Roosevelt's life was among men, and his effectiveness in speaking with them grew out of his repeated experiences in seeking acceptance of his ideas among men.

The emergence of radio as a popular means of communication at about the time of Roosevelt's return to politics in 1928 had much to do with his success as a speaker. Roosevelt was admirably equipped to make use of the new medium. His style of speaking, direct and conversational; his clear pronunciation; his excellent voice; his ability to read orally; and his extrovertive personality were readily adaptable to the microphone. Each listener received the impression that Roosevelt was talking directly to him. Millions of Americans sat at their radios and agreed that they "could practically feel him physically in the room." His voice communicated his expansive personality; it registered what was in him and what he wanted other people to grasp—conviction, sympathy, humility, gravity, humor—in harmony with situations as he saw them.

[184] *F. D. R., His Personal Letters,* I, 431-32.

American Public Address

In his own day, the one aspect of Roosevelt's speaking most often attacked by his critics was his method of speech preparation. There can be little doubt that Roosevelt called upon others to write almost in toto many of his minor efforts such as messages to visiting groups, toasts to visiting dignitaries, and commemorative speeches for minor dedicatory occasions. But it also must be recognized that Roosevelt planned, directed, and supervised carefully the preparation of his major addresses. Moreover, before the address was finished much of his language and his compositional preferences went into the speech. Roosevelt was directly responsible for what he said and how he said it. They were *his* speeches.

Roosevelt knew there was nothing inherently effective about ideas. Ideas could have vitality only insofar as they had relevance to the culture of which they were a part. He had the unique capacity to present ideas in such a way as to give them the vitality of relevance. Language was the instrument through which he gained access to the minds and feelings of other men, and, in turn, transmitted his own ideas and feelings.

His ideas were gained from his own observations and the observations of other men. His mind never wandered far from concrete realities. These realities he had the power to project before the eyes of listeners. It was not a power which was native to him; it was a power which was won, as a study of the many revisions of his speeches would indicate. Clear consciousness of purpose and of means lay behind his success in communication.

Thus, Franklin D. Roosevelt transcended the commonplace and became the inspiring leader whose bold and confident public speaking did much to combat fear, panic, defeatism, and complacency. History seems destined to accept and approve the facts and judgments of Roosevelt's close friend and admirer, Harry L. Hopkins:

More people listened to Franklin Roosevelt's speeches than ever heard the voice of any man. I believe more people read them. . . . Roosevelt's speeches were, as everyone knows, the vehicle by which he set in motion tremendous social and moral forces to combat fear and evil.[185]

SELECTED BIBLIOGRAPHY

Collections

The best source of information about Franklin D. Roosevelt is his collection of Private Papers, deposited at the Franklin D. Roosevelt Library, Hyde Park, New York. The collection includes thousands of letters to and from Roosevelt, speech manuscripts, files of speech materials, scrapbooks, recorded speeches, photographs, motion pictures,

[185] Foreword to *Nothing to Fear, The Selected Addresses of Franklin Delano Roosevelt,* ed. B. D. Zevin (New York: Houghton Mifflin Co., 1946), p. vii.

and recorded interviews of persons who knew Roosevelt. The Papers of Louis McHenry Howe and the Papers of Harry Hopkins are also deposited there.

Published Original Materials

Much original material is available in printed form. The following are indispensable to an understanding of Roosevelt:

F. D. R., His Personal Letters, ed. Elliott Roosevelt. 4 vols. New York: Duell, Sloan & Pearce Co., 1947, 1948, 1950.

The Public Papers and Addresses of Franklin D. Roosevelt, ed. Samuel I. Rosenman. 13 vols. 1928-36, New York: Random House, 1938. 1937-40, New York: The Macmillan Co., 1941. 1941-45, New York: Harper & Brothers, 1950.

The Public Papers of Franklin D. Roosevelt, Forty-eighth Governor of the State of New York. 4 vols. Albany, N. Y.: J. B. Lyon, 1930, 1931, 1932, 1933.

Autobiography, Biography, History

BALDWIN, HANSON W. *Great Mistakes of the War.* New York: Harper & Brothers, 1950.

BEARD, CHARLES A. *American Foreign Policy in the Making, 1932-1940.* New Haven: Yale University Press, 1946.

———. *President Roosevelt and the Coming of the War, 1941.* New Haven: Yale University Press, 1948.

Franklin D. Roosevelt's Own Story, ed. Donald Day. Boston: Little, Brown & Co., 1951.

FARLEY, JAMES. *Jim Farley's Story, The Roosevelt Years.* New York: McGraw-Hill Book Co., 1948.

FLYNN, JOHN T. *The Roosevelt Myth.* New York: Devin-Adair Co., 1948.

FRIEDEL, FRANK. *Franklin D. Roosevelt: The Apprenticeship.* Boston: Little, Brown & Co., 1952.

———. *Franklin D. Roosevelt: The Ordeal.* Boston: Little, Brown & Co., 1954.

GOSNELL, HAROLD F. *Champion Campaigner Franklin D. Roosevelt.* New York: The Macmillan Co., 1952.

GUNTHER, JOHN. *Roosevelt in Retrospect.* New York: Harper & Brothers, 1950.

JOHNSON, GERALD W. *Roosevelt: Dictator or Democrat.* New York: Harper & Brothers, 1941.

LINDLEY, ERNEST K. *Franklin D. Roosevelt.* Indianapolis: Bobbs-Merrill Co., 1931.

———. *The Roosevelt Revolution.* London: Victor Gollancz, 1933.

LUDWIG, EMIL. *Roosevelt: A Study in Fortune and Power.* New York: The Viking Press, 1938.

MOLEY, RAYMOND. *After Seven Years.* New York: Harper & Brothers, 1939.

PERKINS, FRANCES. *The Roosevelt I Knew.* New York: The Viking Press, 1946.

RAUSCH, BASIL. *Roosevelt: from Munich to Pearl Harbor.* New York: Creative Age Press, 1950.

ROOSEVELT, ELEANOR. *This Is My Story.* New York: Harper & Brothers, 1937.

———. *This I Remember.* New York: Harper & Brothers, 1949.

ROOSEVELT, MRS. JAMES [Sara Delano Roosevelt]. *My Boy Franklin.* New York: Ray Long and Richard R. Smith, 1933.

The Roosevelt Omnibus, ed. Don Wharton. New York: Alfred A. Knopf, 1934.

The Roosevelt Treasury, ed. James N. Rosenman. Garden City: Doubleday & Co., 1951.

ROSENMAN, SAMUEL I. *Working with Roosevelt.* New York: Harper & Brothers, 1952.

SHERWOOD, ROBERT. *Roosevelt and Hopkins.* New York: Harper & Brothers, 1949.

TULLY, GRACE. *F. D. R. My Boss.* New York: Charles Scribner's Sons, 1949.

Unpublished Theses

The numerous unpublished efforts of graduate students frequently provide excellent data and interpretations concerning specific aspects of F. D. R.'s public life. More than fifty Ph.D dissertations, and numerous M.A. theses have been published. The following have been particularly useful in preparing this study:

BRANDENBURG, EARNEST. "An Analysis and Criticism of Franklin D. Roosevelt's Speeches on International Affairs Delivered between September 3, 1939, and December 7, 1941." Ph.D. dissertation, State University of Iowa, 1948.

COWPERTHWAITE, LOWERY LEROY. "A Criticism of the Speaking of Franklin D. Roosevelt in the Presidential Campaign of 1932." Ph.D. dissertation, State University of Iowa, 1950.

CROWELL, LAURA. "An Analysis of Audience Persuasion in the Major Campaign Addresses of Franklin D. Roosevelt in the Presidential Campaign of 1936." Ph.D. dissertation, State University of Iowa, 1948.

RAY, ROBERT F. "An Evaluation of the Public Speaking of Franklin D. Roosevelt and Thomas E. Dewey in the Presidential Campaign of 1944." Ph.D. dissertation, State University of Iowa, 1947.

Index

547

Index